Encyclopedia of American Popular Fiction

GEOFF HAMILTON AND BRIAN JONES

ENCYCLOPEDIA OF AMERICAN POPULAR FICTION

Facts On File, Inc.
An imprint of Infobase Publishing
132 West 31st Street
New York NY 10001

Library of Congress Cataloging-in-Publication Data

Hamilton, Geoff.
Encyclopedia of American popular fiction / Geoff Hamilton and Brian Jones.
p. cm.
Includes bibliographical references and index.
ISBN 978-0-8160-7157-9 (hc : alk. paper) 1. Popular literature—United States—Encyclopedias. 2. Popular literature—United States—Bibliography. 3. American fiction—20th century—Encyclopedias. 4. American fiction—20th century—Bibliography. I. Jones, Brian. II. Title.
PS374.P63H36 2009
813'.5409—dc22
2008020662

Facts On File books are available at special discounts when purchased in bulk quantities for businesses, associations, institutions, or sales promotions. Please call our Special Sales Department in New York at (212) 967-8800 or (800) 322-8755.

You can find Facts On File on the World Wide Web at http://www.factsonfile.com

Text design by Lina Farinella
Cover design by Semadar Megged / Takeshi Takahashi

Printed in the United States of America

Bang KT 10 9 8 7 6 5 4 3 2 1

This book is printed on acid-free paper.

Contents

INTRODUCTION

This encyclopedia is intended as a guide to popular contemporary fiction, covering those writers and works that have enjoyed commercial success in the United States but have typically been neglected by guides to more "literary" works. We include entries on writers (American or other) whose work has reached, or consistently come very close to, the annual top ten list of best sellers during roughly the past 30 years (1980 to the present, with a weighting toward the last 15 years), in addition to entries on a representative selection of individual works that have reached top ten best-seller status in a particular year during this period. We consulted several sources in order to determine what counts as "top ten," relying heavily on lists compiled by the *New York Times* and *Publishers Weekly*. Entries cover every major genre in popular fiction, from romance to science fiction to mystery, from crime to fantasy to horror, as well as numerous hybrids. Some works from the 1970s that have enjoyed continuing popularity since their initial publication (such as Erica Jong's *Fear of Flying*) have also been included. While the focus is on fiction for adults, a special case is Dr. Seuss's *The Butter Battle Book*, which was added because of its popularity among children of all ages. Another unusual inclusion is the work of memoirist James Frey, whose *A Million Little Pieces* and *My Friend Leonard* are covered here since they turned out to be fictitious. Best-selling works typically categorized as "literary" rather than "popular" have been excluded.

To indicate a cross-reference, any name or term that appears as an entry elsewhere in the book is printed in SMALL CAPITAL LETTERS (on first appearance in an entry only).

A NOTE ABOUT THE SUBJECT MATTER

Popular fiction, as a term to describe the works discussed here, is at once the most helpful and unhelpful, true and untrue designation possible. These works are certainly fiction and undeniably popular. But so is *War and Peace*. For some readers works of popular fiction are *only* popular, while Tolstoy's text is . . . art, let us say. Too many scholars and critics use the term *popular fiction* both to disparage their object and ennoble themselves. Such critics see themselves as standing before the altar of literary art, like the priests of old, and interceding on behalf of the layperson and the uninitiated in the exploration—and sometimes worship—of the text. If the text can speak to the people directly, critics and scholars are unnecessary, and, if unnecessary, absurd. Popular fiction speaks to the people directly.

Some have suggested that the term *popular fiction*, which at least makes sense in describing the works here, should be replaced by *genre fiction*. But the latter fails even to capture a significant measure of the truth, let alone the worth of the texts. Many works of popular fiction can be placed under the rubric of more than one genre, and some, such as the alternate-world scenarios of Jack Vance or the apocalyptic saga of Jenkins and LaHaye, can be placed under virtually all of them (though the *western*, with its six-shooters, cowboys and Indians, is perhaps somewhat more limited in application). Literary fiction can also be described by these terms: *Pride and Prejudice* is a *romance*; *Crime and Punishment*, a *psychological thriller*; and *War and Peace, historical fiction*.

So, if both Sidney Sheldon and Tolstoy both wrote popular fiction, what *does* distinguish the work discussed in this volume? What makes it matter so much to its audience? What makes it the *best* at what it is doing?

We would suggest that popular fiction is not second-rate fiction but first-rate storytelling. Of course, Tolstoy was also a great storyteller, but many other literary authors are not (they are *just* literary). The authors discussed in this volume are the premier storytellers of our time, and their stories, the premier stories of our time—as stories. These authors are *just* storytellers, and that is a priceless gift.

With this change of perspective comes (or should come) a change of aesthetic. We readers of popular fiction do not seek—and disparage, if we do not find—profound psychological complexity or insight, stylistic originality, striking conceit, esoteric allusion—all the literary hardware that at least since Joyce has proven so attractive to authors and scholars alike. What we seek instead is the spellbinding, atavistic magic of a tale well told.

These are the stories of our time, and these, the storytellers. Narrative skill is what distinguishes them. That is why so many of these authors excel in different media and occupations anywhere that stories are told. Sheldon, for example, won an Oscar and a Tony, was nominated for an Emmy (for *I Dream of Jeannie*), and sold 300 million books. Others among these storytellers are also musicians; visual artists, some of whom, like Dr. Seuss or Kit Williams, illustrate their own stories; teachers, like Eoin Colfer or Pat Conroy, who practiced their craft in the classroom first; journalists and preachers; lawyers and doctors; soldiers and criminals. And their stories, as stories have always done, define the essential shape of our community. In a sense they set the stage for art. These are craftspeople, not artists, and only a culture that has lost its sense of craft and the critical value of craft to culture could mistake them for artists.

In many ways the weaknesses in a modern psychological novel are the strengths of a good story; the death of the one is the life of the other. The two-dimensional characters common to storytelling, for example—the bane of literary fiction—do not *lack* three dimensions. Their essence is completely different. They are purposefully flattened and made smooth, like cartoonish, geometric figures on an Archaic Greek vase. Psychological complexity would merely disrupt that seamless surface and the hypnotic rhythm and pace of the tale. The spell would break, and the spell is everything.

The formulaic repetitiveness of narrative elements, characters, even speech, are the very stuff that storytellers' dreams are made of, like the formulaic composition of the Homeric epics. Thus, Dirk Pitt, the swashbuckling hero of Clive Cussler's marine adventures, for all his outlandish exploits, will always be the same Dirk Pitt, always act the same way, in the same world, with the same villains and heroines; talk the same way to his trusty henchman Al Giordino; and be echoed in countless other tales of similar adventurers, on land, in space, or in time. The copious but idealized detail of these tales, their endless romantic locales, impossible beauties (and beasts), exotic lifestyles, and improbable fortunes—all these elements are also prominent in Greek myth.

Even the suspense of narrative fiction is similar to the paralyzing apprehension of Greek tragedy. There may be no doubt of the ending, or even of the salient features, of the plot: The lovers will always find love; the heroes survive; the villains will be crushed; the victims will be vindicated. But our assurance of these things, which should ruin the suspense, actually permits us to enter the dream more completely, to thrill to its internal and harmless uncertainties, like a child daydreaming in the arms of its father. In the rare cases where this assurance is undermined, as in the acute moral ambivalence of le Carré's morality tales, other elements take its place—such as the cold war formula of the espionage thriller.

This is in no way meant to suggest that these stories are equal to Homeric epics or that their authors rival Aeschylus, merely that they share with those ancient models and preserve, even in our time, a number of key formal elements that set them *both* apart from the modern novel.

Geoff Hamilton and Brian Jones

Absolute Power **David Baldacci** (1996)

Absolute Power is the first novel written by DAVID BALDACCI and one of 10 thus far to make the *New York Times* best-seller list. Like many of his works, it revolves around the struggles of outsiders who are thrust into moral confrontation with corrupt and hypocritical powers-that-be.

Luther Whitney is set to pull off the biggest caper of his long career. Three months of planning and preparation are meant to culminate in one—and his last—night's work. At 65 Luther is one of the most accomplished cat burglars in the Washington, D.C., area and has carefully scouted the layout, occupants, and staff of The Coppers, the name that billionaire Walter Sullivan has bestowed on his multimillion-dollar home in secluded Middleton County, Virginia.

Luther easily defeats the state-of-the-art burglar alarm and locates the hidden vault behind a floor-to-ceiling mirror panel set into the wall. But on entering the six-by-six-foot vault, he is surprised to find a chair situated in front of the mirror panel, facing out. Then, while working quickly to remove two and a half million dollars worth of stamps, coins, negotiable bonds, and jewels, he is interrupted by the sound of cars arriving.

No one is supposed to be home, but suddenly three men and two women appear, leaving Luther trapped inside the vault, with a two-way mirror revealing the room before him. The chair in the vault is apparently installed so that a spectator, no doubt billionaire Sullivan himself, can view the lady of the house entertaining male guests in her bedroom. The man and woman begin to get intimate, but the lovemaking escalates into violence, with the man at last slugging the woman hard enough to dislodge her teeth and dislocate her jaw. She grabs a sharp letter opener and straddles him, at which point:

> The man, seeing his life about to end as the letter opener plunged toward his chest, screamed with every bit of strength he had left. The call did not go unheeded.
>
> His body frozen in place, Luther's eyes darted to the bedroom door as it flew open.
>
> Two men, hair cropped short, crisp business suits not concealing impressive physiques, burst into the room, guns drawn. Before Luther could take another step they had assessed the situation and made their decision.
>
> Both guns fired almost simultaneously (28–29).

Almost immediately, there is an exclamation from the man whose life the two agents have just saved.

> "Jesus fucking Christ!" The President of the United States sat up, one hand covering his limp and damaged privates, the other holding the letter opener that a moment before was to have been the instrument of his death. It had more than just his blood on it now.
>
> "Jesus fucking Christ, Bill, you killed her" (32).

Having witnessed the killing of Walter Sullivan's wife by the Secret Service agents, Luther is forced to remain in the vault during the meticulous cover-up cleaning that follows, as the murder scene is made to look like Christine Sullivan interrupted a burglar in the act of breaking in and stealing her valuables and was killed by the burglar. The work is temporarily suspended when the inebriated and confused President Richman stumbles back into the bedroom and has to be escorted to his car. And in the few confused moments that it takes for the Secret Service men and Gloria to get Richman out of the room, a key piece of evidence is left behind. Luther slips out of the vault, takes up the blood-soaked and fingerprinted letter opener, and escapes through a second-floor window.

Throughout the balance of the tale, Luther is on the run from the police, the Secret Service, and Sullivan's private hitman, while Luther's estranged daughter, Kate, an associate district attorney, and her ex-boyfriend, upscale lawyer Jack Wright, frustrate Luther's plan to train a spotlight of accusation on President Richman and his chief of staff, Gloria Russell. However, Luther's sense of honor and rightness is acutely offended by the callous manner in which the hypocritical president and Russell treat the dead woman, and he finally determines to topple all those involved in Christine Sullivan's death.

A Middleton homicide detective, Seth Frank, is assigned to the case and begins to hunt for Luther, but as he unravels the tangled threads of the mystery, he finds himself not only beginning to doubt Luther's commission of the murder, but also developing a grudging respect for the longtime burglar, as well as Kafkaesque anxieties about his own role in the morally ambiguous but mortally significant circumstances in which he is working.

Compared to the work of some of his contemporaries, such as MICHAEL CONNELLY (*Blood Work, Echo Park,* LINCOLN LAWYER, et al.), Balducci's work is more sparse and restrained in language but shows eminent skill in its sculpting of the action and suspense. Both President Richman and Gloria Russell are convincingly drawn as power-obsessed characters who will stop at nothing, even murder, to protect themselves and their position in the White House; and the subtle interplay of Luther and Frank's tactical and moral struggles is memorable.

The movie *Absolute Power* (1997), starring and directed by Clint Eastwood, significantly departs from the text, and whereas the book is defined by carefully plotted and paced suspense, much of this is lost in the film. The novel's president, for example, is a powerful, charismatic, and multilayered character, but in Gene Hackman's portrayal he is a near caricature of myopic power obsession; in fact, most of the characters in the film, with the exception of Luther Whitney and Seth Frank (played by Ed Harris), lack the depth and realism of those in the book. Moreover, much of the story line seems to drag in the film, and the characters' motivations are either occult or obscure. But Eastwood himself delivers a nuanced, true-to-the-text portrayal of Baldacci's conflicted but ultimately noble master-thief.

Bibliography

Absolute Power. Directed by Clint Eastwood. Columbia Pictures, Sony Pictures Entertainment, Warner Bros, 1997.

Baldacci, David. *Absolute Power.* New York: Warner Books, 1996.

Warren Graffeo

Adams, Douglas (1952–2001)

Adams was a British author and humorist, best known for creating the comic science-fiction series *The* HITCHHIKER'S GUIDE TO THE GALAXY (1979). Although the series began with little fanfare on radio, it quickly became a worldwide cultural phenomenon, spawning a BBC Television adaptation, a computer game, several stage shows, and the publication of five hugely successful novels in what became known as "the increasingly inaccurately named Hitchhiker's Trilogy." A feature film, some 20 years in development, was released in 2005.

Douglas Noel Adams was born in Cambridge and attended Brentwood School in Essex. His first publication, at age 12, was a short story in the

Eagle comic. While at preparatory (junior) school, Adams studied English with a teacher named Frank Halford. The novice writer was profoundly influenced by Halford and famously received the only 10 out of 10 ever awarded by the teacher in his entire career; Halford thought Adams's creative writing exercise was "technically and creatively perfect—a remarkable piece of work for a boy of that age" (Simpson 11). Adams, who suffered from writer's block and frequent crises of confidence, would recall this perfect mark for encouragement throughout his writing career.

Adams was accepted to St John's College, Cambridge, in 1971. The young author's principal reason for applying to this university was to enable him to join the legendary Footlights Dramatic Club, a comedy revue group that had produced several of Adams's comic inspirations, among them Peter Cook, as well as John Cleese, Eric Idle, and Graham Chapman of *Monty Python* fame. However, to his dismay Adams was rejected for membership and instead began to write and perform with a breakaway comic troupe called Adams-Smith-Adams. This initial sense of failure and displacement may have found creative expression in Adams's most famous character—the perpetually bemused and neurotic Arthur Dent of *HHGG*.

Upon graduation with a B.A. in English literature in 1974, Adams made the decision to become a full-time writer and had some minor successes on radio and television (including a small contribution to an episode of *Monty Python's Flying Circus*), forming a promising writing partnership with *Python*'s Graham Chapman. However, freelance writing of this kind paid poorly, and Adams was forced to undertake a range of jobs to make ends meet. As ever, Adams made great use of these experiences in his fiction and his renowned anecdotes, making frequent reference to his stints as bodyguard for a wealthy Arab family, hospital porter, barn builder, and chicken-shed cleaner.

Adams's fortunes began to change when, in 1977, he was commissioned to write a science-fiction comedy radio series, initially titled *The Ends of the Earth*, which would become *The Hitchhiker's Guide to the Galaxy*. An enthusiastic raconteur, Adams would later claim that the idea for the series came to him when he was lying drunk in a field in Innsbruck, Austria, while hitchhiking round Europe as a student (although it became apparent after his death that this story was a typically playful Adams fabrication, chosen for its narrative resonance rather than its historical accuracy). Shortly after this commission, Adams also wrote a number of scripts for the cult BBC science-fiction series *Doctor Who*.

Although he would become most famous as an author of comic SF and advocate of technology, Adams was not particularly well versed in SF literature or history. Later in his career he would express admiration for the absurdist SF writing of Kurt Vonnegut, but for the most part Adams's influences were writers with a traditional comic approach, particularly Charles Dickens and P. G. Wodehouse (Adams would write an introduction to Wodehouse's final novel, *Sunset at Blandings*, reproduced in the posthumous collection, *The Salmon of Doubt*). However, his interest in science, his wit, and his boundless capacity for invention combined to shape a writing style that mixed humor and absurd (though plausible) technological speculation to striking effect.

The success of the radio series led to Adams's authorship of five phenomenally successful Hitchhiker novels—*The Hitchhiker's Guide to the Galaxy* (1979); *The Restaurant at the End of the Universe* (1980); *Life, the Universe and Everything* (1982); *So Long, and Thanks For All the Fish* (1984); and *Mostly Harmless* (1992)—which trace the bizarre and increasingly pessimistic adventures of Arthur Dent, the last surviving Earthman, and his Betelgeusian friend, Ford Prefect. A highly successful BBC Television adaptation was broadcast in 1981, and a movie version was proposed shortly afterward (a project that would not be fully realized until after Adams's death).

Between the final two volumes of the Hitchhiker series, Adams produced two novels that featured a metaphysical sleuth and another selection of memorable supporting characters and oddly plausible coincidences. *Dirk Gently's Holistic Detective Agency* (1987) was described by its author as "a kind of ghost-horror-detective-time-travel-romantic-comedy-epic, mainly concerned with mud, music and quantum mechanics" (Gaiman 169), and was followed in 1988 by the similarly genre-spanning *The Long Dark Tea-Time of the Soul.*

Many of Adams's personal preoccupations are apparent as recurring themes in his work. Apart from his lifelong interest in technological advancement, his self-described "radical atheism" becomes steadily more apparent in the increasingly random and unsympathetic Hitchhiker's universe, and the credulous Electric Monk in *DGHDA* satirizes the anachronistic nature of religious belief in a secular and technologically sophisticated world. Adams was also a passionate amateur musician (once playing guitar onstage with his friend David Gilmour at a Pink Floyd concert), and several novels discourse eloquently on music, from a virtuosic passage on Dire Straits in *So Long, and Thanks for All the Fish* to the use of Bach's music as the basis of a computer algorithm in *DGHDA.* Adams's environmental activism resulted in his teaming up with zoologist Mark Carwardine for *Last Chance to See,* a radio series and book that documented their worldwide search for endangered animals.

Adams died suddenly of a heart attack on May 11, 2001, and was survived by his wife, Jane Belson, and daughter, Polly. An incomplete novel, which may have become either a final Hitchhiker's or Dirk Gently volume, was published posthumously as *The Salmon of Doubt,* collected with a Hitchhiker-related short story ("Young Zaphod Plays It Safe") and a selection of nonfiction pieces focusing primarily on Adams's three major interests—science, religion, and music. His unfinished *Hitchhiker's* screenplay served as the basis for the 2005 Hollywood film, which ended with the dedication, "For Douglas."

Bibliography

Adams, Douglas. *Dirk Gently's Holistic Detective Agency.* London: Pan, 1987.

———. *The Long Dark Tea-Time of the Soul.* London: Pan, 1988.

———. *The Salmon of Doubt.* London: Pan, 2003.

———. *The Ultimate Hitchhiker's Guide: Five Novels and One Story.* New York: Gramercy Books, 2005.

——— (with Mark Carwardine). *Last Chance to See.* London: Pan, 1991.

Gaiman, Neil. *Don't Panic: Douglas Adams & The Hitchhiker's Guide to the Galaxy.* London: Titan Books, 2002.

The Hitchhiker's Guide to the Galaxy. Directed by Garth Jennings. Touchstone Pictures, 2005.

Simpson, M. J. *Hitchhiker: A Biography of Douglas Adams.* London: Hodder & Stoughton, 2003.

Webb, Nick. *Wish You Were Here: The Official Biography of Douglas Adams.* London: Headline, 2004.

Nicholas Dunlop

Albom, Mitch (1958–)

Mitch Albom is the author of nine books, including best sellers *Tuesdays with Morrie* and *The* FIVE PEOPLE YOU MEET IN HEAVEN, and is an award-winning journalist and radio host. Albom was born in Trenton, New Jersey, and graduated from Brandeis University, where he met "Morrie," the sociology teacher Morrie Schwartz. After graduating, Albom set out to become a professional musician but, unable to make a living at it, turned to writing in New York. After completing a master's degree in journalism at Columbia University, he wrote for a number of magazines and newspapers but is best known for his work in the *Detroit Free Press,* where he is the lead sports columnist and has won the Associated Press award for sports editor an unprecedented 13 times. Albom's columns have been collected into four books, beginning with *Live Albom!* in 1987 through to *Live Albom IV* in 1995. Albom is also a contributing editor to *Parade* magazine and has appeared on numerous television shows, including *The Oprah Winfrey Show, Larry King Live,* and *Good Morning America.* He hosts a radio show and is in a band, Rock Bottom Remainders, made up of fellow writers, including Matt Groening, STEPHEN KING, and Amy Tan. His latest novel, *For One More Day* (2006), was an instant *New York Times* best seller.

Tuesdays with Morrie catapulted Albom to fame and has become something of a commercial cult classic. After losing touch with his favorite teacher at Brandeis, Albom met up again with the eponymous Morrie as the latter was dying from ALS

(Lou Gehrig's disease). Albom visited him once a week to listen and record his mentor's views on life and ethics. In 1999 Oprah Winfrey produced a television movie based on *Tuesdays with Morrie,* starring Jack Lemmon and Hank Azaria, which won four Emmy Awards in 2000, including Best Actor (Lemmon).

Albom's first novel, *The Five People You Meet in Heaven,* is the story of Eddie, a maintenance man at a fairground who dies on his 83rd birthday while attempting to save the life of a young girl. The story follows Eddie in the afterlife as he meets five people whose lives he influenced during his life. Like *Tuesdays with Morrie,* Albom's novel was turned into a television film, which enjoyed considerable success on ABC in 2004.

Albom's work is characterized by simple and lucid prose, as well as a concern with ethics and relationships, with the importance of seizing the moment and not living to regret neglected opportunities, and with forging connections to people, even at the expense of ambitious individualism. Although his work is commercially successful, he is not without his detractors. Critics have called his writing excessively saccharine, but his defenders point to his own tireless charity work and the "life-changing" qualities that his books have offered so many.

Bibliography

Albom, Mitch. *The Five People You Meet in Heaven.* New York: Little Brown, 2003.

———. *Tuesdays with Morrie.* New York: Anchor, 2005.

Doug Field

. . . *And Ladies of the Club*

Helen Hooven Santmyer (1982)

. . . *And Ladies of the Club* depicts life in the small midwestern town of Waynesboro, Ohio, over the course of four generations. The novel's events begin in 1868, with the upheaval and anguish of the Civil War still fresh in the minds of both the town's citizenry and the country at large. Historical events will continue to affect life in Waynesboro, including Temperance and the assassination of President Garfield, immersing the reader in a world that feels especially alive as a result of such historical context. Anne Alexander and Sarah "Sally" Cochran appear within the first few pages, and it is the experience of these two women, just 18 at the start, that forms the novel's core. Although many other characters come and go throughout the story, the author returns, as to a touchstone, to the lives of Anne and Sally, both of whom remain in Waynesboro all their lives. Theirs is a lifelong friendship, marked in their youth by gossip and excitement over romantic pursuits and evolving into a sisterly bond capable of weathering even the most profound personal tragedies. Yet Anne and Sally exist as two very distinct women. Sally is the more outgoing of the two, delighting in a house full of rambunctious children and throwing lively parties. Anne, generous and self-sacrificing perhaps to a fault, grows more introspective over the years.

Anne and Sally become charter members of the Waynesboro Women's Club, which meets every two weeks to discuss various literary topics of the day. The club serves as the means by which Anne, Sally, and the other members come together for fellowship, despite their vastly different social standings, religious beliefs, and political leanings. So important is the Waynesboro Women's Club to the narrative thread that the novel's title derives from one of Anne's early interactions with the group, in which she addresses both "Madam President, and Ladies of the Club" (60). The women involved in the club range from the scholarly but aloof Amanda Reid to the spinster Gardiner sisters, to the warmhearted Kitty Edwards, with the story recounting events from the lives of all club members, from youth and marriages to illnesses and death. The start of each chapter lists both current members of the club and, in an "In Memoriam" section, those who have died. As the years roll on, this provides an excellent means for the reader to maintain a sense of the wholeness and integrity of the club as a living thing, noting those who are no longer members, whether through death or leaving Waynesboro.

Helen Hooven Santmyer tackles difficult, even controversial events in the lives of Waynesboro's citizens with grace and tact, defying the notion that women of the 1800s are straitlaced Victorians who lack passion and idly accept society's edict that they should be wives and mothers but little else. Anne, for example, understands too well that women can become trapped by custom. She says of Amanda, whose college degree still does not permit her an academic career, "It must be awful: to have what you aren't equal to thrust upon you, and no chance at all to do what you are equal to" (229). Miss Pinney, suffering from sciatica, ends up tragically addicted to laudanum. Her decline is public and awful; she grows increasingly disheveled and unwashed. Eventually, she cares for nothing but her next fix.

Perhaps the finest example of Santmyer's ability to depict both "the taboo" and the importance of kinship among women occurs when one of the club members dies from childbed fever. Anne and one of her friends prepare the body for the undertaker, bathing her corpse and dressing her in clean clothing. Through this intimate, caring act, they do "the last thing for her that could be done on this earth" (578).

Santmyer's other published novels also explore the themes of small-town life and the intricacies of family relationships. *Herbs and Apples,* published in 1925, features a female heroine who gives up a bustling career in order to return to her small Ohio town to care for her younger siblings after their mother dies. *The Fierce Dispute* (1929) focuses on three generations of women from a family that once enjoyed great wealth. *Farewell, Summer* was published posthumously in 1988 and deals with a tragic love affair. Santmyer also authored essays on life in her hometown of Xenia, Ohio.

There are as yet no film adaptations of . . . *And Ladies of the Club.*

Bibliography

Santmyer, Helen Hooven. *Herbs and Apples.* 1925. Reprint, New York: Harper and Row, 1985.

———. *The Fierce Dispute.* 1929. Reprint, Boston: G.K. Hall, 1989.

———. . . . *And Ladies of the Club.* 1982. New York: Berkley, 2000.

———. *Farewell, Summer.* 1988. Columbus: Ohio State University Press, 2001.

Amy M. Green

Angels and Demons Dan Brown (2000)

Angels and Demons is the first novel by DAN BROWN featuring Robert Langdon, who also appears in the phenomenally successful novel *The* DA VINCI CODE (2003). The plot of *Angels and Demons* is actually quite similar to that of the later work, with Langdon becoming reluctantly embroiled in a murder mystery involving a scientist at the international scientific laboratory CERN, who is killed over a discovery that could have profound religious implications. The murderer is connected to a secret society, the Illuminati Brotherhood, and his calling card is a series of cattle-style brands created in the form of ambigrams, which are words that can be read upside down as well as right side up. There are six ambigrams, one for each of the four elements (earth, air, fire, and water), one for the name of the Illuminati, and the sixth, an enigmatic, unnamed symbol that appears as the mystery is unraveled. The first victim is both a priest and scientist, and his body is mutilated and branded with the Illuminati ambigram. His scientific work is stolen and used to create a time bomb, which is then hidden underneath the Vatican as the conclave of cardinals is gathered to elect a new pope. Langdon and the adopted daughter of the dead scientist have to find the "path of illumination" supposedly hidden throughout Rome by the artist Bernini, portrayed as himself a secret member of the Illuminati. This path will lead to the location of the weapon, which could conceivably wipe out the entire hierarchy of the Catholic Church at one blow. Four cardinals are kidnapped by the murderer, and they are each to be killed along the path, one per hour until the bomb explodes. Each cardinal is branded with one of the ambigrammatic elements of earth, air, fire, and water, and these elements are used as the murder weapons in each case. Langdon must use his arcane knowledge to solve the mystery and save the church officials.

The novel was not nearly as successful as *The Da Vinci Code,* but once that book became popular *Angels and Demons* found a renewed and larger audience through rereleases and special editions. Brown is currently working on another Langdon novel, *The Solomon Key,* set in the United States and involving the Freemasons as the secret society.

The major theme of *Angels and Demons* centers on the conflict between science and religion, especially in the face of the church's lessening importance as science and technology provide answers formerly sought under its purview. But surprising, perhaps, to those only familiar with Brown's work through the controversy over *The Da Vinci Code, Angels and Demons* does not offer any shocking revelations about church doctrine or the continued existence of secret societies like the Illuminati. Instead, characters weigh in on both sides of the debate, some making the case for Enlightenment philosophy and the triumph of science and human reason, while others argue for the necessity of faith in a technological world. The centerpiece of this debate, and perhaps the most moving part of the book, occurs almost two-thirds of the way through the novel when the *camerlengo,* a church official who holds power until a new pope is elected, makes an impassioned speech on worldwide television that stretches over seven pages. "The ancient war between science and religion is over," he exclaims. "You [science] have won" (475). He acknowledges that science now provides the miracles that were formerly the domain of the church, and that, finally, "Science is the new God" (473). But, he asks,

> Who is this God science? Who is the God who offers his people power but no moral framework to tell you how to use that power? What kind of God gives a child *fire* but does not warn the child of its dangers? The language of science comes with no signposts about good and bad. Science textbooks tell us how to create a nuclear reaction, and yet they contain no chapter asking us if it is a good or a bad idea.
>
> To science, I say this. The church is tired. We are exhausted from trying to be your signposts. . . . We ask not why you will not govern yourselves, but how can you? Your world moves so fast that if you stop even for an instant to consider the implications of your actions, someone more efficient will whip past you in a blur. So you move on. You proliferate weapons of mass destruction, but it is the Pope who travels the world beseeching leaders to use restraint. . . . You encourage people to interact on phones, video screens, and computers, but it is the church who opens its doors and reminds us to commune in person as we were meant to do.
>
> . . .
>
> Whether or not you believe in God . . . you must believe this. When we as a species abandon our trust in the power greater than us, we abandon our sense of accountability. . . . With faith we are accountable to each other, to ourselves, and to a higher truth. . . . If the outside world could see the church as I do . . . they would see a modern miracle . . . a brotherhood of imperfect, simple souls wanting only to be a voice of compassion in a world spinning out of control (477–479).

In its dramatic context, the speech becomes a powerful set piece, arguing for a positive view of the church's role in the modern world; and the final unraveling of the mystery compels us to think about the implications of the *camerlengo*'s statement that "Religion is flawed, but only because *man* is flawed" (479).

Many argue that *Angels and Demons* is a better book than *The Da Vinci Code,* and one reason may lie in the greater complexity with which Brown tackles the ancient conflict between religion and Enlightenment thought. *Angels and Demons* does not portray the church simplistically, in either a positive *or* negative light; nor does it definitively point toward the moral superiority of the secular worldview. In addition to this more nuanced outlook, it does not directly contradict orthodox Christian belief as part of its basic premise, another factor contributing to the later novel's livelier appeal. From a purely literary standpoint, however, it weaves its far-reaching themes into fast-paced and tightly plotted action, a blend that many think the later book did not achieve. Finally, the larger questions it raises about the role of faith in a secular world encourage rereading.

A film of *Angels and Demons,* directed by Ron Howard and with Tom Hanks in his role as Robert Langdon, is scheduled for release in 2009 (IMDb).

Bibliography

Brown, Dan. *Angels and Demons.* New York: Simon & Schuster, 2000.

———. *The Da Vinci Code.* New York: Simon & Schuster, 2003.

Internet Movie Database. "Angels & Demons." Available online. URL: http://us.imdb.com/title/tt0808151/. Accessed January 12, 2007.

Julie Brannon

Anita Blake: Vampire Hunter (series)

Laurell K. Hamilton (1993–2007)

Through 15 novels and two short stories, LAURELL HAMILTON has created an enduring character in Anita Blake, heroine of the most prominent and successful series in the new subgenre of *horrorotica.* In her world—the "Anitaverse"—vampires, werewolves, and other creatures of the night do not merely exist but have legal standing; and vampires, though undead, have citizenship in the United States.

In her regular job Anita is an "animator," a necromancer who can raise the dead. This is done mostly for legal purposes as the freshly risen zombies are able to give legal depositions. Mystically forbidden from lying, such zombie witnesses recall the Fair Witnesses in Heinlein's *Stranger in a Strange Land,* who are incapable of speaking untruth and have photographic memories—the ultimate Notaries Public. Anita, then, raises the zombies to resolve their own property settlements and sometimes help solve their own murders; and many of the scars on her forearms are the result of her having to draw her own blood, in lieu of animal sacrifice, to enact the spell of raising.

Because of her notable abilities, she also serves as a consultant to the Regional Preternatural Investigation Team out of her hometown of St. Louis, her education and training in the supernatural making her a valued if sometimes resented member of the squad, called in on the most inexplicable (and often grisly) cases. In addition, Anita holds a special commission as a federal marshal, empowered to perform vampire executions, the only way to discipline a citizen-vampire run afoul of the law. The badge and her license to kill have gained her entrance to law enforcement cases, as well as the nickname "The Executioner" among the vampires.

In this universe the supernatural rules and roles are pretty clear (though Anita herself most prominently breaks them, by means of the abilities she develops over the course of the series); for example, the vampires have a well-articulated hierarchical structure, with family trees recording the creators and lineage of each vampire, much like the meticulous records of the British peerage. The older the vampire, the greater that vampire's powers, especially in mind control. Likewise, the vampire's "family" will be larger, in an increasing pyramid. Moreover, each vampire has an animal to call as a servant, and vampires take human servants in a variety of roles, including feeders or "pommes de sang." Finally, vampires are a tourist attraction, like the Master of the City, Jean-Claude, head vampire of St. Louis, who runs a vampire strip club called Guilty Pleasures, catering to (mostly female) fetishists.

The race of lycanthropes or shapeshifters has a similar structure but is more social than that of the vampires. The werewolves, for example, have a complex pack-structure with an Ulfric, alpha wolf, who leads the pack, partnered with a wolf queen, a Lupa, and rules of challenge when that leadership is disputed. Similar rules exist for the wererats, wereleopards, and werelions, all of whom interact with Anita in some fashion.

Anita's character evolves dramatically over the course of the series, shaped by her actions, interactions, and a constant struggle between her own conflicting desires and impulses; while the series' theme itself evolves from horror adventure with sexual undertones, through stories with equal parts horror and sex, to its latest emphasis on sexuality in a horror setting. A committed Christian who sleeps with a stuffed penguin, Anita is also one of the most lethal fighters in her world, and her dichotomous attitudes extend deep into her personal life as she is drawn into relationships that have lasting effects on her and her powers.

In the first phase of the series, running through the first five books, there is a "courtship period," in which a central romantic triangle emerges between Anita, Jean-Claude (master vampire of the city), and Richard Zeeman (Ulfric of the local werewolf pack). Richard is as conflicted as Anita: If he should be outed as a werewolf, he would lose his job as a schoolteacher, but he also wants Anita to accept his animal side, both emotionally and sexually. Jean-Claude's interest is more straightforward: He wants Anita for his human servant, due both to his attraction and the clout he stands to gain in vampire politics by domesticating the famed Executioner.

With the sixth installment, *The Killing Dance* (1997), this triangle becomes a triumvirate, with each acquiring greater power in their respective discipline by drawing energy from and communicating telepathically with the others. At this point Jean-Claude is firmly in control of the vampire contingent, Richard leads the werewolves, and Anita is a psychic bridge, serving as Jean-Claude's declared human servant and Richard's Lupa (queen) in his pack. With wolves being Jean-Claude's animal-on-call, and with Anita as their queen, Richard's place in the triumvirate is especially important, while the rest of the supernatural community views their powerful alliance with understandable trepidation. It is during this period that Anita is injured during a struggle with werewolves and wereleopards, an injury that, though not immediately subjecting her to transformation in the full moon, will loom large in the evolution of the series.

In the third phase of the series Anita's powers need to be fed, and sexual ardor becomes her controlling impulse. Just as a vampire needs blood, Anita needs sex to maintain her psychic energy (an alternative way that vampires in Jean-Claude's bloodline can feed, awakened in Anita by the latter's seduction of her). Over the course of her adventures she has developed ties to lesser vampires and shapeshifters whose energy fades if Anita is weak, and from whom Anita can draw energy through sex. For a woman who has sought a normal relationship (and thought she might have one with schoolteacher/werewolf Richard), Anita is now forced to acquire such energy from various members of her extended supernatural family, which, though not off-putting to Jean-Claude, who has had a variety of female and male lovers of his own, becomes an acute source of tension with Richard.

The triangle is complicated temporarily in the series' 10th installment, *Narcissus in Chains* (2001), when Micah, the Nimir-Raj (leader) of the wereleopard pard, rapes Anita when they are showering together, physical modesty not being an obstacle for shapeshifters in the series. Anita is pressed into helping lead the local wereleopards and later surrenders to a passionate romance with Micah, serving even as Nimir-Ra to his pard. This prompts Richard to break with Anita for a time, but they are ultimately reunited with an understanding of nonexclusivity, Richard finally being able even to overcome his previous reservations and join Anita and Jean-Claude in a triumvirate that is sexual as well as political.

In the 14th and most recent book, *Danse Macabre* (2006), many of these developments come to a dramatic crisis, with the specter of pregnancy and news that Anita carries several lycanthrope strains (wolf, leopard, lion, and one unknown) in her system, making her potentially a "pan-wer." Moreover, the *ardeur* is beginning to act more like an entity unto itself, seemingly shaping Anita's various lovers into better partners for each other, as well as for her.

At this writing, the series has shifted away from both of her career paths (federal marshal/vampire executioner and animator) to focus almost exclusively on her personal life and relationships. While the pregnancy turns out to be a false positive caused by her unique body chemistry, she is nonetheless forced into a painful reassessment of her various lovers and potential fathers, and finally of her own self and place in the world. Micah, who has had a vasectomy, is the closest thing Anita has to a "boyfriend," but she comes to realize that it is finally the *ardeur* that is controlling her feelings, and the burgeoning number of her partners threatens every sense of geometric proportion upon which her already complicated life has thus far depended. Add to this that as the dominant female in each social group, her choice of lover profoundly affects the power structure of that group and the complex, intensely political world of which it is a part, and a sense of almost baroque distension is felt by even the most seasoned of Hamilton's readers. Vampire hunter, necromancer, lycanthrope, and succubus, all in one, Anita Blake's future would seem thoroughly and intriguingly indeterminate.

Bibliography

Hamilton, Laurell, K. *The Killing Dance.* New York: Berkley, 1997.

———. *Narcissus in Chains.* New York: Berkley, 2001.

———. *Danse Macabre.* New York: Berkley, 2006.

Heinlein, Robert. *Stranger in a Strange Land.* New York: Ace/Putnam, 2005.

Ronald C. Thomas

The Aquitaine Progression

Robert Ludlum (1985)

Beginning in Geneva, but with a tentacular plot that extends to a global scale, *The Aquitaine Progression* is a novel rooted firmly in the thriller genre. With a rich palette of characters, many of whom have allegiances that are often complex and unclear, the novel weaves a thematic concern with political paranoia into a fast-paced narrative of international conspiracy and intrigue.

The very name of its protagonist, Joel Converse, embodies the contradictory nature of his personality; *Joel* suggesting the G.I.'s "Joe," referring to his status as former military personnel, and the service and subsequent imprisonment that he endured in Vietnam; *Converse* highlighting his oppositional and defiant personality, a trait that proves central to the novel's development, as he directly challenges the authority of his superiors in Vietnam and ultimately escapes his imprisonment by the Vietnamese. His conversity is also suggestive of the prospective disintegration of his own mental state, evidenced during his recovery from imprisonment:

> Like most men kept isolated for the greater part of their imprisonment, Converse had examined and re-examined every stage of his life, trying to piece them together, to understand . . . to *like* . . . the cohesive whole. There was much that he did not understand—or like—but he could live with the product of those intensive investigations. Die with it, if he had to; that was the peace he had to reach for himself. Without it the fear was intolerable (13).

The ritualized searching for, isolating, and preserving aspects of his life that his memory retains under severe duress is a way of reconciling his fear and maintaining his own mental stability. By thus drawing on the familiar and by reasserting its validity, Joel is able to create a framework and support capable of resisting and finally overcoming even the torture he had undergone in the camps. ROBERT LUDLUM deftly prefigures this inner struggle and commotion in the opening pages' description of Geneva, a city in perpetual tension and transition; at once

> the old and the new. City of high medieval walls and glistening tinted glass, of sacred cathedrals and less holy institutions. [. . .]
>
> City also of the unexpected, predictability in conflict with sudden unwanted revelation, the violence of the mind accompanied by striking bolts of personal lightning.[. . .]
>
> Geneva. City of inconstancy (9–10).

This sense of contrast and revelation, of facades and hidden agenda, of the straightforward and the unexpected, reflects not only the structural features of Ludlum's novel, but the constant "cross and double-cross" experienced by its characters.

Converse's primary antagonist is General "Mad" George Marcus Delavane, known personally to Joel as "The Butcher of DaNang and Peiku" (30) and "the warlord of Saigon" (30); a tyrannical military figure who condemned Joel to the hopeless air strike, in support of ground assault troops moving into the Tho Valley, which results in his capture and imprisonment. After three failed attempts, Converse is finally successful in escaping and returns home acutely disillusioned with the military establishment. Ironically, it is his very attempt to retire from all such conflict, by becoming a successful attorney for an international company, which draws him into the violence of the Aquitane Progression.

As its title suggests, the novel is oriented around the territory of Aquitaine, "the name first given to a region in southern France that at one time in the first centuries after Christ was said to have extended from the Atlantic, across the Pyrenees to the Mediterranean, and as far north as the mouth of the Seine" (60). The history of this region, like so much in the novel, is both convoluted and controversial. George Delavane views himself as a "student of history—in the tradition of Caesar, Napoleon, Von Clausewitz . . . even Patton" (61), and his interpretation of Aquitaine focuses on the ambiguities of its existence, inconsistencies that emerged out of "political, marital and military miscalculation" (61). In his view Aquitaine could have "encompassed most if not all of Europe" (61), but for the "fundamental law of western civilization [. . .]. You cannot crush then unite by force and rule disparate peoples and their cultures—not for any length of time" (61–62). Nonetheless, as one who aspires to the status of such imperial figures, Delavane (and his group of fellow international military operatives located firmly on the political right) seek to "construct the Aquitaine that never was" (62). By preying on the fears and prejudices of the global populace, through the orchestration of a series of assassinations that will create civil unrest and political vacuums, Delavane and his cohorts intend to ultimately establish a dictatorship that will encompass the world.

Joel's involvement in preventing the success of this plan is prompted by an encounter with a "legal mechanic" (10) from San Francisco, referred to as A. Preston Halliday, who purports to be replacing Aaron Rosen (the lawyer whom Converse has been working alongside on a major technological and financial merger), and who claims to know Converse from their time at university. Halliday makes reference to something called the Aquitaine Progression in their first meeting, but Converse only uncovers the full scale and complexity of the plan when directed to meet an aging academic, Dr. Edward Beale of Mykonos island, known formerly as "The Red Fox of Inchon," a strategist and ally with a prodigious reputation in military service and connected to Converse through mutual encounters with Delavane.

Converse is eventually drawn into a position as double agent—again suggested by his own name—both as a conspirator with Delavane and his organization and as an agent for the "good guys," attempting to win back the trust of his own government and employers. The conspirators employ high-level propaganda in an effort to thwart Converse's efforts, and Delavane's power is found to extend into the darkest corners of the U.S. government, with a level of influence previously inconceivable. At last Converse's dual existence as both hunter and hunted intensifies to such degree that his mental state itself, for all the hardening of his Vietnam experience, begins to disintegrate.

In terms of the Ludlum oeuvre, *The Aquitaine Progression* is a characteristically robust thriller with the proven formula of an international conspiracy, a protagonist on the verge of a mental breakdown, and a host of unexpected plot developments drawn, nonetheless, to a neat and well-orchestrated conclusion. There are striking parallels with Ludlum's own Bourne series, each narrated on an epic, global scale, with protagonists drawn into sinister plots and finally forced to question just whose side they are truly on—and, indeed, whether there are any sides at all.

Bibliography

Ludlum, Robert. *The Aquitaine Progression.* Glasgow: HarperCollins Ltd, 1985.

Martyne J. Colebrook

Asimov, Isaac (1920–1992)

Asimov wrote more than 400 books in his lifetime. The popular claim that he is the only author to have published a book in every category of the Dewey Decimal system is untrue, but this urban legend nevertheless helps capture the tremendous output and breadth of Asimov's writing. While he proved a popular author of nonfiction texts, Asimov is most famous for his contributions to the science-fiction genre, where he is considered one of the three "grand masters" of classic science fiction.

Asimov is perhaps most famous for his use of the "three laws of robotics," a series of guidelines for android behavior that first appeared in his series of robot stories. One of these stories, "The Bicentennial Man," about a robot's quest to be human, was made into a movie in 1999, starring Robin Williams in the title role. 2004's *I, Robot,* starring Will Smith, borrows the title of one of Asimov's robot anthologies and makes use of plot points from Asimov's short stories but is not a faithful adaptation of any one work.

Born in Russia in 1920, Asimov grew up as a precocious member of a family of Jewish immigrants. Since his family moved to America when he was three years old, Asimov retained no Russian, and his feelings toward his family's cultural heritage were ambiguous. Although conscious of his Jewish heritage, Asimov was himself a professed atheist, and he refused to dramatize his family's background. "I have frequently had hotheaded romantics assume that our family fled Russia to escape persecution," he wrote in his autobiography, *I, Asimov,* stating instead that he had no personal "horror tales" to tell of either Russian or American anti-Semitism (19). Believing that "prejudice was universal and that all groups who were not dominant . . . were potential victims," Asimov believed it was pointless to "denounce anti-Semitism unless I denounced the cruelty of man to man in general" (21). This he did in novels such as *Pebble in the Sky* (1950) and *The Caves of Steel* (1954), using far-future settings to explore the problems of social prejudice and oppression.

Asimov became an avid reader of pulp magazines while working in his father's candy store and soon started submitting his own fiction. He sold his first short story when he was 18, an accomplishment he later attributed to the low standards of pulp magazines rather than any personal skill or aptitude for writing. Two and a half years later, he published his 32nd short story, "Nightfall," which became one of the most famous science-fiction stories of all time.

"Nightfall" is set in a world illuminated by six major suns, which has consequently rarely seen darkness or the distant stars. The story follows several characters who slowly realize that the periodic collapse of civilizations on their planet is related to an upcoming phenomenon called nightfall, in which the rare setting of all six suns will plunge their world into darkness. "Nightfall" is considered a quintessential "idea story," a staple of pulp science fiction, in which a simple what-if premise ("what if people had never seen stars before?") is spun into a minimalist plot that brings the premise to its most dramatic conclusion ("they would go insane!").

"Nightfall" represented a turning point for Asimov and helped establish him as a force to be reckoned with in the science-fiction world. For his part Asimov considered "Nightfall" as part of a literary trend that signaled a turn away from the space operas and high-tech devices of older science fiction and was increasingly interested in the dynamics of human societies.

Asimov's next major work, the short stories that would become the Foundation series, was inspired by Asimov's reading of Gibbon's *Decline and Fall of the Roman Empire.* Asimov approached editor John W. Campbell with the idea of writing a future history about the rise and fall of a galactic empire. Campbell persuaded him to write an open-ended series of short stories dealing with this situation. Asimov undertook the project but set it in an all-human universe (an exception in science fiction of the time), because he did not want to have to conform to Campbell's firm notions regarding the superiority of human over alien races. Asimov perceived this science-fiction convention as a metaphor for Aryan superiority over other races, something that as a Jewish writer he wanted no part of.

The original Foundation series follows the fall and rise in fortunes of a galactic empire ruling 25 million planets, colonized by humans in their expansion from Earth. A new science, "psychohistory," allows a psychologist called Hari Seldon to effectively predict the future, including the imminent collapse of the empire and the coming dark ages. Seldon plans for the coming crisis by creating two Foundations, one of scientists and one of psychologists, who will implement a plan to shorten the dark ages to only a thousand years. The series of novelettes that make up the original Foundation trilogy follow the Foundations over the course of

400 years as they meet one crisis after another, following Seldon's plan and preserving humanity.

Since the Foundation stories take place in different time periods, the only consistent character in the series is Seldon, whose filmed image counsels and manipulates members of the Foundation long after he is dead. Seldon thus emerges as a scientific God-figure, a paternal, omnipotent guardian of humanity, who is not above misleading generations of his followers for the good of the human race.

In 1950, Asimov's *I, Robot* was published, gathering together short stories Asimov had written in response to traditional portrayals of robots in science-fiction magazines. Before Asimov the robots that appeared in science fiction were usually mechanical monsters that inevitably turned on their arrogant creators. Asimov considered such portrayals "Faustian" and implicitly slanted against science. Arguing that inventions from knives to electric wiring had usually been accompanied by some kind of safety feature, he instead wrote stories about robots programmed to obey the three laws of robotics:

1) A robot may not injure a human being, or through inaction allow a human being to come to harm.
2) A robot must obey the orders given it by human beings except where such orders would conflict with the First Law.
3) A robot must protect its own existence as long as such protection does not conflict with the First or Second Law. (11)

While Asimov was not the first science-fiction author to use robots as sympathetic characters, he was the first to provide readers with solid, logical grounds for why killer robots were unlikely. The "3 laws of robotics" proved so popular with readers that, since *I, Robot*'s publication, virtually every portrayal of robots in film or literature has had to conform to (or explain away) Asimov's laws.

While Asimov's fiction has proved enormously popular and influential, it is criticized for its spare prose, scarcity of female characters, lack of character development, and preference for reason over emotion. The kinds of "idea stories" Asimov wrote for John W. Campbell ("Nightfall," for example) are not as popular as they used to be; indeed, guidelines for modern science-fiction magazines often go out of their way to dissuade would-be authors from sending them fiction that relies heavily on the conventions of Asimov's early writing days. Nevertheless, Asimov's fiction is still thought of as classic by the science-fiction community. His books and short stories continue to inspire film adaptations, and his famous Foundation series continues in the form of authorized sequels written by authors such as Gregory Benford, David Brin, and Greg Bear.

Asimov died in 1992. Ten years after his death, his widow, Janet Asimov, revealed that he had died of AIDS acquired from a blood transfusion. She claimed that Asimov had wanted to reveal the real nature of his affliction but had been persuaded by his doctors that making his condition public would harm his family.

Bibliography

Asimov, Isaac. *I, Robot*. New York: Doubleday, 1950.

———. "Nightfall." In *The Complete Stories*, vol. 1. New York: Broadway Books, 1990, pp. 334–362.

———. *The Caves of Steel*. New York: Spectra, 1991.

———. *Foundation*. New York: Spectra 1991.

———. *Pebble in the Sky*. New York: Spectra, 1991.

———. *I, Asimov: A Memoir*. New York: Doubleday, 1994.

———. *Bicentennial Man*. London: Gollancz, 2000.

Gunn, James. *Isaac Asimov: The Foundations of Science Fiction*. Rev. ed. Boston: Oxford University Press, 1996.

Siobhan Carroll

At First Sight Nicholas Sparks (2005)

At First Sight, the sequel to NICHOLAS SPARKS's best-selling *TRUE BELIEVER* (published only six months earlier), follows 37-year-old Jeremy Marsh from his flighty bachelor existence in New York to married life in Boone Creek, North Carolina. But whereas *True Believer* ended with the hero's falling in love with Lexie Darnell, the 30-year-old librarian of that small town, *At First Sight* describes the trying months before their marriage, centering on their attempts to start a life together in the parochial South. And thus maturity instead of romance is the focus of the sequel, at the end of which the protagonist at last achieves a hard-won wisdom through the harrowing loss of his wife and his evolving love for their only child.

The novel is framed by a prologue (five years after the main action) that asks "Is love at first sight truly possible?" (1), and an epilogue that reveals Jeremy and his four-year-old daughter, Claire, in the same Boone Creek cemetery where it all began. Attempting to free her from nightmares, Jeremy brings his daughter there to watch the mysterious lights—the same lights he himself had come to Boone Creek to observe five years before, and that her mother had watched when attempting to come to terms with the loss of her parents. The end of the novel suggests that Jeremy, once the great debunker of occult "mysteries," has now learned to accept the supernatural as a necessary part of existence, explaining the lights to his daughter by saying "I think she [Mama] wanted to meet you" (332). The prologue's "Love at first sight," then, refers not only to Jeremy's love for Lexie, but also and more profoundly, at last, to his parental love for Claire, whom he comes to see as the living image of her dead mother.

With Jeremy's arrival in Boone Creek, the blithe romance of *True Believer* begins to sour. His decision to abandon his glamorous New York existence and adapt his lifestyle to a rural and close-knit southern community, as well as the distance to his relatives and his usual work surroundings, leads to a persistent writer's block that threatens his job as a columnist for *Scientific American*. In addition, severe tensions develop in his relationship with Lexie. In a vain attempt to avoid gossip, they maintain separate residences and try to keep Lexie's pregnancy a secret, while preparing their wedding, having their new house renovated, and settling differences in matters as mundane, but potentially explosive, as the purchase of a car. The situation only worsens when Jeremy watches Lexie holding hands with her childhood friend Rodney without telling him about the meeting; and his jealousy and distrust of Lexie escalate dramatically when he receives an anonymous e-mail asking: "HOW DO YOU KNOW THE BABY IS YOURS?" (106). His suspicions are only heightened by the receipt of a second e-mail, which leads to him finding out that Lexie has also failed to tell him about a former pregnancy.

Sparks masterfully augments the suspense by heightening the duress under which Jeremy labors: The renovations dangerously drain his funds; he feels less and less able to write; and the e-mails now target his own masculinity as they remind him of the breakdown of his first marriage, partly caused by a doctor's prognosis that he would never be able to beget children. After a particularly angry row he leaves for New York, ostensibly to celebrate his stag party there, but perhaps never to return (as Lexie fears). The mystery of the poisoned e-mails, however, is suddenly resolved when his best friend, Alvin, admits to having written them in a well-meaning attempt to save his friend from a potentially unhappy marriage. Jeremy returns to Boone Creek shaken but sobered, willing to clean the slate and resume his relationship with Lexie on a basis of mutual trust.

Their renewed closeness, however, does not remain untested for long, as their unborn child is threatened by amniotic syndrome, which could lead to severe deformity and even death. At this point the narrative begins the harrowing trial from which Jeremy will only emerge at the end of the novel. The child is born healthy, but the mother dies in childbirth from an amniotic fluid embolism (303). While at first having great difficulty even accepting, let alone loving a child that has cost his wife's life, Jeremy gradually develops an altruistic love for Claire, who is named after Lexie's mother; and the cycle of love, loss, and the lights, with their intimation of the living presence of the dead, at last closes with Jeremy's aforementioned realization of the timelessness and selflessness of love.

The shocking conclusion to the novel can overshadow, especially on a first reading, the many lighthearted, comic elements in the plot, which paints a picture of small-town America that sometimes borders on parody. Dickensian characters that delighted in *True Believer* reappear: Lexie's aunt, a psychic who can predict the gender of unborn children; Gherkin, the mayor of Boone Creek, a meddling know-it-all, but also a kind and energetic friend when it comes to organizing the wedding in a state park; threatening ex-boyfriends and unfathomables like Jed the taxidermist; all deftly deployed in Sparks's romantic chiaroscuro.

Ultimately, *At First Sight* is a novel about maturation, about how human beings cope with trauma and loss, and about how these both are often, sadly, inseparable in a human life. While written mainly from the perspective of the male protagonist, the novel also provides sensitive insights into the workings of Lexie's mind and the deeper, complex reasons for her sometimes inscrutable behavior. In addition to the two-volume roman à clef, and the sequel's bildungsroman, Sparks's Boone Creek saga inscribes many elements of detective fiction, as well as Pickwickian comedy. But while the mix of romance, comedy, mystery, and melodrama might prove too much for some, especially those of a non-Dickensian temperament, the message of the novel is simple and clear: Family values, and the selfless love in which they are rooted, are to be cherished above all. Thus, once again, Jeremy "fell in love," but now, "wanted nothing more than to hold Claire and keep her safe forever" (315).

Bibliography

Sparks, Nicholas. *At First Sight.* New York: Hachette Book Group, 2005.

———. *True Believer.* New York: Hachette Book Group, 2005.

Heike Grundmann

Auel, Jean M. (1936–)

Auel has achieved worldwide renown for her five best-selling historical-fiction novels set in prehistoric Europe, with a sixth currently in preparation to round out the EARTH'S CHILDREN SERIES. One of five children born to Neil Solomon Untinen and Martha Wirtanen in Chicago, Jean Marie Untinen married Ray Bernard Auel (pronounced "owl") shortly after graduating from high school and has since had five children of her own. Auel earned her M.B.A. in 1976, attending night school while working for an electronics firm in Portland, Oregon. After graduation Auel quit her job with the electronics firm to find work more in keeping with her M.B.A. However, in 1977 she took time to jot down the rough sketch of a story she had conceived while doing her job search, and the fleshing out of this basic story idea eventually evolved into her new career. The sketch, with a working title of *Earth's Children,* was concerned with the childhood of a young Neanderthal girl but developed into a far-reaching and immensely absorbing series that chronicles the dawn of humanity in prehistoric Europe, centering on the character of Ayla, the young girl Auel had first envisioned.

Auel's (and the series's) first novel, *The Clan of the Cave Bear* (1980), was an immediate success, selling more than 1 million copies in a month and remaining on the best-seller lists for months afterward. In 1986 it was adapted into a movie starring Daryl Hannah and Joey Cramer. (To date, there have been no attempts to adapt the other novels of the series for film.)

Even by the often meticulous standards of historical fiction, Auel's research is extraordinary. Beyond her painstaking use of traditional resources, Auel also signed up for instruction in wilderness survival and took several field trips to gain firsthand experience of all sorts, from making ice caves and beds in snow to making fire without matches and fashioning blades out of stone. She learned how to cure and tan hides, how to hunt and gather wild foods using handmade spears and baskets; and she acquired knowledge of the medicinal properties of various plants that would have been around at the time depicted in the series. After the first novel found such success, Auel was able to take more trips to do firsthand research in distant locations, visiting museums and talking with various experts throughout Austria, Czechoslovakia, France, Germany, Hungary, the Soviet Union, and the Ukraine. In the (typically copious) acknowledgments for *The Shelters of Stone,* Auel especially notes the importance, both narrative and imaginative, of her early and repeated visits to the Lascaux, Niaux, and other painted caves in France.

The result, beyond the series's great popularity, has been frequent commendations for her outstanding research. And though recent discoveries and research in the field of archaeology indicate that some details in the series are inaccurate, Auel's ceaseless attention to such details has allowed her to adapt the series in media res. In 1983, for example, a discovery was made that revealed a Neanderthal hyoid bone, which may have allowed Neanderthals to use vocal language, instead of being forced to depend on grunts and body signals. Since this discovery was made long after the original idea for the series and after the publication of the first novels, it might have seemed pointless to try to incorporate the new knowledge into later novels, and Auel was always free to claim poetic license; yet the discovery is deftly integrated into her later novels in the limited capacity of some of the "mixed spirits" to speak (these being half "Flathead" or "Clan," and half "Other" or "Earth Children").

Auel's relatively few novels have taken so long to write that at this printing she is now a grandmother, and devoted readers are still waiting for the last novel of the series. Fans have created a host of Web sites in her honor, but she has an official Web site (http://www.randomhouse.com/features/auel/webroot/index.html) where anyone may access information on the books and view video interviews with the author.

Bibliography

Auel, Jean M. *The Clan of the Cave Bear.* New York: Bantam Books [Random House], 1980.

———. *The Valley of Horses.* New York: Bantam Books [Random House], 1982.

———. *The Mammoth Hunters.* New York: Bantam Books [Random House], 1985.

———. *The Plains of Passage.* New York: Bantam Books [Random House], 1990.

———. *The Shelters of Stone.* New York: Bantam Books [Random House], 2002.

Geraldine Cannon Becker

B

Bach, Richard (1936–)

Richard Bach considers all his books nonfiction in a sense, including the novels. Whether their plot focuses on events from his own life, or those of seagulls or ferrets, each records an intensely personal search for life's meaning. His enthusiasts consider him a sage, while his detractors assign little value to this often overt philosophical dimension in his work. However he be esteemed, his animal stories are well rooted in the tradition of narrative anthropomorphism, reflecting and indirectly questioning the human condition, dating as far back as Aesop and continuing through *Animal Farm* and *Watership Down.*

Bach was born in 1936 in Oak Park, Illinois, to Ruth and Robert Bach, a Protestant minister, and his life was transformed at 17 when he learned to fly, a skill he has avidly practiced ever since. He married Bette Jeanne Franks, his high school sweetheart, when he was 21 and pursued a variety of jobs (mail carrier, jewelry salesman, barnstormer, Douglas Aircraft employee, etc.), none lasting for as long as a year. He also served stints in the Iowa Air Guard and the U.S. Air Force, from 1956 to 1959 and 1961 to 1962, respectively.

Bach spent one year in college (1955, at Long Beach State) and later tried unsuccessfully to support himself as a freelance aviation writer. Between 1961 and 1964 he worked as associate editor, editor, and then West Coast editor of *Flying.* However, between 1965 and 1970 he was back working as an aviation mechanic, charter pilot, flight instructor, and barnstormer in Iowa and the Midwest. During this time he published memoirs of his career as a pilot that achieved modest sales: *Strangers to the Ground* (1963), *Biplane* (1966), and *Nothing by Chance: A Gypsy Pilot's Adventures in Modern America* (1969).

In 1967, now with a wife and six children and in the midst of one of his financial crises—indeed, shortly after the family car was repossessed—Bach had a vision, which had first appeared to him in 1959 at the age of 23. In it a bodiless voice says, "Jonathan Livingston Seagull." Prompted by the reappearance of this vision, Bach completed the manuscript he had begun in 1959, then began a three-year search for a publisher. During this time he became estranged from his family, and he and his wife divorced in 1970. Not long afterward, however, an editor at Macmillan, Eleanor Freide, persuaded the firm to publish the book *Jonathan Livingston Seagull,* and despite a small print run and modest advertising budget, a limited number of reviews, and reviewers' often tepid reactions, sales took off. The first edition went through 29 printings, and the book had sold over 1.8 million copies by the end of 1972. Still in print, it has been translated into 30 languages and has sold more than 30 million copies.

The main character, the eponymous seagull, devotes himself to perfecting flying as an end in itself, rather than solely as a means of obtaining food, eventually experiencing transcendent states in which he escapes the boundaries of time and space. All of this leads the other seagulls to ostracize him, but instead of focusing, then, on his own transcendence he returns to the flock to teach any who will listen. His story, told in only 10,000 words, is accompanied by Russell Munson's seagull photographs.

The book appeared when counterculture movements were common, many emphasizing personal and social transformation through self-transcending mystical states, rather than social engagement. It is not surprising, then, that Bach's work achieved such popularity, despite the negative reaction of mainstream critics, which ranged from dismissive to openly hostile, often expressing distaste for a lack of intellectual content that left readers to assign whatever meaning they wanted. In 1973 Paramount Pictures released a film version with the same title, directed by Hall Bartlett.

Bach's royalties immediately transformed his life. He made large gifts of money to his children and ex-wife, started collecting airplanes, and began traveling the world in an expensive, amphibious live-in aircraft named *Widgeon*. However, unwise investments and more than a million dollars in back taxes forced another dramatic change in lifestyle, and by 1976 he and his companion, actress Leslie Parrish, were living on the road in a 45-foot trailer in remote regions of Arizona, Nevada, and Oregon. As part of his bankruptcy proceedings in 1981, he ceded rights to the royalties of all of his books. However, after he and Parrish got married later that year, she began liquidating her own assets and purchasing his copyrights from the government. And by 1991 the royalty income enabled the couple to support a lifestyle that included residing in a gated estate outside Seattle.

Through it all Bach continued to write and publish. His *Gift of Wings* (1974) collects 46 essays, most relating to aviation. In *Illusions: The Adventures of a Reluctant Messiah* (1977) and *There's No Such Place as Far Away* (1979), he returns to themes concerning the meaning of life and personal fulfillment, through plots involving a fictional messiah. His search for a soul mate is the focus of *The Bridge across Forever: A Lovestory* (1984). He followed this work with a best-selling novel, ONE (1988), in which fictional versions of himself and his wife realize they are time-traveling while on a car trip and discover how their past decisions have affected themselves and others, while at the same time achieving an awareness of the oneness of humanity. *Running from Safety: An Adventure of the Spirit* (1994) consists of an internal dialogue between Bach and his inner child (nine-year-old "Dickie"). He returns to themes of time disjunctions in *Out of My Mind: The Discovery of Saunders-Vixen* (1999), in which the airplane company Saunders-Vixen exists in a parallel universe, a 1920s Britain in which World War I did not happen. More recently Bach has returned to publishing animal parables in a series of books called The Ferret Chronicles, in which ferrets abandon their own utopia to aid the human race.

Bibliography

Bach, Richard. *Strangers to the Ground.* Introduction by Gill Robb. New York: Wilson/Harper, 1963. Reprint, New York: Harper, 1972. Reprint, New York: Macmillan, 1983.

———. *Biplane.* Prelude by Ray Bradbury. New York: Harper, 1966. Reprint with photography by Paul E. Hansen and Bach. New York: Macmillan, 1983.

———. *Nothing by Chance: A Gypsy Pilot's Adventures in Modern America.* Photographs by Paul E. Hansen. New York: Morrow, 1969. Reprint, New York: Macmillan, 1983.

———. *Jonathan Livingston Seagull.* Photographs by Russell Munson. New York: Macmillan, 1970.

———. *A Gift of Wings.* Illustrations by K. O. Eckland. New York: Delacorte, 1974.

———. *Illusions: The Adventures of a Reluctant Messiah.* New York: Delacorte, 1977.

———. *There's No Such Place as Far Away.* Illustrations by Ronald Wegen. New York: Delacorte/Friede, 1979.

———. *The Bridge across Forever: A Lovestory.* New York: Morrow, 1984.

———. *One.* New York: Morrow, 1988.

———. *Running from Safety: An Adventure of the Spirit.* New York. Morrow, 1994.

———. *Out of My Mind: The Discovery of Saunders-Vixen.* Illustrations by K. O. Eckland. New York: Morrow, 1999.

———. *Air Ferrets Aloft.* New York: Scribner, 2002.

———. *Rescue Ferrets at Sea.* New York: Scribner, 2002.

———. *Writer Ferrets: Chasing the Muse.* New York: Scribner, 2002.

———. *Flying: The Aviation Trilogy.* New York: Scribner Classics, 2003.

———. *The Last War: Detective Ferrets and the Case of the Golden Deed.* New York: Scribner, 2003.

———. *Rancher Ferrets on the Range.* New York: Scribner, 2003.

———. *Messiah's Handbook: Reminders for the Advanced Soul.* Charlottesville, Va.: Hampton Road, 2004.

———. *Curious Lives: Adventures from "The Ferret Chronicles."* Charlottesville, Va.: Hampton Road, 2005.

James Kaser

Baldacci, David (1960–)

David Baldacci has been publishing novels since 1996, 14 in all, 12 of them *New York Times* best sellers. Though he has a wide range, even having recently commenced publishing children's books, Baldacci is best known for novels of suspense that explore the theme of the slipperiness of "the truth." He is clearly comfortable writing about the intricacies and intrigues of the D.C. scene, and his protagonists are often "little guys" uncovering scandals of epic proportions (especially involving government corruption), who must struggle to maintain dignity and honor—and to stay alive. The preoccupation with terrorism and national security since 9/11 has provided additional levels of suspense in his more recent novels.

Baldacci was born in Virginia, where he lives today, and his native state, from the farms and foothills of the rural regions to the D.C. suburbs of northern Virginia, is the setting of many of his novels. He studied political science as an undergraduate at Virginia Commonwealth University and received a law degree from the University of Virginia. He practiced trial and corporate law in Washington, D.C., for nine years before turning to writing full time.

In his first novel, *ABSOLUTE POWER* (1996), which quickly became a best seller and was made into a film (directed by Clint Eastwood) a year after its release, Baldacci takes on the formidable task of drawing a fictional U.S. president embroiled in the sleaziest of scandals. It established Baldacci as a writer capable of sustaining high suspense while developing characters who are flawed and believable. In particular, the modest character of Luther Whitney becomes a prototype for several heroes of later novels: people from the wrong side of the tracks, imperfect and even criminal, but ultimately honorable, who witness the sins of the elite and powerful and become involved in larger-than-life dramas. Baldacci's typical subjects—the FBI, hostage rescue teams, the Secret Service, the Supreme Court, the presidency, witness protection programs—lend themselves to gripping suspense, but the plots involving them are always tempered by quieter dramas of romance, and familial love, and conflict. His work thus crosses the boundaries of espionage, legal, and government thrillers, inhabiting a fictional space somewhere between TOM CLANCY and JOHN GRISHAM.

Baldacci does meticulous research to give the scandals and the characters who perpetrate and expose them as much verisimilitude as possible. Because of his experience in the D.C. legal scene, he is also able to get information from sources inside even such enclaves as the Supreme Court. As he said in a 2006 Time Warner Bookmark interview:

> When I research I become a journalist. I do much research from books and written materials, but the best kind of research is person-to-person. . . . You need to interview the people doing the job to see how it's really done. That's where you get the little details, the nuances that make a story fascinating, interesting to read, and appear more realistic.

As a result of this kind of painstaking research, Baldacci is able to provide extraordinary detail when writing about the usually dangerous work his characters do for a living.

In addition to his writing career, Baldacci is an active philanthropist. He and his wife founded the Wish You Well Foundation, which is devoted to encouraging literacy in the United States.

Bibliography

Baldacci, David. *Absolute Power.* New York: Warner Books, 1996.

Rose Shapiro

Barker, Clive (1952–)

Novelist, short story writer, illustrator, playwright, and scriptwriter, Clive Barker may be best known of late as the screenwriter and director of the horror standard *Hellraiser,* which he adapted from his own novella *The Hellbound Heart* (1986), but he is equally famous for the short stories in the six volumes of *The Books of Blood* (1984), with their characteristic and inimitable mix of chilling horror and compelling fantasy. He has also written a children's book, *The Thief of Always* (1992), the urban fantasy *Weaveworld* (1987), and the Hollywood noir ghost story *Coldheart Canyon* (2001). A host of his works have been adapted for film (some with Barker's involvement), most notably *Nightbreed* (from the novel *Cabal*) and *Candyman* (from the short story "The Forbidden"), while others have been adapted into graphic novel form.

Barker was born in Liverpool, England, and grew up a just few streets away from Penny Lane (he claimed that he and his brother were not even aware of this as Beatles fans were always stealing the road sign), attending Quarry Bank High School, John Lennon's old school. From an early age, Barker's eclecticism was evident in his avid interest in art and writing, as well as his love of fairy tales, comic books, and the entire oeuvre of Edgar Allan Poe. A visit by British horror writer Ramsey Campbell to Quarry Bank impressed Barker greatly: "He was very downbeat and I thought 'Oh my gosh, people actually do this as a profession!'" By the time he started at the University of Liverpool, he had already published a magazine at Quarry Bank and taken the lead in writing and directing plays. At the University of Liverpool he continued his involvement in theater and art while studying English and philosophy, and after university he worked with various theater groups in Liverpool and London before embarking on the short stories that became *The Books of Blood.*

Their publication was keenly anticipated, as luminaries such as STEPHEN KING, Peter Straub, and Ramsey Campbell had all spoken highly of them and their author—King going so far as to state: "I have seen the future of horror, and it is Clive Barker." The stories in the six collections were striking for the extremity of their visual imagination and their refusal to moralize, many of them almost resembling fairy tales brought to surreal life. "In the Hills, The Cities," for example, evokes the image of two giants in mortal combat, giants literally composed of the populations of rival towns who have fought in this way from time immemorial. "The Midnight Meat Train" imagines the city fathers of New York as literal monsters requiring the bodies of commuters as tribute. Such intense and visceral evocations earned the tales the epithet *splatterpunk* from one critic; however, several of the stories also subtly stress the transformative power of the artistic imagination itself, a theme that would emerge more explicitly in Barker's later works.

The Damnation Game, Barker's first novel, was published in 1985, and reworks the Faust myth, telling the story of an immortal gambler who seeks to pass on his secret to a willing victim. The novel elaborated many of the themes and techniques found in *The Books of Blood,* such as the appearance of fantastical and horrific elements in a hitherto familiar urban setting (London and postwar Warsaw), but also explores the fragility of the human body, the permeable boundaries between life and death (shown in the grotesque yet matter-of-fact depiction of zombie killers and dogs who drop decaying bits at every appearance), and the conflict between imagination and the void. Nihilism, not forbidden knowledge, is the true evil in Barker's retelling of Faust.

In 1987 Barker directed *Hellraiser,* based on his *The Hellbound Heart,* and both film and novella are cautionary tales, warning of the dangers of getting what one wished for, in this case a life of sensations unknown to mere humans; both display the same flamboyant visual imagination. Yet again the Faustian myth is at work: Frank, the central character, gives up everything to experience a life of sheer sensation and is offered and well schooled in it by the monstrous Cenobites. In the end, like Faust, Frank attempts to escape their hell, but like Faust he is unsuccessful. "Pinhead," the chief Cenobite, became a horror icon, assuming a yet more prominent role in the numerous sequels.

Barker's focus since *Hellraiser* has shifted more toward the fantastic while still inscribing elements of the horrific. *Weaveworld* is an urban fantasy novel written, Barker claims, in reaction to the more pastoral and nostalgic fantasies of Tolkien and C. S. Lewis. It opens in a grimy, run-down section of Liverpool and depicts an alternative world, the Fugue, contained in an elaborate carpet. As Barker cleverly demonstrates over the course of the novel, "the Fugue" is literally composed of stories and figures of the imagination and thus can be remade over and over again; characters may die, but their world renews itself forever. In succeeding novels such as *The Great and Secret Show, Everville,* and *Coldheart Canyon,* this theme constantly recurs, augmented by stories and myths derived from Hollywood, contemporary media, and the forgotten history of the West.

Though famous for such outlandish conceits, for his spectacular plots (which in later novels tend toward the epic), and his belief in the transforming and healing power of the imagination, Barker is also notable for his use of strong female characters. Typical among them is Tesla Bombeck, one of the protagonists in *The Great and Secret Show* and *Everville.* A Hollywood screenwriter, she enters the world of "the Art" and is transformed by her encounters with it, becoming at last a kind of secular shaman, able to manipulate myth and matter to keep the world of the Art alive. *The Art* is Barker's term for a type of transformative magic, integrating myth, sexuality, and imagination; and we use such art, Barker once claimed, as "windows through which to glimpse the miraculous" (Jones 354).

Barker's influence as writer and filmmaker is ubiquitous; evident, for example, in the mix of graphic horror and mundane setting in Peter Jackson's film *Braindead* (as well as his later true crime/fantasy film *Heavenly Creature*), or Danny Boyle and Alex Garland's *28 Days Later.* Such influence stems in part from the way his work never evokes its lurid violence and horror merely to shock but reminds the reader of essential, if often latent, features of the human condition itself. Evil and terror may be prominent in Barker's universe, but he offers his characters and readers alike the means to subvert if not defeat them by the power of myth and imagination.

Bibliography

Barker, Clive. *The Books of Blood.* Vol. 1–3. 1984. New York: Time Warner Books, 2006.

———. *The Books of Blood.* Vol. 4–6. London: Sphere Books, 1984.

———. *The Damnation Game.* 1985. London: Sphere Books, 1986.

———. *The Hellbound Heart.* 1986. New York: HarperPaperbacks, 1991.

———. *Weaveworld.* 1987. New York: Pocket Books, 1988.

———. *The Great and Secret Show.* 1989. New York: HarperPaperbacks, 1990.

———. *The Thief of Always.* 1992. New York: HarperPaperbacks, 1993.

———. *Everville.* 1994. New York: HarperPaperbacks, 1995.

———. *Coldheart Canyon.* 2001. New York: HarperPaperbacks, 2002.

Jones, Stephen, ed. *Clive Barker's Shadows in Eden.* Lancaster, U.K.: Underwood-Miller, 1991.

Alice Palumbo

Be Cool Elmore Leonard (1999)

Be Cool (1999) is the sequel to Elmore Leonard's hugely successful 1990 novel GET SHORTY and follows the continued adventures of Ernest "Chili" Palmer, ex-mobster and loan shark, who became a successful film producer in the first novel but here becomes disillusioned with the film industry after the sequel he made to his original film has flopped.

Chili has a unique approach to developing ideas for films, using the people, places, and events in his own unfolding life; and the tale is populated with a large cast of lively and offbeat characters. When one of Chili's old friends, Tommy Athens, the owner of Nothing To Lose records, is murdered (Chili himself narrowly escaping), the record company passes to Tommy's widow, the attractive Edie, who enlists Chili to help her run it. Coincidentally, Chili's new idea for a film also centers on the music industry, focusing on a young, beautiful, and talented rock singer he has met, Linda Moon. Without a pause he decides to become her manager and see what the music business is like.

Linda likes Chili and believes his uncompromising and unorthodox talents can make her a star; but the matter is complicated by her already having a manager, Raji, an aggressive small-time hood who has placed her in an inferior band, wasting her talent doing cover versions of the Spice Girls. Raji often behaves more like a pimp than a manager, complete with a huge and inseparable Samoan bodyguard, homosexual actor Elliot Wilhelm. When Chili informs Raji that he is replacing him as Linda's representation, the latter sets out for unbusinesslike revenge; at the same time, the Russian Mafia, responsible for Tommy Athens's death, learns that Chili was a witness to the killing and makes plans to have him silenced. However, Chili thrives on such complications, in part because they make such excellent material for his screenplay, which he discusses with the studio executive Elaine Levin as their professional relationship develops into a love affair.

As in all of Leonard books, the characters are just as if not more important than the action itself. "The thing people forget," he notes, "is that I've been trying to do something new and different in my books. My characters are what the books are about: the plot just kind of comes along" (Leonard, 2004).

Yet the plot of *Be Cool* is as intricate and elaborate as any reader could desire, as Chili first outsmarts Raji by promising his bodyguard Elliott a role in a future film and turning him against his homophobic master, while at the same time assisting a police officer in the search for the killers of Tommy Athens. Through it all he confronts with characteristic verve the harsh and cynical realities of the music business, as he had previously done of film, particularly how difficult it is to retain one's artistic integrity in the face of an increasingly commercialized, corporate-driven environment. Finally he realizes that the only way to make Linda a star, despite her abilities, is to entirely compromise her talent and sell out. The climax of the book sees all the narrative strands united, while in addition Linda learns of Chili's betrayal and leaves him to join a more reputable agent. Undeterred, Chili deploys his experiences in the screenplay for his new film, which this time he is sure will be a blockbuster. The book concludes, as does *Get Shorty,* with the hero musing not on the nature of endings but of sequels and how difficult they are to write.

While arguably not one of his strongest works, *Be Cool* is an entertaining mix of Leonard's trademark idiosyncratic characters and memorable situations, while Chili Palmer remains an iconic creation, embodying the sort of wit, intelligence, and self-assurance in all manner of danger that makes for a charismatic and attractive protagonist. Like its predecessor the novel draws a host of unflattering comparisons between the music business and organized crime, with the skills of a gangster seeming effortlessly transferable to the music industry, and with a host of characters occupying both worlds with relative ease. The book lacks something of the satirical edge of *Get Shorty,* owing partly perhaps to Leonard's lack of insider knowledge of the music industry (he spent decades, on the other hand, as a Hollywood writer), and partly to his advancing age (he was in his mid-70s when the book was released). However, the thematic motif of sequels is mined for a number of amusing asides, with Leonard very much aware that he is writing a sequel to a best-selling book, and with Chili himself in a similar situation, the latter having once already made a failed sequel and searching for a second score. Moreover, Leonard is conscious that he is not only following up the narrative of *Get Shorty* but also the hugely successful film.

Be Cool was itself made into a film in 2005, directed by F. Gary Gray, but unlike the film *Get Shorty,* which stayed close to the original text, the sequel makes substantial changes to the narrative, with Linda Moon, for example, becoming a young black singer (played by Christina Milan), and her music pop instead of rock. John Travolta reprises his role as Chili in the film, but the character of Edie is greatly expanded, reuniting Travolta with his *Pulp Fiction* costar Uma Thurman.

Bibliography

Be Cool. Directed by F. Gary Gray. Metro-Goldwyn-Mayer Pictures, 2005.

Get Shorty. Directed by Barry Sonnenfeld. Metro-Goldwyn-Mayer Pictures, 1995.

The Italian Job. Directed by F. Gary Gray. Warner Bros. Pictures, 2003.

Leonard, Elmore. *Get Shorty.* London: Penguin, 1991.

———. *Be Cool.* London: Penguin, 2000.

———. "Detroit Spinner: An Interview with Elmore Leonard." *The Guardian,* 31 July 2004.

The Negotiator. Directed by F. Gary Gray. Paramount Pictures, 1998.

Pulp Fiction. Directed by Quentin Tarantino. Miramax Films, 1994.

Terence McSweeney and Olga Lopatnikova

Benchley, Peter (Peter Bradford Benchley)
(1940–2006)

Benchley is the author of several successful novels evoking the nightmarish, but often mesmerizing terrors of the sea, including *Jaws, The Deep,* and *The Island.* He was born in New York City; his father was the novelist Nathaniel Benchley and his grandfather the humorist Robert Benchley. After graduating from Harvard, Benchley worked as a reporter for the *Washington Post,* then as an editor at *Newsweek* and a speechwriter in the White House for President Lyndon B. Johnson, only later becoming a freelance writer.

Benchley's first novel, *Jaws* (1974), is centered in the fictional coastal town of Amity, Long Island, a summer resort terrorized by a great white shark. Although he had been interested in sharks since his childhood days, Benchley was inspired by an item in the *New York Daily News* about a fisherman who caught a 4,550-pound great white shark off Long Island's Montauk Point in 1964. In *Jaws* the three major characters who ultimately confront the shark are the town's police chief Brody, marine Biologist Hooper, and fisherman and World War II veteran Quint. Also featuring a mayor (Murray Hamilton) who attempts to cover up the dangers of the underwater enemy, *Jaws* resonated for audiences in the 1970s with echoes of the Watergate scandal and met with a stunning reception, remaining on the *New York Times* best-seller list for 44 weeks. It became a publishing phenomenon, rivaling in fame if not quality America's other great marine saga, Herman Melville's *Moby-Dick* (1851) about the search for another monstrous sea creature, a great white whale. More than 20 million copies of *Jaws* were sold, and in 1975 the novel was adapted to film, with screenplay by Benchley and directed by Stephen Spielberg; the film, too, was an instant blockbuster, going on to win three Oscars at the 1976 Academy Awards.

The Deep (1976), Benchley's second novel, is the story of a couple diving in Bermuda who discover sunken treasures and are subsequently targeted by a drug syndicate. *The Island* (1979) posits the intriguing possibility that the descendants of 17th-century buccaneers are responsible for the disappearance of ships in the Bermuda Triangle area. Both were adapted into screenplays (cowritten by Benchley) in 1977 and 1980, respectively, although they failed, unsurprisingly, to meet with the success of *Jaws*. *Girl of the Sea of Cortez* (1982) is Benchley's most critically acclaimed work. It is a fable—with environmental overtones that anticipate the author's future work in oceanic conservation—about a 14-year-old girl who discovers an enchanted underwater world. Benchley's other novels include: *Q Clearance* (1986), *Rummies* (1989), *Beast* (1991), *White Shark* (1994), and *Peter Benchley's Creature* (1997).

In his later years Benchley wrote, narrated, and appeared in a series of television documentaries about marine wildlife. An ardent ocean conservationist, he also served on the national council of Environmental Defense and became a spokesperson for the plight of sharks. Benchley died at the age of 65 from pulmonary fibrosis (progressive scarring of the lungs) at his home in Princeton, New Jersey.

Bibliography

Benchley, Peter. *The Deep.* London: Pan Macmillan, 1977.

———. *The Island.* London: Pan Macmillan, 1980.

———. *Girl of the Sea of Cortez.* London: Corgi Books, 1983.

———. *Jaws.* London: Pan Macmillan, 2004.

———. *Shark Trouble: True Stories about Sharks and the Sea.* London: Random House, 2003.

———. *Shark Life: True Stories about Sharks and the Sea.* Adapted by Karen Wojtyla. London: Random House, 2005.

Quirke, Antonia. *Jaws.* London: British Film Institute, 2002.

Victoria E. Price

***The Big Bad Wolf* James Patterson** (2003)
The Big Bad Wolf, one of JAMES PATTERSON's best-selling Alex Cross novels, introduces its arch-villain the "Wolf" by reputation, commencing with a putative account of his practice of "zamochit," the Russian ritual of breaking every bone in a victim's body, on an East Coast mob boss. The crime has attained near legendary status, but not because of its horrific cruelty; the Wolf carried out this particular crime in a high-security super-max prison and still managed to evade capture.

The crimes that follow, which serve as the central focus of the narrative, are not as sensational but are no less disturbing for their everyday nature. A woman, for instance, is abducted from a local shopping mall. While her status as the wife of a judge initially draws the FBI into the case, the victim is otherwise a typical homemaker, whose greatest concern on the morning of her kidnapping is how to get her other two daughters to a swimming lesson and dentist appointment after her youngest daughter's birthday party that afternoon (the kidnappers even refer to her by the code name "Mom"). But from this single crime, one which could seemingly happen to anyone, anywhere, a nationwide pattern emerges, in which similar women have gone missing in similar circumstances. Thus, the "White Girl" case is opened, and Alex Cross, Patterson's trademark protagonist, freshly inducted into the FBI, is assigned to the task force investigating it.

Cross's freshman status in the bureau provides him with almost as many obstacles as the criminals themselves in his attempt to discover who is behind what turns out to be a white slavery ring, a ring with price tags on potential victims—from $3,500 to $150,000—listed in a catalog:

> The brochure was printed on 8½-by-11-inch glossy paper bound in a clear report cover with a red spine. . . . The colors were electric. The cover looked perfect. The elegance was weird, actually, as if the Wolf were looking at a Tiffany's catalog (95).

It appears to Cross's immediate superiors that the new recruit from the Washington P.D. is receiving special treatment from those higher up in the bureau, and he must pass repeated tests while attempting to catch the Wolf before he takes another victim. Some are brutally plain, as when Cross is trapped in a classroom while the Wolf roams free; others and more subtle, as when he is taken off the White Girl case and sent to Baltimore to try to bring a suicidal cop and his hostages out alive, at the very moment of a second kidnapping—and this one with a witness.

But even when finally allowed by the bureau to turn his full attention to the case, Cross's task is far from easy. First, his reputation and career are threatened when the story hits the press with details only an insider would know, and he is suspected of the leak. When details of yet another victim are posted on an online chatroom, Cross is pulled off the case altogether. But then a 14-year-old girl hacks into the "Den," a Web site run by the Wolf where victims are chosen and bid upon via online auction. When the teenage computer prodigy finally reports her discovery to the authorities, it is passed off as a crank. Only Cross and his partner recognize its relevance to the case, and with this Cross is brought back on. But now the Wolf issues new threats, directed at the agent himself and his family, and here the novel strikes the deepest thematic chord in Patterson's series: the role and significance of family.

Cross is a devoted father to Jannie, Damon, and Little Alex, and Patterson creates a rich and convincing home life for his detective. Like any average family, the Crosses go to the park or to the movies, watch sports on television and root for their favorite teams. Cross's own references to popular culture and current events increase the reader's sense of familiarity, as well as adding realism to the novel. Much of his uncommon strength of character comes from Nana Mama, his grandmother, who lives with the family, and at 82 still insists on climbing a ladder and cleaning the gutters herself. She is also one of the main sources of Cross's emotional support; always loving, always frank, as in her insistence on his needing a woman in his life, a need Cross himself recognizes but can do little to address given the consuming demands of his work and home.

In the middle of the White Girl investigation, a woman from Cross's past returns. But Christine Johnson is not in the capital to resume her role in his life. Instead, Little Alex's mother wants sole custody of the boy and threatens to take him with her to Seattle, where she now lives. Devoted to his son and wanting to do what is best for him, Cross is devastated at the thought of losing him—yet another test he must overcome in his efforts to capture the Wolf.

Characteristically, Patterson's villain is drawn with the same care and nuance as his protagonist. The Wolf is a "modern-day godfather" (60), one who fixes professional sporting events, for example, not for financial gain but to delight his seven-year-old son. He has been KGB and Red Mafiya but is now independent, equally invisible to those who uphold the law and those who break it, with his wealth and charm making for easy movement in celebrity circles under assumed names. His real identity is unknown, but he is respected and feared by all. Chess is one of his passions, and his crimes are played out like a championship match in which his skill is pitted against multiple opponents, and checkmate is death.

It is against criminals like the Wolf that Cross's Ph.D. in psychology is such an asset, and the books in the series gain a greater depth of characterization from his own frequent insights into human nature, both good and evil. But the weapon is double-edged. As Cross's new partner in the bureau puts it:

> Do you know what they say about you, Dr. Cross? That you're close to psychic. Very imaginative. Maybe even gifted. You can think like a killer (101).

Moreover, as Patterson employs the alternating narrative voices characteristic of the Cross series as a whole, the reader is allowed to enter the criminals' minds as well as that of Cross, which, while deepening the sense of character and adding layers of contrast and irony to the tale, in no way diminishes from its suspense. Indeed, the novelist's deft handling of movement within and without, of thought and action, and the reader's efforts to make sense of each, only add to the pleasure.

Bibliography

Patterson, James. *The Big Bad Wolf.* New York: Little, Brown, 2003.

Susan Lynne Beckwith

Binchy, Maeve (1940–)

Maeve Binchy is a prolific author and journalist whose works include short stories, plays, screenplays, novels, and nonfiction, usually centering on the struggles of women in dealing with everyday issues in modern Ireland, such as marriage, divorce, family, and friendship.

Binchy was born in Dalkey, Ireland, about 10 miles from Dublin, and her homeland often serves as a backdrop for her works, for she considers Ireland ". . . a treasure trove on my doorstep" (*Books* 4). Her childhood was a happy one, with a supportive mother, father, and three younger siblings. After schooling at Holy Child Convent in Killiney, County Dublin, Binchy earned a degree in history at University College Dublin in 1960 and began her working life as a teacher of history and Latin at a Catholic school before moving to a Jewish school at which she was a French teacher. The parents of the Jewish school's students were so appreciative of Binchy's teaching that they paid for and sent her on a trip to Israel, from which she sent letters home detailing her travel experiences. Her father typed up these letters and sent them to the *Irish Times* in 1963, and one, a letter about a kibbutz in Israel, launched Binchy's writing career, as its publication by the paper led to a regular column for the author. She continued for a while to teach and maintain the column but gave up teaching in 1968 to devote herself to writing full time, moving from Ireland to London and writing twice-weekly columns about life in that city, some of which were worked into her first major publication, aptly named *My First Book,* in 1970. While in London, she met Gordon Snell, a BBC broadcaster and writer, and they married in 1977, eventually returning to Dalkey, where both continue to live and write. In fact, the couple shares an office in their home, which is close to Binchy's childhood home, and they are in frequent contact with her siblings living nearby.

While her books consistently outsell those of Irish icons Joyce and Yeats, Binchy makes no claims to literary greatness, aware that her strengths are as a popular storyteller. Nonetheless, her works have been translated into 12 languages, and she attributes her popularity to their universal themes, such as love, family, friendship, and betrayal. Lunching once with former first lady and Binchy fan Barbara Bush, she was told, "... you've managed to write about all the vulnerabilities and the innocence of what we had when we were young" (Burns 24).

During her time as a newspaper columnist, Binchy wrote not only about London, but also, deeply and sensitively about the plight of women, especially Irish women constrained by the Catholic Church's stance on abortion and divorce, a concern reflected in her fictional work as well. And while her novels are notable for their humor and warmth, they never shy away from confronting controversial issues such as adultery, divorce, and substance abuse.

Binchy's first novel, *Light a Penny Candle* (1982), chronicles the complex friendship between the English Elizabeth White and the Irish Aisling O'Connor. Sent to Ireland during World War II to escape the bombing, Elizabeth lives with the O'Connors and, while eventually returning to England, keeps in contact with Aisling, the novel exploring the development of their relationship over the next three decades.

Binchy sets most of her novels, such as *Light a Penny Candle* and *Echoes,* in the 1950s and 1960s, a time in Irish history when lack of employment forced many to leave the small towns of their birth and upbringing. *The Lilac Bus,* for example, follows the lives of a set of young people who leave their childhood towns to live and work in Dublin during the week but return home on the weekends; *Circle of Friends* similarly details the friendship of Benny (Bernadette) and Eve as they leave their village to attend university in Dublin; the young in all such works having to negotiate a hybrid existence between the country and city, small and great, old and new. Typical also of a Binchy tale, are major disruptions that have protagonists feeling at sea, eventually forcing them to reevaluate their lives and take control. The heroines of *Evening Class* and *TARA ROAD,* for example, each disappointed and deserted by men, confront and overcome these challenges with courage and humor. Friendship, especially between unlike characters, is also a major theme in her works, as is family and what may constitute such.

To the dismay of fans worldwide Binchy announced her retirement from writing with the novel *Scarlet Feather* in 2000. But in 2002 she was back with *Quentins,* a fictional history of the restaurant featured in some of her previous novels. She has since published two more novels, *Nights of Stars and Rain* and her latest, *Whitethorn Woods.*

A number of her works have been adapted for television and film; among them, *Echoes,* a novel set at an Irish seaside resort, was made into a four-part miniseries for British television, while *The Lilac Bus* was turned into a 90-minute television film. *Tara Road,* a small independent film, has recently been released on DVD in Ireland. The most successful and well-known adaptation of a Binchy work is the major motion picture version of *Circle of Friends* starring Minnie Driver. While she has written dramas and even a screenplay, for which she won an award, Binchy has not adapted any of her own works for the screen.

In addition to her regular writing projects, Maeve Binchy also maintains a Web site, on which she posts short stories and notes to her fans.

Bibliography

Binchy, Maeve. *Light a Penny Candle.* New York: Random House, 1985.

———. *Echoes.* New York: Viking Adult, 1986.

———. *Firefly Summer.* New York: Delacorte Press, 1988.

———. *Silver Wedding.* New York: Delacorte Press, 1989.

———. *Circle of Friends.* New York: Delacorte Press, 1991.

———. *The Lilac Bus.* New York: Delacorte Press, 1991.

———. *The Copper Beech.* New York: Delacorte Press, 1992.

———. "Gold at the Rainbow's End." *Books* 7, no. 4 (July 1993): 4.

———. *The Glass Lake.* New York: Delacorte Press, 1995.

———. *Evening Class.* New York: Delacorte Press, 1997.

———. *Tara Road.* New York: Delacorte Press, 1999.

———. *Scarlet Feather.* New York: Dutton Adult, 2001.

———. *Quentins.* New York: Dutton Adult, 2002.

———. *Nights of Rain and Stars.* New York: Dutton Adult, 2004.
———. *Whitethorn Woods.* New York: Knopf, 2007.
———. maevebinchy.com.
Burns, Mike. *Europe* 345 (April 1995): 22–25.

Karen Bell

Black Order James Rollins (2006)

Black Order is a science-fiction adventure novel featuring Painter Crowe and Grayson Pierce, the Sigma Force operatives first introduced in *Map of Bones* (2005). Sigma Force is an elite special operatives team for the U.S. Department of Defense. The story begins with several seemingly unconnected investigations: a mysterious plague in a Himalayan monastery that results in madness and death, the sale of Charles Darwin's Bible in Denmark, and the tales of a mythological beast that is preying on living beings in South Africa. Rollins seamlessly interweaves these stories and incorporates them into a far-reaching discussion of evolution, intelligent design, genetic experimentation, and quantum physics.

The three story lines all tie into a conspiracy that began at the end of World War II when a Nazi officer, Jakob Sporrenberg, led a military operation to protect a secret project from Russian forces advancing into Breslau, Poland. Rumors of the existence of a hidden lab and a device called the Bell in the Wenceslas Mine began with the villagers reporting torturous screams coming from the lab, along with a mysterious illness that had afflicted those outside the complex. Sanctioned by Heinrich Himmler himself, research evidence was destroyed, and 62 scientists were killed, including the project's lead scientist, Hugo Hirzfeld.

In the present day Painter Crowe discovers that the Bell is being used again at a hidden castle in the Himalayan Mountains. Jakob's granddaughter, Anna Sporrenberg, and other Nazi descendants are trying to continue the project's research, but a series of accidents has spotlighted the covert operation that had been undetected for generations. Painter, while at the village near the monastery, is exposed to the Bell's effects when strange lights appear up in the mountains during the night. Since he was farther away from the site than the monastery, his debilitation is slower, but the diagnosis is still the same as the monks'. He finds that the accident was actually an act of sabotage that destroyed the Bell and exposed the scientists to its effects. They now share the same diagnosis as Painter and the monks. So, "Sigma and the Nazis together" (170) must cooperate to search for a cure.

Painter struggles with the need to cooperate with a detested enemy. Although Anna and the scientists proclaim they are no longer Nazis and want to open their research to the scientific community, they still retain their arrogance and interest in changing the world with their evolutionary experiments. To Painter's disgust they calmly talk about the atrocious human studies they had conducted. Anna notes that they stopped using humans and continued their experiments with DNA testing: "But mostly, we've declined human studies because our interests over the last decade have turned more clinical. We don't see ourselves as harbingers of a new master race. We are indeed no longer Nazis. We believe our work can benefit mankind as a whole, once perfected" (194). But some elements of Nazi philosophy appear to have survived, as she underscores their plan to prevent their research from being "bound by the laws of nations and the ignorant. . . . Science is not a democratic process. Such arbitrary restraints of morality would only slow our progress tenfold. That is not acceptable" (194).

Meanwhile, Grayson Pierce is in Europe investigating a series of black market trades, all pertaining to historical documents that once belonged to Victorian-era scientists. The latest item, the Bible of Charles Darwin, was once owned by Hugo Hirzfeld and is now in the possession of a teenage girl. Grayson and the girl become the target of assassins who want access to the notes and symbols written in the Bible's margins.

Grayson and Painter's investigations at last come together in South Africa, where sightings of a legendary monster are reported near a private estate owned by the Waalenberg family, a well-established dynasty that was a major financial backer of a Nazi research group led by Himmler. There they discover parallel genetic research occurring, aimed at a more sinister result.

The novel speculates on the Nazi quest to create a super race and on what might have happened to related projects after the fall of the Third Reich. In his accompanying notes Rollins provides additional historical information, among which is a description of Nazi attempts to hide or destroy their research and secret labs before Allied forces found them. There is, in fact, evidence of a project at a hidden lab in a mine outside Breslau that was code-named *die Glocke,* or "the Bell," and nearby villagers had indeed reported strange lights and mysterious illnesses and deaths. But when Russian forces reached the mine, they found it deserted, and 62 scientists had been shot. No device was claimed to have been found.

One of the premises of the book is that while the Americans based their atomic bomb research on Einstein's theory of relativity, the Nazis had dismissed his theories because he was Jewish and searched instead for a new energy source based on the quantum mechanics research of German scientist Max Planck. Rollins refers to recent historical findings that suggest the Nazis had achieved some results with quantum models, but only in the past decade has the mainstream scientific community made significant progress in drawing practical applications from the field of quantum physics.

The fast-paced action in *Black Order* is enhanced by underlying questions raised by the theories of quantum physics, evolution, and intelligent design. Rollins has a background in evolutionary biology and believes that evolution is well supported by evidence in nature but formulated in the novel as an encouragement to society to support open debates on controversial scientific thought. Using current-day theories on quantum physics, for example, Rollins employs characters' dialogue to offer his own speculations on evolution and intelligent design. For instance, Anna explains to Painter that the Bell controls evolution—what she calls "quantum evolution," a field that not only offers the strongest support for intelligent design but also indicates that we may ourselves be such designers. In another discussion Grayson proposes an explanation of how prayer may work scientifically.

Bibliography

Rollins, James. *Black Order: A Sigma Force Novel.* New York: William Morrow, 2006.

Donna Smith

Blow Fly Patricia Cornwell (2003)

In *Blow Fly,* the 12th book of Patricia Cornwell's Kay Scarpetta series, the author departs from the formula her readers have come to expect: standalone crimes solved by Virginia's chief medical examiner, Kay Scarpetta, and her strong supporting cast, including FBI profiler Benton Wesley, Richmond police officer Pete Marino, and strong-willed niece Lucy Farinelli, narrated in the first person and describing autopsies and other forensic procedures in great detail. Instead, *Blow Fly* finds Kay, having left law enforcement entirely and working as a teacher and consultant, assigned ad hoc to a team investigating the disappearances of 10 women from the Baton Rouge area. The reader learns early that the killer is Jean-Paul Chandonne, a.k.a. Jay Talley, one of the twin serial killers from the multinational Chandonne crime family who also appear in Cornwell's *Black Notice* (1999) and *The Last Precinct* (2000). Jay is handsome and suave, while his twin, Jean-Baptiste, is known as the "werewolf" because he suffers from hypertrichosis, a rare medical condition leading to facial deformity and excessive hair on the face and body. Both in their way are in love with Kay and want to kill her; and the struggle between the Chandonne brothers and Kay's unofficial team becomes a yet more compelling story line than the serial killer plot itself, which is actually resolved largely offstage.

Blow Fly also marks a significant stylistic departure from the series' formula, employing a third-person narrative instead of the usual first-person Scarpetta voice and alternating between different perspectives, both of which provide readers with unusually vivid insights into secondary characters. Moreover, in only about a quarter of the novel does Kay herself appear and even then is seldom represented in her capacity as a forensics specialist. Chapters are short and fast paced, and the entire narrative unfolds in the present tense, creating a rising sense of urgency as characters get embroiled in multiple subplots. These continually changing perspectives and the large number of chapters create a refracted reality that mirrors the serpentine plot of the novel.

The changes in style accentuate changes in the main characters of the series. Kay has recently dealt with professional disillusionment and continues to struggle with the apparent death of her longtime lover, Benton Wesley, seemingly brutally murdered in *Point of Origin* (1998). Such ongoing grief challenges her previously serene view of the world as a place where good people like herself can eradicate evil through a commitment to science and rationality. Now "she is no longer entirely clinical" (129), no longer able to find solace and control "deep inside the refuge of her analytical mind" (339). In fact, Kay's work in *Blow Fly* occurs almost exclusively outside the lab.

Nor is Kay the only one to question the power of science alone to address horrendous crime. It is revealed early in the novel that Benton is still alive, having faked his own death to protect himself and Kay from the Chandonne family. And like Kay, he has changed dramatically. Once a lead FBI profiler, he now questions the very basis of his former profession, calling it "propaganda and marketing. It is hype" (64). His worldview, too, has changed, grown darker and more ambivalent. Thus, though now convinced that "all kindnesses will be repaid" (138) and "evil will get its ugly reward" (138), Benton blurs ethical lines in ways he never has before. The reader learns, for example, that he has implicated Marino and Lucy, the two other people closest to Kay, in the deception surrounding his death. Such uncharacteristic actions are attributed to his years of isolation, made necessary by the powerful reach of the evil Chandonnes, and ensconce him in a pattern typical of detective fiction: the contamination of good detectives by pervasive evil.

Cornwell explores opposing models of evil through representations of the twin serial killers. The Scarpetta series is famous for its focus on victims instead of criminals, but *Blow Fly* is an exception, devoting several chapters each to Jean-Baptiste and Jay. The monstrous Jean-Baptiste is subtly nuanced, his depravity linked to his horrific physiological condition and sexual impotence. Though his malevolent actions are gruesomely described, his state may evoke pity, as the narrator explains that his "revenge on the world is to cause death and disfigurement, to re-create others in his own image. He is the ultimate embodiment of self-hate" (154).

His twin brother, on the other hand, is pure evil, mendacious and manipulative to the core—a model psychopath: "Jay Talley . . . does not look like what he is. For that reason, he is worse than Jean-Baptiste" (61). Interestingly, Jay's obsession with Kay serves to validate her as a strong and capable woman. He stares at one of his victims, "hoping that somehow her body will become Kay Scarpetta's, and finally becomes furious because it can't, furious because Scarpetta wouldn't be polite, furious because Scarpetta isn't weak. A rabid part of him fears he is a failure because Scarpetta is a wolf and he captures only lambs" (8). Scarpetta herself often feels weak in *Blow Fly*, but the serial killer, and ultimately the reader, discovers the strength at her core.

Both Scarpetta and the secondary characters from Cornwell's long-running series tend to act uncharacteristically in *Blow Fly*, unique both in its form and content. Although it does not stand well alone, with its multiple plots so dependent on previous novels, it serves nonetheless as an important transitional work in the series, providing new and fresh perspectives on ongoing themes such as women's place in law enforcement, the power of science, the genesis of evil, and the possibility of contamination for detectives intimately involved in the fight against crime. It ends with the reunion of Kay and Benton, which cannot help but lead character development in still new directions in the novels to follow.

Bibliography

Cornwell, Patricia. *Point of Origin*. New York: Putnam, 1998.

———. *Black Notice*. New York: Putnam, 1999.

———. *The Last Precinct*. New York: Berkley Books, 2000.

———. *Blow Fly*. New York: Berkley Books, 2003.

Pamela Bedore

Blue Smoke Nora Roberts (2005)

Blue Smoke is the story of Catarina Hale, a woman whose life is shaped by tragedy and by her family's strength. At the age of 11, "Reena" witnesses the arson of her family's restaurant in Baltimore's Little Italy and determines that same night to pursue a career in arson investigation. As she enters college, her life is again touched by catastrophic fire when her first lover is killed in an apartment blaze. She completes her degree and joins the police force. While she is certified to fight fires, her true ambition is to study them—to see how they work and why they were set. She becomes a member of the arson investigation unit and sees firsthand what fire can do.

At the heart of Reena's life and story is her family. The large and loving Italian clan has lived in Baltimore for generations and serves as the hub of the surrounding community. The family restaurant provides a touchstone for Reena as she navigates the ups and downs of adulthood. But when she becomes the target of a psychotic serial arsonist, no one about her is safe. Every man she is involved with is attacked or dies, and she begins to feel that no relationship will ever work for her—until she meets Bowen Goodnight, literally the boy next door. As the intensity of their relationship increases, so does the frequency of the serial arsonist's attacks, and Reena races to uncover the arsonist's identity before everything she loves is destroyed.

The novel is structured in three sections, as she grows from timid tomboy to stubborn, strong-willed woman, each illustrating a significant period in her life, and all serving to link the minute events of that life to a larger pattern of vengeance and hatred. The undercurrent of the novel is the relationship between cause and effect: "Who or what started the fire? Who was changed by it, grieved by it or benefited from it?" (131). The fire at Sirico's drove her to college and a career in arson investigation. At college she met people who changed her life—including Josh Bolton, her first love. Josh's death pushed her to work harder to reach her goal. When she joined the force and passed the fire certification, she paused long enough to begin a new relationship. But when it, too, had an untimely end, she poured herself into her career once again, seldom surfacing long enough to expose herself to the possibility of another such shock. Only her family, stable and unshaken by catastrophe, receives her true affection and loyalty. With them she can love and be loved in return without fear of pain or loss.

Bo Goodnight, however, slips beneath her defense. A carpenter by trade, he has loved Reena for 13 years before they met. After spotting her at a college party, he gave her the nickname of "Dream Girl"—the elusive girl he could never find. Their paths cross two other times, and each time he is left with only the illusion, until she moves in next door. Not intimidated by her job or her boisterous family, Bo acts unlike any of Reena's other lovers, allowing her the freedom she craves. When their relationship is tested by the reemergence of Reena's psychotic stalker, he refuses to let her give in to the temptation to run but instead provides her with a safe place to go when she needs one.

The Hale family itself—from the artistic Bianca and her non-Italian husband, Gib, to their children Francesca, Bella, Reena, and Xander—is a central character in *Blue Smoke.* The novel opens with the family and ends with the beginning of another one. In between we witness their marriages, pregnancies, and family joys, as well as profound troubles and setbacks. But the Hales always rebound with the help of one another. They are a close-knit unit, strong enough not merely to look after their own but to accept strangers as friends.

The importance of family recurs in most of Nora Roberts's romantic suspense novels, acting both as a contextual tool for gaining a better understanding of the main character and as a means of increasing the emotional depth of the work. These characters genuinely care for one another—even to the point of "pounding on each other" as signs of affection. The interaction between husbands and wives, sons and daughters, parents and children, is deftly handled, and the Hale family, like those at the center of Roberts's other novels, while not a perfect unit, is in its very imperfection realistic and believable.

With any suspense novel, the villain plays a crucial role, and in the case of *Blue Smoke,* the identity of the villain is easy to ascertain. The suspense consists in the anticipation of his next move, Roberts offering periodic glimpses into his mind and his calculations for revenge. For him as for the other players in the novel, Roberts draws quickly but surely the lineaments of character. While the Hale family uses affection and a sprinkling of Italian in their speech, and Reena uses carefully chosen diction, the villain's speeches are devoid of any emotion save rage or glee. Also typical of Roberts's suspense writing is her attention to detail, notable in her careful description of investigative techniques, as well as her sensual depictions of fire, adding to the richness and verisimilitude of the tale.

Blue Smoke was adapted to film in 2007. In a television movie for the Lifetime channel, *Blue Smoke* starred Alicia Witt as Reena Hale, Matthew Settle as Bo Goodnight, and Talia Shire as Bianca Hale.

Bibliography

Roberts, Nora. *Blue Smoke.* New York: Putnam, 2005.

Kelly Rivers

The Body Farm Patricia Cornwell (1994)

With *The Body Farm,* Patricia Cornwell offers her readers an unusually grisly look at the world of forensic investigation. When 11-year-old Emily Steiner is found dead, Virginia's chief medical examiner, now acting as a consulting forensic pathologist for the FBI, her partner Detective Pete Marino, and forensic psychologist Benton Wesley are summoned to Black Mountain, North Carolina. To solve the crime, Scarpetta relies on the assistance of the Body Farm, a research facility where decomposing bodies serve as a testing ground for forensic investigators, based on the University of Tennessee's actual Anthropological Research Facility in Knoxville (after the release of Cornwell's novel, the appellation stuck to the UT facility).

The Body Farm is the second installment in a quartet of novels about serial killer Temple Gault and his accomplice, Carrie Grethen, Gault first appearing in 1993's *Cruel and Unusual,* where his identity is discovered but he remains unapprehended. In *The Body Farm,* Cornwell introduces Gault's accomplice, Carrie, who is actually in training at the FBI's Quantico facility with Scarpetta's niece Lucy. Again Gault is still at large at the end of the novel, and it is not until the final pages of *Potter's Field* (1995) that he is finally killed by Scarpetta, while Carrie goes on to create yet more havoc, until she herself is dispatched at the conclusion of *Point of Origin* (1998).

The central thematic thread weaving together the varied characters of *The Body Farm*—victims, criminals, and law enforcement alike—is that of inappropriate, alternative, and even deviant and fatal sexuality. Detective Pete Marino, for example, becomes involved with the victim's mother. Scarpetta embarks on an adulterous affair with married FBI profiler Wesley Benton. Lucy comes to terms with her sexuality and begins a relationship with the murderous Carrie Grethen. A local police officer investigating Emily Steiner's death himself dies from what appears to be autoerotic asphyxiation. And Temple Gault himself, "an exquisitely pretty blond young man" (*Cruel and Unusual* 400), is sexually ambivalent.

Comparisons between Scarpetta and Clarice Starling, the sexually charged FBI agent in THOMAS HARRIS's *The* SILENCE OF THE LAMBS (1988), have been noted by a number of critics, and in a sense Scarpetta may be seen as an aging Starling, one who has already been down the path that the younger agent is just embarking upon. In the opening pages of *The Body Farm,* Scarpetta is completing a run at Quantico, just as Starling is shown doing in the opening scenes of the film version of Harris's novel, and the relationship between Gault and Scarpetta appears to mimic that of Lecter and Starling; however, Gault's evil is more stereotypical than Lecter's, and the relationship he has with Scarpetta, decidedly less complex.

Linda Mizejewski describes Cornwell's novels as "haunted by crises of gender and sexuality" (7); and these crises often draw Scarpetta's attention from her own forensic investigations, garnering the disapproval of some critics and the praise of others. Moreover, Cornwell consistently highlights Scarpetta's personal life in her novels, examining her motives in the light of her many disruptive relationships, and establishing character doublings of almost archetypal proportions. For example, Scarpetta complains that "I was a woman who was not a woman. I was the body and sensibilities of a woman with the power and drive of a man" (341).

The medical examiner profession is dominated by men, and the resistance she faces contributes to the intense ambivalence and sometimes androgynous quality of Cornwell's heroine.

Even more intriguing, in *The Body Farm* she is curiously but clearly affected by an encounter she observes between Lucy and Carrie, revealing a fluidity of gender identification in the novel. However, Lucy is more of a daughter to her than niece, and Scarpetta is cast in the archetypal role of good mother in contrast to the host of bad mothers in the novel, of which her sister, Lucy's mother, is one. Emily Steiner's mother is another, represented as suffering from Munchausen syndrome by proxy, a mental illness in which a woman induces illness in her child to garner sympathy from the medical community (she is later discovered to be the murderer of her own daughter).

The doubling continues with a mirroring of Lucy's sexual awakening as a lesbian and Scarpetta's initiation of an adulterous affair—entering into dangerous relationships with unsuitable partners. Benton Wesley becomes Scarpetta's lover in spite of being married, while Lucy begins a dangerous relationship with Carrie Grethen, the psychopathic accomplice of Gault; and the cool collected Wesley is contrasted to the emotionally messy Marino in his affair with the victim's mother.

Gault himself, a serial killer who tortures and murders children, is the most dangerous character Scarpetta has yet faced. At first glance the death of Emily Steiner appears to be his work. Though the deed is eventually traced to the child's mother, the shadow of Gault hangs heavily over the entire novel, even absorbing, vampirelike, the FBI's Grethen.

Critics have also noted the similarities between Temple Gault and Kay Scarpetta on the one hand, and the characters of serial killer Jack and criminal profiler Samantha Waters in the television series *Profiler* (1996–2000). Like Jack, Gault is a computer genius and veritable chameleon who escapes apprehension by using advanced technological methods. Joy Palmer has noted, in addition, how the mystery detective novel has long been seen as a masculine genre (57) and sees the "invasion" of women into the masculinized arena of forensic work in such characters as Waters and Scarpetta as an important contribution to feminist activism.

The Body Farm is packed with the sophisticated disquisitions readers have come to expect from Cornwell's novels: Readers are treated to a lengthy explanation of the use of superglue to find trace evidence at a crime scene; they learn the intricacies of the manufacture of duct tape; they tour the Decay Research Facility, where bodies are subjected to various climactic and technological experiments. Along with Harris's *Silence of the Lambs*, *The Body Farm* ushered in an era of forensic detective fiction that is only increasing in popularity and influence, with continued releases by Cornwell, Kathy Reichs, and Jeffrey Deavers, and a host of television series such as the *CSI* and *Law and Order* franchises, which feature the skill of medical examiners and other forensic investigators in solving violent and often lurid crimes. But the true success of Cornwell's novels in general, and of *The Body Farm* in particular, lies in their tight interweaving of fascinating scientific detail with the subtle and evolving characterization of the scientist Scarpetta herself.

Bibliography

Cornwell, Patricia. *Cruel and Unusual.* New York: Scribners, 1993.

———. *The Body Farm.* New York: Scribners, 1994.

———. *Potter's Field.* New York: Scribners, 1995.

———. *Point of Origin.* New York: Scribners, 1998.

Mizejewski, Linda. "Illusive Evidence: Patricia Cornwell and the Body Double." *South Central Review* 18, no. 3/4 (autumn/winter 2001): 6–20.

Palmer, Joy. "Tracing Bodies: Gender, Genre, and Forensic Detective Fiction." *South Central Review* 18, no. 3/4 (autumn/winter 2001): 54–71.

Service, Robert F. "Where Dead Men Really Do Tell Tales." *Science* (August 11, 2000): 855+.

Patricia Bostian

Borchgrave, Arnaud de (1926–) and Robert Moss (1946–)

The brief collaboration between award-winning journalists Arnaud de Borchgrave and Robert Moss produced two internationally best-selling novels, *The SPIKE* (1980) and *Monimbo* (1983). *The Spike,* an espionage thriller that has sold 3 million copies and been translated into 19 languages, elicited critical controversy because of its portrayal of Soviet disinformation and its effects in the United States during the turbulent 1960s. *Monimbo,* another spy thriller, depicts Cuban dictator Fidel Castro and his government's attempts to destabilize the United States through race riots, drug dissemination, and terrorist acts. Although the Belgian-born de Borchgrave has published no further fiction, both he and the Australian-born Moss have continued to publish prolifically in their respective careers, the former in journalism and the latter in politics, economics, and, more recently, the field of dream interpretation.

The Spike takes place in Paris, Washington, and New York, roughly from 1967 to 1976, and opens with Berkeley graduate student Bob Hockney, son of a U.S. Navy admiral, taking part in a campus antiwar demonstration. But as the novel unfolds, Hockney, now a journalist, abandons his liberal perspective for an apparently more enlightened one that sees Soviet disinformation as a carefully orchestrated plot to destabilize the United States. As he travels to Vietnam and various European cities, Hockney explores—and eventually writes about—the entire disinformational catalog, from murder, intrigue, moles, trained sex experts, and double agents to those naive Americans whom Lenin called "useful idiots." The novel ends with him helping a Soviet KGB agent to defect and bring charges against his government in the halls of the U.S. Congress. The turning point for Hockney is also the source of the novel's title: Feeling helpless in the face of his newspaper's decision to "spike" his story, merely because the editor disagrees with its politics, he becomes an independent operator.

Arnaud de Borchgrave, the older of the two writers, was born in Brussels in 1926 to Baudouin de Borchgrave, a diplomat, and Audrey Townshend, a writer. Educated in Belgium, England, and the United States, de Borchgrave served in the British Royal Navy from 1942 to 1946. After World War II he worked for United Press International (UPI) in New York and then for *Newsweek* in Paris from 1951 to 1963. From 1959 to 1969 he was married to Eileen Ritschel, then subsequently married the photographer Alexandra Villard in 1969, the same year in which he won the Overseas Press Club award for Best Magazine Reporting from Abroad, the first of six awards for his overseas coverage. De Borchgrave remained with *Newsweek* as chief foreign correspondent from 1963 to 1980, during which time he covered 71 wars and the events in more than 90 countries.

Osborn Elliott, former editor in chief of *Newsweek* and former dean of the Columbia School of Journalism, believes that "de Borchgrave has played a role in world affairs known to no other journalist." Over the course of his career he has interviewed such disparate figures as Egyptian president Anwar Sadat, North Vietnamese prime minister Pham Van Dong, Israeli president Golda Meir, and King Hussein of Jordan and spent seven tours of duty in Vietnam as a war correspondent. In 1981 de Borchgrave received the World Business Council's Medal of Honor, and in 1985 he was awarded the George Washington Medal of Honor for Excellence in Published Works.

He served as editor in chief of the *Washington Times* from 1985 to 1991, and in 1999 was appointed chief executive officer of UPI. After the September 11th attack on the World Trade Center de Borchgrave traveled to both Afghanistan and Pakistan, and recently he has commented publicly on the 2007 political assassination of his friend Benazir Bhutto (Van Susteren). The late 20th-century journalist Theodore H. White wrote that de Borchgrave "is one of America's great foreign correspondents" (Corse 1,279). Arnaud de Borchgrave currently serves as director of the Transnational Threats Project for the Center for Strategic and International Studies, as the CEO of UPI, and as the editor at large for the *Washington Times.* He lives with his wife in Vevay, Switzerland.

Robert Moss was born in 1946 in Australia and graduated from the Australian National University with a first-class honors bachelor of arts degree, which he followed with a master of arts. After working for the *Canberra Times* from 1967 to 1969, Moss moved to London, where he has been associated with the *Economist* ever since. He was editor of the *Economist*'s weekly bulletin, "Foreign Report," from 1974 to 1980 and is currently a syndicated writer for the *London Daily Telegraph.* An authority on political and military matters, Moss exposed the Bulgarian plot to assassinate Pope John Paul II. As a polarizing figure in the worlds of journalism and politics—he has been praised for his insights into disinformation and left-wing governments and criticized for his one-sided approach to these issues—Moss has written seven novels in addition to *The Spike* and *Monimbo.* His first, *Death Beam* (1981), was followed by *Moscow Rules* (1985). Set in Russia and told through the words of a young woman journalist, the latter describes a revolt of Russian citizens against the Communist Party in general and the KGB in particular. *Carnival of Spies* (1987), an espionage novel set in the 1930s, features a Communist Party member named Johnny, who, after losing both his lover and best friend, grows disillusioned and becomes a double agent; *Mexico Way* (1991) tells a sinister tale of oil-rich billionaires whose plan to appropriate Mexico's oil fields is foiled by Jim Kreeger, head of the American CIA mission in Mexico.

In 1991 Moss changed direction and published *Fire Along the Sky,* a tale set during the mid-18th-century French and Indian War as the half-English, half-Irish Shane Hardacre shares adventures and misadventures with various Native Americans. He followed with *The Firekeeper: A Narrative of the Eastern Frontier* (1995), an ambitious and complex tale of the Mohawk and their struggle to maintain their independence, told from the viewpoints of three immigrants, Billy Johnson, Peter Warren, and Catherine "Cat" Wissenberg, which alternate with those of the Native Americans and a particularly charismatic Native American woman. Its sequel, *The Interpreter: A Story of Two Worlds* (1997), is another 18th-century novel that moves back and forth between the Old and New Worlds. It features the youthful German refugee Conrad Weiser, who sails to New York and gradually learns the ways of the Mohawk, with their dream-worship, visions, and spirituality, eventually becoming an Indian agent and then leader of a German colony in Pennsylvania. Moss has also done pioneering work in dream interpretation and published several books on the subject.

Bibliography for Arnaud de Borchgrave

Bunch, Sonny. "Arnaud de Borchgrave Named CEO of United Press International." PR Newswire (December 16, 1998).

The Spike. With Robert Moss. New York: Crown, 1980.

Monimbo. New York: Simon & Schuster, 1983.

"Disinformation documentation." *Washington Times,* 4 October 1999.

Rothmeyer, Karen. "Unindicted co-conspirator? With millions to burn and suspicion to match, Richard Scaife feeds the right's fires." *The Nation* (February 23, 1998).

Van Susteren, Greta. "Interview with Arnaud de Borchgrave." "On the Record," Fox News (December 27, 2007). Available online. URL: http://www.foxnews.com/story/0,2933,318743,00.html.

Bibliography for Robert Moss

Gruson, Lindsey. Review of *Moscow Rules. New York Times,* 17 February 1985.

The Spike. With Arnaud de Borchgrave. New York: Crown, 1980.

Death Beam. New York: Crown, 1981.

Monimbo. With Arnaud de Borchgrave. New York: Simon & Schuster, 1983.

Moscow Rules. New York: Villard, 1985.

Carnival of Spies. New York: Villard, 1987.

Fire along the Sky. New York: St. Martin's, 1990.

Mexico Way. New York: Simon & Schuster, 1991.

The Firekeeper: A Narrative of the Eastern Frontier. New York: Forge, 1995.

The Interpreter: A Story of Two Worlds. New York: Forge, 1997.

Abby H. P. Werlock

The Bourne Identity Robert Ludlum (1980)

The first in ROBERT LUDLUM's immensely popular Bourne series, *The Bourne Identity* is a suspense/international-espionage novel featuring Jason Bourne, a covert operative, who is pulled barely alive from the Mediterranean, with multiple bullet wounds and no idea about his own identity. Over several weeks he is nursed back to health by an alcoholic British expatriate doctor who cannot cure Bourne's amnesia but does provide him with certain clues. The doctor has removed a microfiche from Bourne's hip, which contains the name and account number of a Swiss bank, and has observed Bourne's frequent nightmares and cries of "*Kwa-sah*" in an Asian language. Bourne is referred to simply as "the patient" in the first part of the book, since he has no awareness of his own name or of what activities led him to be shot. The doctor is also able to tell Bourne that previous plastic surgery has toned down some of the sharper features of his face, rendering it more nondescript and that he has often worn contact lenses. His overall appearance, then, is such that he can assume many disguises with only minor alterations to his manner of dress or hairstyle. It is clear that the patient is a man who speaks French, English, and an Asian language fluently, and it soon becomes apparent that when faced with physical attack, he can instinctively employ martial arts like an expert. The novel then follows Bourne as he makes his way to Switzerland, Paris, and New York in a search for both his identity and his own survival.

Offering far more than the usual thriller fare, Ludlum's narratives suggest that the world of covert intelligence operations is linked, sometimes quite directly, as in the Iran-contra affair, to a misuse of power. But the correction of this misuse is a fraught and tenuous occupation, typified by anonymous heroes and serendipitous events. Often in his works, truth—the only real weapon against such misuse—can triumph only if the right information or action can be discovered and deployed in time.

Early in the novel, for example, the protagonist suddenly finds himself ruthlessly hunted. He has no idea who is trying to take his life, but his attempt to withdraw money from his Swiss bank account results in pursuit by armed men. Through his adroit response, Bourne is able to flee in time, only to discover, again just in time, that his hotel has been infiltrated and he has no safe place. Improvising madly, he takes a hostage in the form of one Marie St. Jacques, an economist for the Canadian government, whom he forces to drive him round Zurich as he attempts to collect himself and gather clues to his own crisis. St. Jacques is initially a terrified female, nearly forced into shock by her violent abduction, and when she at last succeeds in escaping, she is immediately captured by the same people hunting Jason. She is raped and about to be killed, when Bourne finds her and saves her from the attacker. At last, and only through these pitiless means, she realizes that Bourne is not merely a cold-blooded assassin:

> "All I really know is that seven hours ago I was underneath an animal, his mouth all over me, his hands clawing me . . . and I knew I was going to die. And then a man came back for me—a man who could have kept running—but who came back for me and offered to die in my place. I guess I believe in him" (132).

By the end of the novel's first section she determines to help Bourne make sense of the mystery, finally becoming his lover and accomplice and playing a critical role in the remainder of the tale.

Typical of Ludlum's oeuvre, *The Bourne Identity* has an intricate, fast-paced, and surprising plot, pausing only briefly before another attempt is made on Bourne's life or another advance in uncovering the many mysteries of his existence. Ultimately, Bourne learns (again) of the notorious Carlos the Jackal, an assassin and mastermind behind countless high-profile hits across Europe, his kills ranging from the faithless underlings of the Verbrecherwelt to prominent ambassadors and political figures. Conspiracy, terrorism, and the ubiquitous but largely invisible force of the criminal underworld are all deftly portrayed. Bourne and Marie find an unexpected ally in the form of General Villiers, an aging member of France's National Assembly and member of the Resistance, whose son was slaughtered by Carlos's men; Villiers articulates one of the novel's principal themes: "A free society is ripe for infiltration, and once infiltrated the changes do not stop until that society is remade into another image. Conspiracy is everywhere; it cannot go unchallenged" (357).

Thus, both in its protagonist and plot, *The Bourne Identity* reaches far beyond the customary limits of its genre, employing that form, rather in the way of JOHN LE CARRÉ, to explore broader philosophical questions, here about the nature of personal identity and its role in the understanding of loyalty and justice.

Ludlum's Bourne novels have been adapted into three films: *The Bourne Identity* (2002), *The Bourne Ultimatum* (2004), and *The Bourne Supremacy* (2007), with Matt Damon as the gifted amnesiac in all three films. Readers of the novel will notice that significant portions of Ludlum's original plot have been completely revamped to incorporate references to contemporary events.

Bibliography

Ludlum, Robert. *The Bourne Identity.* New York: Bantam Books, 2001.

Elizabeth Whitehead

Bradford, Barbara Taylor (1933–)

Barbara Taylor Bradford is one of the most popular romance writers of the 20th century, with sales of more than 75 million copies. Her first book, *A Woman of Substance* (1979), was published to great acclaim and is one of the top ten best-selling fictional works of all time. It is also the first book in the EMMA HARTE SAGA, Bradford's trademark series. Publishing prolifically since 1979, she commenced her most recent series with her 21st novel, *The Ravenscar Dynasty,* in 2006. Many of her works have been adapted to television.

Bradford's life seems at times almost as romantic as her fiction. Born and raised in Leeds, she was encouraged to read widely from a very young age by her mother, a former nurse. In her late teens she began working as a journalist at the *Yorkshire Evening Post,* then moved to London as an editor of *Women's Own* magazine at age 20 and worked successfully in journalism for several years afterward. In 1963 she married an American movie producer, Robert Bradford. Although she did not attend university, Bradford has received honorary doctorates from Leeds University, the University of Bradford, and Tokyo University and is one of the world's wealthiest authors. Her rise from journalist to best-selling author is frequently paralleled in the success of female protagonists in her books, and many of her works are set in Yorkshire, where she grew up. Piers Dudgeon's authorized biography, *The Woman of Substance: The Life and Works of Barbara Taylor Bradford* (2005), offers the most comprehensive and provocative account of the many parallels between Bradford's life and fiction.

Bradford's greatest success may be the Emma Harte Saga, six books chronicling the struggles and achievements not merely of Emma herself but of her friends, as well as their descendants. The first, *A Woman of Substance,* narrates the rise of Emma from lower-class chambermaid to global mercantile tycoon. Along the way she has five children, endures two difficult marriages, and finally falls in love with a wonderful man, although her happiness with him is cut short. The novel is shaped by Emma's contentious relationship with her children and difficult decisions about who will run the empire she has created after she dies. In the following books her granddaughter Paula and great-granddaughter Linnet—the successors to Emma's financial empire—each have a prominent place in the narrative. The saga also includes *Hold the Dream* (1985), *To Be the Best* (1988), *Emma's Secret* (2003), *Unexpected Blessings* (2004), and *Just Rewards* (2005).

Authors such as ROSAMUNDE PILCHER, DANIELLE STEEL, JUDITH KRANTZ, and Penny Vincenzi share Bradford's style of expansive and romantic storytelling, but the latter's specialty lies in staging her tales of strong women juggling careers, children, and romances against sweeping historical backgrounds. *Voice of the Heart* (1983) tells the story of the miraculous rise of resolute actress Katherine, while *Everything to Gain* (1994) explores the tragedy Mallory faces when she loses her perfect family. In *Where You Belong* (2000) photojournalist Val must rediscover herself after her lover is killed, while in *The Triumph of Katie Byrne* (2001), Katie is determined to succeed as an actress in order to satisfy her own dream and honor her childhood friends. Bradford is also known for her sensitive and searching explorations of friendship and relationships between women. *Act of Will* (1986) intertwines stories of three generations of Kenton women, while in *Three Weeks in Paris* (2002) old friends Jessica, Maria, Kay, and Alexandra reunite in Paris after decades apart and renew their tumultuous relationship. Bradford's other novels include: *The Women in His Life* (1990), *Remember* (1991), *Angel* (1993), *Love in Another Town* (1995), *Dangerous to Know* (1995), *A Secret Affair*

(1996), *Her Own Rules* (1996), *Power of a Woman* (1997), and *A Sudden Change of Heart* (1999). Her commercial and critical success puts her at the forefront of women's popular fiction; and she has strongly influenced other authors of that genre.

Ten of Bradford's books have been filmed for television. They include several stories from the Emma Harte Saga: *A Woman of Substance* (1984), *Hold the Dream* (1986), and *To Be the Best* (1992), starring Jenny Seagrove, Deborah Kerr, and Lindsay Wagner. Three other programs, *Voice of the Heart* (1990), *Act of Will* (1989), and *Love in Another Town* (1992), have been filmed starring Victoria Tennant. *Remember* (1993) starred Donna Mills, while *Everything to Gain* (1996) starred Sean Young. *Her Own Rules*, starring Melissa Gilbert, and *A Secret Affair*, starring Janine Turner, were telecast in 1998 and 1999, respectively.

Bibliography

Bradford, Barbara Taylor. Official Web site. 2007 Bradford Enterprises. June 1, 2007. Available online. URL: http://www.barbarataylorbradford.com.

———. *Everything to Gain*. New York: HarperPaperbacks, 1994.

———. *The Triumph of Katie Byrne*. New York: Dell, 2001.

———. *Where You Belong*. New York: HarperCollins, 2001.

———. *Three Weeks in Paris*. New York: Dell, 2002.

———. *Act of Will*. New York: St. Martin's, 2005.

———. *Voice of the Heart*. New York: St. Martin's, 2005.

———. *A Woman of Substance*. New York: St. Martin's, 2006.

———. *The Ravenscar Dynasty*. New York: St. Martin's, 2007.

Dudgeon, Piers. *The Woman of Substance: The Life and Works of Barbara Taylor Bradford*. London: HarperCollins, 2005.

Rachel Mann

Brashares, Ann (1967–)

Brashares is a writer of young-adult fiction targeted at female readers and the author of the wildly successful Traveling Pants series, commencing with *The* SISTERHOOD OF THE TRAVELING PANTS (2001) and continuing through *The Second Summer of the Sisterhood* (2003), *Girls In Pants: The Third Summer of the Sisterhood* (2004), and *Forever in Blue: The Fourth Summer of the Sisterhood* (2007). The first novel in the series was made into a motion picture of the same name in 2005, and a film version of the fourth was released in 2008, featuring the same cast as the original *Traveling Pants* film.

Brashares graduated from Barnard College in 1989 with a degree in philosophy, then worked for 10 years as an editor of children's books (rising to become copresident of Alloy Entertainment alongside Les Morgenstein), during which time she began to think about turning her own hand to children's writing, her first two efforts being biographies for young readers interested in technology, *Steve Jobs: Think Different* and *Linus Torvalds: Software Rebel* (both 2001). During this time Brashares had an important conversation with colleague Jodi Anderson, an editor at Alloy Entertainment, in which Anderson told Brashares about a group of friends who shared a pair of pants, a story from her own college experiences. Brashares has characterized the conversation as a casual storytelling between friends that inspired her to create the Traveling Pants novels, but Anderson has described it instead as a story pitch, claiming that she had written a proposal for the series that was sold to Alloy Entertainment with the suggestion that she would write the series. Anderson was contacted for a sample of the series, but Brashares eventually chose to write the novels herself. While the controversy has dogged Brashares's otherwise bright literary career, the situation appears to be at least publicly resolved. Brashares thanks Anderson in the acknowledgments section of each Traveling Pants book, referring to her in the first book, for example, as "the true muse." Anderson was promoted from assistant editor to editor and granted a small bonus, though denied a story credit on the first Traveling Pants film in 2005 (the sequel was released in 2008). She has since left Alloy Entertainment but published her own young adult novel, *Peaches*, with Alloy in 2005, with a sequel, *The Secrets of Peaches*, released in 2006.

Brashares counts Judy Bloom as a major influence in her work, noting that the success of the Traveling Pants series rests on a similar exploration of the themes of love and loyalty, here revolving around the well-traveled pants. While she says she never set out to write moralizing tales, her young readers are undoubtedly attracted partly by the stories' sensitive depiction of the struggle to maintain friendship and find love in the most challenging circumstances, as well as by their heartening conclusion, that friendship conquers all.

Brashares is married to artist Jacob Collins. The couple has three children.

Bibliography

Brashares, Ann. *The Sisterhood of the Traveling Pants.* New York: Random House, 2001.

Fleming, Michael. "Warner Bros. Stitching New 'Pants.'" *Variety*, 23 April 2007.

Kolhatkar, Sheelah. "Viswanathan-athon: Plagiarizing Writer Fell in Weird Alloy." *The New York Observer* (May 7, 2006).

Literature Online Biography. "Brashares, Ann." 2004. Available online. URL: http://gateway.proquest.com.proxy.hil.unb.ca/openurl?ctx_ver=Z39.88-2003&xri:pqil:res_ver=0.2&res_id=xri:lion-us&rft_id=xri:lion:ft:ref:BIO028621:0

Osterheldt, Jenee. "'Sisterhood' Brings Author and Alumna Ann Brashares Close to Characters." *Contra Costa Times*, 23 May 2005.

Random House: Sisterhood Central. "Meet Ann: The Author of the Sisterhood." Available online. URL: http://www.randomhouse.com/teens/sisterhoodcentral/author_qa.htm.

Brenna Clarke Gray

The Bridges of Madison County

Robert James Waller (1992)

Waller's blockbuster novella centers on a passionate four-day love affair that takes place in August 1965 between Robert Kincaid, a nomadic *National Geographic* photographer, and Francesca Johnson, an Italian-born war bride bored with her husband, Richard, and Iowan farm life. On a photographic assignment, Kincaid gets lost in rural Iowa and stops at the Johnson farm for directions to Roseman Bridge. With husband and children away at a state fair in Illinois, Francesca directs him to the bridge but then spontaneously invites him to a home-cooked dinner. Self-described as "one of the last cowboys," destined for extinction "along with the mountain lion and gray wolf," Robert is the perfect contrast to Francesca's husband (101). Robert indulges in after-dinner brandy and cigarettes, while Richard splurges on cornbread, butter, and maple syrup; Robert eats a vegetarian diet, but Richard raises prizewinning steers for slaughter; and the tools of Robert's trade are Nikon cameras and Kodachrome film, while Richard deals in corn pickers and Allis-Chalmers tractors. Most significant, though, Robert is a poet and artist, while Richard sees no value in such lofty pursuits. Robert rekindles in Francesca a joie de vivre that has lain dormant throughout her many years in Iowa; and while she ultimately makes the painful choice to stay with her family instead of running away with him, the two develop in only four days an indelible bond that leads to both of their ashes being later scattered over Roseman Bridge.

Their love story is framed by the later discovery of their mother's journals by Francesca's son and daughter, journals narrating her love affair with Kincaid. Inspired by this remarkable story, in which a woman chooses the responsibility of children, husband, and farm over passion, soul mate, and freedom, Michael and Carolyn Johnson want to see their mother's story told, so they contact a writer, allowing Waller to indulge in a clever bit of metafiction. When readers first encounter him, the writer is awaiting inspiration, "looking at a blinking cursor on the computer screen" (vii). Later, as Michael and Carolyn share what they know of their mother's story, he implicitly addresses the readers, describing how he recognizes a good story: "I begin to see the images. First you must have the images, then come the words. And I begin to hear the words, begin to see them on pages of writing" (viii).

Another construct within *Bridges* occurs at the end of the novel in the form of a tape-recorded interview with a tenor saxophone player named John "Nighthawk" Cummings, which fills in some of the details of Robert Kincaid's life in the 1980s:

> He started comin' in once a week, always on a Tuesday, always drank beer, but not much of it. . . . After a while we got to know each

> other a little. . . . He was workin' on somethin' where he was tryin' to convert music into visual images (166–167).

Through Nighthawk Cummings also, Waller reifies the profundity of the lovers' experience, demonstrating that Francesca was not just another girl in the proverbial port, and that Robert was not merely whispering sweet nothings to her during those four intense days. Far from a tawdry chronicle of infidelity, Waller's depiction of the relationship between the two is that of a perfect union of two divergent but complementary souls. Kincaid tries to capture its unique reality:

> I think we're both inside of another being we have created called "us." Well, we're really not inside of that being. We *are* that being. We have both lost ourselves and created something else, something that exists only as an interlacing of the two of us. Christ, we're in love. As deeply, as profoundly, as it's possible to be in love (113–114).

At once providential and apocryphal, this perfect union that Robert describes is nevertheless not meant to be. Francesca explains:

> As much as I want you and want to be with you and part of you, I can't tear myself away from the realness of my responsibilities. . . . Don't make me give this up, my responsibilities. I cannot do that and live with the thought of it (116).

Here in Francesca's realization of the paradox between duty and desire lies the great and enduring appeal of the novella itself. While feminist literary critics revile the book for its unassertive female protagonist, who never escapes her 1950s model domestic prison, and while other theorists complain that it fails to effectively consider alternative motivations and points of view, Waller nevertheless tapped in to a popular aesthetic with *Bridges* that kept it on the *New York Times* best-seller list for more than three years. Readers who appreciate bodice-ripping sensuality are not disappointed, but at the same time the book is more lucidly written and substantial than any conventional potboiler and compels its readers to reexamine some of their own moral assumptions. For instance, those who normally place adultery on the dark side of a black-and-white scale are induced to sympathize with Francesca in her dignified grief for all that she has given up and respect her for her courageous recommitment to her husband and children.

In 1995 *The Bridges of Madison County* was adapted to film by Amblin Entertainment, and Hollywood megastars Clint Eastwood and Meryl Streep played Robert Kincaid and Francesca Johnson, respectively. Streep received both Golden Globe and Oscar nominations for best actress, and the film was nominated for the best drama Golden Globe in 1996.

Bibliography

Waller, Robert James. *The Bridges of Madison County.* New York: Warner Books, 1992.

Dana Nichols

Bridget Jones's Diary Helen Fielding (1996)

Bridget Jones's Diary is a novel in the form of a diary, documenting a year in the life of a thirty-something London woman struggling to find "inner poise," job success, love, and the perfect diet (not necessarily in that order). Its immense popularity inspired an entirely new genre, "chick lit," focusing on the friendships, sex, and careers of single women in urban locales. The novel, which emerged from Fielding's column in the *Independent* newspaper, has since spawned a sequel entitled *Bridget Jones: The Edge of Reason* (1999), a film adaptation (2001), and a film of the sequel (2004), and has influenced a wide range of popular culture for women, from "chick lit" itself to assorted merchandise and television shows like *Sex and the City* and *Ally McBeal.*

For all its airy tone the work's profound influence has prompted serious controversy surrounding its attitude to feminism. Because Bridget Jones enjoys the sort of economic and sexual independence won by feminism, yet is still primarily focused on finding a man, the novel is sometimes read as *post-feminist,* a term many critics find troubling as it implies that the feminist movement is effectively dead. The novel begins, for example, with Bridget's resolutions for the new year: She will "Save up money in form of savings" and "Go to gym three times a week not merely to buy sandwich" (3), but will not "Drink more than fourteen alcohol units a week" or "Get upset over men, but instead be poised and cool ice-queen" (2). Most of the novel's diary entries begin with Bridget documenting her progress, or regress, via numbers: weight, calorie count, "alcohol units" consumed, cigarettes smoked. Occasionally she records other vices such as "minutes spent looking at mini-break brochures" or "lottery tickets." Her vital statistics for the day will often include gloss or justification; on Sunday February 19th she writes: "125 lbs. (v.g. but purely through worry), alcohol units 2 (but the Lord's Day), cigarettes 7, calories 2100" (48).

Bridget's obsession with measurement and superficial self-monitoring have led many to read the novel as a satire of modern femininity, where women's magazines, diet plans, and self-help books outline impossible standards in excruciating detail for women's bodies and behavior. Like many women Bridget has internalized these standards yet finds herself unable to live by them, vacillating throughout the novel between an irrepressible appetite for pleasure and rules for appropriate regulation of self provided by magazines such as *Cosmopolitan* and books such as *Men Are from Mars, Women Are from Venus.* Much of the debate surrounding *Bridget Jones's Diary* concerns whether Bridget is a conscious or unconscious victim of this consumerist-oriented women's culture, and whether the novel criticizes or corroborates its construction of women. At times Bridget's unabashed enthusiasm for the latest "anticellulite diet" presents women as the most gullible of consumers, practically unfit to take care of themselves; yet even she is alert to the absurdities of modern feminine regimens, reflecting as she prepares for a date that "Being a woman is worse than being a farmer—there is so much harvesting and crop spraying to be done: legs to be waxed, underarms shaved, eyebrows plucked, feet pumiced, skin exfoliated and moisturized. . . . The whole performance is so highly tuned you only need to neglect it for a few days for the whole thing to go to seed" (27).

Bridget's wavering between self-controlled "inner poise" and the pursuit of pleasure is echoed in her vacillation between contentment as an independent single woman and the desire to find a man. On evenings out with her friends Sharon, Jude, and Tom (a self-described "hag fag"), the four express drunken pride in being "Singletons" and assert their superiority over "Smug Marrieds" who try "pathetically to simulate the thrilling sex enjoyed by Singletons" and buy "ever-more exotic foodstuffs in Marks and Spencer . . . to pretend they're in a lovely restaurant like the Singletons" (213–214). The driving force of the plot, nonetheless, is whether Bridget will form a relationship with her boss, Daniel Cleaver, or his rival, Mark Darcy; while the novel does not end in marriage, it does follow the trajectory of the traditional marriage plot, in which a young person, especially female, negotiates the trials of courtship and romance for marriage's reward.

Indeed, far from denying its 19th-century roots, *Bridget Jones's Diary* consciously models itself on Jane Austen's 1813 classic, *Pride and Prejudice.* Like Austen's heroine, Elizabeth Bennett, Bridget Jones has an embarrassing mother, a loving but detached father, and two prospective beaus, one of whom is Darcy. Through such parallels, Fielding reminds readers both of how much has changed for women since Austen's day and of how much has not. Bridget has economic independence and a flat in the city, while Elizabeth Bennett had to marry just to live, as her father's estate was entailed on the male line. Bridget's mother, however, is just as greedy as Mrs. Bennett to marry her daughter to a rich man; after being introduced to Mr. Darcy by her mother, Bridget wryly comments, "I don't know why she didn't just come out with it and say, 'Darling, do shag Mark Darcy over the turkey curry, won't you? He's *very* rich" (11).

Fielding's allusions to *Pride and Prejudice* mock the ostensibly valuable lessons women have taken from this classic novel. Early in the diary, for example, Bridget decides to develop a "sense of self as woman of substance, complete *without* boyfriend, as best way to obtain boyfriend" (2). Typically postmodern in its penchant for intertextual reference, the novel reveals how Bridget's sense of identity as a woman is shaped by books, movies, and television—life in this way literally imitating art. Watching the BBC version of *Pride and Prejudice,* Bridget feels Darcy and Elizabeth are her "chosen representatives in the field of shagging, or rather, courtship" (215). With both her values and goals modeled on texts such as *Pride and Prejudice, Cosmopolitan,* and the television show *Blind Date,* high culture and low have equal hold on Bridget's psyche, making her, as Darcy himself notes, a "top postmodernist."

Bibliography

Fielding, Helen. *Bridget Jones's Diary.* London: Penguin, 1996.

Gill, Rosalind, and Elena Herdieckerhoff. "Rewriting the Romance: New Femininities in Chick Lit?" *Feminist Media Studies* 6, no. 4 (2006): 487–503.

Marsh, Kelly. "Contextualizing Bridget Jones." *College English* 31, no. 1 (2004): 52–72.

McRobbie, Angela. "Post-Feminism and Popular Culture." *Feminist Media Studies* 4, no. 3 (2004): 255–264.

Elizabeth Carolyn Miller

The Broker John Grisham (2005)

The Broker is a political thriller set in Washington, D.C., and in the historical towns of Italy. With the novel Grisham leaves behind his signature rural Mississippi, peopled with corrupt companies and morally ambiguous heroes, to explore a world of political intrigue and clandestine life in ancient Italian towns, with their foreign language and exotic culture. He also leaves behind the familiar plot elements of the legal thriller that wind their way, through shocking discovery and ingenious exposure, to a predictable culmination in courtroom drama. Abandoning, too, his area of expertise (he is a trained lawyer), Grisham creates a drama of international espionage, high-tech satellites, and political machinations.

At the novel's opening Joel Backman is ruined. A high-powered D.C. broker, he has been convicted of trying to sell to the highest bidders—be they Israeli, Saudi, Chinese, or Russian—software that could access and control satellite surveillance systems. He has been in federal prison for six years and is broke, disbarred, and disgraced. Yet his life is not over. The CIA's legendary director, Teddy Maynard, now almost 80 years old, thinks he could be useful, since the treasonous deal had involved technology more sophisticated and advanced than America's own. He persuades Arthur Morgan, the nondescript outgoing president of the United States, to pardon Backman.

The CIA's plan is to release Backman, give him a new secret identity, place him in another country, have him learn a new language, and then let the intelligence services he dealt with know who and where he is. The country whose assassins get to him will be revealed as the country that operated the system in question. The "broker" is released, only to be used as bait in someone else's dirty deal.

This Backman—whose 52 years has amounted to "bilking clients, chasing secretaries around the office, putting the squeeze on slimy little politicians, working seven days a week, ignoring three surprisingly stable children, crafting the public image, building the boundless ego, pursuing money money money money"—is to be re-created with the help of his male handler, Luigi, and his Italian teacher, Francesca, the middle-aged love interest of the story.

The action formally begins as Backman is pulled from his cell and put on a military cargo plane. He is flown first to Treviso, a town north of Venice, but his CIA handlers shuffle him around to keep him disoriented, scared, and obedient. He is finally settled in Bologna.

To the surprise and disappointment of many fans of Grisham, the novel now plunges into detailed depictions of Italian life and culture, following Backman as he tours the porticoes of the town, samples Italian desserts, and comes to understand cultural trivia; e.g., cappuccino is only to be ordered before 10 A.M. Grisham shows us Bologna's leaning tower, its basilicas, marble crypts, and frescoes. He takes the time to narrate the legend of the Roman god Neptune, whose bronze statue is in Bologna, and details the distinct qualities of Italian clothing. Grisham admits to loving "all things Italian," and it shows.

The story meanders through this architecturally rich town, but as operatives from Israel, China, Saudi Arabia, and Russia converge on Backman, his suspicions are aroused, and the subplot that has prepared for his escape, involving the help of his son Neal, now unfolds, as the broker makes his way to a Swiss bank, then back to Washington.

On arrival Backman sets about the negotiation of his last and most crucial deal: the terms of his own freedom. However, the political scene back in Washington is complicated as a pardon-for-profit scheme is exposed, and Backman once again finds himself implicated. But now he has a hard-won wisdom on his side. After "his miserable mess of a life," he has only a brokered identity—"Joel, or Marco or Giovanni or whatever the hell your name is," he says to himself—but this very shattering of his past allows him to pose the question critical to his future: "For the first time in your rotten life, why don't you do what is right, as opposed to what is profitable?"

Grisham often works out the partial redemption of his lost souls: The Washington lawyer in *King of Torts* recovers a measure of decency and even high-mindedness after helping himself to lots of cash in some dubious legal proceedings; the greedy, self-promoting lawyer in *The FIRM* finally understands the value of family life after he is drawn into the violent machinations of mafia deals; and the undoing of high-level tobacco interests is the subject of *The RUNAWAY JURY*, the novel Grisham claims to care most about. Backman, like other such lost souls, turns his own tainted craft, here brokering, to make the turn (here deal) that will save his life, literally and morally. *The Broker* also includes other familiar Grisham elements: an unusual love story, a father-son rapprochement, as well the betrayal, guns, and chases generic to the thriller.

In style the work resembles most Grisham novels, written in clear and urgent prose, its robust sentences and well-chosen details propelling the story along and keeping the reader engaged. It diverges from his other books, however, in its loving and leisurely detour through Italy, with much local dialogue and even language lessons, always careful, nonetheless, to make this diversion pleasant and accessible to all readers.

In his preface Grisham admits that *The Broker* takes him outside his area of expertise: "[M]y background is law, certainly not satellites or espionage. I'm more terrified of high-tech gadgets today than a year ago . . . I know very little about spies, electronic surveillance, satellite phones, smartphones, bugs, wires, mikes and the people who use them. If something in this novel approaches accuracy, it's probably a mistake." The work is evidently one of fiction, but whether such details are verifiable or not, they are convincing and woven into a compelling story. Grisham's real departure is from courtroom scenes and courtroom logic, which normally focus the themes of his stories and give them a concrete conclusion. From biblical archetypes to the philosophical literature of existentialism to the genre fiction of Perry Mason, the courtroom has offered a literary framework to pose, focus, and address questions of right and power. The vagaries of Washington politics, however, afford no such precision or resolution. Joel Backman can only return to Italy, in the end, and begin his life anew.

Bibliography

Grisham, John. *The Firm*. New York: Dell, 1997.

———. *The Runaway Jury*. New York: Dell, 1997.

———. *The Street Lawyer*. New York: Doubleday, 1998.

———. *The Testament*. New York: Doubleday, 1999.

———. *The Broker*. New York: Doubleday, 2005.

Andrea Sauder

Brown, Dan (1964–)

Dan Brown is an American writer of thrillers, most notably of the spectacularly successful *The DA VINCI CODE* (2003). The international response to Brown's controversial claims about an amorous relationship between Jesus Christ and Mary Magdalene (a central theme of *The Da Vinci Code*) spawned a plethora of books aimed at debunking Brown's "facts." In addition, Brown's novel was a factor in the revival of popular interest in the nature and development of early Christianity.

Brown is the son of Constance and Richard Brown and the eldest of their three children. His mother worked as a church organist, and his father, a respected mathematician who wrote several mathematical textbooks, taught at the prestigious Philips Exeter Academy in New Hampshire. Brown and his siblings grew up around the grounds of the academy and participated in Episcopal Church activities, including the church choir. Brown eventually attended Philips as well and after graduation went to Amherst College, an elite private college in Massachusetts, where he double-majored in English and Spanish. He participated in a range of student activities and continued his singing in the college's glee club.

After graduating from Amherst, Brown self-produced several albums (playing synthesizer and piano) between 1986 and 1995, none of which achieved widespread success. He also lived in Hollywood from 1991 to 1993, where he attempted to break into the singer-songwriter market while teaching at a private school to make ends meet. Eventually, he moved back to New Hampshire with Blythe Newlon, whom he married in 1997, and began teaching at Philips Exeter Academy.

Around the time he started teaching, Brown read a novel by SIDNEY SHELDON and decided that he could produce a better story. With Newlon's research assistance, he began writing (his early efforts included a humor book under the pseudonym "Danielle Brown") and by 1996 decided to quit teaching and devote his full time to pursuing a career as a novelist. His first novel was *Digital Fortress* (1998), which features a brilliant mathematician who must foil a dangerous computer code. His second, *ANGELS AND DEMONS* (2000), centers on a plot by the Illuminati (a legendary international secret society) to destroy the Vatican during a papal conclave and explores the conflict between religion and science. This novel also introduced Robert Langdon, a "symbologist," who is the protagonist of *The Da Vinci Code. Deception Point* (2001) describes the chain of events that unfolds after a meteorite containing an extraterrestrial fossil is discovered in Antarctica, revolving around the efforts by various conspirators to suppress knowledge of its existence due to the fossil's religious ramifications.

With his fourth novel, *The Da Vinci Code,* Brown's combination of fast-paced plot, intricate mathematical codes and puzzles, and a long-standing deception maintained by a secret cabal, struck a chord with the public, and the novel became a tremendous international best seller, as well as the basis of a film adaptation (2006) starring Tom Hanks as the work's protagonist, Robert Langdon. *The Da Vinci Code*'s plot focuses on a sinister conspiracy by the Roman Catholic order Opus Dei to uncover information regarding the location of the Holy Grail (traditionally the wine cup Christ used at the Last Supper), whose true nature threatens the Catholic Church's power. Robert Langdon, the hero of *Angels and Demons,* joins French police detective Sophie Neveu in trying to decipher an elaborate series of clues encoded in Leonardo da Vinci's art, which will guide them to the hiding place of the Holy Grail. After a harrowing quest across France, they journey to London, where the truth about the Grail is finally discovered.

The religious controversy sparked by Brown's claim that all the historical details in *The Da Vinci Code* are factual further promoted interest in the book, as well as a host of works denouncing the heterodox statements in the novel about Christ and Mary Magdalene (a female disciple whom some ancient texts claim Jesus married). Brown made similar claims about historical factuality in each of his preceding novels, though critics have pointed out that his claims are often more tentative or fanciful than certain. Other critics note that his characters tend to lack depth, and that his plots rest on a series of coincidences or feature sophisticated technological jargon, lending verisimilitude to the improbable ideas and conspiracies contained in the novels.

The depiction of Opus Dei as a nefarious, secretive organization, as well as the critical tone the book takes toward the Catholic Church's historical attitude toward women, are further elements prompting outspoken reaction against *The Da Vinci Code,* especially among more orthodox Christian believers. Additional negative criticism focused on the book's discussions of art and architecture, as well as its interpretation of formative historical events in the early history of the Christian Church.

The Da Vinci Code also sparked a lawsuit by Michael Baigent and Richard Leigh, the authors of a 1980s pseudo-history called *Holy Blood, Holy Grail,* which claims that members of the medieval French Merovingian dynasty were the genetic descendants of Christ and Mary Magdalene. The two men claimed that Brown lifted crucial plot elements from their work and even went so far as to name one of the main characters—the Grail researcher, Leigh Teabing—using the last name of one and an anagram of the last name of the other (a point Brown confirmed during trial testimony, though he indicated that this was intended as a tribute to the authors). The London court found Brown innocent of plagiarism, the case conveniently promoting further interest in the books involved and in the film adaptation of Brown's novel, which premiered shortly after the legal proceedings ended.

Following the success of *The Da Vinci Code,* Brown found all his previous novels back in print (now available in 40 languages), while film adaptations are being planned for some. Brown has been listed as one of the most influential people in America by *Time* and *People* magazines and has been featured on a variety of radio and television programs. The film adaptation of *The Da Vinci Code,* directed by Ron Howard, included one of Brown's own musical compositions in the soundtrack and brought further attention to his novel, though critical reception of the film was decidedly mixed.

Brown currently resides in New England, where he is at work on *The Solomon Key,* another thriller featuring symbologist Robert Langdon.

Bibliography

Brown, Dan. *Digital Fortress.* Boston: Thomas Dunne, 1998.

———. *Angels and Demons.* New York: Simon & Schuster, 2000.

———. *Deception Point.* New York: Atria, 2001.

———. *The Da Vinci Code.* New York: Doubleday, 2003.

Joseph Becker

Brown, Sandra (Laura Jordan, Rachel Ryan, Erin St. Claire) (1948–)

Brown has written more than 65 crime thrillers, suspense dramas, and romance novels, appearing on the *New York Times*'s best-seller list more than 50 times since 1990. Her recent best sellers alone include *Ricochet* (2006), CHILL FACTOR (2005), *White Hot* (2004), *Hello, Darkness* (2003), *The Crush* (2002), *Envy* (2001), *The Switch* (2000), *The Alibi* (1999), *Unspeakable* (1998), and *Fat Tuesday* (1997), all of which have placed in the top five spots. *French Silk* was adapted into an ABC-TV movie in 1994, and several other novels have been optioned for feature films or television movies.

Born Sandra Cox in Waco, Texas, Brown grew up in Fort Worth. As a young girl she devoured Nancy Drew mysteries and later developed an appreciation for writers ranging from HAROLD ROBBINS to Tennessee Williams, whom she identifies as her favorite "in terms of mood and setting" (Foege 81). She attended Texas Christian University, Oklahoma State University, and the University of Texas, marrying Michael Brown in 1968.

Both were employed by WFAA-TV in Dallas, but when she lost her television job, Brown's lucrative writing career began. Her background as an English major, her early interest in fiction, and her sheer desire to create led her to try writing, and the results have been prolific. The Browns reside in Arlington, Texas, but she often writes from her second home in Hilton Head, South Carolina.

Her first novels were formulaic romance novels, which she churned out for Harlequin, Bantam Books, and Dell. Although by 1985 she was earning $250,000 annually, Brown wished to break free of the genre's constrictions. She sought to employ more complicated plots and reach a broader audience.

Hiring an agent and refusing to write more romances, Brown signed a contract with Warner Books, receiving a $300,000 advance for *Slow Heat in Heaven* (1988), *Best Kept Secrets* (1989), and *Mirror Image* (1990). Although these were suspense novels, they retained intense love scenes, and Warner capitalized on Brown's reputation by incorporating cover art that mimicked that of Brown's earlier romance novels. The author protested, "No more bosoms and biceps or I'm out of here" (Machan). Warner capitulated and worked with Brown to change her image.

In 2003 Brown signed a contract with Simon & Schuster, whose editor in chief, Michael Korda, praises her versatility and growth: "She doesn't write cookie-cutter books. . . . She's rather like Michael Crichton in that way, and that ability is priceless. The reader comes to each book expecting something different, and she delivers" (Harris).

Her work has evolved, and Brown is now recognized for her complex plot twists, steamy love scenes, and gripping suspense in books that have crossed the gender barrier. The settings range from San Francisco to New York, with many stories based in her native Texas. The events of *Ricochet* (2006) occur in Savannah, Georgia, and *Chill Factor* (2005) frames a story in the hills of North Carolina. Brown's inspiration often comes from her own imagination, but she also gleans ideas from the media, her tales often confirming that truth may indeed be stranger than fiction.

Bibliography

Brown, Sandra. "Frequently asked questions." Available online. URL: www.sandrabrown.net/faq.

Foege, Alec, and Michael Haederle. "Texas Tornado." *People Weekly,* 21 Sept. 1998, 81. Expanded Academic ASAP.

Harris, Joyce Sáenz. "Bound and Determined." *The Dallas Morning News*, 9 March 2003. Available online. URL: www.sandrabrown.net/happenings/dmn_03.html.

Machan, Dyan. "Romancing the Buck." *Forbes,* 2 June 1997, 44–45. Available online. URL: http://search.ebscohost.com.libproxy.ws.edu/login.aspx?direct=true&db=f5h&AN=9705222547&site=ehost-live. Accessed Oct. 17, 2006.

Tyler, James Michael. "Video Interview with Sandra Brown, 2006." Available online. URL: http://www.expandedbooks.com/authorsbooks.php?authorid=118.

Viki Rouse

The Burden of Proof Scott Turow (1990)

After a lackluster nonfiction debut in 1977 with *One L,* Stanton creative writing professor and lawyer Scott Turow reemerged on the literary scene with his first novel, *Presumed Innocent* (1987), and whetted America's appetite for what would become a new genre of popular fiction, the legal thriller. Crime drama is certainly nothing new—Dashiel Hammett, Raymond Chandler, and others turned out hard-boiled detective fiction for decades—but Turow's work is a deliberate departure from these gritty tales, whose narrator is coolly detached from the events he recounts. While Turow's stories contain their fair share of gritty realism, the narrative style is anything but detached, and a hallmark of Turow's fiction is the way in which his often subtly drawn characters not only engage with the events of the story but resonate with the reader.

The Burden of Proof (1990) is Turow's second novel to be set in the fictional Kindle County, which George F. Will compares to Faulkner's Yoknapatawpha County as a "convincing moral landscape"; he opted for this fictional setting because he "didn't want to get stuck with having a geography (he) couldn't alter" (Turow, "Scott Talks About"). One of the pleasures of Turow's storytelling is the way in which he draws his reader into this fictional environment by reintroducing minor characters and creating back stories for them in subsequent works. Sonia "Sonny" Klonsky, for example, who was an avid spectator at the trial of Rusty Sabich in PRESUMED INNOCENT, here serves as a prosecuting attorney in the case against Stern's brother-in-law Dixon Hartnell, then again in *The Laws of Our Fathers* (1996) as the presiding judge; George Mason, a minor character in *Presumed Innocent,* serves as Stern's defense lawyer in *The Burden of Proof* and then narrates *Personal Injuries* (1999), giving voice to a "belief in the value of the law . . . honor, family, tradition, and justice" (Rich) that is an underlying characteristic of many of Turow's leading characters, and, one suspects, of Turow himself.

Alejandro "Sandy" Stern, the protagonist of *The Burden of Proof,* is himself familiar to readers as the soft-spoken lawyer who successfully defends *Presumed Innocent*'s Rusty Sabich. Sabich describes Stern, who will rise to national prominence as a result of handling Sabich's case, as "a reasonable man and judicious" (*PI* 169), with "a look of deep, if practiced, sadness, [. . .] [a] brown-eyed spaniel expression" (*PI* 170) that would seem to belie his "commanding" presence in the courtroom where the soft Spanish accent that Sandy himself sees as a "deficit . . . like a limp" (*BP* 5) and that "lends an intrigue to his speech, and where his considered formalism gives him substance" (*PI* 236). Sabich calls him "the most subtle man I've met" (*PI* 176).

When he discovers his wife of 30 years dead in their garage, Sandy finds himself "lost, the emotional pathways [of his life] hopelessly tangled" (*BP* 6), and so commences a thoroughly unconventional murder mystery. Indeed, the greatest mystery to Stern is his wife herself (ironically named Clara, as she and the motives for her suicide are anything but clear to him). Whereas Rusty Sabich recounted the events surrounding the murder of Carolyn Polhemus, here Turow employs a more flexible and dispassionate third-person narrative, although the perspective is clearly Stern's. Moreover, Stern suddenly finds himself living "Burke's aphorism that law sharpens the mind by narrowing it" (Cole 13). He has been so absorbed in the law that other aspects of his life are as new to him in many ways as they would be to an outsider; the very use of the third-person narration subtly intimates a sense that the life he is coming to terms with belongs to someone else, and he observes it as if from outside.

In the aftermath of Clara's suicide, Sandy must confront the oblique and often strained relations he has developed with each of his three children, bereft as they all are of the buffer that Clara provided while she lived. His eldest child, Peter, arrives at the scene first, and Stern is struck by the overtly emotional reaction of his doctor son but does not yet see that Peter's flamboyant appearance, extreme closeness to his mother, and effeminate behavior may betoken a lifestyle that his father has never seriously confronted or even conceived of.

Stern's relations with his daughters are equally complex. Stern "shares a natural intensity" (*BP* 23) with his middle child, Marta, who like her father practices law and like her older brother is unmarried. Stern's youngest child, Kate, has escaped these polarized family dynamics and, although exhibiting the intellectual and artistic promise of her mother and elder siblings, has chosen to settle down with John, "a sweet, Gentile lunk, an almost laughable prototype, a football player and a paragon of blond male beauty with his apple-pie face and hapless manner" (*BP* 22). Kate and John are expecting their first child, a fact not shared with Clara before her death. That John, who has remained employed by Stern's brother-in-law because of his apparent lack of initiative and acumen, proves to be more clever than anyone thought possible is a surprise to everyone but his admiring wife.

As Stern tries to cope with these unsettling revelations about his offspring, he is at last driven to reflect on his relationship with their mother, and Turow reveals intriguing information about the enigmatic Clara in a series of artful flashbacks characteristic of his nonlinear narrative style. Juxtaposed with these scenes are clues to the mystery of why Clara took her own life. Admittedly liking "complicated stories with lots of turns" (Andleman), Turow situates Clara's death in the midst of the very complicated legal affairs of Dixon Hartnell, who is partly responsible for her suicide, and his experience with the Cook County Board of Tax Appeals during the prosecution of Attorney General Bill Scott for tax fraud further enhances Turow's skillful incorporation of the various thematic elements into a firm and compelling legal tale.

Equally engaging are Sandy's struggles to adapt to life as a middle-aged bachelor. The self-deprecating humor with which Turow narrates these scenes reveal a completely different side of Stern's rather stern character and lend to it a depth that is often poignant and always believable. The women with whom he becomes involved—Fiona, the Sterns' neighbor and wife to the philandering Dr. Nate Cawley; Margy Allison, Hartnell's gritty yet vulnerable CEO; the pregnant and admiring Sonny Klonsky; and the forthrightly sensual divorcee Helen Dudak—are all drawn as individuals worthy of the interests of a man of Stern's complexity.

Turow has expressed concern that he may have "screwed it up" by creating mysteries that were too literary or stories that contained too much mystery to be considered literary (Cole 12). But despite the trouncing that *The Burden of Proof* received from the *New York Times Book Review* (Andleman), the novel, along with *Presumed Innocent,* both of which have been made into films, is widely acknowledged to have been of seminal importance in creating the popular demand for legal thrillers and serves as the defining work in his expanding oeuvre. A 1990 *Times* magazine cover dubbed Turow "the bard of the litigious age" (Cole 9), and his preeminent place, along with John Grisham, in the growing pantheon of legal thriller writers is incontestable.

Bibliography

Andelman, Bob. "The Burden of Innocence." *St. Petersburg Times Online,* Tampa Bay, 23 September 2003. Available online. URL: http://www.andelman.com/ARTICLES/media.html.

Cole, Jeffrey. "An Interview with Scott Turow: Reflections on Law and Life and Other Things that Matter." *Litigation Online: The Journal of the Section of Litigation, American Bar Association* 29, no. 2 (winter 2003).

Murphy, Stephen M. *Their Word Is Law: Bestselling Lawyer-Novelists Talk About Their Craft.* New York: Berkley Books, 2002.

Rich, Colleen Kearney. "The Five-Minute Interview: Arthur Scott Turow." *The Mason Gazette*, 21 February 2007.

Turow, Scott. *Presumed Innocent.* 1987. New York: Warner Books, 1988.

———. *The Burden of Proof.* 1990. Reprint, New York: Warner Books, 2005.

———. Home page. "Limitations." Available online. URL: http://www.scottturow.com/limitations.htm.

———. Home page. "Scott Talks About . . .". Available online. URL: http://www.scottturow.com/scotttalks.htm.

Dawn Ellen Jacobs

The Butter Battle Book

Dr. Seuss (Theodor Seuss Geisel) (1984)

First published in 1984, *The Butter Battle Book* is one of Dr. Seuss's most popular and most political books. The narrative describes the escalating conflict between the Yooks, who eat their bread with the butter side up, and the Zooks, who eat their bread with the butter side down. Each is so appalled by the culinary habits of the other that they thoroughly demonize the contrasting community. A xenophobic poster reading "Yooks Are Not Zooks. Keep Your Butter Side Up!" is visible, for instance, in the background of one scene (7). In addition, the two settlements have constructed a large stone wall between themselves to thwart the entrance of any contaminating influences.

Aside from their butter preferences, the Zooks and the Yooks are identical. Their names sound similar, their citizens look similar, and their societies even have military-industrial complexes that are almost exactly in step with each other. Indeed, the bulk of Seuss's text chronicles how, whenever the Yooks devise a larger, more lethal (and inherently more ridiculous) weapon to better guard the wall and intimidate their enemies, the Zooks counter with an identical or even superior device: They defeat the Yook Triple-Sling Jigger with a Jigger-Rock Snatchems and then foil the Kick-a-Poo Kid with their Eight-Nozzled, Elephant-Toted Boom-Blitz, which "shoots high-explosive sour cherry stone pits" (22).

This petty game of military one-upmanship reaches a crisis point when the Yooks unveil their most sophisticated weapon to date, the Bitsy Big-Boy Bomeroo, a bomb that "can blow all of those Zooks clear to Sala-ma-goo" (34). When the narrator's grandfather climbs the wall with the device and encounters his longtime Zook nemesis, he is shocked to find him holding an identical object. While members of both the Yook and Zook communities file into underground bomb shelters, the two men threaten to drop their respective Bomeroos. As they teeter on the brink of self-annihilation, the narrative ends with provocatively unanswered questions:

> "Grandpa!" I shouted. "Be careful! Oh, gee!
> Who's going to drop it?
> Will *you* . . . ? Or will *he* . . . ?"
> "Be patient," said Grandpa. "We'll see.
> We will see. . ." (42).

From the initial publication of *The Butter Battle Book* in the symbolic year of 1984, critics, parents, and teachers recognized its obvious connections to the nuclear arms race between the United States and the Soviet Union. Suggestive echoes ring throughout, from the Yook and Zook strategies for buttering bread, satirizing the opposing political systems of American democracy and Soviet communism, to the Berlinlike wall that divides the two Seussian communities.

While many readers would connect *The Butter Battle Book* with Dr. Seuss's other politically minded narratives—most notably *Yertle the Turtle* (1958), about political dictatorship, and *The Lorax* (1971), about environmental pollution—a smaller number might realize that these issues predated his career as a children's author/illustrator. During World War II, Dr. Seuss—born Theodor Seuss Geisel—worked as a staff artist for *PM*, a left-wing political newspaper in New York City, contributing more than 400 political cartoons in a span of less than two years. Akin to *The Butter Battle Book,* many of these works offered a sharp commentary on the ever-escalating threat of fascist dictators and the horrifying power of nuclear weaponry.

The Butter Battle Book, however, signaled a milestone not merely in the career of Dr. Seuss but in the history of American picture books. As Philip Nel has discussed, the 1984 narrative "inspired intense interest [in] the politics of his work" (Nel 12). From Roger Sutton's "Children's Books: Yooks, Zooks and the Bomb" (Sutton 197) to John Cech's "Some Leading, Blurred and Violent Edges of Contemporary Picture Books" (Cech 22), an array of articles explored the way in which this genre, which had previously eschewed complex political problems, was now embracing them. Many of these studies rightly grouped Seuss's *The Butter Battle Book* with other politically charged children's narratives released during this era, including David Macaulay's *Baaa* (1985), Judith Vigna's *Nobody Wants a Nuclear War* (1986), and Raymond Briggs's *The Tin-Pot Foreign General and the Old Iron Woman* (1984).

The Butter Battle Book still resonates with readers, even in the wake of the collapse of the Soviet Union and the dismantling of the Berlin wall. Although the nuclear arms race between the cold war superpowers has ended, dangerous games of military one-upmanship have not. Indeed, in today's more globalized world, *The Butter Battle Book*'s cautionary tale about the often petty origin of international conflicts and the hazards of nuclear proliferation remains, rather sadly, as relevant today as it did more than two decades ago when Seuss's narrative first appeared.

Bibliography

Briggs, Raymond. *The Tin-Pot Foreign General and the Old Iron Woman.* Hamish Hamilton Ltd, 1984.

Cech, John. "Some Leading, Blurred, and Violent Edges of Contemporary Picture Books." *Children's Literature* 15 (1987): 197–206.

Seuss, Dr. *Yertle the Turtle and Other Stories.* New York: Random House, 1958.

———. *The Butter Battle Book.* New York: Random House, 1984.

———. *The Lorax.* New York: Random House, 1971.

Sutton, Roger. "Children's Books: Yooks, Zooks and the Bomb." *New York Times,* 22, February 1987, 22.

Macaulay, David. *Baaa.* Boston: Walter Lorraine Books, 1985.

Minear, Richard H. *Dr. Seuss Goes to War: The World War II Editorial Cartoons of Theodor Seuss Geisel.* New York: The New Press, 1999.

Nel, Philip. *Dr. Seuss: American Icon.* New York: Continuum, 2004.

Seussville. Available online. URL: http://www.seussville.com.

Vigna, Judith. *Nobody Wants a Nuclear War.* Morton Grove, Ill.: Albert Whitman, 1986.

Michelle Ann Abate

Caldwell, Ian (1976–) and Thomason, Dustin (1976–)

Ian Caldwell and Dustin Thomason emerged on the literary scene in 2004 with their debut novel, *The* RULE OF FOUR. This engaging thriller intertwines art, history, mystery, and academia, transforming scholarship into detective work. On its publication many reviewers drew comparisons to DAN BROWN's wildly successful novel *The* DA VINCI CODE and Donna Tartt's intelligent best seller *The Secret History*.

Caldwell and Thomason are childhood friends who wrote their first play together at the age of eight. In their college years Caldwell studied history at Princeton, while Thomason studied anthropology and medicine at Harvard. On their graduation in 1998 Thomason won the Hoopes Prize for writing and Caldwell's academic excellence was reflected by his membership in the Phi Beta Kappa Society.

The writing project that would evolve into *The Rule of Four* began in the basement of the Caldwell family home in the three months following their 1998 graduation. Over the next six years the authors endured a process of consultation and drafting via e-mail and telephone to bridge their geographical separation. In 2003 Thomason received his M.D. and M.B.A. from Columbia University, and a year later *The Rule of Four* was published.

Friendship and collaboration are central themes of *The Rule of Four,* and inevitable comparisons between the novel's protagonists and its young authors followed on its publication, emphasizing that the university backdrop of the novel is Princeton, Caldwell's alma mater. The novel's title refers primarily to a mathematical code used to unlock the centuries-old secrets of a mysterious Renaissance text, the *Hypnerotomachia Poliphili,* but also to the evolving friendship between the four young male protagonists; the coming-of-age narrative suggests influences ranging from F. Scott Fitzgerald's *This Side of Paradise* to Rob Reiner's film *Stand By Me.*

The Rule of Four traverses several centuries of history, literature, and culture, combining murder and betrayal with a more philosophical meditation on the nature of power, creation, obsession, friendship, and loss. It is also a highly intertextual novel, reflecting Caldwell and Thomason's academic backgrounds, its scholarly milieu constructed with references to romantic writers such as Shelley, Blake, and Keats, appearing alongside Victorians such as Browning and Dickens. Moreover, the work frequently juxtaposes canonical works, such as those by Plato and Shakespeare, with feature films such as *Breakfast at Tiffany's* and *My Fair Lady.*

Dustin Thomason now resides in New York City, and Ian Caldwell lives in Newport News, Virginia. Future collaborative writing projects between the two authors are anticipated.

Bibliography

Brown, Dan. *The Da Vinci Code.* New York: Doubleday, 2003.

Caldwell, Ian, and Dustin Thomason. *The Rule of Four.* New York: Dell, 2004.

Alison Jacquet

California Gold John Jakes (1989)

According to its author, *California Gold* was written to demonstrate why California is "the world's paradigm of hope and opportunity," and how this came about, describing "the flavorful and exciting history of the state as it changed from the old frontier to a modern society" (747). Although California is fundamentally American, it is treated as a universal and magnetic symbol, "with its visions of sunshine and surf, palm trees and movie glamour, indolence and escape and renewal" (747).

In his preparation JOHN JAKES read countless books, articles, statistics, news clippings, and other materials related to the history of California, finding two books by Dr. Kevin Starr particularly helpful: *Americans and the California Dream, 1850–1915* and *Inventing the Dream: California through the Progressive Era.* He also conducted extensive on-site research with the assistance of a Californian associate (753).

While Jakes's Kent Family Chronicles and NORTH AND SOUTH SERIES are set in the American Revolutionary War and Civil War periods, respectively, *California Gold* focuses on the years 1886 through 1911, chronicling the adventures of a penniless young man from Pennsylvania, James Macklin Chance, who seeks his fortune in California. The son of a poor miner whose own dream of success in California during the Gold Rush ended in failure, Mack is determined to pursue the gold of his time in the Golden State: black oil, farming, golden citrus, movies, and the railroads.

At age 18, in 1886, he leaves his home carrying a copy of T. Fowler Haines's *The Emigrant's Guide to California & Its Gold Fields* (1848), which is more than a mere guidebook—almost a talisman for his long and arduous journey. Suffering from hunger, thirst, and every conceivable form of hardship, Mack makes his way on foot through the Midwest, the Great Plains, and the Rocky Mountains before finally reaching his promised land.

On arriving in the Golden State, however, Mack immediately encounters fierce hostility toward outsiders in general and himself in particular. Otto Hellman, for example, the largest landowner in the state, threatens to shoot him for having drunk water from a stream on his (vast) private property. In San Francisco Mack is brutally beaten up by Detective Lon Coglan for having stood up against C. P. Huntington, a railroad tycoon who runs the Southern Pacific Cooperation. Walter Fairbanks is a haughty lawyer who challenges Mack throughout the novel—in sports, politics, and personal relationships.

Finally warned to leave San Francisco within 24 hours, Mack journeys to Southern California on a mule, initially residing among the "Escrow Indians," a "tribe" of real-estate promoters and developers known for their greediness and deception. Mack briefly serves as a partner to Wyatt Paul, a real-estate businessman from Kansas whom he met on the way to California, then works as a tunnel digger and a roughneck, eventually acquiring a thorough knowledge of the oil industry. Through perseverance, hard work, and good fortune he rises to become a famed oil tycoon as well as orange grower, who pursues wealth without sacrificing human decency.

Mack is romantically involved with two women, Carla Hellman and Nellie Ross. Carla, Otto Hellman's daughter, enchants the youthful Mack with her sensual beauty and vivacious lifestyle. Although wary of her licentious ways, Mack impetuously marries her, and a son is born, but their relationship ends abruptly with her sudden departure. Soon after, Mack meets Nellie, an independent and courageous reporter for the *San Francisco Examiner,* and their long friendship evolves at last into a deep and loving relationship founded on mutual trust and respect, the novel ending with their happy marriage in August 1911.

California Gold revolves around the theme of the Californian and by extension American dream. During the Gold Rush, Mack's father fell victim to the lure of this dreamt-of California, the reality being that only a few forty-niners found gold, and most of those who did eventually lost it (2). Nor has time changed much; the promises of California are still elusive and empty for many. The business world of California is marred by deception, intimidation, and bribery; an oil-company proprietor in financial distress commits suicide at Santa Monica; Bao Kee, a native Californian whom Mack calls "[a] decent harmless Chinese who just want[s] the right to earn in living" (135), is brutally killed by those who think that Chinese Americans should not be allowed to compete with white men. But by virtue of his innate decency and persistence, Mack achieves wealth and fame in the place where his father had failed.

As a historical novel, *California Gold* is enlivened by its many vividly drawn portraits of well-known historical figures, including Randolph Hearst, Harrison Gray Otis, Leland Stanford, Ambrose (Bitter) Bierce, Jack London, John Muir, and Theodore Roosevelt; its occasional inclination to melodrama is offset by the author's rigorous and measured descriptions of historical events such as immigration, the assassination of President William McKinley, the Thalia riot, and the suffragist movement. The result is not merely an entertaining tale but a highly instructive insight into the mores and movements of turn-of-the-century California.

Bibliography

Jakes, John. *California Gold.* New York: Ballantine Books, 1989.

John J. Han

The Camel Club David Baldacci (2005)

DAVID BALDACCI dedicates his 11th best-selling novel to the men and women of the United States Secret Service. Published in 2005, the novel is set in an America menaced by terrorists and plagued by its own foreign policy errors. The Washington insiders who gather information on terrorists, as well as those who develop the international strategies to contain them, prove to be naive, cynical, or worse.

The Camel Club opens with three shady Middle Eastern characters driving the back roads of Virginia, armed and seemingly en route to a political crime. Suddenly a helicopter arrives, and in the apparent confusion one of the men kills the other two. Then from the unmarked chopper two grim Americans appear, carrying an unconscious man in a body bag. They fake the murder of the unconscious man by one of the dead Middle Easterners, plant the identification of the initial murderer on the corpse and fly off. So begins a complicated tale involving officially dead assassins, ex-CIA men, members of the Secret Service, and the head of national security, all revolving around a conspiracy to kidnap the president and redirect the course of international policy.

Four Washington outsiders, marginal characters with an obscure past, ambiguous legal standing, and peculiar expertise, meet regularly to monitor and thwart just this kind of activity: Rueben Rhodes, a six-foot-four graduate of West Point Academy and distinguished CIA operant; Caleb Shaw, holder of twin doctorates and librarian at the Library of Congress; Milton Farb, aging prodigy with obsessive-compulsive disorder, a photographic memory, and a way with numbers; and Oliver Stone, a man with no home, no phone, and no identity registered on any governmental data base. In the course of one of their meetings, held late at night at the Roosevelt monument, they witness a suspicious murder arranged to look like a suicide. Observed by the killers and followed on their row back across the Potomac, they are in immediate danger. Having been shot at and tracked to their homes, having had their friends targeted and lovers kidnapped, they finally decide to put the killers in their own crosshairs, enlisting the help of two Secret Service agents, a lawyer for the Department of Justice, a White House cook, an aging Washington socialite, and a seemingly deranged pro-life activist. With a girlfriend held hostage and no idea who can or cannot be trusted in the FBI, CIA, or National Intelligence Center, the club members, led by the self-named Oliver Stone, take on the conspirators themselves.

The plot thickens when the president himself is poisoned, his doctor and guards shot, his route to the hospital sabotaged, and he is then finally taken into the hands of kidnappers, whose tactics and demands are as confusing as the abduction itself. When the dust clears, the president is gone, but his doctor, attendants, and guards get up and walk away, having been shot with tranquilizer guns; the only carnage on the scene is a heap of Middle Eastern bodies, each bearing a clean identity—seemingly suicide assassins but with no indication of who or why they have undertaken this well-planned but costly attack.

Behind these events, perplexing in themselves, the club discovers at their peril a complex organization of assassins—all officially dead—organized by two Americans: the first, Captain Jack, working for money, and the second, Hemmingway, motivated by the impossible ideals of his own murdered father. The assassins, too, have their stories, some surprisingly sympathetic. Djamila, for example, impersonating a nanny so as to be able to drive the sedated president in the back of her van through any roadblock, is intelligent, shrewd in her analysis of American policy in her native Iraq, and compelling in her critique of American decadence. Although knowing she will die, she still saves the young lives in her charge and even spares their "whoring" mother, whom the children will need. The ideals of Hemmingway, and the myriad wrongs committed by Americans in the Middle East—both at the level of policy and at the level of covert operations—help explain the televised demands of those holding the president: to give Islam the respect it deserves, to match aid to Israel with aid to Palestine, to withdraw from Iraq and Afghanistan, to return oil profits to those living in resource-rich territories, to accept responsibility for political and social problems plaguing those territories, and to renounce state-sponsored violence in the area. The reader is finally driven to question what real patriotism is, whether power is inherently corrupting, and whether ideals of peace, honesty, and open government can survive the cynicism both of the bureaucrats who administer institutions and of those who wish to subvert them.

Set in Washington, D.C., the action of *The Camel Club* takes the reader to many important landmarks of the American capital, from the Washington Monument to the Library of Congress, from the obscure Mt. Zion cemetery to Roosevelt Island in the middle of the Potomac River, with Baldacci supplying vividly detailed historical descriptions of all. The reader learns, for example, that the United Methodist Church cemetery (Mt. Zion) was owned by the oldest black congregation in the city and had been an important stop on the underground freedom railroad.

But in the end this Washington is really that of its central character. Like many action heroes, Oliver Stone is a loner, trained as a crack commando but disguised as a homeless man, with keen intelligence and a deep compassion for the marginal and outcast: leaving an intolerant cabbie, for example, with a $20 tip and a stern admonition, "the regulations under which you operate do not allow you to discriminate on any basis." His personal history of grief and loss—an opening dream sequence recounts the death of his wife and the disappearance of his baby girl—give him insight and empathy as well as an educated wariness of those in power, Baldacci reminding readers not only that appearances can be deceiving but also that the truest Americans may be invisible and unrewarded outsiders.

Bibliography

Baldacci, David. *The Camel Club.* New York: Grand Central, 2005.

Andrea Sauder

The Celestine Prophecy: An Adventure

James Redfield (1993)

Appearing on the *New York Times* best-seller list for more than three years, *The Celestine Prophecy* attracted a great deal of popular attention during the 1990s. Variously classified as a New Age novel, a metaphysical tale, and an occult adventure story, Redfield's work follows the familiar fictional trajectory of the mysterious lost manuscript. Here the protagonist searches for "the Nine Insights" into the meaning of life, found in a document written in Aramaic around 600 B.C.E. and reportedly hidden somewhere in Peru.

The adventurous first-person narrator is contacted by an old friend, Charlene, who tells him about the Manuscript (always capitalized in the book). Reportedly, as soon as news of the document's discovery was made known, the church and government authorities suppressed it as the insights it contained could threaten their power. The narrator had recently taken time off work as an adolescent counselor to find some meaning in his own life and is intrigued enough by Charlene's story to begin the quest, aided the next morning by a fortuitous cancellation on a flight leaving in three hours.

In another apparent coincidence the narrator discovers on the plane that a college professor, Wayne Dobson, is traveling for the same purpose, and after Dobson reveals to him the Second Insight, the narrator decides to join forces with him in the quest. Though they are later separated, this proves only one of a host of such serendipitous meetings, as the protagonist journeys through Peru with the aid of other ardent seekers of the Insights. The church and the Peruvian government are the narrator's chief antagonists, responsible for a series of thefts, murders, accidents, and disappearances as he endeavors to bring the Manuscript to light. Eventually, he is able to connect with a group of like-minded seekers, but the problems do not end here, as the group itself faces further persecution.

The First Insight is revealed in a prefatory author's note: "It begins with a heightened perception of the way our lives move forward. We notice those chance events that occur at just the right moment, and bring forth just the right individuals, to suddenly send our lives in new and important directions." There really is no coincidence, says the Manuscript; everything has a purpose. Seemingly chance meetings, unusual coincidences, and fateful choices—all plot devices Redfield himself employs—underscore this Insight. At one point a fellow seeker admonishes the narrator: "Get it into your head. Everyone who crosses our path has a message for us. Otherwise they would have taken another path, or left earlier or later. The fact that these people are here means that they are here for some reason" (207). Even the work itself is structured into nine chapters, each division serving as a vehicle for revealing one of the Nine Insights, while reinforcing the importance of coming to understand them sequentially.

Throughout the novel the narrator is enthralled by what he learns of the Manuscript and suffers only the vaguest of misgivings about his quest, with every question he raises about the validity of the Manuscript or the worth of his pursuit being quickly answered. In the first chapter, for example, he questions Charlene:

> "You know, all this sounds awfully sophisticated for a Manuscript written in 600 B.C."
>
> "I know," she replied. "I raised the question myself. But the priest assured me that the scholars who first translated the Manuscript were absolutely convinced of its authenticity. Mainly because it was written in Aramaic, the same language in which much of the Old Testament was written" (8–9).

Later, he asks Father Carl how he can continue on his search when he is so afraid, and the Father answers, "You must understand what is at stake. The truth you are pursuing is as important as the evolution of the universe itself, for it enables evolution to continue" (149).

Enhancing both the reader's interest and the verisimilitude of the tale, the narrator frequently and deftly describes his own astonishment and growing sense of wonder, his own evolution, as he contemplates the unfolding Manuscript, its Insights, and the answers it can provide for humanity:

> I had come to Peru with a mild curiosity and now I found myself in hiding, an unwitting fugitive who didn't even know who his pursuers were. And the strangest thing of all was that at this moment, instead of being terrified, totally panicked, I found myself in a state of excitement. . . . As I considered my options, I realized that in reality I had no choice. The Second Insight had ended any possibility of going back to my old preoccupations (37).
>
> I suddenly realized that the Ninth Insight was going to reveal where we humans were going with this revolution. I had wondered how humans would be acting toward each other as a result of the Manuscript, and that question had been answered with the Eighth Insight, and now the logical next question was: where is all this going to lead, how will human society change (217)?

The work is populated by a host of colorful and well-drawn minor characters, each of whom propel the narrator forward on his journey in some way; however, in keeping with the genre, he is the only significant character and his sensibility the touchstone for the reader's own understanding. The novel is above all a story of one man's search for spiritual fulfillment in an increasingly impersonal, material, and technological world. For the narrator, and presumably Redfield himself, this is a journey that must and will be made in the new millennium by each individual, leading to a peaceful world of new reality, with a "new consciousness [. . .], a new awareness that can only be called transcendent, spiritual." He offers *The Celestine Prophecy* as a step toward the "culture that has been the goal of history all along." Therefore, the work, like Pirsig's *Zen and the Art of Motorcycle Maintenance,* is at once a novel and self-help manual; the individual, if he will only embrace the Nine Insights, will be a contributing part of this new reality. In fact, the back cover of the 1994 paperback edition published by Warner Books calls the book "a guidebook that has the power to crystallize your perceptions [. . .] and to direct your steps with a new energy." Moreover, again like Pirsig's *Zen, The Celestine Prophecy* may be considered a spiritual autobiography of sorts, for while the search in Peru is clearly a literary device, the unnamed first-person narrator is strikingly similar to Redfield.

The Manuscript containing the Ninth Insight mentions a Tenth, serendipitously providing the author with an opportunity for a follow-up work—thus Redfield's *The Tenth Insight* in 1997. But even before this appeared, the author had collaborated with psychologist Carol Adrienne to produce *The Celestine Prophecy Experiential Guide,* a workbook for individuals or groups who want to achieve the higher consciousness offered by the Nine Insights. In 1995 Redfield also published *A Pocket Guide to the Nine Insights.* In addition to these, the novel has spawned numerous workshops, seminars, and Web sites.

A film adaptation of *The Celestine Prophecy,* described by its producers as "a spiritual adventure film" was released in 2006, directed by Armand Mastroianni and with Redfield collaborating on the screenplay.

Bibliography

Redfield, James. *The Celestine Prophecy: An Adventure.* New York: Warner Books, 1993.

Jean Shepherd Hamm

Cell Stephen King (2006)

Cell, STEPHEN KING's take on the "zombie apocalypse" genre, follows a string of films such as *28 Days Later* (2002), the remake of George Romero's *Dawn of the Dead* (2004), and the comedic parody *Shaun of the Dead* (2004), which have signaled a renewed cultural interest in the figure of the zombie. King actually dedicates *Cell* to Romero as a tribute to this early master of the genre but complicates the traditional zombie story in a number of ways, exploring broader (and more realistic) cultural fears such as dependence on technology and the threat of terrorism.

The novel opens in Boston with Clayton Riddell, a novelist who has just sold his first book, walking back to his hotel, where he plans to call his estranged wife and share with her the good news. Clay decides to stop for an ice-cream cone, destined not to get it, for King, who never allows his audience to relax for long in such idyllic scenes, cuts the moment short with a horrific sequence of violent images. People who only moments before had been chatting casually on their cell phones suddenly begin attacking those around them, using their teeth to tear at jugulars, impervious to any damage done to themselves. Clay watches in shock as a man in a business suit bites the ear of a dog. At the same time chaos seems to erupt all over Boston; cars slam into buildings and one another, and explosions sound in the distance. Clay quickly realizes that only those who had been talking on cell phones have turned murderous and flees back to his hotel.

He is eventually joined by two others, the phlegmatic Tom McCourt and Alice Maxwell, a teenage girl whose quick thinking and decisiveness establish her as the leader of the group (a nod to the rise of adolescence, hybridizing with computers, typical of the novel). The three take stock of their situation in Clay's hotel and decide that together they will venture to Kent Pond, Maine, to try to find Clay's wife, Sharon, and his son, Johnny.

Clay's quest marks the central irony of the novel; before catastrophe struck, "his major object in life had been reaching Sharon on the phone" (22). Now, when that object has become even more imperative, reaching anybody by phone has become impossible. The mode of communication people reflexively rely on to make things work has become not only inaccessible but the enemy. Anyone who uses a cell phone is struck by "the Pulse," a signal that damages the brain in some horrendous way—the very ubiquity of cell phones making them the perfect vehicle for causing mass destruction:

> "the insidious thing is that when people see things going wrong all around them. . . . Their first impulse is to reach for their cell phones and try to find out what's causing it," said Tom (59–60).

Moreover, King blurs the line between human and machine by highlighting parallels between the mind and computers. Clay, Tom, and Alice meet two others, Jordan, a high school student at an upscale academy, and Charles Ardai, the school's headmaster. Jordan, a self-professed computer geek, explains, "What do you think a brain is? . . . . A big old hard drive. Organic circuitry. No one knows how many bytes" (204). The Pulse, they realize, simply wipes the brain's hard drive clean; as the "phone-crazies" rest each night, they have new programs transmitted to them. It takes Jordan's technological savvy to puzzle out how the effects of the Pulse might be reversed, and in the end it is only through his extraordinary (and unsettling) grasp of the similarities between the human mind and the computer program controlling the Pulse that Clay can save his son, who has been affected by a weakened version of the cell-phone madness. The end of the novel finds Clay about to put all his trust into the same technology that rests at the root of the story's evil.

While it is never made clear who originated the Pulse—characters speculate that it was a terrorist group, but it could just as easily have been computer hackers working out of their garage—King deftly exploits its effects to explore issues at the root of the terrorist phenomenon: a vulnerable people's perception of threat from some greater power and tensions between their respective ideologies. The phone-crazies initially start out as a deadly rabble, turning on each other as readily as they turn on others. However, the computer system controlling them continually adds to their programming until they begin to operate as cohesive "flocks," similar to our notion of terrorist "cells." These flocks gradually gain mastery of themselves and the world around them, while through their newly acquired telepathic powers they are able to influence those not affected by the Pulse.

In response Clayton and his group, perceiving their own vulnerability to the zombies' growing power, destroy a flock with explosives while it sleeps, killing thousands—an act of such extreme violence as to blur the line between monster and hero, terrorist attack and righteous war. Clay's group is labeled insane, not only by the phone-crazies themselves, but by the regular people hoping to cooperate with them, suggesting the unsettling possibility at the margins of moral thinking that definitions of right and wrong, sane and insane are not fixed, but instead based upon the whims of majority opinion.

Further, the destruction perpetrated by the protagonists highlights King's long-standing concern with the violent tendencies latent in us all, reminding us that it does not take a brain-scrambling signal to bring out the worst and most dangerous in people. When Clay, Tom, and Alice are fleeing Boston, Alice is harassed by a religious zealot. Without thinking, Clay punches the woman and is immediately horrified by his action, only to be more surprised by the mild-mannered Tom threatening to strike her again. King writes, "[Tom] held his fist before her eyes, and although Clay had already concluded that Tom was an educated man, civilized, and probably not much of a puncher under ordinary circumstances, he could not help feeling dismay at the sight of that small, tight fist, as if he were looking at an omen of the coming age" (85)—an age announcing its arrival yet more clearly in the later, senseless murder of Alice, not by phone-crazies but by "regular" people.

In the end the Pulse is destroyed from within by a computer virus. Clay and his group manage to kill most of the phone-crazies, while those who remain may possibly be rehabilitated. But King carefully and subtly avoids any happy ending, leaving exposed contradictions and malignancies latent in modern society, and leaving the reader profoundly uncertain what—beyond mere hope—may be appealed to in attempting to remedy them.

Bibliography

Dawn of the Dead. Directed by Zack Snyder. Universal, 2004.

King, Stephen. *Cell.* New York: Pocket Star, 2006.

Shaun of the Dead. Directed by Edgar Wright. Universal, 2004.

28 Days Later. Directed by Danny Boyle. 20th Century Fox, 2002.

Jan Cadwallader

Chill Factor Sandra Brown (2005)

Chill Factor is a romance/suspense novel set in the wintry mountains of small town Cleary, North Carolina, a place of secrets, lies, and murder. Five women have vanished from the community over the last two years, and a serial killer known as Blue has just kidnapped and killed his latest victim. The town fears Blue is one of their own.

The action centers on Lilly Martin, the only character not harboring a secret or masking her identity, and as her name suggests, a figure of regeneration and new life. A successful magazine editor, Lilly is in Cleary to close her mountain cabin and make final her divorce from Dutch Burton, Cleary's chief of police, whose brutish and destructive nature prompts a chain of events with grave consequences.

Lilly's attempts to leave Cleary and her ex-husband behind are thwarted by a raging storm that effectively foreshadows the violence to follow. Driving down the icy mountain road, Lilly's car skids and hits a hiker whom she recognizes as Ben Tierney, the man she met and flirted with while on a white-water rafting trip the previous summer. Trapped with Tierney in her cabin until the storm passes, Lilly senses that his true identity is something other than the professed adventure writer. She distrusts this "stranger" and wonders if he is somehow linked to Blue. Tierney, though, disavows any connection to the serial killer and urges Lilly to face her feelings for him, saying, "if you think we're strangers, then you're not remembering the day we met the same way I remember it" (48).

Tierney is characterized as an intriguing mix of danger and romance, "the kind of man women throw panties at" (52). On the novel's first page he is seen holding a shovel and standing over the open grave of the most recent victim. Something sinister is secreted in his hotel room. His initials appear in the diary of the most recent victim, and he has handcuffs and a gun in his backpack, both of which he will use. Yet this dangerous man also tenderly administers to Lilly during her crippling bouts of asthma. Lilly senses this paradoxical undercurrent in Tierney and battles with her own growing attraction to him, even as she fears him.

Suspicion, though, does not rest on Tierney alone. As in other SANDRA BROWN novels, including *Ricochet* and *Temperature's Rising,* most of the men in *Chill Factor* are psychologically or physically abusive, especially to women. Wes Hamer, responsible for Burton's position as chief of police and Dutch's best friend, bullies his son Scott, forces him to take steroids, and cheats on his wife. William Ritt, the town pharmacist, treats his sister like a servant and blackmails many of the town's residents. Scott Hamer dated the latest victim, Millicent Gunn, before her disappearance. The timing of the murders also coincides with Burton's tenure as chief of police, and his obsession to save Lilly from suspected serial killer Tierney borders on the pathological. Any of these men might be Blue.

The failures of Cleary's police force to apprehend Blue are countered by the "good guys," FBI officer Charlie Wise and Special Agent in Charge Kent Begley. In stark contrast to Burton's vigilantism, Begley is focused and fair. Although out of the field for years, he is keen to capture this killer of young women, his daughter being the same age as the most recent victim. Children's vulnerability is a key subplot in the novel: Two of the victims are teenagers; Lilly's daughter Amy dies from a brain tumor; Tierney himself suffers the death of a child; and the anguish of the parents of the most recent victim, Millicent Gunn, is heartbreakingly transparent.

For the women of Cleary, to find Blue is, in the end, to find truth, strength, and renewal. Initially characterized as victims, they end up as victors and saviors. Dora Hamer, married to the morally corrupt Wes, is fiercely protective of her son Scott; Marilee Ritt, considered by most to be a lonely spinster, has a latent core of extraordinary strength that is revealed at the novel's conclusion; Lilly herself, having long battled depression over the loss of her daughter and the failure of her marriage, finally confronts the serial killer, saving both herself and her town.

Bibliography

Brown, Sandra. *Chill Factor.* Simon & Schuster, New York: 2005.

Susan Amper

The Christmas Box Richard Paul Evans (1995)

The Christmas Box is a holiday tale about the importance of family, a lesson that narrator RICHARD EVANS learns from MaryAnne Parkin, a wealthy, elderly widow who welcomes Richard, his wife, Keri, and their young daughter, Jenna, into her home as a kind of surrogate family as well as domestic help. As Richard spends ever more time away at his new business, he begins to have recurring dreams, accompanied by a beautiful melody, about an ethereal angel who turns into stone, which finally lead him to a Christmas box in the attic, where he finds a handful of unsigned love letters. At the same time, Mary, who is dying of cancer, quietly attempts to educate him in the meaning of Christmas; but he only begins to understand after coming upon the tombstone of Mary's dead child—the stone angel in his dreams—and learning that the love letters have been written, in mourning, to this child, her daughter, Andrea. Richard comes to realize that the first gift of Christmas is a parent's love for a child and is at last able to reassure Mary of his understanding, hearing as he does the melody from his dreams, as she herself, murmuring, "My angel," joins her daughter in the afterlife (116).

While Richard narrates the tale and experiences the story's epiphany, Mary emerges as the strongest and most dynamic character, as her past suffering is revealed and her wisdom passed on. Living by her teachings, she spends a great deal of time with Richard's little girl, Jenna, instilling the importance of family and home. In a typical exchange Jenna asks:

> "Is work better than home?"
> "No. No place is better than home."
> "Then why does Daddy want to be there instead of here?"
> Mary paused thoughtfully. "I guess sometimes we forget," she answered and pulled the little girl close (116).

Despite her love for Jenna, Mary never discusses Andrea, whose presence yet haunts the last pages of the novel; but the other two books in The Christmas Box trilogy, *Timepiece* (1996) and *The Letter* (1997), relate Mary's earlier life with the child and her husband, David.

In all three works characters receive a second chance to prioritize their lives anew and reconnect with their families and deepest selves; the effortful maintenance of faith, both in a higher power and other people, through difficult and cynical times, is another theme running through the trilogy. Richard begins *The Christmas Box,* reflecting:

> It may be that I am growing old in this world and have used up more than my share of allotted words and eager audiences. Or maybe I am just growing weary of a skeptical age that pokes and prods at my story much the same as a middle-school biology students pokes and prods through an anesthetized frog to determine what makes it live, leaving the poor creature dead in the end. Whatever the reason, I find that with each passing Christmas the story of the Christmas box is told less and needed more (15–16).

The Christmas Box was adapted into a television movie with the same title in 1995, also highly successful, but the story behind the novel, which Evans shares in *The Christmas Box Miracle* (2001), has become almost as famous as the story itself. He wrote *The Christmas Box* for his first two daughters, and after the book was well received by family members and friends, he and his wife, Keri, decided to publish it nationally, investing all of their resources in the endeavor. With the book not selling and his family fortunes looking bleak, Evans experienced what he describes as divine inspiration and offered the book up to God. Shortly thereafter it became a national phenomenon, the first book to be a number one best seller simultaneously in hardcover and paperback on the *New York Times* best-seller list. But Evans himself considers the book's success to be far more than financial, believing that, through the experience,

> [God] gave me the chance to know that both Keri and I were doing this, not for money or acclaim, but because it was the right thing to do—even if it cost us everything we owned. He gave both Keri and me one of the greatest gifts we can hope to receive in this life. He gave us a chance to see our own souls (Canfield 210–211).

Bibliography

Evans, Richard Paul. *The Christmas Box.* New York: Simon & Schuster, 1995.

———. *Timepiece.* New York: Simon & Schuster, 1996.

———. *The Letter.* New York: Simon & Schuster, 1997.

———. *The Christmas Box Miracle: My Spiritual Journey of Destiny, Healing and Hope.* New York: Simon & Schuster, 2001.

———. "The Christmas Box." In *Chicken Soup for the Writer's Soul: Stories to Open the Heart and Rekindle the Spirit of Writers.* Edited by Jack Canfield, Mark Victor Hansen, and Bud Gardner. Deerfield Beach, Fla.: Health Communications, 2000, pp. 204–211.

Ramona Caponegro

The Chronicles of Thomas Covenant, The Unbeliever **Stephen Donaldson** (1977–2004)

On the surface The Chronicles of Thomas Covenant, The Unbeliever seems a typical fantasy trilogy, pitting the forces of good and evil in an almost cartoonish struggle, with the good finally and inevitably victorious. The protagonist, Thomas Covenant, is questing in a parallel realm known simply as "the Land"; in the first volume, *Lord Foul's Bane,* he is disconsolate, estranged from his wife and inexplicably jettisoned from normal reality. In a nebulous underworld he struggles with the forces of evil, finally regaining his home, apparently in triumph, a pattern that is repeated in the following two installments, *The Illearth War* and *The Power That Preserves.* The narration is linear and male characters dominate. Beneath this superficial conservatism, however, ambiguities and enigmas proliferate, complicating The Chronicles' high-fantasy status. Offering, in addition, no happy resolutions, the trilogy searchingly explores issues of isolation, desertion, and identity, themes also informing Donaldson's two other fantasy series, *Mordant's Need* and *The Gap.*

The trilogy's first peculiarity lies in its choice of protagonist. Thomas Covenant is a leper, already having lost two of his fingers. Abandoned by his wife and son and shunned by the community, he seems consumed by rage and mentally unbalanced, more an anti-hero than the traditional fantasy protagonist questing to become a more fully realized being. Nevertheless, it is Covenant who is chosen to save the Land.

Donaldson's Land too is problematic, with no defined borders and obscure means of entrance and departure. In *Lord Foul's Bane* Covenant simply slips into this reality after being accosted by a beggar who tells him he is "in perdition" and admonishes him to "be true." Covenant, in fact, refuses to accept its reality, convinced it is just another delusion. Though it, too, like its potential savior, is under threat, Covenant will not act on its behalf, his denial reflected in the title he bestows upon himself: The Unbeliever. Initially readers are inclined to agree with Covenant, understanding the Land as a symbolic emanation of his disturbed mind, but as the story develops, it becomes increasingly real and significant, and Covenant eventually undertakes the task of saving it.

It remains, nonetheless, difficult to know whether he acts on his own volition or is being used as a pawn, tossed about by the forces of good and evil, represented by the Creator and Foul, respectively. The Creator, located in Covenant's "real" world, is the maker of the universe, and Foul, his corrupt counterpart, Lord of the underworld. Both these entities claim to have summoned Covenant, Foul treating him as no more than a "groveller" (1.44) called to the Land to serve the dark forces; the Covenant as "my unwilling son" (3.554), sent into the darkness, much like Jesus, in order to overcome it. As the story evolves, Covenant is increasingly torn between these two characters, as well as the roles in which they have cast him.

His first task upon arrival in the Land is assigned to him by Foul: to deliver a message to the Lords, the benevolent stewards of the Land who govern by way of magic, a cohesive group, able to meld their minds. Once authoritative leaders, their rule has been undermined by the loss of the Staff of Law, an emblem of their true power, and hampered by an Oath of Peace to which they are bound. "Unhomed" Giants in ancient times made an alliance with the Lords and still continue to help them, while the latter are further protected by 500 Haruchai warriors, a band of interlopers who have sworn an oath to serve the Lords unstintingly; they are "the Bloodguard," semi-immortal, never sleeping or growing old.

The message entrusted to Covenant informs the Lords that Foul's minion, Drool Rockworm, has unearthed the Lord's lost Staff of Law, and In *Lord Foul's Bane* a questing party manages to wrest the Staff from Drool. But in *The Illearth War* the Staff is once again dramatically lost, and in *The Power That Preserves* is used against the Lords themselves by one of their own deceased. The parties that quest after the lost Staff always include several Bloodguards, the Giant Saltheart Foamfollower, and the Lords. Covenant, though an unwilling participant, is vital to these quests as he alone possesses the ultimate power, a bizarre force that inexplicably and inadvertently explodes from within his white-gold wedding band at crucial, life-saving moments, rather like the Ring in the Tolkien saga. Though, like Tolkien's Frodo, Covenant is unable to explain this power, equally reluctant both to understand it and better use it. He will not give away the band, and its amazingly destructive power renders him a necessary but potentially lethal helper.

As the quest unfolds, Donaldson reveals the richness of his underworld. As well as defiling swamps and ominously threatening forests, the Land includes the idyllic magical woodland of Andelain, a place of concentrated goodness and strength. There is also Revelstone, the marvelous rock citadel and ancestral seat of the Lords. On bleak plains the questers face and combat Foul's strange and formidable army made up of ur-viles, Demondin, Ravers, and *kresh,* victory always very much in doubt. On the more salubrious Plains of Ra the Lords are assisted by a superior race, the Ramen, who tend the great horses, the Ranyhyn. The questers also meet with the keeper of the sentient forests, Caer-Caveral.

The Chronicles can be read as a manifold confrontation between the forces of good and evil, as well as an investigation into the nature of evil itself, grounded in a series of creation stories that the Lords relate to Covenant. In many respects Donaldson's mythology parallels that of the Bible, but with critical variations: Where the latter, to the consternation of scholars, never accounts for the existence of evil, Donaldson attempts to explain its origin and anatomize its nature; and where the God of the Bible is a transcendent being, omniscient and omnipotent, Donaldson's Creator is a vulnerable, corporeal tramp located in the physical world and continually threatened by his counterpart, Foul.

Some critics argue that The Chronicles is a derivatively Tolkienesque work, merely following in the footsteps of *Lord of the Rings* (1954), and there are certainly parallels, beyond the Ring itself: Donaldson's Andelain is akin to Tolkien's Lothlórien, his Ravers and Giants similar to Tolkien's Nazguls and Ents; but Donaldson is also innovative and original. The communities of the Woodhelvennin and the Stonedowners are unique and memorable, with no parallels in Tolkien's text. And where Tolkien's Middle Earth may be seen as backward-looking, more representative of a medieval English utopia, Donaldson's Chronicles may be read as a challenge to many assumptions that inform the contemporary Western world. Rather than promoting the romantic notion of the realized hero, for example, the trilogy highlights the problems promoted by cynicism, despair, and disbelief. Its ending, too, is profoundly ambivalent in comparison to that of the Ring trilogy.

Donaldson has plans to extend The Last Chronicles, with four more books expected, of which two, *The Runes of the Earth* (2004) and *Fatal Revenant* (2007) have been published thus far.

Bibliography

The Chronicles of Thomas Covenant, The Unbeliever:

Donaldson, Stephen. *Lord Foul's Bane.* New York: Holt, 1977.

———. *The Illearth War.* New York: Holt, 1977.

———. *The Power That Preserves.* New York: Holt, 1977.

The Second Chronicles of Thomas Covenant:

———. *The Wounded Land.* New York: Del Rey Books, 1980.

———. *The One Tree.* New York: Del Rey Books, 1982.

———. *White Gold Wielder.* New York: Del Rey Books, 1983.

The Last Chronicles of Thomas Covenant:

———. *Runes of the Earth.* London: Gollancz, 2004.

———. *Fatal Revenant.* London: Gollancz, 2007.

Mordant's Need:

———. *The Mirror of Her Dreams.* London: Collins, 1987.

———. *A Man Rides Through.* London: Collins, 1988.

The Gap Series:

———. *The Real Story: The Gap into Conflict.* London: Collins, 1990.

———. *Forbidden Knowledge: The Gap into Vision.* London: HarperCollins, 1991.

———. *A Dark and Hungry God Arises: The Gap into Power.* London. HarperCollins, 1992.

———. *Chaos and Order: The Gap into Madness.* London: HarperCollins, 1994.

———. *This Day All Gods Die: The Gap into Ruin.* London: Voyager, 1996.

Short Stories

———. *Daughter of Regals.* New York: Grant, 1984.

———. *Reave the Just and Other Stories.* New York: Spectra, 2000.

Mystery Novels

———. *The Man Who Killed His Brother.* New York: Ballantine, 1980.

———. *The Man Who Risked His Partner.* New York: Ballantine, 1984.

———. *The Man Who Tried to Get Away.* New York: Ballantine, 1990.

———. *The Man Who Fought Alone.* New York: Tor/Forge, 2001.

Kate Simons

The Cider House Rules John Irving (1985)

JOHN IRVING's sixth novel is not easy to classify. One is tempted to describe it as a coming-of-age novel, but the protagonist comes of age midway through, though not fully mature until the end. One might consider it a family saga, but the main characters, while intricately intertwined, do not constitute a traditional family. Whereas Irving's earlier work was clearly if at times blackly comic, here it is genuinely difficult to decide whether one is dealing with comedy or drama—perhaps one might describe it as "a problem comedy." On one level it is a very serious book, dealing with very serious topics of morality and mortality; yet on another level it is a raucous read, though still somewhat muted by Irving's standards.

Irving reveres the work of Charles Dickens and believes a novel should be "as complicated and involved as you're capable of making it" (Herel). Yet the novels of both authors are for the most part straightforward in structure. This work, characteristic of Irving's oeuvre, proceeds in chronological order, with a few long flashbacks, ultimately spanning a period of some 80 years, from the late 19th to mid 20th century; it, too, is set in Maine and narrated in the third person.

The author once told interviewer Suzanne Herel that when he set out to write *The Cider House Rules* he saw it as being about a father-son relationship but wanted that relationship to be "closer, more conflicted, and ultimately more loving, than most" (Herel). And thus instead of writing about a biological family, he created a relationship between the director of an orphanage and an unadoptable orphan. The director of the St. Cloud's orphanage is the kindly Dr. Wilbur Larch. Women come there to give birth to the babies they will give up for adoption. However, Larch does more than deliver babies and watch over the orphans. He also secretly provides safe abortions, thereby breaking the law as abortion was universally prohibited early in the 20th century. But Larch feels morally obliged to offer the service. When still a young man, just starting work as an obstetrician in a big city, he had once turned away a woman who wanted an abortion; when she reappeared on his doorstop to die, he became painfully aware of both the inevitability and the dangers of backstreet abortions.

The unadoptable orphan is Homer Wells, offered for adoption by his mother at birth. When still small, Homer is actually adopted, and by more than one family. But something always goes wrong, and he returns to St. Cloud's and the ever-welcoming Dr. Larch. Every night Larch reads aloud to the orphans—Dickens's *David Copperfield*—and every night, as he concludes the reading and goes to turn out the dormitory light, he delivers his signature phrase: "Good night! Good night—you princes of Maine, you kings of New England!" (72). Over time, however, he develops a particular affection for Homer, whom he decides will follow in his footsteps, one day running the orphanage and performing the abortions.

To this end Larch starts giving Homer medical training at a very early age, and by the time the boy becomes a teenager he is perfectly capable of delivering babies on his own. He lives by one of Dr. Larch's most important rules, that everyone has the moral duty to "be of use" (80). But while Homer accepts the fact that women come to St. Cloud's to have abortions, he decides that he himself will not perform them. This creates conflict between Homer and Dr. Larch and eventually leads to Homer's running away from St. Cloud's.

The second half of the book revolves around Homer's new life. He goes to live and work at the Ocean View Orchard, an apple farm run by the Worthington family. (Wally Worthington and his girlfriend, Candy, met Homer when they came to St. Cloud's in order for Candy to have an abortion.) At Ocean View Homer finds an entirely new and fulfilling way to be of use, and when Wally goes off to fight in World War II, Homer is placed in charge of the orchard, including the migrant workers who come to pick the crop every fall. The book's title refers to the list of avuncular rules that is posted on their bunkhouse wall, such as PLEASE DON'T OPERATE THE GRINDER OR THE PRESS IF YOU'VE BEEN DRINKING (281). After the family finds out that Wally's plane has been shot down over Burma, Homer and Candy begin an affair that results in her being pregnant. She goes away for a time, but Homer eventually goes after her, and they return with a baby boy named Angel. They do not reveal to the Worthington family, however, that the boy is actually theirs—instead Homer pretends he has adopted Angel through St. Cloud's. The situation is complicated tremendously when it turns out that Wally was not in fact killed in his plane crash and returns to the farm.

Wally's return forces Homer to confront profound and baffling questions about the nature of a family, and at the same time, Angel's budding friendship with a girl who is being sexually abused by her father forces Homer reevaluate his stance on abortion. Ultimately he returns to St. Cloud's to run the orphanage and perform abortions, just as Dr. Larch has always wished.

The Cider House Rules is a complex and multifaceted novel. Although deceptively simple in its plot, it is searching and subtle both in theme and development of character. Dr. Larch, for example, is at the same time the avuncular head of St. Cloud's and an ether addict. Homer is sweet by nature yet wrestles with an amazing capacity to lie. The book's main subplot involves an orphaned girl named Melony, who for much of the tale is cast as a villain but is ultimately sympathetic. And all is encompassed by provocative, ultimately unanswerable questions of how and why humans develop rules to govern their lives, exploring what happens when people realize the rules that are imposed upon them—whether it be by government, society, or an employer—must be broken.

When *The Cider House Rules* appeared in 1985, it was well received by critics. *New York Times* reviewer Christopher Lehmann-Haupt, for example, hailed it as superior to Irving's earlier work. Although he noted Irving drove home his point—that society always has multiple sets of rules—with his usual "sledgehammer effect," he regarded the book as streamlined and controlled, with a good resolution. Other reviewers praised Irving for creating lovable characters and thought-provoking dilemmas, and today academics consider it one of three Irving novels likely to become classics, the others being his earlier blockbuster *The World According to Garp* and *A Prayer for Owen Meany*.

The reading public, however, had mixed feelings toward the book. Irving is a popular author with many avid fans, and the book rapidly attained best-seller lists. But its searching exploration of the morality and perceptions of abortion made it controversial for some. Pro-life groups such as the U.S. Conference of Catholic Bishops were dismayed, while the National Women's Caucus gave

Irving a Good Guy Award for the novel, claiming it championed the rights of women. Irving was of course pleased to accept the award but noted that he did not write the novel in order to send a political message.

The Cider House Rules was made into a popular movie in 1999—10 years in the making, starring Michael Caine, Tobey Maguire, and Charlize Theron. John Irving had a cameo and also wrote the screenplay. The movie received an astonishing total of 26 Oscar nominations and won four awards, with Irving himself receiving the Best Adapted Screenplay award and Caine being named Best Supporting Actor. In 2000 John Irving published a nonfiction book called *My Movie Business,* which was about his involvement in the making of the movie.

Bibliography

Herel, Suzanne. "John Irving," *Mother Jones* (May/June 1997). Available online. URL: http://www.motherjones.com/arts/qa/1997/05/outspoken.html.

Irving, John. *The Cider House Rules.* New York: Bantam, 1986.

Lehmann-Haupt, Christopher. "The Cider House Rules, by John Irving." *New York Times,* 20 May 1985. Available online. URL: http://query.nytimes.com/gst/fullpage.html?res=990DE2DE133BF933A15756C0A963948260.

Ann Graham Gaines

Clancy, Tom (1947–)

Insurance broker turned novelist, Tom Clancy achieved early success when his first work, *The* HUNT FOR RED OCTOBER, became a best seller in 1984 after President Reagan praised it publicly. Similar to the stir created when President Kennedy announced his fondness for Ian Fleming's James Bond series, the Clancy "franchise" was thus launched with a presidential impetus. Although often referred to as the father of the technothriller, Clancy himself awards that title to Michael Crichton of *The Andromeda Strain,* while also suggesting that the genre itself is faux and ought to be considered part of fiction as a whole.

The core of the Clancy phenomenon is the series of books featuring *Red October*'s lead character, Dr. Jack Ryan, tracing his rise from CIA analyst to president of the United States, and the "Ryanverse" ultimately provides a window on the entire political and military milieu in America from the cold war of the 1980s to the post-9/11 present and near future. Moreover, though the order of release (and writing) of the Ryan books does not track in a perfect line through the Clancy bibliography, the collection nonetheless forms a sort of trunk from which all of the latter's major branches emerge.

Viewing the Ryan books as a series, *The Hunt for Red October* (1984) introduces readers to the hero through his involvement in the defection of a Soviet nuclear submarine. Next comes *Patriot Games* (1987), in which Ryan is embroiled in conflict with the Irish Republican Army. In 1988's *The Cardinal of Kremlin,* Ryan is instrumental in defections from the highest level of the Soviet KGB. Then, in something of a pastiche of the Iran-contra scandal, *Clear and Present Danger* (1989) sees him rise to deputy director of the CIA and interact with the White House, presaging a wider role for Ryan in the books to come. *The Sum of All Fears* (1991) places him in the aftermath of nuclear terrorism at the Super Bowl and an attempt to avert a misdirected U.S. nuclear strike against Iran. In DEBT OF HONOR (1994), he becomes national security advisor as an economic clash with Japan turns into a shooting war, and, in an explosive climax that foreshadowed 9/11, is suddenly vaulted from vice president to president. Assuming the presidency in 1996's *Executive Orders,* Ryan deals with a united Iran and Iraq, who together launch biological terrorism against the United States, while domestically he must deal with a constitutional controversy over the legitimacy of his own presidency, somewhat foreshadowing the 2000 election. President Ryan is then found next to the central character in *The Bear and the Dragon* (2000), in which the United States acts as an ally to the Russian Federation to avert a war with China over newly discovered oil and gold in Russia, and then appears in a flashback adventure, *Red Rabbit* (2001), describing the real-life assassination attempt on Pope John Paul II in 1981. The "Ryanverse" continues to unfold, however, now a generation later, in *The Teeth of the Tiger* (2003), in which the now-grown Jack Ryan Jr. begins his career in post 9/11 counterterrorism.

Throughout this series and its spin-offs Clancy maintains a remarkably (and persuasively) coherent worldview: There is right and wrong in the world, and the United States should always act in the right. Ryan serves as the moral compass for the series, providing an (exceptional) everyman's view into the messy world of geopolitics, much as earlier generations looked through Jimmy Stewart's eyes in the movies. Ryan has thus far been portrayed in four film adaptations, *The Hunt for Red October* in 1990 with Alec Baldwin, *Patriot Games* (1992) and *Clear and Present Danger* (1994), both with Harrison Ford, and *The Sum of All Fears* (2002) with Ben Affleck—with the last neither as faithful nor successful as the first three.

A second tier of novels feature John Clark, a supporting character in several of the Ryan books. With smaller roles in *Patriot Games* and *The Cardinal of the Kremlin,* Clark becomes a featured character in *Clear and Present Danger,* running the counterdrug special operations force in Colombia and becoming closely allied with Ryan. By *Sum of All Fears,* Clark is in charge of Ryan's close protection detail, which includes Ding Chavez, a member of the Colombian special ops team from *Clear and Present Danger.* In *Debt of Honor* Clark and Chavez conduct an operation in Somalia, while Clark himself stars in *Without Remorse* (1993), which tells the story of his life as John Kelly, before his CIA recruitment. A former Navy SEAL, he takes vigilante action against the drug gang that killed his fiancée, which puts him in conflict with Baltimore Detective Lt. William Ryan, Jack Ryan's father. Faking his own death, Kelly is reborn as Clark in the CIA. In *RAINBOW SIX* (1998) Clark and Chavez are sent to England to start a multinational counterterrorism unit that Clark then leads to foil a biological attack on the Sydney Olympics.

Clancy's second novel, *Red Storm Rising* (1986), the tale of a conventional, nonnuclear war between the United States and Soviet Union, was coplotted with Larry Bond (who would become a successful military thriller writer in his own right), and the book's scrupulous research and verisimilitude provided readers with a preview of stealth aircraft in a combat role. It also lent its name to the video game and electronic entertainment company, Red Storm Entertainment, which produces the popular Clancy computer and console games.

The practice of working with a collaborator has led to additional successful series for Clancy. With Steve Pieczenik he cocreated *Tom Clancy's Op Center* (1995), a series of novels set in their own narrative universe, in which Op Center is the U.S. crisis operations center, headed by Paul Hood; it was made into a television miniseries (rereleased in a shorter movie version) starring Harry Hamlin in 1995. In like manner Clancy and Pieczenik cocreated *Tom Clancy's Net Force* (1999), set in 2010. Net Force is a special unit within the FBI tasked with cybercrime, and part of the Net Force adventures take place in virtual reality. Net Force was also adapted to the small screen that same year in a miniseries starring Scott Bakula as director Alex Michaels. Both series had successful paperback runs, and Net Force spun off a version for younger readers featuring the teenaged "Net Force Explorers."

Another cocreated series, this time with Martin Greenberg, was *Tom Clancy's Power Plays,* whose plots center more on global economics and politics. An interesting case of media convergence was presented by the first book in the series, *Politika* (1997), as this was based on an extant computer strategy game. *Politika* itself spawned and was actually packaged with a board game as well. The Power Plays series, too, had a successful paperback run of several episodes.

The gaming connection is strong with the surge in computer combat and strategy gaming itself. *Rainbow Six* inspired a whole series of tremendously popular PC and console games featuring squad level counterterrorist operations. Termed *first-person shooters,* they allow the player to operate as one of the characters in an unfolding narrative; and some of the *Rainbow Six* characters, like Ding Chavez, make the transition to the games intact. The base game spawned numerous sequels and add-ons, while a new game franchise, *Splinter Cell,* features near-future counterterrorist Sam Fisher and has itself spawned several sequel games, as well as a novel. However, the first *Splinter Cell* (2004) novel is notably only "created by Tom Clancy," and written by David Michaels, which marks a decisive transition for Clancy into a powerful and generic brand name all to himself.

Clancy's success in military fiction has given him remarkable entrée into the real-life military-industrial complex, and he has written a popular series of nonfiction "guided tour" books, such as *Fighter Wing: A Guided Tour of an Air Force Combat Wing* (1995), which have the look of his novels but are instead highly detailed profiles of extant military units and equipment. In addition to these efforts, he has coauthored several military nonfiction books with notable commanders, such as *Every Man a Tiger* (1999) with General Chuck Horner, USAF (ret.), who was the U.S. and coalition air commander for Operation Desert Storm.

A native of Baltimore, Clancy continues to reside in the Maryland area featured so prominently in his books.

Bibliography

Clancy, Tom. *The Hunt for Red October.* Annapolis, Md.: Naval Institute Press, 1984.

———. *Debt of Honor.* New York: G.P. Putnam's, 1994.

———. *Fighter Wing: A Guided Tour of an Air Force Combat Wing.* New York: Berkeley, 1995.

———. *Rainbow Six.* New York: G.P. Putnam's, 1998.

Clancy, Tom, and Martin Greenberg. *Tom Clancy's Power Plays: Politika.* New York: Berkeley, 1997.

Clancy, Tom, and Chuck Horner. *Every Man a Tiger.* New York: G.P. Putnam's, 1999.

Clancy, Tom, and Steve Pieczenik. *Tom Clancy's Op-Center.* New York: Berkeley, 1995.

———. *Tom Clancy's Net Force.* New York: Berkeley, 1999.

———. *Tom Clancy's Net Force: The Deadliest Game.* New York: Berkeley, 1999.

Greenberg, Martin, ed. *The Tom Clancy Companion.* Rev. edition. New York: Berkeley, 2002.

"In Depth with Tom Clancy." C-SPAN (Feb. 23, 2002).

Michaels, David. *Tom Clancy's Splinter Cell.* New York: Berkeley, 2004.

Tom Clancy's Rainbow Six. Morrisville, N.C.: Red Storm Entertainment, 1996.

Ronald C. Thomas Jr.

Clark, Mary Higgins (1929–)

Dubbed the "Queen of Suspense," Mary Higgins Clark is the author of more than 20 best-selling novels. Born in 1929, Clark came of age during the Great Depression and World War II. Her family struggled after her father died in 1939, and she herself would face single parenthood after the sudden death of her first husband in 1969. Her fiction features strong, independent women who protect and nurture their families despite having their lives invaded by crime and violence.

Clark's work has been overwhelmingly successful, and she herself has become an icon of popular suspense fiction. The *Mary Higgins Clark Mystery Magazine* appeared on newsstands from 1996 to 2000, and Simon & Schuster launched an annual Mary Higgins Clark Award in 2001. She has won numerous literary awards and honorary doctorates and has served as president of the Mystery Writers Association of America. Her fiction is especially well received in France, where she was named a Chevalier of the Order of Arts and Letters in 2000. In addition, her work in the Catholic Church has earned her papal honors.

In the early 1950s, while attending classes at New York University, Clark began writing short stories and became a founding member of the Adams Round Table writing group. She had been producing radio scripts when her first novel, *Where Are the Children,* appeared in 1975, followed three years later by *A Stranger Is Watching,* both of which were made into feature films and remain among her most popular works, even after 30 years of best-selling novels and successful TV movies. The characters, themes, and techniques in her novels have been consistent since her style and formula solidified with her fourth novel, *Stillwatch* (1984), which features not one but two of her signature heroines. She has produced one or more books a year since 1989.

Clark has consistently found inspiration in current events and true crime. Her first novel drew its material from recurrent headlines concerning crimes against children, and her second, which considers the ethics of capital punishment, was occasioned by a Supreme Court ruling on a capital case. Several novels have dealt with bioethical issues such as artificial insemination, genetic manipulation, and plastic surgery, while many others have evolved out of her interest in the FBI, including PRETEND YOU DON'T SEE HER (1997), which tells the story of a woman in the witness protection program.

All of Clark's novels feature a strong, resourceful, and self-reliant heroine, the one possible exception being *A Cry in the Night* (1982), in which the female protagonist allows her trust in a handsome stranger to endanger her family. Clark's usually male villains are most often mobsters or sexual predators. These characters and their settings become increasingly upper class and urban in her middle and later work, and her best critical reception has been for the novels set in New York. However, as Linda Pelzer comments, a self-confident and successful heroine does not necessarily equate to a socially liberal or radically feminist perspective, and indeed most of Clark's novels feature a conventional resolution in which the protagonist finds the true love of a good man and family and society are restored to order.

Most of her heroines are confronted with the task of finding, saving, or avenging a child, and her plots are driven by recurring threats to women and children. Even when a young child is not on hand, most of the crimes are viewed through the eyes of grieving parents, both fathers and mothers. Many stories feature mothers who champion their own immediate family, but just as often the child at stake is a niece or nephew.

Clark's fiction is marked by a strong, optimistic dualism between good and evil. The roles of heroine and villain are immediately recognizable, and the line between them never blurs with doubt or sympathy. Yet despite incidences of extreme criminal behavior, Clark's books remain "clean" and "cozy." She consistently avoids graphic sex, violence, or profanity and attributes this to a traditionally conservative point of view, preferring the "Hitchcock way" of dealing with sex and violence indirectly. The restrained and dignified treatment of horrible crimes also lends her work an ironic tone, James Broderick describing her style as "a mix of normalcy while restless phantoms hover just beyond the page" (62). He continues:

> That's Clark's method: take a Norman Rockwell painting and start scratching the canvas to reveal a darker portrait underneath. She portrays an idyllic life and then interrupts it, sometimes subtly, sometimes with extreme prejudice (63).

This instantly recognizable moral scheme has contributed to Clark's popularity. Her novels are widely enjoyed for their restrained and subtle treatment of otherwise sensational material, and their readability is enhanced by the appeal of Clark's recurrent theme: admirable women refusing to fall victim to the evils that threaten themselves and their families.

While Clark's best-selling suspense novels follow a reliable pattern, she has authored several books that stand apart from these. With 2000's *Deck the Halls* she began an ongoing collaboration with her daughter, Carol Higgins Clark. Her 1969 biography of George Washington was rereleased as *A Mount Vernon Love Story* in 2002 to critical acclaim. And that year also saw the publication of her memoir, *Kitchen Privileges*.

Clark's work has been most often placed in context with Agatha Christie and Alfred Hitchcock, primarily for her discreet treatment of sex and violence, but also for her use of suspense and anxiety to propel readers through the story. The most common criticism leveled against her is that her stories are formulaic, but Clark herself cites her highly refined formula as a factor in her success. Critics, too, are occasionally disappointed that Clark's novels are not strictly mysteries in the whodunit tradition, there being usually no uncertainty as to the nature of the crime or the identity of the killer. Instead, the reader's (often considerable) suspense hangs on whether the criminal will be stopped before he can kill again or on just how the heroine will manage to reconstruct a normal life despite repeated trauma.

Bibliography

Broderick, James F. *Paging New Jersey: A Literary Guide to the Garden State.* New Brunswick, N.J.: Rutgers University Press, 2003.

Clark, Mary Higgins. *Where Are the Children?* New York: Simon & Schuster, 1975.

———. *A Stranger Is Watching.* New York: Simon & Schuster, 1978

———. *A Cry in the Night.* New York: Simon & Schuster, 1982.

———. *Stillwatch.* New York: Simon & Schuster, 1984.

———. *Pretend You Don't See Her.* New York: Simon & Schuster, 1997.

———. *Deck the Halls.* With Carol Higgins Clark. New York: Simon & Schuster, 2000.

———. *Kitchen Privileges: A Memoir.* New York: Simon & Schuster, 2002.

———. *A Mount Vernon Love Story: A Novel of George and Martha Washington.* New York: Simon & Schuster, 2002.

Pelzer, Linda C. *Mary Higgins Clark: A Critical Companion.* Westport, Conn.: Greenwood Press, 1995.

Charles Tedder

Clarke, Arthur C. (1917–2008)

Clarke is one of the most famous authors of science-fiction novels and short stories and is also renowned for his nonfiction essays on scientific issues, but is probably best known for his collaboration with filmmaker Stanley Kubrick on the 1968 film *2001: A Space Odyssey.* Clarke was knighted in 2000.

Arthur Charles Clarke was born in Minehead, Somerset, and his interest in genre fiction and science was evident from a young age—he recalls the seismic effect that Olaf Stapledon's science-fiction classic, *Last and First Men,* had upon him at age 12. His father died when Arthur was 13; subsequently, Clarke attended school, worked alongside his mother tending the family farm, and devoted his spare time to astronomy and collecting American science-fiction magazines. Unable to afford a university education, he took up a Civil Service post and moved to London in 1936. During World War II Clarke served with the Royal Air Force as a radar training instructor (significantly in light of his later work, he insisted that his religious views be categorized as "pantheist" when he enlisted), and upon his demobilization in 1946 took a first-class degree in mathematics and physics at King's College, London.

Clarke's interest in writing and science continued to flourish in the postwar period. He served as chairman of the British Interplanetary Society 1946–47 and 1950–53. As early as 1945 he proposed the novel concept of geostationary satellites as a means of global communication; the geostationary orbit that now constitutes the principal element of worldwide communications systems is sometimes referred to as the Clarke Orbit in his honor. Around the same time he was beginning to find a market for his speculative fiction, which, although imaginative, was rooted firmly in robust scientific methodology. His first published story was "Loophole," which appeared in the magazine *Astounding Science Fiction* in April 1946, though his first sale was "Rescue Party," which appeared in the same publication the following month. In 1948 Clarke wrote a short story for a BBC competition. The story, "The Sentinel," was rejected for publication but nonetheless remains one of the most significant works of his career. It outlines the discovery of a mysterious alien artifact, created by a highly advanced extraterrestrial race, on Earth's Moon. This simple concept would eventually evolve into the script for *2001: A Space Odyssey.*

Following the publication of *Interplanetary Flight* (a nonfiction work on space travel), his first two novels, *Prelude to Space* (written in 20 days) and *The Sands of Mars,* and stints as science adviser for the classic British comic serial "Dan Dare" and assistant editor of *Physics Abstracts,* Clarke devoted himself to writing full time from 1951 onward. The success in the United States of another nonfiction work, *The Exploration of Space,* provided him with the necessary financial freedom to continue to experiment with science fiction. Although his career as a writer and scientific figurehead was beginning to blossom, Clarke's personal life was somewhat unconventional. In May 1953 he met and within three weeks had married a young American divorcee, Marilyn Mayfield, who had a young son from her previous marriage. The couple separated after six turbulent months, though their divorce was not finalized until 1964. In 1956 Clarke immigrated to Sri Lanka (then called Ceylon), where he lived until his death.

Clarke's major novels—*Childhood's End* (1953), *The City and the Stars* (1956), *Rendezvous with Rama* (1973), and the Odyssey series (*2001: A Space Odyssey* [1968], *2010: Odyssey Two* [1982], *2061: Odyssey Three* [1988], and *3001: The Final Odyssey* [1997])—reveal a major recurring thematic contradiction that is at the heart of much of his phenomenal written output, both fiction and nonfiction. In some ways Clarke's work is the epitome of the "hard," realistic, technically feasible, technologically savvy and methodically extrapolated science fiction also practised by such giants of the genre as Robert A. Heinlein and ISAAC ASIMOV (the other two members of the SF "Big Three"); his scientific background is clearly apparent within even his most imaginative pieces (famously, one short story, "Jupiter Five," required some 20 to 30 pages of scientific calculations to ensure narrative accuracy). Paradoxically, however, Clarke's fiction also reflects an obsession with the paranormal, the metaphysical, and the mystical, with several of the novels depicting scientific progress and alien intervention as parallel with human advancement or even transcendence. In Clarke's work—particularly *Childhood's End* and the Odyssey series—advanced alien races appear as benign father figures (perhaps reflecting Clarke's own loss as a boy), alongside which humanity is little more than a curious, shortsighted, and occasionally petulant child. For many, this pseudo-religious allegorical aspect of Clarke's fiction sits uneasily with the scientific rationalism he displays elsewhere.

The theme of transcendence through evolution, heavily influenced by Stapledon, is perhaps most visible in both the film and novelization of *2001: A Space Odyssey.* Alongside meticulous scientific realism, the screenplay (coauthored by Clarke and Kubrick, though the novel is credited to Clarke alone) posits a highly advanced race of superintelligent beings who use the mysterious artifact known as the Monolith to guide and shape human destiny. The biblical parallels are evident, though to the film's credit, never overstated; Clarke's point is that technological, scientific, and mental evolution can render intelligent beings akin to gods. Dave Bowman's transformation into the Star Child, and his further interaction with unevolved humanity in the later novels, blurs the distinction between god and man, between science and metaphysics, and further supports one of Clarke's most famous aphorisms: "Any sufficiently advanced technology will be indistinguishable from magic." The success of Kubrick's lengthy, complex and challenging film brought Clarke recognition as possibly the most important SF writer of the past century, and although much of his later work (some of it coauthored with Gentry Lee) failed to maintain the rigorous twin vision of science and mysticism that made his name, Clarke continued to be a hugely important and influential voice in both contemporary SF and science in popular culture.

Bibliography

Clarke, Arthur C. *Childhood's End.* London: Pan Books, 1956.

———. *The Exploration of Space.* Harmondsworth: Penguin, 1958.

———. *Rendezvous with Rama.* London: Pan Books, 1974.

———. *Prelude to Space.* New York: Ballantine Books, 1976.

———. *2010: Odyssey Two.* London: Granada, 1982.

———. *Interplanetary Flight.* New York: Berkley Group, 1985.

———. *The Sands of Mars.* New York: Bantam Books, 1991.

———. *2061: Odyssey Three.* London: Voyager, 1997.

———. *3001: The Final Odyssey.* London: Voyager, 1997.

———. *2001: A Space Odyssey.* London: Orbit, 1999.

———. *The City and the Stars.* London: Victor Gollancz, 2001.

McAleer, Neil. *The Authorised Biography of Arthur C. Clarke.* London: Victor Gollancz, 1992.

2001: A Space Odyssey. Directed by Stanley Kubrick. MGM, 1968.

Nicholas Dunlop

Clavell, James (1924–1994)

Perhaps most notable for his six epic novels collectively known as the Asian Saga, Clavell also worked as a successful writer, producer, and director in Hollywood. The British author was born in Sydney, Australia, in 1924, but became a naturalized American citizen in 1963. His father was a member of the British Royal Navy, and Clavell followed his father's example, joining the British Royal Artillery in 1940 at the age of 16. Two years later, in 1942, Clavell was captured and held in the notorious Japanese prison camp Changi. The three years he spent in Changi had a significant influence on him, and his experiences as a POW during World War II served as both catalyst and material for his major body of work. After his release from Changi Clavell returned to Britain and while on leave was involved in a motorcycle accident that left him with a limp and, ultimately, resulted in his discharge from service in the British Royal Artillery.

In his late 20's Clavell moved to Hollywood, where he began a career as a screenwriter, working on such notable films as *The Fly* (1958) and *To Sir, With Love* (1966), which he also produced and directed. In 1960, during a screenwriter's strike, Clavell found himself out of work and began what would become the first novel of his Asian Saga, *King Rat* (1962); the others are *Tai-Pan* (1966), *Shogun* (1975), *NOBLE HOUSE* (1981), *WHIRLWIND* (1986), and *Gai-Jin* (1993).

The complex and compelling confrontation of East and West is a trademark of the saga, which explores the interaction between people from vastly different cultures, whose social, political, and even religious systems are often in conflict with one another, conflict whose resolution provides endless narrative and philosophical opportunities for the author. And while the action often takes place on a grand scale, Clavell's memorable characterization explores humankind's personal conflicts, questions of loyalty and belonging, both to oneself and to others, the challenging of long-accepted values, and, perhaps most important, the simple struggle to survive.

The novels are distinguished by cinematic dialogue, large and often complex casts of characters, and carefully detailed descriptions of the culture and scenery of the foreign lands in which the narratives take place. Also typical is the recurring appearance of certain characters, the exploration of political themes, and heroes who exemplify the sort of individualism that Clavell himself prized. Finally, Clavell, who thought of himself primarily as a storyteller, is noted for his deft use of historical personalities and events as the basis for his stories, adding vivid authenticity to the tales.

The partially autobiographical *King Rat,* first in the series, takes place in a World War II Japanese prison camp, and it is here that the character of Peter Marlowe, Clavell's fictionalized counterpart, first appears (he will reappear later in *Noble House* as a novelist doing research for a book about Hong Kong). In addition to its exploration of political themes common to such prisoner-of-war tales, *King Rat* is a detailed and sensitive essay in the anatomy of survival, and its protagonist, a kind of enslaved capitalist, is the quintessential Clavellian hero, self-reliant, enduring, cynical, but principled in his self-serving way.

Following the success of *King Rat,* Clavell released *Tai-Pan,* set in Hong Kong in 1841, just after the end of the first Opium War and Britain's capture of the Chinese port. The central character is Dirk Struan, the head of a major trading company, whose family's corporate empire itself reappears in several of the other novels in the saga. As with *King Rat,* but here on a more global scale, *Tai-Pan* explores political themes arising from the clash of East and West; Struan's resilient struggle to survive and indeed thrive in the fraught atmosphere of British Hong Kong echoes many aspects of Marlowe's own struggle in the prison camp—same struggle, just a larger camp. *Shogun,* which takes place in feudal Japan in the early 1600s, is chronologically the first of the novels, though the third in the series, and tells the story of English sailor John Blackthorne, who is taken captive following a shipwreck on the coast of Japan; here the political exploration of the first few novels is complicated and deepened by religious conflict.

In *Noble House,* Struan's trading company reappears, this time under the leadership of Ian Dunross, who is fighting to keep the company alive. The novel is set in Hong Kong in the early 1960s, and though more than 1,000 pages in length takes place within the time span of a single week, a testament to Clavell's maturing gift as a storyteller. The leader of the Noble House is seeking a partnership with an American investor and must deal not only with the internal struggles of his company but also with a host of outside factors, including, among other things, the influential criminal underground in Hong Kong, Soviet spies, Chinese communists, and a stock market crash.

Whirlwind, the fifth novel in the series, shifts the focus to Iran, revolving around the struggle of a group of pilots, again part of Struan's empire, who are living and working in Iran as the Islamic Revolution of 1979 breaks out. While not as critically acclaimed as the other novels in the series, *Whirlwind* was equally popular and explored many of the same themes, while the structure of the novel, with its immense but well-integrated cast of characters and its compressed time span, is vintage Clavell. *Gai-Jin,* the final novel in the Asian Saga, takes place in Japan in 1862, 20 years after *Tai-Pan,* and tells the story of another Struan, Malcolm, whose challenging existence as a *gai-jin* (foreigner) in the "hermit kingdom" reveals in an intensified form the political and religious conflicts that shape the saga as a whole.

While several of the novels were adapted for film, such as *King Rat* in 1965, and *Tai-Pan* in 1986, the novels' extraordinary length and profusion of detail are perhaps best suited to the miniseries format, and two of the most popular Clavell adaptations are those of *Shogun,* a 12-hour television miniseries starring Richard Chamberlain released in 1980, and *Noble House,* adapted into a miniseries in 1988 starring Pierce Brosnan. (The latter film was skillfully updated to the 1980s from the original 1960s time frame of the novel.)

In addition to his Asian Saga Clavell wrote two works for children, *The Children's Story* (1980) and *Thump-O-Moto* (1986), which was illustrated by George Sharp. In 1983 he also published a translation of Sun Tzu's famous *The Art of War,* and in 1994 he released *Escape,* which was a shorter novel containing the love story from the novel *Whirlwind.* Suffering from cancer, Clavell died of a stroke in 1994 at the age of 69.

Bibliography

Clavell, James. *King Rat.* New York: Little, Brown, 1962.
———. *Tai-Pan.* New York: Atheneum, 1966.
———. *Shogun.* New York: Dell, 1975.
———. *Noble House.* New York: Delacorte Press, 1981.
———. *Whirlwind.* New York: W. Morrow, 1986.
———. *Gai-Jin.* New York: Delacorte Press, 1993.

Angela Craig

Coelho, Paulo (1947–)

Paulo Coelho, actor, theater director, journalist, lyricist, and novelist, has sold more than 85 million books in more than 150 countries and that have been translated into 62 languages but is best known for *The Alchemist* (1988), whose first edition sold only 900 copies and was not reprinted by the original publisher but has now sold 11 million copies worldwide.

Coelho was born in 1947 in Rio de Janeiro to Pedro (an engineer) and Lygia Coelho de Souza. He was raised in a middle-class Catholic home and attended Jesuit school where he discovered his talent for writing but was discouraged from this vocation by his parents. Despite this, Coelho started a magazine called *2001* and began collaborating as a lyricist with Raul Seixas, a music producer, together writing such popular songs as *Gita* and *Al Capone.* From his earliest adulthood Coelho was a passionate spiritual searcher, profoundly influenced by the teachings of the controversial English mystic Aleister Crowley. Coelho traveled broadly through the Americas, Europe, and North Africa and became involved in the creation of a group in Brazil called the Alternative Society, based on Crowley's dictum: "Do what thou wilt' shall be the whole of the Law." (Coelho would later adopt Catholicism but preserve this teaching.) Along with other members Coelho was imprisoned and, allegedly, repeatedly tortured for his participation in the group.

Coelho published his first book, *Hell Archives,* in 1982 to little success, followed by a contribution to the *Practical Manual of Vampirism,* which he later tried to take off store shelves, claiming it was of bad quality. He continued to write prolifically, however, his efforts culminating finally in the tremendous international success of *The Alchemist,* which describes the fabular journey of self-discovery (like Coelho's own pilgrimage to Santiago de Compostela) of a boy named Santiago in his symbolic search for hidden treasure near the pyramids of Egypt.

Coelho's mix of spiritual passion, narrative simplicity, and fablelike language are highly esteemed by a broad range of readers, from Umberto Eco and Nobel laureate Kenzaburo Oe to pop star Madonna. He has received a plethora of national and international awards, including France's National Legion of Honor (1999) and induction into the prestigious Brazilian Academy of Letters (2003). He even has his own drink, hot chocolate with orange, an honor bestowed by the Hotel Le Bristol's bar in Paris, where much of his recent work, *The Zahir: A Novel of Obsession,* takes place.

Coelho published his latest novel, *The Witch of Portobello,* in 2007.

Bibliography

Coelho, Paulo. *The Alchemist.* New York: HarperCollins, 1993.

———. *Zahir: A Novel of Obsession.* Translated by Margaret Jull Costa. New York: HarperCollins, 2005.
———. *The Witch of Portobello.* New York: HarperCollins, 2007.

Rebecca Housel

Colfer, Eoin (1965–)

Eoin Colfer was born in Wexford, Ireland, in 1965. The son of two teachers, he followed his parents' career path and taught at the primary level for many years. Colfer loved teaching and particularly enjoyed reading to his students, improvising when the class's attention appeared to be waning: "Sometimes, when their attention flagged, I would add a bit here and embellish a slow passage there. Eventually I discarded the books altogether and was telling stories from memory. It was only a short step from there to writing down my own stories" (Eccleshare). This interest in storytelling was one Colfer carried with him from his childhood: "While the other kids were out playing sports or climbing trees, I was inside writing plays and drawing comics" (Wotmania.com).

Colfer rose to international fame with the publication of his Artemis Fowl series, books aimed at children but which also have a wide following among adults: *Artemis Fowl* (2001), *Artemis Fowl: The Arctic Incident* (2002), *Artemis Fowl: The Eternity Code* (2003), *Artemis Fowl: The Opal Deception* (2005), *Artemis Fowl: The Lost Colony* (2006), and the companion book, *The Artemis Fowl Files* (2004). It is expected that Colfer will write one more Artemis Fowl book.

Described as "*Die Hard* with fairies," Artemis Fowl is a fantasy series that draws upon a wide range of influences, including Irish fairy lore, American detective novels, spy novels, film noir, and big budget action movies. The series' protagonist, Artemis, is an intelligent, sophisticated, and often ruthless antihero, in stark contrast to the stereotypical, rural, and unrefined character that previously dominated representations of Irishness.

The worlds of the fairies and humans have been kept separate for millennia, only occasionally colliding and always with disastrous effects. However, Artemis's dastardly deeds lead to a crossing of the interworld divide, which results in a calamitous confusion of humans and fairies. Holly Short, a member of LEPrecon, an elite police organization, is the chief fairy character in the series. Magical elements are a strong feature and, as a result, the collection has drawn comparisons with J. K. ROWLING's Harry Potter series, though the former typically incorporates more elements of modern technology.

In 2001 Miramax bought the rights to *Artemis Fowl,* expecting to release a film adaptation of it in 2004. Fraught with preproduction problems, however, the film has yet to be completed. Irish director Jim Sheridan is currently working with Colfer on the screenplay and is now expected to direct the movie, whose new release date is 2009.

Following the worldwide success of *Artemis Fowl,* Colfer has had a number of other children's books published. *The Supernaturalist* (2004), a science-fiction novel, sees a group of orphans battling a force of life-sucking creatures called the Parasites, while *Half Moon Investigations* (2006) is a detective novel drawing strongly on Raymond Chandler's Philip Marlowe mysteries; both are aimed at a young-adult audience. Two further books, *The Legend of Spud Murphy* (2004) and *The Legend of Captain Crow's Teeth* (2006), are aimed at six- to eight-year-olds.

In October 2006 Colfer presented a successful West End show in London, *Fairies, Fiends and Flatulence,* which blended stand-up, family stories, and tales that inspired *Artemis Fowl.* He has also written short stories and plays for adults, none of which have achieved the success of his children's books.

Colfer currently lives in Wexford with his wife, Jackie, and his sons, Finn and Seán.

Bibliography

Colfer, Eoin. *Benny and Omar.* Dublin: The O'Brien Press, 1998.
———. *Benny and Babe.* Dublin: The O'Brien Press, 1999.
———. *Going Potty.* Dublin: The O'Brien Press, 1999.
———. *Ed's Funny Feet.* Dublin: The O'Brien Press, 2000.
———. *The Wish List.* Dublin: The O'Brien Press, 2000.
———. *Ed's Bed.* Dublin: The O'Brien Press, 2001.
———. *Artemis Fowl.* London: Viking, 2001.
———. *Artemis Fowl: The Arctic Incident.* London: Puffin, 2002.

———. *Artemis Fowl: The Eternity Code.* London: Puffin, 2003.
———. *The Artemis Fowl Files.* London: Puffin, 2004.
———. *The Legend of Spud Murphy.* London: Puffin, 2004.
———. *The Supernaturalist.* London: Puffin, 2004.
———. *Artemis Fowl: The Opal Deception.* London: Puffin, 2005.
———. *Artemis Fowl: The Lost Colony.* London: Puffin, 2006.
———. *Half Moon Investigations.* London: Puffin, 2006.
———. *The Legend of Captain Crow's Teeth.* London: Puffin, 2006.
———. *The Legend of the Worst Boy in the World.* London: Puffin, 2006.
Eccleshare, Julia. "Dispatches from Fairyland." *The Guardian*, 9 March 2002.
Wotmania. "Eoin Colfer Interview" Available online. URL: http://www.wotmania.com/fantasymessageboard showmessage.asp?MessageID=149730. Downloaded January 11, 2007.

Sinead Carey

Collins, Jackie (1937–)

Born Jacqueline Jill Collins in 1937, Jackie Collins is the author of 25 novels to date, has sold more than 400 million books, and has enjoyed a varied career spanning more than five decades.

Collins is more than a novelist—she is a modern popular culture phenomenon. Beyond her talents as a writer of lengthy action-packed novels, which are frequently themselves foundations for series that grow and change over decades, often becoming movies and television series, she is known for her numerous television appearances. She has hosted a series for E! Entertainment Television called *Jackie Collins Presents* and had a short-lived chat show, *Jackie Collins' Hollywood.* She has also gained fame for her flamboyant lifestyle, with her brassy fashion choices and lavishly decorated Beverly Hills mansion, and is widely considered as a key player in the modern invention of novel writing as, and of, show business. Developing a signature black panther brand and appearing in garish outfits such as animal-print suits, Collins successfully occupies some of the same spotlight inhabited by the real-life show business elite who inspire her characters, and she does not exaggerate when saying that she "chronicles the real truth from the inside looking out" (www.jackiecollins.com).

Collins was born in Bayswater, London, to Joseph "Will" William and Elsa Bessant Collins (a theatrical agent and a dancer, respectively). When the teenaged Jackie showed a disinclination to stay at school, her parents swiftly recognized the advantages of moving her out to America to try her luck living with her older sister, actress Joan Collins. Jackie tried acting and made largely unexceptional appearances in films and television series, including *The Saint* and *Barnacle Bill.* But unlike *Dynasty* star Joan, whose late efforts at novel writing were most remarkable for an expensive lawsuit between the star and her publishers, Jackie soon made an extremely successful switch from the screen to the page, enjoying a hit with her first book, *The World Is Full of Married Men* (1968). And although the sisters' talents diverged, they have formed a formidable team over the years, their most impressive successes coming by way of film and television adaptations of Jackie's books. Jackie is thought to have written *The Stud,* for example, with the explicit intention of casting her sister as its heroine, Fontaine, an intention realized in 1978, when the sisters collaborated with director Quentin Masters on a raunchy and successful film version of the novel.

Such spirited raunchiness, combined with Collins's strong female characters, lightning pace, and adventurous approach to genre, have always attracted controversy. Her books consistently play about the borders of the world's two most popular genres—romance and pornography—and anticipated the advent of the "sex and shopping" novel by several decades. *The World Is Full of Married Men* caused scandal in England and was banned in Australia, with Barbara Cartland calling it "nasty, filthy and disgusting," and adding, "Miss Collins, you are responsible for all the perverts in England" (Butler). Such violent antipathy may be partly attributed to the simple fact that Collins's first ventures in fiction were made in a time before women had access to such popular erotica series as Black Lace or were even supposed to be interested in reading about sex. Her books introduced frank sexual description and interest in sex for its own sake, which were missing from women's fiction at the time, turning the tables on romance and (unlike most pornographic books) delivering a coherent and compelling narrative at the same time. A model, as ever, may be found in *The Stud,* whose titular character, Tony, like the novel's other soulless husbands and lovers, is objectified by powerful women and used by them for superficial erotic pleasure. With *The Stud* Collins offered an open challenge to the mainstream romance industry. Minor character Alexandria seeks happiness in the customary way, through a romantic connection with a powerful man, but is tragically blind to his total inability to fulfil that role for her or for anybody else. Thus Daphne Watson has written:

> Mary Stewart, for example, writes about brave and independent-minded women who struggle on behalf of the forces of good but who find no real problem in sinking back finally, with a happy sigh of relief, into the protective arms of the hero. Collins . . . seem[s] uncomfortable with [her] awareness of the changing nature of late twentieth-century woman, and the fact that for her the hero's arms are not enough. Or rather . . . that it should not be enough; that a fulfilling job is better than an unequal and dependent role as a mere wife; that women can be as aggressive, as hero-like, as any man (Watson, 1995: 95–96).

This type of Collins character, a woman seeking fulfilment along socially conservative lines, is constantly hurt and disappointed by the more streetwise people who surround her. She is typically contrasted to one of Collins's trademark "bitch" characters (the most famous of which is the phenomenally popular Lucky Santangelo), women of an often natively loving disposition who have learned the hard way that the world is stacked against them and choose to fight back. Lucky, certainly the most important of Collins's characters, first surfaces in the popular *Chances* (1981), before receiving star-billing in *Lucky* (1985) and then reappearing in *Lady Boss* (1990), *Vendetta: Lucky's Revenge* (1997), *Dangerous Kiss* (1999), and *Drop Dead Beautiful* (2007). A "poor little rich girl" daughter of an Italo-American gangster, Lucky lives a fraught existence: while rich, powerful, and resourceful in her own right, she is nevertheless constantly oppressed by less than moral, misogynistic male characters.

Collins reworks and complicates Lucky's "bitch" brand of survival in several different characters. Fontaine, of *The Stud,* is powerful only while she remains married. Montana, a protagonist in the blockbuster *HOLLYWOOD WIVES* (1983), is a talented screenwriter whose husband cannot stop philandering (and eventually dies) and whose career is continually stalled by powerful men. She achieves a token revenge upon one of these men, but the novel provides her with no happy ending. This often searching interest in the complications attached to women's survival and success mingles, often indiscriminately, with Collins's inexhaustible fascination with sex and brand labels.

Drop Dead Beautiful sees the return of the perennially popular Lucky, and the author promises a whole new generation of such adventures as she now takes up the life of Lucky's daughter, Max, here age 16. Jackie Collins herself has three children: Tracy, with Wallace Austin (whom she divorced after only a few years of marriage owing to his neglect and substance abuse), and Tiffany and Rory, with Oscar Lehrman. Collins survives Oscar, who had adopted Tracy, and whom she lost in 1992 after 26 years of marriage. She appears regularly on the *New York Times* best-seller list (most recently for *Married Lovers,* in 2008) and has been featured on the Sunday *Times* Rich List.

Bibliography

Butler, Diane. "An Enduring Star." *The Courier Mail,* M27, 19 May 2007.

Collins, Jackie. *The World Is Full of Married Men.* New York: Pocket Books, 1968.

———. *The Stud.* New York: Simon & Schuster, 1969.

———. *Chances.* New York: Warner, 1981.

———. *Hollywood Wives.* Suffolk: Pan, 1984. First edition, Collins, 1983.

———. *Lucky.* New York: Simon & Schuster, 1985

———. *Lady Boss: A Novel.* New York: Simon & Schuster, 1990.

———. *Vendetta: Lucky's Revenge.* New York: HarperCollins, 1997.
———. *Dangerous Kiss: A Novel.* New York: Simon & Schuster, 1999.
———. *Lovers and Players.* New York: St. Martin's, 2006.
———. *Drop Dead Beautiful.* New York: St. Martin's, 2007.
Watson, Daphne. *Their Own Worst Enemies: Women Writers of Women's Fiction.* London and Boulder, Colo.: Pluto Press, 1995.

Anne Brumley

Collins, Larry (1929–2005) and Dominique Lapierre (1931–)

Best known for the terrorist thriller *The* FIFTH HORSEMAN, as well as six nonfiction books written in an alert, engaging style, Collins and Lapierre confessed to be interested in "the great modern epics of humanity," considering themselves "historian[s] using the modern technique of investigative journalism." They spent roughly two years collecting data for each of their books, and the resulting works are as "thoroughly and seriously researched as the most serious history books." The authors' engaging style, as well as their dramatic subject matter, have made even their nonfiction, such as *Is Paris Burning?*, *O Jerusalem,* and *Freedom at Midnight,* popular with the general public.

John Lawrence Collins Jr. was born in 1929 in Hartford, Connecticut, and studied at Yale University, where in 1951 he obtained his B.A. in economics, having attended numerous courses in history and English. He married the Egyptian Princess Nadia Hoda Sultan and had two children. Until 1964, when he devoted himself to researching and writing full-length books, Collins worked as a journalist for United Press International (UPI) and *Newsweek,* and while at UPI was a correspondent in Paris (1956), news editor in Rome (1957), and Middle East correspondent (1957–59). After three years as Middle East correspondent for *Newsweek* (1959–61) he was appointed chief of the Paris bureau (1961–64).

Under the name Larry Collins he published two novels: *Fall from Grace* (1985) and *Maze: a Novel* (1989), and three nonfiction books: *Black Eagles* (1995), *Tomorrow Belongs to Us* (1998), and *Le Jour du Miracle: D-Day Paris* (1994). In 2005, while working at his home in the South of France on a book about the Middle East, he died of a cerebral hemorrhage.

Dominique Lapierre was born in 1931, in Chatelaillon, France, the son of Jean (a diplomat) and Luce (Andreotti). He married Aliette Spitzer in 1952 and had one child, Alexandra, herself an accomplished writer. He attended the Institut des Sciences Politiques, Paris, and Lafayette College, where he got his B.A. in 1952. From 1953 he worked for *Paris Match* (magazine) as a war correspondent in Korea and then as an editor between 1954 and 1967. In 1967 he quit journalism and turned exclusively to book writing, becoming a critically acclaimed and commercially successful author of historical documentary nonfiction. Apart from the books written with Collins, and *Il était minuit cinq à Bhopal* (*Five Past Midnight in Bhopal,* 2001), coauthored with Javier Moro, he wrote *La Cité de la joie* (*The City of Joy,* 1985), *Plus grands que l'amour* (*Beyond Love,* 1990), which chronicles the epic story of the discovery of the AIDS virus, *Mille soleils* (*A Thousand Suns,* 1999), and an event-based autobiography, *Il était une fois l'USSR,* (*Once Upon a Time in the USSR,* 2006). He is often praised as one of the pioneers of the "subjective news story," and his compassionate interest in his subjects is reflected in his founding of the City of Joy, a charity aimed at aiding impoverished inhabitants of Calcutta slums.

Thus, both Collins and Lapierre were journalists turned writers. They met in 1954, when both were assigned to the Supreme Headquarters of Allied Powers in Europe outside Paris, and their friendship deepened during Collins's time as UPI correspondent in Paris, where Lapierre was an editor for *Paris Match. Is Paris Burning?* (1965), their first collaborative project, has a strong Franco-American theme, and critics were unanimous in praising the skillful arrangement of its complicated material. The team of Collins-Lapierre strove vigorously for accuracy in their nonfiction and verisimilitude in their fiction. Collins described their unique method of manuscript preparation:

> We do a very detailed outline before beginning the writing. Then Dominique may

> take the first section and write it in French. I'll take the second and write it in English. Then we read them to each other. I'll translate his French into English, while he's doing the reverse to my draft. Next we come back to each other and recast the sections into our own languages again (*Contemporary Authors,* 1999: 130).

As a result of their writing technique, two manuscripts, one in English and one in French, were produced, leading often to near simultaneous publication of English and French versions of their work.

Through their six nonfiction efforts, their individual works of fiction, and above all the tremendous success of *The Fifth Horseman,* they established an international reputation for meticulous research and historical accuracy enhanced by an astonishing capacity for empathy and compassion, their prose often resembling the classic fictional whodunit in which "the events follow upon one another with a heart-stopping cadence" (Bernard Frizell, *Life,* quoted in 1999:130), flashes of tragedy and comedy alternating with passages of tenderness and love. After *The Fifth Horseman* the authors engaged in individual projects, resuming their collaboration with *Is New York Burning?* shortly before Collins's death in 2005.

Although holding the film option for *The Fifth Horseman,* Paramount never produced a movie with this title for fear that terrorists might try to emulate the chilling scenario described so vividly in the book.

Bibliography

"Dominique Lapierre." Available online. URL: http://en.wikipedia.org/wiki/Dominique_Lapierre.

"Dominique Lapierre: Bestselling Writer Turns Philanthropist." Available online. URL: http://www.cityofjoyaid.org/bio_lapierre.html.

Peacock, Scot, ed. *Contemporary Authors.* New Revision Series, vol. 77. Detroit, San Francisco, London: Gale, 1999.

Swaim, Don. "Interview with Larry Collins." 1985. Wired for Books, Ohio University. Available online. URL: http://wiredforbooks.org/larrycollins.

Alexandra Dumitrescu

A Common Life Jan Karon (2001)

A Common Life, the sixth work in the Mitford series, is a pastoral novel set in North Carolina that depicts the rustic and rural segment of a larger society that is evidenced in small towns all over the country. Father Tim Kavanagh, an Episcopal priest, his dog named Barnabas, Cynthia Coppersmith, Miss Sadie, Emma, a boy named Dooley Barlowe, and their friends reflect the author's appreciation for routine life experiences and faith in humanity. In Mitford people's prayers are simple and pious, not polished, and solitude and reflection intermingle with the chaos and intensity of lived life.

The series explores relationships and the intersection of the ordinary and extraordinary events that occur across a lifetime. Sixty-two-year-old Father Tim struggles between his fears of marriage and his love for Cynthia Coppersmith, while balancing his personal interests with those of Mitford's residents, who consider him their personal responsibility, a task that involves removing lint from his shoulder, remembering his birthday, baking his wedding cake, and pondering how the 60-something priest will be able to fit husbandly duties into his schedule.

Father Tim's proposal and announcement of Cynthia's acceptance are a case in point, as he weighs the dignity of announcing the engagement in church against possibly offending friends who learn that the announcement has been made in the pew bulletin before they hear it on the street. Father Tim fidgets, wondering what Miss Sadie and Louella will think as he accepts their offered lemonade. Louella pragmatically asks, "You itchy?" and realizing he has been read like a book, the Father confesses, "I'm getting married!" (26).

Questions of flower arrangements, allergies, and what the matron of honor will wear with her luggage rerouted to Charlottesville plague Mitford. Father Tim hopes he has effectively declined the offer of extra music and a choir that would leave only standing room for himself and his bride in the small quarters of nave and chancel. Hessie Mayhew, *Mitford Muse* reporter, Presbyterian, and gifted flower arranger, frets that people do not consider growing seasons when planning weddings but commits herself nonetheless to scouring the local meadows and pastures. She explains to

Cynthia that her options primarily involve pods, seeds, and berries—unless she wants mums; after Cynthia's offhand suggestion of "dozens of roses and armloads of lilacs," Hessie reflects, on behalf of the community, on the implications of "that kind of money" (53).

Esther Bolick, meanwhile, imagines baking the Father's wedding cake, crowned with calla lilies and scattered edible pearls (hoping they would not break anyone's fillings), then realizes that she has not been asked to bake a wedding cake. She argues with herself that it is only a matter of time, especially with the Father raving about her orange marmalade for years, even after two pieces nearly killed him (47).

Like jigsaw puzzle pieces, the wedding details come together by the end of the novel. Cynthia regrets that her nephew, probably still in the Congo, is her only family, leaving no one to fill "the bride's side," while Father Tim, asked what he intends to do for the wedding other than showing up, replies, "I'm doing the usual. I'm baking a ham!" (50). The anticipated premarital interview with his bishop should give Father Tim few concerns, given their friendship, but his anxiety, nonetheless, tempers the warm custard contentment and joy that Cynthia brings to his life and makes him feel vulnerable as he questions his fitness for the intimacy of marriage. Surprisingly, the issue is eclipsed by another matter that his bride and his bishop seem to consider an even greater concern.

The honeymoon involves a negotiation of space. Cynthia's house is "too small to cuss a cat, no offense to Violet," and Father Tim's bed "is so small"; but these problems are solved by "drawing straws," and the rings are a simple matter of agreement (59). The question, however, of whose car they will drive on the parkway or whether to visit the bishop is more significant.

Uncle Billy is also anxious about the approaching celebration, praying that the Lord won't mind providing "a good joke for th' preacher" (78), while Barnabas, the large dog who has adopted the priest, and Dooley, the boy whom Father Tim has adopted, are concerned about potential changes in their settled lives. Dooley wants to be happy for Father Tim and Cynthia, but in his memory, "when people lived together under the same roof: They yelled and screamed and fought and said terrible things to each other" (85). When Cynthia asks Dooley to sing a cappella, he wishes for loud trumpets and prays that his voice won't crack. The bride, who ate like a canary at the bridal luncheon, asks for a moment alone, and is soon 20 minutes late for perhaps the most celebrated event in Mitford in decades. Guests stir in the pews, while in the front row Dooley feels conspicuous and wonders if his worries have truly been for nothing. He prays again that he won't "mess up." Father Tim, meanwhile, sprints from Lord's Chapel down Old Church Lane to find Cynthia, and make her his wife after all.

Mitford, like GARRISON KEILLOR's Lake Wobegon, provides a vivid slice of ordinary, small-town life, moral values, and routine humor and compassion. First published by a small press with a limited distribution, JAN KARON's series went on to debut on the *New York Times* best-seller list. *At Home in Mitford,* the first novel in the series, was nominated for an ABBY by the American Booksellers Association in 1996 and 1997. The novels are also available in audio format.

Bibliography

Karon, Jan. *At Home in Mitford.* New York: Penguin, 1994.

———. *A Light in the Window.* New York: Penguin, 1995.

———. *These High, Green Hills.* New York: Penguin, 1996.

———. *Out to Canaan.* New York: Penguin, 1998.

———. *A New Song.* New York: Penguin, 1999.

———. *A Common Life: The Wedding Story.* New York: Penguin, 2001.

———. *In This Mountain.* New York: Penguin, 2002.

———. *Shepherds Abiding.* New York: Random House, 2003.

———. *Light from Heaven.* New York: Viking Penguin, 2005.

Stella Thompson

Connelly, Michael (1956–)

Michael Connelly exploded onto the mystery novel landscape with the publication in 1992 of his first book, *The Black Echo,* featuring detective

Harry Bosch; the novel being warmly received by critics and readers alike and winning the Edgar Award for Best First Novel by the Mystery Writers of America. Fascinated by the crime noir world of Raymond Chandler's Los Angeles, Connelly decided to be a crime beat reporter in order to learn his craft, and after a story of his about a plane crash in Florida was short-listed for a Pulitzer, he landed a job writing for the *Los Angeles Times.* While still working as a reporter, he wrote *The Black Echo,* based on a true crime. Three more Bosch books rapidly followed, *The Black Ice* (1993), *The Concrete Blonde* (1994), and *The Last Coyote* (1995), with *Echo Park* (2006) the 12th installment in the series.

Hieronymus (Harry) Bosch is named for the 15th-century Dutch painter whose nightmarish canvases are peopled with grotesque figures against a backdrop of violent landscapes, all echoed in Bosch's own cases and his often hellish-seeming Los Angeles. The detective himself is not modeled on any one police officer with whom Connelly worked but is composed of traits drawn from both real and fictional detectives, among the latter, Chandler's Philip Marlowe and Ross McDonald's Lew Archer, along with the film icon Dirty Harry. Connelly's plots are inspired by his years working the crime beat as well as from current events, and their tightness and ingenuity have been compared to those of such craftsmen as JAMES PATTERSON, Robert Parker, and James Lee Burke.

In *The Poet* (1996) Detective Jack McEvoy fails to apprehend a serial killer named Robert Backus; Backus slinking away into the darkness until Bosch returns in *The Narrows* (2004) to track him down. *LINCOLN LAWYER* (2005) is Connelly's first courtroom drama, focusing on the dilemma faced by a cynical and self-serving lawyer when his defense of a rich playboy goes violently wrong. In *Echo Park* (2006) Bosch is out of retirement, working cold cases, only to see his whole career as a cop thrown into question when a jailed serial killer confesses to the killing of a woman whose murder Bosch had failed to solve 13 years ago—a failure that has made possible nine other murders in the meantime. In 2006 Connelly released *Crime Beat,* a nonfiction collection of his reportage.

In Connelly's Bosch novels the author succeeds above all in creating a real man performing a real job, flawed and sometimes tortured by his flaws, but admirable for his honest confrontation with them and for the hard-won peace he gains thereby.

Bibliography

Connelly, Michael. *The Black Echo.* New York: Little, Brown, 1992.

———. *The Black Ice.* New York: Little, Brown, 1993.

———. *The Concrete Blonde.* New York: Little, Brown, 1994.

———. *The Last Coyote.* New York: Little, Brown, 1995.

———. *The Poet.* New York: Little, Brown, 1996.

———. *The Narrows.* New York: Little, Brown, 2004.

———. *The Lincoln Lawyer.* New York: Little, Brown, 2005.

———. *Echo Park.* New York: Little, Brown, 2006.

———. *Crime Beat: A Decade of Covering Cops and Killers.* Little, Brown, 2006.

Patricia Bostian

Conroy, Pat (1945–)

Conroy is the author of two memoirs, five novels, and an intriguing storyteller's cookbook, transforming a life marked by adversity and suffering into a host of richly human best-selling novels, with the dysfunction of his family and the resulting emotional turmoil throughout his life being consistently portrayed with sympathy and humor. Conroy was born the oldest of seven children in Atlanta, Georgia, but his family moved 23 times before he was 18 due to his father's career as a military pilot, and Conroy describes himself as the quintessential military brat. In his cookbook, which features autobiographical stories, Conroy more broadly describes himself as a southerner (he raised his own family there as well), and his novels are fictionalized and often intensely exaggerated, almost caricaturish accounts of his own life. Conroy has admitted that members of his own family refused contact with him because of his novels and describes his parents as types of Zeus and Hera, at war for his psyche (1996). He was a basketball player and a graduate of the Citadel Military College and is currently married to popular novelist Cassandra King.

His first novel, *The Boo* (1970), was self-published after being rejected by numerous publishers. Conroy then wrote *The Water Is Wide* (1972), an openly autobiographical novel based on his experience teaching semiliterate children on Daufuskie Island, South Carolina, after being fired for his unconventional teaching style. His firing earned some press attention, and one reporter recommended him to literary agent Julian Bach. Unable to type, Conroy asked his neighbors and friends to each type a chapter of *The Water Is Wide,* and the manuscript was submitted to Bach on many different types and colors of paper, some even the personal stationery of his friends.

His first novel as a professional writer and his breakthrough work was *The Great Santini* (1976), a coming-of-age story about high school senior Ben Meecham and his siblings as they weather the trials of a military and Roman Catholic family in the Deep South. Their publicly affable yet privately abusive father, Bull Meecham, calls himself the Great Santini, and Conroy made no secret of the fact that the narrative was based on his relationship with his own father. Surprisingly, publication of the book created a new bond with his father, who was delighted to see the book filmed and even signed copies of his son's novel as "The Great Santini." *The Lords of Discipline* (1980) is a fictionalized account of a military school cadet, who is charged with protecting the institution's first African-American student. More even than his previous books, which do not stint in their depictions of visceral brutality, *Lords* is graphic in its portrayal of bigotry and torturous behavior, especially during the college hazing. One of Conroy's relatives claims she could not read past the fourth page due to the graphic descriptions and sexual references (2004).

Conroy states that after reading Gabriel Garcia Márquez's *One Hundred Years of Solitude* and JOHN IRVING's *The World According to Garp,* he realized how much he had been holding back as a writer, and this revelation resulted in his most celebrated and controversial novel, *The* PRINCE OF TIDES (1986). The story follows an out-of-work southern teacher, Tom Wingo, who travels to New York to help in the rehabilitation of his twin sister, who has attempted suicide. This time, however, the overt similarities between the fictional sister and Conroy's real-life sister, poet Carol Conroy, caused serious rifts in his family. The novel was both critically acclaimed and chastised for its style. Richard Eder, in the *Los Angeles Times Book Review,* declared that "inflation is the order of the day. The characters do too much, feel too much, suffer too much, eat too much, signify too much, and above all talk too much" (2004); yet that very "inflation" of feeling is what many fans and critics of Conroy enjoy most about his works, delighting in their baroque intensity and drama. It was the pinnacle of Conroy's career, spawning an acclaimed movie and acutely heightening demand for his next novel.

Beach Music (1995) followed almost 10 years later, and here again Conroy would mine the hardships of his own life, this time to enrich the story of an American expatriate in Rome who returns to South Carolina for the death of his mother, further developing his signature theme of strong personalities conflicting in emotionally charged situations. *My Losing Season* (2002) is a more formal memoir focusing on his senior year at the Citadel, during which he played in the longest game in the history of college basketball (a quadruple-overtime win over rival VMI).

The movie version of *The Prince of Tides* was nominated for seven Academy Awards, including best picture, best actor for Nick Nolte, and best adapted screenplay for Pat Conroy and Becky Johnston. *The Water Is Wide* was produced as a movie twice, once under the title *Conrack* in 1974, distinguished by Jon Voight's moving portrayal of the eponymous teacher, and once as a made-for-television move in 2006. Other movie versions of Conroy's works include *The Great Santini* in 1979, starring Robert Duvall, and *The Lords of Discipline* in 1983.

Bibliography

Book Report. "Interview with Pat Conroy." Available online. URL: http://www.geocities.com/SoHo/7315/conroy.html.

Conroy, Pat. *The Boo.* Verona, Va.: McClure Press, 1970.

———. *The Water Is Wide.* Boston: Houghton Mifflin, 1972.

———. *The Great Santini.* Boston: New York, 1976.

———. *The Lords of Discipline.* Boston: Houghton Mifflin, 1980.

———. *The Prince of Tides*. Boston: Houghton Mifflin, 1986.

———. *Beach Music*. New York: Nan A. Talese/Doubleday, 1995.

———. *My Losing Season*. New York: Nan A. Talese/Doubleday, 2002.

Conroy, Pat, and Suzanne Williamson Pollack. *The Pat Conroy Cookbook: Recipes of My Life*. New York: Nan A. Talese/Doubleday, 2004.

Gale Reference Team. *Biography of Pat Conroy*, 2004.

Internet Movie Database. Available online. URL: http://www.imdb.com.

Morgan Adams

Contact Carl Sagan (1985)

Contact is the story of Eleanor Arroway, a brilliant but misfit astronomer who has spent her career at work on SETI, the Search for Extraterrestrial Intelligence. Growing up in Wisconsin in the 1960s, Ellie loses her father at an early age and is estranged from her mother but becomes absorbed in radios and electronics; a child of the space age, she makes radio astronomy her career. At first a conventional researcher, she finds herself drifting into the less-reputable SETI work. She borrows radio telescope time to listen for signals from intelligent life elsewhere in the universe and eventually manages to get funding for her own Project Argus, an array of radio dishes in New Mexico designed to systematically scan the entire northern sky.

After years of watching their computers steer the dishes around the sky and periodically scrambling to interpret false alarms, Ellie's team is alerted to yet another unusual signal from the vicinity of the star Vega. It is a series of pulses, each group representing prime numbers—numbers divisible only by themselves and one—and there is no known way for natural phenomena to produce this kind of pattern. With growing excitement they get confirmations from other observers around the world. The press and government officials descend on the remote location, among them presidential science adviser Ken der Heer, with whom Ellie becomes romantically involved. But the signal is not merely a simple semaphore. Embedded in the pulses is a copy of an old television transmission from Earth, broadcast in the 1930s and spreading out through space ever since. There is also a data transmission buried in the signal—huge amounts of data, a total of 30,000 pages, received piece by piece over a period of months—and there are diagrams.

Worldwide interest in the "Message" rises to a feverish pitch. Governments attempt to keep its contents secret, but since no one receiver has the entire Message (half the world is always facing away from Vega), they have to cooperate. Religious sects are divided about whether the Message is from God or the Devil. Agnostic and with a thoroughly scientific outlook, Ellie nevertheless finds herself debating theology with popular preacher Palmer Joss.

Even before the Message is decrypted, many think it looks like a construction plan; for instance, one of the diagrams seems to include five armchairs inside an open space, the chairs perfectly proportioned for human beings. At this point brilliant engineer turned eccentric industrialist S. R. Hadden appears. Wanting to build the Machine seemingly described in the Message and intrigued by the decryption problem, he helps find the primer that in turn allows the rest of the Message to be understood; indeed it is a construction plan, complete down to the test procedure to use for each part before assembling. Yet, in all its 30,000 pages there is no hint of what it will do, the fearful imagining a doomsday device or perhaps an easy way to collect human specimens for an interstellar zoo. In the end human curiosity gets the better of caution, and a multinational consortium spends years building two Machines, one in Wyoming and one in Russia.

Unknown saboteurs destroy the Wyoming machine, and things appear to have taken a step backward as the Russian Machine is even less advanced and making little progress. It turns out, however, that Hadden and his corporate partners have quietly constructed a third Machine on the Japanese island of Hokkaido as part of experiments in understanding the alien technologies; a crew of five scientists, including Ellie, accept his offer to try it out. The Machine proves to be a vehicle, and the remainder of the novel describes the extraordinary events of their journey and return to Earth.

Carl Sagan was famous as an astronomer with a talent for explaining science to the general public, both in books and the popular TV program *Cosmos*. *Contact* is his only novel, and in many ways a personal statement of his lifelong dream to find proof of life elsewhere in the universe. Ellie herself is loosely based on real-life SETI researcher Jill Tarter, while the portraits of minor characters draw upon Sagan's career in the scientific community. Each scientific concept is thoroughly enunciated in the story, with great care taken to ensure that everything is consistent with present-day science. But Sagan's gift lies more in exploring concepts than character; dozens of characters appear, act out standard roles, and are little changed by the momentous events of the story, even though there are regular statements about how humanity as a whole begins to come together as a result of the Message. Ellie herself is really the only one profoundly affected by her experience, even being healed of the lingering hurt from the loss of her father, but the novel ends with only hints as to what her future holds.

The conflict between religion and science is a central theme of the novel. In keeping with his personal views, Sagan is firmly on the side of the scientists, to whom he offers challenges they easily dispatch. For instance, Ellie responds to the issue of prophecy in the Bible by pointing out that the predictions are all vague and asks why the Bible never asserts a single fact that the people of 3,000 years ago could not have known or any of Newton's or Einstein's laws. Thoroughly agnostic, she wants scientific proof of God's existence.

In general, however, the story is immensely optimistic. Written in the last decade of the cold war, with no one imagining it would soon come to an end, *Contact* depicts the Message as a powerful force for peace and reconciliation. Even though the Machine experience proves disappointing in some ways, it still holds out hope for humankind's future. The few evildoers in the story are simply misguided and fearful, looked upon with pity as unable to see the bright possibilities ahead. Most optimistically of all, the novel sees the centuries-old conflict of faith and science being solved by the insights gleaned from Message and Machine, perhaps the most poignant and personal statement of all.

The film version of *Contact*, directed by Robert Zemeckis and featuring Jodie Foster and Matthew McConaughey in the lead roles, was released in 1997.

Bibliography

Sagan, Carl. *Contact*. New York: Simon & Schuster, 1985.

Contact. Directed by Robert Zemeckis. Warner Bros, 1997.

Stan Shebs

Cook, Robin (1940–)

Born in New York in 1940, Cook studied medicine at Columbia and did postgraduate medical study at Harvard. In the 1970s he began writing fiction based on his medical knowledge, and following the success of his second novel, *Coma* (1977), took a leave of absence from practicing medicine. When asked whether he is more of a writer or a doctor he replies, "I think of myself more as a doctor who writes, rather than a writer who happens to be a doctor" (MacDonald 7). He is currently on leave from the Massachusetts Eye and Ear Infirmary and divides his time between homes in Boston and Florida.

Cook is a prolific writer, often credited with originating the medical thriller. Linda Badley, in her book *Film, Horror and the Body Fantastic*, describes him as nothing less than the "inventor" of the "subgenre of medical horror" (Bradley 24), leading the way for other authors such as Michael Crichton. Although he has published more than 26 novels to date, many of which have spent weeks on the *New York Times* best-seller list, his first book, *The Year of the Intern* (1972), was neither a thriller, nor successful. Cook methodically set about researching what makes a best seller before his next attempt, the hugely popular *Coma*. Throughout subsequent novels, he engages with many of the moral issues inherent in medical science, always writing in a way that ensures popularity with the widest nonspecialist audience. Issues of fertility treatment, in vitro fertilization, stem cell research, drug research, organ donation, genetic engineering, disease in beef production, and organ transplantation have all been explored in his work. Therefore, although some critics see him as a subpar writer, there is little doubt that his books, scrupulously researched, play a serious role in a world of ever-increasing medical science and, by extension, ever-increasing anxieties over what humans are capable of. His 1999 work, *Vector,* for example, detailed a series of anthrax bioterrorist attacks in New York City, two years before the anthrax poisonings across the United States.

His books have been frequently adapted for film or television. *Coma,* a 1978 feature film starring Genevieve Bujold and Michael Douglas (with Tom Selleck and Ed Harris in minor roles), was in fact adapted and directed by fellow doctor and writer Michael Crichton. Among TV adaptations of his work are *Harmful Intent* (1993), *Mortal Fear* (1994), *Virus* (adapted from *Outbreak,* 1995), *Terminal* (1996), and *Invasion* (1997).

When asked in an interview to comment upon the public's interest in his fiction, Cook replied, "The main reason is, we all realize we're at risk. We're all going to be patients at some time. You can write about great white sharks or haunted houses, and you can say I'm not going in the ocean or I'm not going in haunted houses, but you can't say you're not going to go in a hospital" (MacDonald 7).

Bibliography

Badley, Linda. *Film, Horror and the Body Fantastic.* Westport, Conn.: Greenwood Press, 1995.

Cook, Robin. *The Year of the Intern.* New York: Signet, 1973.

———. *Outbreak.* 1987. New York: Berkley, 1988.

———. *Mortal Fear.* 1988. New York: Berkley, 1989.

———. *Harmful Intent.* 1990. New York: Berkley, 1991.

———. *Terminal.* 1993. New York: Berkley, 1994.

———. *Coma.* New York: Signet, 1997.

———. *Invasion.* New York: Berkley, 1997.

———. *Vector.* 1999. New York: Berkley, 2000.

MacDonald, Jay. "What a Shock: Robin Cook Fuses Stem Cells with a Suspenseful Tale." *BookPage* 15, no. 189 (September 2001): 7.

Julie Barton

Coonts, Stephen (1946–)

Thriller and science-fiction novelist Stephen Coonts is the author of 20 novels, of which 17 have been on the *New York Times* best-seller list. He was born in Buckhannon, a small coal-mining town in West Virginia. In 1968 he graduated with a B.A. in political science at West Virginia University and immediately after graduation enrolled in the U.S. Navy, earning his flight wings in 1969. He flew two combat tours as an A-6 bomber pilot at the end of the Vietnam War, then served as a flight instructor before leaving active duty in 1977. He then moved to Colorado, working briefly as a taxi driver and police officer, before studying law at the University of Colorado. In 1979 he received his law degree and returned to West Virginia to practice law, specializing in oil and gas issues.

Coonts's first novel, *Flight of the Intruder* (1986), became his first best-seller, enjoying 28 weeks on the *New York Times* list. *Intruder* is the first in the Jake Grafton series, which totals 10 novels drawing heavily on the author's own experiences as an attack pilot. Though Grafton is in many ways not a typical hero, he is archetypical in always doing the right thing with no regard for consequences. The novel's success permitted Coonts to dedicate himself to writing full time. In 1991 Paramount Studios made a major motion picture based on *Flight of the Intruder* starring Danny Glover, Willem Dafoe, and Brad Johnson. Coonts's other fiction includes the Deep Black, Tommy Carmellini, and Saucer series.

Though renowned for his fiction, his nonfiction books are also worthy of notice. *The Cannibal Queen* (1992), for example, is an account of Coonts and his son David's travels in an old Stearman open-cockpit plane, as they circumnavigate the United States in a search for their own country.

His latest effort, *The Assassin,* appeared in 2008. Coonts currently lives in Nevada with his wife, also an avid pilot, who accompanies him on his many pleasure flights in one of their four planes.

Bibliography

Coonts, Stephen. *Flight of the Intruder.* Annapolis, Md.: Naval Institute Press, 1986.

———. *The Cannibal Queen.* New York: Pocket Books, 1992.

———. *The Assassin.* New York: St. Martin's Paperbacks, 2008.

Gabriella Villagran

Cornwell, Patricia (1956–)

Although preceded by medical detective mysteries such as P. D. James's *Death of an Expert Witness* (1977) and Susan Dunlap's *Pious Deception* (1989), Patricia Cornwell's *Postmortem* (1990) opened the floodgates on "forensic mystery," a genre so popular that it has extended beyond novelistic fiction into such successful television series as *C.S.I.* and *Bones*. Forensic mysteries focus on science's role in solving crimes: pathology, anthropology, toxicology, and behavioral profiling, among a host of interrelated specialties. High-tech investigative techniques are employed to solve otherwise refractory crimes, but the novels conjoin to such technical detail scenes of visceral gore, in the form of autopsies and reconstructions of the crime, amounting to a potent mix of the intellectual and sensational. Cornwell's mysteries revolve around the life and work of Kay Scarpetta, chief medical examiner for the state of Virginia, an exceptionally talented woman—too talented in the eyes of some critics who question her plausibility: forensic pathologist, lawyer, expert marksman, and skilled scuba diver.

Cornwell's first published book was a work of nonfiction, *A Time for Remembering* (1993), a biography of her friend Ruth Bell Graham, wife to evangelist Billy Graham. Turning to fiction, however, Cornwell called on her background as a reporter, augmenting this experience with a period of work in the medical examiner's office in the Richmond, Virginia, morgue. The result was her first Kay Scarpetta mystery.

In *Postmortem* Scarpetta, the 43-year-old unmarried chief medical examiner of Virginia, races to discover the identity of a serial rapist/killer, while at the same time battling chauvinistic colleagues and superiors and raising her young niece, Lucy. Readers are introduced to detailed forensic procedure as Scarpetta tracks down the killer through clues she uncovers with her office's sophisticated equipment and talented staff. The novel won almost every award given to mystery writers, including the Edgar, the Anthony, and the Macavity awards. However, none of her novels since has garnered the same level of praise from critics, although Cornwell's loyal readers keep her consistently on the best-seller list.

Her second novel, *Body of Evidence* (1991), explores Scarpetta's complicated relationships with colleagues (particularly Pete Marino), with men, and with Lucy as she once again must solve a crime based on small and seemingly scattered bits of evidence. Reviewers consistently praise Cornwell's knowledge and depiction of the world of forensic science; however, they frequently fault her emphasis on Scarpetta's messy personal life. There are times, indeed, when the personal takes up more of the plot than the solving of the crime itself, a proportion unheard of elsewhere in mystery literature.

In *Cruel and Unusual* (1993) Cornwell creates a character as chilling as Harris's Hannibal Lecter. As with Lecter and his pursuer, Clarice Starling, Temple Gault, a highly intelligent serial killer preying mostly on young children, forms a highly complex relationship with Scarpetta. The specter of Gault hovers, too, over the proceedings in *The* BODY FARM (1994), its tangled plot including the murder of an 11-year-old girl, the supposed death by autoerotic asphyxiation of an FBI agent, and the dangerous relationship between Marino and the young girl's mother. Gault appears again in *From Potter's Field* (1995), haunting New York's subway system and stalking Scarpetta as she herself is hunting him. He is finally dispatched by her in a face-to-face confrontation in her home.

Cause of Death (1996) explores the computer world of Scarpetta's brilliant niece, Lucy, and as the series' storyline unfolds, Lucy plays an ever increasing role, more like a daughter to the childless Scarpetta than a niece. Marino is also close to Lucy and is unable to reconcile the fact that she is a lesbian; Lucy's sexual orientation becoming an issue in later books as her lover, Carrie Grethen, an accomplice of Gault's, threatens both Lucy's career with the FBI and her life.

Internal strife in the medical examiner's office and threats to Scarpetta's position are at the center of *Unnatural Exposure* (1997), which features a series of deaths in Ireland that seem linked to similar deaths in Virginia.

Black Notice (1999), *The Last Precinct* (2000), and BLOW FLY (2003) form a minitrilogy as Scarpetta battles a strange werewolflike killer. The case takes her to Paris, where she learns that more is at play than a killer suffering from a strange physical disorder. Ousted from the medical examiner's office, she is asked to help Lucy in cases investigated by a private detective agency called the Last Precinct. In *Blow Fly* the narration shifts from the first to third person, and Scarpetta has moved to Miami as a forensic consultant to heal from the grief of losing both her lover, FBI agent Benton Wesley, and the loss of her position as medical examiner.

Scarpetta returns to Richmond in *Trace* (2004), and the writing once again focuses on forensic investigation; but in *Book of the Dead* (2007) she is on the move again—this time to Charleston, South Carolina, where she opens a private forensic pathology practice that she operates with Marino and Lucy. The new team's battles with public agencies while investigating murder cases has Cornwell's fans anticipating her return to the high-action plots of earlier books.

Cornwell displays a lighter side in her series about Andy Brazil, a reporter assigned to ride with the Charlotte, North Carolina, police force. Brazil is introduced in *Hornet's Nest* (1997), where readers also meet chief of police Judy Hammer and deputy Virginia West. The book was not well received, however, with *Publishers Weekly* describing its characters as "preternaturally competent automatons, obsessive and utterly devoid of self-awareness." In *Southern Cross* (1999) Brazil is now a police officer and accompanies Hammer and West to Richmond, Virginia, to investigate corruption in the police department. The novel fared better with critics, who appreciated Cornwell's humor and her departure from the grim Scarpetta series. The third installment in the Brazil series recalls Carl Hiaason's darkly humorous novels set in Florida. The locale for *Isle of Dogs* (2001) is Tangiers, an island off the coast of Virginia, where Brazil stirs up trouble with his Web site Trooper Truth, frankly answering the public's questions about law enforcement and offering sidelights into southern history. The island of Tangiers eventually secedes from Virginia in this humorous romp.

At Risk (2006) introduces new characters to Cornwell's fans. Massachusetts State Police detective Winston "Win" Garano is asked by Tennessee district attorney Monique Lamont to solve a 20-year-old Knoxville crime, Lamont desiring to display the capabilities of the cutting-edge technology used by her At Risk crime initiative. The success of the program will propel her into the governor's office.

Cornwell also found success with a nonfiction title about Jack the Ripper. *Portrait of a Killer: Jack the Ripper—Case Closed* (2002) is a result of the research Cornwell has done into the unsolved murders of prostitutes in Victorian London, Cornwell's theory being that a sexually dysfunctional Victorian painter, Walter Sickert, was responsible for the murders. Whether her theory is correct remains debatable, but the book was praised for its powerful writing and meticulous research.

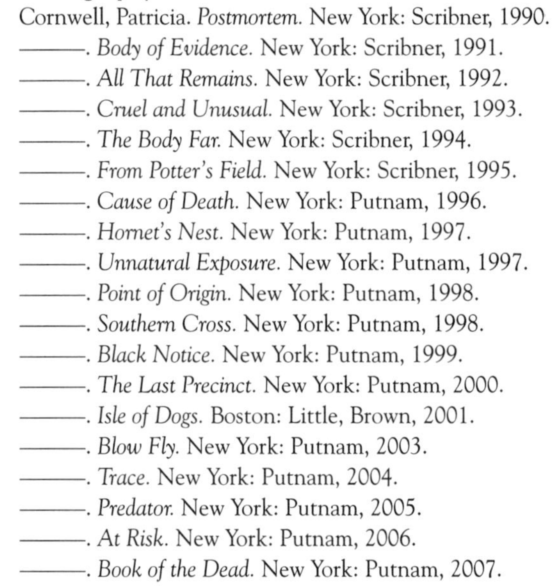

Bibliography

Cornwell, Patricia. *Postmortem*. New York: Scribner, 1990.

———. *Body of Evidence*. New York: Scribner, 1991.

———. *All That Remains*. New York: Scribner, 1992.

———. *Cruel and Unusual*. New York: Scribner, 1993.

———. *The Body Farm*. New York: Scribner, 1994.

———. *From Potter's Field*. New York: Scribner, 1995.

———. *Cause of Death*. New York: Putnam, 1996.

———. *Hornet's Nest*. New York: Putnam, 1997.

———. *Unnatural Exposure*. New York: Putnam, 1997.

———. *Point of Origin*. New York: Putnam, 1998.

———. *Southern Cross*. New York: Putnam, 1998.

———. *Black Notice*. New York: Putnam, 1999.

———. *The Last Precinct*. New York: Putnam, 2000.

———. *Isle of Dogs*. Boston: Little, Brown, 2001.

———. *Blow Fly*. New York: Putnam, 2003.

———. *Trace*. New York: Putnam, 2004.

———. *Predator*. New York: Putnam, 2005.

———. *At Risk*. New York: Putnam, 2006.

———. *Book of the Dead*. New York: Putnam, 2007.

Patricia Bostian

The Covenant **James A. Michener** (1980)

In a prologue and 13 character-rich, action-driven chapters, JAMES MICHENER's 850-page *The Covenant* presents an epic overview of the geography and cultural history of the southern portion of the African continent, from the region's habitation by Stone Age hunters and gatherers some 13,000 years before the Common Era until its domination by the apartheid-plagued, Afrikaner-dominated society of the late 1970s. Perhaps more profoundly than any of his previous works, the novel explores the contradictory nature of human impulses; juxtaposing the positive value of maintaining racial and cultural heritage against the horrors of racial prejudice and cultural bigotry; juxtaposing the humanistic importance of the pursuit of religious faith against the evils of religious persecution; and depicting South Africa—with its stunning ecological uniqueness, complex racial and cultural diversity, immense economic potential, and radical humanistic inequities—as a microcosm of planet Earth itself. By including in his narrative scheme memorable and sympathetic characters from many races, religions, continents, and phases of cultural development, Michener portrays the social and political struggle occurring in South Africa in the 1970s, the time of his writing of *The Covenant,* as a global and international crisis, implicating all of humanity both in its creation and its solution.

While renowned for the extensive research he conducted in writing his historical novels, Michener spent an exceptionally long time preparing to write *The Covenant.* At least as early as 1971, almost a decade before the publication of the novel, Michener began interviewing South Africans and assembling background information for his novel, and he undertook several research trips to South Africa. Having spent a decade developing an understanding of modern-day South African life, Michener attempted to explain in the novel how, why, when, and by whose influence the seminal elements of that culture came into being, suggestively associating each of the chapters and each stage in the historical evolution of South Africa with a different mammal (successively the eland, rhinoceros, hippopotamus, leopard, hyena, wildebeest, lion, sable antelope, zebra, Basuto pony, springbok, elephant, Cape buffalo and giraffe). He also implies that just as diverse fauna coexist in interdependence upon one another, the staggeringly varied peoples and cultures that contribute to the formation of the 20th-century South African state (whether black, white, brown, yellow, "colored," African, European, Asian, animist, Muslim, Catholic, Protestant, Hindu, San, Xhosa, Zulu, Portuguese, Dutch, English, French, Indian, Chinese, hunter and gather, warrior, slave, servant, outlaw, farmer, rancher, miner, wine producer, tradesman, industrialist, youth, or adult) must all develop some yet-to-be-achieved formula for productive coexistence.

A brief summary of *The Covenant* attests to both the grandeur of its scope and the vivid color of its local detail. In chapter I, entitled "Prologue," the San people, the prehistoric hunters and gatherers who would come to be called Bushmen, live in a tenuous but intimate balance with nature, surviving by killing wild game and searching for natural water sources. For the San animist religious ritual and the production of cave art enrich the rawness of their Stone Age life. In "Zimbabwe" the narrative leaps forward some 15,000 years to scenes of the 15th-century flourishing of the great southern African city of Zimbabwe. And in depicting the Old World "discovery" of this southern Africa, first by Middle Eastern Muslim Arabs, and later by Christian Europeans, Michener introduces what will be a central theme of the work: the refusal of foreign invaders and immigrants to recognize or appreciate the remarkable cultural expressions of indigenous black South Africans. In "A Hedge of Bitter Almond," set in the 1650s, Portuguese, English, and Dutch adventurers and traders struggle to establish control over the South African region. Biblical associations and references recur throughout the novel, and here the Christian newcomers seize upon biblical texts to justify their subjugation of the native black "Hottentots" and their lands. Indeed, the novel's title is derived from the religious hegemony of the Dutch settlers, who see South Africa as the "Promised Land" given by God's covenant to the Dutch, "God's chosen people." In "The Huguenots" French Protestants, driven from their homeland in the late 1600s by religious persecution, immigrate to South Africa. As the Christian Europeans battle to establish themselves by suppressing the native "Bushmen," their establishment of vineyards and wine production begins to transform the natural landscape. In "The Trekboers" two rival rural cultures, immigrant Dutch farmers and native Xhosa tribesmen, compete during the 1800s for the same vast land area. Ironically, though speaking different languages and worshiping different gods, the Boers and the Xhosa bear remarkable resemblance to each other in their use and love of the land. In "The Missionary" the English, who by the early 1800s had solidified their political control over the South African Cape Colony, attempt to promote a peaceful coexistence between the native peoples and the increasingly restive Boer settlers. "The Mfecane" presents perspectives of the native black peoples. Unified under the leadership of the great Zulu king Shaka and determined to preserve their historic control over southern Africa, a coalition of black peoples wages a war of survival against the more technologically advanced white invaders. In "The Voortrekkers" the white Boers revolt when in 1833 the English rulers of South Africa abolish slavery. Convinced that they have been appointed by God to enslave the native blacks, they undertake the Great Trek to escape English control and found the Boer republics of Transvaal and the Orange Free State in the 1850s. In "The Englishmen" the English imperialist Cecil Rhodes works to make South Africa a formal part of the British Empire. The English wage war to control the Zulus and Boers alike, and the European invaders temporarily unite to finally crush the native Zulus in 1879. "The Venloo Commando" recounts the great cruelty, suffering, and loss of life resulting from the English wars against the Boers in the 1880s and 1890s; while in "Education of a Puritan" the Boers, though defeated militarily, recast themselves as "Afrikaners" and work during World War I to gain social and political control over South Africa. In "Achievement of a Puritan" they solidify their political control over the South African government. In "Apartheid," set after World War II, the notorious system of racial segregation or "apartness" is institutionalized throughout South Africa, creating radical social inequities and international outrage. In the final chapter, "Diamonds," the Afrikaner-dominated South Africa of 1979 is being forced to confront a future of social, political, religious, and ecological alternatives. Rather like the rough stones that with skill and care can be fashioned into brilliant gems, Michener's novel proposes—prophetically, as it turned out—that the strife-torn South Africa of 1979 must in time be carefully cut and shaped into a well-formed and polished nation.

The Covenant explores racism and cultural prejudice in complex ways, allowing readers to understand and even sympathize in so far as possible with the religious and social imperatives used to justify genocide, slavery, and Apartheid, employing a third-person narrator who seems reliable but is far from omniscient. A reasonable man with Western, liberal sympathies, he seems genuinely interested in understanding the conflicting perspectives, beliefs, and goals of virtually all the characters he depicts but is not necessarily approving of all the ideas his characters promote, keenly aware that such contradictory impulses as his characters represent simply cannot coexist peacefully or productively. In the end Michener's humanist ethic and his intense admiration for the diversity and variety of human cultural expression ground a stubborn faith that the crisis of 1970s South Africa will be resolved. Indeed, his resounding belief in human equality would anticipate, and itself to some extent foster, the revolutionary political and social changes that occurred in South Africa in the decades following the book's publication.

Bibliography

Michener, James A. *The Covenant.* New York: Random House, 1980; New York: Fawcett Crest, 1982 (paperback).

Cliff Toliver

Crichton, Michael (1942–2008)

Crichton was a prolific thriller writer and film producer/director. His books have been translated into 36 languages, and 13 have been made into films. He helped to invent the techno-thriller genre, in which new technologies go terribly wrong, the best known example being *JURASSIC PARK,* which became a blockbuster film under the direction of Stephen Spielberg; others include *Westworld, The Lost World, Prey,* and *Next.* His books and films also include historically based novels (*The Great Train Robbery, Eaters of the Dead*) and general contemporary-interest stories (*DISCLOSURE, Rising Sun*). In addition, Crichton has two computer games to his credit and was the creator and coproducer of the television medical drama *ER.*

In his early career writing and directing seemed of equal importance, and Crichton often directed work from other authors' screenplays (such as the excellent 1978 thriller *Coma*). In his 60s, however, he appeared to have become a full-time novelist for the first time in his life, not having directed a movie since 1989, and his last screenplay was *Twister* in 1996. But his own lack of cinematic activity has not stopped Hollywood from mining his work. The 1976 historical novel *Eaters of the Dead,* for example, based loosely on the Old English poem *Beowulf,* appeared in 1999 as *The 13th Warrior,* starring Antonio Banderas, and Crichton's work continues to translate well to the big screen.

Born in Chicago in 1942, Michael Crichton trained as a doctor, graduating with his M.D. from Harvard Medical School, then for a time followed an academic research career, first as a postdoctoral fellow at the Salk Institute for Biological Studies and then as a visiting fellow in anthropology at Cambridge University, pursuing interests in the computer modeling of medical and anthropological data that have figured prominently in his thrillers about medicine, genetic research, and the pernicious involvement of business and the law in these areas. His knowledge of computing also helped in the development of the first computer-generated special effects for the movies, seen in the 1973 film for his own *Westworld.*

These interests developed in parallel with his career as a writer. Even at medical school Crichton was writing thrillers, partly to fund his studies, under the pseudonyms John Lange and Jeffrey Hudson, and his work is distinguished by its meticulous, topical, and cutting-edge research, often explicitly acknowledging the scientists and scientific literature he has consulted (*STATE OF FEAR,* for example, describing a particularly involved scientific crisis, has an extensive annotated bibliography). Nonetheless, his novels are unmistakably thrillers, briskly and surely paced, suspenseful, and obviously indebted to 19th-century adventure novelists such as Arthur Conan Doyle and H. Rider Haggard. Indeed, *Congo,* as Crichton had acknowledged, is a contemporary version of Haggard's 1885 imperial adventure yarn *King Solomon's Mines.*

The most successful of the early thrillers, *The Andromeda Strain,* appeared in the year of the first Moon landing, 1969, and was filmed two years later. Echoing British author Nigel Kneale's 1953 television play and 1955 screenplay *The Quatermass Experiment,* Crichton's thriller deals with attempts to control a deadly viral disease brought to Earth by a returning satellite. Crichton would later return to the theme of the alien unknown in 1987 in *Sphere,* which echoes Stanislaw Lem's influential 1961 novel *Solaris,* and which itself is echoed in James Cameron's 1989 movie *The Abyss.*

The Andromeda Strain is a model Crichton techno-thriller, with its secret government departments with official contingency plans and secret underground laboratories, and its lethal and uncontrollable nonhuman enemy—a threat to humankind as a whole—which must somehow be destroyed before it gets loose, here through the heroic actions of a small, isolated group of people. This—the few racing against time against a sophisticated scientific threat to the many—is the essential plot that Crichton perfected over his many novels and films: in *Westworld* a cybernetic being in a theme park, in *Jurassic Park* genetically engineered dinosaurs, in *Prey* the nightmarish microrobots of nanotechnology.

But it is rarely the nonhuman enemies who are the true bad guys. The real villains of *Terminal Man, Jurassic Park, The Lost World, Prey,* and *Next* are the naive scientists, the greedy businessmen—including the industrial spies of *Jurassic Park* and *Airframe*—and the aggressive lawyers who combine to develop new technologies with insufficient humility in the face of the complexity of the natural world (as *Jurassic Park*'s "chaos mathematician" Ian Malcolm explicitly puts it); while in *The State of Fear* the threat to humankind comes from environmental extremists. Crichton does not merely inform readers who the bad guys *are,* but *why.* Thus, in *Jurassic Park,* Ian Malcolm's long speeches force readers to step back from the faced-paced storytelling and reflect on the inadequate scientific principles and business malpractices that have created the catastrophe in the park.

Indeed, Malcolm appears to be given this role (and a leading role in the sequel, *The Lost World,* despite his apparent death in *Jurassic Park*) because he is a spokesman for Crichton himself. *State of Fear* has a similar figure, though his target here is not big business but its often equally dangerous opponents. Over the course of the novel John Kenner skeptically engages various characters in discussions about global warming, acknowledging that the world is growing warmer but challenging the increasingly held view that this global warming is potentially catastrophic for the future of humanity—all while striving to defeat a global conspiracy by environmental groups who are trying to engineer environmental catastrophes in the Antarctic and the Pacific in order to demonstrate their own beliefs about global warming and thereby obtain further research funding.

Such a turn away from the usual targets of the techno-thriller delighted conservatives, especially in America, while the patriotism of *Rising Sun* and the sexual politics of *Disclosure* suggested a possible shift in Crichton's customary perspective. However, his customary attack on the unscrupulous combination of academic science, business, and the law was vigorously renewed in his most recent novel, *Next* (2006), a hostile exposé of the patenting of human DNA. Crichton died of cancer on November 4, 2008.

Bibliography

Crichton, Michael. *The Andromeda Strain.* New York: Knopf, 1969.

———. *The Terminal Man.* New York: Knopf, 1972.

———. *The Great Train Robbery.* New York: Knopf, 1975.

———. *Westworld* (Screenplay). New York: Bantam Books, 1975.

———. *Eaters of the Dead.* New York: Knopf, 1976.

———. *Congo.* New York: Knopf, 1980.

———. *Sphere.* New York: Knopf, 1987.

———. *Jurassic Park.* New York: Knopf, 1990.

———. *Rising Sun.* New York: Knopf, 1992.

———. *Disclosure.* New York: Knopf, 1994.

———. *The Lost World.* New York: Knopf, 1995.

———. *Airframe.* New York: Knopf, 1996.

———. *Twister* (Screenplay, with Anne-Marie Martin). New York: Ballantine Books, 1996.

———. *Timeline.* New York: Knopf, 1999.

———. *Prey.* New York: Harper Collins, 2002.

———. *State of Fear.* New York: HarperCollins, 2004.

———. *Next.* New York: HarperCollins, 2006.

Trembley, Elizabeth. *Michael Crichton* (Critical Companions to Popular Contemporary Writers). New York: Greenwood Press 1996. Available online. URL: http://www.crichton-official.com

Andrew Blake

Cussler, Clive (1931–)

The career of Clive Cussler would appear to add new meaning to the phrase "Life imitates art," so closely does it mirror that of Dirk Pitt, the hero of many of his best-selling adventure novels. Like Pitt, Cussler collects classic cars and works for the National Marine Underwater Agency (NUMA). But in an uncanny overlap Cussler created this very agency for his novels, then in 1979 created a real-life version, which he still directs and funds with royalties from his writing. Cussler even leads expeditions to locate and recover long-lost shipwrecks, lending credence to his claim that "there are many things I'd rather be doing than writing a book" (Straub 101).

Born in Aurora, Illinois, Cussler grew up in Alhambra, California, and attended Pasadena City College for two years before enlisting in the Air Force, where he served as an aircraft mechanic and flight engineer. While in the Military Air Transport Service, he did a great deal of scuba diving, hunting for shipwrecks off-shore. After his discharge he wrote and produced radio and television commercials and is credited with creating the famous Ajax "White Knight" commercials. Several of his advertising spots won awards, including one at the Cannes Film Festival.

In 1965 Cussler began writing novels to pass the time while his wife worked nights, and in 1973 he brought his diving experience and lifelong fascination with unsolved mysteries to bear in writing *The Mediterranean Caper,* the first Dirk Pitt novel. In 1997 his first work of nonfiction, *The Sea Hunters,* which details his real-life experiences hunting for shipwrecks, earned him a doctor of letters from the Maritime College, State University of New York—the first time such a degree was awarded.

Originally, Cussler's distinctive brand of fiction was seen as unmarketable, and he received numerous rejections before finally getting a manuscript accepted through a ruse worthy of Dirk Pitt, sending recommendations from a fictitious West Coast agent to various New York publishing houses. Critical opinion of his work has improved since then, but a recurring criticism is that his plots are implausible and his writing style riddled with clichés. However, all agree it is nearly impossible to put down a Cussler book.

The majority of his novels feature Dirk Pitt and his sidekick, Al Giordino, who work for the fictional NUMA and are continually embroiled in a series of swashbuckling adventures, facing off against evil arch-villains and rescuing beautiful women. Pitt has been described as having "the archaeological background of Indiana Jones and the boldness of James Bond. He is as skilled and comfortable underwater as Jacques Cousteau, and like Chuck Yeager, he can fly anything with wings" (Straub 103). But Pitt is not infallible; he often makes errors in judgment, though he has an uncanny ability to turn a negative situation into a positive one. Despite the similarities in their lives, Cussler insists Pitt is not based on anyone in particular but rather was built block by block, though he is named after Cussler's son, Dirk, taking his last name from the former prime minister of England. "One syllable names are much easier to work with," Cussler notes. "It's much easier to write 'Pitt did this' and 'Pitt did that' than to write 'Shagnasty climbed the fence'" (Straub 101).

Like Pitt Cussler collects classic cars, which he restores and showcases in photos on the back of each novel. Further blurring the distinction between art and life, Cussler writes himself into the novels in cameo appearances, where he gives Pitt and Giordino key information or a helping hand when they need it most.

Though Cussler's real-life version of NUMA is perhaps less swashbuckling than the fictitious agency, the nonprofit organization dedicates its resources to preserving American maritime history and to uncovering and exploring historically significant shipwrecks. Initially, Cussler rejected the decision to name the organization after the NUMA of his novels, but the board of directors overruled him. The author makes no claim to being an archaeologist, describing himself as "a dilettante who loves the challenge of solving a mystery" (NUMA homepage). The NUMA Web site lists more than 60 shipwrecks that NUMA and Cussler claim to have either discovered or surveyed and positively identified, though some of these claims are disputed, including his discovery of the Confederate submarine *Hunley*. NUMA donates all the artifacts it finds to state and federal authorities and museums.

Cussler's interest in preserving the past is a major element in his fiction, historical themes being usually introduced in a prologue describing a past event about which there is some air of mystery or unresolved question. The connection to the book's main plot gradually becomes clear, and in the epilogue the loose ends are tied up and the historical event's relevance revealed. Such historical occurrences range from the sinking of the *Titanic* or the disappearance of a Viking ship in New York to a strange submarine that might have been the inspiration for Jules Verne's *Twenty Thousand Leagues under the Sea*.

Though Cussler's protagonist is often compared to Ian Fleming's James Bond, Pitt is unabashedly American, as are his colleagues in NUMA, and in fact all of the "good guys" in the books. The villains, on the other hand, rarely hail from the United States, and good always triumphs through the ingenuity and persistence of Cussler's heroes. While the NUMA novels are considered action-adventure, the futuristic and improbable nature of Cussler's premises sets them apart from other, more realistic works such as those of TOM CLANCY.

Cussler branched out from his Dirk Pitt novels in 1999 to create a younger protagonist, Kurt Austin, who also works for NUMA. In 2003 he started a completely new series, *The Oregon Files,* which features a NUMA-like organization called The Corporation, dedicated in part to righting the wrongs of others. Cussler has also adapted several Pitt novels for younger readers and recently wrote *The Adventures of Vin Fiz,* a children's book. Two of Cussler's novels have been realized as films, *Raise the Titanic* (1980), which was a box-office and critical failure, and *Sahara* (2005), a comparative success. For *Sahara* Cussler negotiated for and won casting and script approval; however, he was still unhappy with the results and is suing the film company, charging that they violated the agreement. He has no plans to approve future film adaptations of his work until that lawsuit is settled.

Bibliography

Cussler, Clive. *The Mediterranean Caper.* New York: Simon & Schuster, 1976.

———. *Raise the Titanic.* New York: Bantam Books, 1979.

———. *Sahara.* New York: Simon & Schuster, 1993.

———. *The Adventures of Vin Fiz.* New York: Puffin Books, 2006.

———. *Plague Ship.* New York: Putnam, 2008.

———, and Craig Dirgo. *The Sea Hunters: True Adventures with Famous Shipwrecks.* New York: Pocket Books, 1997.

National Underwater Marine Agency. Available online. URL: http://www.numa.net. Accessed January 5, 2007.

Straub, Deborah, ed. *Contemporary Authors New Revised Series.* Vol. 21. Detroit: Gale Research, 1987, pp. 101–105.

Patti J. Kurtz

D

Daddy Danielle Steel (1989)

Daddy is an uncharacteristically complex romance, but one revolving around DANIELLE STEEL's customary focus on family values and dynamics, and specifically on all that it can mean, in a world bereft of traditional supports and conventions, to be a daddy. Oliver and Sarah Watson have a seemingly ideal marriage, three wonderful children, and a comfortable lifestyle, but it soon becomes apparent that Sarah has become uncomfortable with her stay-at-home role, chaffing at the lost career opportunities she gave up after college. Thus far the reader's sympathies rest firmly with her, but as the story switches from Sarah's point of view to that of Oliver, the tale rapidly increases both in subtlety and complexity.

Oliver's narrow world is shaken when Sarah decides to return to college, and her further decision, to attend school in another state, shatters the seemingly solid family structure, its repercussions commencing with the youngest son, nine-year-old Sam, who begins to wet his bed and insists on sleeping with his dad after Sarah leaves. Fifteen-year-old Melissa blames her father for the disruption of the family; 17-year-old Benjamin seeks solace in the arms of a girl he hardly knows. Set in a contemporary setting, with a husband working a successful job, and the family living comfortably in the suburbs, Steel gently but implacably anatomizes the fragile nature of the American Dream. As each member of the nuclear family staggers in the aftermath of Sarah's departure, Oliver, himself now the object of sympathies, must negotiate the inevitable confusion, hurt, anger, resignation, and finally resolution to live without Sarah.

In addition to his own suffering, Oliver is encompassed by tribulation. His mother, Phyllis, is suffering from Alzheimer's, and weakened as he is, Oliver must somehow be a source of strength to his distraught father. The sense of what a father is, should be, and *can* be are all brought into question as his struggle with the new developments in his own parents' relationship, as much as their physical and mental health, strains Oliver's resources to the breaking point.

Unsupported by a wife, Oliver must now, in a sense, be twice a father, for as his own parents are struggling with the second childhood of senility, his eldest son, Benjamin, is floundering in the first. When Sarah leaves the family home to attend school in Boston, Benjamin retreats into his own world. He begins dating a girl and in his own emotional turmoil incautiously seeks solace in her arms and bed. The youthful ardor unsurprisingly proving incapable of bearing such weight, Benjamin's life begins to disintegrate from the inside out; he skips school, jeopardizes his college entrance, and then finds that his girlfriend is pregnant. Determined to do the right thing, he quits school and begins working multiple jobs to support her and, ultimately, his own son after the baby is born. But for all its dissimilarities to his father's miasmic American Dream, Benjamin's trial ends with much the same result. After three children, increasingly unwanted by his increasingly estranged wife, he is left trying to be a daddy, against all odds.

In the 1991 film adaptation of the same name, the nuanced description of the first marriage is dispensed with, the film commencing with the wife's departure. And Sarah's important presence-as-absence is severely circumscribed, with no intimation either of the great internal struggle she goes through while making her decision to leave for college or of her feelings after leaving. Thus the sympathy for her so critical to the delicate moral balance of the novel is forsaken.

In the end *Daddy* is, above all, a study in balance—balance and imbalance, a cautionary tale about the hubris of contemporary imbalance and the vain confidence in the capacity of material possessions and quotidian technique to protect people from themselves. Helplessly ensconced both in a family of troubled fathers and in the contemporary problematic of fatherhood itself, Oliver's dogged and ultimately noble struggle culminates at last in nothing more nor less than a reminder of the daunting world within the simple word *daddy*.

Bibliography

Daddy. Directed by Michael Miller. NBC Home Video, 1991.

Steel, Danielle. *Daddy*. New York: Dell, 1989.

Linda Dick

The Da Vinci Code Dan Brown (2003)

The Da Vinci Code is a mystery/thriller involving Harvard professor Robert Langdon, the hero of DAN BROWN's earlier novel *ANGELS AND DEMONS* (2000). The novel became Brown's first best seller and spawned a heated religious controversy with its claim that Jesus of Nazareth and Mary Magdalene were married and bore a child whose descendants still exist. The book also depicts a widespread conspiracy on the part of the real-life Catholic religious order Opus Dei (Work of God) to hide the truth about the early history of Christianity in order to preserve the Catholic Church's power. Brown's bold statement at the novel's outset that the ideas regarding the nature and development of the early Christian church presented in the novel are "true" inspired numerous books rebutting its claims.

The novel commences with the mysterious death of Jacques Saunière, the curator of the Louvre, at the hands of Silas, a fanatically pious monk in the Roman Catholic Opus Dei movement (in fact, Opus Dei does not have a monastic order per se). Before Saunière expires, he manages to leave several written and visual clues. His body (arranged in the likeness of da Vinci's *Vitruvian Man*) is discovered near some of Leonardo da Vinci's artworks; among the messages found near it, one states, "P.S. Find Robert Langdon." This leads police detective Bezu Fache to telephone Langdon and ask him to come to the crime scene, purportedly to try and interpret Saunière's puzzles, but in fact to arrest him for his murder.

After viewing Saunière's body and the other clues, Sophie Neveu, Saunière's granddaughter, a respected police cryptologist, warns Langdon that Fache suspects him of committing the murder and tells him that her grandfather left clues specifically directed to her, which may help them understand the circumstances of his death. After getting rid of a tracking device that Fache has planted on Langdon, they escape from the Louvre and set out themselves to uncover the meaning of Saunière's riddles. Langdon quickly ascertains that the "P.S." in Saunière's message could stand for the "Priory of Sion," which he explains is an organization committed to the preservation of goddess-centered worship as well as the protection of an ancient secret related to the Holy Grail, about which Langdon happens to be writing at the time. After managing to solve a couple of puzzles embedded in Saunière's messages, they locate a bank vault in which a cryptex (a secure message carrier originally designed by Leonardo da Vinci) created by Saunière has been stored. The cryptex must be opened by a secret code, and Langdon suggests they visit a renowned Grail expert, Sir Leigh Teabing, for assistance in discovering it.

The Opus Dei monk Silas, meanwhile, appears in an important subplot, as he himself seeks the location of the Holy Grail based on information Saunière gave him just before he shot him. After the murder Silas telephones a person he knows as the "Teacher," who directs him to continue his search for the Grail based on Saunière's information, and he proceeds to a church where, after killing a nun, he discovers that Saunière's statements were merely a ruse designed to throw him off the trail.

Langdon and Neveu manage to reach Teabing's residence outside Paris, and the Grail historian describes how the Catholic Church is, in fact, largely a political construct created by the Emperor Constantine, explaining that the key doctrinal elements of Christianity were fabricated by the early church leaders to exclude women from positions of power and to hide the fact that Jesus Christ was not divine. Teabing also reveals that Christ was actually married to Mary Magdalene with whom he had a child. Teabing suspects Saunière was killed because the Priory of Sion was planning to unveil the truth about Christ and Mary Magdalene, and Opus Dei will do anything to prevent this from happening.

At this point Silas shows up and accosts Teabing, but the scholar is rescued by Langdon and Neveu, and Teabing suggests they head to London, where a church built by the Knights Templar may contain further information that will help them discover where the Holy Grail is hidden. The final portion of the novel intertwines with the main narrative a number of subplots involving, variously, the efforts of Silas's superior in Opus Dei to return the maligned order to papal favor, the identity of the Teacher, and Silas's ultimate fate. The story culminates in a skillfully unified conclusion in which the contents of the cryptex, the bearers of the bloodline of Christ and Magdalene, and the true hiding place of the Holy Grail are all revealed.

The novel offsets a noticeable lack of character development by keeping readers in relentless suspense. In particular, the deft mix of action and intellection, from the protagonists' constant pursuit by police and villains to the cryptological puzzles the characters must strive to solve and the controversial discussions of early Christian history, keeps the novel moving, sometimes at a breathless pace.

The controversy inspired by the novel was principally driven by Brown's insistence (which he includes in all his works) that his historical data are strictly accurate and that the Priory of Sion and the cryptic features of Leonardo da Vinci's artwork (especially his paintings of *The Madonna of the Rocks*, *The Last Supper*, and the *Mona Lisa*) do indeed contain the secrets as depicted in the novel. But it was Teabing's vehement assault on orthodox Christian beliefs (especially the divinity and celibacy of Christ), as well as some other grand claims made in the novel—in addition to a couple of outright historical inaccuracies—which caused the most intense debate, usually along sectarian lines. The Catholic Church considered the novel an outright anti-Catholic attack, and Opus Dei quickly set out to counter the negative image of the movement portrayed in the novel.

But the novel also found praise precisely, if ironically, because the controversy it inspired helped generate a renewed interest in early Christian history, in the role of women in the Christian church, and in the conflict between orthodox and heterodox interpretations of religious texts and imagery. For instance, Brown, via Langdon and Teabing, draws attention to the conflict between literalist and metaphoric interpretations of sacred texts and emphasizes that most people with sufficient faith will be able to handle the truth about Christ (i.e., that he was married) without losing the core elements of their faith (e.g., loving one's neighbor, etc.). The role of women in Western religion is highlighted by the Priory of Sion's mission to preserve devotion to the Goddess and to honor the important role of Mary Magdalene as both female disciple and wife. Finally, the novel depicts the ongoing conflict between mainstream orthodox beliefs and the potential challenge from heretical alternatives. While Silas believes he is helping quash a heretical sect and preserve the true Catholic faith, the Priory of Sion seeks to maintain an alternate path to religious devotion, even though, by so doing, its members risk death at the hands of orthodox believers.

Whatever its weaknesses or strengths, there can be no doubt, however, that the novel's readers are encouraged, with all the persuasive force of good storytelling, to seek a more profound meaning beneath the unexamined surface of their lives.

Bibliography

Brown, Dan. *Angels and Demons*. New York: Simon & Schuster, 2000.

———. *The Da Vinci Code*. New York: Doubleday, 2003.

Ehrman, Bart. *Truth and Fiction in The Da Vinci Code: A Historian Reveals What We Really Know about Jesus, Mary Magdalene, and Constantine.* New York: Oxford University Press, 2006.

Joseph E. Becker

Debt of Honor **Tom Clancy** (1994)

The eighth and penultimate novel in TOM CLANCY'S Jack Ryan series, *Debt of Honor* follows Clancy's reluctant hero out of semiretirement and into public life—and eventually, in the aftermath of the novel's surprising climax, into the Oval Office itself. The novel is openly didactic in its aims, not only in the sense familiar to Clancy's readers—full of instructive digressions, detailed accounts of the workings of mutual funds, U.S. Treasury notes, computer trading software, and the like—but also in a more urgent sense. *Debt of Honor* offers a warning to its audience: The cold war has ended, and a few spies have come in from the cold, but new enemies are lurking, and the United States is ill-prepared to confront them.

At the novel's outset Jack Ryan reflects on the then controversial notion of an "end to history" (6), which was most fully elaborated by American political economist Francis Fukuyama in his 1992 book *The End of History and the Last Man,* shortly after the fall of the Berlin Wall and the collapse of the Soviet Union. Fukuyama argued that those events marked the victory of Western liberal democracy in an ideological struggle that was now ended for good, and Clancy's novel, detailing the destruction of the last remaining nuclear missiles held by the United States and Russia, features the strange spectacle of former cold warriors from both sides of the Iron Curtain learning to work together in a common cause. Ryan, however, a historian by training, is skeptical of history's reported demise, and events quickly prove him right. The very notion is dangerous because it breeds complacency, and complacency, in turn, breeds vulnerability.

Debt of Honor returns repeatedly to the diminished power of the U.S. military, the conspicuous result of a deliberate strategy to channel government funds to "more pressing" causes. Bart Mancuso, one of many recurring characters in the series, reflects with mixed emotions on his ascendancy to the esteemed position of commander of the Submarine Force, U.S. Pacific Fleet, recognizing that his is "a dying business" (35). The submarines that once engaged in the sort of life-and-death struggle chronicled in *The* HUNT FOR RED OCTOBER (1984) are now relegated to tracking the movements of whales, and "his country, as it had done so many times in the past, had rewarded its warriors by forgetting them" (36). For the avidly pro-military Clancy, of course, this new attitude represents a significant failure on the part of the nation, both moral and strategic.

While Mancuso reflects with melancholy on the decline of American military power, Jack Ryan does so with deep and restless concern. "We've cut back too much," he warns the president, who has brought him to the White House as his new National Security Advisor, "Our people are strung out very thin" (44). Ryan's warning proves prescient when the badly weakened United States is drawn into a military conflict with an unexpected enemy, a resurgent imperial Japan. As the threat of the former USSR recedes, a new one arises in the east, not only from Japan, but also India, with the specter of China eventually joining these two in a formidable three-way alliance of eastern powers.

While the nominal enemy is Japan, Clancy takes pains to distinguish between the real instigators of the conflict—a handful of powerful Japanese businessmen—and the actual government and people of Japan, who remain largely ignorant of the undeclared and secret war. Clancy's Japan is not a democracy so much as a corporate oligarchy, a nation run by a behind-the-scenes collective, the *zaibatsu,* a group of "twenty or thirty men elected by no one but their own corporate boardrooms" (651). The most powerful of this group, Raizo Yamata, nurses a deep hatred of the United States—a hatred born in 1944, when all of his family were killed during the American seizure of the Pacific island of Saipan. Yamata's grudge is not merely personal, however, but informed by a widespread resentment of the United States among Clancy's Japanese characters. After a military exercise in which the United States has won yet another victory, a Japanese military commander imagines the thoughts of his demoralized men: "*Again,* they thought, the Americans have done it to us *again*" (390). This resentment over past defeats mingles with a powerful sense of superiority over *gaijin*, American and otherwise, to fuel a hostility that quickly escalates from a trade dispute into war when the Japanese aggressors seize the opportunity handed to them by a careless U.S. government. "Instead of merely maintaining their power" following the collapse of the Soviet Union, Yamata thinks, "the Americans had cast it aside at the moment of its ascendancy . . . and in the dimming of two formerly great powers lay the opportunity for a country that *deserved* to be great" (99). To guarantee this Japanese ascendancy, Yamata has secretly commissioned 20 nuclear missiles of his own.

The conflict begins with a seemingly unrelated pair of surprise attacks by the Japanese, a circumstance explicitly linked to the 1941 bombing of Pearl Harbor that drew the United States into World War II. During a supposedly friendly military exercise in the Pacific, the Japanese target and sink two American submarines and badly damage two of the navy's four aircraft carriers, thus severely compromising America's capacity to respond to the subsequent Japanese invasion and occupation of Guam and Saipan. The other attack, initially the more alarming of the two, is on the U.S. economy. By purchasing a controlling interest in the Columbus Group, the "cornerstone of the mutual-funds community" (66), Yamata has positioned himself to single-handedly influence financial markets. Taking advantage of the vulnerabilities created through automated computer trading, Yamata invisibly engineers a stock-market crash that threatens to leave the U.S. economy in a state of chaos. Meanwhile, the Indian navy, confident that the United States is too preoccupied with its economic crisis and the undeclared war with Japan to police the Indian Ocean, plans an opportunistic strike against Sri Lanka, and U.S. president Roger Durling faces a political crisis at home arising from a pending rape charge against his philandering vice president, Ed Kealty.

Fortunately for the Americans, Jack Ryan is a "good man in a storm" (884), as his president notes. The financial crisis is contained with the assistance of the Columbus Group's former head and the cooperation of all the major North American and European financial organizations, while the military crisis is resolved owing largely to the creativity and determination of Clancy's warriors. As Yamata's scheme unravels, former Japanese prime minister Koga notes that Yamata has badly misunderstood his American opponents, whose "roots are found in ideals" (790). The message of *Debt of Honor*, though, is that ideals alone do not make the world a safe place; they require the protection and backing of political will and military strength. When a frustrated Jack Ryan asks, "when did we stop being the United States of America?" (646), the novel's answer is obvious: when the nation lost the will and the ability to "project real power" (813) throughout the world. Ryan accepts an interim term as Durling's vice president on the understanding that the military will once again receive the attention he feels it deserves. In the novel's final, cataclysmic moments, when a rogue Japanese pilot manages to eliminate President Durling and most members of Congress, there seems little doubt that the new president, Jack Ryan, will steer the country through the chaos and back into "the power-projection business" (495).

Bibliography

Clancy, Tom. *Debt of Honor.* 1994. Reprint, New York: Berkley, 1995.

Fukuyama, Francis. *The End of History and the Last Man.* New York: Free Press, 1992.

Garson, Helen S. *Tom Clancy: A Critical Companion.* Westport, Conn. and London: Greenwood Press, 1996.

Brian Patton

The Devil's Alternative

Frederick Forsyth (1981)

FREDERICK FORSYTH's fourth novel, as the title suggests, ultimately concerns a morally impossible choice. The pivotal force is a ruthless, aging, and brilliant Russian president who masterminds a geopolitical chess game played out near the end of the cold war. Forsyth introduces the key players in a characteristically deliberate manner: seven dedicated Ukrainian terrorists who want to embarrass the mighty Soviet Union, the president of the

United States with his team of top advisers, the British prime minister and her cabinet, members of the British secret service, the Russian Politburo, and the general secretary of the Communist Party. A Swedish shipping magnate, a Norwegian captain, and several Western and Eastern European leaders are minor characters, some of whom play pivotal roles, nonetheless, as in many Forsyth novels.

While its narrative is painted with broad strokes, employing a host of stock situations and believable though two-dimensional characters, the novel also, typically, inscribes a plethora of telling and scrupulously researched details, adding an almost documentary feel to the fanciful tale. We are provided, for example, with a wealth of information about the latest weapons technologies, satellite imaging, flight capabilities, details of every narratively significant edifice in the three principal countries, and an insider's view both of the Politburo and the U.S. president's cabinet. The technical details fit perfectly with the action, and Forsyth entertains and informs the reader simultaneously. Moreover, the use of real-life characters as the basis for some of the major characters—the willful British prime minister (Margaret Thatcher), the moderate U.S. president (Jimmy Carter), and his two chief advisers—gives the novel a quasi-historical feel, vividly depicting a Soviet Union unstably poised on the brink of the glasnost and perestroika of the '80s, and even presaging its disintegration in the '90s, an inconceivable thought in 1981, the year of the novel's publication.

The narrative spans a full year, from April 1982 to April 1983, and explores the implications of two seemingly unrelated events—the picking up of a sailor adrift in the Black Sea and the CIA's clandestine discovery of a major crop failure in the USSR—which eventually converge on the eponymous "alternative" that threatens the world's security.

The novel opens with the report of an unidentified man being rescued from the Black Sea, an innocuous-seeming event that nonetheless leads at last to the assassination of the head of Russia's KGB. The second plot strand is both more complex and more global in scope, emerging from the failure of the Russian winter wheat crop due to a freak valve malfunction and overdose of a deadly pesticide to the seed grain—an event noticed by American spy satellites even before the Russian Politburo. The U.S. president William Matthews and his aides shrewdly anticipate a move from the USSR to acquire grain from the Western nations to avoid famine, and this inspires them to seek a treaty on arms concessions from the Russians, a move of benefit both to the U.S. president and to the world (when the deadly plans of reactionaries within the Politburo are revealed). The president invokes the Shannon Act to secure all the excess grain on the American market, and his aides draft the negotiation plans.

As expected, the Russians attempt to cover up the disaster, and their leader, General Secretary Maxim Rudin, reluctantly negotiates the sale of grain to his country on favorable terms in the face of strong opposition from half the Politburo. In order to foil his enemies, the moderate Rudin then initiates an intricate double plot that is not revealed until the closing pages. The success of his plan becomes imperative as his chief opponents, party theoretician Vishnayev and Defense Minister Marshal Kerensky, propose to invade and subjugate the populations of Western Europe and Asia to provide land and food for the Russian people.

A minor but critical subplot unfolds when a coincidence forces the British agent in Moscow to leave and be replaced by Adam Munro, a prototypical Forsythian protagonist with an independent streak, a military and journalistic background, and expertise in foreign languages. On his arrival in Moscow a charming Russian secretary (an ex-girlfriend and the love of his life) approaches him and provides explosive information, the transcripts of the Politburo's emergency meetings. Munro relays these to London, where they are shown to the British prime minister, Joan Carpenter, who promptly shares them with the U.S. president. The documents of Munro's "spy," code-named "Nightingale," reveal just what the failure of the negotiations would mean for Russia and the rest of the world.

During the negotiations, which are held on neutral territory in Ireland, the two countries vigorously spy on one another but keep up the charade of ignorance about the other's vulnerabilities. Many details of the negotiations are reminiscent of the arms negotiations between the United States and the Soviet Union in the '80s and '90s.

In the concluding section of the novel its two central strands intertwine and become one as the global negotiations are acutely and perilously complicated by disagreement about the fate of the captured assassins of the KGB head. Munro's importance then increases until he becomes one of Forsyth's most memorable heroes, shuttling from Carpenter and Matthews to Rudin, and effecting a subtle yet radical bilateral solution to the crisis, involving a grand and dangerous finesse on the part of each leader in their relations with their own governments.

While some of the plotting stretches the imagination, and the characterization is serviceable but comparatively uninspired, the novel's genuinely disturbing conclusion reveals Forsyth's ambiguous moral and political vision at its most subtle and penetrating. Though the Russians are, for the most part, stereotypically depicted as ruthless cynics, the Western leaders, overtly benevolent, are themselves opportunists, willingly coopted into helping the Russians. Indeed, if any characters elicit the reader's sympathy in this uncompromising study in realpolitik it would be the assassinators of the KGB head, a devoted and doomed group of underdog Ukrainian extremists whose desperation in the face of long-standing and relentless persecution seems almost to justify their murderous action, if only for its sincerity.

Bibliography

Forsyth, Frederick. *The Devil's Alternative.* New York: Viking, 1981.

Abha Patel

Dirk Gently's Holistic Detective Agency

Douglas Adams (1987)

Dirk Gently's Holistic Detective Agency is described by its author as "a thumping good detective-ghost-horror-whodunnit-time-travel-romantic-musical-comedy epic," in a quote that has appeared on the jacket of each paperback edition to date. This tongue-in-cheek authorial description neatly sums up the difficulty of placing Adams's eclectic and capricious fiction within neat generic boundaries. Adams is best known for his comic science-fiction saga *The* HITCHHIKER'S GUIDE TO THE GALAXY, but the Gently franchise offered scope for further flights of imagination within a less constrained format—Adams asserted that the Gently stories would be "recognisably me but radically different—at least from my point of view" (Simpson 231). Adams's new project was eagerly awaited both by ardent fans of the existing four Hitchhiker's books and a publishing industry that hoped to re-create the earlier publishing phenomenon.

The intricate plot of the novel is almost impossible to synopzise, including as it does references to time travel, the works of Samuel Taylor Coleridge, ecological disaster, an Electric Monk that believes things for other people to save time, fractal physics and quantum mechanics (including allusions to Schrodinger's cat), the choral music of Bach, alternative timelines, parallel universes, Oxbridge academia, and the dawn of life on Earth. What ultimately connects this Moebius strip of disparate themes is the appropriately whimsical and lateral-thinking Dirk Gently (aka Svlad Cjelli), an antiheroic private detective who in Nick Webb's words is "so cool that his mind owed more to Heisenberg's Uncertainty Principle than traditional deduction" (258).

The mysterious, pizza-devouring, chain-smoking Gently, who specializes in "missing cats and messy divorces" (111), espouses an approach to detection that recognizes "the fundamental interconnectedness of all things," describing his philosophy to his clients in this way:

> I do not concern myself with such petty things as fingerprint powder, telltale pieces of pocket fluff and inane footprints. I see the solution to each problem as being detectable in the pattern and web of the whole. The connections between causes and effects are often much more subtle and complex than we with our rough and ready understanding of the physical world might naturally suppose (115).

Suitably warned that the search for a lost cat, for example, may involve several months of research on a Bahaman beach, the reader gradually becomes aware that all the irreconcilable elements of plot and genre are part of a much larger panoptic view of how things operate; as the novel progresses, its many threads entwine in a coherent narrative strand inscribing the novel's central theme of holism and interconnectivity.

Typical of Adams, many of his own enthusiasms made their way into the work. He had recently become interested, for example, in chaos theory, in particular James Gleick's *Chaos: Making a New Science,* and his burgeoning fascination with ecological issues and the threat of species extinction manifests itself in a time-traveling jaunt to Mauritius to see the last of the dodos. There is also a wonderfully plausible-sounding academic article on "Music and Fractal Landscapes," which outlines, among other things, an algorithm for converting financial spreadsheets into corporate anthems—the ultimate transmogrification of commerce into art.

In addition to these fresh ideas, Adams (who despite his undoubted wit and originality found coming up with new ideas a tortuous process) characteristically recycled a range of older material that he felt had not yet fulfilled its potential. Thus, in *Dirk Gently,* parts of the narrative borrow heavily from two episodes of the British SF series *Doctor Who,* which Adams had written. The time-traveling don of the fictional St. Cedd's College, Reg (or, to give him his full title, Professor Urban Chronotis, the Regius Professor of Chronology) was originally a retired Time Lord in the never-broadcast *Doctor Who* episode "Shada," while the plot element of alien intervention in the creation of life in the primeval past is recycled and tweaked slightly from an episode entitled "City of Death."

The appearance of both Samuel Taylor Coleridge and Johann Sebastian Bach in the novel opens a rich vein of intertextuality, and their presence dovetails neatly with Adams's use of the parallel universes theory of modern physics. In the novel's original timeline, for example, the music of Bach does not exist; the time-traveling Professor Chronotis salvages an excerpt from an alien starship that generates it algorithmically and attributes it to the previously unknown composer. Similarly, at the outset of the narrative Coleridge not only attends St. Cedd's College, Cambridge (rather than Jesus College, his actual alma mater), but manages to complete his epic *Kubla Khan* without interruption by the famed "person from Porlock" (who, once the chronology has been restored to its familiar state, turns out to have been none other than Dirk Gently). There are further references to Gently's role in altering literary history, as we learn that his continual references to albatrosses finally convince the poet that his newest work, *The Rime of the Ancient Mariner,* should perhaps not be about an asteroid strike after all. There is a final piece of delightful wordplay when a deposed editor of a literary magazine raves to one of three hapless wedding guests about his desire to kill the man who has usurped him—one Albert Ross.

Tonally, the novel is characteristically uneven, careening from one generic convention to another, from the almost noirish opening line—"This time there would be no witnesses"—to the weirdly persuasive faux-academic essay on fractals, all infused with a generous mix of Adamsian wit, bathos, and misdirection (in particular, a moment near the outset when Reg asks two questions but answers three, which turns out to be hugely important and further underlines the novel's thematic concern with the relevance of seemingly negligible details). However, despite these inconsistencies of tone, the novel is delicately and deliberately structured, with layers of narrative continually interlocking then separating again in a way that maintains the reader's sense of suspense and dislocation while revealing just enough about the various elements to maintain dramatic coherence.

In many ways *Dirk Gently's Holistic Detective Agency* represents a more significant literary achievement than any of the Hitchhiker's novels. Although it may lack what Webb calls "the same joke quotient per line" (271), and although the range of ideas may be slightly more limited, the unprecedented depth with which these ideas are explored and the more persuasive characterization (Dirk himself is a far more interesting and enigmatic protagonist than Hitchhiker's Arthur Dent, who is for the most part a mere cipher, more happened to than happening) combine to create a novel that stands alone on its own merits. A sequel, *The Long Dark Tea-Time of the Soul,* was less successful both creatively and commercially but continued to engage with similar themes, particularly the nature of religious belief and the possibility of other universes overlaid on this one, within the framework of a slightly more traditional and linear murder mystery. At the time of his death Adams was working on *The Salmon of Doubt,* a book that may have become either a sixth Hitchhiker's or a third Dirk Gently novel (the incomplete manuscript was published as part of the eponymous posthumous collection).

In October 2007 BBC Radio broadcast a six-part radio series based on the novel starring British comedian Harry Enfield in the title role.

Bibliography

Adams, Douglas. *Dirk Gently's Holistic Detective Agency.* London: Pan, 1987.

———. *The Long Dark Tea-Time of the Soul.* London: Pan, 1988.

———. *The Salmon of Doubt.* London: Pan, 2003.

Simpson, M. J. *Hitchhiker: A Biography of Douglas Adams.* London: Hodder & Stoughton, 2003.

Webb, Nick. *Wish You Were Here: The Official Biography of Douglas Adams.* London: Headline, 2004.

Nicholas Dunlop

Disclosure Michael Crichton (1993)

Disclosure is suspense author MICHAEL CRICHTON's 17th novel and met with success similar to earlier blockbusters such as STATE OF FEAR and JURASSIC PARK. It tells the story of a cataclysmic week in the life of Tom Saunders as he struggles to salvage his reputation in light of a sexual harassment accusation placed against him by his recently appointed boss, Meredith Johnson. As an employee at Digicom—a CD-ROM producing corporation—Saunders manages technical productions from the head office in Seattle and was responsible for the establishment of various outsourcing factories, including one in Kuala Lumpur, Malaysia. On the opening day of the narrative (Monday) Digicom is rumored to be announcing a merger that would place Saunders in position for a promotion. However, upon arriving at work, Saunders learns that the position he anticipated winning has been granted to Johnson—owner Bob Garvin's personal favorite and, worse, Saunders's former lover. That evening in her office, Johnson makes sexual advances on Saunders, who reluctantly complies—stopping just before consummating the act. Humiliated, Johnson attacks Saunders and screams threats at him as he dresses and stumbles out of the office. The following morning he learns that Johnson has filed a sexual harassment claim against him within Digicom, and as punishment he will be transferred to Texas—a peripheral site rumored to be closing in the near future. Saunders spends the remainder of the tale challenging the allegations, in the course of which he discloses more sinister motives for Johnson's behavior, namely, the machinations of a far-reaching and destructive corporate conspiracy of which she is a part.

Subtly anatomized in a host of different relationships, sexuality and gender are a dominant theme in the novel. Saunders himself is depicted as a hypermasculine figure, found limping on his way to work after a grueling football weekend in which he scored the "winning touchdown. Crossed the end zone in glory. And then I got creamed" (11). Despite his enlightened facade, Saunders is irritated by the control that Johnson gains over him, and like many of the male characters in the novel, he speculates that only her having a sexual affair with Garvin (or some other important executive) could account for her success in the corporation.

Meanwhile, Johnson lives up to her femme fatale persona, attempting to seduce Saunders in her office after reminiscing about their previous sexual relationship, crossing and uncrossing her legs like Catherine Tramell in Verhoeven's *Basic Instinct.* An enigma to the various men in the office, Johnson exudes a "masculine" corporate drive that contrasts with her "feminine" sexuality. At one point Saunders finds himself gazing at her, taking inventory of her feminine qualities:

> Her eyes were light blue, almost grey. He had forgotten that, as he had forgotten how long her lashes were. Her hair fell softly around her face. Her lips were full. She had a dreamy look in her eyes (86).

Throughout the novel Johnson's complicated gender performance enables the male employees at Digicom to simultaneously lust after, sympathize with, and villainize her.

Johnson's ability to manipulate her employees and colleagues with her femininity is contrasted by other primary female characters in *Disclosure,* who equal her in diligence, and sometimes in success, but who are understood as merely sexless or even masculine by the male characters. Stephanie Kaplan, for example, another Digicom executive, is noted for her skill and commitment to the corporation but is overlooked for promotion, partly because of her superior golfing skills. Saunders's assessment:

> She was a tall, bony, awkward woman who seemed resigned to her lack of social graces [. . .] Colorless, humourless, and tireless, her dedication to the company was legendary; she worked late every night and came in most weekends (53).

Yet, while Johnson is perceived as dangerous for her use of feminine sexuality to control the men at Digicom, Kaplan is seen as equally dangerous for her *lack* of feminine sexuality, dubbed the "stealth bomber" (53) by the male employees. Likewise, the attorney that Saunders employs to pursue his countercharge of sexual harassment against Johnson epitomizes the model of the cold, working woman:

> She was a tall woman in her thirties, with straight blond hair and a handsome, aquiline face. She was dressed in a pale, cream-coloured suit. She had a direct manner and a firm handshake. [. . .] She wasn't at all what he had expected. She wasn't sweet and demure at all (134).

Another significant theme inscribed in *Disclosure*'s narrative is the global problematic of outsourced labor. Digicom's conspiracy surrounds their factory in Malaysia, a typical third-world environment exploiting cheap labor under the guise of "free-trade" and the mal-logic of "Buy American." The employees at Digicom, even including Saunders, who initiated and supervises the operation (at a comfortable distance), do not recognize the effects of the corporation's presence in Malaysia and the position Digicom maintains in relation to the exploitative practice of sweatshop production.

Disclosure further reflects the turn-of-the-century technical revolution, the dot.com era and the fetishistic tendencies of capitalist culture. And like the science fiction–influenced novels of Crichton's earlier career (such as *Congo* [1980], *Sphere* [1987], and *Jurassic Park* [1990]), the tale features incredible scientific accomplishments—this time in the form of virtual reality portals. Here again the unscrupulous marriage of high technology and corporate greed threaten to run roughshod over both the human and natural world.

Disclosure, however, also interests itself in the legal battles and corporate politics that seethe under the smooth surface of large corporations, recalling the legal thrillers of SCOTT TUROW and JOHN GRISHAM. Indeed, in a retrospective note about the novel, Crichton explains that *Disclosure* is based on a true story told to him by a lawyer friend familiar with a case regarding "corporate governance" in 1987 ("Disclosure." MichaelCrichton.com). In the same note Crichton challenges the negative, feminist response to *Disclosure,* claiming that any such reading "had not read the book" and stressing that many female readers had, in fact, identified with Johnson as an empowered and successful working woman.

A film adaptation of *Disclosure* was released in 1994 directed by Barry Levinson and produced by Warner Bros. The film featured Michael Douglas as Saunders and Demi Moore as Johnson.

Bibliography

Crichton, Michael. *Congo.* New York: Knopf, 1983.

———. *Electronic Life.* New York: Knopf, 1983.

———. "Electronic Life." MichaelCrichton.com. Available online. URL: http://www.michaelcrichton.net/books-electroniclife.html.

———. *Jurassic Park.* New York: Knopf, 1990.

———. *Disclosure.* New York: Alfred A. Knopf, 1993.

———. "Disclosure." MichaelCrichton.com. Available online. URL: http://www.michaelcrichton.net/books-disclosure.html.

Disclosure. Directed by Barry Levinson. Warner Brothers, 1994.

Jenny Hei Jun Wills

Dolores Claiborne Stephen King (1992)

In many ways, STEPHEN KING's *Dolores Claiborne* is unique in his oeuvre. A transcript of the life story of a woman told into a tape recorder at the local police station, the novel nonetheless forms a single, continuous, intensely idiomatic narrative whose few interruptions—questions posed by the officers and requests for drinks—merely offer tactical pauses in this solitary account; "[S]till your jawin and listen to me for awhile," Dolores Claiborne instructs her audience, "I got an idear you're gonna be listenin to me most of the night, so you might as well get used to it" (1).

The story, which Claiborne is "gonna start in the middle and just kinda work both ways," "front to back and back to front" (5), revolves mainly around two women, herself and one Vera Donovan. Set on Little Tall Island, a small land mass off the coast of Maine, Dolores "start[s] with this: twenty-nine years ago, when Police Chief Bissette here was in the first grade and still eatin the paste off the back of his pitchers, I killed my husband, Joe St George" (3), a detail that "folks on the island" know already (2), though her motive and means remain unclear. As she explains, "an island's not a good place to kill *anybody*, I can tell you that. Seems like there's always someone around, itching to get his nose into your business when you can least afford it" (6); still, she has "come down here on [her] own hook" to unravel her "foul life" (5) on tape, and confirm that she "didn't kill that bitch Vera Donovan" (2).

Among its many uncharacteristic touches, the novel reveals no spatial anomalies attracting sinister forces, like the burial ground in *Pet Sematary* (1988), for example, or the interred spaceships of *The Tommyknockers* (1987); nor does it involve a small town gradually slipping into homicidal psychoses, a staple of King's fiction. Rather, it disseminates its atrocities into less remarkable situations and on a much smaller scale. Gory disasters are replaced with near invisible and relatively bloodless tragedies, often developing because of almost unconscious choices and happening within family units. Such muted terrors, however, are "hungry" nonetheless, "eatin" the afflicted "alive" (89), the "way bat'try acid will eat a hole in your clothes or your skin if you get some on you" (139). Well into her narrative, for example, Dolores reflects on the events leading up to her disastrous marriage, "the biggest mistake of my life" and "the only mistake that really mattered, because it wasn't just me that would end up payin for it," struggling to understand "how we had gotten from the Junior-Senior Prom at the Samoset Inn" to wedlock, and finding that she "couldn't do it. It was like bein in a magic forest where you look back over your shoulder and see the path has disappeared behind you" (108). The only "love part" she remembers, the single incident she succeeds in isolating as a cause for her "spendin the best years of my life with that old rumpot," is Joe's "nice forehead"; how "smooth" it was and "without a single pimple on it" (54), how it looked in "period seven study-hall when the light came slantin in on it" (55). For all its uniqueness, however, the novel illustrates King's usual penchant for linking his novels with thematic and even literal connections, here recalling his *Gerald's Game* (1992), which contains a scene that flashes on Dolores, with "a whiff of stale air" (202), of a little girl watching the solar eclipse "sittin on her father's lap" (184)—a seemingly innocuous revery that will prove critical to the shape of novel as a whole.

As the tape recorder and the narrative spin forward, parallels between Dolores and Vera emerge—"two bitches livin on a little chunk of rock off the Maine coast, livin together most of the time in the last years" (301), sharing beds as well as secrets. In Vera Donovan's huge house, with most of its gloomy rooms shut off, its guest beds stripped and the sheets "wrapped in plastic and put away in the linen closet" (22)—hints of exile and denial that are later made explicit—Dolores reflects that "[m]aybe I picked up a little of her fear and made it my own" (53).

Against this repressed and inchoate background the figure of the solar eclipse acts as a vivid thematic and narrative motif. A traditional source of social disruption and strangeness, it effectively empties the town—"the streets were so empty it was spooky" (175)—and temporarily alters the nature of its many shadows, which take on "a funny *thin* kind of look" (184). For Dolores, it seems an outward expression of her "inside eye," an expression of malignant aversion as well as utter misery, which "had gotten free of [her] somehow" (197) and is now "hangin in the middle of things," causing everything to appear "off-kilter and out of place" (198). Yet as its very malignancy draws people toward the docks and onto boats, "stopped dead in the middle of the reach between the mainland and the island" (159) to observe the sky, it intimates a weird sense of hope, providing a glimpse of "what wasn't gonna happen again in their lifetimes" (171). As such, it manifests a double nature—as do many elements in this ambivalent tale—intimating a sense of what survives, even when the world itself is eclipsed, together with the laws that govern it.

"I was there and the law wasn't," says Dolores (193), whose often sympathetic, almost fabular story constantly returns to systemic failures of regulations, failures that exacerbate their inherent indifference to the "inside of families" (291) and unjustly favor "the man of the house" (127). Harmful blindspots exist that the law never sees, as it notices only "the top of things" (132) while missing "the things underneath" (132), which surface out of "shallow wells" (201) and rise out of holes in the ground. And while people stand "around with their necks craned back" (159), these things underneath always manage, sooner or later, to snake their way into and secure their hold on the imagination.

Dolores Claiborne was adapted for the screen in 1995 starring Kathy Bates and Jennifer Jason Leigh.

Bibliography

King, Stephen. *The Tommyknockers.* New York: G.P. Putnam's: 1987.

———. *Dolores Claiborne.* London: Hodder and Stoughton: 1993 (1992).

———. *Gerald's Game.* London: Hodder and Stoughton: 1993 (1992).

———. *Pet Sematary.* London: Hodder and Stoughton: 2000 (1988).

Fabienne Collignon

Donaldson, Stephen (1947–)

Donaldson is best known for a series of novels, The CHRONICLES OF THOMAS COVENANT, alternately described as fantasy and science fiction. The first six volumes are organized into two trilogies. Translated into a host of different languages, both series have been best sellers. A final Covenant Series is currently in process, this time a quartet of which only two volumes have to date been published. The first and second trilogies have both won awards.

The Covenant series was followed by the two-volume, award-winning fantasy series, Mordant's Need, and The Gap series, a five-volume science-fiction "space opera," heavily influenced by Richard Wagner's *The Ring.* These series also made the best-seller lists.

Donaldson was born in Cleveland, Ohio. His father, James Donaldson, was a medical missionary working with lepers; his mother, Mary Ruth Reeder, a prosthetist. At the age of four Donaldson accompanied his parents to India, where he remained until the age of 16, and he claims his unique Indian upbringing had a direct influence on his writing career, making his fiction "romantic, religious, exotic, and grim." Back in America he entered the College of Wooster (Ohio), where he earned his B.A. in 1968. The following two years were spent as a conscientious objector doing hospital work in Akron. After the Vietnam War he attended Kent State University, receiving his M.A. in English in 1971. At 30 he abandoned his Ph.D. studies to become a full-time writer.

Donaldson's fantasy is notable for its intricate plots incorporating complex parallel worlds. The Covenant trilogies are focused on "the Land," a mysterious place critics have aligned with Tolkien's Middle Earth, Frank Herbert's *Dune* and Lewis's Narnia. As well as containing all manner of fantastical beings, the Land is underpinned and sustained by a rich and interesting mythological past. The realm of Mordant from Mordant's Need is medieval in nature, complete with a sprawling gothic castle. The Gap series exploits the unlimited possibilities of outer space.

As a storyteller Donaldson's style is traditional, but he deviates from the norms of high fantasy in his powerful characterization. In particular, his male protagonists, with the exception of Geraden from Mordant's Need, are portrayed in vivid, even visceral terms and are often depraved, repulsive, and extraordinarily violent, more antiheroes than heroes. Thomas Covenant himself is a leper who refuses to be healed. In spite of his poor condition and the heinous rape that he commits, he is chosen to save the Land. The Gap series offers a Janus-faced male lead in the form of two men, Angus Thermopyle and Nick Succorso. Both are sadistic multiple rapists contending for and brutalizing the same woman. In the Mordant volumes Geraden is outwardly socially acceptable, but his alter egos, Eremis and Gilbur, are characterized as cruel and sexually obsessed.

Such dark, morally ambivalent protagonists make Donaldson's fantasy compelling and thought-provoking; their alienation, despair, and loss as well as their struggle with tyranny, betrayal, and cynicism add intense poignancy to the fantasy narratives. In spite of the sweeping breadth of Donaldson's fantastical worlds, the lead actors are never allowed to transcend the narrow confines of their self-centered existence. Instead, they are stifled and contained. This contrast, this feeling of restriction in the vast expanses of Donaldson's parallel worlds, produces much of the excitement and explosiveness in his writing.

Donaldson's other works include two volumes of short stories, as well as four mystery novels, three of which were initially published under the pseudonym of Reed Stephens. In an interview with Cindy Lynn Speer, Donaldson admits to producing these works when exhausted, after having completed his "big stories," so it is not surprising that they are somewhat melodramatic and clichéd. While self-contained, they are linked by their protagonists, Mick "Brew" Axbrewder and his partner, Ginny Fistoulari, both of them seedy characters who suffer horrendously. In the first book the characterization and gruesome material, particularly the excessive amount of rape, can be seen as foreshadowing The Gap series. Donaldson's mystery novels can be read as an attempt to undo the tidy, class-conscious, drawing-room mysteries of Agatha Christie.

Bibliography

The Chronicles of Thomas Covenant, The Unbeliever:

Donaldson, Stephen. *Lord Foul's Bane.* New York: Holt, 1977.

———. *The Illearth War.* New York: Holt, 1977.

———. *The Power That Preserves.* New York: Holt, 1977.

The Second Chronicles of Thomas Covenant:

———. *The Wounded Land.* New York: Del Rey Books, 1980.

———. *The One Tree.* New York: Del Rey Books, 1982.

———. *White Gold Wielder.* New York: Del Rey Books, 1983.

The Last Chronicles of Thomas Covenant:

———. *Runes of the Earth.* London: Gollancz, 2004.

———. *Fatal Revenant.* London: Gollancz, 2007.

Mordant's Need:

———. *The Mirror of Her Dreams.* London: Collins, 1987.

———. *A Man Rides Through.* London: Collins, 1988.

The Gap Series:

———. *The Real Story: The Gap into Conflict.* London: Collins, 1990.

———. *Forbidden Knowledge: The Gap into Vision.* London: HarperCollins, 1991.

———. *A Dark and Hungry God Arises: The Gap into Power.* London. HarperCollins, 1992.

———. *Chaos and Order: The Gap into Madness.* London: HarperCollins, 1994.

———. *This Day All Gods Die: The Gap into Ruin.* London: Voyager, 1996.

Short Stories

———. *Daughter of Regals.* New York: Grant, 1984.

———. *Reave the Just and Other Stories.* New York: Spectra, 2000.

Mystery Novels

———. *The Man Who Killed His Brother.* New York: Ballantine, 1980.

———. *The Man Who Risked His Partner.* New York: Ballantine, 1984.

———. *The Man Who Tried to Get Away.* New York: Ballantine, 1990.

———. *The Man Who Fought Alone.* New York: Tor/Forge, 2001.

Kate Simons

The Earth's Children Series

Jean M. Auel (1980–2002)

The Clan of the Cave Bear (1980), a historical novel set in prehistoric Europe, is the first book of JEAN M. AUEL's groundbreaking Earth's Children Series, a unique epic of imaginative reconstruction, telling the story of the rise of *Homo sapiens*. The main character, a young Cro-Magnon girl named Ayla, around the age of five loses her family in an earthquake and is found on the verge of death by a group of people known by some as "flatheads," although they call themselves Clan (Neanderthals). Instead of being left to die, Ayla is taken up and cared for by the medicine woman, Iza. Societal restriction is a major theme in the series, and this is the first significant instance of a female character stepping out of the bounds of the expected.

Ayla is allowed to live with Iza and Creb, the Clan Mo-gur (shaman), and begins to learn the ways of the Clan. Unlike Clan members, however, who are born with ancestral memories, Ayla has to find ways to remember what they expect her to know, memorizing as much as possible. With excellent skills of organization, an uncanny ability to comprehend even abstract details, and unique ways of using Clan knowledge, she is eventually accepted as a healer by most of the Clan. However, the leader's son, Broud, who will one day be a leader himself, can barely control his anger toward Ayla, whom he sees as a foul offspring of "the Others." This leads to brutal confrontations and outbursts of fierce desire, jealousy, envy, and revenge. Critical but brittle boundaries are strained to the point of rupture, until at last Ayla knows she must leave the Clan, the only family she has ever really known, and seek out the Others. Auel's first novel became an instant success, selling more than 1 million copies in its first month and remaining on the best-seller lists for months afterward. In 1986 it was adapted for film starring Daryl Hannah and Joey Cramer.

An accidental writer whose reading had consisted mostly of romance novels and some science fiction, Auel was never happy with the typical roles for women in fiction or in life, and the latter is cited as a greater and more decisive influence on her writing than fiction. She is renowned for the time and care she spends in researching her novels, and a distinguishing trait of Auel's work, even in the realm of historical fiction, is her meticulous attention to factual detail, merged with her field notes and firsthand experiences. A great variety of research helps shape each of the novels in the Earth's Children Series, and as the latter incorporates many elements of other genres, it is almost impossible to place in the pantheon of popular fiction, as much romance as action/adventure, as much mystery/thriller as historical re-creation, with considerable fidelity to the latest developments in academic research.

The Valley of Horses is the second novel in the series and finds Ayla continuing to demonstrate a fierce propensity for countering the expected roles of females in her known society. She sets out on her solitary way from the prehistoric Clan (Neanderthals) members who had raised her in search of the Others (Cro-Magnon), first finding lasting shelter in a valley cave where she begins to prepare for the longer journey. Her solitary existence in the valley is lonely but productive, recalling the quiet but compelling heroism of Defoe's Robinson Crusoe; she trains a horse as a pack animal and eventually learns to ride him; she rescues an infant cave lion, teaching it to hunt and share. Meanwhile, the narrative turns to the adventure of two Others, half brothers Jondalar and Thonolan, who journey along "the great river" until one day Ayla, riding her horse, hears a horrible scream. She arrives in time to see her cave lion attacking the men, restrains the beast and rescues the surviving man, then buries the other and takes the survivor back to her cave, where she also delivers a foal to her mare. Ayla cannot speak the Other's language (carefully reconstructed by Auel, along with the others spoken in her saga), and he thinks she works magic; but as she patiently nurses Jondalar, she learns his language and they exchange skills and knowledge.

Jondalar has been taught to think of "flatheads" as akin to animals and is taken aback when he discovers that Ayla was raised by them and has practiced their healing methods on him. Even more disturbing, she allowed a "flathead" to come to her, leading to her contamination and abomination; here the theme of religious and social prejudice, a critical element in the series, makes a powerful early appearance. At first Jondalar is disgusted that he has shared Ayla's bed, but as he grows to love her he realizes the stupidity of his prejudice and accompanies her when she at last leaves the valley.

In the *The Mammoth Hunters,* the third book of the series, Ayla and Jondalar leave the sheltered valley with a group of people known as the Mammoth Hunters, or Mamutoi, and are invited to stay with their Lion Camp. When the Mamutoi see how skilled Ayla is with hunting and training animals, including a lone wolf cub, they allow her to study with Old Mamut, their wisest shaman.

Ayla, however, is still depicted as naive, and her increasing understanding of communication and sexual relations is a major theme in the novel. Raised by the Clan (Neanderthals), she was taught to present herself for access when signaled to by males in order to relieve their needs. Before Jondalar, she had never known sexual pleasure; but in the valley Jondalar had shown her what he called "first rights" of shared pleasure, and in *The Mammoth Hunters* she shares her bed with a brown-skinned man named Ranec, alienating Jondalar, who is confused and jealous. She loves Jondalar and does not understand what she has done wrong.

Meanwhile, though knowing how she was raised, the Mamutoi still wish to adopt Ayla into their tribe, and before the ceremony she returns to the valley to pick up some things she has made to give as gifts. The Mamutoi are surprised at her wealth, and Ayla of no people becomes Ayla of the Mammoth Hunters, even accepting an offer of marriage from Ranec. However, she breaks her promise to Ranec when she and Jondalar, finding themselves alone, are finally able once again to communicate the way they had once done in the sheltered valley. The pair at last resume their journey together across the plains toward Jondalar's people.

The Plains of Passage, fourth in the series, finds them on their trek across the European plains, with Ayla's confidence growing stronger as she is accepted as a powerful healer, having great spiritual prowess, especially over animals. Ayla continues to learn more about herself and others from each new cultural exchange, even as she continues to stretch the boundaries of what is traditionally thought appropriate for females. She has been using contraceptives throughout the journey and partakes in discussions about childbirth with a number of women throughout the novel. The common idea of conception is that the Great Mother of All combines the spirits of all the people who mate, honoring her while taking pleasure with one another. She then selects a spirit to put into a chosen woman, who then has a child that could have been fathered by any man who had honored the Mother of All but would be cared for by the man of the hearth. Ayla first questioned the purpose of mating when she lived with the Clan (Neanderthals), where, again, such questioning was entirely unexpected and untraditional. Since the act itself was not then a pleasurable experience for her, she had surmised that the main purpose must be to make babies, and she had noted that some offspring had features clearly reminiscent of those who had recently coupled.

Jondalar and Ayla are now invited to become Sharamudoi and to stay with this group of people forever, but Jondalar has started wondering more about his half brother's spirit, and here the series extends its study of restriction, ignorance, and enlightenment into the sphere of religiosity.

In *The Shelters of Stone,* fifth in the series, the couple arrives back among the Zelandonii, Jondalar's people, and he relates the death of Thonolan and his rescue by Ayla. Obviously, the two love each other, and Ayla is pregnant, not having had the ability to make a fire to brew her contraceptives on the last part of their journey across the ice. The Zelandonii, overcoming their initial prejudice on learning of her upbringing, accept Ayla, and she shares her knowledge and skills with them, especially with the One Who Was First—the spiritual leader who helped Jondalar become a man, training him in first pleasures.

Here a number of other themes developed earlier are conjoined in an extensive exploration of the upbringing and care of children. Calling upon early teachings of her "flathead" upbringing, Ayla demonstrates that an infant can be nursed to health by more than one woman when its own mother cannot or will not take care of it; by the end of the novel Ayla's spiritual powers appear to overtake those of the One Who Was First. Long able to see into the past, thanks to Creb, the Mog-ur of the Clan (Neanderthal), she now shows signs, enticing to the countless fans of the series, of taking on a truly prophetic role in the next and projected last novel in the saga.

Bibliography

Auel, Jean M. *The Clan of the Cave Bear.* New York: Bantam Books [Random House], 1980.

———. *The Valley of Horses.* New York: Bantam Books [Random House], 1982.

———. *The Mammoth Hunters.* New York: Bantam Books [Random House], 1985.

———. *The Plains of Passage.* New York: Bantam Books [Random House], 1990.

———. *The Shelters of Stone.* New York: Bantam Books [Random House], 2002.

Geraldine Cannon Becker

Edwards, Kim (1958–)

The oldest of four children, Kim Edwards was born in Texas and raised in Skaneateles, in the Finger Lakes region of Upstate New York. She received her bachelor's degree from Colgate University and her master's degrees from the University of Iowa. She has an M.A. in linguistics, an M.F.A. in fiction, and is a graduate of the Iowa Writer's Workshop. Although Edwards knew she wanted to write from a young age, she spent time teaching in Malaysia, Japan, and Cambodia to broaden her life experience and find her own authorial voice. These travels not only provided settings for her later stories but actually sharpened her sensitivity to the English she heard rarely and often as a second language. She is now an assistant professor in the English Department at the University of Kentucky in Lexington, where she lives with her husband.

Edwards's first publication was a collection of short stories entitled *The Secrets of a Fire King,* which was an alternate for the 1998 PEN/Hemingway Award; one of these, "The Story of My Life," was broadcast on public radio, read by Holly Hunter. Edwards has also received the Nelson Algren Award for her short story "Sky Juice" in 1990 and a Whiting Writers' Award in 2002. Reviewers of these short stories remarked that their broad narrative sweep gave them the scope of a novel.

Edwards's next work was indeed a novel: *The* MEMORY KEEPER'S DAUGHTER. It was a number one *New York Times* best seller, receiving a Barnes & Noble Discovery Award and the Kentucky Literary Award for Fiction in 2005. Published first by Viking Press in June 2005 and then by Penguin, the novel is a family drama tracing the profound consequences of Dr. David Henry's decision to give away his newborn daughter, who is afflicted with Down syndrome, after delivering his twins in a late winter snowstorm in 1964. It has become exceptionally popular with college students and community book groups since the summer of 2006, when it gained fame through word-of-mouth praise.

Although Edwards structures her stories intuitively, she does research elements of her writing in some detail. Her work with mentally challenged adults and interviews with parents who have raised children with Down syndrome gives her character of Phoebe real veracity. At the same time Edward's keen interest in the art and theory of photography lends her treatment of that theme depth and credibility. She spent time at the Eastman Kodak Museum in Rochester and studied Susan Sontag's seminal essay *On Photography* to complement her experience in friends' photographic studios and darkrooms.

Kim Edwards is currently at work on a new novel, *The Dream Master*, set in the Finger Lakes of her childhood.

Bibliography

Edwards, Kim. *The Memory Keeper's Daughter*. New York: Penguin, 2005.

Cynthia M. Vansickle

Emma Harte Saga

Barbara Taylor Bradford (1979–2005)

Barbara Taylor Bradford's Emma Harte Saga details the extraordinary career of determined businesswoman Emma Harte, as well as the stories of her many descendants and their relationships with two other families, the O'Neills and the Kallinskis, persistently questioning whether women can find at once both personal and professional success. Each installment returns to themes of finding—and keeping—love, overcoming adversity, withstanding tragedy, and creating family. Emma's children—Edwina, Kit, Robin, Elizabeth, and Daisy—all play important parts. Daisy's daughter, Paula, eventually marries Blackie O'Neill's grandson, Shane, and the three families hope that Paula and Shane's daughter, Linnet, will unite all the descendants by marrying Julian Kallinski. Other pivotal players include Robin's conniving son Jonathan, Paula's eldest daughter Tessa, Emma's great-nephew Gideon, and Edwina's son and granddaughter, Anthony and India. Although the books are all deeply interrelated, it is possible to read each independently, or out of order; to aid in this, each includes a comprehensive family tree.

The saga commences with *A Woman of Substance* (1979), beginning and ending in the 1960s, as Emma struggles to determine who will inherit her empire; however, the majority of the story takes place in flashbacks explaining her effortful ascent from poverty to wealth. While working as a chambermaid in the Fairley household, Emma becomes pregnant after an affair with Edwin Fairley. Coldly rejected by Edwin, she moves to Leeds to make her fortune and calculate her revenge, starting as a humble tailor but slowly purchasing her own series of shops and then buying into a department store, which ultimately becomes Harte Enterprises, her numerous relationships with rich men helping at last to extend her financial empire over several continents and into real estate, art, and oil.

The next two installments focus on Paula, Emma's favorite grandchild, with *Hold the Dream* (1985) exploring the consequences of Emma's decision to leave to her alone the majority of control over her business empire. Paula fights to keep Harte Enterprises afloat while contending with her jealous cousin Jonathan, who is plotting a takeover. Meanwhile, Paula's marriage to Jim Fairley seems to help bury an old feud, but their relationship soon falters. She falls in love with Shane O'Neill and plans to divorce Jim when a tragic accident robs her of many family members. She must then overcome both professional and personal adversity to justify her grandmother's faith and discover that she, too, is a woman of substance.

To Be the Best (1988) commences in 1981, 11 years after Emma's death, and focuses mainly on the third-generation Hartes, following Paula from London to Australia and Hong Kong as she works to sustain and expand her family's mercantile empire. Her husband, Shane, deals with an unexpected crisis at their Australian hotel, while her cousin Sandy reveals a tragic secret. Meanwhile, Paula's cousin Jonathan makes a return appearance, crafting another sinister plan to take over the Harte dynasty, and his implacable cruelty forces Paula to finally question what a family truly is. The novel also introduces Paula's assistant Madelana and her fateful meeting with Philip, Paula's brother.

Emma's Secret (2003) brings the saga to the present day, with Linnet, Paula's second daughter, planning a fashion retrospective to honor Emma and hiring a young woman, Evan Hughes, to assist her. From the moment he sees her arrive at Harte Enterprises, Gideon, Linnet's cousin, finds Evan—who bears a stunning resemblance to Emma—irresistible. While planning the retrospective, Linnet and Evan stumble across a cache of Emma's old diaries, and with this the narrative flashes back to the 1940s, providing a glimpse into Emma's life during the war years, revealing both how she coped with the death of her dearest lover and a mystery buried in Evan's past.

The fifth installment, *Unexpected Blessings* (2004), picks up where *Emma's Secret* left off by focusing on four female Harte descendants. Evan is continuing her romance with Gideon but must choose whether to tell her father the family secret she recently discovered. Linnet and her half sister, Tessa, battle for control of the family business but must set their differences aside when Tessa's young daughter, Adele, mysteriously vanishes during the middle of Tessa's divorce proceedings. Finally, their cousin India comes up against family obstacles when she falls in love with an unsuitable man, a poor artist named Dusty.

Just Rewards (2005) appears to conclude the saga and sees Linnet struggling to keep the Harte department stores successful while Tessa, trying to renew her life after a painful divorce, steps aside from the business when she discovers her new lover is in danger. When Paula is struck down by a mysterious illness, Linnet must find the strength to guide the family business while remaining true to her great-grandmother's ideals. Meanwhile, India's impending wedding to Dusty may be thwarted by the presence of her fiancé's past. And amid all this, outstanding villain Jonathan returns to cause the Hartes more grief—this time with a powerful ally, Evan's adopted sister, Angharad.

Fans of the series, however, will be relieved to know that while *Just Rewards* seems to conclude the Harte story, Bradford may not be entirely finished with its characters. She states on her Web site that while she had planned to end the saga with this text, she is still contemplating possible new story lines and may yet add to the saga: "I could see a number of potential storylines that could continue in a future book [. . .]. I certainly wouldn't mind revisiting the Hartes in a few years."

Bradford's historically grounded chronicles about women rising from poverty to power as they struggle to balance romances, careers, and families places her firmly in the company of authors such as DANIELLE STEEL, Penny Vincenzi, Belva Plain, and ROSAMUNDE PILCHER. Her non-Harte works share many similar traits with the popular saga: meticulous research and grandeur of scope, sumptuous romantic settings, searches for happiness amid personal tragedies, and repeated assaults on religious discrimination and traditional class standing. Nonetheless, though her protagonists succeed by force of personal initiative, most of her work portrays the struggles of wealthier families, and their dramas are played out against the backdrop of beautifully furnished and lavishly described estates.

In 2006 Bradford returned to the saga format with the commencement of The Ravenscar Dynasty, a series paralleling the Harte saga both in theme and style.

The first trilogy of the Harte saga was filmed for television, with the first two installments, *A Woman of Substance* and *Hold the Dream*, sharing the same cast. *A Woman of Substance* (1984) starred Deborah Kerr and Jenny Seagrove as Emma, and Liam Neeson as Blackie, while *Hold the Dream* (1986) starred Jenny Seagrove as Paula and Stephen Collins as Shane, with Kerr and Neeson reprising their roles. *To Be the Best* (1992) starred Lindsay Wagner as Paula, Christopher Cazenove as Jonathan, and Sir Anthony Hopkins as Jack Figg. Bradford has mentioned plans to develop *Emma's Secret* as another television miniseries.

Bibliography

Bradford, Barbara Taylor. *A Woman of Substance.* New York: Doubleday, 1979.

———. *Hold the Dream.* New York: Doubleday, 1985.

———. *To Be the Best.* New York: Doubleday, 1988.

———. *Emma's Secret.* New York: St. Martin's Press, 2004.

———. *Unexpected Blessings.* New York: St. Martin's Press, 2004.

———. *Just Rewards.* New York: St. Martin's Press, 2005.

———. Official site. 2007 Bradford Enterprises. Available online. URL: http://www.barbarataylorbradford.com.

Rachel Mann

Erdman, Paul E. (1932–2007)

Paul Emil Erdman, an economist and financial commentator, is the author of nine financial thrillers and four nonfiction titles. His books have been translated into 32 languages, and his novels of international finance have spent a combined total of 152 weeks on the *New York Times* best-seller list.

Erdman was born in Ontario, Canada, in 1932. He attended Concordia College in St. Louis, Missouri, as well as the Georgetown University School of Foreign Service, graduating with a bachelor's degree in 1955. After graduation he worked briefly for the *Washington Post,* then attended the University of Basel in Switzerland, where he earned a master's degree, as well as a Ph.D. in economics. He married in 1954 and had two daughters. Erdman has lived in Healdsburg, California, since 1973.

Following his education, Erdman joined the Stanford Research Institute as an economic consultant to American and European companies and in 1962 became vice chairman of Salik Bank in Basel, Switzerland. It was here that his somewhat inadvertent career as a novelist began. When Salik was purchased by United California Bank in 1969, unexpected market fluctuations led to the bank's collapse, leaving UCB with more than $40 million in losses. As chief executive of the bank, Erdman was imprisoned for nine months in Basel, Switzerland, and it was in jail that he began to write, not the nonfiction book he had always intended, but a novel, *The Billion Dollar Sure Thing.* As he told the *New York Times Book Review,* "I had no research facilities, so I decided to try [writing a book] in novel form." Eventually cleared of all charges related to the collapse of UCB, Erdman left Switzerland and returned to the United States to finish his novel.

The Billion Dollar Sure Thing was published by Scribner in 1973. It explored the effect on U.S. currency of international manipulation of the price of gold. In it Erdman relied heavily on his knowledge of world economics and international markets, employing a heightened realism and detail rarely seen before in financial fiction. As critic Oliver Hancock wrote, "When published in the summer of 1973, [the book] contained more truth than fiction." Critical and popular approval followed, with the novel earning an Edgar Award for Best First Mystery from the Mystery Writers of America.

Erdman's second novel, *The Silver Bears,* confirmed his growing status as a master of financial fiction. Released in 1974, the book dealt with dramatic fluctuations in the price of silver, something that had in fact occurred in 1968. Reviewers were impressed with Erdman's ability to blend stories of intrigue, politics, and espionage with complex financial details in a way that readers could understand. In 1978 *The Silver Pears* was adapted into a movie starring Michael Caine and Cybill Shepherd.

His reputation as a writer both topical and prescient was assured with the release of his third book, *The Crash of '79,* in 1976. The story line centered on U.S. dependence on foreign oil and the increasing amount of Arab monetary deposits in U.S. banks. It went on to sell more than 3 million copies, a testament both to Erdman's popularity and his reputation as a financial insider. "What I do is write anticipatory novels," Erdman told *Esquire*; "I regard *The Crash* as a teaching tool." Daniel Yergen of *Esquire* agreed: "An astonishing number of people professionally involved with foreign policy, energy, finance and arms have been reading the book."

Subsequent novels continued to intrigue and inform readers. Erdman's 1992 release, *The Swiss Account,* for example, is credited with launching an investigation by the World Jewish Council into assets that were deposited into Swiss banks by Jews before World War II. His most recent novel, *The Set-up,* was published in 1997. In addition to his novels and nonfiction titles, Erdman was also a contributor to the *Washington Post* and *New York Times* and a host on San Francisco's KGO Radio. He was also a financial news columnist for CBS's MarketWatch.com since 1998.

Bibliography

Contemporary Authors Online 2005 Literature Resource Center. "Paul E(mil) Erdman." Available online. URL: http://galenet.galegroup.com. Accessed November 21, 2006.

Davies, Roy. "The Financial Fiction Genre: Banker-novelists and Modern Financial Thrillers." Available online. URL: http://www.ex.ac.uk/~RDavies/bankfiction/bigbang.html.

Erdman, Paul E. *The Billion Dollar Sure Thing.* New York: Scribners, 1973.
———. *The Crash of '79.* London: Pocket Books, 1978.
———. *The Silver Bears.* London: Arrow, 1987.
———. *The Swiss Account.* New York: Tor Books, 1992.
———. *The Set-up.* New York: St. Martin's, 1997.
Kilduff, Paul. "Favourite (other) books." Available online. URL: http://www.paulkilduff.com/favourites.htm. Accessed January 4, 2007.
PRNewswire.com. "Economist & Author Paul Erdman Joins CBS.MarketWatch.com as Columnist." Available online. URL: http://www.prnewswire.com. Accessed January 4, 2007.
Ridpath, Michael. "Questions and Answers." Available online. URL: http://www.michaelridpath.com/qanda.html. Accessed January 4, 2007.

Debra Hoffmann

Evanovich, Janet (1943–)

Evanovich is a romance and mystery writer best known for her creation of the plucky Stephanie Plum, low-end lingerie buyer turned incompetent bounty hunter, the protagonist of a popular series of comic detective novels chronicling Plum's crime-fighting exploits in a working-class neighborhood in Trenton, New Jersey, called "the burg."

Born in South River, New Jersey, in 1943, Evanovich first pursued a career in art, studying at Douglass College, part of Rutgers University in New Jersey. After four years of art school Evanovich turned her attention to writing. However, after nearly 10 years of rejection from publishers, she gave it up and found work as a temporary secretary, a career mercifully shortened by the acceptance of one of her romance manuscripts, *Hero at Large* (1987), for publication, which earned Evanovich $2,000 and encouraged her to pursue writing as a full-time career. Evanovich wrote several romances for the "Second Chance at Love" series under the pseudonym Steffie Hall and teamed up with coauthor Charlotte Hughes for a number of the novels in the "Full" romance series.

After writing 12 romances, Evanovich declares that she "ran out of sexual positions and decided to move into the mystery genre" (White). She was inspired to write a novel about a bounty hunter after watching the engaging film *Midnight Run* starring Robert DeNiro and Charles Grodin. In the words of her official Web site her research for the first Plum novel, *One for the Money* (1994), took the form of two years of "drinking beer with law enforcement types, learning to shoot, [and] practicing cussing" ("Evanovich"), but the move into the mystery genre has proven to be an immensely successful one for Evanovich, who now claims a large and loyal audience. The fifth novel in the Plum series, *High Five,* became her first hardcover best seller, and she has won several awards from the Crime Writers Association, including the John Creasy Memorial, the Last Laugh, and the Silver Dagger Award. She has also been recognized by the Independent Booksellers Association and Left Coast Crime, and Tristar has purchased the film rights to *One for the Money.* In 2004 Evanovich combined her skill in mystery writing and her fascination with NASCAR in *Metro Girl,* the first novel in a new series featuring a female protagonist named Alex Barnaby. In 2006 she released a nonfiction work entitled *How I Write,* in which she discusses her writing process.

Though her early paperback romances quickly went out of print, Evanovich's STEPHANIE PLUM MYSTERY SERIES has experienced sustained popularity, showcasing as it does her ability to create a diverse cast of appealing eccentrics engaged in delightfully madcap plots. The author rejects the notion that Stephanie Plum—a big-hair and trash-mouthed Jersey girl who devours pizza and pineapple upside-down cake but can still squeeze into a spandex miniskirt—is an autobiographical character, though she does admit to "knowing where she lives." Though Evanovich's oddball characters have been criticized by some as over-the-top caricatures, merely deployed for laughs, others have praised this same Dickensian quality in her work and celebrated the appeal of her smart and self-deprecating heroine. The *Los Angeles Times Book Review*'s Charles Champlin, for example, found the first novel in the Plum series "funny and ceaselessly inventive" and attributed much of the enjoyment to "Stephanie's voice, breezy and undauntable" (Champlin). In addition, Evanovich shows a deft and humorous touch in describing the ever-changing romantic and sexual tensions between Stephanie, her sometimes boyfriend, Trenton cop Joe Morelli, and her sometimes bounty-hunting partner, the mysterious Ranger. Stephanie's bounty-hunting sidekicks include the ex-prostitute Lula and even, occasionally, Stephanie's irrepressible Grandma Mazur, either of whom can turn any carefully planned criminal apprehension into a complete disaster in seconds. The cast is rounded out by Vinnie, Stephanie's employer and sexually deviant cousin, the dysfunctional members of the Plum family, Joe Morelli's intimidating mother and grandmother, and a host of misfits and eccentrics from the burg whom Stephanie must track and apprehend for their failure to appear in court.

The success of the Plum series (2008's *Fearless Fourteen* reached the *New York Times* best-seller list) has prompted a second release of a number of Evanovich's earlier paperback romances. The author resides in Hanover, New Hampshire, with her husband, Peter. She has two grown children, Peter and Alex, both of whom work for the family business, Evanovich, Inc.

Bibliography

Champlin, Charles. Review of *One for the Money*. *Los Angeles Times Book Review*, 20 November 1994.

Janet Evanovich Home Page. Available online. URL: http://evanovich.com.

Nadell, Martha Jane. "Comic Mysteries and Cookbooks." *Chronicle of Higher Education* 51, 6 May 2005.

White, Claire E. "A Conversation with Janet Evanovich." *Writers Write: The Internet Writing Journal*. Available online. URL: http://www.writerswrite.com/journal/jan99/evanovich.htm.

Young, Earni. "Writing While: An Unprecedented Number of Black Characters Inhabit Today's Mainstream Fiction Best-seller Lists, but Few of Them Are Created by Black Authors." *Black Issues Book Review* 6 (July/August 2004): 26–28.

Michelle Greenwald

Evans, Nicholas (1950–)

Evans is the author of four popular novels, *The* HORSE WHISPERER (1995), *The Loop* (1998), *The Smoke Jumper* (2001), and *The Divide* (2005).

He was born in Worcestershire, England, and studied law at Oxford University. After graduation he worked for the Voluntary Service Overseas (VSO), spending much of his time in Africa, an experience he would often return to in his novels. On returning to England, he became a journalist, first in print and then on television, where he produced documentary films about politics and art. In 1983 he met David Lean, the renowned director of such award-winning films as *Bridge on the River Kwai* (1956) and *Lawrence of Arabia* (1962). Lean became a mentor and friend, and encouraged Evans to write fiction. About him Evans has said, "His films had always had a great impact on me—that of intense human drama set against a huge backdrop. I wanted to write a book that had that same kind of epic feel" (Evans 2005b).

An accidental meeting with a blacksmith provided the inspiration for what would be his first novel. *The Horse Whisperer* (1995) is a romantic melodrama set in an evocatively realized Montana landscape, the plot focusing on a love triangle between Tom Booker (the "horse whisperer"), a man with the mysterious power to heal traumatized horses, an uptight English woman named Annie Graves, and her husband, a lawyer from New York. After her daughter is injured in a serious horse accident, Annie becomes convinced the young girl's recuperation is somehow connected to the fate of the physically and psychologically damaged animal. She contacts Tom Booker and against her better judgment eventually embarks on an affair with him.

The novel is unashamedly sentimental, its juxtaposition of country and city, responsibility and passion being two themes that will run through all of Evans's work. Booker is a romanticized figure, a man at one with nature and himself, and an embodiment of an old-fashioned cowboy ideal distinctly at odds with 21st-century life. Through him Annie comes to better understand her relationship with her daughter and learns some essential truths about herself. Comparisons are inevitable to the other, similarly themed best seller of the 1990s, *The* BRIDGES OF MADISON COUNTY (1992) by ROBERT JAMES WALLER.

Evans's love for the Montana country is evident in his passionate prose. What is peculiar is that he is an Englishman writing about quintessential American landscapes and themes. Evans registers this: "A lot of people find it odd that an English guy should be writing about the American West. The truth is I have always been obsessed with the place. Long before I got a chance to travel there, the images of that landscape had a great influence on me" (Evans 2005b).

The Horse Whisperer became one of the publishing sensations of the decade, selling more than 15 million copies worldwide and was later adapted into a critically and commercially successful film directed by and starring Robert Redford.

Evans's second novel, *The Loop* (1998), like its predecessor, is set in the American Midwest and explores the conflict between humanity and nature, using the relationship between animals and humans as a central motif. Its main character, too, is a young woman with emotional problems: Helen Ross is a biologist specializing in the behavior of wolves; she becomes embroiled in clashes between the government and farmers over the rights to protect their cattle from predators, many of which are endangered species. One of the reasons for the success of Evans's novels is undoubtedly his ability to create strong and vibrant roles for such female characters.

One can see the influence of writers such as Jack London, Cormac McCarthy, and Ernest Hemingway most clearly in *The Loop* and his third book, the compellingly titled *The Smoke Jumper* (2001).

The Smoke Jumper is the most David Lean–like of all his narratives, spanning several continents as it moves from Montana to Rwanda and Sarajevo. It is also his second novel to feature a love triangle at its core. Connor Ford and Ed Tully are best friends and "smoke jumpers," airborne firefighters who parachute into danger areas to contain forest fires and prevent devastation. After a tragic accident leaves one of them disabled, the other feels so guilty about his attraction to his best friend's wife that he travels the world from war zone to war zone, seeking to lose himself in other people's grief and forget what he has left behind.

Evans's most recent novel, the ambiguously titled *The Divide* (2005), is arguably his finest but also his least commercially successful. When a dead body is found frozen on the top of a mountain, a divorced couple are forced to reflect on the events that lead to the destruction of their marriage as well the illegal ecoterrorist activities of their beloved daughter. Thematically it reflects his predilection for ecological narratives, fractured families, and rich descriptions of the Montana landscape; the title would appear to refer as much to the rupture of the Cooper family (once happy but destroyed by betrayal and death) and the broader lack of understanding between men and women as to the idyllic ranch near the Continental Divide, where the Coopers used to vacation when their children were younger.

Like many popular writers, it seems Evans will be forever identified with his first book, *The Horse Whisperer,* one of the very few novels to capture the imagination of the American public in 1995. As of writing there is no word on Evans's next project. He lives in Devon, England, and is married to the singer Charlotte Gordon Cumming.

Bibliography

The Bridge on the River Kwai. Directed by David Lean. 1956.

Lawrence of Arabia. Directed by David Lean. 1962.

Evans, Nicholas. *The Horse Whisperer.* New York: Corgi, 1995.

———. *The Loop.* New York: Corgi, 1998.

———. *The Smoke Jumper.* New York: Corgi, 2001.

———. *The Divide.* New York: Time Warner, 2005.

———. "An Interview with Nicholas Evans." (2005). Available online. URL: http://www.nicholasevans.com/author/interview.asp. Accessed January 1, 2007.

The Horse Whisperer. Directed by Robert Redford. 1998.

Waller, Robert James. *The Bridges of Madison County.* New York: Warner, 1992.

Terence McSweeney & Olga Lopatnikova

Evans, Richard Paul (1962–)

Evans is the author of 10 novels, two nonfiction works for adults, and five picture books for children. Four of his books have been adapted into television movies. His most famous work, *The* CHRISTMAS BOX (1995), became the first book to be a number one best seller in both hardcover and paperback simultaneously, and all his novels for adults have appeared on the *New York Times* bestseller list.

Before commencing his writing career, Evans worked in advertising. He wrote *The Christmas Box* as a story for his first two daughters and initially published the book himself. Since then he has won the Storytelling World Award for his children's books three times, as well as the American Mother's Book Award. He has also won the *Washington Times* Humanitarian of the Century Award and the Volunteers of America National Empathy Award for the work done by the Christmas Box House International, an organization of shelters that Evans established in 1997 to aid abused and neglected children.

The Christmas Box, his first and most popular work, teaches that the first gift of Christmas was a child, a lesson that Richard, a distracted father, learns from MaryAnne Parkin, an elderly woman who lost her own child years ago and wants to ensure that Richard does not miss his own daughter's fleeting childhood. Evans's next two books, *Timepiece* (1996) and *The Letter* (1997), describe MaryAnne Parkin's earlier life, particularly her marriage and the life and death of her daughter. In addition to *The Christmas Box* trilogy, Evans's other holiday books include *The Christmas Candle* (1998) and *The Light of Christmas* (2002) for children, and *Finding Noel* (2006) for adults.

Evans is known not only for his holiday books, however, but also for the sensitive treatment of themes of love, family, and redemption that characterize all his work. Characters are given second chances at loving, in romances and in families, when they come to value their relationships more than individual success and security, with religious faith often playing a central role in this transformation. Social injustices, such as racism in *Timepiece* and *The Letter;* wrongful accusations and incarcerations in *The Locket* (1998), *The Looking Glass* (1999), and *The Last Promise* (2002); and the mistreatment of children in *The Sunflower* (2005) also form an important background to Evans's stories, all such injustice being challenged and overcome by his characters, albeit sometimes at great personal cost. The general tone throughout his work is one of hope, quietly but insistently affirming that love can indeed triumph over evil.

Bibliography

Dickens, Charles. *The Christmas Carol.* London, 1843.

Evans, Richard Paul. *The Christmas Box.* New York: Simon & Schuster, 1995.

———. *Timepiece.* New York: Simon & Schuster, 1996.

———. *The Letter.* New York: Simon & Schuster, 1997.

———. *The Christmas Candle.* New York: Simon & Schuster Children's Publishing, 1998.

———. *The Locket.* New York: Simon & Schuster, 1998.

———. *The Looking Glass.* New York: Simon & Schuster, 1999.

———. *The Last Promise.* New York: Simon & Schuster, 2002.

———. *The Light of Christmas.* New York: Simon & Schuster Children's Publishing, 2002.

———. *The Sunflower.* New York: Simon & Schuster, 2005.

———. *Finding Noel.* New York: Simon & Schuster, 2006.

———. *The Gift.* New York: Simon & Schuster, 2007.

———. *Grace.* New York: Simon & Schuster, 2008.

VanLiere, Donna. *The Christmas Shoes.* New York: St. Martin's, 2001.

Ramona Caponegro

Fast, Howard (1914–2003)
Fast's publishing career spanned 70 years and more than 80 books, including several best sellers, the most famous of which, partly owing to the extraordinary film by Stanley Kubrick, was *Spartacus* (1951).

Fast was born into poverty in Manhattan. Until his mother's death, when he was eight, she protected the Fast children from this poverty, but after her passing his father fell into depression and was often unemployed so that Fast and his brothers were essentially on their own. Growing up in New York, Fast was troubled by the great difference between the lifestyles of the rich and the poor but could not articulate his disaffection until he discovered Shaw's *The Intelligent Woman's Guide to Socialism and Capitalism,* after reading which he became a lifelong philosophical socialist and joined the Communist Party in 1944. He was called before the House Committee on un-American Activities in 1948 but refused to name names, and in 1950 he served three months in prison for contempt of Congress. In 1956, after Khrushchev revealed the atrocities committed under Stalin, Fast publicly quit the party.

He was introduced to the world of books through working at the New York Public Library and never considered another career than writing. Publishing his first novel in 1933 at the age of 19, he wrote steadily and at a consistently high level until the end of the century, winning critical and popular acclaim for his historical fiction, including *Conceived in Liberty: A Novel of Valley Forge* (1939), *The Last Frontier* (1941), *The Unvanquished* (1942), *Citizen Tom Paine* (1943), *Freedom Road* (1944), *Spartacus* (1951), and *April Morning* (1961), all still in print, some still regularly assigned in history classes around the country. But his output was vast and eclectic, from short stories and novels to plays, film scripts, children's books, biographies, poetry, and histories. When no publisher would take his books during the Red Scare, he started a publishing house, Blue Heron Press, and began writing under the pseudonym E. V. Cunningham, producing a group of lighter novels bearing women's names, as well as several works featuring the Japanese-American detective Masao Masuto. He also published two memoirs: *The Naked God* (1957) and *Being Red* (1990). While blacklisted in America, his novels did well enough abroad for him to live on the royalties. In fact, he has always been popular internationally, and his books have been translated into an astonishing 82 languages. Several of his novels have been adapted for television and movies, most notably *Spartacus* in 1960 starring Kirk Douglas.

His later output was dominated by the Immigrant series. Comprising *The Immigrants* (1977), *The Second Generation* (1978), *The Establishment* (1979), *The Legacy* (1980), *The Immigrant's Daughter* (1985), and *An Independent Woman* (1997), the series tells the sprawling story of the Lavette, Levy, and Cassala families in San Francisco over the century from the 1880s to the 1980s, centering on the life of Barbara Lavette, who serves almost as Fast's alter ego, with many incidents from his own memoirs appearing here as fiction. Hardly a single significant movement or event in the history of the United States or California goes unexplored in the series. But while witnessing what happens to people caught up in the events of the time gives a human face to history, that these three families should be so intimately connected with nearly every movement of the century often strains credibility, and the series at times takes on an allegorical feel. Regardless, it was immensely popular and sold more than 10 million copies.

Fast's style has been called journalistic because of its dispassionate approach not only to events but to the emotions and aspirations of his characters, the prose neither daring nor memorable in itself, but eminently serviceable, aiming for transparency, a window on its world. Reviewers sometimes criticized him for churning out so many works, intimating that if he took his time he could produce more literary fiction, a sentiment Fast acknowledged, but pointed out that writing was the way he made his living, and he knew enough of poverty to want to avoid it.

His fiction is notable in its attempt to give voice to the disenfranchised, espousing a liberal viewpoint, and critics have commented on the irony of his producing middlebrow fiction of the radical left for popular consumption. But as a college dropout, modest in his intellectual pretensions, Fast may well have countered that such translation of the radical into the accessible and the resulting popularity of the message was the highest service of which he was capable.

Bibliography

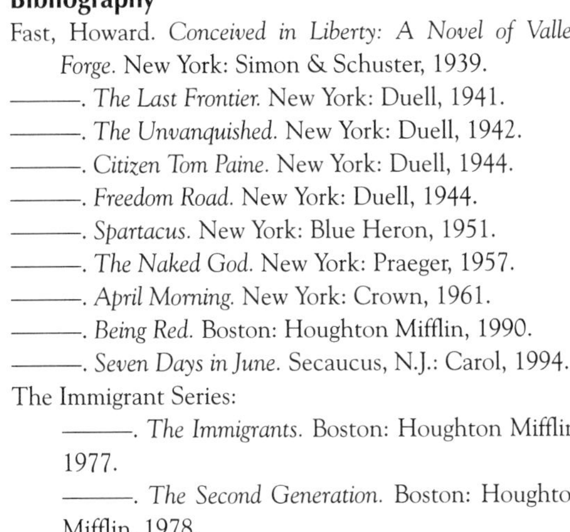

Fast, Howard. *Conceived in Liberty: A Novel of Valley Forge.* New York: Simon & Schuster, 1939.

———. *The Last Frontier.* New York: Duell, 1941.

———. *The Unvanquished.* New York: Duell, 1942.

———. *Citizen Tom Paine.* New York: Duell, 1944.

———. *Freedom Road.* New York: Duell, 1944.

———. *Spartacus.* New York: Blue Heron, 1951.

———. *The Naked God.* New York: Praeger, 1957.

———. *April Morning.* New York: Crown, 1961.

———. *Being Red.* Boston: Houghton Mifflin, 1990.

———. *Seven Days in June.* Secaucus, N.J.: Carol, 1994.

The Immigrant Series:

———. *The Immigrants.* Boston: Houghton Mifflin, 1977.

———. *The Second Generation.* Boston: Houghton Mifflin, 1978.

———. *The Establishment.* Boston: Houghton Mifflin, 1979.

———. *The Legacy.* Boston: Houghton Mifflin, 1981.

———. *The Immigrant's Daughter.* Boston: Houghton Mifflin, 1985.

———. *An Independent Woman.* New York: Harcourt Brace, 1997.

MacDonald, Andrew. *Howard Fast: A Critical Companion.* Westport, Conn.: Greenwood Press, 1996.

Shaw, George Bernard. *The Intelligent Woman's Guide to Socialism and Capitalism.* Garden City, N.Y.: Garden City Publishing [ca. 1928].

Jacque Roethler

Fear of Flying Erica Jong (1973)

Fear of Flying is ERICA JONG's partially autobiographical first novel, which details the sexual liberation of its protagonist, Isadora White Wing. The novel principally charts the progression of Isadora's adulterous affair with English psychoanalyst Dr. Adrian Goodlove. Over the course of their developing relationship Isadora is forced to consider her attitudes toward the social conventions around her—particularly social conventions about women—which have contributed to her dissatisfaction with her married life. The title of the novel refers not only to Isadora's literal fear of flying, which is detailed in the first chapter, but to a metaphorical fear of freedom, a fear of letting go of the combination of social expectations, culture, and gender that dictates to her what she should be and which she has thoroughly internalized. By the time Adrian leaves her, she is ready to analyze herself and accept the freedom of life without a man, a prospect that she formerly found terrifying.

Jong's novel is essentially a picaresque adventure, in which Isadora reconsiders her life, her relationships, and her work as a poet. Writing is depicted as the ultimate liberating act for a woman, but in many ways Isadora finds it as terrifying as she does flying. Isadora's writing is intimately connected to her sense of self. Writing poetry is much easier for her when she has a strong sense of her place in society, but her attempt to view herself as a poet is frequently at odds with her view of herself as a woman. She wrestles with the initially intractable problem of being either a poet (and unpartnered) or being a woman (and partnered). Neither option, to Isadora, seems inherently satisfying.

Fear of Flying was first published in 1973 as the second wave of Anglo-American feminism gathered momentum. Kate Millet had published *Sexual Politics* four years earlier, Germaine Greer's *The Female Eunuch* came out in 1970, and Shulamith Firestone's *The Dialectic of Sex: The Case for Feminist Revolution* was published in the same year. Feminists were radically reenvisioning female sexuality, and *Fear of Flying* was considered a revolutionary novel at the time, partly due to Isadora's frank musings about sex. Her fantasy of the "zipless fuck"—a spontaneous sexual encounter with no strings attached—is perhaps the most notorious:

> [T]he incident has all the swift compression of a dream and is seemingly free of all remorse and guilt; because there is no talk of her late husband and his fiancée; because there is no rationalizing; because there is no talk at all. The zipless fuck is absolutely pure. It is free of ulterior motives. There is no power game. The man is not "taking" and the woman is not "giving." No one is attempting to cuckold a husband or humiliate a wife. No one is trying to prove anything or get anything out of anyone. The zipless fuck is the purest thing there is (14).

The zipless fuck, with its focus on freedom and equality, represents Isadora's ideal encounter between the sexes, but it also introduces the central question that permeates both the book and Isadora's consciousness: What does it mean to be a woman in the 1970s?

Isadora's accounts of her family illustrate the socially conservative construction of womanhood: Her three sisters are all married with children, and her mother has had to give up being an artist in order to be a wife and mother. Isadora's own marriages—which she recounts to the reader during her affair with Adrian—illustrate the difficulties she has with a paradigm that insists all women must be partnered with men in order to be socially acceptable; her first husband, Brian, is a schizophrenic, and her second husband, Bennett, is emotionally aloof.

Finding neither relationship fulfilling, Isadora examines the contemporary social construction of femaleness in relation to sex and creativity, asking why women should be forced to choose between art and family. She concludes that the most important thing in art—and in life—is honesty, although she is well aware that she is frequently unable to live up to her own standards of honesty, particularly in her relationships with men.

Isadora initially relies upon her adulterous affair with Adrian to liberate her, although he is well aware that only she can liberate herself since it is in her psyche that many of the limits on her behavior lie. He espouses a form of "existentialism"—living entirely in the moment, without thought for consequences or for the future, the principal way in which he attempts to reshuffle Isadora's fundamentally conventional approach to gender and relationships. When she leaves her husband Bennett to tour Europe with Adrian, he insists that she act as though the future does not exist in order to break down the boundaries of what she can endure. He represents a direct challenge to the mores by which Isadora has constructed her life:

> Unless he could break at least two taboos with one act, he wasn't interested at all. What really would have turned him on would have been the opportunity to bugger his mother in a church (183).

She finds the lifestyle exhilarating, if terrifying, and is therefore incensed when she discovers that Adrian plans to leave her in order to meet his girlfriend and children, and moreover that the plan has existed for some time, in total contradiction to the existentialist principles he has espoused.

It is only at this point in the novel that Isadora begins to analyze *herself.* This analysis is significant since all the other analysts she has worked with throughout the novel have been male. For the first time she stops blaming herself for everything that has happened to her and begins to adjust to life without a man for the first time. When she discovers that Bennett is in London, she crosses the Channel to meet him, and the novel ends as he walks in on her taking a bath in his hotel suite; but Jong gives the reader no clues as to whether she is planning to resume life as his wife, and if she is, under what terms she will consent to return.

A movie adaptation of the novel was planned in the mid-1970s but never materialized and eventually became enmeshed in lawsuits as Jong sued the movie producers in an unsuccessful attempt to retrieve the rights of the novel. Isadora Wing also appears in Jong's subsequent novels *How to Save Your Own Life* and *Parachutes and Kisses.*

Bibliography

Firestone, Shulamith. *The Dialectic of Sex: The Case for Feminist Revolution.* New York: Morrow, 1970.

Greer, Germaine. *The Female Eunuch.* London: Flamingo, 1993.

Jong, Erica. *Fear of Flying.* New York: Holt, Rinehart and Winston, 1973.

———. *How to Save Your Own Life.* New York: Holt, Rinehart and Winston, 1977.

———. *Parachutes and Kisses.* New York: New American Library, 1984.

———. "Erica Jong." Available online. URL: www.ericajong.com. Accessed on February 27, 2007.

Millett, Kate. *Sexual Politics.* Urbana: University of Illinois Press, 2000.

Claire Horsnell

Fielding, Helen (1958–)

Fielding is the author of several books that helped establish and popularize the genre known as "chick lit," among them the best sellers *BRIDGET JONES'S DIARY* (1999), *Bridget Jones's Guide to Life* (2001), and *Bridget Jones: The Edge of Reason* (2001). Two of the Bridget Jones books have been adapted to film and have helped make the title character an icon in popular culture.

Fielding was born in Morley, West Yorkshire, and devoured books as a teenager, sometimes reading four a week—her favorites Pat Barker and Jane Austen, with the latter exerting a strong and overt influence on her work (*Bridget Jones's Diary*, in particular). An Oxford education with concentration in English landed her several jobs in journalism and the BBC, leading eventually to columns in several prominent newspapers.

Her first novel, *Cause Celeb* (1994), a satire set in Africa, emerged from Fielding's own involvement with Comic Relief, for which she produced documentaries in Africa, hence its blend of serious social issues like starvation with comic satire. After finishing the novel, she began writing an anonymous column about a character she had developed earlier and originally targeted for a sitcom, sensing, as she puts it, that "English newspapers are really keen about [materials] about women." Her prototype for Bridget Jones livened the pages of *The Independent,* and Fielding admits she was embarrassed that her character, worrying about trivial things like panty hose, appeared side by side with the politics and serious debates covered by the paper. But fans responded warmly, and eventually Fielding admitted she was the author of the column, reciprocating with one of the great comedic novels of recent years, *Bridget Jones's Diary.* She followed with *Bridget Jones: The Edge of Reason, Bridget Jones's Guide to Life,* and most recently, *Olivia Joules and the Overactive Imagination,* a spy-novel parody in which the leading lady is romantically involved with a terrorist.

In *Bridget Jones's Diary* readers meet the title character and her two love interests, Daniel Cleaver and Mark Darcy, and Fielding openly admits to using the basic plot of Jane Austen's *Pride and Prejudice* as the foundation for the book. But while the plot's structure is unoriginal, the novel's quirky confessionary format is unique and charms the reader into following and sympathizing with its heroine's quotidian struggles through direct access to her diary.

The diary is characterized by short, crisp, and simple sentences, often with whimsical gaps and twists in the logic connecting them. But the simplistic sentence structure does not equate to simplistic content. Fielding builds from these varied and irregular shards a broad and subtle mosaic of self-image, aging, and relationships with romantic interests, friends, and family.

As one of the founders of the "chick lit" movement, Fielding is often accused, especially by feminists, of creating and sustaining a genre in which women are dependent, self-obsessed, and weak. Bridget Jones is a "singleton" and almost always confused, worrying more about her caloric intake and "ciggies" than world events. Her work methods are haphazard; she speaks without thinking and constantly indulges her cravings for nicotine, liquor, and sex. She *can* be silly; she *is* regularly shallow; she is *always* insecure. But Fielding's star character is, for all that, endearing and realistic. For many, the writer commonly referred to as the "Godmother of chick lit" broke new ground by creating a blundering female character who proves grace, discipline, and feminism are not necessarily required to become a successful and happy woman. In contrast, her lead character in *Olivia Joules and the Overactive Imagination* is talented, quick-witted, and not so obsessed with her appearance.

Renée Zellweger's performance as Bridget Jones earned her an Oscar nomination for best actress. With costars Hugh Grant (Daniel Cleaver) and Colin Firth (Mark Darcy), the film versions of *Bridget Jones's Diary* (2001) and *Bridget Jones: The Edge of Reason* (2004) became blockbuster comedies and solidified Bridget's presence as an icon in popular culture.

Bibliography

Fielding, Helen. *Cause Celeb.* New York: Viking, 1994.

———. *Bridget Jones's Diary.* New York: Penguin, 1999.

———. *Bridget Jones's Guide to Life.* New York: Penguin, 2001.

———. *Bridget Jones: The Edge of Reason.* New York: Penguin, 2001.

———. *Olivia Joules and the Overactive Imagination.* New York: Penguin, 2005.

Guardian Unlimited. 2007. "Author Page: Helen Fielding." Available online. URL: http://books.guardian.co.uk/authors/author/0,,-203,00.html. Accessed May 10, 2007.

Weich, Dave. "Helen Fielding Is Not Bridget Jones." Available online. URL: http://www.powells.com/authors/fielding.html. Accessed May 10, 2007.

Karley Adney

The Fifth Horseman

Larry Collins and Dominique Lapierre (1980)

The first novel by Collins-Lapierre revolves around the time-honored thriller theme of two disparate civilizations engaged in a mortal clash, here revolving around an attempt by Lybian president Quadhafi to drive the Israelis from the West Bank (and thereby demonstrate his inspired leadership) by orchestrating a terrorist nuclear attack on New York. His principal henchmen are three brothers, Laila, Whalid, and Kamal Dajani, descendants of Jerusalem's Arab elite, who seek to avenge their father's death by killing 8 million New Yorkers, whose guilt lies in belonging to a nation that has supported the formation of the State of Israel.

In the face of a 48-hour ultimatum, the American president summons his councillors and then mobilizes all available national and local agencies in order to look for and deactivate a hydrogen bomb hidden on the island of Manhattan; at stake, not merely the lives of the people but the very values upon which the American people as a whole have built their existence and prosperity, symbolized by a Christmas tree lit by the president despite the threat hanging over the city. But the enemy to America is only partly from without, as the novel intimates that the massive, inefficient, and often self-serving bureaucracies of the West can be, for all their good intentions, insidiously complicit in the weakening and even betrayal of the very culture they are designed to serve.

The novel skillfully inscribes a welter of characters, motivations, and actions into a narrative time of several hours, with explanatory flashbacks to Quadhafi's astonishing rise to power and the yet more extraordinary developments that have lead to his producing a nuclear device. It also provides brief but telling insights into the lives of prominent officials and scientists, as well as sketches of less visible Americans, Palestinians, and Israelis. Thus, alongside the president's and Mayor Abe Stern's intense but futile attempts to reason with the terrorists, Detective Angelo Rocchia enjoys an autumnal love affair with successful journalist Grace Knowland. Scientist-turned-terrorist Whalid Dajani alternates between exultation and despair, his brother Laila between the Spartan world of international terrorism and the glittering allure of American show business. All are interspersed with vivid scenes of quotidian life and anonymous tragedy, such as in the depiction of Rocchia's Down syndrome daughter at play with her mates.

Given its atmosphere of biblical cataclysm, the novel fittingly begins with a passage from the book of Revelation (whence the Fifth Horseman) and ends with a quote from the Koran (403), while its plot revolves around the central leitmotif of death itself, death as fact and perception, as event and apprehension, indifferent to race, creed, occupation, and welfare. Judeo-Christians and Muslims, terrorists and scientists, American administrators and journalists, policemen, FBI agents, and junkies—all are forced to face death, fear or defy it, meditate upon it, and contemplate the prospect of it touching the ones they love. Indeed, as in Nevil Shute's apocalyptic thought experiment in *On the Beach,* the sheer imminence of death exposes all for what they are, whether it be servants of duty, caring parents, killing machines, or fanatical ideologues. The contemplation of its frightening inexorability humanizes even the terrorists, as Whalid soliloquizes:

> Don't think, they had told him. Don't think of anything but your mission. But how did you not think? How did you force your mind from what you'd seen: the faces, the seas, and seas of faces, old faces, young faces, faces of mysery and indifference, faces of laughter and happiness. [. . .] the crowds, the buildings, the rushing cars, the lights that represent so many lives (47)?

Recalling age-old thematic tensions, such as between duty and affection, the novel constantly returns to and orients itself through contrast: that between the crowded, complex world of consumerist New York, spiritual center of "the most powerful, the richest, the most wasteful, the most envied and imitated nation on earth" (13) and the barren asceticism of the Libyan desert; between the media's insatiable hunger for spectacle and public officials' need to conceal disturbing facts from the public; between affiliation (to office or enterprise) and attachment (to people, works of art, ideas, doctrines, or indeed, life itself).

But such intense and ubiquitous contrast in the end cautions against contrast itself as the novel explores and exposes the dangers inherent in any fanaticism or extremism—be it of asceticism or indulgence, of excessive thinking or ignorance, of passion or indifference—especially in a world so interconnected and vulnerable to the force of technique. Ultimately, however, *The Fifth Horseman,* like the Christian work it recalls, is a tale of love in all its forms—from passionate romance to the most banal family attachment—the great but elusive panacea for morbidities of contrast.

Explaining what has moved them to write fiction after a decade and a half of collaborative nonfiction projects, Collins declared, "We spent the last fifteen years looking back, tacking up important points of history. . . . [Then] we decided to apply the same intensive research, the same journalistic methods to a very contemporary problem." Much like Balzac, who hoped to be the archivist of his times, Collins and Lapierre wished to "become historians of the present, even of the future" (Peacock 132). Nor was their aspiration entirely vain; besides its tremendous literary success, the novel prompted the French to cancel the imminent sale of nuclear reactors to Libya. Paramount Pictures, which bought *The Fifth Horseman* outright, at last abandoned the aim of adapting it for film, fearing that fanatics might try to emulate the scenario in real life.

Bibliography

Collins, Larry, and Dominique Lapierre. *The Fifth Horseman.* London, Toronto, Sydney, New York: Granada, 1980.

Peacock, Scot, ed. *Contemporary Authors. New Revision Series,* vol. 77. Detroit, San Francisco, London: Gale, 1999.

Watson, Tracey, ed. *Contemporary Authors. New Revision Series,* vol. 125. Detroit, New York: Thompson Gale, 2004.

Alexandra Dumitrescu

The Firm John Grisham (1991)

JOHN GRISHAM's second legal thriller poses and presses a conundrum of divided loyalties between family, profession, and country, and sharpens this conundrum to the point of murder and the betrayal of all. It is a fast-moving legal drama that also draws on gumshoe plots, Mafia thrillers, peroxide blondes, and luxury brand names to sustain its complicated exploration of moral and material success. Its unrelenting tension between conscience and survival, as well as the glimpse it affords into the mystery of legal maneuverings, captivated a worldwide audience after the disappointing sales of Grisham's first book, *A Time to Kill*. It launched Grisham's stellar career, with the film rights actually sold before the book manuscript, and Grisham has since maintained a book-a-year best-seller publication record.

The hero of both novel and film is young, struggling law student Mitch McDeere, "good-looking, athletic-looking, a man's man with a brilliant mind and a lean body" (30). Mitch is an optimist and an innocent when we first meet him in his cross-country search for the first job in his promising legal career. Born into trailer-park poverty, he has his demons—his father is dead, he has lost touch with his waitress mother and uncaring stepfather, his brother Ray is in jail for murder, and a third brother died in Vietnam—but his own conscience is clear, and he has great drive and big dreams. Through hard work, a football scholarship to play quarterback, and his own blistering intelligence, Mitch has thrived in college and is about to graduate from Harvard Law in the top five. Though he and his high school sweetheart (now wife), Abby, are struggling financially, he feels sure that if he works hard he can make their American dream come true. To that end Mitch is considering a number of offers from top firms on Wall Street and almost does not bother to interview for the small Memphis firm of Bendini, Lambert and Locke. His interest is swiftly piqued, though, when this rich and clearly exclusive firm offer him a salary that far outclasses those offered by the Wall Street firms—as long as he can maintain strict confidentiality.

Divulging firm business, the new associates are told, could delay the awarding of the holy grail, a partnership. Nothing leaves the fortress on Front Street. Wives are told not to ask or are lied to. Associates are expected to work hard, keep quiet, and spend their healthy paychecks, and do, without exception.

With 41 lawyers the firm is the fourth-largest in Memphis, but its members do not advertise or seek publicity. Intensely clannish, they do not even fraternize with other lawyers. Their wives play tennis and bridge and shop among themselves. Bendini, Lambert and Locke is a big family of sorts and a very rich one (18).

With hardly a second thought Mitch and Abby pack up their raggedy possessions and mutt Hearsay and drive down to Memphis. Initially the two glory in their first taste of wealth and are in awe of the even greater prosperity that the older lawyers enjoy: "Surrounded by eminently successful lawyers, all millionaires, in their exclusive, lavishly ornamented dining suite, [Mitch] felt as if he was on hallowed ground" (29). Although he has to work long hours, this vision keeps him and Abby going as they enjoy the gleaming BMW and Peugeot, new clothes, good food and rare wine, their first house, and the security of knowing the firm has made full payment on Mitch's student loan—their biggest conflict arising from the fancy dinners that Abby can now afford to cook but which Mitch works too hard to enjoy.

While vividly portraying these pleasures and tensions in the young life of affluence, Grisham gradually reveals the unsavory underbelly of all the prosperity: Bendini, Lambert and Locke is a front for the Mob, and every move the McDeeres make, at work, in the car, and in the home, is being monitored by unconscionable killers like DeVasher, the sadistic ex-cop head of security, Nathan Locke, a hood from his youth, and Oliver Lambert, who likes to watch surveillance footage of his employees in bed with their wives. The Mob's idea is simple: New hires at the firm are imperceptibly implicated as they are unwittingly put to work on illegal firm business; by the time each lawyer is told the horrible secret (five or six years after signing), they are trapped and silenced. Mitch now learns that Bendini, Lambert and Locke can either implicate him in court or creatively arrange for his disappearance, yet he has started a family whose safety he must ensure, and children are "easy targets"(240). An FBI agent cooly anatomizes his position:

> "The next time you see Mr. Lambert around the office, try to remember that he is a cold-blooded murderer. Of course, he has no choice. If he didn't cooperate, they'd find

> him floating somewhere. They're all like that, Mitch. They started off just like you. Young, bright, ambitious, then suddenly one day they were in over their heads with no place to go" (238–239).

Each lawyer must protect his family, but in so doing must be complicit in threats to the others' families. And even the families are engineered by the firm, as in this tactical conversation between two of the mobsters:

> ". . . Lazarov instructed me to get her pregnant."
>
> "McDeere's wife?"
>
> "Yep. He wants them to have a baby, a little leverage. She's on the pill, so we gotta break in, take her little box, match up the pills and replace them with placebos" (268).

Abby is the first to sense that something has gone wrong, as she is subtly but firmly encouraged not to work and instead to breed. In this respect *The Firm* echoes the claustrophobic and vacantly consumerist atmosphere of *The Stepford Wives,* as well as the searching social commentary of John Steinbeck, both of which are noted as influences by Grisham. Mitch and Abby's big mistake, of course, is to let the glitter of a large paycheck blind them to problems that were obvious from the time of the interview, like the firm's policy against hiring women or African-American men ("He commented on the absence of blacks and women, but it didn't seem to bother him" [39]).

While the fate of Mitch's kind colleague and friend Lamar Quin is unambiguous as he resolutely puts his wife and children's welfare before everything, the novel's thrilling climax leaves readers profoundly unsure about the status of Mitch's actions, and by extension, those of an America as vulnerable to the lure of unquestioning material prosperity as he himself has been.

The Firm was made into a 1993 Sydney Pollack film starring Tom Cruise and Gene Hackman and was closely followed by the equally successful *Pelican Brief.*

Bibliography

Grisham, John. *The Firm.* New York: Doubleday, 1991 (reissued Dell, 2003).

Anne Brumley

A Fistful of Charms Kim Harrison (2006)

KIM HARRISON'S *A Fistful of Charms* is the fourth in the Hollows series, a cycle of dark fantasy novels following the exploits of Rachel Morgan—witch, bounty hunter, and alpha (female leader) of a very small Were (werewolf) pack. In the cycle, set in contemporary Cincinnati, Harrison has created an alternative reality in which humans have never been the only sentient life form. Instead, the nonhuman community of Inderland, composed of Were, vampires, witches, pixies, and other supernatural beings, has always lived side by side but unrecognized by the much larger human population. A viral pandemic, however, triggered in 1966 by genetically altered tomatoes, eradicated a large portion of the human population, providing the Inderland citizens with an opportunity to announce their existence in a historic event identified as the "Turn." Since the Turn, humans and nonhumans have—more or less cooperatively—shared the world.

Typical of the series as a whole, *A Fistful of Charms* is a fast-paced, multilayered tale, interweaving a host of plots, subplots, and themes. The action begins with Rachel's discovery that her seemingly practical and uneventful position as the alpha of a two-person Were pack is neither as practical nor uneventful as she had thought. First, Were politics press her to either deal with local Weres as a wolf and not witch or lose her life. Then she learns that her ex-lover, Nick, has persuaded her partner Jenks's eldest child, Jax, to join forces with him in stealing a priceless Were relic. This latter serves as the overarching story line of the novel, offering a chance for Rachel to mend her broken relationship with Jenks (as described in the series' third installment, *Every Which Way but Dead*) and travel with him to the wilds of Michigan to retrieve Jax and the relic. Her best friend, Ivy (a living vampire, child of a human and a vampire, who will become one of the undead upon her death), soon joins them. They find Jax and learn that Nick and the relic must be rescued from a werewolf with a god-complex, who has discovered that the artifact can be used to unify the usually chaotic Were packs into a force capable of wresting control from the vampire elite. Jax, Nick, and the relic are all retrieved, but in the process Rachel learns of Nick's betrayal, finally putting an end to their long and troubled relationship.

To make the trip safely, Jenks must transform from pixie to human size, requiring Rachel to employ dark magic, which she does, illicitly, hoping that her benign intent will diminish the cost to her immortal soul. Her hopes are not realized.

> My aura had turned the usually red sheen of everafter to black. Hidden in it was a shimmer of gold from my aura, looking like an aged patina (101).

This choice, like the others she makes in the novel to use the black arts, only adds to the shadows already gathering about her soul, recalling a key theme in *A Fistful of Charms* as well as the other novels in the Hollows series. When faced with the choice of harming herself or those she loves, Rachel Morgan always chooses the former. But whether she does so for noble reasons or, as Jenks and her lover Kisten (also a living vampire) tell her, because she is an adrenaline junkie, or, most frightening to Rachel herself, because she is only telling herself "a lie of convenience—one that would delude me into believing I had the right to flaunt the rules, that I lived above them" (420), remains intriguingly unresolved.

The trip to rescue the pixie child and artifact also deepens the problematic friendship between Rachel and Ivy. Rachel's failure to understand the complex combination of sex and blood involved in many vampire/human relationships leads to an almost catastrophic end when she offers to find a blood balance with her friend. During the process Ivy loses control, drawing nearly enough blood from Rachel to kill her. Frightened by her weakness, Ivy increasingly withdraws from her friend but is warned by Kisten:

> You opened the door. . . . And if you don't walk her through it, she'll find someone who will. I don't have to ask your permission. And unless you tell me right now that someday you're going to try to find a blood balance with her, I will if she asks me (495).

Unsurprisingly, the novel ends with this and other key issues unresolved: How Rachel, a human witch, can act as alpha for a Were pack; how much damage her dabbling in the dark arts has done to her immortal soul; whether she and Ivy can find a nonsexual blood balance; how her intense relationship with Kisten will respond to such pressures. The saga continues in the series' fifth and sixth installments, *For a Few Demons More* and *The Outlaw Demon Wails*.

Bibliography

Harrison, Kim. *Every Which Way but Dead.* New York: HarperTorch, 2005.

———. *A Fistful of Charms.* New York: HarperTorch, 2006.

———. *For a Few Demons More.* New York: Eos, 2007.

Laura Colmenero-Chilberg

Five Days in Paris Danielle Steel (1995)

Five Days in Paris tells the dramatic tale of Peter Haskell, farm-boy-turned-president of a pharmaceutical company, who is developing a miracle cancer drug named Vicotec, and opens in Paris with Peter waiting to hear from one of his most rigorous researchers. The news is not good: Vicotec could be a killer instead of savior. As Haskell awaits the rest of the test results, there is a bomb scare at his hotel, the Ritz, and in the course of the evacuation he again comes across the beautiful Olivia Thatcher, wife of Senator Andy Thatcher, whom he has noticed on and off for the last several days. He watches her slip away from the crowd and her bodyguard and follows her, winding up having coffee and talking until the early hours of the morning, commencing an intense five-day affair in which each realizes how the other is trapped in their life and circumstances and how unhappy they themselves have become.

Born on a farm in Wisconsin but married into money, Peter must constantly struggle to overcome the stigma that he has been effectively bought by his father-in-law, to whom his wife appears closer and more loyal than to him, tending to the widower's every need and otherwise engaged in an incessant round of social activities. Peter has remained with her because he loves her and their three sons but has been hitherto ignorant of how miserable he really is.

Olivia Thatcher, on the other hand, was born into a political and moneyed household. She marries a lawyer, and they are committed to staying out of politics until Andy's brother, a senator at the time, is assassinated, at which point Andy enters politics and is transformed for the worse, absent even through the cancer and death of their young son. Olivia has never forgiven him but remains with him out of a misguided sense of loyalty.

The tales of both illustrate a common and immensely popular theme in DANIELLE STEEL's fiction, in which characters have imperceptibly come to accept a quotidian state of misery that is exploded by unforeseen romance. Typical also is her use of topical issues both for verisimilitude and suspense, here the machinations of the pharmaceutical industry in its search for exorbitant profits from wonder drugs. Peter wants Vicotec to be inexpensive and easy to administer so that anyone can use and afford it; his father-in-law wants it to be expensive, like a designer drug, with the company poised for a windfall from its sale alone. The price of drugs has been a hot topic in Congress and the news media in recent years, especially because of the aging of the baby boomers.

Steel also reflects on the malignant effect of the paparazzi, especially when manipulated for cynical ends. At one point, for example, Olivia is in a serious boating accident, and her husband tries to use her injuries, as well as the deaths of her sister-in-law, niece, and nephew, for his own political gain. Ethics in the pharmaceutical industry and the media's often invasive place in people's lives are also explored.

In common with all her fiction, however, the novel abounds in romantic clichés and exotic locales, as well as cultural conceits such as references to famous British mystery author Agatha Christie and her mysterious disappearance for 10 days in 1926 or to *An Affair to Remember,* the 1957 film starring Cary Grant and Deborah Kerr, in which two people on a cruise meet, fall in love, then leave each other to sort out their lives, agreeing to meet six months later. But while that film ended in typical Hollywood style, with the new couple settling down happily ever after, *Five Days in Paris* concludes with much greater realism and pathos. Though they, too, cherish the thought, on returning to their respective families, of one day reuniting, Peter and Olivia both come to face squarely the much harder but perhaps nobler task of saving what they had all but lost.

Bibliography

Steel, Danielle. *Five Days in Paris.* New York: Dell, 1995.

JJ Pionke

The Five People You Meet in Heaven

Mitch Albom (2003)

The Five People You Meet in Heaven is a novel about Eddie—a grizzled war veteran who works in a fairground in a small town in America—but begins with his death as he tries to save a young girl from an accident on his 83rd birthday. He wakes up in the afterlife, where he learns that heaven, far from being a place of unimaginable beauty nestled in the clouds, is one of meditation on and confrontation with the meaning of his own life. "There are five people you meet in heaven," he is told: "Each of us was in your life for a reason. You may not have known the reason at the time, and that is what heaven is for. For understanding your life on earth" (37).

MITCH ALBOM structures the novel through a series of flashbacks that begin with a countdown to Eddie's death, interspersed with seemingly innocuous encounters with the five fated characters, always on his birthday, from a young boy to an old man, developing a vivid chronological picture of the protagonist's life. The first person he meets is the Blue Man, whom Eddie does not at first recognize but who relates that as a child Eddie's actions had unintentionally and unknowingly led to his death. With each of his encounters Eddie finds himself in a very different place, often unsure even where he is, in what era, and how each person he meets is connected to him. But each encounter marks a move from confusion to understanding as he learns how the person has played an important part in his life story; each ends with some form of ennobling resolution as he progresses toward a clearer and more synoptic understanding of his life. At the same time he begins to see how all actions are connected and that there is no such thing as a random or inconsequential moment in life.

Among his journeys in the afterlife, Eddie is taken back to the Philippines, where he had served as soldier and been held as a prisoner of war. There he meets his former captain and learns shocking details about his time as a soldier, fundamentally altering the way he has conceived of his life and friendships. Musing on war, injury, death, and loss, Eddie begins to understand that "[s]ometimes when you sacrifice something precious, you're not really losing it. You're just passing it on to someone else" (98). After leaving the captain, he moves further back in time to the 1930s, where he meets a woman whose husband died in a fire at the fairground before Eddie was even born. Initially at a loss why he should even meet Ruby, he is told, "[t]hings that happen before you are born still affect you," and "people who come before your time affect you as well" (130). Ruby then reveals hitherto unseen aspects of the father with whom he had had a long, troubled, and distant relationship. Albom glosses: "All parents damage their children [. . .]. The damage done by Eddie's father was [. . .] neglect" (109). But through Ruby's tutelage Eddie learns to forgive his father and begins to find peace.

His journeys then take him through a meeting first with his wife, Marguerite, who had died at 47, and then an encounter with a child, Tala, whom Eddie had had a profound influence on during the war. The novel ends in calm and sure resolution as Eddie is given the final piece in the all-encompassing puzzle of his own existence, allowing him to find peace and harmony forever in the afterlife.

The Five People You Meet in Heaven is written in clear, lucid, and modest prose, reminiscent of Albom's first book, the best-selling *Tuesdays with Morrie,* with short chapters conducive to meditation structured around Eddie's celestial encounters. The tale is peppered with Albom's characteristically heartening philosophical maxims, most of which center on how all things in life, whether positive or negative, happen for a reason; the reader is induced to journey with Eddie as he gains a fuller insight into the (reassuringly benign) meaning of life. Like *Tuesdays with Morrie, Five People* was been made into a successful TV film (2004) starring Jon Voight and with screenplay by the author.

Bibliography

Albom, Mitch. *Tuesdays With Morrie.* New York: Doubleday, 1997.

———. *The Five People You Meet in Heaven.* New York: Hyperion, 2003.

Douglas Field

Follett, Ken (1949–)

Follett is the author of 27 novels, most of them spy thrillers distinguished by painstaking research and complex plotting. He has also authored one work of nonfiction.

He was born in Cardiff, South Wales, in 1949, and his family moved to London when he was 10. He attended University College, London, where he studied philosophy and became involved in left-wing politics for the first time, an interest that has continued throughout his life. After working as a journalist for some years Follett began to write fiction in 1973, publishing 11 novels under a series of pseudonyms; the best known, *The Modigliani Scandal* (1976) and *Paper Money* (1977), were both written under the pen name of Zachary Stone, and both later republished under Follett's own name, with a preface by the author emphasizing that they are "early works" (on his Web site, he notes, self-effacingly, "I was almost good when I wrote *The Modigliani Scandal* and *Paper Money*").

Follett's first big success, however, came with *Eye of the Needle* (1978), like FREDERICK FORSYTH's *Day of the Jackal* (1971), a riveting tale of espionage surrounding the D-day invasion in World War II. It was published in 1978 and in 1979 won the Edgar Allan Poe Award for Best Novel. He followed this success with four more spy thrillers: *Triple* (1979), *The Key to Rebecca* (1980), *The Man from St. Petersburg* (1982), and *Lie Down with Lions* (1986), all of them working interesting variations on the traditional spy thriller, especially in their choice of antihero protagonists (the Russian anarchist in *The Man from St. Petersburg,* for example, or the Nazi agents in *Eye of the Needle* and *The Key to Rebecca*). In 1983, having been approached by Ross Perot, whose wife had been impressed by *Eye of the Needle,* Follett published *On Wings of Eagles,* a work of nonfiction chronicling the efforts of the American rescue team in the Iranian hostage crisis.

Follett then began a number of historical novels, the first of which was the phenomenally successful *The PILLARS OF THE EARTH* (1989), an epic tale, considered by some his best work, describing the struggle of a 12th-century prior to organize and secure the building of a cathedral. A sequel to *The Pillars of the Earth* entitled *World without End* was published in 2007.

Like those of his contemporary, Frederick Forsyth, Follett's books are meticulously researched and often feature copious and intriguing details both of the methods and the reasoning employed by their protagonists in the pursuit of their ambitious goals. In addition, there are vast amounts of technical information, from code theory, architecture, and engineering to analyses of the make of weapons and personalities alike. But Follett's fiction is especially notable for his ability to complicate conventionally simple dichotomies of good and evil, his characters (with a few notable exceptions) rarely representative of one or the other in any simple way. For example, *The Pillars of the Earth* frequently pits the "good guys" against one another by exploring their complex and often conflicting interests; Aliena, its displaced-noble heroine, for example, is initially helped but ultimately hindered in the pursuit of her goals by Philip, the virtuous prior, whose primary interest is the well-being of the Priory of Kingsbridge. Likewise, the Nazi agent Faber in *The Eye of the Needle,* a memorably heartless technician, is ultimately undone by his uncontrollable affection for the novel's heroine, Lucy, who is withering in a loveless marriage to an embittered former RAF fighter pilot. The novels are also notable for their refusal to whitewash unpalatable historical truths about the political cultures they depict. In the same work, for example, the search for Faber takes Bloggs, a British policeman, to a house where the agent had formerly boarded, where he attempts to solicit information from its reticent new owners. "Why is the old man frightened of the police?" he asks when the father abruptly disappears, to which the daughter impassively replies:

> "My father-in-law is a German Jew. He came here in 1935 to escape Hitler, and in 1940, you put him in a concentration camp. His wife killed herself at the prospect [. . .]."
>
> Bloggs said, "We don't have concentration camps."
>
> "We invented them. In South Africa. Didn't you know? We go on about our history, but we forget bits. We're so good at blinding ourselves to unpleasant facts" (86).

In keeping with this more nuanced and unconventional approach to their protagonists, Follett's novels often focus on desire and sexuality as complicating, often dangerous forces in their lives, with consequences often extending far beyond the personal arena, forces indifferent to political or military affiliation as much as to the goodness or evil of their aspirations.

Four of Follett's novels have been adapted into film: The 1981 adaptation of *Eye of the Needle* with Donald Sutherland and Kate Nelligan, *The Key to Rebecca* (1985) with Cliff Robertson and David Soul, *Lie Down with Lions* (1994) featuring Timothy Dalton, and *The Third Twin* (1997) with Kelly McGillis and Jason Gedrick. *On Wings of Eagles* was adapted into a five-hour TV miniseries in 1986. Follett himself fulfilled a lifelong dream in 1997, when he made a cameo appearance as a manservant in *The Third Twin.*

Bibliography

Follett, Ken. *The Modigliani Scandal.* London: Collins, 1976.

———. *Paper Money.* London: Collins, 1977.

———. *The Eye of the Needle.* London: Futura, 1978.

———. *Triple.* London: MacDonald, 1979.

———. *The Key to Rebecca.* New York: Morrow, 1980.

———. *The Man from St. Petersburg.* New York: Morrow, 1982.

———. *On Wings of Eagles.* New York: Morrow, 1983.
———. *Lie Down with Lions.* New York: Morrow, 1986.
———. *The Pillars of the Earth.* New York: Morrow, 1989.
———. *World without End.* New York: Penguin, 2007; London: Macmillan, 2007.
———. *The Eye of the Needle.* New York: HarperCollins, 2005.
Forsyth, Frederick. *The Day of the Jackal.* London: Hutchinson, 1971.
"Ken Follett." Available online. URL: http://en.wikipedia.org/wiki/Ken_Follett. Accessed April 4, 2007.
"Ken Follett." Available online. URL: www.kenfollett.com. Accessed April 4, 2007.

Claire Marie Horsnell

Forsyth, Frederick (1938–)

Frederick Forsyth is a groundbreaking thriller writer whose best work is distinguished by a steady and implacable buildup of momentum and suspense. His early novels transformed the genre and transferred well to the big screen—*The Day of the Jackal,* for instance, has been filmed twice. Influenced by writers such as John Buchan and Geoffrey Household, in his turn Forsyth has influenced those like TOM CLANCY, who share his love of detailed descriptive realism. A lifelong Conservative, he is reportedly the favorite modern author of Margaret Thatcher.

Forsyth was born in Ashford, Kent, in 1938, shortly before his father began service in World War II, and was educated at Tonbridge School and the University of Granada, Spain. Following national service in the RAF, he became a journalist, training as a cub reporter on a small local newspaper before joining international news firm Reuters in 1961. In 1965 he joined the BBC and from July to September 1967 covered the civil war between the would-be independent state of Biafra and Nigeria, becoming such a firm supporter of the Biafran cause that he was forced to leave the BBC, which considered his reports biased. The dispute ended in defeat for the rebels, but in 1969 Forsyth's first book, *The Biafra Story,* gave a stirring account of the rebellion and the horrors attending the Biafran defeat.

Forsyth then turned to fiction with *The Day of the Jackal* (1971), a blockbuster political thriller adapted to the screen in 1973 and starring Edward Fox as the Jackal (a pastiche of the plot was filmed in 1997 as *The Jackal,* starring Bruce Willis). The novel is a model both of Forsyth's method and style, employing meticulous journalistic research technique and matter-of-fact prose to describe his characters' working methods in vivid detail and rooting fictional characters in the real world in a tale involving topical political issues—here a genuine assassination attempt on the president of France, General Charles de Gaulle, in 1962. Typical of a Forsyth protagonist, the hired assassin (the Jackal) zealously researches his task, skillfully procures identities and armaments, painstakingly chooses the location for the attempt, and implacably pursues his end.

Forsyth's research has often brought him into contact with dangerous people, from the special ops soldiers, mercenaries, and contract killers who act—some of whom are actually named in his pages—to the rich, powerful, and influential figures who shape the world of that action. Such contact has unsurprisingly led to controversy, with the *Sunday Times* even claiming that Forsyth had been involved in a real conspiracy to overthrow a minor African state while working on *The Dogs of War* (1974), which chronicles a conspiracy to overthrow a minor African state. Forsyth countered that his contacts with "real" plotters had merely been a part of the thoroughness of his research for the book, in which a businessman hires a band of mercenaries to kill the psychotic tyrant of Zangaro, intending to substitute a favorable regime that will give him the right to exploit its spectacular deposits of platinum. Much of the book is given over to prosaic descriptions of the preparations for the attack (as usual, the product of Forsyth's meticulous research), but the narrative is so tight and the mounting conspiracy so convincing that the novel builds with extraordinary force to the exciting firefight and surprising twist at its conclusion. The novel was filmed in 1981 starring Christopher Walken as mercenary Cat Shannon.

Thirty years after its publication, journalists would point to uncanny *post-facto* parallels with this same novel, when a group of alleged mercenaries was arrested in Zimbabwe in 2004. It was believed they had intended to assist in overthrowing the government of Equatorial Guinea in exchange for mineral rights, and yet again it was alleged that the conspirators had some connection with Forsyth. (If so, they failed to heed his novelistic advice: Shannon explicitly advises against the use of flights such as the one that resulted in their capture.)

However uncanny be its mimetic force, Forsyth's realism has strict limits. Unlike the similar work of his contemporary KEN FOLLETT, his are action stories with little psychological depth, subtlety, or development. The novels all have male protagonists at their center, with women, Bond-style, in supporting roles at best. Romance and sex in their rare occurrences are essentially servants of the plot, as are beliefs and values, which are described with often questionable economy. Readers never really learn, for example, why Islamic fundamentalists or Ukrainian nationalists want the world changed. Forsyth gives crisp descriptions of such people and then lets them get on with it. The plots become denser as Forsyth learns his trade, but the realism stemming from detailed research and reverence for plot remains a trademark of the Forsyth thriller.

The intricate plot of *The Odessa File* (1972) is arguably his best. More original than *The Day of the Jackal* with its echoes of Geoffrey Household's 1939 thriller *Rogue Male*, it describes a German reporter's hunt for a psychopathic former SS officer still working in Germany, who is being protected by the ODESSA organization, which is developing weapons for the Egyptian opponents of Israel. It was filmed in 1977 starring Jon Voight as journalist Peter Miller.

The DEVIL'S ALTERNATIVE (1979), the longest and most densely plotted Forsyth novel thus far, weaves together several complex stories against a cold war backdrop. Forsyth would revisit this territory in 1984 with *The Fourth Protocol*, in which hawkish elements within the Soviet Union plan to explode a nuclear bomb at an American airbase in the United Kingdom, while the British Secret Service tries to prevent the explosion. It was filmed with a pre-Bond Pierce Brosnan and Michael Caine as the Russian and British protagonists, respectively. *The Negotiator* (1989) weaves the death of a president's son into plots and counterplots involving the cold war and the Middle East, while *The Deceiver* (1991) examines the career of a British agent as the Secret Service forces him to retire from active service, forming a kind of literary memorial to the cold war.

Like JOHN LE CARRÉ, Forsyth now looked elsewhere for the topical, finding it in the Islamic world and the post-Soviet states. *The Fist of God* (1994) features Mike Martin, a John Buchanesque British hero who can pass as Arab and is therefore chosen to foil Saddam Hussein's intentions in the first Gulf War. In 1996's *Icon*, post-Soviet Russia is on the verge of becoming a fascist state. *Avenger* (2003) features a lawyer and Vietnam vet's attempt to bring a Serbian killer to the United States for trial despite the efforts of the CIA, which wishes to exploit the killer's talents. In *The Afghan* (2006) the shadowy plan for an attack that will exceed the impact of 9/11 is discovered, and Mike Martin is again enlisted, here to substitute for an Afghan Taliban commander being held at Guantánamo Bay. Martin, who it turns out can speak Pashtun as well as Arabic, sets out to prevent a hijacked oil tanker from sinking the *Queen Mary II*, which is acting as host to the G8 summit of world leaders.

The movie of *The Fourth Protocol* appeared in 1987 and is so far the last film of a new Forsyth work, reflecting a general view that his best work is behind him. For some reviewers *The Afghan* was a return to form, while others were unconvinced, finding the topicality and realism of detail overwhelmed by such improbabilities as the substitution itself, upon which the entire plot turns.

Bibliography

Cabell, Craig. *Frederick Forsyth, a Matter of Protocol.* London: Robson Books, 2001.

Forsyth, Frederick. *The Biafra Story.* Harmondsworth: Penguin, 1969.

———. *The Day of the Jackal.* London: Hutchinson, 1971.

———. *The Odessa File.* London: Hutchinson, 1972.

———. *The Dogs of War.* London: Hutchinson, 1974.

———. *The Shepherd.* London: Hutchinson, 1975.

———. *The Devil's Alternative.* London: Hutchinson, 1979.

———. *No Comebacks.* London: Hutchinson, 1982.

———. *The Fourth Protocol.* London: Hutchinson, 1984.
———. *The Negotiator.* London: Bantam, 1989.
———. *The Deceiver.* London: Bantam, 1991.
———. *The Fist of God.* London: Bantam, 1994.
———. *Icon.* London: Bantam, 1996.
———. *The Phantom of Manhattan.* London: Bantam, 1999.
———. *The Veteran and Other Stories.* London: Bantam, 2001.
———. *Avenger.* London: Bantam, 2003.
———. *The Afghan.* London: Bantam, 2006.

Andrew Blake

Freeman, Cynthia (1915–1988)

Beatrice Cynthia Freeman Feinberg, who wrote as romance novelist Cynthia Freeman, is the author of nine books, including *A World Full of Strangers, Come Pour the Wine, Seasons of the Heart,* and *The Last Princess,* characteristically exploring the struggles faced by Jewish immigrants, as well as her own Jewish heritage. Her novels have sold more than 20 million copies worldwide and have been translated into 33 languages.

Freeman was born in New York in 1915 and was moved to San Francisco when she was six months old. Her formal education stopped in the sixth grade at her own insistence. "My parents obviously were not thrilled, but my mother, a well-educated English lady, realized what I needed," Freeman said in a 1986 interview with the *Los Angeles Times.* "I had a tutor, and my mother gave me a lot of her time. I was reading Shakespeare at age eleven." At 15 she decided she was ready for college and attended Berkeley as an unofficial student. "I didn't register but I took every course I wanted and got a very liberal education for free," Freeman told the *Times.*

She never set out to be a writer. At 18 she married 33-year-old Herbert Feinberg, her grandmother's physician. Freeman gave birth to a son and a daughter and embarked on an interior decorating career when her children started school. Her career as a decorator lasted 25 years until a rare intestinal disorder made it impossible for Freeman to work. She was sidelined by the illness for five years.

When Freeman recovered, she found she was no longer up to the rigors of interior decorating. Using a portable typewriter, Freeman, now age 50, wrote *A World Full of Strangers,* based on a story she had written 20 years earlier. "I probably never would have turned to writing had I not been critically ill," Freeman told the *Times.* She then wrote a personal appeal to two dozen literary agents ("a hysterical letter, humble but positive," she recalled) and received 19 requests to see the manuscript. *A World Full of Strangers* was published by Arbor House Publishing when Freeman was 55.

Though reviewers were not generally kind to *A World Full of Strangers,* the public responded favorably, eventually buying more than a million copies of the book. Audiences equally embraced Freeman's subsequent novels (whose themes tended to revolve around the struggle Jewish immigrants faced as they tried to hold on to their traditions), even as critics dismissed them. *Washington Post Book World* critic Maude McDaniel summed up Freeman's appeal: "You have learned to like these silly, one dimensional people [referring to Freeman's characters] and you want to be in on everything that happens to them."

Freeman faced her own share of tragedy in her life. Her husband died in 1986 after a battle with Alzheimer's disease, and she lost her daughter in an auto accident in 1985. Freeman died of cancer on October 22, 1988.

Bibliography

Collins, Glenn. "Cynthia Freeman Is Dead at 73; Writer of Best-Selling Romances." *New York Times,* 26 October 1988, B12.
Folkart, Burt. "Novelist Cynthia Freeman; Her Books Explored Jewish Heritage." *Los Angeles Times,* 27 October 1988, B34.
Freeman, Cynthia. *A World Full of Strangers.* New York: Arbor House, 1970.
———. *Come Pour the Wine.* New York: Arbor House, 1980.
———. *Seasons of the Heart.* New York: Putnam, 1986.
———. *The Last Princess.* New York: Putnam, 1987.
Stix, Harriet. "Novelist Cynthia Freeman: It's Never Too Late." *Los Angeles Times,* 12 June 1986, E6.

Debra Hoffmann

Frey, James (1969–)

Frey is the author of two best-selling "memoirs": *A MILLION LITTLE PIECES* (2003) and *MY FRIEND LEONARD* (2005). Questions concerning the factual status of these books began to multiply in early 2006, when the online magazine thesmokinggun.com revealed that Frey had apparently wholly fabricated or seriously exaggerated large portions of his work. Defending himself on *Larry King Live,* Frey dismissed his critics and insisted that his books represented the "essential truth" about his life. Near the end of the show Oprah Winfrey called in to voice her own continuing support. However, several weeks later she hosted Frey for the second time on her own show, berating him for lying about the authenticity of his work, misleading vulnerable readers, and embarrassing her. Under intense pressure, Frey admitted that he had lied in representing his recollections as entirely factual.

Frey's major themes are the destructive influence of drugs and alcohol, and the redemptive power of heterosexual love and male bonding. His books emphasize the importance of self-reliance and reject what he considers "victim-centered" accounts of addiction, in particular the 12-Step approach to recovery favored by Alcoholics Anonymous. *AMLP* is notable for its extreme stylistic experiments—among them the irregular capitalization of nouns, the absence of paragraph indentation, a frequently poetic or stream-of-consciousness form, and numerous repetitions of certain words and phrases. *MFL* employs a prose style that is still deliberately eccentric, though less so than that of *AMLP.* The capitalization of some nouns has been abandoned here, although the occasional turn to stream-of-consciousness effects as well as unconventional grammar remains. The influence of famous American authors known for their macho posturing—above all, Ernest Hemingway and Norman Mailer—is palpable in Frey's writing.

Frey was born in Cleveland in 1969, moving to St. Joseph, Michigan, with his parents in 1981. In his books, as well as in interviews before the 2006 scandal, Frey describes himself as a troubled youth who continuously acted out because of feelings of social alienation. He claims to have been an extremely active juvenile delinquent who became notorious in his school and community for a variety of antisocial acts. Though he has suggested that he was arrested multiple times before the age of 19, little evidence has been uncovered to corroborate these contentions. Perhaps the most distasteful falsehood in *AMLP* involves Frey's claim to have been blamed for the death of a teenage girl in a train accident in 1986. In his book Frey recalls that he was ostracized in his hometown and interrogated by the police for helping the girl meet up with an older student whom her parents had forbidden her to see. Betraying his insistence that he rejects the status of victim, he constructs himself as a deeply wounded scapegoat in this tragedy. In fact, Frey did not know the girl well and was never blamed in any way for her death.

Frey attended Denison University, a liberal arts college located in Granville, Ohio. While there he was a member of the Sigma Alpha Epsilon fraternity. Frey's wealthy parents—his father is a corporate lawyer—supported him with a generous allowance during these years. Though Frey has claimed to have been heavily abusing a variety of illicit substances while at Denison, including crack cocaine and glue, he graduated on time in 1992. Later that year Frey was arrested for parking in a restricted zone and driving while intoxicated. He was held for several hours by the police and then released when a friend posted bail. The arresting officer, who has since been interviewed by journalists, reported that no drugs were found on Frey and that the arrestee was well behaved and cooperative at all times. This minor incident was spun by Frey in his books and media interviews into a drug-crazed melee with police, resulting in a series of extremely serious charges and a three-month stay in jail. These lies proved most disastrous to Frey's reputation, since both his books depend on his incarceration in jail for critical plot twists, as well as for the "street cred" of the author himself.

In late 1993 Frey's parents paid for him to enter Hazelden, an expensive drug and alcohol rehabilitation center in Minnesota. His time here, which has been confirmed, formed the basis for *AMLP.* However, many of the incidents that Frey relates in the book—including his endurance of dental surgery without anaesthetic, his rescue of another patient from a crack house, and his befriending of a cast of rather stereotyped characters—have met with great skepticism, especially since the details of the author's other fabrications have surfaced. Since almost all the characters in the book other than Frey himself have, he insists, either died or disappeared, confirming the factual truth of many parts of the author's version of events has been impossible.

In 1996 Frey began to write *AMLP,* which he originally shopped to publishers, unsuccessfully, as a novel. The narrative follows Frey's six-week stay at Hazelden as he struggles with his addiction, falls in love with a troubled young woman named Lily, and befriends a mobster named Leonard. By the end of the book Frey has gained control of his aggressive and self-destructive impulses and has prepared himself to live a sober life. As the protagonist of the book, Frey emerges as a fantastically brave—and, indeed, dangerous—young man. *AMLP* was published as a "memoir" in 2003 and became a best seller. It rose to superbook status in 2005, when Oprah Winfrey selected it for her book club. A sequel, *My Friend Leonard,* was published in 2005 and also became a best seller. It follows Frey during the period immediately after he left rehab. Both books now contain disclaimers alerting readers to the inclusion of fabrications, though publishers have continued to list them as nonfiction.

Though disgraced as a memoirist, Frey published a novel, *Bright Shiny Morning,* in 2008. He has made tens of millions of dollars from sales of his books and now lives in New York City with his wife.

Bibliography

Frey, James. *A Million Little Pieces.* New York: Doubleday, 2003.

———. *My Friend Leonard.* New York: Riverhead, 2005.

Geoff Hamilton

Gabaldon, Diana (1952–)

Diana Gabaldon is best known for her Outlander series, commencing in 1991 with *OUTLANDER* (also known as *Cross Stitch*), and including *Dragonfly in Amber, Voyager, Drums of Autumn, The Fiery Cross,* and *A Breath of Snow and Ashes* (which won a Quill Award in 2006), accompanied by *The Outlandish Companion* (a nonfiction handbook to the series). Though distinctive and uniformly well written, the series defies categorization, having elements of romance, science fiction (principally in its time travel), fantasy, adventure, and historical fiction.

Although her familiarity with Scottish history and lore has convinced many readers that she is Scottish or of Scottish descent, Gabaldon's ancestry is in fact English and Mexican. Born in 1952 in Flagstaff, Arizona, she was raised there by schoolteacher parents, attending university in Arizona and California and receiving her B.A. degree in zoology, an M.A. in marine biology, and a Ph.D. in ecology. She then worked as a research ecologist for 12 years at Arizona State University.

Gabaldon's move from science to fiction writing was a happy accident. While browsing through Web sites on the Internet, she came across the CompuServe Literary Forum site and decided to try her hand at fiction but was initially at a loss for a subject. Inspired by a Scottish character in an episode of *Dr. Who,* set in 18th-century Scotland, she began writing stories of warring clans, and the addition of a female character, an Englishwoman or "outlander," rounded out the essential elements for her series. In a *January Magazine* interview Gabaldon said of the new character:

> [T]he minute I put her in, she refused to talk like an 18th-century person. She immediately started making smartass modern remarks and she also started telling the story herself. And I said, "Well, if you're going to fight me all through this book, go ahead and be modern and I'll figure out how you got there later" (Richards).

Gabaldon's science background, however, has not gone to waste. She attributes her mastery of Scottish culture and history to the research abilities she honed as an academic.

In the series Claire Randall, an Englishwoman on honeymoon in Scotland, 1945, walks through a Stonehenge-like stone circle and emerges in Scotland, 1743. There in the Highlands she braves dangers from many sources: her husbands' ancestor, a sadistic English officer who thinks she is a spy for the Highland lairds; the Highland lairds, who think she is a spy for the English; and the locals, who suspect she is a witch. Her adventures are complicated by her entanglement with the colorful Jamie Fraser, a Highland farmer, warrior, and occasional criminal.

In addition to the Outlander series, Gabaldon has commenced a spin-off series centered on a minor but important character in the main series, Lord John. The works here are more conventional historical mysteries, shorter and more focused, with the largest being the novel *Lord John and the Private Matter.* Gabaldon expects to shortly publish a second work in this series, *Lord John and the Hand of Devils,* consisting of three shorter pieces, *Lord John and the Hellfire Club, Lord John and the Succubus,* and *Lord John and the Haunted Soldier.* She has just completed a second Lord John novel, *Lord John and the Brotherhood of the Blade.*

Gabaldon, her husband, and children live in Scottsdale, Arizona.

Bibliography

Gabaldon, Diana. *Outlander.* New York: Dell, 1991.

People. "Plaid to the Bone." Available online. URL: www.lallybrock.com/LOL/peoplemag.html. Accessed November 13, 2006.

Richards, Linda. "Diana Gabaldon." Available online. URL: www.januarymagazine.com/profiles/gabaldon.html. Accessed November 13, 2006.

LuAnn Marrs

Garner, James Finn (1960–)

James Finn Garner was born in Detroit to Irish-Catholic parents and grew up in Dearborn, Michigan, where he attended the Divine Child High School. He graduated from the University of Michigan with a degree in English literature and criticism in 1982. As a university student he was honored with a Hopwood Award for a short play.

After graduating, Garner moved to Chicago, where he worked in odd jobs and took acting classes, eventually performing as a comedian at nightclubs such as the Elbo Room, where he created his "Theatre of the Bizarre." Among his best known stage projects are "The Waveland Radio Playhouse," "McCraken After Dark," and the art comedy troupe "JazzPoetry . . . TRUTH!" His fresh and witty performances in the "Theatre of the Bizarre" included humorous variations of classic fairy tales—altered by a politically correct tone—that became material for the author's later best seller, *POLITICALLY CORRECT BEDTIME STORIES.*

Garner has written for a number of journals and periodicals, including the *New York Times, Playboy,* the *Wall Street Journal,* and for three years wrote a monthly column for *Chicago Magazine* entitled "The Garner Report," a satiric analysis of local and national issues.

Politically Correct Bedtime Stories was published in 1994 and remained for 64 weeks on the *New York Times* best-seller list, eventually selling 2.5 million copies in the United States and translated into 20 languages. Its topicality and universal appeal have spawned TV pilots, calendars, and computer games, as well as two full-length sequels, *Once Upon a More Enlightened Time* (1995) and *Politically Correct Holiday Stories* (1995). The first takes up other classic fairy tales, while the second revises Christmas stories, with such titles as "Twas the Night Before Solstice" and "Rudolph the Nasally Empowered Reindeer," extending the season's "good will" to "womyn, pre-adults and companion animals."

In 1997 Garner published *Apocalypse Wow!: a Memoir for the End of Time,* satirizing the history of apocalyptic prophecy and millennial anxieties, and ranging in its search for prophetic guidance from crop circles and harmonic convergence to boiled tea leaves, crystal balls, and severed donkey heads.

Garner has also contributed to the award-winning essay collection *HOME: American Writers Remember Rooms of Their Own.*

He lives in Chicago with his wife and two children.

Bibliography

Garner, James Finn. *Politically Correct Bedtime Stories.* New York: Macmillan, 1994.

O'Conner, Patricia T. "Politically Correct Bedtime Stories." *New York Times Book Review,* 15 May 1994.

Tabor, Mary B. W. "At Home with James Finn Garner: On Pens and Needles." *New York Times,* 28 September 1995.

Rafael R. Pleguezuelos

Get Shorty Elmore Leonard (1990)

Get Shorty is one of crime writer Elmore Leonard's most popular and highly regarded novels. Published in 1990, it was later turned into a critically and commercially successful film directed by Barry Sonnenfeld in 1996; a sequel, *BE COOL,* appeared in 1999 with many of the same characters and with much of the successful formula intact.

The story concerns a charismatic loan shark, Ernest "Chili" Palmer, nicknamed originally for his explosive temper in childhood but now for his composure in the dangerous situations in which his line of work places him. When a plane crashes, apparently killing a man who owes Chili money, he is suspicious and soon discovers that the man is in fact still alive; so he sets out to reclaim the debt. His search takes him from Miami to Las Vegas and then Los Angeles, where he meets a small-time movie director named Harry Zimm, who has made a career out of low-budget exploitation films with names like *Grotesque* and *Slime Creatures* but has aspirations to make it big. In talking with Harry, Chili is taken with the thought of being in show business himself and already has an idea for a film—about a loan shark searching for a man who has apparently died in a plane crash but is in fact alive.

The narrative follows Chili's dual roles as mobster and aspiring film producer partnered with Harry Zimm. Harry himself has a screenplay for what he believes could be his big break—a legitimate big budget Hollywood melodrama called *Mr. Lovejoy*—but knows that any chance of a deal with a major film studio would require a big star. Luckily the famous Michael Weir, a very short, self-obsessed method actor, is interested in the project but is equally famous for his inability to commit to a role. To complicate matters, Chili becomes romantically involved with actress-turned-producer Karen Flores, who is not only Harry Zimm's ex-girlfriend but Michael Weir's ex-wife. Also, Chili is not the only one interested in coproducing *Mr. Lovejoy;* some less reputable investors of Harry's earlier films also want to be involved. All of which encourages Chili to bring his previous loan-sharking skills to bear on the film industry.

The work is full of vivid characters, typical of Leonard's style, which he himself describes as "about character and dialogue, it's about letting people talk" (Leonard 1996). Another Leonard trademark is the nonlinear plot, with the novel briskly moving backward and forward in time, revealing details about Chili's past as they become relevant to the evolving story.

Leonard's status as a Hollywood insider informs much of the novel's darkly satirical and cynical account of the film industry, and a host of suggestive parallels are drawn between the machinations of the Hollywood establishment and those of the criminal underworld. But Leonard's affection for the cinema is palpable throughout; the book is full of film trivia, and characters constantly talk about movies, discuss stars and directors, and even quote lines of dialogue. During a potentially explosive face off between Chili and a rival gangster, for example, the hero corrects the hood about a John Wayne film playing in the background, a passage revealing both Chili's cool working demeanor and his—and the novel's—fascination with cinema, especially cinematic icons of masculinity:

> "Robert Mitchum was the drunk in *El Dorado,* Dean Martin in *Rio Bravo,* practically the same part. John Wayne, he also did the same thing in both. He played John Wayne." Chili couldn't tell if Catlett believed him or not, but it was true. He had won five bucks off Tommy Carlo one time betting which movie Dean Martin was in (282).

Leonard's Hollywood is a cynical, mercenary, and superficial place, more a factory of nightmares than of dreams, and in this world of hype and insubstantiality Chili's directness proves to be his greatest asset. Leonard satirizes Hollywood superstars through his depiction of the egotistical Michael Weir, the "Shorty" of the title, widely regarded as a thinly veiled portrait of Dustin Hoffman, whom Leonard had worked with on a script of one of Leonard's previous novels, *La Brava,* and found imperious and self-serving. In a 1993 interview with *The Guardian,* Leonard stated:

> Finally I said to them [Hoffman and Scorsese]: "Look, it's OK for you guys but I'm not getting paid for this." Hoffman said: "Don't worry, you'll be paid retroactively." My agent is rolling on the floor laughing when I tell him this. He said: "They'll never make the picture" (Leonard 1993).

The book climaxes in exuberant complication, with both of Chili's worlds coming together as he evades various attempts on his life from his enemies, and the film star Michael Weir becomes interested not merely in *Mr. Lovejoy* but in the story of the charismatic loan shark that is Chili. Small wonder, then, that Leonard concludes the story with his protagonist musing on how difficult it is to end one: "Chili didn't say anything, giving it some thought. Fuckin endings, man, they weren't as easy as they looked" (292).

In the film Chili is played by John Travolta, capitalizing on the remarkable success of his comeback with *Pulp Fiction,* a film itself heavily influenced by the work of Elmore Leonard; Danny DeVito gives a masterly performance as self-absorbed Michael Weir. The film won several awards, including a best actor Golden Globe for John Travolta.

Bibliography

Get Shorty. Directed by Barry Sonnenfeld. Metro-Goldwyn-Mayer, 1995.

Leonard, Elmore. *Get Shorty*. London: Penguin, 1991.

———. *La Brava*. London: Penguin, 1992.

———. *Rum Punch*. New York: Delacorte, 1992.

———. *Out of Sight*. London: Viking, 1998.

———. *Be Cool*. London: Penguin, 2000.

———. "An Interview with Elmore Leonard." *Time Out* (London) February 1996, 21–28.

———. "Then You Find Out It Is Not as Simple as It Looks: An Interview with Elmore Leonard by Adam Sweeting." *The Guardian* (October 17, 1993).

Terence McSweeney and Olga Lopatnikova

The Glitter Dome

Joseph Aloysius Wambaugh, Jr. (1981)

In his sixth novel, *The Glitter Dome,* JOSEPH WAMBAUGH gives readers an in-depth and often unsettling look at police work in the Los Angeles metropolitan area, adhering to the narrative pattern he established in previous books such as *The New Centurions* (1971) and *The Blue Knight* (1972), while also deploying valuable comic elements, as in *The Choirboys* (1975) and *The Black Marble* (1978). Named after a raucous bar frequented by off-duty members of the Los Angeles Police Department, *The Glitter Dome* highlights the investigation of four pairs of police officers into the shooting death of Nigel St. Claire, a Hollywood film studio executive. As the author recounts the sometimes less-than-successful efforts of the police to investigate the case, he incorporates biographical details from the officers' lives, mixes stories of excessive drinking with those of scandalous sexual encounters, adds negative images of police bureaucracy, and provides an often stinging social commentary on the people of Hollywood.

Far from being paragons of virtue, the four pairs of officers are depicted with all-too-human weaknesses and strengths, willing to bend the rules and, at times, feeling decidedly lackadaisical about their work. The Ferret and the Weasel are bearded motorcycle types who serve on a narcotics detail; Schultz and Simon act like bumbling, sentimental, obese clowns; and Buckmore Phipps and Gibson Hand, nicknamed the street monsters, are ribald, gluttonous officers who enjoy violence. The chief investigators, Aloysius "Al" Mackey and Martin Welborn, are a study in contrast: Mackey is sloppy, irreverent, and obsessed with alcohol and sex; Welborn, a neatness fanatic, is haunted by past cases, acting at times as if the weight of the whole world rested on his shoulders. Searching for St. Claire's murderer takes the police on a madcap tour of Hollywood and Beverly Hills, with Wambaugh providing amusing descriptions of bizarre locales, including homes of the rich and not-so-rich, a skating rink, a pornographic bookstore, a massage parlor, and a highbrow film industry party. In the end the murder turns out to have been an accident; the bullets that struck St. Claire were meant for someone else. But in order to appease department administrators primarily concerned about closing—not solving—cases, Mackey, who speaks no Vietnamese, forces a confession from a dying Vietnamese thug who barely knows English. The actual perpetrator, whose identity is finally discovered by Welborn, will not face time in prison, as Welborn does not believe that justice would be served by revealing his name. In the minds of the police administration and the public the case is closed, but the solution to the case and its lessons about society and the human condition increasingly torment Welborn and finally lead to his suicide as the novel ends.

Many readers respond first to the text's varied, clever, and often telling humor. The novel abounds in memorable, comic scenes ranging from conversation laced with sexual innuendo to tales of official incompetence. Wambaugh jokes, for example, about the extreme measures officers take to find a sexual partner or to get an erection and even describes how an unidentified individual sneaks drugs into the pipe tobacco and coffee of Captain Roger "Whipdick" Woofer, a pompous administrator, turning him into a hallucinating madman who accuses a meek secretary initially of "letting the caterpillars conquer the kingdom" (84) and later of "[letting] the ladybugs loose in the castle" (299). The humor is double-edged, however. Wambaugh spices his narrative with jokes and incidents that both amuse and yet embarrass readers, causing them to confront their own human weaknesses and encouraging them to become more tolerant when passing judgment on the police—an almost Socratic practice, refined in later works such as *The Delta Star* (1983), *The Golden Orange* (1990), *Fugitive Nights* (1992), *Finnegan's Week* (1994), and *Hollywood Station* (2006).

Beyond its comedy *The Glitter Dome* explores the often cynical tactics employed by the police in order to clear, if not solve, their cases. One might be tempted to label the novel a police procedural, and it does indeed describe the quotidian activities of the police as they go about interviewing suspects and collecting clues. In addition, the settings—whether an interview room at the police station, a stakeout, or the scene of a crime—resemble those commonly found in police procedurals. Furthermore, as frequently occurs in such fiction, the text has an episodic format, interweaving narrative threads that relate incidents from the officers' personal lives and tales of on-the-job exploits. However, Wambaugh is less interested in describing the organizational workings of a 20th-century police force than in detailing the emotional and psychological effects that this police work has on patrolmen and detectives as they carry out their responsibilities day after day. In fact, though following department procedure might bring Mackey and Welborn close to determining the identity of the murderer, the solution and explanation come as a result of sheer coincidence.

For all their antics, crudeness, vulgarity, and bravado, Wambaugh's police are tied to their job by deep and serious bonds of camaraderie, responsibility, and curiosity that they cannot break. Close relationships to other members of the police force and the exhausting demands of their work alienate them from the rest of society, often leading to despair and resulting in a gradual yet implacable transition from idealistic recruits intent on saving the world to disillusioned, disgruntled veterans who occasionally choose to "chew on" their off-duty gun (26). In the case of Martin Welborn, *The Glitter Dome* functions as a study of how one detective who seemingly has control of his professional life and does not acquire the callous behavior common to other officers succumbs nonetheless to the disappointment, disorientation, and disillusionment that confront all members of the force. Welborn does not have the safety valve of vulgar humor, indiscriminate sex, random violence, or petty graft to relieve his frustration and prevent his final desperate act of self-destruction.

In *The Glitter Dome* Wambaugh creates a realistic, at times laughable portrait of the Los Angeles Police Department, eschewing the one-dimensional detectives of 1950s-style television and radio series. Plagued by personal and professional problems, his officers do not act as secular saints, their hearts filled with love for the citizens they are paid to protect. But at the same time he exposes and assails the cynicism and lack of trust that the general public feels toward the police. The dialogue, characterizations, and descriptions of setting reveal Wambaugh's sharp eye for detail, while his use of humor shows more restraint than in earlier novels such as *The Choirboys* and none of the sentimentality found in later novels such as *The Secrets of Harry Bright* (1985).

In 1984 the *The Glitter Dome* was adapted for cable television. Stanley Kallis wrote the teleplay, and Stuart Margolin directed an all-star cast featuring James Garner, Margot Kidder, and John Lithgow. Critical reception was lukewarm, with many feeling that it failed to capture Wambaugh's macabre sense of humor, but Garner and Lithgow earned praise for their performances.

Bibliography

Wambaugh, Joseph. *The New Centurions.* Boston: Little, Brown, 1970.
———. *The Blue Knight.* Boston: Little, Brown, 1972.
———. *The Choirboys.* New York: Delacorte, 1975.
———. *The Black Marble.* New York: Delacorte, 1978.
———. *The Glitter Dome.* New York: Morrow, 1981.
———. *The Delta Star.* New York: Morrow, 1983.
———. *The Secrets of Harry Bright.* New York: Morrow, 1985.
———. *The Golden Orange.* New York: Morrow, 1990.
———. *Fugitive Nights.* New York: Morrow, 1992.
———. *Finnegan's Week.* New York: Morrow, 1993.
———. *Hollywood Station.* New York: Little, Brown, 2006.

David Witkosky

Gorky Park Martin Cruz Smith (1981)

Gorky Park is the first book in what became known as the Arkady Renko series, six crime/thriller novels featuring comrade Arkady Vasilevich Renko, who in *Gorky Park* is Moscow's chief homicide investigator with the Soviet militia (later with the Russian police), the proletarian police force of the Ministry of Internal Affairs. The plot involves an intriguing combination of detective work and espionage. Vividly re-creating the suffocating Kafkaesque oppression and paranoia of the late 1970s Soviet Union, the novel begins with the discovery of three long-dead and mutilated bodies found in the famed Gorky Park in central Moscow, their faces and fingertips cut off, their identity unknown.

Sparked by a *Newsweek* article on Soviet scientist Mikhail Gerasimov's memoir *The Face Finder* (1968), Smith constructed the novel around the work of facial restoration, and Gerasimov appears in the book as Professor Andreev, a dwarf anthropologist who reconstructs the face of one of the victims, a Siberian girl named Valerya Davidova: "[she] was alive again. Her eyes sparkled, blood coursed through her cheeks, her lips were red and parted with anxiety, she was about to speak" (208). As the bodies begin to "speak," they are gradually identified—two of them Soviet citizens, Valerya and a bandit called Kostia Borodin, the third an American, James Kirwill, whose identity is determined through dental work unique to America—and with this the investigation becomes an international concern.

The attention of Renko turns foremost to an American, John Osborne, a fur broker who has been trading with the Russians for 30 years, buying a million dollars' worth of furs every year. Even with his background as a capitalist, Osborne moves graciously in the Soviet circles, having helped them in the antifascist war in Murmansk and during the Leningrad siege during World War II. Regarded by the Russian authorities as a friendly foreigner, he also acts as an informer for the KGB. Another suspect is a German national, Hans Unmann, who has connections with Osborne. The American connection is augmented by a violent encounter between Renko and the American victim's policeman brother, William Kirwill, who has come in search of his brother's killer and who eventually and grudgingly collaborates with Renko in solving the crime.

Despite chronic harassment, deflection, and abuse from his superiors, Renko doggedly pursues the investigation, resisting even the allure of the West, as when he laconically refuses a sable fur hat offered by Osborne: "I can't accept it. There are regulations about gifts" (153). Such intrepidity and integrity motivate his efforts, together with a keen interest in criminology, frustration with his failing marriage, his budding affection for the actor Irina Asanova, and his rage over of the murder of one of the detectives working for him, Pasha Pavlovich. The investigation is further complicated by a tug-of-war between the KGB and the militia over whether the murders are of political significance, a conflict only exacerbated by deep-seated personal enmity between Renko (of the militia) and the KGB's Major Pribluda.

Throughout the novel, again reminiscent of Kafka, there are constant but muted and indirect criticisms of the Soviet state. "THE SOVIET UNION IS THE HOPE OF ALL MANKIND! GLORY TO THE COMMUNIST PARTY OF THE SOVIET UNION!" (128) reads a huge red sign passed by Renko early in the tale; later "Hooligans had kicked down all the words of the red sign except for one: HOPE" (170). Renko himself is a classic Kafkaesque study yet is equally defined by the most indomitable elements of American individualism, utterly passive in the face of official authority but constantly resisting and undermining such authority in the pursuit of his investigation. Thus, though as Peter Osnos (1981, 4) comments, "Most novels about the Soviets tend to caricature them into sinister stick figures: spies, dissidents, generals, political commissars," Renko emerges as a morally reliable and humane character, sympathetic and engaging, whose success and fate are of real interest to the reader.

The narrative is rich in historical and local detail, replete with minute and skillfully deployed particulars about everyday objects and life, food and drink, cultural artifacts, speech patterns, geography, and Soviet politics, earning Smith a reputation as a Russian specialist though remarkably he spent only two weeks in Moscow. There are also numerous literary allusions that increase its air of authenticity. Renko, for example, a voracious reader of his native literature, immediately recognizes a reference Andreev makes to Tolstoy's *Anna Karenina* (142), while Osborne reminds him that "almost no one in the West reads Mandelstam. He's too Russian. He doesn't translate" (148).

The novel is centered in Moscow, where Renko tries to establish a motive for the murders, only making strategic, and highly significant, forays from the capital. As such executions are virtually unknown in the Soviet Union, Renko has little or no precedent to go on, but the foreign connection proves decisive, though at first mistaken for counterfeiting or the smuggling of icons and religious chests. Frustrated in these speculations, but as patient as a chess player (a game he loves), Renko eventually traces the motive to an attempt to break the age-old Soviet monopoly on the sable market, especially that of the precious, imperial Barguzin variety.

After a final shoot-out on Staten Island, most of the novel's central players have died. Irina is saved and decides to seek refuge in the United States. Her lover does not: "I'm Russian," Renko says. "The longer I'm here, the more Russian I am" (363). In the final scene, instead of shooting the precious sables as he was ordered to do, he releases them into the wild: "He thrilled as each cage door opened and the wild sables made their leap and broke for the snow—black on white, black on white, black on white, and then gone" (365). Thus are popular icons born.

Gorky Park has been translated into a host of foreign languages. In Soviet times, unsurprisingly, Smith was regarded as an enemy of the state and the book was banned, becoming nonetheless an underground hit. Other books in the Arkady Renko series are *Polar Star* (1989), *Red Square* (1992), *Havana Bay* (1999), *Wolves Eat Dogs* (2004), and *Stalin's Ghost* (2007).

The novel was adapted into a successful film of the same title in 1983 with screenplay by Dennis Potter and directed by Michael Apton and starring William Hurt as Arkady Renko, Joanna Pacula as Irina Asanova, Lee Marvin as John Osborne, and Brian Dennehy as William Kirwill. Due to the novel's disfavor in the USSR, the film was shot in Helsinki, Finland.

In 2005 *Gorky Park* was shortlisted for the prestigious Crime Writers' Association 50th anniversary first crime-fiction prize, the Dagger of Daggers (the award went to JOHN LE CARRÉ's epochal work *The Spy Who Came in from the Cold*, 1963).

Bibliography

Osnos, Peter. "Three Faceless Corpses." *Washington Post, Book World*, 29 March 1981, 4.

Pascoe, David. "Moscow Rules." *Sunday Times*, 27 September 1992.

Smith, Martin Cruz. *Gorky Park*. London: William Collins, 1981.

Suplee, Curt. "The Master of *Gorky Park*." *Washington Post*, 10 April 1981.

Joel Kuortti

Grafton, Sue (1941–)

Sue Grafton is the author of a popular detective-fiction series featuring a female private investigator named Kinsey Millhone, a series whose titles follow the letters of the alphabet. The first, *A Is for Alibi*, was published in 1982, and Grafton has produced a new one almost yearly, the most recent being *T Is for Tresspass* (2008). Kinsey's complex sensibility reflects that of her author in some respects, and her life is of sufficient interest to readers that Natalie Kaufman and Carol Kay have actually published a scholarly but readable biography of the fictional character, *G Is for Grafton: The World of Kinsey Millhone.*

Born in Louisville, Kentucky, where she still maintains a residence, Grafton currently lives in Montecito, California. But it is nearby Santa Barbara where Grafton lived for several years that serves as a model for the Santa Teresa where Kinsey lives and works. Grafton's father was C. W. Grafton, himself a crime novelist (and lawyer), and her mother was a high school chemistry teacher. Grafton began writing at a young age, publishing two novels while in her 20s, *Keziah Dane* (1967) and *The Lolly-Madonna War* (1969), both focusing on the struggles of poor, rural families and neither meeting with much success. Eventually divorce forced her into writing television scripts and screenplays in order to make a living, and while she did not enjoy this writing, she credits the experience with her skill in plotting out and structuring her later novels.

After her second marriage, to Stephen Humphrey in 1978, she was able to settle down and write full time, introducing her readers to Kinsey Millhone in 1982, the mystery series having been partly inspired by her father's works. Her rage during a very ugly custody battle provided the impetus for the plot of the first Kinsey novel; however, in order to write a detective series, Grafton had to research the particulars of the criminal world, as well as the finer points of investigation and criminology—a habit she has scrupulously maintained throughout her subsequent work, meticulously researching and keeping an extensive journal for each novel. She begins a journal as a way of keeping track of ideas, but in time the journal itself articulates the specific shape of the coming book. For example, Grafton notes on her Web site that *R Is for Richochet,* which was 500 double-spaced manuscript pages, involved no less than nine such journals, each containing 500 single-spaced pages—journals she later shared with Kaufman and Kay when they were researching Kinsey's biography.

Grafton's novels, along with their gritty heroine, have been compared to the hard-boiled detective mysteries of Raymond Chandler and Dashiell Hammett. She, along with other female authors of the genre such as Sarah Paretsky, is credited with offering an updated alternative to traditional female detectives like Miss Marple or Nancy Drew. Moreover, as in Chandler and Hammett, many of Kinsey's investigations revolve around dysfunctional families and the secrets they hide. However, she also tackles social ills, a common trait among female mystery authors, Kaufman and Kay noting that "female detectives normally challenge many societal constraints simply by proving themselves to be competent, effective problem solvers operating in a resistant, male-dominated profession" (49). Class structure and the inherent problems associated with a divisive society are the most prominent themes in her novels, with many focusing on corruption within the established systems of government, justice, or health care. Ageism, too, is an issue she targets both directly and indirectly in her work.

Grafton and her novels have won numerous awards from various societies devoted to detective fiction and mystery, including the Mysterious Stranger Award, the Cloak and Clue Society Award, and the Private Eye Writers of America Award. She has also been president of the Private Eye Writers of America and of the Mystery Writers of America.

Bibliography

Kaufman, Natalie Hevener, and Carol McGinnis Kay. *G Is for Grafton: The World of Kinsey Millhone.* New York: Henry Holt, 1997.

Kay, Carol McGinnis. "Sue Grafton." In *DLB: American Hard-Boiled Crime Writers,* edited by George Parker Anderson and Julie B. Anderson. Detroit: BCL-Gale, 2000, 175–187.

Reddy, Maureen T. "The Female Detective from Nancy Drew to Sue Grafton." In *Mystery & Suspense Writers: The Literature of Crime, Detection, and Espionage,* edited by Robin Winks. New York: Scribners, 1998.

Walton, Priscilla L. "'E' Is for En/Gendering Readings: Sue Grafton's Kinsey Millhone." In *Women Times Three: Writers, Detectives, Readers,* edited by

Kathleen G. Klein. Bowling Green, Ohio: Popular Press, 1995, 101–115.

Susie Scifres Kuilan

Grisham, John (1955–)

As a child John Grisham dreamed of a career in Major League Baseball, but happily for millions of readers worldwide he never realized the dream (though he is a Little League commissioner with six ball fields on his expansive Mississippi property). Instead, he became the most popular and renowned author of the "legal thriller." Recognized by *Publishers Weekly* as the top-selling author of the 1990s, Grisham currently has more than 235 million books in print, with translations in 29 languages. Nine of his novels and one original screenplay have been made into films.

Born the second of five children to working-class parents in Jonesboro, Arkansas, in 1955, Grisham lived in various places across the South before his family settled permanently in Southaven, Mississippi, in 1967. After high school he attended Northwest Mississippi Community College and Delta State College (where he was cut from the baseball team), before completing an accounting degree at Mississippi State University in 1977. He then enrolled in law school at the University of Mississippi, intending to pursue tax law, but soon opted for the greater drama of criminal defense litigation. Passing the bar in 1981, Grisham married childhood friend Renee Jones and joined a small practice in Southaven, where he achieved notable success in both criminal defense and civil personal injury cases, and in 1983 he was elected to the Mississippi House of Representatives, where he served until resigning in 1990.

Always an avid reader, with favorites in the unlikely but telling pair of John Steinbeck and JOHN LE CARRÉ, Grisham attempted two novels, finishing neither, before completing *A Time to Kill* in 1987. Struck by the 1984 case of a 12-year-old rape victim he had observed in the DeSoto County courthouse, Grisham rose every day for three years at 5:00 A.M. to write before his workday began, exploring what might have happened if the rape victim's father had murdered the rapist. The novel was rejected by numerous publishers before being accepted by Wynwood Press, which printed a mere 5,000 copies in 1989, many of which Grisham purchased himself. Undaunted, he began a second novel, chronicling a Harvard Law grad's eventful experience in a seemingly ideal law firm that hides a host of devastating secrets; and *The* FIRM (1991) created a stir in the publishing industry when Paramount Pictures paid $600,000 for film rights before it was even accepted for publication. It spent 47 weeks on the *New York Times* best-seller list in hardback, and 90 weeks on the *Publishers Weekly* paperback list, 38 at number one. The Oscar-nominated Sydney Pollack movie, starring Tom Cruise, Jeanne Tripplehorn, Gene Hackman, and Holly Hunter, was itself a blockbuster success in 1993, and Grisham's writing career was well under way. He retired from practicing law in 1991, and from *The Firm* forward he has produced an average of one novel a year. *The Pelican Brief* (1992) reached the top of the *New York Times* best-seller list, and *The Client* (1993) debuted at number one, while each of his subsequent books has quickly achieved international best-seller status. In addition to having nine novels adapted into film, Grisham created the story idea for *The Gingerbread Man* (1998) and wrote the original screenplay for *Mickey* (2004). His only nonfiction work, *The Innocent Man* (2006), is also a best seller. In 1994 he became publisher and co-owner of *The Oxford American,* a respected literary magazine that features southern writing, and in 1996 he returned to the courtroom to honor a preretirement commitment to represent the family of a railroad brakeman killed by being crushed between two railcars. Grisham won the case and won his clients the largest dollar-amount verdict of his career, $683,500. He divides his time with wife Renee and their children, Ty and Shea, between his Mississippi and Virginia farms.

The mainstay of the Grisham ouevre is the legal thriller. Arising directly from his own experiences as a practicing lawyer, *A Time to Kill* may be taken as a model both of his style and of the genre as a whole. The novel is tightly structured around the trial of Carl Lee Hailey, a black man accused of shooting two white men, who had raped and beat his daughter, as they are about to be convicted of a lesser charge. Jake Brigance, Hailey's lawyer, becomes embroiled in dangerous confrontations with Ku Klux Klansmen. Crusading on the side of right (with the aid of an attractive young female assistant) against an establishment of hardened bigots in the racially volatile Deep South, Brigance is an idealistic young protagonist pitted against powerful forces—an establishment institution—rife with sinister corruption beneath a veneer of respectable normalcy.

Indeed, perhaps the most predominant theme of Grisham's law-related books is a mistrust of the system, whether legal, political, economic, or social. In *The Firm* Mitch McDeere discovers that the perfect-seeming Memphis firm he joins fresh out of law school has deeply rooted ties with the Mafia. Partners and associates who threaten to expose the truth about the firm wind up dead, and Mitch must skillfully gather evidence for the FBI while escaping harm from the firm's "security team" and the powerful mobsters behind them. In *The Pelican Brief* Tulane law student Darby Shaw risks her life to expose oil tycoon Victor Mattiece (a longtime friend of the president), who has commissioned the assassinations of two Supreme Court justices to protect his drilling rights in oil-rich Louisiana swampland. In *The Client* 11-year-old Mark Sway witnesses a suicide and learns where a murdered U.S. senator is buried. Mark and his down-on-her-luck lawyer, Reggie Love, are pursued by both the FBI and the Mafia, the latter hoping to silence the boy before he reveals their part in the senator's assassination. In *The Rainmaker* (1995) the enemy is the insurance industry, big tobacco companies in *The* RUNAWAY JURY (1996), real estate developers (and their legal representatives) in *The Street Lawyer* (1998), and pharmaceutical companies in *The King of Torts* (2003).

In several works Grisham turns a critical eye on aspects of the legal system itself, exposing the greed of large, upscale law firms in *The Firm, The Partner* (1997), and *The Street Lawyer,* and anatomizing the mendacity of class-action civil lawyers in *The King of Torts,* wherein the central character, Clay Carter, initially a public defender, is brought to the verge of moral ruin by the allure of massive verdict awards. In *The Runaway Jury* Grisham demonstrates the vulnerability of the trial-by-jury system when juror number 2, Nicholas Easter, and his female accomplice, Marlee, succeed in manipulating a jury, both for vengeance against tobacco companies and to squeeze millions from crooked attorneys in exchange for a guaranteed verdict. Two Grisham books take up the death penalty: *The Chamber* (1994) portrays a young lawyer requesting a stay of execution for his grandfather, Sam Cayhall, who is innocent of the murder he was convicted of but assuredly guilty of numerous other hate crimes while a member of the Ku Klux Klan; *The Innocent Man* relates the true story of Ron Williamson, a failed minor league baseball player wrongfully convicted and sentenced to Oklahoma's death row for the 1982 rape and murder of 21-year-old cocktail waitress Debbie Carter.

In more recent years Grisham has ventured farther afield. Both *The Brethren* (2000) and *The* BROKER (2005) are novels of political intrigue. In the former three imprisoned judges conduct a scam blackmailing closeted gay men, and one of their targets is a defense-friendly presidential candidate supported clandestinely by the head of the CIA. *The Broker* is essentially a spy novel in which the CIA secures the pardon of Joel Backman, a lobbyist convicted of attempting to sell classified defense secrets to unknown foreign enemies. Backman is freed and relocated to Italy, where U.S. agents follow him in hopes he will be assassinated, an act they expect will reveal information about both the initial source of the leak and Backman's intended buyers. *A Painted House* (2001), Grisham's most lyrical work, drawing on recollections of his Arkansas childhood, explores the lives of rural cotton farmers, centering on seven-year-old Luke Chandler, who awakens from childhood innocence to confront a variety of harsh truths as he is caught up in a host of intrigues involving his family and neighbors. *Skipping Christmas* (2001) is a comedic novella in which Luther and Nora Krank try to avoid the typical Christmas shopping, decorating, and entertaining by taking a Caribbean cruise; but when their daughter Blair announces her surprise return from Peace Corps service in Peru, the Kranks cancel their plans and rush to arrange all the usual Christmas traditions in the four hours remaining before Blair's arrival. Grisham's love of sports is evident in *Bleachers* (2003), which portrays former high school football players revisiting their love/hate relationship with legendary coach Eddie Rake as they gather for his funeral. His latest, *Playing for Pizza* (2007), chronicles the cultural misadventures of a failed third-string NFL quarterback who moves to Italy to play for the Parma Panthers. Grisham's passion for baseball in particular is evident in the *Mickey* screenplay, inspired by his experiences as a Little League coach, depicting a boy and his father in hiding from the IRS, which discovers their secret when the boy's team reaches the Little League World Series.

Among the more notable film adaptations of Grisham novels, in addition to *The Firm*, are *The Pelican Brief* (1993) starring Julia Roberts, Denzel Washington, Sam Shepard, and John Heard; *The Client* (1994) featuring Susan Sarandon, Tommy Lee Jones, and Mary-Louise Parker; *A Time to Kill* (1996) starring Matthew McConaughey, Sandra Bullock, Samuel L. Jackson, and Kevin Spacey among others; *The Rainmaker* (1997) directed by Francis Ford Coppola and starring Matt Damon, Danny DeVito, Claire Danes, and Jon Voight; *The Runaway Jury* (2003) with John Cusack, Gene Hackman, Dustin Hoffman, and Rachel Weisz; and, based on his novel *Skipping Christmas*, *Christmas with the Kranks* (2004) featuring Tim Allen, Jamie Lee Curtis, and Dan Ackroyd.

Bibliography

All editions below except *A Time to Kill* are the hardback editions published by Doubleday in New York.

Grisham, John. *A Time to Kill*. New York: Wynwood Press, 1989.

———. *The Firm*. 1991.

———. *The Pelican Brief*. 1992.

———. *The Client*. 1993.

———. *The Chamber*. 1994.

———. *The Rainmaker*. 1995.

———. *The Runaway Jury*. 1996.

———. *The Partner*. 1997.

———. *The Street Lawyer*. 1998.

———. *The Testament*. 1999.

———. *The Brethren*. 2000.

———. *A Painted House*. 2001.

———. *Skipping Christmas*. 2001.

———. *The Summons*. 2002.

———. *The King of Torts*. 2003.

———. *Bleachers*. 2003.

———. *The Last Juror*. 2004.

———. *The Broker*. 2005

———. *The Innocent Man*. 2006.

———. *Playing for Pizza*. 2007.

Chip Rogers

H

Hailey, Arthur (1920–2004)

Hailey is best known as the author of a series of meticulously researched novels, typically involving characters who wage dramatic struggles within the complex, sometimes sinister workings of industrial systems. He also wrote extensively for television and film and is often credited as inaugurating the disaster movie genre.

Born in Luton, England, Hailey moved to Canada in 1947 after serving as a flight lieutenant in World War II, to the United States in 1965 after enjoying huge commercial success with his novel *Hotel,* and finally, in flight from exorbitant taxes, to the Bahamas in 1969. He died there in 2004, still married to his second wife, Sheila Dunlop, who penned an often unflattering portrait of him in *I Married a Bestseller* (1978).

Hailey began his career as a fiction writer in the 1950s, coauthoring adventure novels that often drew on his military experience. After writing television and film scripts about an imperiled cross-country commercial flight (the pilots poisoned by tainted food), Hailey turned the story into the novel *Runway Zero-Eight* (1958). The melodramatic narrative of disaster narrowly averted was parodied several decades later in the movie *Airplane!* (1980). Next came the novels *The Final Diagnosis* (1959), which explores professional life at a large hospital, *In High Places* (1962), a political thriller involving Canadian-American relations and the threat of nuclear war, and the breakout commercial hit *Hotel* (1965), a work in part inspired by the film *Grand Hotel* (1930), itself based on Vicki Baum's German best seller about the inner workings of a luxury hotel, *Menschen im Hotel* (1929).

With his next series of novels Hailey established himself as one of the preeminent popular chroniclers of big business, "instruct[ing] Americans," as John Sutherland puts it, "about how modern America worked" (Sutherland 69). With *Airport* (1968, adapted to film in 1970), *Wheels* (1971, adapted as a TV miniseries in 1978), *The Moneychangers* (1975, adapted as a TV miniseries in 1976), *Overload* (1979), and *Strong Medicine* (1984, adapted as a TV movie in 1986), Hailey explored the airline, automotive, banking, power, and health care industries. More recently, and with somewhat reduced commercial success, he turned his attention to journalistic practices with *The Evening News* (1991) and criminal investigations with *Detective* (1998, adapted as a TV movie in 2005).

Key to the appeal of these novels was their expository perspective on whatever subject they took up, promising both a meticulously detailed education in regard to technical processes and the subtleties of behind-the-scenes power-brokering, along with potentially shocking revelations about the actual functioning of familiar industries. Here, for instance, is Hailey writing about the relationship between parts manufacturers and the major automakers in *Wheels*:

> The world, when it thinks of Detroit, does so in terms of name-famed auto manufacturers, dominated by the Big Three. The impression is correct, except that major car

makers represent the portion of the iceberg in view. Out of sight are thousands of supplemental firms, some substantial, but most small, and with a suprising segment operating out of holes-in-the-wall on petty cash financing. In the Detroit area they are anywhere and everywhere—downtown, out in suburbs, on side roads, or as satellites to bigger plants. Their work quarters range from snazzy compages to ramshackle warehouses, converted churches or one-room lofts. Some are unionized, many are not, although their total payrolls run to billions yearly. But the thing they have in common is that a Niagara of bits and pieces—some large, but mostly small, many unrecognizable as to purpose except by experts—flow outward to create other parts and, in the end, the finished automobiles. Without parts manufacturers, the Big Three would be like honey processors bereft of bees (211).

Dudley Jones allies Hailey with FREDERICK FORSYTH as an author primarily interested in "professionalism," or in other words a concern for bringing a documentarian's rigorousness to his research, and for revealing, in a narrative largely concerned with summarizing that research, the subtleties of contemporary professions themselves. A common criticism of Hailey is that his tendency to put his erudition on display sometimes gets in the way of good storytelling; Jones furnishes the following examples:

> In a skillfully prepared, tense scene towards the end of *Airport,* the saboteur succeeds in detonating the bomb in the airliner. With the passengers facing death through oxygen starvation, Hailey, instead of conveying the necessary information in a few sentences, suspends the narrative to insert a lecture on the inadequacy of the regulations concerning oxygen masks. A page further on, with disaster still imminent, the reader is given an account of the way simulators prepare pilots for this kind of emergency (166).

Critics of Hailey's writing often also point to his formulaic plotting and two-dimensional characterization. Few readers would argue that Hailey is particularly skilled as a stylist or psychologist. His great strength, attested to in sales that extend into the tens of millions, lies in his alluring mimesis of the intricacies of modern business, which he manages to make unusually accessible to readers.

Hailey's emphasis on technical description links him, according to Clive Bloom, with other preeminent "men's fiction" writers, among them JACK HIGGINS, PETER BENCHLEY, JOHN GRISHAM, and JAMES CLAVELL, who share an interest in "the truth of technology" (54–55). Indeed, the reverence demonstrated before the products of contemporary engineering means that at times it is not simply Technos and Logos that merge, but Eros too, as in this encounter between Nimrod, the hero of *Overload,* and Karen, his wheelchair-bound paramour:

> Using the electric wheelchair's blow-sip tube control, and with a speed and dexterity which amazed him, Karen maneuvered herself from the living room, down a small hallway, and into a bedroom.
>
> "[You're] strong Nimrod, you can lift me in your arms."
>
> He did so, gently but surely, aware of the warm softness of her body, and afterward followed instructions which Karen gave him about her breathing apparatus. He switched on a small Bantam respirator already at the bedside; at once he could hear it cycling—a dial showed fifteen pounds of pressure; the rate was eighteen breaths a minute. He put a tube from the respirator into Karen's mouth; as she began breathing the pressure went to thirty. Now she could dispense with the pneumo-belt she had been wearing beneath her clothes.
>
> "Later," Karen said, "I'll ask you to put a chest respirator on me. Not yet, though" (258–259).

Bibliography

Bloom, Clive. *Bestsellers: Popular Fiction Since 1900.* Houndsmills: Palgrave MacMillan, 2002.

Hailey, Arthur. *The Final Diagnosis.* Garden City, N.Y.: Doubleday, 1959.

———. *In High Places.* New York: Doubleday, 1962.
———. *Hotel.* New York: Dell, 1965.
———. *Airport.* New York: Dell, 1968.
———. *Wheels.* New York: Doubleday, 1971.
———. *The Moneychangers.* Toronto: Doubleday, 1975.
———. *Overload.* Toronto: Doubleday, 1979.
———. *Strong Medicine.* New York: Doubleday, 1984.
———. *The Evening News.* New York: Doubleday, 1990.
———. *Detective.* New York: Crown, 1997.
Jones, Dudley. "Professionalism and Popular Fiction: The Novels of Arthur Hailey and Frederick Forsyth." In *Spy Thrillers: From Buchan to le Carré.* New York: St. Martin's, 1990.
Sutherland, John. *Bestsellers: A Very Short Introduction.* Oxford: Oxford University Press, 2007.

Geoff Hamilton

Hamilton, Laurell, K. (1963–)

Laurell Hamilton has firmly established herself as a master of "horrorotica," or erotic horror fiction, most notably through her ANITA BLAKE: VAMPIRE HUNTER series. In 2002 she added to this the Merry Gentry series about a faerie princess turned private investigator. Beyond these, she has published a novel, *Nightseer* (1992); a collection of short fiction, *Strange Candy* (2006); and stories in the collections *Bite* (2005) and *Cravings* (2004).

Hamilton was born in Heber Springs, Arkansas, but raised in Sims, Indiana, by her grandmother after her mother died in an automobile accident in 1969. Her grandmother's tales of southern horror legends, along with her own reading of heroic sword-and-sorcery stories and assorted works concerning the vampire mythos, formed her earliest influences.

"Two things I do well in books are sex and violence," Hamilton states on her Web site, ". . . only as graphic as need be. And never included unless it furthers the plot or character development." Indeed, her work well illustrates Bruce Franklin's dictum that good science fiction requires a "coherent fictional speculation," or, in more modern terms, "world-building." There are rules established for how magic works, how vampires gain strength or can be defeated, and so on, scrupulously followed within and between her individual works, and evolving organically with the evolution of the world itself. The reader is thus rewarded with a sure and always mounting sense of the integrity of that world.

Her work also mixes genres to create layered and subtly nuanced narratives. The already rich background of her series' protagonists, for example, is augmented by the trappings of detective fiction. Merry Gentry is a Los Angeles–based private investigator, while Anita Blake is a "vampire executioner," a special kind of federal marshal in the Anita-verse, and is attached to the Regional Preternatural Investigation Task Force out of St. Louis (where Hamilton lives in real life with her husband, Jonathon Green, and daughter, Trinity).

Enjoying great commercial success in hardcover and paperback, Hamilton's work is also being adapted into comic book form, with the Anita Blake series being produced by Marvel Comics.

Bibliography

Franklin, H. Bruce. *Future Perfect: American Science Fiction of the Nineteenth Century—An Anthology.* New Brunswick, N.J.: Rutgers University Press, 1995.
Hamilton, Laurell K. *Nightseer.* New York: New American Library, 1992.
———. *Strange Candy.* New York: Berkeley, 2006.
———, et al. *Cravings.* New York: Jove Books, 2004.
———, et al. *Bite.* New York: Jove Books, 2005.

Ronald C. Thomas

Hannibal Thomas Harris (1999)

THOMAS HARRIS's fourth novel, *Hannibal,* is the third involving the cannibalistic psychiatrist Hannibal Lecter, after *RED DRAGON* (1981) and *The SILENCE OF THE LAMBS* (1988). Where *The Silence of the Lambs* explored the initial interplay between Lecter the prisoner and Clarice Starling, FBI trainee, *Hannibal* catches up with them seven years after Lecter's escape and Starling's graduation. Lecter's skill at languages and his scholarship in medieval and Renaissance Italian history have brought him to the library of the Palazzo Capponi as curator. Publicly he is Dr. Fell, respected by his fellow scholars and invited to lecture on pre-Renaissance Italian art and literature; privately he delves into the story of one of his 12th-century ancestors, all the while observing the frustrated career of Agent Starling.

Starling has been caught in lateral moves within the agency, battling "the glass ceiling like a bee in a bottle" (27). Though responsible for catching and killing the notorious "Buffalo Bill" (in *The Silence of the Lambs*), the trainee has made serious enemies within the FBI, including Deputy Assistant Inspector General Paul Krendler. *Hannibal* begins with Starling's involvement in a public relations disaster. The media, having been tipped off by criminals, appear just in time to film Starling's shootout in a meth lab drug bust. One of her victims, Evelda Drumgo, is photographed slumped over the baby she was using as a shield. Harris then anatomizes FBI and law enforcement politics and misbehavior as Starling deals with the death of her fellow officers, including her well-respected friend John Brigham, while resisting the agency's attempt to sacrifice her in the name of public relations. This strain between ethical action, justice, and revenge emerges as a dominant theme within the novel, questioning traditional categories of good and evil.

Hounded by the press and awaiting subpoena for an investigation into her killing of five people during the drug raid, Starling receives a letter of encouragement from Lecter. Starling brings out her evidence gloves and alerts Behavioral Science to Lecter's written presence. She also reads the letter, inappropriate as it might be, and takes comfort from Lecter's assessment of her ethics compared to those of the bureaucracy in which she works.

Assigned to Behavioral Sciences, she is once more on the trail of Lecter. Starling's old friend Jack Crawford's last-minute phone call temporarily saves her from the machinations of a law enforcement tribunal that includes Paul Krendler, but Starling is now drawn into the ugly world of Lecter's old victim, Mason Verger. Verger is the inheritor of his father's vast meatpacking empire and as coldly manipulative of the human beings around him as his business is of the animals it slaughters. Nineteen years earlier Lecter drugged Verger and convinced him to feed his face to his starving dogs; now Verger plans to allow specially bred killer swine to eat Lecter alive.

Meanwhile, Lecter's courteous literary impulse draws the attention of the global watchdogs. The letter he sent to Clarice offers Behavioral Sciences a clue in its postal meter, and the novel's action now alternates between the American and Italian search for Lecter, exploring law enforcement's ambiguous engagement with lesser criminals in attempting to gain access to a larger, supposedly more dangerous criminal. Florence's chief investigator, Rinaldo Pazzi of the Questura, the descendant of a man hanged from the very building in which Lecter works, slowly and creatively comes to recognize the identity of Lecter's Dr. Fell. A dirty cop, however, Pazzi sells Lecter's information to Verger's contacts, even as FBI agent Starling shares information with Verger in order to gain the political clout to continue her search. Ironically, Verger, paralyzed in his bed on Muskrat Farm in Maryland, effectively manipulates police and government officials to accomplish his malicious ends.

Harris draws suggestive comparisons between Verger and Lecter in the quantity and quality of malice. But at the same time readers cannot help but sense affinities between this same Lecter and the sympathetic Starling, both in their keen ethical sense and in their experience as targets of revenge. They finally meet when Lecter narrowly escapes the Italian operatives sent to kidnap him and comes to America, both as fugitive and pursuer, victim and fiend. Lecter seeks out Clarice with an anonymous gift, and again, as with his original letter, it is his own courtesy and affection that lead to his discovery—a pattern of obsessional vulnerability mirroring that which encompassed Will Graham in Harris's first novel.

Captured by Verger's minions, Lecter awaits torture and death. Alerted to the danger in which Lecter has placed himself, Starling attempts to rescue him. With this act she places herself firmly outside the law that has been her life's guiding principle but stays true to the sense of justice underlying that principle; while in yet another reversal Lecter becomes Starling's savior, freeing her from both the human and porcine killers on the farm. From the first shooting to the climactic scene at Muskrat Farm, each act of violence must be read in context. When a monster such as Lecter exerts benign control over other monsters and helps to protect the innocent, the reader is hard put to clearly distinguish the good from the bad.

In the midst of this convoluted drama Lecter begins to unravel Starling's emotional trauma over her father's death. After saving her from the violence on Muskrat Farm, he treats her tranquilizer dart wound and begins to psychoanalyze her using drugs and hypnosis, but he shares in the process his own pain over the death of his baby sister at the hands of cannibalizing Russian soldiers during World War II. Blending psychiatry, philosophy, and physics, Lecter hopes to create a space within Starling's mind for the presence of his lost sister, Mischa. Harris thus intimates Lecter's own victimization and pain along with his intellect and a certain integrity as the characters grow closer both emotionally and psychologically.

At last, Lecter invites Starling to an exquisitely prepared feast, the first course of which is Starling's FBI nemesis Paul Krendler, whose brain Lecter serves in delicate slices on broad croutons. The peculiar dinner party is part graduation ceremony for Starling, who has completed her psychotherapy, and part entrée into Lecter's world of refined aesthetic finesse, beyond law and conventional mores. In a startlingly intense conclusion Starling not only joins Lecter in the consumption of her enemy but returns his admission of desire with physical intimacy—she no longer an unambiguous representative of the law, he far from an unambiguous villain.

The 2001 MGM/Universal production of *Hannibal* directed by Ridley Scott offered both a substantially different ending to the story and the replacement of actor Jodie Foster with Julianne Moore as Clarice Starling. Anthony Hopkins once again played Dr. Hannibal Lecter.

Bibliography

Harris, Thomas. *Black Sunday.* New York: Bantam, 1976.

———. *Red Dragon.* New York: Bantam, 1981.

———. *The Silence of the Lambs.* New York: St. Martin's, 1988.

———. *Hannibal.* New York: Random House, 1999.

Hannibal. Directed by Ridley Scott. MGM/Universal, 2001.

Frances Auld

Harris, Thomas (1940–)

Harris is the author of five crime thrillers, each of which has been successfully adapted to film: *Black Sunday*, RED DRAGON, *The* SILENCE OF THE LAMBS, HANNIBAL, and HANNIBAL RISING. The last four of these involve the notorious serial killer Dr. Hannibal "the Cannibal" Lecter, who has become a pop-culture icon.

Harris was born in Jackson, Tennessee, but lived in several parts of Mississippi while growing up. His mother was a high school biology teacher. Harris majored in English literature at Baylor University in Waco, Texas, graduating in 1964. As an undergraduate he covered the crime beat part time for the local newspaper. Harris went on to work for the Associated Press in New York from 1968 to 1974, sometimes covering stories in Mexico. He now divides his time between New York, Florida, and Mississippi. Harris keeps a low public profile, and very little is known about his personal life.

In order to research his Lecter novels, Harris visited the FBI's famed Behavioral Science Unit (BSU) in Quantico, Virginia, several times during the 1980s. He met practicing criminal profilers there and was given access to the case files of actual serial killers such as Edmund Kemper, Richard Chase, and Ed Gein. Robert Ressler, a former FBI profiler who was responsible on one occasion for showing Harris around the BSU, claims to have introduced the author to the sole female agent then working for the organization. If this is true, this agent may have helped to form the basis for the character Clarice Starling in Harris's third novel (Simpson 71).

Black Sunday, Harris's first novel, was published in 1975. Inspired by the murder of 11 Israeli athletes at the 1972 Munich Olympics, it involves a plot by an agent of the Palestine Liberation Organization and an unhinged Vietnam veteran to crash a blimp into the Super Bowl. *Red Dragon* (1981) introduces Hannibal Lecter, an exceptionally cultured psychiatrist and serial killer who assists the investigator Will Graham in tracking a disfigured killer named Francis Dolarhyde. *The Silence of the Lambs* (1988), generally considered Harris's best novel, deepens Lecter's story as the gifted but deranged inmate of the Chesapeake State Hospital for the Criminally Insane is called upon by rookie FBI agent Clarice Starling to help in another serial killer investigation. *Hannibal* (1999) takes place seven years after the previous novel and sees Lecter free, having escaped the confines of the hospital. He is pursued by FBI Special Agent Starling, as well as by one of his former victims, who is now bent on revenge and would like to feed his nemesis to a herd of boars he has bred for the purpose. *Hannibal Rising* (2006) explores Lecter's early life and the formative influences on his evil character.

Harris is known for his gripping plots, terrifying and ornate scenes of carnage, occasional moments of black comedy, and an extraordinary attention to detail in descriptions of forensic procedures. Among the most recurrent themes in his work is the disturbing affinity between violent criminals and the ostensibly normal. Hannibal Lecter's key message to those who seek his help is that the line separating the law-abiding from the grossly criminal, the civilized from the barbaric, is disturbingly hard to maintain. What makes it difficult for those who encounter Lecter to dismiss him as merely a quack is his superior intellect, which like his physical strength is of almost superhuman proportions. Such gifts are common to Harris's killers, who are often constructed as monstrous aesthetes intent on using the bodies of their victims to express grotesque personal visions. Also prominent in Harris's writing is a meticulous exploration of the techniques employed by experts to profile and capture deviant individuals. Well versed in the specifics of law-enforcement procedures, the author makes these procedures essential to his plots.

Harris has been extraordinarily prescient in terms of his subject matter. *Black Sunday* offers the first fictional treatment of a terrorist attack involving an Islamic extremist on American ground, while *Red Dragon* was in the vanguard of popular interest in serial killers and criminal profilers. As Philip L. Simpson remarks:

> It is little exaggeration to say that Thomas Harris, for all practical purposes, created the current formula for mainstream serial killer fiction back in 1981 with the publication of *Red Dragon*. His 1988 follow-up, *The Silence of the Lambs*, solidified the formula (controlling Gothic tone, two killers, a dark and troubled law-enforcement outsider in uneasy alliance with a murderer) and ensured his status as the foremost writer of serial killer fiction (70).

Countless other fiction writers, as well as television dramas such as *Profiler* and the *CSI* franchise, have been heavily influenced by Harris's memorable representations of criminals and those who hunt them.

Anthony Hopkins's representation of Lecter in three wildly successful films has secured the character's prominent and enduring place in pop culture. The film version of *The Silence of the Lambs* starring Hopkins and Jodie Foster appeared in 1991 and went on to garner five Academy Awards. *Hannibal*, released in 2001, was also a commercial success, with Julianne Moore taking on the role of Starling. *Red Dragon*, which had been filmed under the title *Manhunter* in 1986, appeared in 2002 and starred Edward Norton. *Hannibal Rising* was released in early 2007.

Bibliography

Harris, Thomas. *Black Sunday*. New York: Bantam, 1976.

———. *Red Dragon*. 1981. New York: Dell, 1990.

———. *The Silence of the Lambs*. New York: St. Martins, 1991.

———. *Hannibal*. New York: Dell, 2000.

———. *Hannibal Rising*. New York: Delacorte, 2006.

Simpson, Philip. *Psycho Paths: Tracking the Serial Killer through Contemporary American Film and Fiction*. Carbondale: Southern Illinois University Press, 2000.

Geoff Hamilton

Harrison, Kim (1966–)

Harrison has written seven novels, all recounting the exploits of witch and bounty hunter Rachel Morgan, with some titles punning on Clint

Eastwood films: *Dead Witch Walking* (2004), *The Good, the Bad and the Undead,* and *Every Which Way but Dead* (both published in 2005), *A* FISTFUL OF CHARMS (2006), and *For a Few Demons More* (2007), her first hardcover edition. She has joined a burgeoning category of authors writing hybrid genre novels, combining elements of fantasy, science fiction, romance, and mystery, a group including such well-known authors as LAURELL K. HAMILTON and Charlaine Harris.

An exceedingly private person, Harrison releases few facts of her personal life, though maintaining an active and sociable online relationship with her fans. Born in the 1960s, she grew up a midwesterner in "Tornado Alley," attending high school and college in the 1980s—a significant decade since she sees herself as "forever marked by its music" (Hamilton), citing inspiration from such diverse musical groups as Duran Duran and Nine Inch Nails (Harrison Web site). On her Web site she explains, "My muse exists in music. Logic maps the story, but music gives it its soul and sends my characters in directions that surprise even me."

Harrison's earliest plans had nothing to do with writing. She majored in biology and minored in chemistry at a small state university, planning a career in the sciences, but her second minor, art, held hints of a direction change. Although she deliberately stayed away from English courses, she was a voracious reader, citing Ray Bradbury and Grimm fairy tales as motivations for her writing (Gentle). Frustration with the quality of the books she was finding to read sparked her first unplanned efforts as an author (Farrell). She has been writing since 1995, and for the past few years it has been her full-time job.

The world Harrison creates is an alternative history grounded on the premise that a pandemic caused by genetically manipulated tomatoes has killed a significant portion of the world's human population. Inderlanders, an unrecognized and much smaller nonhuman populace made up of vampires, werewolves, witches, and other supernatural beings, have always lived side by side with but unknown to humans. With humanity decimated by the pandemic, these nonhumans announce their existence to humankind and social reality becomes complex and hybrid, humans sometimes sharing their power and sometimes serving as prey. Rachel Morgan, the central character in all of Harrison's novels, is a citizen of this new world. As a human witch she walks the border between humans and nonhumans, never fully part of either community. About her a core group of characters—living vampire, Ivy, her best friend and roommate; her friend, partner, and pixie, Jenks; and her living vampire lover, Kisten—work, love, play, and battle the bad guys and, in the case of some, try not to become the bad guys themselves.

The novels are multilayered. On the surface they appear to be little more than simple, entertaining action stories, but beneath one inevitably detects her universal concerns: racial and sexual diversity; the obligations and responsibilities of friendship; the nature, temptations, and costs of evil; and the just use of power.

Bibliography

Adams, John Joseph. "Demons Goes Darker." Available online. URL: http://www.scifi.com/scifiwire/index.php?category=0&id=39107&type=0. Accessed December 7, 2006.

Farrell, Shaun. "Shaun Farrell Interviews Kim Harrison." Shaun's Quadrant (June 2005). Available online. URL: http://www.farsector.com/quadrant/interview-kimharrison.htm. Accessed December 7, 2006.

———. "Shaun Farrell Interviews Kim Harrison (New Interview)." Shaun's Quadrant (May 2006). Available online. URL: http://www.farsector.com/quadrant/interview-kimharrison2.htm. Accessed December 7, 2006.

Gentle, Dee. "Witchy Women: Spotlight on Witch Featured Romance." *PNR Paraphernalia* (October 2006). Available online. URL: http://www.writerspace.com/ParanormalRomance/KimHarrison06.htm. Accessed November 13, 2006.

Harrison, Kim. *Dead Witch Walking.* New York: HarperCollins, 2004.

———. *Every Which Way but Dead.* New York: HarperTorch, 2005.

———. *The Good, the Bad and the Undead.* New York: HarperCollins, 2005.

———. *A Fistful of Charms.* New York: HarperCollins, 2006.

———. *For a Few Demons More.* New York: Eos, 2007.

———. "Re: Kim Harrison Bio." E-mail to the author. November 29, 2006.

———. "Hollow's Music" and "Kim's Bio." *Kim Harrison* (December 2006). Available online. URL: http://www.kimharrison.net. Accessed December 18, 2006.

Laura Colmenero-Chilberg

Harry Potter and the Sorcerer's Stone

J. K. Rowling (1998)

Harry Potter and the Sorcerer's Stone (released as *Harry Potter and the Philosopher's Stone* in the U.K.) is a fantasy children's work that introduces the title character as a young orphan boy being raised by his aunt and uncle, who on his 11th birthday is informed that he is a wizard and must attend Hogwarts School of Witchcraft and Wizardry. Harry is "small and skinny for his age" with a "thin face, knobby knees, black hair, and bright green eyes," and he wears eyeglasses taped in the middle; "the only thing Harry liked about his own appearance was a very thin scar on his forehead that was shaped like a bolt of lightning" (20). *Sorcerer's Stone* introduces readers to a space where the magical and nonmagical (or Muggle) world exist side by side—the Muggle world none the wiser—and forms the first in a seven-part series, each novel taking place during a subsequent year at Hogwarts. Harry's coming of age unfolds, like many hero tales, as a journey toward an ultimate confrontation with a great evil, here a wizard named Lord Voldemort. For Harry is the only survivor of an attack by Voldemort—"You Know Who" as he is called in the wizarding world—which killed Harry's parents when Harry was just a year old. It was Lily Potter's sacrifice of her own life to protect her infant son that prevented Voldemort's curse from killing Harry, and the backlash of that spell blasted Voldemort so badly that he disappeared for 10 years, existing only in a kind of half-life. The blast also left Harry with the lightning bolt scar on his forehead, marking him as "the Boy Who Lived," revered by wizards and witches even as he grows up wholly ignorant of his fame. Each year at Hogwarts is fraught with more danger as Harry becomes increasingly hard pressed to withstand the mounting power of Voldemort. The final novel in the series, *Harry Potter and the Deathly Hallows* (2007) concludes his adventures as he reaches his majority (which in the wizarding world occurs at age 17).

But it is *Sorcerer's Stone* that sets the stage for all that is to come, and for many fans it remains the definitive and favorite installment. As the novel opens, Harry has been horribly treated by his Muggle Aunt Petunia and Uncle Vernon Dursley, as well as by their repellent son, Dudley, and has been kept completely ignorant of his magical heritage. So he is startled just prior to his 11th birthday to receive an invitation, dropped off by a large owl, to begin his education. Suddenly the strange things that have happened when he has been upset now make sense. For example, Aunt Petunia once "cut his [unkempt] hair so short he was almost bald except for his bangs, which she left 'to hide that horrible scar'" (24). But Harry so feared how he would be teased at school next day that his hair grew back overnight.

The Dursleys go to great and comical lengths to keep Harry from his birthright, including rowing out to a dreary, rain-swept island in the middle of nowhere in an attempt to suppress the increasing number of owls delivering invitations. But finally late at night the family is startled by the appearance of a giant figure come personally to bring Harry to Hogwarts: Hagrid, the Hogwarts Gamekeeper and friend of the headmaster, the great wizard Albus Dumbledore. On the Hogwarts Express, a special train that leaves from Platform 9¾ at King's Cross Station, Harry meets Ron Weasley, son of a large, poor, and loving wizarding family, and Hermione Granger, daughter of a Muggle family of dentists, and the three become best friends who see one another through many dangerous adventures. In *Sorcerer's Stone* Harry and his friends discover a secret that may allow Voldemort to return, a magical item kept at Hogwarts for safekeeping but which Voldemort has found a way to steal. Harry, along with Ron and Hermione, must work together to prevent Voldemort from getting this item and returning to full life. Through courage and magical adventure, Harry is victorious and Voldemort once again banished.

As this epic plot unfolds, readers are introduced to a whimsical world full of quirky and arcane knowledge, magical creatures and potions, and the wondrous game of Quidditch, a blend of rugby, soccer, and lacrosse, played on flying broomsticks. Harry must take courses on Potions, Herbology (the study of magical plants), Care of Magical Creatures, and the seemingly hard-to-staff Defense Against the Dark Arts, among others. The school is divided into four houses, each reflecting the virtues of the four wizards who founded Hogwarts: Gryffindor (courage), Slytherin (ambition), Hufflepuff (loyalty), and Ravenclaw (intelligence). The first-year students are separated into their houses by an enchanted Sorting Hat, which determines by sitting on the student's head which house he or she will be sorted into. In Harry's case the hat hesitates, wondering whether Harry should be in Slytherin or Gryffindor. Because all of the dark wizards have come from Slytherin, and Harry's nemesis Draco Malfoy has just been sorted there, Harry doubly wishes to avoid the place. The scene is interesting in its intimation of telling conflicts both within the later novels and within Harry's character itself:

> The last thing Harry saw before the hat dropped over his eyes was the hall full of people craning to get a good look at him. Next second he was looking at the black inside of the hat. He waited.
>
> "Hmm," said a small voice in his ear. "Difficult. Very difficult. Plenty of courage, I see. Not a bad mind either. There's talent, oh my goodness, yes—and a nice thirst to prove yourself, now that's interesting. . . . So where shall I put you?"
>
> Harry gripped the edges of the stool and thought, *Not Slytherin, not Slytherin.*
>
> "Not Slytherin, eh?" said the small voice. "Are you sure? You could be great, you know, it's all here in your head, and Slytherin will help you on the way to greatness, no doubt about that—no? Well, if you're sure—better be GRYFFINDOR!" (121).

This minor-seeming confusion over Harry's house becomes a central issue in the second novel, *Harry Potter and the Chamber of Secrets,* as Harry shows evidence of being Slytherin's heir in his ability to talk to snakes—also presaged in *Sorcerer's Stone* when Harry is able to communicate with a large Brazilian python at the zoo. Harry, too, is here first associated with the evil Voldemort, who also spoke Parselmouth (snake language); many of the wizards and witches at the school begin to fear Harry, as several people are struck down by a mysterious creature, supposedly let loose by Slytherin's heir to clear the school of Mudbloods (derogatory slang for people not of pure wizard families). The connection is explained away by Dumbledore as the result of the blast that destroyed Voldemort when he tried to kill Harry, but its shadow broods over the later novels as Voldemort's power increases and Harry begins to have dreams that share Voldemort's own experience.

With the later novels becoming progressively darker, it is the first that remains the whimsical favorite for many fans. Harry's wide-eyed wonder at this new world is shared by the audience. J. K. ROWLING's decision to keep Harry ignorant of the wizarding world and its history enables her to educate the reader as part of the narrative and avoids bogging down the plot with digressions. The first book is, very simply, fun; Rowling's descriptions of this intricate world, enchanting. Consider her description of the unique candies of the wizarding world, which Harry discovers on his train trip to Hogwarts:

> He had never had any money for candy with the Dursleys, and now that he had pockets rattling with gold and silver he was ready to buy as many Mars Bars as he could carry—but the woman didn't have Mars Bars. What she did have were Bertie Bott's Every Flavor Beans, Drooble's Best Blowing Gum, Chocolate Frogs, Pumpkin Pasties, Cauldron Cakes, Licorice Wands, and a number of other strange things Harry had never seen in his life (101).

With the great popularity of the Harry Potter franchise, many of these candies can now be bought in stores, although the Chocolate Frogs don't jump. Bertie Bott's Every Flavor Beans are produced by the Jelly Belly jellybean company and, as Ron tells Harry, "When they say every flavor, they *mean* every flavor—you know, you get all the ordinary ones like chocolate and peppermint and marmalade, but then you can get spinach and liver and tripe. George reckons he had a booger-flavored one once" (103–104). Jelly Belly indeed produces a booger-flavored bean, as well as vomit, grass, dirt, and earwax. Recent additions to the flavors include rotten egg and spaghetti.

Thematically, such fantasy is employed to explore, often quite deftly, many searching issues of childhood. Most of *Sorcerer's Stone* centers on Harry coming to understand his past and the burdens of this knowledge. The opening scenes of his mistreatment by the Dursleys underscore Harry's feeling that he does not belong anywhere, a common theme of preadolescent literature. He is further challenged by his own growing power and sense of self as he learns that magic, far from solving all his problems, may simply cause more and more grievous ones, particularly as his connection to Voldemort emerges. Harry's increasing maturity and the difficult decisions such maturity engenders reflect in many ways the journey all adolescents must make, only heightened here and nuanced by the magical dimension.

The 2001 film starring Daniel Radcliffe as Harry, with Maggie Smith and Richard Harris, grossed almost a billion dollars, making it the fourth most successful film in history.

Bibliography

Rowling, J. K. *Harry Potter and the Sorcerer's Stone.* New York: Scholastic, 1998.

———. *Harry Potter and the Chamber of Secrets.* New York: Scholastic, 1999.

———. *Harry Potter and the Deathly Hallows* New York: Scholastic, 2007.

Julie Brannon

Highsmith, Patricia (1921–1995)

Highsmith is the author of 22 novels and 10 collections of short stories. She became famous after Alfred Hitchcock adapted her first novel, *Strangers on a Train,* to the screen in 1951, but her subsequent popularity has primarily rested on five novels written over a span of four decades that feature the character Tom Ripley. She is notable also as the author of a groundbreaking lesbian novel, *The Price of Salt,* originally published under a pseudonym in 1952 and later republished as *Carol* under her own name in 1990.

Highsmith's fiction is often categorized as mystery or suspense, but while this designation is often appropriate, she, in fact, resented it. When she started her career, these genres were considered pulp fiction, insignificant as art and barely significant as literature, while Highsmith herself most admired canonical writers such as Poe, Dostoevsky, Proust, and Kafka and wished that her fiction be considered in the tradition of serious literature. While not usually considered to be in such company, she has grown in importance since her death and was not without critical acclaim during her lifetime. She was often nominated for the Edgar Allan Poe Scroll and won in 1956 for *The Talented Mr. Ripley* (1955); she won several European awards, including Great Britain's Silver Dagger Award in 1964 and the Officier dans l'Ordre des Arts et des Lettres from the French Ministry of Culture in 1990.

Highsmith was born Mary Patricia Plangman in 1921 in Forth Worth, Texas. Her parents had divorced nine days earlier, and she did not meet her biological father until she was 10. Highsmith's mother, Mary Coates, married Stanley Highsmith three years later, and for much of her childhood Highsmith was shuttled between her parents in New York City and her grandparents in Fort Worth. Highsmith attended Barnard College in New York City after graduating from high school in 1938 and there worked for the *Barnard Quarterly,* which published her first story, "Quiet Night," in 1939, and nine more before she graduated with a B.A. in 1942.

For six years starting in 1942 Highsmith wrote stories for two comic book publishers, the first collection for Michel Publishers, featuring narratives about historical figures such as Oliver Cromwell and Albert Einstein, and the second for Fawcett, specializing in adventure tales such as "Spy Smasher" and "Pyroman." Although she loathed the work, it allowed her time to write her own fiction, and her first success came when her short story "The Heroine" was included in the *O. Henry Memorial Award Prize Stories of 1946.* On the strength of this story and Truman Capote's recommendation, Highsmith was granted a two-month residency in 1948 at Yaddo, a community of artists and writers in Upstate New York, where she wrote her first novel, *Strangers on a Train.* Published in 1950 and made into a movie a year later, *Strangers* launched Highsmith on her literary career.

Recalling in some ways the more famous work of Ernest Hemingway, Highsmith's writing is marked by two qualities standing in interesting contrast: complex psychological and philosophical themes, written in sparse, readily accessible prose; themes such as identity, consciousness, sexuality, morality, justice, criminality, and the individual's relationship with society. In addition, her fiction frequently challenges definitions of normative behavior and relishes protagonists who reject social mores, with Highsmith usually emphasizing her antihero's point of view, encouraging readers to sympathize—or at least empathize—with these criminal characters. Highsmith herself rejected the mode of narrative that traditionally held up criminals and their punishment as moral examples. It was almost scandalous that her most popular character, Tom Ripley, was able to murder with impunity. In 1966 Highsmith published a book about her writing process, *Plotting and Writing Suspense Fiction,* in which she boldly espoused the relativity of social mores: "I find the public passion for justice quite boring and artificial, for neither life nor nature cares if justice is ever done or not" (51).

This is not to suggest that Highsmith was unconcerned with social justice. She was briefly a member of the Communist Party in her 20s and was later actively involved in Amnesty International, while in her work she would become more and more interested in exploring inequalities of American society and the imperialist tendencies of her country's foreign policy. By the late 1960s, for example, Highsmith regularly voiced her vehement opposition to the Vietnam War and America's support of Israel, and *The Tremor of Forgery* (1969), perhaps her most political novel, utilizes the Arab-Israeli Six Day War of 1967 as a backdrop for the clash of two opposing characters with opposite views on the Vietnam War. This was written in the middle of a 13-year stint in Europe, where Highsmith moved in 1963, and during the political upheavals of 1968, when she lived in France. In his study of the political import of Highsmith's writing, Russell Harrison suggests that Highsmith's stay in Europe provided a unique vantage point on the troubles back home, but her status as an expatriate also hampered her critical perspective by removing her from the immediacy of the people she wrote about (Harrison 59).

Homosexuality is another important theme in Highsmith's work. *The Price of Salt* (1952), with its radical suggestion that two female lovers could have a happy ending, broke away from the standards of popular fiction, which stressed unhappy conclusions for unsanctioned relationships. Highsmith herself was a lesbian who occasionally had male lovers, and the events of *The Price of Salt* were inspired by her own experiences. "Homosexuality, its theory as well as practice," notes her biographer Andrew Wilson, "informed all of Highsmith's writing. In each of her [journals] she would introduce her observations on the subject under the heading, N.O.E.P.S.—Notes On Ever Present Subject" (Wilson 99). From her first novel, *Strangers on a Train,* with its undertones of sexual attraction between Bruno and Guy, to her last, *Small g: a Summer Idyll* (1995), with its explicit dramatization of Zurich's gay scene, themes of homosexuality are consistently and searchingly addressed.

Any definitive collection of Highsmith's novels must include, however, a selection from what many fans call the "Ripliad," five novels written between 1955 and 1991 about the nefarious Tom Ripley, beginning with *The Talented Mr. Ripley.* Like all of the Ripley novels and most of her other work, *Talented* meditates on amorphous identities, alienated individuals, ambiguous realities, and the absence of moral constants. Tom is a brilliant but impoverished man in his mid-20s hired by the wealthy Herbert Greenleaf, who wants his son, Dickie, to return from an extended vacation in Europe and start his career. Tom meets Dickie and soon falls in love with him and his affluent lifestyle. When their relationship falters, Tom kills Dickie and assumes his identity for a brief period. Dickie's girlfriend, his father, and a private detective all come to suspect Tom, but eventually accept his version of events, which include the finding of a will (forged on Dickie's typewriter) that grants his inheritance to Tom. The novel concludes with Tom rich and free in Greece.

The next installment, *Ripley under Ground,* was published in 1970, and again Highsmith dramatizes themes of false identities and fluid realities. Tom is now in his early 30s, married, and living in France, managing a painter who forges new paintings by a dead artist. *Ripley's Game* (1974) takes place shortly after the events of *Ripley under Ground* and situates Tom, his ill neighbor Jonathan, and his delinquent American friend, Reeves, in a complex plot of murders and countermurders. Tom plays the role of the active observer, Reeves the old criminal hand, and Jonathan the hapless innocent caught up in the swirl of violence. *The Boy Who Followed Ripley* (1980) departs significantly from its predecessors as Ripley exhibits compassion and indulgence toward 16-year-old Frank, who turns to Tom for help after committing patricide. They travel to Berlin together; Frank is kidnapped and rescued by Tom, returns to France guilt-ridden, and finally commits suicide. The final installment of the Ripley novels, *RIPLEY UNDER WATER* (1991), the last novel Highsmith published in her lifetime (the last novel she wrote, *Small g: A Summer Idyll,* was published a month after her death), is in some ways a return to form. Tom, urbane and wealthy, is contrasted with his loutish stalker, David Pritchard, who knows about Tom's crimes. David, unassisted by Tom, eventually drowns in his own pond, leaving Tom as free as he thought he was before David's arrival.

Highsmith's fiction, and especially the Ripley series, has inspired many film adaptations: Hitchcock's *Strangers on a Train* (1951) starred Robert Walker as Bruno and Farley Granger as Guy; *The Talented Mr. Ripley* was filmed by René Clement as *Purple Noon* (1960) and starred Alain Delon as Tom; Dennis Hopper played Tom in Wim Wenders's version of *Ripley's Game,* titled *The American Friend* (1977); in 1999 Matt Damon played the lead in Anthony Minghella's version of *The Talented Mr. Ripley.*

Highsmith died of aplastic anemia in Switzerland in 1995 and bequeathed her entire estate to Yaddo, the artists and writers community that had facilitated the completion of her first novel almost 50 years before.

Bibliography

Harrison, Russell. *Patricia Highsmith.* New York: Twayne, 1997.

Highsmith, Patricia. *Strangers on a Train.* 1950. Reprint, New York: W.W. Norton, 2001.

———. *The Price of Salt.* 1952. Reprint, New York: W.W. Norton, 2004.

———. *The Talented Mr. Ripley.* 1955. Reprint, New York: Vintage, 1992.

———. *Plotting and Writing Suspense Fiction.* 1966. Reprint, New York: St. Martin's, 2001.

———. *The Tremor of Forgery.* Garden City, New York: Doubleday, 1969.

———. *Ripley under Ground.* 1970. Reprint, New York: Vintage, 1992.

———. *Ripley's Game.* 1974. Reprint, New York: Vintage, 1999.

———. *The Boy Who Followed Ripley.* 1980. Reprint, New York: Vintage, 1993.

———. *Ripley under Water.* 1991. Reprint, New York: Knopf, 1992.

———. *Small g: A Summer Idyll.* Bloomsbury: London, 1995.

Wilson, Andrew. *Beautiful Shadow: A Life of Patricia Highsmith.* New York: Bloomsbury, 2003.

Michael Mayne

The Historian Elizabeth Kostova (2005)

The Historian is constructed around the search by an unassuming and unnamed female narrator for the answer to a great historical mystery: Who was Vlad Ţepeş, better known to the world as Dracula? After stumbling across a collection of letters in her father's library, each addressed to "My dear and unfortunate successor . . .", the young girl unwittingly inherits the role of Dracula historian and begins a quest to unearth the truth about the 15th-century Romanian villain, whom she discovers to her amazement may still be alive (5).

The novel opens with a cryptic epilogue written by the protagonist in 2008, then shuffles readers back in time to Amsterdam in 1972, whence the 16-year-old heroine begins her journey, probing the archives, libraries, and even grave sites of Europe. Her father, Paul, a diplomat, gradually passes on the secrets of the letters and the accompanying nearly blank book that he inherited from his mentor, a professor Bartholomew Rossi; the novel traces the efforts, too, of these and other "unfortunate" historians whose search for Dracula led them to thrilling and finally disastrous ends.

The book is structured in three main parts, divided according to time periods, although the narrative of the heroine remains nested throughout the story. The first, set in 1930, focuses mostly on the biography of Professor Rossi and his Dracula research. The second chronicles the efforts of a young Paul when in 1954 he took on the research of his predecessor. In the third the reader is returned to the narrator's present, 1972, and the beginning of her own historical quest. The plot builds gradually, meandering over 642 pages, encompassing the protagonist's discovery of letters and scholarly literature in Budapest, Istanbul, Amsterdam, and Vlad's historical homeland of Wallachia and incorporating her reconstruction of the Dracula stories her father had told her in her childhood. The author's stylistic use of epistolary exchanges, historical drama, and several different time settings creates further layers in an otherwise largely straightforward narrative.

As the story nears its climax, the heroine's historical sleuthing of the vampiric Vlad Ţepeş intertwines with the mysteries of what happened to Professor Rossi during his research up to his mysterious disappearance in the 1950s and of a secret society—the Order of the Dragon—dedicated to preserving the secrecy of the Dracula legend. As a confrontation with Dracula becomes inevitable, the heroine also finds herself confronted with her own family's connection to the famous vampire and the realization that it might not be accidental that she became the historian. When the answers to all these mysteries begin to take shape, the reader is reminded of the narrator's suggestive warning in her opening remarks: "As an historian, I have learned that, in fact, not everyone who reaches back into history can survive it" (5).

One of the most noteworthy elements of the book is the author's extraordinary fidelity to descriptive detail in each of her varied settings, which also partially accounts for the novel's considerable length. Kostova provides readers with vivid accounts, for example, of the sights, sounds, and smells of each library the characters visit, each city they travel to, and each historical episode referenced, with the result that much of the novel, especially the introductory chapters to each section, reads like an actual textbook of eastern European history. And unlike the vampire novels of ANNE RICE, or even Bram Stoker's *Dracula*, *The Historian* is not crafted as an occult gothic saga. Gory as the vampire legend is, Kostova's novel is more light than dark, with an accessibility more akin to DAN BROWN's thriller *The DA VINCI CODE* than Stoker's *Dracula*.

Thematically, beyond a gentle romanticizing of the often quotidian work of historians, the novel's principal concern is the heroine's quest to discover the truth of her own history in her effort to solve the Dracula mystery, colored by the subtle irony that such historical inquiry is inextricably personalized around the historian herself. The author is also keen to deconstruct the stereotypical depictions of Dracula as an immortal bloodsucking monster, instead evoking a villain who in many ways resembles the protagonist, a fellow historical truth seeker who, in the words of the count, "became an historian in order to preserve my own history" (576); the novel's climax partly centers on the historian's discovery that what she is studying is also studying her.

ELIZABETH KOSTOVA famously spent 10 years writing the novel, her first, devoting much of her time to historical research in European libraries and archives. Her earlier work studying the folk cultures of Bulgaria is also on display in the novel's many descriptive passages of Eastern Europe. Like her unnamed character, Kostova's father brought her up with Dracula tales that ultimately inspired her to spin a literary work of her own. While completing her M.F.A. at the University of Michigan, Kostova won the university's Hopwood Award for a novel-in-progress for her manuscript of *The Historian*, and when it was finally released in June 2005, the novel's successes—a bidding war by publishing houses, translation into at least 28 languages, a quick ascent to number one on the *New York Times* best-seller list—attested as much to the author's intense and skillful labor as the current popularity of such historical thrillers. *The Historian* is slated for a film adaptation by Sony Pictures Entertainment.

Bibliography

Guthmann, Edward. "Vampires Lurk in Our Collective Imagination, as 'The Historian' Author Can Tell You." *San Francisco Chronicle*, 25 July 2005. Available online. URL: http://www.sfgate.com/cgi-bin/article.cgi?f=/c/a/2005/07/25/DDGBKDS8DC1.DTL &type=books. Accessed April 30, 2007.

Kostova, Elizabeth. *The Historian*. New York: Little, Brown, 2005.

Maslin, Janet. "Scholarship Trumps the Stake in Pursuit of Dracula." *The New York Times*, 13 June 2005. Available online. URL: http://query.nytimes.com/gst/fullpage.html?res=9C03E5D91E38F930A25755C0A96 39C8B63. Accessed April 30, 2007.

Rice, Anne. *Interview with the Vampire*. New York: Ballantine, 1976.

Stoker, Bram. *Dracula: The Author's Cut*. London: Creation Books, 2005.

Younge, Gary. "Bigger Than Dan Brown." *Guardian*, 18 July 2005. Available online. URL: http://books.guardian.co.uk/departments/generalfiction/story/0,6000,1530568,00.html. Accessed April 30, 2007.

Richard Alexander Johnson

The Hitchhiker's Guide to the Galaxy

Douglas Adams (1979)

The Hitchhiker's Guide to the Galaxy is a comic science-fiction novel, the first in a phenomenally successful and culturally significant series by the British humorist DOUGLAS ADAMS. The narrative combines aspects of Swiftian satire, absurdist humor, and surrealism with a more traditional approach to the parent genre, resulting in an affectionately parodic and self-referential mode of SF that remains hugely influential some 30 years after the novel first appeared.

It began life as a radio serial for the BBC, having been commissioned in 1977 and broadcast the following year; Adams's adaptation of his original scripts into book form incorporated a range of new ideas and some tweaking of the story but retained the episodic flavor of the series (much of Adams's later work would eschew this kind of linear storytelling for a more complex narrative approach, as in his *DIRK GENTLY'S HOLISTIC DETECTIVE AGENCY*).

The plot centers on the experiences of Arthur Dent, a hapless 30-something everyman who discovers on the same day that his best friend is an alien and that the Earth has been scheduled for demolition to make way for a hyperspace bypass. The novel takes its title from the publication for which Dent's friend Ford Prefect is a researcher, a pre-Internet electronic encyclopedia with the words "DON'T PANIC" inscribed in large, friendly letters on the front cover. Armed with the eccentrically edited and occasionally extremely unreliable guide, Arthur and Ford end up traveling the galaxy along with its eccentric president, the three-armed, two-headed Zaphod Beeblebox, his assistant Trillian (formerly Tricia McMillan of Earth), and Marvin, a clinically depressed robot (or "Paranoid Android") with a "brain the size of a planet" (74) and a dysfunctional personality to match. The characters travel to the mythical supposedly lost planet of Magrathea and discover that the recently vaporized Earth was in fact a massive organic computer constructed by the planet-building Magratheans to ascertain the Question to the Ultimate Answer (which is already known to be "Forty-Two" [128]). The "hyper-intelligent pan-dimensional beings" (119) behind this scheme turn out to be Frankie and Benjy, Trillian's pet mice, who plan to harvest Arthur's brain—the last remaining part of the Earth's 10-million-year program. The mismatched heroes escape and head for the Restaurant at the End of the Universe—the title of the next novel in the series—but the novel's rather abrupt ending leaves some of the key narrative strands conspicuously unresolved, the reason for which has often baffled readers. In his official biography of Adams, however, Nick Webb suggests it was simply a case of Pan Books finally losing patience with the author's famously cavalier approach to publishing schedules. Adams himself notes, "[T]hey said, very pleasantly and politely, that I had already passed ten deadlines, so would I please finish the page I was on and let them have the damn thing" (Webb 148).

The novel as a whole, then, is strongly influenced in its structure by the creative and economic circumstances surrounding its construction. This is not necessarily to its detriment, however, as its sprawling, episodic nature, carried over from the radio (and ultimately Dickensian) serial, lends the novel a page-turning momentum of suspense and narrative drive, while even the sudden conclusion merely served as an appetizer for sequel-hungry fans and arguably helped to fuel the *Hitchhiker's* hysteria already apparent at the end of the decade. It is easy to see the reasons for the novel's appeal. Although (contrary to initial assumptions among the fan fraternity) Adams was not steeped in either literary or cinematic SF traditions, his imagination, wit, and inventive take on the clichés of the genre offered an accessible and immensely attractive hybrid of genuine comedy and speculative fiction.

Thematically, the novel sets the reader adrift in a random and frequently ridiculous universe, mocking the pretensions of humankind to any kind of privileged position within the cosmos. Arthur, although a rather colorless and passive protagonist, serves as a transparent window through which one can observe frailties, neuroses, and impotence when faced with an uncaring world (or worlds). But rather than lamenting the unpredictability and plurality of the universe, *The Hitchhiker's Guide to the Galaxy* celebrates this randomness in its depiction of contemporary life as a perpetually surprising adventure while subtly exploring issues of religious faith in its revelation of that evolutionary marvel the Babel fish (which offers "final and clinching proof of the non-existence of God" [52]) and the philosophical blockbusters of the sceptical Oolon Colluphid (16). Although Adams had not yet fully embraced the radical atheism that would become explicit in his later books, his rejection here of any teleological, ordered cosmos is early evidence of what would become an obsession toward the end of his life.

Some of the book's conceptions—the Infinite Improbability Drive, for instance—demonstrate Adams's ability to combine boundless imagination with surprisingly rigorous and plausible technological speculation, but rarely are they deployed merely to demonstrate the breadth of Adams's scientific imagination; instead they are used, in a manner recalling Swift's *Gulliver's Travels,* as a means of satirizing contemporary concerns. The galactic scale and high-blown, Carl Sagan-esque delivery of the opening paragraphs, juxtaposed with the myopic and parochial perspective of humanity, offers a useful insight into this satirical strategy:

> *Far out in the uncharted backwaters of the unfashionable end of the western spiral arm of the Galaxy lies a small unregarded yellowsun. Orbiting this at a distance of roughly ninety-two million miles is an utterly insignificant little blue-green planet whose ape-descended life forms are so amazingly primitive that they still think digital watches are a pretty neat idea.*
>
> *This planet has—or rather had—a problem, which was this: most of the people living in it were unhappy for pretty much of the time. Many solutions were suggested for this problem, but most of these were largely concerned with the movements of small green pieces of paper, which is odd because on the whole it wasn't the small green pieces of paper that were unhappy* (15, italics original).

Similarly, the novel's Vogons symbolize a race whose technological advancements far outweigh their capacity to use that technology wisely, resulting in a boorish, philistinic (their poetry is "the third worst in the universe" [55]), and astonishingly bureaucratic culture. This makes them the ideal civil servants for the Imperial Galactic Government, and it is they who set the events of the novel into motion with their thoughtless (though frighteningly efficient) destruction of the Earth. It is this binary opposition between order and chaos—the conflict between the tin-pot bureaucracy of Prosser and the Vogons and the shambolic improvisation of Zaphod and Ford—which is at the heart of *Hitchhiker's* thematic structure; it is the novel's shameless embracing of the latter that accounts for much of its anarchic appeal.

The Hitchhiker's Guide to the Galaxy was followed by four books in the series, each one becoming slightly darker and more sophisticated, while perhaps unavoidably losing some of the kinetic energy and naïveté that had lent the original such charm (the final novel in the series, *Mostly Harmless,* is widely regarded as the most pessimistic novel in Adams's oeuvre). At the time of his death Adams was working on *The Salmon of Doubt,* which could have become either a sixth Hitchhiker's novel or a third Dirk Gently book. Since the novel was never completed, however, the end of *Mostly Harmless* marks a surprisingly downbeat conclusion to the series.

A film adaptation of *The Hitchhiker's Guide to the Galaxy* was released to mixed reviews in 2005. The novel has also been adapted to the stage on several occasions.

Bibliography

Adams, Douglas. *The Salmon of Doubt.* London: Pan, 2003.

———. *The Ultimate Hitchhiker's Guide: Five Novels and One Story.* New York: Gramercy Books, 2005.

Gaiman, Neil. *Don't Panic: Douglas Adams & The Hitchhiker's Guide to the Galaxy.* London: Titan Books, 2002.

The Hitchhiker's Guide to the Galaxy. Directed by Garth Jennings. Touchstone Pictures, 2005.

Simpson, M. J. *Hitchhiker: A Biography of Douglas Adams.* London: Hodder & Stoughton, 2003.

Webb, Nick. *Wish You Were Here: The Official Biography of Douglas Adams.* London: Headline, 2004.

Nicholas Dunlop

Hollywood Wives **Jackie Collins** (1983)

JACKIE COLLINS may not have coined the words *you can never be too rich or too thin,* but they could have been averred by any one of her ambitious blond female characters. Collins has earned worldwide fame for her evocation of these rich and beautiful "bitches," as well as her use of gossip magazines, pornography, and romance fiction as source material for her racy sex and shopping plots. While *Hollywood Wives* is no exception, the novel also explores how the lives of the "losers" play out in Hollywood's shallow and shiny plastic world. In a long and twisting tale of very different women and the men who love or use them (or both), secrets haunt the seemingly perfect world of Beverly Hills, acting as a dark backdrop to the personal dramas of characters whose lives seem to revolve around tanning appointments and clandestine affairs.

As the title suggests, the novel focuses on a group of three women. Angel, Elaine, and Montana are all married to Hollywood players. Angel, a sweet, lovely, and innocent Hawaiian blonde, falls in love with, marries, and swiftly becomes pregnant with the devastatingly handsome Buddy Hudson. Buddy has silver screen ambitions, and real talent, but has exaggerated his success to his new wife and is desperate to make his claims come true before she finds out she is in fact not married to a rising superstar. Elaine Conti's husband, Ross, has been much more successful than Buddy but is now relying on past successes, forgetting his lines and starting to look like a has-been. Elaine, perfectly groomed but preoccupied by the stress of hiding her rough childhood, would do anything to revive his career but is feeling rejected and looking for solace. Meanwhile, her husband is seeking excitement with young actresses, leaving Elaine to wonder if it is time to swap hairdressing appointments and aerobics for the arms of another man. The young and talented writer Montana, on the other hand, has lifted her once-great actor husband, Neil, out of a seedy Paris gutter, stood loyally by his side, and encouraged him; they are determined to rebuild his reputation. Unlike Elaine, however, Montana intends to stand beside her partner, not behind him, as a Hollywood powerhouse in her own right. The respective struggles of Angel, Elaine, and Montana provide the novel's central story lines, and the tale of each becomes increasingly interwoven with the others' as the plot grows in complexity.

However, the *Hollywood Wives* narrative palette is far from exhausted by the tales of its three heroines. Buddy has his own demons to contend with. Abused as a boy and desperate for vengeance on a world which, until Angel's appearance, had dealt him nothing but blows, he must somehow justify her trust and prove himself a breadwinner before he can think of himself as whole—all the while seeking a measure of revenge on the side. More poignant still are the voices of the women who never get to be Hollywood wives and the men whom the camera has left behind. Sadie LaSalle, for example, is the town's best agent, and it seems can have anyone (male or female) that she wants. But she wants no one, and readers learn why in learning more about Buddy and Ross, whose fates are inextricable from her own.

Indeed, the book begins not even near the rich compounds or secure mansions inhabited by the wives but in the suburbs where their husbands' films play on TV; here in the flickering glow of a television screen the ugly and rejected Deke Andrews violently murders three people:

> Sobs began to shake him violently. Strange silent sobs which convulsed his body as he wielded the machete. Dealing with all three of them equally. Indulging in a frenzy of grisly death blows.
>
> The television drowned out the sounds of the carnage. Archie Bunker. Canned laughter.
>
> And the machete continued to whirl and slash as if powered by some demonic force (10).

Deke's trail of fear finally and astonishingly becomes the link between all the wives, their husbands, and a host of other minor characters whose smaller-scale lives play out far from a camera's lens.

As with all of Collins's best sellers, *Hollywood Wives* is peppered with talk of shallow sex, gossip, popular songs, and movie stars, its characters always striving to speak and think purely in terms of the hermetic ethos of Beverley Hills; witness the "perfect" but dissatisfied Elaine: "Over the years she had changed. The nose was now retroussé, cute. A perfect Brooke Shields in fact . . . Her teeth were capped. White and even. A credit to Charlie's Angels" (14). But there are human touches to the tale as well. The wives come to realize that life can be lived on very different terms and that extraordinary and unforeseeable compromises may be exacted by love. Success and stardom are sometimes achieved, in fact, when no longer frenziedly sought, in a sober and mature recognition of the importance of familial affection, for example. The reader will, however, be more than a little surprised to find out just who is family to whom in the fast-paced climax. There are also moments, however rare, of human kindness. Gay hairdresser Koko and his partner, Adrian, for example, provide a surrogate family and home for a pregnant and desperate Angel, suggesting that even Collins's Hollywood has a heart, merely buried, perhaps, and well concealed within the realms of the powerful and ambitious.

Hollywood Wives was followed by the matching tale of *Hollywood Husbands*.

Bibliography

Collins, Jackie. *Hollywood Wives:* Suffolk: Pan, 1984. First edition Collins 1983.

———. *Hollywood Husbands:* London: William Heinemann, 1986.

Anne Brumley

Hooper, Kay (1957–)

Kay Hooper is the prolific author of richly textured popular crime fiction and mystery romances. She has authored five book series, including the Bishop/Special Crimes, the Quinn/Thief, the Men of Mysteries, the Once Upon a Time, and the Hagan series. Some of her best-selling novels include *Chill of Fear, Elusive, The Delaney Christmas Carol, Lady Thief,* and *Sleeping with Fear.* Hooper's trademark characters are investigators or romantic leads who exhibit some form of paranormal ability.

She was born in 1957 in California at the air force base where her father was stationed, but soon after, Hooper's family moved to North Carolina, where she and her younger brother and sister spent their childhood. On graduating from East Rutherford High School, Hooper attended Isothermal Community College in Spindale, North Carolina, where she soon learned that the business education she was pursuing did not spark her interest. Instead, she began taking history and literature classes, reading everything from Shakespeare, Agatha Christie, and Dorothy Sayers to Stephen King and Terry Pratchett; it was during the literature classes that she discovered her love for writing. After receiving a typewriter one Christmas, Hooper undertook her first serious writing project, a romance novel entitled *Lady Thief,* which she eventually published as a Regency Romance for Dell Publishing in 1980. She was 22 years old.

Hooper's stock and trade is romance, whether classical, with a paranormal slant, or ensconced in mystery and suspense; but she has also written numerous psychological and paranormal crime thrillers. Among her most notable works are the Hagen series, about a spymaster and his quest for the top position within his agency; the Once Upon a Time series, a collection of romantic mysteries; the Men of Mysteries Past, a mystery romance series; and her most famous, the Bishop/Special Crimes Unit series, which consists of nine novels beginning with the Shadows Trilogy (2000—*Stealing Shadows, Hiding in the Shadows* and *Out of the Shadows*). The series follows the investigations of an FBI special crimes unit under the direction of special agent and profiler Noah Bishop, but Hooper adds her own unique twist on the investigative techniques of the unit by weaving in paranormal abilities as part of each character, their skills ranging from telepathy and telekinesis to clairvoyance and psychometrics.

Hooper has written more than 60 novels and novellas and has contributed short stories to a variety of anthologies. She has also published three compilations of her early novels, including the most recent, *The Real Thing* (2004), by the Berkley Publishing Group, which is a reissue of two novels: *Enemy Mine* (1989) and *The Haviland Touch* (1991). She lives in a small town in North Carolina, and when not writing or reading she spends time with her seven beloved cats and two dogs. She loves baseball and movies and is active in her community, promoting literacy and working for the safe harbor and humane treatment of pets.

Bibliography

Hooper, Kay. *Elusive.* New York: HarperCollins, 1999.

———. *Hiding in the Shadows.* New York: Bantam, 2000.

———. *Stealing Shadows.* New York: Bantam, 2000.

———. *Out of the Shadows.* New York: Bantam, 2000.

———. *The Real Thing.* New York: Penguin, 2004.

———. *Enemy Mine.* New York: Penguin, 2005.

———. *The Haviland Touch.* New York, Penguin, 2005.

———. *Chill of Fear.* New York: Bantam, 2006.

———. *The Delaney Christmas Carol.* New York: Bantam, 2006.

———. *Lady Thief.* New York: Penguin, 2006.

Debbie Clare Olson

Hornby, Nick (1957–)

Hornby is the British author of the best-selling soccer memoir *Fever Pitch* (1992) and four novels, *High Fidelity* (1995), *About a Boy* (1998), *How to Be Good* (2001), and *A Long Way Down* (2005). He has also edited a short story collection, *Speaking with the Angel* (2001); penned an essay collection, *Songbook* (2003); and published two anthologies of his columns for *Believer* magazine, *Polysyllabic Spree* (2004) and its sequel *Housekeeping vs. The Dirt* (2006). He writes a monthly column for *Believer* called "Stuff I've Been Reading" and is also a frequent contributor to *The New Yorker* as a music critic.

Hornby was born near London into a middle-class English family in 1957. His father, a successful businessman, left the family for another woman, and Hornby grew up fatherless. He studied English literature at Cambridge University. After graduating, he worked as an English teacher and a freelance journalist in Cambridge and then London, writing for publications such as *Time Out, Literary Review, Esquire,* and *GQ.* His attraction to some of his early literary influences—Anne Tyler, Raymond Carver, Richard Ford, and Lorrie Moore—prompted him to try his hand at screenwriting and eventually novels.

By his own account Hornby did not believe he would be a successful writer when he began to pen *Fever Pitch* in his early 30s. A memoir of his childhood and young-adult life as it revolved around his beloved Arsenal football club, the book was a surprising hit in England and made Hornby an instant star. The book was noted especially for challenging two conventions: first, that an adult football fanatic was necessarily some kind of social deviant who could not find meaning in *real* life, and second, that young men could not be introspective and inquisitive of their emotional selves. *Fever Pitch* also established the trademark Hornby style—fluent, informal, and unadorned.

Thematically, the perpetually distressed child inside Hornby continued to grow in his first two novels, *High Fidelity* and *About a Boy.* Hornby continued to explore the frontiers of the male psyche with two successive main characters, one a record store owner, the other a do-nothing heir, each approaching middle age, struggling both with relationships and with the very idea of looking inward at himself. As Hornby later told an interviewer, these "first two [novels] couldn't have been written twenty-five years ago. Men writing about how they feel would not have been tolerated" (McGuigan). Separately, the novels tell us something else about the author. *High Fidelity* reveals Hornby's passion for music as both obsessive hobby and metaphor, similar to what soccer was for him in *Fever Pitch.* In *About a Boy,* in which the protagonist "adopts" a troubled kid in order to date single mothers, Hornby tepidly navigates themes of fatherhood and parenting formerly lacking in his portrayal of men.

In his two recent novels Hornby departs from traditional modes of storytelling. *How to Be Good*—a comic tale of a foul-mouthed father and husband who goes to absurd lengths to find spiritual rejuvenation—is narrated by a female character, a voice Hornby strove to authenticate by having countless women read his drafts. Engaging more mature themes that revolve around family rather than self—around parenthood rather than soccer—is terra incognita for Hornby. In terms of both sales and iconic status his recent novels have not had the success of his earlier work.

In *A Long Way Down* the story is told by four alternating narrators—three despondent Brits and one American likewise, each of whom has grown up to be a failure of some kind—who plan to commit suicide together. Once again Hornby employs a frank and humorous style to explore the depths of his characters' emotional distress.

Hornby's earliest literary success coincided with the birth of his son, Danny, who is autistic. In 1997 Hornby cofounded the TreeHouse Trust, a charity that works to provide education for children with autism. He created the short story collection *Speaking with the Angel* with the participation of 11 other writers to raise money and awareness for autism and his foundation.

Hornby won the William Hill Sports Book of the Year award for *Fever Pitch* (1992). He has received the E. M. Forster Award from the American Academy of Arts and Letters (1999) and Writer's Writer Award from the Orange Word International Writers Festival (2003). Though he has been favorably compared with Charles Dickens in his embracing humanism, Hornby's writing is more often mentioned in relation to that of HELEN FIELDING (*BRIDGET JONES'S DIARY*), Zadie Smith (*White Teeth*), and Martin Amis (*London Fields*).

Two of Hornby's novels have been adapted to film. *High Fidelity* (2000) with John Cusack and Jack Black transplanted the book's setting to the United States and was a minor box-office success. *About a Boy* (2003) with Hugh Grant was a major commercial success.

Before Hollywood fell in love with Hornby's prose, Britain's Channel Four Films adapted *Fever Pitch* to the screen in 1997, with Hornby penning the screenplay and Colin Firth playing the lead role. A limited U.S. release in 1999 grossed about $113,000. In 2005 the American filmmaking brothers Bobby and Peter Farrelly adapted *Fever Pitch* into a movie about the Boston Red Sox baseball team (2005, starring Drew Barrymore and Jimmy Fallon), though the brothers admit to not having read Hornby's book before they made the film. The latter *Fever Pitch* had a worldwide gross of $50 million.

Bibliography

Hornby, Nick. *Fever Pitch.* London: Gorancz, 1992.

———. *High Fidelity.* London: Riverhead, 1995.

———. *About a Boy,* London: Riverhead, 1998.

———. *How to Be Good.* London: Viking, 2001.

———. *Songbook.* London: Viking, 2003.

———. *A Long Way Down.* London: Viking, 2005.

McGuigan, Patrick. "Gender Trouble." Available online. URL: http://www.spikemagazine.com/0501nickhornby.php. Accessed January 5, 2007.

Richard Alexander Johnson

The Horse Whisperer Nicholas Evans (1995)

The Horse Whisperer, NICHOLAS EVANS's debut novel, was an immediate publishing sensation, earning the author a huge advance and with a 600,000-copy first printing. It spent 38 weeks on the best-seller list of *Publishers Weekly,* going on to sell 15 million copies worldwide and translated into 36 languages. The film rights were snapped up by Robert Redford for $3 million, which in 1994 was the largest amount ever paid for rights to a first novel. The story's mass-market appeal is immediately evident, encompassing as it does an old-fashioned tale of forbidden love within the day-to-day dynamics of family life, enmeshed in the trauma of a horrific road accident and a physically and psychologically damaged horse and young girl.

Young teenager Grace Maclean sets out for a ride on her horse, Pilgrim, with her best friend, Judith, on a beautiful snowy morning in rural Upstate New York; but a shortcut proves disastrous as both horses and riders find themselves hurtling down a steep slope, in effect an ice sheet masked by the newly fallen snow, and ultimately careening headlong into the path of a 40-ton truck. Judith and her horse are killed outright; Grace has a partial leg amputation and remains traumatized, unable to come to terms with the horror of the accident. The story now turns to the severely injured horse, Pilgrim, who instead of being put down is kept alive on the orders of Grace's mother, workaholic magazine editor Annie Maclean, for whom the accident proves to be a wake-up call to prioritize her life. She quickly comes to understand that the salvation of her daughter somehow lies in the physical and mental recovery of the horse.

Thus begins the search for a savior to work what amounts to a miracle on the damaged animal, a search taking the mother and daughter away from New York and lawyer husband/father, Robert, across the continent of North America and finally to the Montana ranch of Tom Booker, where, under the watchful eyes of the "horse whisperer," the scars—both physical and mental—of Pilgrim and Grace begin to heal.

It now becomes the turn of the mother, Annie, to confront her own personal issues as she and Booker fall in love. When her husband finally arrives in Montana after an absence of several weeks to see the progress made by his daughter, Evans produces a compelling denouement in keeping with the quasi-mystical, redemptive tone of the novel.

Three main thematic concerns dominate the novel: trust, love, and the dynamics of family relationships. At its start the Maclean family is already dysfunctional and untrusting, but as the tale unfolds, the physical effects of the accident on both family and horse are eclipsed by its spiritual effects, beginning with Annie's seemingly unreasonable, even foolish desire not to have Pilgrim put down: "Perhaps this need she felt to keep Pilgrim alive, to find someone who could calm his troubled heart, wasn't about Grace at all. Perhaps it was about herself" (101). The real healing, then, is ultimately a spiritual one: "It wasn't only Pilgrim's fate that was to be determined today by this stranger, it was the fate of all of them. Grace's, Robert's and her own" (133).

So begins the journey of self-discovery for Annie that leads her to the door of Tom Booker, who "understood the languages of horses in the same way he understood the difference between colors or smells" (112). With Booker Evans introduces a mystical element to the novel: "[Tom] felt himself simply part of a pattern, a cohesion of things animate and inanimate, to which he was connected both by spirit and by blood" (124). The impression given is that Booker is not quite of this world, that he is essentially different from other men and therefore not bound by their commonplace rules and conventions.

Nor is the choice of the horse's name an arbitrary one: "It was then [Annie] noticed, among the pile of books and magazines [. . .] the copy of *Pilgrim's Progress* Liz Hammond's cousins had given her" (284). This book by John Bunyan, first published in 1678, is an allegorical novel that sees its protagonist Christian (whose name was previously "*Grace*less") journey from the "City of Destruction" (Earth) to the "Celestial City" (Heaven). And in the story of the horse's gradual recovery from his terrible injuries, readers may note a similar kind of allegory, here ending in the healing of the Maclean family, body and soul, not so much in a traditional religious sense, but rather with the aid of the New Age Tom Booker as their salvation. Thus, it was the memory of Bunyan's book that led Annie "to call Diane to ask if she and Grace could come to church. However, the urge [. . .] had little, if anything to do with religion—it had to do with Tom Booker" (285).

In its latter stages the novel takes on an almost fatalistic quality, with the characters assuming a puppetlike stature, so implicit is their trust in Booker and so total, if subtle, is his influence. Annie is the only character other than Booker himself who senses that events are beginning to exceed anyone's deliberate control, and that sheer trust is the key to salvation: "It seemed to Annie, and would always seem, that in what followed there was no element of choice" (311). Her growing love for Tom is juxtaposed with guilt over betraying her husband, yet the power to turn away from Tom is beyond her: "And in the sharing quiet of that moment Annie knew she could not leave this man" (375).

In 1998 Robert Redford directed and starred in the lead role of the film, which also featured Kristen Scott Thomas as Annie, Sam Neill as Robert, and a young Scarlett Johansson as Grace. The film was a commercial success, grossing $187 million worldwide, with even hostile critics acknowledging the beauty of its cinematography, depicting the visually stunning Montana landscape so well evoked in the novel. At nearly three hours in length it gave Redford the opportunity to explore most of the novel's plot and themes but with a curiously more pedestrian and depressing ending than is found in the novel.

Evans has published three further novels since *The Horse Whisperer*—*The Loop* (1998), *The Smoke Jumper* (2001), and *The Divide* (2005), which have all been international best sellers.

Bibliography

Evans, Nicholas. *The Horse Whisperer:* New York: Delacorte, 1995.

———. *The Loop:* New York: Delacorte, 1998.

———. *The Smoke Jumper:* New York: Delacorte, 2001.

———. *The Divide:* New York: Putnam, 2005.

Gerri Kimber

The Hotel New Hampshire

John Irving (1981)

On the surface *The Hotel New Hampshire* is an eccentric, sometimes blackly comic family saga told at a madcap pace. Beneath this turbulent surface, however, it is a thoughtful and nuanced meditation on one family's resourceful, stubborn, and ultimately noble capacity to survive. In structure the book is straightforward. Plot-driven, vast, and often Dickensian in tone, the tale is narrated by John Berry, the family's middle child. As an adult, looking back on his childhood, he feels the need to "set the record straight, or nearly straight" and believes that he is the one to do it because, in his estimation, he is the "least opinionated" (1).

His chronological narrative begins with a favorite family story, that of his parents' charmed romance. In the summer of 1939 two teenagers go to work at Arbuthnot-on-the-Sea, an inn on the coast of Maine. Winslow Berry and Mary Bates do not know each other, despite hailing from the same hometown, Daisy, New Hampshire. Temperamentally unsuited to each other—he prone to dreaming, she to practicalities—they share two extraordinary experiences on the very day they meet: First, they are captivated by a man they will come to refer to as "our Freud," a Viennese Jew who travels about on a motorcycle with a performing bear; later that same evening they are sitting on the inn's dock when a yacht suddenly appears and a man in a white dinner jacket holds a brief conversation with them, then disappears after warning them that "[Soon] the *world's* going to be no place for *bears*!" (14).

Despite this warning, Win and Mary soon settle down and start a family, their first three children, Frank, Franny, and John, born in quick succession ("Bang! Bang! Bang!" as the children later describe their arrival). Then come Lilly and Egg ("Pop and Fizzle" [2]), and for a time the family's life is relatively normal. Everything changes, however, when Win persuades his wife that they should buy an abandoned girls' school and make it into what they call the Hotel New Hampshire; henceforth the family will subsist in a perpetual domestic half-life in an unending succession of hotels. Although refurbishing the first proves challenging, the family thrives until the three older children become adolescents, when the plot distends more than thickens. First, the family finds out that Lilly, who they always thought just small for her age, is actually a dwarf; then a barely pubescent John loses his virginity to a much older woman, even as he falls in love with his sister; then Franny is gang-raped, and the tone of the novel, as if suspended thus far by some false illumination, becomes abruptly darker.

"Our Freud" reenters the picture, writing to beseech Win to move his family to Vienna in order to help run yet another hotel, and ever the dreamer, Win talks Mary into going. Mary and Egg die en route, the latter having to die, according to the author in an interview, because she was the only adult with a "firm grip on reality" (*New York Times on the Web*); had she made it to Vienna, she would have realized at once that Freud's hotel—which renamed will be the second Hotel New

Hampshire—is both a brothel and home to a pod of radical malcontents and would have had her family turn round and return to the United States.

Without her, the rest of the family simply settles in, making do, as ever, making sensible madness out of the raw material. Frank, Franny, John, and Lilly finish their schooling and go to college, spending a great deal of time coming to terms with their sexualities; Franny and John being well aware of the dangers of their relationship, and Frank wrestling with his homosexuality. Lilly's time, on the other hand, is consumed by writing a coming-of-age novel, which suddenly becomes highly prized after the family foils a dastardly plot to blow up the Vienna Opera House, becoming celebrities.

The sudden reversal of their fortunes means they can now return to the United States, where they move into New York's luxurious Stanhope Hotel. Here they begin at last, each in their way, to confront the recalcitrant truths of the quotidian world, with a profoundly comic credo, worthy of the author of *Tom Jones:* "The way the world worked—which was badly—was just a strong incentive to live purposefully, and to be determined about living well." In a fitting conclusion to the novel's weirdly classical plotline, John purchases Arbuthnot-by-the-Sea and turns it into a rape-crisis center (his now blind father believing, however, that it is serving as a third Hotel New Hampshire).

Like Dickens, with whom for all his postmodern contemporaneity he has much in common, Irving is a novelist most noted for his storytelling ability, once telling an interviewer from *Mother Jones*: "I believe a novel should be as complicated and involved as you're capable of making it." And certainly *The Hotel New Hampshire* inscribes many surprising and daunting elements, including a great deal of foreshadowing, snatches of Donald Justice's poetry, multiple allusions to *The Great Gatsby,* and a welter of unresolved leitmotifs, such as speculations on the meaning of sorrow and references to passing open windows. But for many readers it is the strange but persistent afterglow of his characterization that lingers on in memory.

The Hotel New Hampshire was John Irving's fourth novel, written during the period when his third, *The World According to Garp,* appeared on the best-seller list and made him famous. His earlier novels had achieved critical success but only small sales. *Garp* was both wildly popular and well received by critics; thus *The Hotel New Hampshire* was highly anticipated, with *Time* magazine devoting a six-page spread to Irving on the eve of its publication. Its reception, however, was and remains profoundly mixed, some critics complaining about its rambling length and apparent fascination with the bizarre, others highly praising it, including one of Irving's favorite living writers, Robertson Davies. Irving himself takes great pride in the novel, which he considers more significant than *Garp,* likening the latter work to a fairy tale in its evocation of a world unto itself, complete with its own rules and logic, much like that of Dickens's *Pickwick Papers,* which once entered is never truly left behind. Such worlds house this one, instead of the other way round.

As is the norm for popular fiction, readers paid little attention to the critics in any case, embracing *The Hotel New Hampshire* with enthusiasm, many noting that its plot was much like the one T. S. Garp—the protagonist of *The World According to Garp*—planned to write near the end of his life and delighting in elements reminiscent of Irving's earlier fiction, from talismanic bears to prep schools, New England, and Vienna. The novel quickly became a best seller and soon appeared in paperback, as well as being picked up by the Book-of-the-Month Club. In 1984 it was made into a popular movie starring Jodie Foster, Rob Lowe, and Beau Bridges.

Bibliography

Herel, Suzanne. "John Irving Interview." Available online. URL: http://www.motherjones.com/arts/qa/1997/05/outspoken.html. Accessed November 17, 2006.

Ann Gaines

How Stella Got Her Groove Back

Terry L. McMillan (1981)

How Stella Got Her Groove Back is the fourth novel by best-selling African-American novelist TERRY MCMILLAN. The highly successful novel sparked a rise in tourism to Jamaica by black women, spawned a money-making 1998 Twentieth Century Fox movie starring Angela Bassett, Taye Diggs, and

Whoopi Goldberg, and introduced "get your groove back" to the lexicon.

Forty-two-year-old Stella Payne yearns to "put the fizz back" into her life. The recently divorced, highly successful Payne feels numb. Having recently packed her son, Quincy, off for a summer visit to his father, Stella decides to slow down the hectic pace of her life and take a breather. As the book begins, Stella is trying to "run the vacuum through my mental house and chill out," but fails, focusing instead on the tasks she can accomplish during her son's absence. Exhausted by the thought of trying to get her life on track, Stella collapses into a chair. There she sees a tourism ad harkening, "Come to Jamaica," and makes a decision with profound consequences.

The novel begins in stream of consciousness, a literary technique characterized by intensely immediate, first-person internal narration of the character's thoughts and feelings. While some commentators criticized the opening chapter as self-indulgent and clumsy, others praised it as an evolution in McMillan's realist style, allowing her reader even more and more intimate access to Stella's mind. McMillan irreverently employs the same technique to parrot her critics:

> [. . .] I don't know what all the hoopla is about and why everybody thinks she's such a hot writer because her shit is kind of weak when you get right down to it and this book here has absolutely no literary merit whatsoever at least none that I can see and she uses entirely too much profanity. Hell, I could write the same stuff she writes cause she doesn't exactly have what you'd call a style but anyway I can sort of relate to some of her characters [. . .] (60).

According to McMillan, the story grew in part out of her own difficulty finding a compatible black man for a significant romantic relationship. Worn out by the success of *Waiting to Exhale,* her effort to write a screenplay adaptation of the novel, and the deaths of both her mother, Madeline Tillman, and lifelong friend, Doris Jean Austin, McMillan decamped to Jamaica for a well-deserved, "first real" vacation. While there she met and became infatuated with 20-year-old Jonathan Plummer. The relationship blossomed, and Plummer moved to the United States. In 1998 McMillan and Plummer married; the union ended dramatically in 2005 with the revelation of Plummer's homosexuality but left a profound impression on McMillan's work.

Stella Payne is a classic McMillan heroine, a smart, attractive, highly capable, successful financial analyst who drives a BMW M-5 racing car and lives in a spacious Phoenix home filled with funky furnishings and one-of-a-kind art. She has also been bruised and battered by the effort to build a successful relationship: "I know God didn't have some master plan when we were supposed to fall in love and then work our asses off to make it work and then it doesn't and then we end up feeling worse longer than we felt good" (12). Exhausted by the effort required to hold her life together, Stella decides to heed that ad. Youngest sister, Vanessa, mother of teenage Chantel, enthusiastically urges Stella to get out and get on with her life. The settled middle sister, Angela, pregnant by her second husband whom she "worships" (22) warns Stella against leaving her highly successful job for an impromptu nine-day vacation in Jamaica. Vanessa, however, prods her on: "I just want you to know that I'm proud of you, Sis, for finally doing something spontaneous and doing something for *you.* It's about damn time" (33).

Soon after she arrives at the sun-drenched all-inclusive Castle beach resort in Negril, Jamaica, Stella encounters Winston Shakespeare, a soon-to-be 21-year-old college student angling for an internship in the kitchen at the hotel. Over lunch they chat, and Winston invites Stella out, much to her amazement: "Is he flirting with me? No, he couldn't be flirting with me. I'm old enough to be his mother! And what could he possibly want from me that he can't get from some young chicks around here, like that fox over there, for instance? On the other hand, he's right. I came here to have some fun, so why not have some?" (53). Soon Stella, for all her age and experience, is thoroughly smitten. She spends the night with Winston, only to learn the next day that he has to leave the resort to start his cooking job at another hotel. "Whenever things feel too good to be true it's usually because they are," she dryly remarks (128). Deeply wounded, Stella overcomes her disappointment to see Winston once more before she leaves. Like other McMillan heroines Stella is tough and accomplished but realizes that she has to revise her attitude and expectations or risk losing her chance at this unconventional romance.

After she returns from Jamaica, Stella learns that she has been downsized yet still cannot shake Winston's spell. Instead, reinvigorated by the blossoming romance, she decides to pursue her artistic career, long ago abandoned in favor of a high-paying analyst job. About a month later she returns to the island with her son and niece in tow, and while there she shares her newfound purpose with Winston:

> I want to find my place in the world [. . .]. I want to love a man so hard it feels soft and I want him to know that it ain't over till the fat lady sings. I want to see how far I can go alone and how far I can go with someone else. I want to be smarter. I want to be the best mother friend sister lover I can be (243).

When the trip reveals that Stella and Winston still have strong feelings for each other, they decide to take a chance. Winston's own three-week visit ends with a proposal and the promise of a new life together.

Like many of McMillan's novels *How Stella Got Her Groove Back* follows the heroine's transformation from emotional exhaustion to renewal. Many African-American women identified with Stella's "superwoman syndrome," her striving to balance home, work, and family without breaking a sweat. However, in order to allow her love with Winston to develop, she must become vulnerable and willing to defy the very conventions that have hitherto shaped her life. The novel concludes on a cautiously optimistic note, suggesting that while a groove can be misplaced, it is never entirely lost.

Bibliography

McMillan, Terry. *How Stella Got Her Groove Back.* New York: Viking, 1996.

Rychetta Watkins

The Hunt for Red October

Tom Clancy (1984)

The Hunt for Red October, TOM CLANCY's first novel, was something of a surprise best seller (it was the first work of fiction published by the specialist Naval Institute Press). However, its tale of cold war intrigue at sea caught the nation's zeitgeist, and the book became enormously popular, claiming among its enthusiastic readership then U.S. president Ronald Reagan and launching the eventful fictional career of Jack Ryan, a military historian who in subsequent books ascends through the CIA to the White House. It also spawned a new genre to describe the distinctive qualities of Clancy's work: the techno-thriller.

The *Red October* is a Soviet missile submarine, the first of its kind, which features a new propulsion system dubbed "the caterpillar," rendering it almost invisible to detection by conventional methods. The submarine's commander, Marko Ramius, is a star in the Soviet navy, the highly regarded "test pilot of submarines" (38). However, he is also a man with a lifelong grudge against the Soviet system, who has conspired with his senior officers to defect to the United States while striking a blow against the Soviet Union by stealing its latest technological prize. In order to ensure that his superiors fully understand the gesture, Ramius leaves behind a letter revealing his plan, thus prompting a pursuit involving virtually all of the Soviet Union's Atlantic fleet—activity that eventually comes to the attention of the British and American authorities. Jack Ryan, a CIA liaison based in London, is uniquely placed to engineer the Western allies' response to the crisis, and thus an erstwhile academic finds himself thrust into the hunt, trying first to read Ramius's intentions and then to ensure that both commander and submarine arrive safely into American hands.

When readers first encounter Jack Ryan—naval historian and family man—he seems an unlikely action hero. However, no stranger to intrigue, Ryan had earlier stumbled upon a terrorist plot in London (a story Clancy later tells in *Patriot Games*), and his conduct on that occasion earned him an honorary knighthood and the attention of the CIA, for whom he became a member of a joint American-British liaison group. Earlier still, Ryan had earned an officer's rank in the U.S. Marines, although his career was cut short by a helicopter crash that left him with a lingering fear of flying. Plucked from his desk job and plunged into a world of adventure and danger, Ryan is an insider-outsider, a courageous patriot whose military past earns him the respect and admiration of his fellow cold warriors.

On the other side of the cold war divide is Marko Ramius, who commands the *Red October.* So embittered by Soviet life that he is driven to a spectacular act of treason, Ramius is the primary vehicle through which Clancy presents his view of a hopeless and inhumane Soviet system. Ramius's father, a Lithuanian, was a Communist hero of the Stalin era owing to his role in the purge of anti-Soviet dissidents in his native country following the 1940 Soviet invasion. In his son's eyes the elder Ramius's betrayal of his people is a source of shame, and the hypocrisy underlying his father's heroic reputation opens his eyes to a more general hypocrisy, alienating him from his familiar world: "As a boy, Ramius sensed more than thought that Soviet Communism ignored a basic human need. In his teens, his misgivings began to take a coherent shape. The Good of the People was a laudable enough goal, but in denying a man's soul, an enduring part of his being, Marxism stripped away the foundation of human dignity and individual value" (31). When Ramius's beloved wife, Natalia, dies—the victim of an inept and corrupt Soviet medical system—Ramius is finally driven to his act of revenge.

The failure of Soviet communism, a principal theme in the novel, is articulated through a series of military and diplomatic contests between East and West—although the overwhelming superiority of the West is never seriously in doubt. Thus, while the Soviet's caterpillar drive is portrayed as an impressive advance, the *Red October* is nonetheless quickly detected by Ronald Jones, the sonar operator aboard the USS *Dallas.* Technically, Jones has violated navy regulations in order to make his discovery, but his success is rewarded with praise and promotion. Time and again the West prevails because of its encouragement and reward of just such individual and often unpredictable initiative. Among Clancy's Soviets, however, the picture is very different. Initiative is stymied by a bureaucratic system in which "every worker is a government worker" (22), and the culture is one of surveillance, suspicion, and fear; the Party has eyes and ears everywhere in the form of political officers as well as undercover agents aboard every ship. The USSR is represented as a virtual prison, standing in gray, ugly contrast to Clancy's rosy depiction of the United States.

Though his politics may be rather simple, Clancy's narrative method is complex, featuring multiple, parallel strands, with frequent jumps from one locale and one set of characters to another. Thus, while the novel follows a tight time line, with its events unfolding over 18 days, the narrative shifts rapidly between Moscow, Washington, and Britain, as well as American planes, ships, and submarines at various points in and over the Atlantic Ocean. The effect of this structure, typical of Clancy's fiction, is to represent the military itself as a kind of organic presence in the novel, comprising and encompassing countless individuals who contribute to an enterprise greater than them all. The all-embracing nature of the military is also suggested through the novel's style, with its extensive use of the jargon of military bureaucracy, including a plethora of acronyms that leave some readers bewildered but heighten the realism of the tale. The overall effect is to establish and normalize the perspective of a military insider, achieving at points an almost documentarylike quality—a quality further enhanced by the attention Clancy devotes to the workings of military technology itself, the tendency that led to the coining of the term *techno-thriller.*

The world of the novel is an emphatically masculine one; female characters are few in number and relegated to minor roles. Both Ramius and Ryan are presented as devoted husbands, but the book is far more concerned with relationships between men, who bond with one another as surrogate fathers and sons. This father-son dynamic informs the relationship between Ryan and his superior and mentor, CIA Deputy Director for Intelligence Vice Admiral Greer, as well as that of Bart Mancuso, commander of the USS *Dallas,* with the young sonar operator Ronald Jones. Ramius, too, had his surrogate father, a former officer in the czar's navy who taught the young Ramius the basics of seamanship that would eventually lead to his distinguished naval career. And Ramius, in turn, has two surrogate sons: his navigator and coconspirator, Grigoriy Kamarov, and the Soviet loyalist who is his most determined pursuer, Viktor Tupolev. This emphasis on homosocial networks, combined with the novel's uncomplicated patriotism, suggests a link between *The Hunt for Red October* and the tradition of masculine romance. For all its emphasis on modern technologies, Clancy's first novel has antecedents among the thrillers of Henry Rider Haggard and John Buchan.

A successful 1990 film adaptation of *The Hunt for Red October* was directed by John Tiernan and starred Sean Connery as Ramius and Alec Baldwin as Jack Ryan. Both the book and subsequent film were adapted as video games released in 1988 and 1991.

Bibliography

Clancy, Tom. *The Hunt for Red October.* 1984. Reprint, New York: Berkley, 1985.

Garson, Helen S. *Tom Clancy: A Critical Companion.* Westport, Conn. and London: Greenwood Press, 1996.

Greenberg, Martin H., ed. *The Tom Clancy Companion.* New York: Berkley, 1992.

Brian Patton

I

The Icarus Agenda Robert Ludlum (1988)
The Icarus Agenda explores themes familiar to readers of political thrillers: the fraught relationship between the Arab world on the one hand, and Israel and the United States on the other; the responsibility of individuals in the midst of dangerous political currents; and the complications arising from the presence of secret organizations operating within a supposedly open and democratic society. The book begins in the midst of an international crisis that echoes a then recent historical event, the seizure of American hostages by Iranian radicals in Tehran in 1979. Ludlum's crisis erupts in Masqat, Oman, where 247 Americans have been taken hostage in the American embassy. Their Arab captors are demanding the release of thousands of prisoners belonging to organizations including the Red Brigade, the PLO, the Baader-Meinhof, and the IRA and have already demonstrated their readiness to execute their prisoners. As the novel opens, the hostage takers have suspended these executions for one week, two days of which have already passed when the central character, Evan Kendrick, appears on the scene.

A rookie congressman for Colorado's Ninth District, Kendrick is an atypical Washingtonian but typical thriller protagonist. Unshaven, unbathed, and dressed for his annual solitary wilderness expedition, he has just learned of the hostage crisis and hastened back to the capital to offer his services. His experience of Southwest Asia is vast, owing to his former role as head of the Kendrick Group, "the American wonder boys in the Emirates" (13), a handful of young architects and engineers responsible for projects ranging from water systems and bridges to housing developments. Four years earlier, the Kendrick Group was devastated by an apparent accident: An explosion caused a cave-in during the celebration of a new project, killing 70 people, including nearly all of the company's partners, employees, and their families. The sole survivors were Kendrick and his irascible mentor, an octogenarian Bronx Jew named Manny Weingrass, a brilliant architect and former Mossad agent. Weingrass saw the accident for what it was, an early sign of a new force in the region—an operative who had taken on the messianic name of "the Madhi," like the Muslim leader whose army drove the British from Khartoum in 1885. However, in the wake of so many deaths, Kendrick had no desire to stay and confront an enemy whose existence he did not recognize. Now however, convinced that the Mahdi is behind the Masqat crisis, Kendrick is ready to return and fight. Disguised in local costume and with his skin artificially darkened, Kendrick is able to penetrate deeply into the Mahdi's organization, gain access to the captured embassy, and—with the assistance of Weingrass, the elite Israeli Masada Brigade, and the beautiful and highly skilled CIA operative Adrienne "Khalehla" Rashad—bring down the self-styled Mahdi in the climax of the first of the novel's three major sections.

The novel's second book is set one year later, with Kendrick back in Washington working out his congressional term in virtual anonymity until his secret service in Masqat is discovered by the members of Inver Brass, a secret cabal that Ludlum introduced in *The Chancellor Manuscript* (1977). The five members of Inver Brass are self-appointed guardians of the republic, a supposedly disinterested extra-governmental group devoted to the betterment of the nation and the world. Collectively, they decide that the nation needs Evan Kendrick, whom they will quietly promote as the next vice president, a position from which he will step into the Oval Office itself. In their clandestine campaign to reveal Kendrick's qualities to the populace, however, they also reveal his hitherto secret activities in the Gulf of Oman and galvanize the political opposition, the wealthy supporters of the corrupt vice presidential incumbent, Orson Bollinger. Bollinger's supporters, who stand to benefit from the large arms contracts that Bollinger's policies would guarantee, work covertly to bring Kendrick's Arab enemies into the United States, where they stage a series of deadly attacks on Kendrick's associates but fail to eliminate Kendrick himself. Drawn once again into the world of covert operations and secret organizations, Kendrick again manages to discover and root out the source of corruption.

The shorter third book returns to the Middle East, where a new threat has arisen in the wake of the Mahdi's defeat: Abdel Hamendi, an arms dealer working in league with Bollinger's former backers, whose apparent aim is to sustain a profitable state of chaos in the Middle East. Working with some of the Mossad agents he first encountered in Oman, Khalehla, and the Sultan of Oman himself, Kendrick disrupts a major arms deal, leaving "the king of the court of international arms merchants" (664) dead and utterly discredited.

The novel's title invokes the Greek myth of Icarus, the son of the inventor and architect Daedalus, who engineered their escape from King Minos of Crete by fashioning wings from feathers and wax. Despite his father's warning that they must take care to fly midway between the sun and the sea, the young Icarus flew too close to the sun, which melted his wings and sent him plummeting to his death. Ludlum reframes this allegory about the dangers of human ambition within a political context. Having selected Kendrick as the nation's next vice president (and eventual president), Inver Brass assign him the code name "Icarus, to be taken as a warning . . . that he will not, as so many of his predecessors have done, try to fly too close to the sun and crash into the sea" (242). However, while Kendrick remains uncorrupted by the allure of power, the members of Inver Brass are themselves guilty of overreaching in operating as an unelected "government within the government" (502). While the aims of most of their membership are benevolent, their means of achieving those ends are clearly at odds with democratic principles. Manny Weingrass describes the cabal as "a bunch of servants running the master's house" and urges Kendrick to "find the bastards and rip them *out*" (502). Ironically, the novel itself seems less certain of its absolute commitment to the democratic ideal. The *demos* as portrayed by Ludlum is very easily influenced, and in the end, regardless of their questionable methods, the ultimate goal of Inver Brass—to steer Kendrick into the vice president's office—has been achieved and is seen by all as a positive outcome.

ROBERT LUDLUM attempts a balanced and liberal view of the Arab/Israeli conflict, suggesting that neither group has a monopoly on suffering, and working throughout the novel to individualize and personalize the broader historical narrative offers glimpses into the private lives of characters who have been variously shaped by this ongoing dispute. Cross-cultural communication and understanding are proffered as the long-term means to a solution, and Ludlum offers a series of progressive models, including Khalehla, Manny, and the American-educated Sultan of Oman and his white American wife. The epitome of cross-cultural understanding, though, is Kendrick himself, who is described at one point as "a modern-day Lawrence." Like the Orientalist adventurers of the imperial thrillers of a century ago—figures like Sandy Arbuthnot in John Buchan's *Greenmantle* (1916), who knows those Arab Others as they know themselves and so can merge seamlessly into their society—Kendrick's superior understanding of the Muslim world allows him to enter secret enclaves and win the love and trust of those who have every reason to be suspicious of the West. Ludlum's portrait of the benevolent capitalist working to bring peace and order to the Arab world recalls those earlier, discredited British imperial fantasies and resuscitates them in a contemporary American context.

Bibliography

Buchan, John. *Greenmantle.* 1916. Reprint, London: Thomas Nelson and Sons, 1922.

Ludlum, Robert. *The Icarus Agenda.* 1988. Reprint, New York: Bantam, 1989.

Macdonald, Gina. *Robert Ludlum: A Critical Companion.* Westport, Conn. and London: Greenwood Press, 1997.

Brian Patton

I'll Take Manhattan Judith Krantz (1986)

I'll Take Manhattan is a romantic and often sensational romp that follows the struggles and successes of the story's heroine Maxime Amberville. The energetic, flamboyant, and "unpardonably pretty" Maxi is the daughter of magazine mogul Zachary Amberville (7). Already divorced three times by the age of 29, she still manages to live a carefree life of pleasure and indulgence. However, this all changes after her father's sudden death when Maxi faces hardship for the first time. Though her widowed mother, Lily Amberville, is left in control of the family empire, she hastily marries Zachary's brother (Maxi's uncle) Cutter. Long jealous of his more successful brother, Cutter manipulates Lily and secretly initiates a strategy to break up and sell the company. Unwilling to watch her father's lifework be destroyed and aware of Cutter's true character, Maxi rallies her two brothers, Toby and Justin, along with several loyal employees, in protest of Cutter. Though he folds three magazines immediately, Cutter reluctantly allows Maxi to take over her father's first publication, the now struggling *Buttons and Bows.* Shedding her immature ways, Maxi reinvents herself *and* the magazine, making the revamped *B&B* an instant hit. Soon after, Lily learns of Cutter's true motives and his role in Zachary's death. She divorces him and decides that instead of selling the company, she will put Maxi in charge of it.

JUDITH KRANTZ's fiction most often revolves around a flawed but lovable heroine. However, as the title of her autobiography, *Sex and Shopping: The Confessions of a Nice Jewish Girl,* might suggest, glamour and lust also play key roles in her work. Her novels are structured in a way that makes them easily adaptable into television miniseries, as with *I'll Take Manhattan,* in 1987. They generally have a large, closely related cast; include detailed and connected subplots; and follow a format in which a conflict is introduced early on, followed by an extended exposition, a turning point, and ultimately an epiphany or revelation with a happy ending; in all of which respects *I'll Take Manhattan* is perfectly typical. The novel's title is a play on the Rodgers and Hart song "Manhattan," from 1925. The line "We'll have Manhattan, the Bronx and Staten Island too" is frequently misquoted, as Krantz is well aware, and the song is even often referred to today as "I'll Take Manhattan" (Groce 19). It is this inaccurate version of the song that a young ambitious Zachary Amberville sings when he first arrives in New York City: "I'll take Manhattan, the Bronx and Staten Island too" (29). A classic rags to riches story follows, as Zachary quickly creates Amberville Publications and is already a millionaire many times over before meeting Lily. However, the main narrative focuses on Maxi, and her story is meant to echo that of her father's. She even sings the same "I'll take Manhattan" lyrics—the lyrics as he taught them to her—after she takes over *B&B* (121). Of course the obvious difference between Maxi and her father is that she starts off unthinkably rich and highly *un*motivated. It is the latter, *figuratively* destitute state that foreshadows her evolution toward the more mature Maxi, who concludes the novel enriched with a sense of purpose and drive.

While the story is meant to be fantastic and somewhat escapist, the challenge Krantz is faced with is making the reader identify and even empathize with the privileged heiress. To overcome this, Krantz creates a reversal and has Maxi identify with "the common woman," the turning point coming when Maxi must decide what sort of magazine she wants *B&B* to be. While flipping through dozens of her former favorite publications, she becomes disgusted by the trend she observes in the images: "Almost nobody can look like that; wear those damn clothes; use that crazy new makeup; have houses like that . . . they're selling putdowns" (242). The irony is that Maxi *can* look like that, wear those clothes and that makeup, and have those houses. In fact, she does. However, in a sudden revelation, she asks, "God damn it to hell, isn't there a single magazine a woman can buy that loves her just the way she is?" (246). Since there is not, Maxi creates one—*B&B*—with articles the likes of "Living Well: Eating, Drinking and Having Sex" (265).

It should be noted that Krantz worked for several major fashion and lifestyle magazines before becoming an author. However, she seems hesitant to pursue Maxi's criticism of her former industry, and this theme regarding the images of women presented in the media is for the most part abandoned. Still, the scene brings the larger-than-life Maxi down to a relatable level (where she remains for the rest of the novel), while also serving the greater purpose of the novel—to entertain. Like *B&B*, *I'll Take Manhattan* is all about allowing imperfection and "exists for your pleasure and *only* your pleasure" (246). However, the success of the novel depends on whether or not Maxi's early acts of "extracting the greatest amount of fun that could still be found of the planet Earth" are redeemable (15). For example, she gives herself sexually to a customs inspector in exchange for a quick pass at the airport. Also, with her daughter from her first marriage still a toddler, she rashly remarries twice while on extravagant vacations around the world. The reader is asked to find amusement in these episodes—as Maxi does—and excuse them in light of her eventual transformation. The sensational quality of the work as a whole and the well-constructed loving relationships between Maxi and her family make this possible.

The novel, like its heroine, has flaws. While a feminist reading could focus on Maxi's success in a male-dominated industry, it must necessarily question whether this is not undermined by the emphasis placed on her physical beauty and charms, an emphasis seemingly echoed in the very magazine images of women she herself criticizes. In addition, there is the swift reunion between Maxi and her first husband, Rocco Cipriani, which concludes the novel. Though their relationship is developed throughout the story as he helps Maxi start *B&B*, the remarriage is surprising. Maxi had vowed "never, ever to marry *another* man"; but clearly this is Krantz's means of creating a playful loophole that ultimately allows her to marry the same man twice (original emphasis, 227). Still, their love story pales in comparison to the romance developed between Toby, who is blind, and Maxi's best friend, India West, a beautiful actress. In any case, by the novel's end "Maxi Amberville had become a woman," and this conclusion seems to suggest that she is incomplete until being happily married (379). Since the strength of the novel lies precisely in its fantastic and romantic aspiration to "have your cake and eat it too," such paradoxical perfection would appear effectively inescapable.

Bibliography

Groce, Nancy. *New York: Songs of the City.* New York: Watson-Guptill, 1999.

Krantz, Judith. *I'll Take Manhattan.* London: Book Club Associates, 1986.

———. *Sex and Shopping: The Confessions of a Nice Jewish Girl.* New York: St. Martin's, 2000.

Thomas Chandler Haliburton

An Indecent Obsession

Colleen McCullough (1981)

An Indecent Obsession is a psychological novel set in a South Pacific army hospital near the end of World War II, thematically concerned with the social effects of homosexuality (or fear of it) and the conflict between love and duty that is common to many of COLLEEN MCCULLOUGH's novels. As a study in mental abnormality, the novel introduces elements of mystery as well and deploys several rapid and mostly unexpected twists to reach to its somewhat predictable conclusion.

In August 1945 a dedicated nurse, Sister Honour Langtry, cares for a group of five men with physical and psychological ailments in a ward "thrown together from the bits left over, parked like an afterthought down on the perimeter of the compound" (5). In Part 1 Ward X receives a new patient, Sgt. Michael Wilson, whose arrival quickly disrupts the equilibrium she has worked so diligently to maintain. Unlike the other patients, Michael's diagnosis is vague; he "is suspected of unsound mind following an unsavory incident" (42), for nearly killing an officer in a fight while defending a tormented friend. Part 2 sets Wilson against another patient, the "acid-tongued bastard" Sgt. Lucius Daggett, who with Iago-like villainy verbally abuses and physically batters those he perceives are weaker and more privileged than himself. Parts 3 and 4 develop the escalating confrontation between Wilson and Daggett and the increasing attraction between Langtry and Wilson. While she resists her feelings for Michael, Langtry warns another nurse, the young and shallow Sister Sue Pedder, not to become involved with Luce, as he is vindictive and sadistic. To retaliate, an incensed Luce falsely accuses Wilson of homosexuality, inaccurate information Luce has surreptitiously read on Wilson's medical chart. He taunts Wilson and tries to goad him into a fight in the ward's shower. Guilt-ridden Captain Neil Parkinson, previously Sister's confidant and possible suitor, grows jealous of Michael but undertakes to protect Langtry from both Luce and Wilson.

To separate Wilson and Daggett, Langtry sends Luce to the ward, and takes Michael to her quarters, where their mutual sexual attraction soon leads them into each other's arms. In Part 5 Luce is found dead from a presumed (and bloody) suicide; Part 6 follows the breakup of the camp and the startling discovery that Luce was murdered by one of the other patients. Part 7, an afterward of sorts, resolves the various plots as Langtry, now a nurse to the mentally ill, discovers what became of her wartime patients, the circumstances of Luce's death, and the truth of her relationship both with Michael and her profession.

Told as a third-person narrative, *An Indecent Obsession* follows the common dramatic structure of balanced rising action, climax, falling action, and conclusion. Its primary focus, however, is less on action than on the psychological motivations of the characters and the shifting relationships among them. Competent, dedicated, intelligent, and attractive, Honour Langtry became a nurse and volunteered for military service following a love affair that ended badly. As a nurse and a woman, she seeks an elusive balance between a need for romantic love and her responsibilities to those assigned to her care. Very much reflecting her care, her patients depend on her and to varying degrees love her. She is close to, but professional with Neil; she nurtures blind Matthew (Matt) Sawyer and hypochondriac Nugget Jones; and rightly worries about her most damaged patient Benedict (Ben) Maynard who suffers from dementia praecox. Despite her professionalism, Langtry falls in love with Michael who, tormented by his own past, chooses to protect the most disturbed of Sister's patients, Ben.

McCullough has stated that *Indecent Obsession* was about duty. But in fact duty and love, epitomized in Sister Langtry's struggles, are the novel's twin themes. Langtry constantly debates between her professional responsibilities and her love for Michael:

> Now here she was, trying to wear two hats at once, love and duty, both donned for the same man. The same patient. The job *said* he was a patient. It didn't matter that he didn't fit that description at all. For there was duty. There was always duty. It came first; not all the love in the world could change the ingrained habit of so many years (195).

These conflicting themes resolve in an oddly stereotypical way for a late 20th-century novel, as Langtry begrudgingly accepts Michael's choice to protect Ben essentially because men have reason and women have feelings that are irrational. For her, "the void between reason and her own feminine feelings was unbridgeable" (197). She sobs to Michael that she only wants to share a life with him: "Living with you! Keeping your home, having your babies, growing old together" (240). Nevertheless, it is Michael who cares for someone else—a traditional female role—and Langtry who returns to nursing, a more feminist decision than even she is aware of. In the end she gains an "understanding of herself. . . . And [an] understanding that duty, the most indecent of all obsessions, was only another name for love" (279).

In 1985 the independent film company PBL produced a small-budget version of *Indecent Obsession,* starring Wendy Hughes, Gary Sweet as Michael, and Richard Moir as Luce Daggett; the film was nominated for three Australian Film Institute awards—best actor in a lead role, best actor in a supporting role, and best screenplay adaptation—and won an AFI award for best original music score.

Bibliography

McCullough, Colleen. *An Indecent Obsession.* New York: Harper & Row, 1981.

LynnDianne Beene

Irving, John (1942–)

Irving is one of America's best-selling contemporary novelists and has achieved the unusual combination of critical acclaim and mainstream popularity for his literate, yet accessible fiction. He is perhaps best known for his novels *The World According to Garp* (1978), *The* HOTEL NEW HAMPSHIRE (1981) and *The* CIDER HOUSE RULES (1985), each of which has been successfully adapted for film (Irving won an Oscar for the screenplay of the last).

He was born John Wallace Blunt Jr. in New Hampshire, his parents divorcing before he was born. Although named for his biological father, whom he never met, Irving's name was changed by his mother to John Winslow Irving when she married history teacher Colin Irving six years later. Irving's new stepfather taught at the prestigious Philips Exeter Academy, an exclusive prep school to which the young Irving was admitted as a student. Although unexceptional academically (principally due to undiagnosed dyslexia), it was at this institution where the young author-to-be developed his twin lifelong passions of writing and wrestling. After Exeter Irving briefly attended the University of Pittsburgh on a wrestling scholarship, dropping out after a year to travel to Vienna. Returning to New England, he graduated from the University of New Hampshire in 1965 and undertook his master's degree at the prestigious Iowa Writer's Workshop. His thesis, submitted in 1967, was revised and published a year later as his debut novel, *Setting Free the Bears.*

This initial effort was met with lukewarm reviews and modest sales but displayed many of the characteristics for which Irving would later become famous: eccentric yet sympathetic characters, combined with a convoluted and unfashionably plot-driven narrative, which together establish him as an heir to the Dickensian tradition of populist grotesquery and old-fashioned storytelling. His next two novels were in a similar vein, with their unique mix of keen social observation and sexual farce, simultaneously old-fashioned in form and sharply contemporary in content. *The Water-Method Man* (1972), an explicitly comic novel about a frustrated writer with urological difficulties, was followed by 1974's *The 158-Pound Marriage,* which weaves Irving's obsession with wrestling into a colorful mid-1970s narrative of wife swapping.

It was only with the publication of his fourth novel in 1978, however, that Irving made the leap from academic obscurity to literary celebrity. *The World According to Garp* was an immediate publishing phenomenon, capturing the zeitgeist with a mix of anxieties and themes that, although Irving had addressed them in his previous works, seemed in this work to gel perfectly for the first time. *Garp* is an unusual and challenging novel in many ways, adopting a range of literary forms (including embedded short stories and extracts from Garp's novels, faux autobiography, and epistolary interludes) to relate a pan-generational saga of misfits, writers, wrestlers, transsexuals, academics, and feminists, each one idiosyncratic yet empathetic as they encounter self-mutilation, adultery, oral castration, or assassination. It is a sprawling narrative, revealing many similarities with Gunter Grass's *The Tin Drum* and the engaging mixture of realism and caricature he had found in Dickens (Irving's essay "The King of the Novel," in *Trying to Save Piggy Sneed,* explicitly acknowledges his debt to Dickens and his admiration for 19th-century literary form). *Garp* transformed its author's career: shortlisted for the prestigious American Book Award, winning the National Book Foundation's award for paperback fiction, and adapted into a successful film starring Robin Williams and Glenn Close (with Irving himself in a cameo as a wrestling referee).

Having attained the upper reaches of literary success, it is perhaps unsurprising that Irving met with a critical backlash of sorts with his follow-up novel, 1981's *The Hotel New Hampshire.* Another complex and sophisticated saga of family life, and once again articulating Irving's preoccupations with sex, violence, Vienna, and the capriciousness of middle-class existence (with incest added for dramatic spice), the novel sold well despite being unpopular with critics, who saw it as a mechanical attempt to recapture its predecessor's charm. In addition, the film adaptation (starring Rob Lowe and Jodie Foster) lacks the effervescence of the cinematic version of *Garp,* emphasizing farcical sex scenes and broad comedy over the poignancy and occasional profundity of the original work.

The Cider House Rules (1985) was hailed, almost without exception, as a triumphant return to form for Irving. Set like his previous two novels in New England, the novel is another Dickensian epic, this time focusing on the life of Homer Wells, an orphan destined to live his entire life at St. Clouds Orphanage. Homer's mentor, Dr Wilbur Larch—based in part on Irving's physician grandfather, Frederick C. Irving—divides his life's work into that of the Lord (delivering and finding homes for unwanted children) and the Devil (performing abortions), and hopes Homer will carry on his twin missions. Although it addresses controversial issues and continues to explore notions of sex, incest, and infidelity, *The Cider House Rules* marked a new period of authority and maturity in Irving's work, downplaying the black comedy and moments of outright farce that characterize the earlier works in favor of a more socially conscious exploration of character development and growth. Fittingly then, unlike the quick cash-ins of *Garp* and *The Hotel New Hampshire,* the film adaptation was in development for more than a decade, and the finished movie (starring Michael Caine and Tobey Maguire) gained several Academy Award nominations, as well as the screenwriting award for Irving himself.

The final novel in the New England Quartet was 1989's *A Prayer for Owen Meany,* which maintained Irving's serio-comic tone and distinctive authorial voice but revealed also his increasing politicization, dealing with still-raw wounds in the American psyche, especially the Vietnam War and the draft. In addition to his political convictions, Irving introduced religion as a central theme for the first time, the novel's eponymous protagonist (who, in a classic Irving narrative flourish, speaks only in capital letters) believing he is chosen by God for a higher purpose. In many ways *A Prayer for Owen Meany* represents the apex of Irving's attempts to fuse form and content. It became his best-selling novel after *Garp* and remains a critical favorite. A film adaptation, *Simon Birch,* was a disaster, and Irving strove to distance himself from it, requesting that the character names be changed throughout.

The 1990s were less successful for Irving; two novels, *A Son of the Circus* (1994) and *A Widow for One Year* (1998), met with lukewarm critical and commercial response, though the latter was successfully adapted to film in 2004 as *The Door in the Floor,* starring Jeff Bridges and Kim Basinger. In many ways Irving's most interesting writing over the last 15 years has been a succession of nonfiction books. *Trying to Save Piggy Sneed* (a collection of essays and short fiction), *My Movie Business* (an entertaining account of his experiences with Hollywood), and *The Imaginary Girlfriend* (a supposed memoir focusing almost exclusively on his lifelong love affair with wrestling) each reveal a humorous, intelligent, and insightful sensibility, with little sign of the tragedy that seems to underpin his imaginative work. His most recent novels, 2001's *The Fourth Hand* and 2005's *Until I Find You,* have been criticized by some as a lamentable continuation of his midcareer doldrums but show signs of moving toward a potentially intriguing, more introspective late period wherein comedy (however black) has no place.

Irving's literary status remains a topic of debate among scholars, but his technical skill, topical insights, plot-heavy narratives, and wide readership lend credence to the claim that he is indeed a major American novelist. He may always remain inextricably linked in the popular imagination with the New England Quartet (and with *Garp,* in particular), but the sense of progression throughout his writing career and his undoubted talent as a master storyteller offers the tantalizing possibility that his best work is yet to come.

Bibliography

Campbell, Josie P. *John Irving: A Critical Companion.* Westport, Conn.: Greenwood Press, 1998.

The Cider House Rules. Directed by Lasse Hallstrom. Miramax, 1999.

Davis, Todd F. and Kenneth Womack. *The Critical Response to John Irving.* Westport, Conn.: Praeger, 2004.

The Door in the Floor. Directed by Tod Williams. Focus Features, 2004.

The Hotel New Hampshire. Directed by Tony Richardson. Orion, 1984.
Irving, John. *Setting Free the Bears.* New York: Random House, 1968.
———. *The Water-Method Man.* New York: Random House, 1972.
———. *The 158-Pound Marriage.* New York: Random House, 1974.
———. *The World According to Garp.* New York: Dutton, 1978.
———. *The Hotel New Hampshire.* New York: Dutton, 1981.
———. *The Cider House Rules.* New York: Morrow, 1985.
———. *A Prayer for Owen Meany.* New York: Morrow, 1989.
———. *A Son of the Circus.* New York: Random House, 1994.
———. *Trying to Save Piggy Sneed.* New York: Arcade Books, 1996.
———. *A Widow for One Year.* New York: Random House, 1998.
———. *My Movie Business.* New York: Random House, 2000.
———. *The Fourth Hand.* New York: Random House, 2001.
———. *The Imaginary Girlfriend.* New York: Random House, 2002.
———. *Until I Find You.* New York: Random House, 2005.
Simon Birch. Directed by Mark Steven Johnson. Buena Vista, 1998.
The World According to Garp. Directed by George Roy Hill. Warner Bros, 1982.

Nicholas Dunlop

It **Stephen King** (1986)

It is a novel overtly concerned with water or, more accurately, with its passage through drainage constructions whose blueprints are missing. The tale begins with a flood in 1957, with a boat made from a sheet of newspaper floating down a gutter swollen with rain, that "bobbed, listed, righted itself again, [and] dived bravely through treacherous whirlpools" (15). The boat is, however, quickly pulled into the "long, dark semicircle" (24) of a drain, out of which the overflowing water "pried fingerholds in the paving and then snatched whole greedy handfuls" (16).

By any account an exceptional opening, and one that, for all its apparent simplicity, through its careful choice of words and imagery establishes the fundamental movements and energies, the dynamic leitmotifs of this long and complex novel. The newspaper boat's trajectory, "floating" into the "terrible darkness" of a drain (26), through "nighted chambers and long concrete hallways that roared and chimed with water" (27), anticipates the downward itineraries of the book's main characters into the intricate underground structures occupied by "the dark entity which exist[s] in and below Derry" (809).

Such descents into regions below ground level, as well as the existence of portals into "the nightside of Derry" (438), form the novel's basic thematic premises. The troubled relations between surfaces and their hidden depths dominate the work, which functions almost as an extended exercise in narrative archaeology, compelled by some inner logic to excavate what lies concealed. The opening descriptions of the streets' ruptured foundations, the consequence of a flood in this preliminary instance, are echoed in countless other configurations throughout the entire town. The deterioration of the surface crust, having "contract[ed] and grow[n] brittle" due to "endless water erosion" (200), undermines the antithesis, so fundamental to civilized life, between the above and the underneath; the mingling of surface and substrata results at last in a strange geological occurrence: "the earth" appears as if it "meant to hatch something" (200).

It is situated within a formidable body of STEPHEN KING's work, whose story lines often descend into lower, concealed topographies of the mind as much of the world, such as those of *Carrie, The Shining,* and *The Tommyknockers.* Like those other narratives, the story of *It* is constantly responding to eruptions, disturbances that develop "underground," beneath the levels of ordinary perception. In this case adults are blind to the real causes and provenance of the murderous goings-on in town, though King more than once suggests that this sightlessness is an active component, a necessary prerequisite of the atrocities committed. Subsurface and shell, then, behave as partners-in-crime, their complicity providing a chilling commentary not only on the corollaries of ignorance but on the extreme tenuousness of innocence. Rushing through the pipes, "coming up from Its own foul runs and black catacombs under the earth" (853), It, both as entity and novel, "hatches" the substantiation of an "invisible world" (531). It's "special place[s]," the "station[s]" from which It is "able to find Its way into the overworld" (846), indicate areas where the surface effects, the elaborate structure of civilized appearance grows thin, allowing the undertow of existence, of political practices, of historical and topographical plots to rise up into view. Indeed, one could argue that *It* intimates the corrupt undercurrents of the Reagan administration, during which the novel was written and published, or indeed, of the democratic process as a whole.

As is so often the case in King's writing, the wider implications and interpretations of the tale stem from a sharply delimited location. The narrative rarely passes beyond the town limits of Derry, Maine, a community whose original settlers all disappeared without a trace between June and October 1741, an event unmentioned in history books of the region, whose "*quiet,*" as local researcher Mike Hanlon notes, "fits the pattern, too" (161). Compiling "interlude segments" on the town's unauthorized history, on its "unpleasant stories" (159), Hanlon asks, "Can an *entire* city be haunted?" His notes, diary entries unearthing Derry's past horrors, report on a strange "cycle" of 26 or 27 years, at the end of which "the rate of disappearance [of children] shoots nearly out of sight" (166). What emerges from the journal—a virtual chronicle of aberration—is a kind of sinister envelope, a shape echoed throughout the narrative, from smells and "curtain[s] of quiet" (161) to the weird weather patterns that hold over Derry alone.

Topographies operating as focal points of malevolent energy and forces enfolding specific areas are common features of King's work. Recalling the claustrophobic menace of *The Shining, Salem's Lot,* and *Pet Sematary,* Derry is described as a "*bad* place" (42), whose very "soil" seems somehow conducive to "hurtful things" (447), and whose territory welcomes whatever forms and manifestations the baleful It assumes. Though It arrives from "outside" (750), from "the spaces between the stars" (928), It "has been here so long . . . that It's become a part of Derry, something as much a part of the town as the Standpipe, or the Canal, or Bassey Park, or the library. Only It's not a matter of outward geography, you understand. Maybe that was true once, but now It's . . . inside. Somehow It's gotten inside" (499). As It seeps into "the hollow places" (891) and vacant parts of Derry, the city, in a sort of tacit, even unconscious Faustian bargain, thrives, its prosperity directly linked to the "unspeakable living light" (1,055), like a perverted sun, that It, unmasked, finally is.

Typical of King's fiction, the tenuous, human forces of good in the novel seldom approach the strength—and indeed, the appeal—of the malevolent It. The individual members of the Losers Club, seven classmates in the local school, fit "neatly against each other's edges" (306), their combined existence producing a "closed body" (1,092) that captures a form of love which "come[s] in waves so clear and so powerful that no one can stand against its simple imperative" (180). Here an "exhilarating kind of energy" accumulates (722), an opposing envelope to that of the cyclical sleeping and feeding of It; it is this opposition, all the more striking for being so rare and ephemeral, that most distinguishes the novel amid King's extensive oeuvre.

It was adapted for television in 1990 directed by Tommy Lee Wallace and starring Annette O'Toole, Jonathan Brandis, and Seth Green.

Bibliography

King, Stephen. *Carrie.* London: New English Library, 1999 (1974).

———. *Salem's Lot.* London: New English Library, 1993 (1975).

———. *The Shining.* London: New English Library, 2001 (1977).

———. *It.* London: New English Library, 1987 (1986).

———. *The Tommyknockers.* New York: Putnam's, 1987.

———. *Pet Sematary.* London: New English Library, 2000 (1988).

Fabienne Collignon

J

Jakes, John (1932–)

A masterful storyteller particularly known for his Kent Family Chronicles ("American Bicentennial" series), the NORTH AND SOUTH TRILOGY, and the Crown Family Saga, Jakes has authored more than 70 mass-market books and 200 short stories, encompassing a variety of genres: historical fiction, fantasy, suspense, westerns, nonfiction for young readers, and science fiction. He is credited with producing more than 16 consecutive *New York Times* best sellers, and more than 60 million copies of his fiction have been sold.

Based on extensive textual and on-site research, his historical fiction narrates a host of seminal events in American history, including the American Revolution, the Civil War, the Spanish-American War, and the California gold rush, bringing to imaginative life such varied historical icons as Abraham Lincoln, William T. Sherman, General Grant, Allan Pinkerton, D. W. Griffith, William Randolph Hearst, Ambrose Bierce, Leland Stanford, Teddy Roosevelt, and Charlie Chaplin. Jakes is notable for his deft use of colorful details, engaging plots and subplots, and colorful elements of romance and adventure.

He was born in Chicago in 1932, and while still a freshman at Northwestern University he sold his first story to a fantasy and science-fiction magazine for $25. As a sophomore he transferred to DePauw University, where he earned a B.A. in creative writing in 1953, and in the following year he earned his M.A. in American literature at Ohio State University. While working in the advertising industry from 1954 to 1971, he published dozens of books for both adults and children, including *The Texans Ride North: The Story of Cattle Trails* (1952), *A Night for Treason* (1956), *When the Star Kings Die* (1967), and *Master of the Dark Gate* (1970), with some of his early works published under pseudonyms such as Jay Scotland, Alan Payne, and William Ard.

His first literary fame came with the publication of the enormously popular Kent Family Chronicles, which comprises eight volumes: *The Bastard* (1974), *The Rebels* (1975), *The Seekers* (1975), *The Furies* (1976), *The Titans* (1976), *The Warriors* (1977), *The Lawless* (1978), and *The Americans* (1980); all narrate the struggles, heroism, triumphs, and passions of the four generations of a fictional family in early America.

Jakes's focus shifted to the Civil War period in his North and South Trilogy, *North and South* (1982), *Love and War* (1984), and *Heaven and Hell* (1987), the last of which became his 11th consecutive best seller. The novels portray the often tragically ironic nature of the Civil War by focusing on the parallel tales of two families, the Mains (Carolina plantation owners) and the Hazards (Pennsylvania industrialists).

The 1990s saw the publication of two Crown family novels set in 20th-century Chicago. The central characters of *Homeland* (1993) are the Crowns, German-American immigrants who create a large beer company at the turn of the 20th century in a nation experiencing a surge in immigrant population, the famous Pullman Strike, the birth of movies, and the Spanish-American War.

In *American Dreams* (1998), which focuses on the second generation of the Crowns, the major characters pursue varied aspirations, but all typical of their time: Fritzi becomes an actress, Carl an aviator, and Paul a moviemaker.

Other notable historical novels by Jakes include CALIFORNIA GOLD (1989), the story of a poor Pennsylvanian's pursuit of the California dream; *On Secret Service* (2000), concerned with espionage during the Civil War; *Charleston: A Novel* (2002), the story of the Bell family of Charleston, South Carolina, from the Revolutionary period through Reconstruction; *Savannah, Or, A Gift for Mr. Lincoln* (2004), which describes General Sherman's conquest of Savannah, Georgia, in 1864; and *The Gods of Newport* (2006), the story of the Gilded Age of the 1890s.

In addition to fiction, Jakes created play productions for *A Christmas Carol* (1989) and *Great Expectations* (2001), both based on the Charles Dickens's novels, and also served as coeditor (with Martin H. Greenberg) of *New Trails: Twenty-three Original Stories of the West from Western Writers of America* (1994) and as editor of *A Century of Great Western Stories* (2000). His novels *The Bastards, The Rebels, The Seekers, North and South, Love and War,* and *Heaven and Hell* have all been made into successful television miniseries.

Among his many awards are the National Cowboy Hall of Fame's Western Heritage Literary Award, a dual Celebrity and Citizen's Award from the White House Conference on Libraries and Information, and the Medal of the Thomas Cooper Society. He also holds honorary doctorates from DePauw University, Wright State University, Winthrop College, the University of South Carolina, and Ohio State University.

Bibliography

Jakes, John. *The Texans Ride North: The Story of the Cattle Trails.* Philadelphia: Winston, 1952.

———. *A Night for Treason.* New York: Bouregy & Curl, 1956.

———. *When the Star Kings Die.* New York: Ace, 1967.

———. *Master of the Dark Gate.* New York: Lancer, 1970.

———. *The Bastard.* New York: Pyramid, 1974.

———. *The Rebels.* New York: Pyramid, 1975.

———. *The Seekers.* New York: Pyramid, 1975.

———. *The Furies.* New York: Pyramid, 1976.

———. *The Titans.* New York: Pyramid, 1976.

———. *The Warriors.* New York: Pyramid, 1977.

———. *The Lawless.* New York: Jove, 1978.

———. *The Americans.* New York: Jove, 1980.

———. *North and South.* New York: Harcourt, 1982.

———. *Love and War.* San Diego: Harcourt, 1984.

———. *Heaven and Hell.* San Diego: Harcourt, 1987.

———. *California Gold.* New York: Random House, 1989.

———. *Homeland.* New York: Doubleday, 1993.

———. *American Dreams.* New York: Dutton, 1998.

———. *On Secret Service.* New York: Dutton, 2000.

———. *Charleston: A Novel.* New York: Dutton, 2002.

———. *Savannah, Or, A Gift for Mr. Lincoln: A Novel.* New York: Dutton, 2004.

———. *The Gods of Newport: A Novel.* New York: Dutton, 2006.

———, adaptation. *A Christmas Carol,* by Charles Dickens. Montgomery, Ala., Shakespeare Festival, 1989.

———, adaptation. *Great Expectations,* by Charles Dickens. Chester, Conn., Goodspeed Musicals, 2001.

———, ed. *A Century of Great Western Stories.* New York: Forge, 2000.

———, and Martin H. Greenberg, eds. *New Trails: Twenty-three Original Stories of the West from Western Writers of America.* New York: Bantam, 1994.

John J. Han

Jenkins, Jerry (1949–) and Tim LaHaye (1926–)

> I myself have been a forty-five year student of the satanically-inspired, centuries-old conspiracy to use government, education, and media to destroy every vestige of Christianity within our society and establish a new world order. Having read at least fifty books on the Illuminati, I am convinced that it exists and can be blamed for many of man's inhumane actions against his fellow man during the past two hundred years.
>
> (Tim LaHaye in *Rapture under Attack*)

This is not a conviction one would tend to associate with an immensely successful author of popular fiction. Yet so skillful is the narrative craft of LaHaye and his longtime collaborator, Jerry Jenkins, and so powerful the undercurrents of Christian fervor in 21st-century America, that the pair have produced a string of best-selling novels relating the cosmic saga born of this conviction. Indeed, Jenkins and LaHaye hold ninth place in Amazon.com's 10th Anniversary Hall of Fame, outselling all but eight authors in Amazon's reckoning over the last decade.

Inaugurated with the astonishing *Left Behind: A Novel of the Earth's Last Days* (1995), and apparently ending in 2007 with the publication of *Kingdom Come: The Final Victory,* Jenkins and LaHaye's evangelical masterwork, the LEFT BEHIND SERIES, conceives the past, present, and future as aspects of one timeless messianic "dispensation" of God's unfolding covenant with man, which will finally be fulfilled in the *literal* reign of Jesus Christ for a thousand years on his second coming. A staggering amalgam of disparate genres, from fantasy and science fiction to thriller, melodrama, and romance, the series is fused into one indissoluble narrative by its authors' uncommon skill and singular vision. The first novel alone sells an average of 8 million copies a year and has sold 58 million copies to date. The Web site reportedly receives more than 25 thousand hits a day.

Jerry Bruce Jenkins was born the son of a police chief in Kalamazoo, Michigan, in 1949, and little is known of his personal life, until he emerged on the scene as the self-described "most famous writer no-one's ever heard of." He was educated at the Moody Bible Institute from 1967 to 1968, Loop College in 1968, and William Rainey Harper College 1968–70. During his student days he worked as a news editor at a Chicago radio station and as a sports reporter, first in Chicago and then, upon graduating, in Kennewick, Washington. In 1971, as LaHaye was planting the seeds with Jerry Falwell of the Moral Majority, Jenkins became the editor of religious publisher Scripture Press Publications, in Wheaton, Illinois, later becoming vice president for publishing, and currently the writer-at-large for Chicago-based Moody Press, owned by the same Moody Bible Institute, where his studies as a boy had begun.

He is the founder and director of the Christian Writer's Guild, with worldwide membership of 2,000, devoted to cultivating and promoting writers with a Christian perspective; he is the owner of Jenkins Entertainment, a media company that produced the 2002 film *Hometown Legend.*

He has written more than 150 books, principally in four genres: biography, most notably the told-to stories of Hank Aaron, Orel Hershiser, Walter Payton, and Nolan Ryan (Jenkins also assisted Billy Graham with his memoir *Just as I Am*); marriage and family, about which Jenkins is also an extensive speaker; children's fiction, most notably the series *Left Behind: The Kids,* a children's version of the Left Behind series; and popular fiction, often with a Christian bent, typified by the famous series he penned with Tim LaHaye.

He and his wife, Dianne, have three grown sons and currently live in Colorado.

About the early life of Tim LaHaye, one of America's most influential evangelicals, more is known. He was born in Detroit in 1926 to Frank LaHaye, a Ford auto worker, and Margaret Palmer. When the Depression struck, Margaret was also forced to take a job in a Ford auto factory, and the stress on the family would soon tell. Frank died suddenly of a heart attack in 1936, and the nine-year-old boy was devastated until he heard the minister at his father's funeral effectively articulate what would become the central core of the Left Behind creed:

> This is not the end of Frank LaHaye; because he has accepted Jesus, the day will come when the Lord will shout from heaven and descend, and the dead in Christ will rise first and then we'll be caught up together to meet him in the air.

"All of a sudden," recalls LaHaye, "there was hope in my heart I'd see my father again."

Coming of age in the Depression years, LaHaye worked to help put himself through college, and it was during a stint as a lifeguard in a Christian summer camp that he decided to become a preacher, enrolling in the conservative Bob Jones University in Greenville, North Carolina, where he met his future wife, Christian activist Beverley Davenport. In 1944 he enlisted in the air force at the age of 17 and served as a machine gunner aboard a bomber in the war, returning to complete his B.A. in 1950. He also holds a doctor of ministry degree from the Western Seminary and a host of honorary degrees.

In 1958 LaHaye and his family moved to San Diego, California, where he became the preacher at the Scott Memorial Baptist Church (now, the Shadow Mountain Community Church), in El Cajon and served there for almost a quarter-century, using it as a base for his increasingly nationwide ministry. In 1971 he founded the San Diego Christian College. While in San Diego, LaHaye hosted a radio program with his wife, Beverly, on Christian values entitled *The LaHayes on Family Life* (which later returned as a television program) in the mid-1950s, and he began to write his influential nonfiction, now numbering more than 50 books.

In 1970, with the help of his wife, friend Jerry Falwell, and others, LaHaye began to shape the so-called Moral Majority, lobbying vigorously in support of traditional family values, pro-life legislation, and strong national defense, and fundamentally reshaping the face of American culture. In 1981 he founded the Council for National Policy, a lobbying organization that has been called "the most powerful conservative organization in America you've never heard of" (Goldberg), and later, the Institute for Creation Research along with Henry Morris, the American Coalition for Traditional Values, and the Coalition for Religious Freedom. In 1988 he took a more direct role in the American political scene, becoming the vice chairman of Jack Kemp's presidential bid, but he lasted only four days in the job when his anti-Catholic views became known. In 1998, after the success of the early installments in the series, he founded the somewhat ominous-sounding Pre-Tribulation Research Centre along with Thomas Ice. In 2000 he returned to his more traditional indirect means of influence and was instrumental in delivering the religious right to the successful campaign of George Bush; in 2007 he endorsed the bid of Mike Huckabee for president. In 2001 the *Evangelical Studies Bulletin* named him the most influential Christian leader of the last quarter-century.

LaHaye currently lives with his wife, Beverley, in the L.A. area and has four grown children.

Long aspiring to articulate in an accessible form his belief in the dispensational premillennialism that would later inform the Left Behind series, LaHaye—not himself a fiction writer—was delighted to be introduced through a literary agent to Jerry Jenkins in 1992, and the two became fast friends, with the first installment in the series published only three years later. LaHaye conceives of and creates the plots for the novels and sends his outlines to Jenkins, who answers with a first draft that is then vetted for theological correctness and revised by LaHaye.

Bibliography

Goldberg, Michelle. "Fundamentally Unsound." Available online. URL: http://dir.salon.com/story/books/feature/2002/07/29/left_behind/index.html.

Nemo Ouden

Jong, Erica (1942–)

Erica Jong is the author of nine novels, six books of poetry, and five books of nonfiction, including two memoirs. The most famous of these is her debut novel *FEAR OF FLYING,* which was first published in 1973.

Jong was born and grew up in New York City. Her father gave up being a professional musician in order to sell household ornaments to support his family, and her mother gave up being a painter because of social expectations that demanded she attend full time to her husband and three daughters (Erica is the second). The sacrifice of both her parents affected Jong deeply—especially that of her mother:

> When she won the bronze medal [instead of the National Academy of Design's prestigious Prix de Rome] and was told—quite frankly (no one was ashamed to be sexist them)—that she hadn't won the Prix de Rome because, as a woman, she was expected to marry, bear children, and waste her gifts, she was enraged. That rage has powered my life [. . .]. (*Fear of Fifty,* 27)

Jong speculates that her mother made her father give up show business on the grounds that "he would have to make the same renunciation that she had made" (28). Encouraged by her mother, Jong began to learn about feminist ideas in high school—when she discovered Simone de Beauvoir's *The Second Sex*—and would go on to become a significant figure in the women's movement of the 1970s, due to her frank writings about sex and women's sexuality. She heard Dorothy Parker—whom she describes as "my idol" (*Seducing the Demon* 114)—read in New York when she was 15 and has also frequently emphasized the influence that the writings of Sylvia Plath and Anne Sexton have had on her own work. In an imaginary letter to Sylvia Plath, she writes:

> What interested me when I first read the *Ariel* poems was how you broke out of the decorous good-girl role. You confronted the world directly with your own searing rage. It was about time a woman raged on the page. And you gave us all the courage to do it (65).

She never met Plath but knew Sexton before her death in 1974 and describes her as "a generous mentor" (60).

Jong attended Barnard College as an undergraduate and, later, Columbia University, where she studied 18th-century fiction. She has commented on the lack of women writers on the syllabus at Barnard when she was a student there: "[W]e did not study women poets and novelists," she says in *Fear of Fifty* (1994). "The atmosphere was full of encouragement for young women, but we felt we had been born, like Venus, from the foam. There were no role models" (77). She published two books of poetry before the appearance of *Fear of Flying,* which brought her instant celebrity and was reviewed favorably by established literary writers such as John Updike and Henry Miller. It also introduced the world to Jong's most famous character, Isadora Wing, heroine not only of *Fear of Flying* but of two other of Jong's novels, *How to Save Your Own Life* (1977) and *Parachutes and Kisses* (1984).

Isadora's forthright and explicit sexuality was revolutionary when it first appeared in print. Many of the key events in Isadora's story, however, are also key events in Jong's own life: her first marriage—while still in college—to a man who developed schizophrenia; her second marriage to a Chinese-American psychoanalyst; her affair with a radical English analyst while in Europe; her residency for several years in Heidelberg, Germany—all appear in *Fear of Flying.*

Jong has developed a reputation over the years not only for her explicit writing about sex and the relationships between men and women but for her rambunctious private life. Her two memoirs, *Fear of Fifty* and *Seducing the Demon: Writing for My Life* (2006), detail numerous affairs, and she married two more times after divorcing her analyst husband. Her third husband, writer Jonathan Fast, is also the father of her daughter, Molly Jong-Fast, who is now also a writer. Her most well known tryst, however, is detailed in *Seducing the Demon*: her now-infamous affair with Andy Stewart, then-husband of celebrity caterer Martha Stewart, at the Frankfurt Book Fair in the early 1980s. Jong was subsequently blamed by Stewart for the breakup of her marriage.

Jong has also wrestled with bouts of alcohol abuse throughout her career, which is reflected in her novel *Any Woman's Blues* (1990), about a New York artist, Leila Sand, who is struggling with creativity and addiction. Jong also talks briefly about her experience with the recovery movement in *Seducing the Demon,* although she emphasizes her deliberate and conscious nonabstinence:

> You cannot quote Omar and drink Diet Coke. You cannot quote Omar and drink San Pellegrino. Wine is demanded. Wine is essential. You cannot be in love and not drink wine. Or I can't, anyway (120).

She devotes a lengthy section of *Seducing the Demon* to considering the relationship in American literary history between alcoholism and creativity and also details her experience of being arrested for driving under the influence in California in 2004.

Although Jong has stated frankly that she believes sex and creativity to be inherently connected (*Fear of Fifty,* 125), her writing deals with many aspects of women's lives. She explores women's writing, for example in *Sappho's Leap,* a fictionalization of the life of the Greek lyric poet, and women's spirituality in a nonfiction book entitled *Witches,* which analyzes the transformation of the witch-figure in the popular imagination. Her other novels include *Fanny: Being the True History of Fanny Hackabout-Jones* (1980), a reworking of the central character from John Cleland's 18th-century novel *Fanny Hill; Shylock's Daughter* (also published under the title *Serenissima* in 1987), a fantasy oscillating between the present-day reality of Venice and Shakespearean London; and *Inventing Memory* (1997), a family saga dealing with four generations of Jewish women in the United States. She has also written *Megan's Two Houses*, a children's book about divorce (originally published as *Megan's Book of Divorce* in 1984, after the breakup of Jong's marriage to Jonathan Fast), and *What Do Women Want?* (1998), a reflection on the women's movement and its successes and failures.

Erica Jong now lives in New York City and Weston, Connecticut.

Bibliography

De Beauvoir, Simone. *The Second Sex.* New York: Knopf, 1953.

Jong, Erica. *Fear of Flying.* New York: Holt, Rinehart and Winston, 1973.

———. *How to Save Your Own Life.* New York: Holt, Rinehart and Winston, 1977.

———. *Fanny: Being the True History of the Adventures of Fanny Hackabout-Jones.* New York: New American Library, 1980.

———. *Witches.* New York: H.A. Abrams, 1981.

———. *Parachutes and Kisses.* New York: New American Library, 1984.

———. *Serenissima: A Novel of Venice.* New York: Houghton Mifflin, 1987.

———. *Any Woman's Blues.* New York: HarperCollins, 1995.

———. *Fear of Fifty: A Midlife Memoir.* New York: HarperCollins, 1994.

———. *Megan's Two Houses: A Story of Adjustment.* New York: Dove Kids, 1996.

———. *Inventing Memory.* New York: HarperCollins, 1997.

———. *What Do Women Want? Bread, Roses, Sex, Power.* New York: HarperCollins, 1998.

———. *Sappho's Leap.* New York: W.W. Norton, 2003.

———. *Seducing the Demon: Writing for My Life.* New York: Penguin, 2006.

———. "Erica Jong." Available online. URL: http://www.ericajong.com. Accessed February 27, 2007.

Plath, Sylvia. *Ariel.* London: Faber and Faber, 1965.

Claire Marie Horsnell

Jurassic Park Michael Crichton (1990)

Jurassic Park is a present-day science-fiction novel—and in a sense a morality tale—about a failed attempt to construct a park furnished with cloned dinosaurs. Exploring one of the central motifs in MICHAEL CRICHTON's oeuvre, that of science gone disastrously awry, the novel can be read as a loose reworking of the *Frankenstein* and *The Island of Dr. Moreau* stories. John Hammond, the owner of International Genetic Technologies Inc., has turned an island off Costa Rica into the eponymous Jurassic Park, a zoo stocked with dinosaurs that his specialist Dr. Wu has cloned by means of a breakthrough genetic engineering technology involving the manipulation of DNA. Donald Gennaro, Hammond's lawyer, is concerned about the safety of the park and brings famed palaeontologist Alan Grant, paleobotanist Ellie Sattler, and mathematician Ian Malcolm to tour the island in an attempt to determine whether the place is suitable for visitors.

While Gennaro, Grant, and Sattler's pessimism is initially assuaged by what Hammond and InGen have achieved, Malcolm remains convinced that the island is doomed, making repeated reference to the idea that nature cannot be predicted or controlled by man and intimating an even greater concern, latent throughout the novel, that by its very nature "[Scientific] Discovery is always a rape of the natural world" (284). Hammond's belief that "you get the engineering correct and the animals will fall into place" (140) is revealed to be woefully naive as the story progresses and the dinosaurs run amok.

The novel also assails the pernicious influence that corporate interests have exerted on contemporary scientific development, claiming at its start that while previous scientists were "free of contaminating industry ties" and, therefore, worked for the benefit of all mankind, the commercialization of science has given rise to a situation in which scientific research "is done in secret, in haste, and for profit" (9). The catastrophic effects of the "privatization" of science are typified by the self-seeking actions of Dennis Nedry, the computer technician who designed the park's complicated computer network. Unbeknownst to Hammond and the others, a rival bioengineering company has paid Nedry to steal 15 dinosaur embryos from the island for their own purposes. Jurassic Park has been designed to run with only a minimal number of staff, with much of the park operating on automated, computer-driven technology and machinery; when Nedry temporarily disables the park's security system in order to steal the embryos, virtually all of the park's other systems begin to malfunction, while Nedry's own classic death-by-one's-own-creation leaves the island deprived of the only person capable of easily rectifying his mistake.

Meanwhile, the breakdown leaves Grant, Malcolm, the park publicist Ed Regis, and Hammond's two grandchildren, Tim and Lex, stranded in their electric tour vehicles just outside the Tyrannosaurus Rex paddock; the T-Rex breaks through the now unelectrified fence, devours Regis and severely injures Malcolm. Grant and the children are forced to flee into the nighttime park on foot. The park's game warden, Robert Muldoon, joins with Gennaro to search for them, but they initially discover only the injured Malcolm, consigning him to the care of Sattler and the park's veterinarian, Dr. Harding.

Eventually, Arnold has the computer system running again and the power back up. Malcolm, however, warns that according to chaos theory, things will soon get much worse. Muldoon and Gennaro venture out again to try and contain the T-Rex, while Grant and the children make their way back to the visitor center, narrowly escaping some flying pterodactyls and the T-Rex again. Grant then finds dismaying evidence that the dinosaurs have in fact been breeding, though the park scientists have ensured that the dinosaur eggs were engineered to create only females.

By the time they get back to the lodge, the power has gone down again, and the velociraptors—surprisingly intelligent and vicious small carnivores that hunt in a pack—are loose on the island, killing Arnold while he tries to turn on the generator and, in a riveting action sequence, laying siege to the lodge where Malcolm, Sattler, Harding, Wu, Muldoon, and Hammond are trapped. In rapid sequence Grant is forced to leave Tim and Lex in the cafeteria while he goes to turn on the power; Wu is killed helping Sattler distract the raptors from Grant; Grant finds Gennaro, who had disappeared, and turns on the generator; and a raptor stalks the children in the cafeteria but is at last cleverly locked in the freezer.

With everyone familiar with the computer system now dead, the computer-savvy Tim now tries to reactivate the electric fences himself, managing to do so just as the raptors are about to penetrate the electrified bars on the lodge skylight. Tim then calls the island's supply ship, which is about to dock in Costa Rica, and Gennaro commands the ship to turn around because velociraptors have jumped aboard. Grant, Gennaro, Sattler, and Muldoon now venture out to find the velociraptor nest, hoping to determine how many raptors there are and whether any more have gotten off the island. While walking outside the lodge, Hammond trips and falls down a ravine, where he is attacked and eaten by a group of small dinosaurs. Malcolm also dies from complications from his earlier injury. Finally, the Costa Rican National Guard arrive, evacuate the survivors, and literally blow up the island, seemingly annihilating the threat, despite Malcolm's dire prophecies. Grant, waiting for the Costa Rican officials to release him, is approached by a stranger who relates a queer story about some suspicious unidentified lizards that have recently been seen traveling in packs through the jungle on mainland Costa Rica. The lizards have since fled deep into the jungle and vanished.

While several of the characters perform what may traditionally be seen as heroic acts, the novel's focus is fixed on the animals and the astonishingly fragile technology that created and controlled them and on their largely passive almost tragic creator, John Hammond. The eccentric yet childlike Hammond can be read as a modern variation on the mad scientist, and the novel self-consciously and playfully alludes to this resemblance at several points, with Grant joking about Hammond's status as "the evil arch villain" and suggesting that he is "about as sinister as Walt Disney" (42), while Malcolm condemns him for forgetting his creations "are alive [and] have an intelligence of their own" (306). Hammond's most similar precursor is Wells's Dr. Moreau, but where the latter experiments with vivisection, dissecting living matter, Hammond's exploration and attendant risk go much deeper, into the very essence of lie itself; both, however, are driven by the same scientific hubris, attempting to usurp God's power as the creator of life by tampering with nature, and both suffer the nemesis of destruction by their own creation. Hammond believes that science's impressive logic and mechanical integrity can overcome the organic, often chaotic forces of nature, but human weakness, vulnerabilities in the technology, and above all the female dinosaurs' unanticipated development of asexual reproduction all serve as a cautionary tale for our time.

Crichton's novel was adapted by director Steven Spielberg in 1993 into a film of the same name, currently the 11th-highest grossing film ever. Spielberg also filmed a less successful sequel based upon Crichton's *The Lost World* in 1995 and served as executive producer for a third film in 2001, *Jurassic Park 3*.

Bibliography

Crichton, Michael, *Jurassic Park*. London: Arrow Books Limited, 1991.

Jurassic Park. Directed by Steven Spielberg. Universal Pictures, 1993.

Jurassic Park III. Directed by Joe Johnston. Amblin Entertainment, 2001.

The Lost World: Jurassic Park. Directed by Steven Spielberg. Amblin Entertainment, 1997.

Shelley, Mary. *Frankenstein*, ed. by M. K. Joseph. Oxford: Oxford University Press, 1998.

Wells, H. G. *The Island of Doctor Moreau*, ed. by Brian Aldiss. London: Orion, 2000.

David Simmons

K

Karon, Jan (1937–)

Jan Karon is the author of the Mitford series, novels depicting the daily lives of a likeable Episcopal priest and his colorful friends and neighbors, set in a quaint little North Carolina town. Since the publication of *At Home in Mitford* in 1994, she has written 14 more Mitford books (eight novels, a cookbook, two books of quotations, two small Christmas tales, and a bedside companion), three children's books, and an inspirational picture book. The prolific Mitford series first established a niche in the Christian literature genre but quickly crossed over to mainstream fiction and now boasts sales of more than 25 million copies, two of its more prominent titles being A COMMON LIFE (2001) and LIGHT FROM HEAVEN (2005).

Jan Karon (formerly known as Janice Meredith Wilson) grew up in Lenoir, North Carolina. Her love for writing developed early when she wrote a novel at age 10 and won a writing contest for a short story that same year. She quit school in eighth grade and later had a baby (Candace) at 16. Before 20 she had married and divorced.

By 18 she was a receptionist for an advertising firm in North Carolina. Her creativity and perseverance propelled her forward in the advertising world, and her career as an advertising writer took her from North Carolina to New York and finally California. She worked 32 years in advertising, becoming creative vice president of an advertising firm, and won awards for her television commercials and magazine advertising.

At age 50 Karon traded her successful career for a cottage in Blowing Rock, North Carolina, where she could pursue her dream of writing. For the next two years she worked to develop a story and then arranged to have segments of it published weekly in the local paper, *The Blowing Rocket*. Each week for two years her story about a tiny town called Mitford was featured in the newspaper and generated a strong local following. In 1994 this serial became the book *At Home in Mitford* and was issued by Lion Publishing, a Christian publisher. Several years later, Viking/Penguin became her exclusive publisher, and her books began appearing in the mainstream fiction market.

Karon's Mitford series recounts the life of a sexagenarian Episcopal priest (Father Tim Kavanagh) and a host of local characters in Mitford, a cozy town similar to television's Mayberry or that of a Norman Rockwell painting. The vibrant citizens of Mitford include Father Tim with his dog, Barnabus, Dooley Barlowe (an underprivileged boy befriended and nurtured by Father Tim), Cynthia Coppersmith (Father Tim's attractive next door neighbor and a children's book author), Puny Bradshaw (Father Tim's housekeeper and cook), and a whole community of eccentric yet loveable folk. The novels are seasoned with biblical scripture, mouthwatering foods, infectious humor, and the rustic charms of a small town.

In all, Jan Karon has written 15 books related to Mitford. Her children's books include *Miss Fannie's Hat* (1998), *Jeremy: The Tale of an Honest*

Bunny (2000), and *Violet Comes to Stay* (2006). She has also written a picture book targeting all ages, entitled *The Trellis and the Seed* (2003).

Karon began a three-book series recounting the travels of Father Tim (to Mississippi, England, and Ireland), with *Home to Holly Springs* in 2007.

Bibliography

Crist, Renee. "Jan Karon: The Good Life in Mitford." *Publishers Weekly* 244, no. 21, 26 May 1997: 60–61. Available online. URL: http://www.ebscohost.com. Accessed December 1, 2006.

Hellmich, Nanci. "Jan Karon Finds Redemption in Rural Virginia." *USA Today*, 18 November 2005. Available online. URL: http://www.ebscohost.com. Accessed December 2, 2006.

———. "Karon's Father Tim to Leave Mitford." *USA Today*, 10 November 2005. Available online. URL: http://www.ebscohost.com. Accessed December 2, 2006.

Karon, Jan. *At Home in Mitford*. Oxford: Lion Publishing, 1994.

———. *A Light in the Window*. New York: Penguin, 1996.

———. *These High, Green Hills*. New York: Viking, 1996.

———. *Out to Canaan*. New York: Viking, 1997.

———. *Miss Fannie's Hat*. Minneapolis: Augsburg, 1998.

———. *A New Song*. New York: Viking, 1999.

———. *Jeremy: The Tale of an Honest Bunny*. New York: Viking, 2000.

———. *A Common Life: The Wedding Story*. New York: Viking, 2001.

———. *The Mitford Snowmen*. New York: Viking, 2001.

———. *Patches of Godlight: Father Tim's Favorite Quotes*. New York: Viking, 2001.

———. *Esther's Gift: A Mitford Christmas Story*. New York: Viking, 2002.

———. *In This Mountain*. New York: Viking, 2002.

———. *Shepherds Abiding: A Mitford Christmas Story*. New York: Viking, 2003.

———. *The Trellis and the Seed: A Book of Encouragement for All Ages*. New York: Viking, 2003.

———. *Jan Karon's Mitford Cookbook and Kitchen Reader*. New York: Viking, 2004.

———. *A Continual Feast: Words of Comfort and Celebration Collected by Father Tim*. New York: Viking, 2005.

———. *Light from Heaven*. New York: Viking, 2005.

———. *Cynthia Coppersmith's Violet Comes to Stay*. New York: Viking, 2006.

———. *Mitford Bedside Companion*. New York: Viking, 2006.

Nelson, Marcia Z. "Lights Out in Mitford." *Publishers Weekly* 252, no. 42, 24 October 2005: 30–31. Available online. URL: http://www.ebscohost.com. Accessed December 1, 2006.

Stanton, Luke A. *Current Biography Yearbook*, ed. by Clifford Thompson. New York: H.W. Wilson, 2003.

Mary Chesnut

Keillor, Garrison (1942–)

Writer, musician, and Radio Hall of Fame personality, Keillor is recognized for his numerous magazine and newspaper articles, radio programs, and books. In *A Prairie Home Companion: The News from Lake Wobegon*, podcasts provide weekly updates regarding the little town where "all the women are strong, all the men are good looking, and all the children are above average," while *The Writer's Almanac* offers a weekly update of literary notes and poetry. A bookstore owner and voiceover artist, Keillor is best known for articles in *The New Yorker* and *The Atlantic Monthly* and for the radio programs *The Writer's Almanac* and *A Prairie Home Companion*.

Gary Edward Keillor was born in Anoka, Minnesota, and his upbringing reflected Scottish and Norwegian heritage and religious values, which, along with his own lively political views and regional experience, form the underpinnings of Keillor's literary monologues. In 1966 he earned an English degree at the University of Minnesota, where he also began his broadcasting career as a student; but both his public radio and writing career, launched in 1969 and 1970, respectively, are closely associated with the evolving format of *A Prairie Home Companion*, a variety radio program with live music.

Keillor's witty reflections on local and global issues have engaged audiences for more than three decades, bringing him recognition as one of the familiar voices of America. Spoof commercials and creative treatment of historical persons and events poke fun at social values and regional paradigms, exposing common foibles and illogical conventions. As a popular cultural critic, he is renowned for making light of individuals and institutions that become too self-important, including himself. In 1970 Keillor was writing for *The New Yorker*, paying rent on a farmhouse, and living what he considered "a princely life." He describes himself at that stage as not "a very good writer at all," with "no idea how to construct a novel" and "a poor ear for dialogue"; as "pretentious and arrogant in all sorts of ways," but still cautious enough not to take his good luck for granted (Bolick). Three decades after his long association with *The Atlantic Monthly* began—as a failed job interview in 1966—Keillor responded in a commemorative interview with typical humor when asked how it felt to have become a national icon: "It's not a dignified life, the archetypal life, but we seem to serve a useful function as landmarks, like the Chrysler Building or the pier at Santa Monica" (Bolick).

In 1994 Keillor was inducted into the Radio Hall of Fame at the Museum of Broadcast Communications in Chicago. His advice column, titled "Mr. Blue," hosted on Salon.com, blends practical observations and humorous comments on such topics as love, marriage, writing, and politics. Sample titles include: "If love's not there to begin with, is it ever gonna be?" "Does love have to be a five alarm fire?" and "Can you fall in love based on someone's writing?" In a 2004 article titled "Every dog has his day," Keillor announced his resignation following a heart attack.

In addition to his more satirical topics, Keillor's themes frequently involve love and home. In the column "Ask Mr. Blue," and again in *Love Me* (2003), he gives advice to lovers, blending storytelling, humor, and compassion to talk about ambition, love, and loss. Love and home are also themes in the monologues collected in *Leaving Home* (1987). Keillor's fictional home, Lake Wobegon, is an approximate and humorous representation of life in the region, and Wobegon leave-taking appropriately includes graduations, career changes, joining the army, and retirement, characteristically discovering the humor and nostalgia related to commonplace events of small-town life. Fatherhood, one of Keillor's themes, is further explored in *Daddy's Girl*, an illustrated book and CD commemorating in rhyme and music the daily interactions of parenting.

At age 55, Keillor described time as no longer moving like "molasses" but as "greased lightning" (Bolick). An "Old Scout" article titled "Older man collapses at home, in satisfactory condition," dated June 20, 2006, announces summer and describes "white custardy clouds in the blueberry sky" and lying "sprawled on a chaise on the porch" with "ambition leaking out," "like water through cupped hands." Another article titled "The Withering Glare of the Spotlight," dated January 30, 2007, reflects on a completed "journey," with "no cameras, no microphones," and no press waiting to hear about the experience, and observes "what a great thing it is to have real work to do." Keillor further notes that "when you fall off the A-list, you simply return to your work, whatever it may be, and that rescues you from insanity."

Describing himself as "culturally quite conservative," Keillor calls being a writer "the purest form of entrepreneurship there is," acknowledging being "a sort of conservative Democrat" that Republicans find "odd." *Homegrown Democrat* (2004), a collection of political essays, has been called Keillor's love letter to liberalism. "Old Scout" articles titled "Needed: More Caribou, Fewer Holsteins" (February 6, 2007) and "Out with the Old" (December 26, 2006) discuss politics, change, and civility: Keillor comments that while "You discard yards and yards of old jazz and folk . . . the Beethoven piano sonatas are as moving today as when you first heard them" and concludes that while such sentiments may conflict with ideological revolution, they leave "Beethoven's moon still shin[ing] brightly." In seeming contradiction to these political and cerebral musings, Keillor defines his primary purpose for writing as to make readers "laugh out loud" even on airplanes experiencing turbulence. He calls this purpose "a revolt against piety" (Bolick). Literary and political critics call Keillor's style of humor in the American tradition that of a "cracker-barrel philosopher" or "yarn-spinner" who has adopted "modes and played roles" not practiced by earlier counterparts (Wroe).

In 1990 Keillor presented a live broadcast from the Mark Twain Memorial in Hartford, Connecticut. The broadcast of music and humor evoked memories of Twain's legacy of satirical genius.

Keillor's Lake Woebegon and accounts of life in the fictional small midwestern town are alternately humorous and poignant, producing Twain-like humor and a platform for the satirical presentation of sterner topics. In poetry as in prose Keillor's staple themes frame the extraordinary experience of ordinary moments. *The Writer's Almanac* program and published collections of poetry are another example of Keillor's poking at dominant trends, and public response to Keillor's poetry suggests that, contrary to the apparent general resistance to poetry, there is an audience for poetry that broadly addresses contemporary life.

The *Prairie Home Companion* radio program and overarching theme of Keillor's work minutely depict the interactions of Lake Woebegon's colorful fictional residents. The movie adaptation, scripted by Keillor and directed by Robert Altman in 2006, depicts a fictional final broadcast of the renowned radio program with a cast that includes: Keillor, Meryl Streep, Lindsay Lohan, Lily Tomlin, Woody Harrelson, John C. Reilly, Kevin Kline, Virginia Madsen, and Tommy Lee Jones. Critics describe the visual adaptation of *A Prairie Home Companion* as whimsical, gentle, and profound.

Bibliography

Bolick, Katie. Garrison Keillor Interview. "It's Just Work." *Atlantic Online*. Available online. URL: http://www.theatlantic.com/doc/199710u/keillor. Accessed February 13, 2007.

Keillor, Garrison. *Happy to Be Here*. New York: Antheneum, 1981.

———. *Lake Wobegon Days*. New York: Viking, 1985.

———. *Leaving Home: A Collection of Lake Wobegon Stories*. New York: Viking, 1987.

———. *We Are Still Married: Stories and Letters*. New York: Viking. 1989.

———. *WLT: A Radio Romance*. New York: Viking, 1991.

———. *A Visit to Mark Twain's House* (audio). Minneapolis: Highbridge Audio, 1992.

———. *The Book of Guys*. New York: Penguin, 1993.

———. *The Old Man Who Loved Cheese*. Boston: Little-Brown, 1996.

———. *The Sandy Bottom Orchestra*. (with Jenny Lind Nilsson). New York: Hyperion, 1996.

———. *Cat, You Better Come Home*. UK: Puffin Reprint, 1997/1995.

———. *Wobegon Boy*. New York: Viking, 1997.

———. *Mother Father Uncle Aunt: A New Monologue Collection*. Minneapolis: Highbridge Audio, 1998.

———. *Me, by Jimmy Big Boy Valente*. New York: Viking, 1999.

———. *Lake Woebegon Summer 1956*. London: Faber & Faber, 2001.

———. *Good Poems*. New York: Viking, 2002.

———. *Love Me*. New York: Viking, 2003.

———. *Homegrown Democrat*. New York: Viking, 2004.

———. *Daddy's Girl*. (book with CD). New York: Hyperion Books for Children, 2005.

———. *Good Poems for Hard Times*. New York: Viking, 2005.

———. "A Prairie Home Companion: The News from Lake Wobegon." American Public Media Web site. Available online. URL: http://prairiehome.publicradio.org/about/podcast. Accessed February 13, 2007.

———. "A Prairie Home Companion: The Old Scout." 2007. American Public Media Web site. Available online. URL: http://prairiehome.publicradio.org/features/deskofgk/2007/01/02.shtml. Accessed February 13, 2007.

———. "The Writer's Almanac." American Public Media Web site. Available online. URL: http://writersalmanac.publicradio.org/. Accessed February 13, 2007.

Lee, Judith Yaross. *Garrison Keillor: A Voice of America* (Studies in Popular Culture). Jackson: University of Mississippi Press, 1991.

Wroe, Nicholas. "Minnesota Zen Master." *The Guardian*, 6 March 2004. Profile. Available online. URL: http://books.guardian.co.uk/print/0,,4872965-99930,00.html. Accessed February 13, 2007.

Stella Thompson

Kellerman, Jonathan (1949–)

Kellerman is best known for 25 crime-fiction novels featuring the well-known character Dr. Alex Delaware.

Jonathan Kellerman was born in New York but raised in Los Angeles, where he received his B.A. in psychology from UCLA, followed by a Ph.D. in psychology from USC at the age of 24. While at UCLA, he worked as an editorial cartoonist, columnist, editor, and freelance musician.

Though winning the Samuel Goldwyn Writing Award for fiction in his senior year at UCLA, it would be 15 years before he would turn to writing for a living. Instead, he first embarked on a successful career in clinical psychology. Kellerman has been married to fellow novelist Faye Kellerman for 34 years, and they have four children, the eldest of whom, Jesse Kellerman, is also a writer. They live in Los Angeles.

Drawing from his experience as a psychologist, Kellerman's first novel, *When the Bough Breaks* (1985), introduces the character of Dr. Alex Delaware, a still young but retired child psychologist in Los Angeles, who becomes involved in a homicide investigation when it is discovered that the only witness to the murder of a psychiatrist is a seven-year-old girl. The novel also introduces Delaware's best friend, Milo Sturgis, an openly gay detective with the Los Angeles Police Department; Robin Castagna, Alex Delaware's love interest; and Dr. Rick Silverman, Milo Sturgis's lover. The novel earned Kellerman the Edgar Award and the Anthony Boucher Award for best first novel in 1986, and its success would be equaled by his follow-up effort, *Blood Test* (1986). Whereas Delaware has overt similarities to the author, Sturgis was a completely original creation of Kellerman's in response to the official line taken by the LAPD that there were no gay officers in the department—to "create a certain amount of tension," as the author said in a 2002 interview. Though profoundly unorthodox for its 1980s milieu, the pairing of the straight Delaware and the gay Sturgis was for the most part well received by readers and critics alike.

Blood Test continues the narrative of *When the Bough Breaks,* with Delaware now in retirement as an occasional police consultant. Following the trail of a couple who kidnap their child from the hospital and subsequently disappear, Delaware is caught up in a solitary investigation that almost leaves him dead.

Exploring issues of greed, exploited genius, and schizophrenia, *Over the Edge* (1987) is still dominated by psychology and not police work, but in his following novel Kellerman takes a break from Delaware, if not his violent and often sordid world. In *The Butcher's Theatre* (1988) a serial killer is loose in Jerusalem, and it is up to Police Chief Inspector Daniel Sharavi to put a stop to him. Sharavi returns in *Survival of the Fittest* (1997), but here as a foil to Delaware and Sturgis in the investigation into the death of a diplomat's handicapped daughter in Los Angeles.

Resuming the Delaware series, Kellerman continued to expand and nuance his own investigation into the psychological dimensions of crime, analyzing the mind and actions of major and minor characters alike: Munchausen-by-proxy syndrome in *Devil's Waltz* (1993), obsessive-compulsive disorder in *Obsession* (2007), the effects of early childhood development in *Bad Love* (1994) and *The Clinic* (1997), phobias and anxiety in *Private Eyes* (1992), child psychopathology in *Rage* (2005), and pseudopsychology ("pop-psychology") in *Therapy* (2004). Killing in order to live out morbid fantasies or to re-create killings from the past are also recurring themes in his work.

Influenced by Ross McDonald and Raymond Chandler, Kellerman considers himself to be a "second-generation South California hardboiled writer" (*Under Interrogation,* 2006), exploring "the deterioration of quality of life and the uneasy coexistence of conflicted lifestyles" (Hartlaub, 2001), but part of his enduring appeal also lies in his ability to produce ever new and strong characters, varying and extending the successful Delaware formula. Five of Kellerman's novels are not part of the Delaware series: *The Butcher's Theatre, Billy Straight* (1998), *The Conspiracy Club* (2003), *Twisted* (2004), and *Double Homicide* (2004) (cowritten with his wife, Faye Kellerman). But even here readers find extended relations: Petra Conner, for example, appearing first in *Survival of the Fittest* (1997) in a minor role alongside Sturgis and Delaware, and receiving a larger role in *Billy Straight,* is the central character in *Twisted,* where she has to solve a seemingly unrelated string of murders before the killer strikes again. Interestingly, whereas Conner's characterization is relatively subtle and convincing, Delaware himself often takes on a sort of comic-book patina, a weakness of the series noted by critics and readers alike.

When the Bough Breaks was adapted into a successful TV movie in 1986 starring Ted Danson as Alex Delaware.

Bibliography

Barnes and Noble: Meet the Writers. "Interview with Jonathan Kellerman." Available online. URL: http://www.barnesandnoble.com/writers/writerdetails.asp?z=y&cid=90088#interview.

Hartlaub, Joe. "Review: 'Dr. Death.'" Available online. URL: http://www.bookreporter.com/reviews/0679459618.asp.

Kellerman, Jonathan. *When the Bough Breaks.* New York: Random House, 1985.

———. *Blood Test.* New York: Little Brown, 1986.

———. *Over the Edge.* New York: Atheneum, 1987.

———. *The Butcher's Theatre.* New York: Bantam, 1988.

———. *Private Eyes.* New York: Bantam, 1992.

———. *Devil's Waltz.* New York: Bantam, 1993.

———. *Bad Love.* New York: Bantam, 1994.

———. *The Clinic.* New York: Bantam, 1997.

———. *Survival of the Fittest.* New York: Bantam, 1997.

———. *Billy Straight.* New York: Random House, 1998.

———. *A Cold Heart.* New York: Ballantine, 2003.

———. *The Conspiracy Club.* New York: Random House, 2003.

———. *Double Homicide.* New York: Warner Books, 2004.

———. *Therapy.* New York: Random House, 2004.

———. *Twisted.* New York: Ballantine, 2004.

———. *Rage.* New York: Ballantine, 2005.

———. *Obsession.* New York: Ballantine, 2007.

Penguin UK Authors. "Jonathan Kellerman under Interrogation." Available online. URL: http://www.penguin.co.uk/nf/Author/AuthorPage/0,,1000007341,00.html?sym=QUE.

Victoria Nagy

The Key to Rebecca Ken Follett (1980)

A spy thriller set in Egypt during World War II, *The Key to Rebecca* primarily deals with the efforts of a British officer, Major William Vandam, to catch the Nazi agent Alex Wolff, who has been feeding crucial information about Allied battle plans to German forces in the region. Wolff was also responsible for Vandam's greatest failure earlier in the war (which occurred before the novel begins): He was the agent who helped the Iraqi prime minister, Rashid Ali, escape Allied agents (including Vandam), murdering a female agent in the process. Vandam feels responsible for her death and cannot forgive himself; when he realizes that Wolff is back, he enlists the help of a young Jewish woman, Elene Fontana, in a desperate bid to catch him.

Among the novel's characters appear several fictionalized versions of key military figures of the time (notably German field marshal Erwin Rommel), and KEN FOLLETT has said on his Web site that the plot is based on a true story he came across while researching his earlier novel, *Eye of the Needle*:

> There was a spy ring based on a house boat in Cairo in 1942 which involved a belly dancer and a British major she was having an affair with. The information at stake was crucial to the battles going on in the desert. The code used by the spies was based on one of the great suspense novels of all time, *Rebecca,* by Daphne du Maurier. (Follett)

A striking feature of *The Key to Rebecca* is its attention to detail—not merely in the taut, complex plotting but in the careful depiction of the military strategies of both German and Allied forces and of the actual function of the code that provides the novel with its title. The "key" is a formula used by Wolff to create coded messages using a combination of the date on which the message will be sent and a copy of Daphne du Maurier's novel:

> Today was May 28. He had to add 42—the year—to 28 to arrive at the page number in the novel which he must use to encode his message. May was the fifth month, so every fifth letter on the page would be discounted. He decided to send: HAVE ARRIVED. CHECKING IN. ACKNOWLEDGE. Beginning at the top of page 70 of the book, he looked along the line of print for the letter H. It was the tenth character, discounting every fifth letter. In his code it would therefore be represented by the tenth letter of the alphabet, J. Next he needed an A. In the book, the third letter after the H was an A. The A of HAVE would therefore be represented by the third letter of the alphabet, C. There were special ways of dealing with rare letters, like X (38).

Follett contrasts such scenes of intelligence and military calculation with the sexual tactics of his protagonists. The consequences of sex with the wrong person can be devastating and even fatal, sex itself being a kind of weapon employed in the shadows of the war.

Follett develops this theme by placing the espionage plot in the context of two sexual relationships—one conventionally romantic (the developing attraction between Vandam and Elene), the other cold and, in conventional terms, dysfunctional (between Wolff and the famous belly dancer Sonja, both of whom use sex only as a means to an end). However, this parallel is complicated when Vandam—despite his fascination with Elene, a former courtesan—asks her to "befriend" Wolff in order to find out how he is receiving his information. When she asks what he means by "befriend," he replies simply, "That's up to you. Just as long as you get his address" (104). Ironically, Wolff is exploiting Sonja's own sexuality in order to get his information, promising to find someone to reenact her favorite sexual fantasy (of abuse and group sex) if she will seduce a British officer carrying Allied battle plans in his briefcase. Sonja is especially happy to do so because she is a proud Egyptian nationalist who hates the British, although she has no strong feelings for Wolff beyond basic sexual attraction.

Follett also complicates the simplistic opposition of "good" Allies and "evil" Nazis by unpacking colonial tensions existing in Egypt at the time, using the struggles of his Egyptian characters to demonstrate that colonization and occupation are necessarily oppressive to an occupied people, no matter which power rules. Follett's Nazis are in no way sympathetic, but the racism of the British colonials is also jarring, and the author makes no attempt to sanitize or gloss over it. For example, on one occasion, when Wolff is posing as a South African officer in a club in Cairo, the grumbling of the English officer next to him makes the Nazi agent seem the more politically sensitive and informed individual:

> Smith complained about the poor food, the way the bars kept running out of drinks, the rent of his flat and the rudeness of Arab waiters. Wolff itched to explain that the food was poor because Smith insisted on English rather than Egyptian dishes, that drinks were scarce because of the European war, that rents were sky-high because of the thousands of foreigners like Smith who had invaded the city, and that the waiters were rude to him because he was too lazy or arrogant to learn a few phrases of courtesy in their language (83).

In contrast, Wolff's superior knowledge of human psychology is emphasized, along with his sophisticated sense of style. His love of good food, wine, and beautiful women fascinates Vandam, a widowed single parent. The glamour of Wolff is repeatedly contrasted with Vandam's mundane and often awkward existence, and it is difficult for a reader to avoid comparison between Follett's portrayal of Alex Wolff and Ian Fleming's portrayal of uber-British secret agent James Bond—even when Wolff kills in cold blood.

The book was adapted into a made-for-TV movie in 1985 starring Cliff Robertson as Major William Vandam and David Soul as Alex Wolff.

Bibliography

Du Maurier, Daphne. *Rebecca.* London: Victor Gollancz, 1973.

Follett, Ken. "Ken's View." Available online. URL: http://www.ken-follett.com/bibliography/rebecca.html. Accessed February 27, 2007.

———. *The Key to Rebecca.* New York: Morrow, 1980.

Claire Horsnell

Kidd, Sue Monk (1948–)

The author of two novels, three memoirs, a collection of writings, and a host of articles and essays, Kidd began writing after an early career as a nurse, turning first to nonfiction and then to memoir before publishing her first novel in 2002.

All of Kidd's work reflects her abiding interest in contemplative spirituality, an interest arising while the author was in her 30s. Originally working freelance producing nonfiction pieces of a personal nature, Kidd's spiritual education lead to three memoirs: *God's Joyful Surprise* (1987), *When the Heart Waits* (1990), and *The Dance of the Dissident Daughter* (1996), the last a very personal journey of self-discovery toward a less traditional, more feminist spirituality. This also describes the experience of the adolescent Lily in Kidd's successful first novel, *The* SECRET LIFE OF BEES (2003). Developed from a short story written in 1993 and following intense study at various courses and conferences, the novel became a *New York Times* best seller and winner of various awards, including the 2004 Book Sense Paperback Book of the Year, inspiring its readers, particularly women, with a sense of identification and spiritual solace. A film of the novel was released in 2008.

Set in South Carolina against a backdrop of emerging civil rights, *The Secret Life of Bees* draws on the author's own childhood in southwest Georgia, telling the story of the motherless Lily and her search for reparation, both for that loss and for the pain inflicted by her cold and cruel father. Lily's search takes her, along with her nanny, Rosaleen, to the bee farm of the Boatwright sisters, where she discovers not only the love and companionship of strong women but also spiritual self-knowledge and identity. Moreover, both Rosaleen and the sisters are black, while Lily is white, adding an additional historical and racial dimension that affects the lives of the characters in a host of significant ways.

Kidd's best-selling second novel, *The Mermaid Chair,* was published in 2005, winning the Quill Award for general fiction. It deals with themes and issues similar to those of *The Secret Life of Bees,* but its heroine is older and more complex. Jessie Sullivan's midlife restlessness and dissatisfaction lead finally to adultery and a personal awakening when she returns to her childhood home to look after her disturbed mother. The fictional island of Egret, located in salt marshes like those around Kidd's own South Carolina home, offers a symbolic setting for Jessie's relationship with one of the monks from the island monastery. Like Lily, she must come to terms with her past, in this case the death of her father in a boating accident when she was nine; for both, sexual discovery and the uncovering of the past lead to a new sense of identity, inflected with a feminine spirituality.

Given her interest in the feminine and the spiritual, it is not surprising that symbols of womanhood figure prominently in Kidd's fiction. The Black Madonna, for example, a maternal image of both divinity and empowerment, is at the heart of the creative spirituality of the Boatwright sisters in *The Secret Life of Bees,* while the mermaid of the *The Mermaid Chair* is a living emblem of the capacity to dive down within oneself and discover a new, deeper life. The novels, too, share a common belief in the importance of communities of women, like those who support and educate Lily and Jessie, bringing them to a realization of their own strength as women.

Kidd's latest publication, *Firstlight* (2006), is a collection of her "early inspirational writings."

Bibliography

Kidd, Sue Monk. *God's Joyful Surprise: Finding Yourself Loved.* San Francisco, Harper & Row, 1989.

———. *When the Heart Waits: Spiritual Direction for Life's Sacred Questions.* San Francisco: Harper & Row, 1990.

———. *The Dance of the Dissident Daughter.* New York: HarperCollins, 1996.

———. *The Secret Life of Bees.* London and New York: Penguin, 2003.

———. *The Mermaid Chair.* London: Headline Review, 2005.

———. *Firstlight: The Early Inspirational Writings of Sue Monk Kidd.* New York: GuidepostsBooks, 2006.

"Sue Monk Kidd." Available online. URL: http://www.suemonkkidd.com.

Sarah Falcus

King, Stephen (1947–)

Referred to variously as the "Master of Horror" or the "King of Terror," Stephen King is one of the most successful novelists in the world. More than 300 million copies of his novels are in publication and have been translated into 33 languages. With more than 40 novels, scores of short stories and articles, and a list of film and television adaptations of his work that has reached triple digits, an American who has not come into contact with King's work would be a rare find.

King was born in Portland, Maine. His parents, Donald and Nellie, separated in 1949, when

Donald abruptly deserted his wife and two young sons. Nellie, a young mother with sole custody of Stephen and his older brother, David, moved the family a number of times before settling in Durham, Maine, in 1958. Here King attended Lisbon Falls High School before going on to the University of Maine at Orono, where he earned a B.A. in English in 1970. At the University of Maine King was active in campus politics and a writer for the school newspaper. He also met Tabitha Spruce, whom he married in 1971.

The Kings struggled financially through their first years of marriage, with King working at a variety of odd jobs to pay the bills while he worked on his fiction. His first published short story, "The Glass Floor," was accepted in 1967, and King followed this with a number of other stories later collected along with it in *Night Shift* (1976). Of the sale of these early stories King writes, "[T]he checks sometimes came just in time to avoid what the power companies euphemistically call 'an interruption in service'" (*Night Shift*, xxii).

Life improved for the Kings after Stephen began teaching high school English at Hampden Academy in Hampden, Maine. King's high school teaching career was short-lived, however, for in 1973, after the lucrative sale of his first novel, *Carrie*, about a bullied high school student with telekinetic powers, King gave up teaching to devote himself fully to his writing career.

A number of King's best-known and most highly regarded novels came out of this early period: *Salem's Lot* (1975), a modern vampire story influenced by Bram Stoker's *Dracula*; *The Shining* (1977), about a family isolated in a haunted hotel (later made into a successful film of the same name starring Jack Nicholson); and *The Stand* (1978), King's apocalyptic tale of germ warfare.

Though professionally successful, King has had demons to battle in his personal life. In *On Writing* (2000) he candidly discusses his addictions to alcohol and cocaine: "My nights during the last five years of my drinking always ended with the same ritual: I'd pour any beers left in the refrigerator down the sink. If I didn't, they'd talk to me as I lay in bed until I got up and had another. And another. And one more" (96–97). Tabitha King organized a group of family and friends to confront her husband about his addictions, an action that convinced King he needed to change his lifestyle. He has been sober and drug-free since the late 1980s.

In June 1999 King was struck by a van while walking along the shoulder of a road near his Lovell, Maine, home, and the resulting injuries, which included a shattered leg, broken hip, and collapsed lung, required five separate surgeries and a three-week hospital stay. King's injuries also made sitting for long periods of time uncomfortable, a situation that slowed his writing output for a time.

When asked about the inspiration for his work, King once responded, "I have the heart of a young boy . . . in a jar, on my desk," a seemingly flippant retort, but one that, in fact, points to a seminal influence: Robert Bloch, best known for his novel *Psycho* (the basis for Hitchcock's film), who originated King's gruesome joke. Bloch is one of "six great writers of the macabre" to whom King dedicated his critical work, *Danse Macabre* (1981). What King prizes in Bloch's works are the characters, like Norman Bates, who embody what he terms the "Apollonian/Dionysian conflict," a version of the Dr. Jekyll/Mr. Hyde split (*Danse Macabre* 83), which typifies his characters from the very earliest works, like the narrator of "Strawberry Spring" (1975) or *The Shining*'s Jack Torrence.

King's youthful fascination with the horror genre began when he found a box of his father's old books, a cache of science-fiction and horror stories that included the "pick of the litter": an anthology of H. P. Lovecraft's stories (*Danse* 101). While Lovecraft's were not the first horror stories King had encountered, he notes that it was the first time he had met with a horror writer who "took his work seriously . . . Lovecraft—courtesy of my father—opened the way for me, as he had done for others before me" (*Danse* 102).

Even Lovecraft's subject matter has served as inspiration for King, who praises the former's "mythos," noting that the great evils at work in his fiction "make us feel the size of the universe we hang suspended in, and suggest shadowy forces that could destroy us all if they so much as grunted in their sleep" (*Danse* 72)—forces well illustrated in King's *IT* (1986), for example. However, King has drawn material for his work from nearly every aspect of his life: A job at an industrial laundry after graduating from college led to the well-known story "The Mangler" (1972); a stay at the Stanley Hotel in Estes Park, Colorado, was the initial inspiration for *The Shining;* witnessing a friend killed by a freight train when King was four would later figure in "The Body" (1982).

Many of King's protagonists are social outcasts, bullied children, or down-on-their-luck adults who struggle sometimes for justice, sometimes for revenge. King's own childhood, the author notes, has a lot to do with this character type: "My mother was a single parent . . . and she went through a lot of menial jobs. We were dragged from pillar to post and there was none of this equal opportunity stuff going on at the time. . . . And I got a sense of who was being taken advantage of and who was lording it over other people. A lot of that sense of injustice stayed. It stuck with me, and it's still in the books today" (O'Hehir).

King has never minded being labeled a "horror novelist" and thus not being treated as a "serious" writer. He is known for referring to his work as the literary equivalent of a "Big Mac and fries" and has said, "I recognize terror as the finest emotion . . . and so I will try to terrorize the reader. But if I find that I cannot terrify him/her, I will try to horrify; and if I find that I cannot horrify, I'll go for the gross-out. I'm not proud" (*Danse* 37). This attitude, only somewhat tongue-in-cheek, belies the seriousness with which some of his more recent work has been treated. King's short story "The Man in the Black Suit," for example, was awarded the 1996 O. Henry Award, while its author received the 2003 National Book Award for Distinguished Contribution to American Letters.

The National Book Foundation's choice drew some criticism from academic circles. Yale professor and literary scholar Harold Bloom, for example, wrote in a *Boston Globe* article that the choice was "another low in the shocking process of dumbing down our cultural life." King himself recognized the foundation's choice as unusual but saw it instead as a positive step for American literature, noting in his acceptance speech that the foundation "took a huge risk in giving this award to a man many people see as a rich hack. For far too long the so-called popular writers of this country and the so-called literary writers have stared at each other with animosity and a willful lack of understanding. . . . But giving an award like this to a guy like me suggests that in the future things don't have to be the way they've always been. Bridges can be built between the so-called popular fiction and the so-called literary fiction."

King's 2006 novel, *Lisey's Story,* has also helped bridge this gap. Though it contains the supernatural elements King is known for, the novel, about a widow's nostalgic look at 25 years of marriage, has received praise for its literary merit, one reviewer noting that with it, "King has crashed literary fiction's exclusive party, and he'll be no easier to ignore than Carrie at the prom" (Charles).

King's best-known novels include *Cujo* (1981), *Christine* (1983), MISERY (1987), DOLORES CLAIBORNE (1992), *Bag of Bones* (1998), *The Girl Who Loved Tom Gordon* (1999), and the seven novel Dark Tower series (1982–2004). Although most of his novels and many of his short stories have been adapted for the screen, the most critically acclaimed adaptations include Brian De Palma's *Carrie,* Stanley Kubrick's *The Shining,* Rob Reiner's *Stand by Me,* and Frank Darabont's *The Shawshank Redemption.* King has also published six novels under the pseudonym Richard Bachman.

Bibliography

Bloom, Harold. "Dumbing Down American Readers." *Boston Globe*, 24 September 2003.

Charles, Ron. "Stephen King Gets Literally Literary." *Orlando Sentinel*, 5 November 2006.

King, Stephen. *Night Shift.* New York: Doubleday, 1976.

———. *Danse Macabre.* New York: Everest House, 1981.

———. *On Writing.* New York: Scribner, 2000.

———. "Acceptance Speech." *National Book Awards 2003.* Available online. URL: http://www.nationalbook.org/nbaacceptspeech_sking.html.

O'Hehir, Andrew. "The Stephen King Interview." *Salon* (24 September 1998). Available online. URL: http://www.cnn.com/books/news/9809/24/king.interview.salon.index2.html?eref=sites earch.

Jen Cadwallader

Kingsolver, Barbara (1955–)

Barbara Kingsolver is the author of five novels: *The Bean Trees* (1988), *Animal Dreams* (1990), *Pigs in Heaven* (1993), *The* POISONWOOD BIBLE (1998), and *Prodigal Summer* (2001).

Kingsolver grew up on a farm in rural Kentucky, the daughter of a physician and a health worker whose work took them to Africa and the Caribbean during Kingsolver's childhood. She studied biology and earned degrees from DePauw University in Greencastle, Indiana, and the University of Arizona. She also has an honorary doctorate in letters from DePauw, awarded in 1995. Her writing is known to amalgamate her childhood penchant for storytelling with her scientific talents, which include a methodical approach to researching her novels and a strong knowledge of the natural world.

One of the most common themes in her work can best be described as uprootedness—a sense of purposeful displacement. She has been commended for creating lush images of disjuncture and disorientation in the individual, the family, and society while still celebrating the triumph of the human spirit. Kingsolver uprooted herself from a slew of jobs and travels between America and Europe to become a freelance journalist in Tucson, Arizona, in 1985. She won an Arizona Press Club award for her journalism and, emboldened with that success and her first short story publication "Rose-Johnny," she embarked on a new career in fiction writing.

Her first novel, *The Bean Trees,* is a story of a young woman from a Kentucky farm who displaces herself, eventually to Tucson. The protagonist, Taylor Greer, learns to embrace humanity as well as her own abandonment during an eventful odyssey across the American West. The *New York Times Book Review* lauded Kingsolver's "vivid language and use of scene . . . [a book] that contains more good writing than most successful careers" (DeMarr 11). The novel was praised for its poignancy and accessibility to a wide audience, and HarperCollins rewarded its lasting success with a 10-year anniversary edition in 1998.

Kingsolver vaulted into literary stardom with 1998's *The Poisonwood Bible,* an international best seller for which she was nominated for the Pulitzer Prize and the PEN/Faulkner Award, and for which she received the U.S. National Humanities Medal (2000). The novel, her fourth, tells the story of an American Southern Baptist missionary family in the Congo in the 1960s and is narrated in competing turns by each of the four daughters in the family. In researching the book, Kingsolver traveled in Central Africa and immersed herself in its languages and cultures, as well as the turbulent modern history of European colonialism and its legacy on the African continent.

Kingsolver also has a reputation as an activist on social issues. Crossing over many genres, her writing is marked by sustained concern for humanity's instability and often explores the oppression of women and of the natural world: "The stories of Kingsolver's women connect them strongly to place . . . and for most of them nature is or becomes a teacher" (DeMarr 21).

Her passion for engaging readers and audiences with these issues led her to found, with HarperCollins, the Bellwether Prize for Fiction, which supports socially-engaged literature. Awarded biannually, the prize grants $25,000 to the writer of an unpublished work and guarantees a minimum printing of 10,000 copies.

Bibliography

DeMarr, Mary Jean. *Barbara Kingsolver: A Critical Companion.* Westport, Conn.: Greenwood Press, 1999.

Kingsolver, Barbara. *The Bean Trees.* New York: HarperCollins, 1988.

———. *Animal Dreams.* New York: HarperCollins, 1990.

———. *Pigs in Heaven.* New York: HarperCollins, 1993.

———. *The Poisonwood Bible.* New York: HarperCollins, 1998.

———. *Prodigal Summer.* New York: HarperCollins, 2001.

Richard Alexander Johnson

Klein, Joe (1946–)

Klein is a journalist and novelist whose work is concerned with individuals and events of note in contemporary American and international politics. A member of the Council on Foreign Relations and former Guggenheim Fellow, he has worked as a left-of-center political correspondent but is best known for his roman à clef *Primary Colors,* which focuses on the political life of President Bill Clinton.

Born in New York City, Klein attended the University of Pennsylvania, where in 1968 he earned a degree in American civilization. During the next three decades he was affiliated variously with the *Peabody Times*, Boston's WGBH-TV, *The Real Paper, Rolling Stone, New York* magazine, CBS News, and *The New Yorker*; he won a National Headliner Award for his *Newsweek* column "Public Lives." By the time he published his first political novel, Klein had already established a solid journalistic reputation through his coverage of the U.S. presidential elections from 1980 to 1992.

Revisiting the 1992 election in fiction, Klein created his best-known work, *Primary Colors: A Novel of Politics*, in 1996. Attributed to "Anonymous," the novel enjoyed enormous popularity, partially fueled by speculation concerning its authorship. Its enigmatic hero, Jack Stanton, is a charismatic southern politician modeled on Clinton, and its narrator, Henry Burton, escapes a midlife crisis by joining Stanton's campaign staff. On the campaign trail he admires Stanton's ability to inspire intimacy, hide a fierce intellect behind a facade of disarming provincialism, and analyze a crowd so deftly that he can instantly appear as its ideal candidate. But as the exercise and refinement of these very capabilities begin to subtly erode Stanton's personal and political convictions, the campaign becomes plagued by scandals, providing Burton with some painful but instructive lessons in the uneasy relation between the ideal and the real. The novel spent 25 weeks on the *New York Times* best-seller list and was adapted to film in 1998. After much speculation and his own protestations to the contrary, Klein claimed authorship of the best seller.

In 2000 he published *The Running Mate*, featuring the fictional campaign of Charles Martin, who is loosely based on Arizona senator John McCain. Running against Stanton, Martin faces the sort of obstacles typically explored in Klein's work: media-hyped scandals, degrading smear tactics, and poll-driven policies. Whereas *Primary Colors* was frequently likened by critics to Robert Penn Warren's *All the Kings Men*, one *New York Times* reviewer described *The Running Mate* as a made-for-TV rendering of *State of the Union* (Kakutani). Klein then returned to his trump suit with a best-selling biography in 2002, *The Natural: The Misunderstood Presidency of Bill Clinton*.

Since 2003 Klein has been part of *Time* magazine's team of senior correspondents along with Margaret Carlson, Michael Kinsley, Charles Krauthammer, Joel Stein, and Andrew Sullivan. He frequently contributes to political blogs such as *Swampland* and appears on televised news programs such as *Meet the Press*. In 2006 he revisited the theme of poll-driven politics with his sixth book, *Politics Lost: How American Democracy Was Trivialized by People Who Think You're Stupid*.

Bibliography

Kakutani, Michiko. "Books of the Times; The 'Anonymous' Joe Klein Tackles a New Candidate." Review of *The Running Mate*, by Joe Klein. *New York Times*, 18 April 2000. Available online. URL: http://query.nytimes.com/gst/fullpage.html?res=9E06EFDE1531F93BA25757C0A9669C8B63. Accessed June 16, 2007.

Klein, Joseph. *Primary Colors: A Novel of Politics*. New York: Random House, 1996.

———. *The Running Mate*. New York: Dial, 2000.

———. *The Natural: The Misunderstood Presidency of Bill Clinton*. New York: Doubleday, 2002.

Primary Colors. Directed by Mike Nichols. Universal Studios, 1998.

Royce Carlton. "Joe Klein: Speaker Press Kit." Available online. URL: http://www.roycecarlton.com/speaker/Joe-Klein-Infokit. Accessed June 13, 2007.

Time.com. "Joe Klein: Biography." Available online. URL: http://www.time.com/time/columnist/klein/article/0,9565,490843,00.html. Accessed June 16, 2007.

Priscilla Glanville

Koontz, Dean (1945–)

Dean Koontz is the author of more than 50 novels, including 10 number one hardback best sellers. While best known for horror-suspense fiction, his output has been widely varied. He began in science fiction and gothic romance, then developed his own genre-crossing brand of thriller, romance, crime, and horror fiction. His works have also included children's books and several volumes of poetry.

Koontz married his wife, Gerda, in 1966 just as he was beginning a career as an English teacher.

After the publication of *Star Quest* (1968), Gerda agreed to support him for five years while he became an established writer. She would eventually leave her job to help handle her husband's career. Koontz's legendary work habits are described in terms of eight- to 10-hour workdays, six or seven days a week. Despite his prolific output, Koontz reports working through dozens of drafts, and he has become known for surprising invention and rich details.

Several aspects of Koontz's fiction stem from his childhood and his troubled relationship with his father, well described in Katherine Ramsland's detailed and intimate biography of 1997. Born in 1945 in Pennsylvania, he lived through a childhood of poverty and abuse, finding refuge in books. His father, Ray Koontz, would be diagnosed and treated for alcoholism and schizoid personality disorder near the end of his life. After his father's death in 1991, Koontz dropped the middle initial *R* from his byline. Many of his villains suffer from some form of mental disorder, and his heroes struggle as often with internal issues as they do with external adversity. Familial happiness and mental health are at stake in most of his fiction.

Koontz's career can be sketched as a rise from early prodigious output in a variety of genres, through a period of increasing focus and success, to a recent trend toward serialization. Beginning as a science-fiction writer, Koontz quickly started publishing under various pen names in order to branch out to gothic romance and other genres without damaging his marketability. Known pseudonyms are Deanna Dwyer, K. R. Dwyer, Aaron Wolfe, David Axton, Brian Coffey, John Hill, Leigh Nichols, Owen West, Richard Paige, Leonard Chris, and Anthony North. He would later regret this practice and attribute it to "bad advice" (Munster 6). Working this way throughout the 1970s, he produced each year an average of three to four books, described as "hackwork . . . not without interest" (Hlavaty 1). All but five of his pre-1975 novels remain out of print. Several early books have been rereleased under his own name, sometimes with new titles and extensive revisions.

The publication of *Whispers* (1980) marked the beginning of greater success for Koontz, and he stopped publishing pseudonymously by 1988. The next year saw the first publication of a scholarly essay collection in which editor Bill Munster explains Koontz's appeal: "It's his looking at the tenuous nature of life and the tissue-thin barrier that separates us from sudden terror and tragedy that gives his books such power and enjoyment" (ix–x). This measure of critical success coincided with a new level of popularity; in 1989 *Midnight* became the first in a string of five consecutive number-one hardback best sellers.

Although Koontz has often resisted calls for sequels or recurring characters, he is currently producing two ongoing series. The series beginning with *Odd Thomas* tells the story of an investigator who speaks to the dead and can see otherwise invisible evil spirits. *Dean Koontz's Frankenstein*, now through its third volume, is a coauthored series originally developed for television. His popular children's book *Santa's Twin* (1996) has also received a rare sequel.

Koontz's novels are most often praised for their intricate characters, twisting plots, and fast pace. Commentary is less unanimous regarding his dense descriptions, hopeful resolutions, and dark humor. The emotional realism of Koontz's characterizations were enhanced by his personal encounters with modern psychology and health practices in caring for his father. Almost all of his characters are well-rounded, with a full psychological and personal history, and he is especially known for strong female protagonists. Both heroes and villains are often given ironic or thematic names, such as the visionary medium Odd Thomas or the mad circus clown Punchinello Beezo. Koontz's labyrinthine plots turn on surprising coincidence and revelation, and he is celebrated for his ability to keep readers turning pages. Criticism of his lighter notes usually stems from his departure from generic norms, many readers finding humor and happy endings at odds with typical horror or suspense fiction, but Koontz has made a career of thwarting such rigid expectations.

Although the body of his work continues to defy easy summation, the major novels, while always suspenseful, seem to alternate between fast-paced thrillers and off-beat dark comedies, while a more sober and unsettling tone has often characterized his most commercially successful work, as in best sellers *Intensity* (1995) and *The Husband* (2006). From early on Koontz would often supply haunting epigraphs to his books from an invented volume, *The Book of Counted Sorrows,* whose short poems were collected together and published under that title as an e-book in 2001. Elements of humor and irony become increasingly present after the occasionally autobiographical *Mr. Murder* (1993), reaching fuller maturity in *Ticktock* (1996) and the nearly vaudevillian LIFE EXPECTANCY (2004). Koontz's zany side can also be found in the first of two collections of whimsical verse, *The Paper Doorway* (2001).

Although often labeled a horror writer and having even once served as president of the Horror Writers of America, Koontz defies this and other categorizations in several ways. Having begun his career in science fiction, for example, he often provides material explanations for seemingly supernatural phenomena in such forms as extraterrestrials, genetic quirks, or psychological aberrations. In interviews Koontz has drawn a thematic distinction between himself and more conventional horror/suspense writers, noting that mainstream fiction tends toward "empty cynicism," while he has "always had a strong belief in the basic goodness of most people and humankind's potential for growth, progress, and eventual transcendence" (De Lint 15).

Bibliography

De Lint, Charles. "Dean R. Koontz." *Fantasy Review* 10 (1987): 14–16, 31.

Hlavaty, Arthur D. "Dean Koontz: Hometown Boy Makes Good." *The New York Review of Science Fiction* 118 (June 1998): 1, 4–5.

Koontz, Dean. *Star Quest.* New York: Ace Double, 1968.

———. *Whispers.* New York: Putnam, 1980.

———. *Midnight.* New York: Putnam, 1989.

———. *Mr. Murder.* New York: Putnam, 1993.

———. *Intensity.* Franklin Center, Pa.: Franklin Library, 1995; New York: Knopf, 1996.

———. *Santa's Twin.* New York: Harper Prism, 1996.

———. *Ticktock.* New York: Ballantine, 1997.

———. *The Book of Counted Sorrows.* New York: Barnes & Noble, 2001.

———. *The Paper Doorway: Funny Verse and Nothing Worse.* New York: HarperCollins, 2001.

———. *Odd Thomas.* New York: Bantam, 2003.

———. *Life Expectancy.* New York: Bantam, 2004.

———. *Dean Koontz's Frankenstein. Book One: Prodigal Son.* With Kevin J. Anderson. New York: Bantam, 2005.

———. *The Husband.* New York: Bantam, 2006.

———. *My Heart Belongs to Me.* New York: Bantam, 2008.

———. *Odd Hours.* New York: Bantam, 2008.

Munster, Bill. *Sudden Fear: The Horror and Dark Suspense Fiction of Dean R. Koontz.* San Bernardino, Calif.: Borgo Press, 1989.

Ramsland, Katherine M. *Dean Koontz: A Writer's Biography.* New York: HarperPrism, 1997.

Charles F. Tedder

Kostova, Elizabeth (1964–)

Elizabeth Kostova is the author of the best-selling historical novel *The* HISTORIAN (2005) and coauthor with Anthony Lord of the travel memoir *1927: The Good-Natured Chronicle of a Journey* (1995).

Born in New London, Connecticut, Kostova spent her youth living in various places in the United States but often traveled with her father, a historian, to eastern Europe, where she cultivated a fascination with the region from an early age. It was her father, she claims, who sparked her interest in the legends of Vlad the Impaler (the inspiration for Bram Stoker's *Dracula*) by telling her stories while on these trips, and *The Historian* is a fictional search for the origins of the Dracula legend.

Kostova graduated from Yale University in 1988 with a degree in British Studies, and while there she won the Wallace Prize for fiction writing from the department of English. In 2004 she completed an M.F.A. from the University of Michigan.

Shortly after graduating from Yale, Kostova toured Bulgaria on a personal research trip to record local folk music, and while there she met her future husband, Georgi Kostov, shortly after the communist regime of Todor Zhivkov fell during Bulgaria's Velvet Revolution. The tour rekindled her childhood interest in Dracula, and in 1995 she began work on the manuscript for *The Historian*, which would take her 10 years to complete, during which time she taught fiction writing at the University of Michigan, completed her M.B.A., and won the Hopwood Award for a novel-in-progress. The attenuated production of the novel was owing in part to Kostova's meticulous research in libraries and archives, both in the United States and eastern Europe, and in part simply to her lack of spare time; she could often write only early in the morning or late at night, on one occasion even writing several pages in longhand while waiting at a doctor's office.

In 2004 Little, Brown won a publishers' bidding war for *The Historian* at a reported $2 million, and the novel hit bookstores on June 14, 2005, reaching number one on the *New York Times* best-seller list just three weeks later. Sony purchased the film rights to the book for $1.5 million, and screenwriter David S. Magee (*Finding Neverland*) is reportedly adapting the novel for film with producer Douglas Wick (*Memoirs of a Geisha*).

When released, *The Historian* immediately drew comparisons to the work of DAN BROWN, at which Kostova bristled. As she told one interviewer, "*The Da Vinci Code* hugely increased public interest in the idea of historical research as a detective tale, and that has a lot to do with why my book sold as well as it did. However, none of my approach to writing is commercial" (*Yale Alumni Magazine*). Others have likened the novel's impact and literary success to Jonathan Safran Foer's *Everything Is Illuminated* and Donna Tartt's *The Secret History*, while Kostova herself lists Henry James's *The Portrait of a Lady* as her most influential work.

At present she is reportedly at work on a second historical novel.

Bibliography

Danford, Natalie. "Two-Million-Dollar Baby." Available online. URL: http://www.yalealumnimagazine.com/issues/2005_05/arts.html. Accessed April 22, 2007.

Guthmann, Edward. "Vampires Lurk in Our Collective Imagination, as 'The Historian' Author Can Tell You." Available online. URL: http://www.sfgate.com/cgi-bin/article.cgi?f=/c/a/2005/07/25/DDGBKDS8DC1.DTL&type=books. Accessed April 22, 2007.

Kostova, Elizabeth. *1927: The Good-Natured Chronicle of a Journey*. Asheville, N.C.: The Captain's Bookshelf, 1995. (Out of print.)

———. *The Historian*. New York: Little, Brown, 2005.

———. Interview with Hayley Whitlock, *BookPl@ce* magazine online (date unspecified). Available online. URL: http://www.thebookplace.com/bookends/be_interviews_kostova.asp?TAG=&CID=. Accessed April 22, 2007.

Maslin, Janet. "Scholarship Trumps the Stake in Pursuit of Dracula." *New York Times*, 13 June 2005. Available online. URL: http://query.nytimes.com/gst/fullpage.html?res=9C03E5D91E38F930A25755C0A9639C8B63. Accessed April 22, 2007.

Michigan State University Web site. "2006 Distinguished Alumni Award." Available online. URL: http://www.cal.msu.edu/portals/stansell.htm. Accessed April 22, 2007.

Younge, Gary. "Bigger Than Dan Brown." *Guardian*, 18 July 2005. Available online. URL: http://books.guardian.co.uk/departments/generalfiction/story/0,6000,1530568,00.html. Accessed April 22, 2007.

Richard Alexander Johnson

Kotzwinkle, William (1938–)

Kotzwinkle is a highly prolific author of everything from science fiction and fantasies to detective stories and fairy tales for children. He has produced almost 50 children's books, novels for adults, and collections of short stories, typically characterized by zesty wordplay, wit, dark humor, magic realism, and incisive satire on greed and human folly. His fiction has been translated into a dozen languages.

Born in Scranton, Pennsylvania, in 1938, Kotzwinkle attended Rider College in New Jersey and then Pennsylvania State University. After working as a cook, editor, and part-time writer, he took up writing full time in the 1960s, his first published book, *The Firemen* (1969), a children's story based on the author's firefighter grandfather. This strand of his oeuvre was continued in works such as *The Day the Gang Got Rich* (1970), *Elephant Boy: A Story of the Stone Age* (1970), *The Ship That Came Down the Gutter* (1970), *Return of Crazy Horse* (1971), *Up the Alley with Jack and Joe* (1974), *The Leopard's Tooth* (1976), *The Ants Who Took Away Time* (1978), *Dream of Dark Harbor* (1979), *The Nap Master* (1979), *The World Is Big and I'm So Small* (1986), *The Empty Notebook* (1990), and *The Million-Dollar Bear* (1995). From 2001 to 2007 Kotzwinkle has also published six children's books in the Walter the Farting Dog series. All of his children's books offer amusement as well as lessons about loving kindness, peace, and acceptance of differences.

One of Kotzwinkle's most important novels for adult readers is *E.T., the Extra-Terrestrial: A Novel* (1982). Adapted from the screenplay by Melissa Mathison, it became a number-one best seller in 1982, selling more than 3 million copies. Its sequel, entitled *E.T., the Book of the Green Planet: A New Novel,* came out three years later. Other well-received novels include *The Fan Man* (1974), the story of a New York hippie's wanderings in the 1970s; *Doctor Rat* (1976), an indictment of animal experimentation; *Fata Morgana* (1977), which describes a Paris detective's pursuit of a killer and his fortune-telling machine; and *The Bear Went Over the Mountain* (1996), the story of a bear's rise to literary stardom.

Bibliography

Graham, Mark. "Silliness Can't Keep Author's Surprising Sci-fi Farce Grounded." *Rocky Mountain News*, 27 October 2005. Available online. URL: http://www.rockymountainnews.com/drmn/books/article/0,2792,DRMN_63_4192782,00.html. Accessed March 14, 2007.

Kotzwinkle, William. *The Firemen*. New York: Pantheon, 1969.

———. *The Day the Gang Got Rich*. New York: Viking, 1970.

———. *Elephant Boy: A Story of the Stone Age*. New York: Farrar, 1970.

———. *The Ship That Came Down the Gutter*. New York: Pantheon, 1970.

———. *Elephant Bangs Train*. New York: Pantheon, 1971.

———. *The Oldest Man and Other Timeless Stories*. New York: Pantheon, 1971.

———. *Hermes 3000*. New York: Pantheon, 1972.

———. *The Fan Man*. New York: Avon, 1974.

———. *Nightbook*. New York: Avon, 1974.

———. *Up the Alley with Jack and Joe*. New York: Macmillan, 1974.

———. *Swimmer in the Secret Sea: A Novel*. New York: Avon, 1975.

———. *Doctor Rat*. New York: Knopf, 1976.

———. *The Leopard's Tooth*. New York: Seabury Press, 1976.

———. *Fata Morgana*. New York: Knopf, 1977.

———. *The Ants Who Took Away Time*. Garden City, N.Y.: Doubleday, 1978.

———. *Herr Nightingale and the Stain Woman*. New York: Knopf, 1978.

———. *Dream of Dark Harbor*. Garden City, N.Y.: Doubleday, 1979.

———. *The Nap Master*. New York: Harcourt, 1979.

———. *Jack in the Box*. New York: Putnam, 1980.

———. *Christmas at Fontaine's: A Novel*. New York: Putnam, 1982.

———. *E.T., the Extra-Terrestrial: A Novel*. New York: Putnam, 1982.

———. *Queen of Swords*. New York: Putnam, 1983.

———. *Superman III: A Novel*. New York: Warner, 1983.

———. *E.T., the Book of the Green Planet: A New Novel*. New York: Putnam, 1985.

———. *The World Is Big and I'm So Small*. New York: Crown, 1986.

———. *The Exile*. New York: Dutton, 1987.

———. *The Hot Jazz Trio*. Boston: Houghton, 1989.

———. *The Midnight Examiner*. Boston: Houghton, 1989.

———. *The Empty Notebook*. Boston: Godine, 1990.

———. *The Game of Thirty*. Boston: Houghton, 1994.

———. *The Million-Dollar Bear*. New York: Knopf, 1995.

———. *The Bear Went over the Mountain*. New York: Doubleday, 1996.

———. *Return of Crazy Horse*. New York: Farrar, 2001.

———. *The Amphora Project*. New York: Grove Press, 2005.

John J. Han

Krantz, Judith (1928–)

Judith Tarcher Krantz is a best-selling author of women's fiction and romance. Born in New York City, she was raised in an upscale environment—her parents a journalist and lawyer—and graduated from Wellesley College, where she read voraciously and was active in extracurricular concerns. In 1948 she moved to Paris, where she became involved in the fashion industry and journalism, and continued to maintain a busy social life. Returning to New York City the following year, she began a career in magazine journalism, and in 1954 she married Steve Krantz.

A Wellesley professor's criticism of her poor spelling, and the B she received for the course, dampened Krantz's enthusiasm for writing, but in 1976, encouraged by her film- and television-producer husband, she rediscovered her earlier fascination with fiction and began to write in earnest. Her first novel, *Scruples,* was published in 1978 and became a *New York Times* best seller. Subsequent novels expanded on this success, generating blockbuster sales, cinematic adaptations, and translations into more than 50 languages.

Krantz credits the success of her novels not to any particularly literary skill but to a respectful and intuitive understanding of her primary audience, and her advice to would-be novelists is to live before trying to write, stressing the importance to her own novels of her earlier social activity and various jobs, especially the considerable research and interviews she did for magazine articles published in *Cosmopolitan, Ladies' Home Journal, McCalls,* and similar publications. Her dominant theme is the working woman succeeding in a man's world, and her fictional response to women's issues, including money, power, fashion, identity, and family is well rooted in the realities of her own rich and varied life.

Though her work is not highly esteemed by critics, her popularity in large part speaks for itself, and she was a resourceful and innovative groundbreaker in the world of celebrity authorship, fundamentally changing the publishing industry through participation in national tours and prepublication advertisement—a "superstar of fiction."

The Scruples trilogy, including *Scruples* (1978), *Scruples Two* (1992), and *Lovers* (1994), chronicles the rise, struggles, and search for meaning of the young and beautiful Billy Ikehorn among the glitterati of Paris and Beverly Hills. A 1980 miniseries adapted from the novel, *Scruples* featured Lindsay Wagner and Efrem Zimbalist, Jr. and was followed by a TV-movie sequel in 1981. In *PRINCESS DAISY* (1980) Princess Marguerite Alexandrovna Valensky, daughter of a Russian prince and American celebrity, is born to staggering wealth and limitless prospects but must confront and surmount a host of harsh realities. It was released as a teleplay in 1983, written by Diana Hammond.

In *MISTRAL'S DAUGHTER* (1982) Krantz's characters are similarly steeped in glamour, the women beautiful, passionate, and driven, and their lives, like that of Princess Daisy, influenced by legacies and secrets, fashion, and love. A melodrama of the same title was released in 1984, directed by Kevin Connor and starring Stefanie Powers, Stacy Keach, Timothy Dalton, and Lee Remick.

I'LL TAKE MANHATTAN (1986) is often seen as Krantz's best work, perhaps because it is the one most firmly rooted in her own impressive experience, with Maxi Amberville, socialite and writer, energetically pursuing a life that must somehow reconcile the most contradictory forces inherent in love and journalism. In 1987 a television miniseries based on the novel was produced by the author's husband, Steve Krantz.

Till We Meet Again (1988) reveals a rich palette of unconventionality, centered on the unrepentant risks of Eve de Lancel. Freddy, Eve's younger daughter, defying both convention and his family's wishes, learns to fly during World War II and bravely pursues love. Delphine, Eve's older daughter, views life from the backdrop of clubs and gambling, and a relentless love that ignores reason and subverts judgment—all in all a grand novelistic soap opera of love, hatred, betrayal, rape, war, birth, and death. The made-for-television movie was released in 1989 by Steve Krantz Productions.

In *Dazzle* (1990) prominent photographer Jazz Kilkullen is comfortably ensconced in her glamorous element until her father's death when, returning to her home on a cattle ranch, she must somehow protect the (suddenly vulnerable) family property and her father's legacy. The movie, directed by Richard A. Colla and released in 2003, features Lisa Hartman, Cliff Robertson, James Farentino, Dixie Carter, and Bruce Greenwood.

Spring Collection (1996) further illustrates Krantz's keen understanding of the underpinnings of the fashion industry and its icons. Francesca Severino, chaperone, and three unknown and contrasting American models chosen for the debut spring collection of designer Marco Lombardi, discover the magic of Paris and romance.

Krantz explores the mother-daughter relationship in *The Jewels of Tessa Kent* (1998), a novel set in the height of elegance and glamour in New York and Hollywood. Maggie, Tessa's illegitimate daughter, is raised by her grandparents, Tessa busy becoming an international figure. But at age 18 Maggie's awe of her "sister" is shattered by the truth, a crisis that provokes Tessa to restore the relationship. The auction of an extraordinary collection of jewels seems the only option in an apparently hopeless situation.

Sex and Shopping: The Confessions of a Nice Jewish Girl (2000) is Krantz's influential autobiography, chronicling the life of surely her most fascinating, provocative, and spontaneous creation. Its title reflects its tone: candid and humorous, yet informed by a subtle and unpretentious understanding of the character and life of one important type of female sensibility.

A DVD video, the *Judith Krantz Collection,* released in 2004, consists of four television miniseries adapted from the novels, *I'll Take Manhattan, Dazzle, Princess Daisy,* and *Till We Meet Again,* and features Courteney Cox, Hugh Grant, Bruce Boxleitner, Valerie Bertinelli, and Lisa Hartman.

Bibliography

Huseby, Sandy. "Judith Krantz: Life Is Even Better Than Fiction." Interview. *BookPage* (May 2000). Available online. URL: http://www.bookpage.com/0005bp/judith_krantz.html. Accessed March 27, 2007.

Krantz, Judith. *Scruples.* New York: Crown, 1978.

———. *Princess Daisy.* New York: Crown, 1980.

———. *Mistral's Daughter.* New York: Crown, 1982.

———. *I'll Take Manhattan.* New York: Crown, 1986.

———. *Till We Meet Again.* New York: Crown, 1988.

———. *Dazzle.* New York: Crown, 1990.

———. *Scruples Two.* New York: Crown, 1992.

———. *Lovers.* New York: Crown, 1994.

———. *Spring Collection.* New York: Crown, 1996.

———. *The Jewels of Tessa Kent.* New York: Crown, 1998.

———. *Sex and Shopping: The Confessions of a Nice Jewish Girl.* New York: St. Martin's, 2000.

Ruark, Liz. "Judith Tarcher Krantz '48." Profile. *Person of the Week* (February 12, 2001). Available online. URL: http://www.wellesley.edu/Anniversary/krantz.html. Accessed March 27, 2007.

Stella Thompson

L

Lake Wobegon Days

Garrison Keillor (1942–)

Shaped as a fictional history, *Lake Wobegon Days* is actually an extended exploration of universal themes and familiar eccentricities. Though the themes may seem random at times, they are deeply, if implicitly, informed by the novelistic region's distinctive values and customs and unfold in a natural, chronological manner. Like Mark Twain, Keillor gently parodies both the light and serious moments that define everyday life in small towns, and, like JAN KARON's contemporary fiction (the Mitford series) and Twain's fictional communities, his work indicates considerable autobiographical influence, with the author himself becoming a virtual character.

Thus the prefatory introduction:

> In the spring of 1974, I got $6000 from the *New Yorker* for writing a piece about the Grand Ole Opry, the most money I had ever seen, and so my wife and small son and I left home in St. Paul and got on the Empire Builder and headed for San Francisco to visit our friends, not knowing that this windfall would be most of my earnings for the year (*v*).

In his extended preface Keillor deftly connects the reader, the narrator, and the "history" of Lake Wobegon, narrating the loss of two works-in-progress, accidentally left in a men's room in a Portland train station, and explaining that on reflection the lost manuscripts seem to become the author's "best work" (*vi*). Attempts to re-create the stories have produced only a formless collection of notes and outlines written on three-by-five cards, one titled "Lucky Man," the story of an individual "who feels fortunate despite terrible things that happen to him," and another, the "Lake Wobegon Memoir."

In the chapter titled "Home" Keillor carefully deploys realistic historical and geographical data, establishing his "Lake Wobegon" in Minnesota on the shore by Adams Hill, which looks "east across the blue-green water to the dark woods" (1). Descriptions of concrete Grecian grain silos, a "SLOW CHILDREN" sign, and the town's only stoplight humorously evoke a timeless, inconic rural town to which "a breeze off the lake brings a sweet air of mud and rotting wood" (2). Lake Wobegon, first named New Albion, is incorporated but omitted from the map. Later renamed from an Indian phrase meaning either "Here we are!" or "We sat all day in the rain waiting for [you]," Lake Wobegon becomes at last the county seat of "phantom" Mist County, in the "heartland" (9).

In the chapters "New Albion," "Forebears," and "Sumus Quod Sumus," Keillor provides the kind of information a reader would expect to find in a descriptive history of the region: genealogical data, landmarks, notable personalities, and historical events. But he also explains how "in 1933 a legislative interim commission proposed that the state recover the lost county by collapsing the square mileage of several large lakes" (91), why Judy Ingqvist doesn't sing "Holy City" on Sunday morning, and why "a minister has to be able to read a clock" (97).

Lake Wobegon is a place where people come to visit or to find their way out of an unplanned detour. Recognizing necessity, or rather economy, as the mother of invention, residents have learned to use what is available, as in the case of "the Living Flag," created from Herman Hochstetter's overstock of red, white, and blue caps. The Knutes support this economy by addressing an inventive series of annual threats to the flag's existence, such as enshrining a "no-look" rule in the municipal ordinance.

Lake Wobegon's theological underpinnings, like its political and geographical foundations, are minutely detailed. The residents worship in the most catholic manner, "listening to rain on the roof, distant traffic, a radio playing from across the street," and the sounds of children on bikes and dogs barking, as they wait for "the spirit to inspire" them. Other worshippers plan fashionable "feasts or ceremonies" to lure more stay-at-home residents, like those who regularly gather in Uncle Al's and Aunt Flo's living room on Sunday mornings, engaged in a "plain meeting" and singing "without even a harmonica" to provide the pitch (103).

The chapter detailing these observances, titled "Protestant," also illustrates Keillor's facility with language, from the plebian drollery of "Our family was dirt poor, which I figured out as a child from the fact that we had such a bad vacuum" (101), to the epic sweep of:

> A town with few scenic wonders such as towering pines or high mountains but with some fine people of whom some are over six feet tall, its highest point is the gold ball on the flagpole atop the Norge Co-op . . . from which Mr. Tollefson can see all of Mist County . . . to raise the flag on national holidays . . . when the blue cross of Norway is flown (9).

Other luminous family events, including evenings on the porch, are described in the chapter titled "Summer." Such proceedings are "formal and genteel," a time when people do not "bolt" their food or leave the table until the slowest eater, who hates "all vegetables except pickles," is finished. The common porch is 30 feet long and almost the width of the house, enclosed with screens and furnished with brown wicker chairs, rockers, and a couch. Neighbors frequently stop to chat but understand the code for when to cordially accept and when to casually decline the polite invitation to "come up and sit" (130).

Lake Wobegon's less genteel summer memories include residents' crushed aspirations and reflections on nature's unfairness. A "champ" tomato destined for a blue ribbon prize, checked twice a day for bugs and nursed through a lightning storm, suddenly disintegrates before the official weigh-in (138); while suffering through hot summers without air-conditioning and winter cold below -30° prompts philosophical reflections on the injustice of nature, and the stoic suggestion, by way of counteracting such injustice, to just sit on the deck and secretly wish for a tornado (140).

School is a "quiet pool of imagination," where dreams are "interrupted by teaching" (170), as each new generation repeats the familiar cycle of beginnings, middles, and ends. The memories of Lake Wobegon residents, of life, war, and death, cluster round here, in the schoolchildren, whose nine-week "marks" mingle with Arbor Day, owning black Keds, and getting chosen for baseball.

Bibliography

Karon, Jan. *A Common Life: The Wedding Story*. New York: Penguin, 2001.

Keillor, Garrison. *Lake Wobegon Days*. New York: Penguin, 1985.

Twain, Mark. *Adventures of Huckleberry Finn*. New York: Penguin, 1986 (Harper, 1884).

Stella Thompson

L'Amour, Louis (1908–1988)

Louis L'Amour once wrote, "Usually I am characterized as a western writer. I do not mind the term, but it is not strictly correct. To me, and to many others, I am a writer of the frontier, not only in the West but elsewhere" (*Education* 136). Undeniably he was a gifted storyteller, and with a total output of 90 novels and hundreds of short stories he is one of the most prolific of all American authors. Moreover, with more than 200 million copies of his books in print nearly 20 years after his death, he remains one of the top-selling authors in the world.

Louis L'Amour was born Louis Dearborn LaMoore in 1908, in Jamestown, North Dakota, the son of Emily Dearborn, who had studied to be a teacher, and Louis LaMoore, a veterinarian who also served as deputy sheriff, policeman, and alderman. L'Amour's formal education ended at 15, when he left school for a series of colorful jobs. Work as a merchant seaman took him around the world. He did stints on farms, ranches, and mines in the West, and even spent time as a professional boxer. (While there are gunfights aplenty in his stories, the bad guys often get their comeuppance from the hero's fists.) Throughout this period of adventure, however, L'Amour read widely, a self-education he recounted in a memoir published after his death, *Education of a Wandering Man* (1989). When he came to write, then, L'Amour could draw on a wealth of experience; later, as a well-known author, he could exploit his colorful past for publicity.

L'Amour worked hard at writing for more than 10 years before he saw significant success. In 1935 his first published story appeared in a magazine called *True Gang Life,* in which he first used *L'Amour,* reclaiming the name's original French spelling. He went on to publish many adventure stories in pulp fiction magazines, a market that demanded he write quickly and get right to the action, habits he maintained throughout his writing life. Wartime military service interrupted his career, with L'Amour entering the army in 1942 and serving with the transportation corps in Europe. On his return to civilian life in 1946 he moved to Los Angeles and began writing westerns using the pen name Jim Mayo, editors considering his own name not "tough" enough. As Tex Burns he also wrote four books as work-for-hire for the Hopalong Cassidy series. His first novel, *Westward the Tide,* was published in England in 1950 but received little attention.

L'Amour's fortune changed with the publication of a short story, "The Gift of Cochise," in *Collier's* magazine in 1952. John Wayne purchased the movie rights and starred in the film version, which had a screenplay by James Edward Grant. L'Amour in turn readapted the screenplay to produce the novel *Hondo,* published by Fawcett Gold Medal in 1953.

In *Hondo* L'Amour hit on the elements that would come to define his own influential version of the western genre: the lone hero, the valiant woman beset by villains, the appeal of land and family, and a plotline of nonstop action. Set in Arizona in the 1870s, *Hondo* tells the story of Hondo Lane coming to the defense of Angie Lowe and her son, who have been abandoned by Angie's no-good husband in the midst of an Apache uprising. Typically, while the characters are straightforwardly drawn, frontier life is complex; the Apaches may be the enemy, but their way of life is as nuanced and legitimate as that of the white man.

The book and movie versions of *Hondo* came out on the same day, and the success of both laid the foundations for L'Amour's subsequent career. As Hondo, John Wayne came to embody the typical hero, and L'Amour himself, in his author photos, would pose in western wear holding a rifle, displaying Wayne-like star power. From 1955 on he was under contract with a new publisher, Bantam, to produce two to three novels a year.

Among L'Amour's best-known works are those of the Sackett family saga, 17 in all, beginning with *The Daybreakers* (1960). Through the Sacketts' story L'Amour tells a complete fictional history of western settlement, originating in 1599 with the first Sackett crossing the Atlantic to encounter a new frontier on the East Coast. *The Sackett Companion* (1988) is L'Amour's nonfiction companion to the series. In shorter series L'Amour told the tale of the Chantry family (five books) and the Talon family (three books). He planned a total of 50 books in all three series, with story lines that would have the families cross paths, but did not live to see the plan fulfilled.

L'Amour is known not only for his intrepid western heroes but also for his detailed and accurate depictions of the landscapes of the West, particularly the areas of Arizona, New Mexico, Colorado, and Utah. His novels were published with maps, which heightened the sense of authenticity and historical accuracy. He famously stated, "When I write about a spring, the spring is there and the water is good to drink" (Keith 22). The settings also possess symbolic meaning, lending depth to what might otherwise have been formulaic story lines. Indeed, reflecting the seriousness with which L'Amour is now approached, one critic, recalling L'Amour's lone heroes wandering through stark desert landscapes, calls his work "pulp fiction existentialism" (Mills 34).

To critics who found his characters and plots formulaic, L'Amour had a ready reply: He was writing about heroes, and heroes have a universal quality; the people and stories of the American frontier have the grandeur of epic poetry. In *The LONESOME GODS* (1983) a character states this directly: "You will find that our Homers will sing of the plains, the deserts, and the mountains. Our Trojans may appear in feathered war bonnets . . ." (116).

Most of L'Amour's books were published as paperbacks, and as his reputation grew, early books published under the names Tex Burns and Jim Mayo were reissued under his own name. Many of his magazine stories have been collected in book form, most recently in the four volumes of *The Collected Short Stories of Louis L'Amour* (2003–2006). However, not until 1983 did Bantam begin publishing his books in hardcover. Among these later works are novels that show his interest in frontiers beyond the 19th-century American West. *The Walking Drum* (1984) tells of the adventures of a 12th-century traveler through Europe and the Middle East. In *LAST OF THE BREED* (1986) a captured American Indian air force pilot uses native skills to escape the Soviets and survive in the Siberian wilderness. In *The Haunted Mesa* (1987) a man from the modern Southwest stumbles onto a passageway in time leading to the ancient Anasazi civilization. Although not traditional westerns, each book reflects L'Amour's penchant for depicting lone heroes and the clash of cultures in a challenging landscape.

Writing in the second half of the 20th century, L'Amour built on a tradition established by earlier western writers such as Owen Wister (*The Virginian*, 1902) and Zane Grey (*Riders of the Purple Sage*, 1912). Although his writing received little respect from the literary establishment, his characterization and style share a kinship with the work of more notable authors, from Ernest Hemingway to Dashiell Hammett, and his influence can be clearly seen in writers of the more literary western, such as Cormac McCarthy, author of *All the Pretty Horses*.

In addition, L'Amour's work has influenced countless film and television westerns, as well as inspiring adaptations of his own stories. Among the movie versions of his novels are *Heller in Pink Tights* (1960), based on *Heller with a Gun; Shalako* (1968); *The Sacketts* (1979), a two-part television miniseries based on *The Daybreakers* and *Sackett* (1961), which the Cowboy Hall of Fame called the most authentic western of the 1970s; and *The Quick and the Dead* (1987). His books have also been produced in dozens of audio versions. His works have been translated into at least 20 languages, and more than 120 of his books are still in print.

L'Amour received many honors later in life. In 1972 the self-taught writer who had dropped out of high school received an honorary doctorate from Jamestown College in his North Dakota hometown. In 1977 two of his books, *Hondo* and *Flint* (part of the Sackett series), were included on the Western Writers of America's list of the best 25 western novels. In 1983 he received a Congressional National Gold Medal for lifetime literary achievement, the only other writer receiving this honor being the poet Robert Frost. In 1984 he received the Medal of Freedom, the U.S. government's highest civilian honor, presented by President Ronald Reagan, who was a great fan of L'Amour's work.

Throughout his career L'Amour kept to a rigorous writing schedule, producing five to 10 pages a day, seven days a week. In 1956 he married Katherine Adams, an actress who had played roles in TV series such as *Gunsmoke*. They had a son, Beau Dearborn L'Amour, and a daughter, Angelique Gabrielle L'Amour. L'Amour died on June 10, 1988, in Los Angeles.

Bibliography

Gale, Robert L. *Louis L'Amour*, rev. ed. Twayne's United States Authors Series. New York: Twayne, 1992.

Grey, Zane. *Riders of the Purple Sage*. New York: Harper, 1912.

Hall, Hal W. *The Work of Louis L'Amour: An Annotated Bibliography and Guide*. Bibliographies of Modern

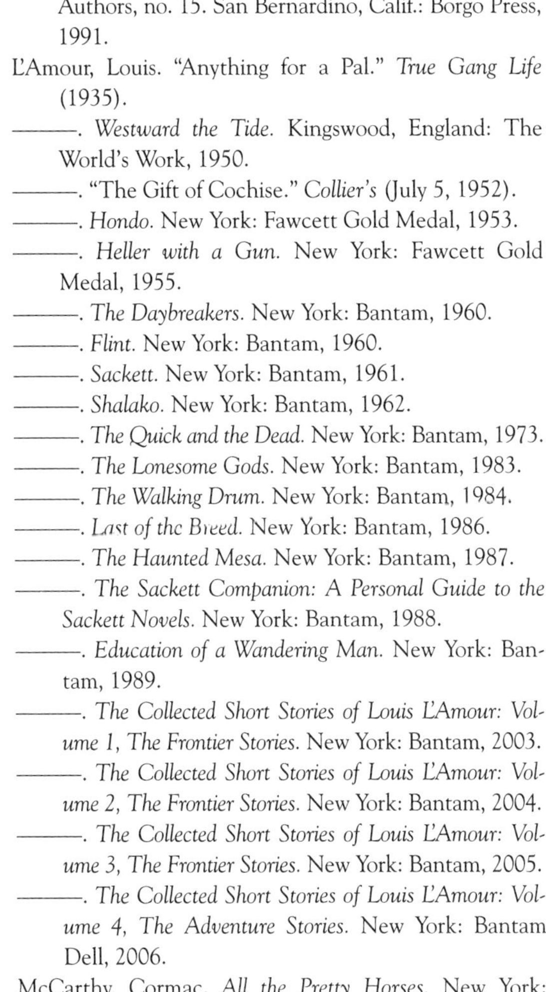
Authors, no. 15. San Bernardino, Calif.: Borgo Press, 1991.

L'Amour, Louis. "Anything for a Pal." *True Gang Life* (1935).

———. *Westward the Tide.* Kingswood, England: The World's Work, 1950.

———. "The Gift of Cochise." *Collier's* (July 5, 1952).

———. *Hondo.* New York: Fawcett Gold Medal, 1953.

———. *Heller with a Gun.* New York: Fawcett Gold Medal, 1955.

———. *The Daybreakers.* New York: Bantam, 1960.

———. *Flint.* New York: Bantam, 1960.

———. *Sackett.* New York: Bantam, 1961.

———. *Shalako.* New York: Bantam, 1962.

———. *The Quick and the Dead.* New York: Bantam, 1973.

———. *The Lonesome Gods.* New York: Bantam, 1983.

———. *The Walking Drum.* New York: Bantam, 1984.

———. *Last of the Breed.* New York: Bantam, 1986.

———. *The Haunted Mesa.* New York: Bantam, 1987.

———. *The Sackett Companion: A Personal Guide to the Sackett Novels.* New York: Bantam, 1988.

———. *Education of a Wandering Man.* New York: Bantam, 1989.

———. *The Collected Short Stories of Louis L'Amour: Volume 1, The Frontier Stories.* New York: Bantam, 2003.

———. *The Collected Short Stories of Louis L'Amour: Volume 2, The Frontier Stories.* New York: Bantam, 2004.

———. *The Collected Short Stories of Louis L'Amour: Volume 3, The Frontier Stories.* New York: Bantam, 2005.

———. *The Collected Short Stories of Louis L'Amour: Volume 4, The Adventure Stories.* New York: Bantam Dell, 2006.

McCarthy, Cormac. *All the Pretty Horses.* New York: Knopf, 1992.

Mills, Joseph. *Reading Louis L'Amour's* Hondo. Western Writers Series, no. 153. Boise, Idaho: Boise State University, 2002.

Weinberg, Robert, ed. *The Louis L'Amour Companion.* Kansas City, Mo.: Andrews and McMeel, 1992.

Wister, Owen. *The Virginian.* New York: Macmillan, 1902.

Erica Olsen

Last of the Breed **Louis L'Amour** (1986)

A thriller set in the Soviet Union of the 1980s, *Last of the Breed* is a very different kind of novel by LOUIS L'AMOUR, an author famous for his westerns. But as L'Amour himself wrote in his autobiography, *Education of a Wandering Man,* he was above all "a writer of the frontier" (136), and few frontiers have dominated the Western imagination like this one. In addition to the political dimension, however, in *Last of the Breed* L'Amour takes his hero across a physical and psychological frontier that divides the 20th century from a long-lost and elemental form of life.

As the novel begins, Joseph Makatozi (aka Joe Mack), a pilot in the U.S. Air Force, is a captive in a Soviet prison camp in Siberia, having been forced down over the Bering Sea in an experimental aircraft. The U.S. military believes he died in an accident, so there is no one to help him but himself—a fate common to L'Amour's protagonists. What his captors do not know is that Mack is an American Indian—his ancestry is Sioux, Cheyenne, and white—who grew up testing his survival skills in the mountains of Idaho; nor do they know that Mack is a former decathlon star. These qualities give him the will, the ingenuity, and the sheer physical strength to escape. Where the guards see a length of pipe in a stack of construction material, Mack sees a pole vault for the camp's electrified fence, initiating an extraordinary odyssey that continues through the long, harsh Siberian winter. On his trail are Colonel Arkady Zamatev, the man responsible for his capture, and Alekhin, an expert tracker. Along the way Mack gets help from a number of Soviets outside the pale (who conveniently speak a little English), including Yakov, a renegade who draws a map to show Mack the way, and a community of former exiles who live as trappers in the forest. A Lithuanian exile, Stephan Baronas, and his beautiful daughter, Natalya, provide friendship, hope, and Russian lessons. The novel alternates between Mack's point of view and that of his pursuers.

Even before he escapes, Mack relies on his ancestral roots to envisage a way to freedom:

> To the north lay the Arctic, to the east and northeast a vast stretch of taiga, tundra, and extremes of weather. Beyond it was the Bering Sea and Alaska. If the anthropologists were correct, his own people had once followed that migration route, pursuing the

> game that led them across the then-existing land bridge to America. If they had done it, he could do it (14).

While Zamatev underestimates his quarry, Alekhin is a Yakut, an indigenous Siberian who understands Mack's capabilities. When Zamatev insists, "He is a civilized man! An officer in his country's air force!" Alekhin replies, "He is an Indian" (37). And it is Alekhin, investigating a helicopter crash, who realizes that the arrowheads in the wreckage are not ancient artifacts but the work of the Indian who has brought down the best of Soviet technology with prehistoric weapons.

The novel's principal theme centers on the emergence of its hero's ancestral character, hitherto hidden under a veneer of civilization; and how this provides him with the will and means to survive and ultimately, to fight back. Alone in enemy territory and with no survival gear, Mack crafts a bow and arrows and kills mountain sheep. He forages, traps, and hunts, covering his tracks like Ishi, the legendary last "wild" Californian Indian of the early 1900s. Eventually, his hair grows so long he wears it in braids. "*All you need now,*" he told himself, "*is a necklace of bear claws*" (270). One critic has aptly described the novel as an "eastern Siberian western" (Gale 71).

Historians might dispute L'Amour's assertions about a universal human character, but the novel nonetheless makes for a timeless adventure story. When Zamatev observes Mack and Alekhin's confrontation, he feels as if "a page of history had rolled back. Suddenly, in his small, bare office, two savages faced each other [. . .]" (8). While *savages* is not the politically correct term, it is clear that the author admires these two far more than the "civilized" Zamatev. *Savage* is a compliment, for L'Amour, and Mack's journey an epic:

> When morning came again, he arose and walked upon the mountain, and the ghosts of Red Cloud and Gall walked beside him. Perhaps the ghosts of even older Indians were there also, those who first followed this same trail to America, following the game out of Asia and into what we foolishly call the New World (50).

L'Amour balances this serious tone with moments of humor. In one scene Mack matter-of-factly kills a bear with bow and arrow, skins it, and roasts the meat—all the while longing for a good cup of coffee.

The land and weather of Siberia are depicted as characters themselves, sometimes helpful, sometimes adversarial. Mack must constantly negotiate the terrain: "He moved along under the pines, looking again across the valley toward the bleak ridges, the massed battalions of the other pines where darkness and shelter might wait or enemies to kill or maim him" (219). He traverses precipitous mountains, icy rivers, taiga (the dense Siberian forest), and tundra, most of the time with only the vaguest idea of his location; his journey often uncannily resembling the experience of early explorers of the American West.

L'Amour's knowledge of woodland skill is everywhere in evidence: how to build a snow cave, how to outwit trackers by walking in moccasins with elk hooves attached to the soles. But the novel also recalls his literary influences. A sympathetic Russian, for example, "had read everything he could find written by Jack London, and because of that he had strong sympathy for that lone American out there in the taiga" (198). Mack himself recalls

> [. . .] the story of the Apache, the Indian Massai, who had been deported to Florida after Geronimo's surrender in 1886. He had escaped from the train after they had left St. Louis, and he had worked his way across country, returning to Arizona without being seen except by a friendly Indian to whom he revealed himself. Two thousand miles or more he had traveled [. . .] (270).

That story is told in Frederic Remington's short story "Massai's Crooked Trail" (1898).

Last of the Breed is one of several novels late in L'Amour's career in which he explored a wider range of fictional worlds and frontiers: 12th-century Europe and the Middle East in *The Walking Drum* (1984); the contemporary Southwest and Anasazi prehistory in *The Haunted Mesa* (1987); and just as no one would refuse to read a western because the U.S. Army is no longer fighting the Apaches, *Last of the Breed* can still be enjoyed after the end of the cold war. Indeed, in one scene Mack speculates on future relations between the Soviet Union and the United States: "If Russia would [. . .] tear down the Berlin Wall, and build more good hotels, we Americans would be all over your country spending money [. . .]" (306). That prospect must have seemed unlikely to readers in 1986, yet only three years later the wall came down. Unfortunately, L'Amour did not live to see it happen.

Bibliography

Gale, Robert L. *Louis L'Amour*, rev. ed. Twayne's United States Authors Series. New York: Twayne, 1992.

L'Amour, Louis. *The Walking Drum*. New York: Bantam, 1984.

———. *Last of the Breed*. New York: Bantam, 1986.

———. *The Haunted Mesa*. New York: Bantam, 1987.

———. *Education of a Wandering Man*. New York: Bantam, 1989.

Remington, Frederic. "Massai's Crooked Trail." 1898. In *The Collected Writings of Frederic Remington*. Edited by Peggy and Harold Samuels. Garden City, N.Y.: Doubleday, 1979.

Erica Olsen

le Carré, John (David John Moore Cornwell) (1931–)

When David Cornwell wanted to publish his first novel, he faced an unusual dilemma: His employer, the British Secret Service, encouraged his writing but would not let him use his name. Hence in the year the Berlin Wall was erected, Cornwell, a junior operative with MI5, searching for additional income and recognition as a serious novelist, became John le Carré, author of the detective-espionage novel *Call for the Dead* (1960). In 1963 le Carré gained international success and financial independence with *The Spy Who Came in from the Cold*. Now, after more than 20 books, countless other writings, numerous awards (including two Edgar awards, a Golden Dagger, and a Diamond Dagger), the enigmatic pseudonym still agrees with this highly literate, psychologically complex, and politically astute writer.

Cornwell's upbringing shapes le Carré's writing. Born in Poole, Dorset, the younger son of Olive and Richard ("Ronnie") Cornwell, the young David Cornwell experienced betrayal and chicanery. Ronnie, an epic con artist, crooked businessman, and womanizer, avoided service to country and family throughout his life, employing his sons in all sorts of fraudulent schemes and, when convenient, palming them off on various "lovelies" (mistresses). Olive, daughter of a Congregationalist minister, deserted her philandering husband and her children for one of Ronnie's swindling partners. With Ronnie jailed for insurance fraud, David was dumped on his mother's unforgiving family and was soon sent without tuition money to St. Andrew's Preparatory, site of James Hilton's *Goodbye, Mr. Chips* (1934). After his release Ronnie remarried and had two more children, Rupert (now Washington bureau chief of *The London Independent*) and Charlotte, an actress and the model for the character of Charlie in *The* LITTLE DRUMMER GIRL (1983).

Le Carré's fiction effortlessly incorporates the duplicities to which Cornwell was subjected as a youth. In the main his characters are lonely, isolated, and although they search for emotional satisfaction, and security, unable to create loving, sustained relationships. To compensate, they join institutions where reality and illusion are indistinguishable. No one walks away an unambiguous victor in a le Carré novel. In particular, Ronnie Cornwall's Micawber-like character reappears wherever public morality mimics private reality. Ronnie charmed and defrauded his family and associates as surely as Rick Pym does in the autobiographical *A Perfect Spy* (1986), but he is equally present as Uncle Benny (*The Tailor of Panama* 1996), as Hugo Cassidy (*The Naive and Sentimental Lover* 1971), or as Salvo's wayward Catholic father (*The Mission Song* 2006). So, too, does Olive's betrayal lurk behind the questionable Marie Ostrakova of *Smiley's People* (1980), the evil mother in *Single & Single* (1999), and the cuckolding Lady Ann Sercombe Smiley. The youthful Cornwell's headmasters serve as models for bigoted sycophants whose stern reprimands and cruel punishments—such as Felix D'Archy (*A Murder of Quality* 1962)—confirm readers' growing suspicion of institutions.

As a student of German at Berne University, Switzerland, Cornwell first encountered intelligence operatives, whose outlines would later appear in his writings. And as a Foreign Service operative in Europe, and later at MI6, Cornwell was exposed to an institution that he saw as a "loony bin" thriving on "inside-out thinking." Through these experiences he acquired firsthand knowledge of international politics, inspired amateurism, global treachery, and the bureaucracy and intrigue that underlie all his novelistic organizations, particularly the "Cambridge Circus," le Carré's designation for the British secret services.

On the more positive side Cornwell's youth gave him his most enduring cold war hero, the reluctant spy George Smiley, who is featured in *Call for the Dead*; *A Murder of Quality*; *Tinker, Tailor, Soldier, Spy* (1974); *The Honourable Schoolboy* (1977); *Smiley's People* (1980); and present in three other novels. A German scholar and spymaster, Smiley is based largely on Cornwell's MI5 colleague Lord Clanmorris. Unlike James Bond, the sadistic agent as a man of fashion, Smiley's unshapely wardrobe and pathetic demeanor conceal a brilliant mind and resolute heart.

Smiley joins the secret service during World War II, marries his boss's secretary, and proceeds through a series of enforced and voluntary separations from the agency to become its director. As the new Control Smiley coerces his professional and personal doppelgänger, Karla, to defect. This triumph highlights his career but costs him his moral authority, for he has embraced Karla's totalitarian methods to achieve his laudable Western ends. Smiley's last appearance explains his resilience and hints at why le Carré so easily moved from cold war themes into his later work. Smiley reassures the service's new recruits that "as long as there are bullies and liars and madmen in the world, we shall spy. For as long as nations compete, and politicians deceive, and tyrants launch conquests, and consumers need resources, and the homeless look for land, and the hungry for food, and the rich for excess, your chosen profession is secure, I can assure you" (*The Secret Pilgrim* 1991).

The cold war set up a convenient dichotomous landscape of West-East, democracy-totalitarianism, decency-immorality for le Carré, and with its end some critics wondered if le Carré would change his writing. He did not because his themes easily continue. Le Carré read the subtleties of the cold war era with more precision than other writers and uses the same skills of discernment to find ample material in contemporary politics. His post–cold war fiction continues to mine the character types and rich themes of his earlier work. The individual versus the institution, means versus ends, belief versus skepticism, and loyalty versus honor now appear woven into the headlines of corporate power, underdevelopment, and globalization. *The Night Manager* (1993), for example, rediscovers the cold war spy in a businessman-as-gunrunner and secret lover, as it laments how the most human of traits—the capacity for love—can become a fatal flaw. *Our Game* (1995) spies, Timothy Cramer and his protégé Dr. Larry Pettifer, joined by Cramer's mistress, Emma, smuggle drugs and embezzle Soviet millions while trying to save themselves from themselves. *Single & Single* brings back Ronnie, this time as Tiger Single, a rogue banker that the *Financial Times* calls "the knight errant of Gorbachev's New East."

The protagonist of *The Constant Gardener* (2001) seeks the truth behind his activist wife's murder, but what he finds, and ultimately dies for, is an international conspiracy of corrupt bureaucracy and pharmaceutical money. This global search for the truth puts the character exactly where le Carré prefers his readers to walk: in the midst of a journey toward love that necessarily forces them to face evil for honor. Similarly, *Absolute Friends* (2003) recalls cold war propaganda to denounce American neoimperialism, George W. Bush's administration, and the uncritical support of Prime Minister Tony Blair.

Economics and politics dominate *The Mission Song* (2006), le Carré's 20th novel. Although set in Africa and lacking the bureaucracy of formal espionage agencies, it, too, hearkens back to le Carré's cold war thrillers, in which ordinary people—like George Smiley or Liz Gold in *Spy*—try but fail to reconcile moral codes with institutional morass. They are tripped up not just by international forces but by absent fathers, missing mothers, and duplicitous spouses. Awaiting deportation from Britain, *Mission*'s protagonist Salvo reflects, "home as a concept confused me. It still does." David Cornwell would agree on one level, John le Carré on two, adding to the domestic a complex world of politics and terrorism.

Early in le Carré's career James Bond dominated the best-seller lists, but le Carré turned genre fiction into mainstream literature using unwitting betrayal and an individual's relationship with himself, his family, and his country as his themes. His protagonists are three-dimensional; his novels unflinchingly engage institutions and morals in altogether more realistic manners; and his positions on duty, life, and fortune are markedly unglamorous. As le Carré has said of his espionage career, "I entered [British Intelligence] in the spirit of John Buchan and left it in the spirit of Kafka." But when asked why he does not quit writing, le Carré less philosophically snaps back, "I have become an angry old man waiting as impatiently as a young man for the world to develop further. And the world in its current situation could anger a fossil."

When he left MI6 to become a full-time writer, le Carré bought a cliff-top home at Tregiffian, near St Buryan, in Cornwall, England, where he lives today.

Bibliography

Hindersmann, Jost. "'The right side won, but the wrong side won': John le Carré's Spy Novels before and after the End of the Cold War." *Clues* 23, no. 4 (summer 2005): 25–37.

le Carré, John. *Call for the Dead.* London: Gollancz, 1961.

———. *A Murder of Quality.* London: Gollancz, 1962.

———. *The Spy Who Came in from the Cold.* London: Gollancz, 1963.

———. *The Looking-Glass War.* London: Heinemann, 1965.

———. *A Small Town in Germany.* London: Heinemann, 1968.

———. *The Naive and Sentimental Lover.* London: Hodder & Stoughton, 1971.

———. *Tinker, Tailor, Soldier, Spy.* London: Hodder & Stoughton, 1974.

———. *The Honourable Schoolboy.* London: Hodder & Stoughton, 1977.

———. *Smiley's People.* London: Hodder & Stoughton, 1980.

———. *The Little Drummer Girl.* London: Hodder & Stoughton, 1983.

———. *A Perfect Spy.* London: Hodder & Stoughton, 1986.

———. *The Russia House.* London: Hodder & Stoughton, 1989.

———. *The Secret Pilgrim.* London: Hodder & Stoughton, 1991.

———. *The Night Manager.* London: Hodder & Stoughton, 1993.

———. *Our Game.* London: Hodder & Stoughton, 1995.

———. *The Tailor of Panama.* London: Hodder & Stoughton, 1996.

———. *Single & Single.* London: Hodder & Stoughton, 1999.

———. *The Constant Gardener.* London: Hodder & Stoughton, 2001.

———. *Absolute Friends.* Hodder & Stoughton, 2004.

———. *The Mission Song.* Hodder & Stoughton, 2006.

———. *A Most Wanted Man.* Hodder & Stoughton, 2008.

Saler, Michael. "John le Carré's allegiances." *TLS: Times Literary Supplement*, 20 September 2006. Available online. URL: http://tls.timesonline.co.uk/article/0,,25339-2367283,00.html.

LynnDianne Beene

Left Behind Series

Tim LaHaye and Jerry B. Jenkins (1995–2007)

In its entirety the Left Behind series consists of 12 novels (1995–2004), three prequels (2005–2006), and a sequel (2007), envisaging on a grand scale the apocalyptic years before the Second Coming of Christ. Conceived by Reverend Tim LaHaye and written by Jerry B. Jenkins, the novels seek to reinforce the beliefs of evangelist readers and move non-Christian readers toward salvation, combining countless proven elements of popular genres (action thriller, science fiction, melodrama, romance) with equally proven techniques of evangelist preaching, and supported by many spin-off products, including a children's series, graphic novels, movies, a radio drama, and a video game.

The series is rooted in an evangelical theology called premillennialist dispensationalism, which argues that believers will not suffer through the tribulation period but will be "raptured" before it begins, and in the expansive view of LaHaye and Jenkins conversions are still possible even after the rapture. The novels take biblical prophecy as "an accurate history of the world, much of it written in advance" (*The Remnant* 228), and advocate belief in a comprehensive, single God and religion, rejecting equally Catholicism, Judaism, Islam, and ecumenism.

The politics of the series are largely fundamentalist, proposing a strict either/or and denying the validity of nonevangelical positions: "There is right and wrong, there are absolute truths, and some things cannot and should not ever be tolerated," preaches the charismatic Ben-Judah, minister to a congregation of a billion members (*Apollyon* 189). The UN is ridiculed as the "Global Community," its political ideals (world peace, universal health care, eradication of poverty) presented as a ploy of Satan to alienate people from God—an Old Testament God, loving toward his followers and wrathful toward his enemies. Abortion and homosexuality are sinful practices of self-centered individuals who deserve extermination.

In some respects, however, the novels depart from the fundamentalist line. While traditional gender roles are affirmed and feminism on the whole rejected (Rayford, a central protagonist is a natural leader; Buck, the head of his family), women like the heroine Chloe play a central role. She leads an international co-op, takes part in the adventures, and dies as a martyr. The "Tribulation Force," God's earthly militia, is racially inclusive (Dr. Floyd is African American; Al B. and Abdullah Smith are Arabic; Ming Toy and Chang Wong are Chinese), even though ultimate power lies with white American men.

Also atypical of rapture fiction, the novels glorify technology. Here it is not Satan's tool but a miracle for the use of the Tribulation Force. Ben-Judah teaches a billion-strong cybercongregation, and the prime weapon against the apostate Carpathia is information technology (laptop computers, solar-powered cell phones, hacking).

Critics of the Left Behind series have argued that LaHaye and Jenkins follow a pick-and-choose approach to Bible exegesis, linking isolated passages of the Old and New Testament and subjecting the prophecies to a literalist reading. Key concepts such as the rapture, tribulation, and Antichrist are presented as biblical truths, but they are neither supported by most religious scholars nor embraced by mainstream Christians. In addition, the novels have been accused of being undemocratic, racially and religiously intolerant, excessively violent, and employing scare tactics to sway people to conversion.

The series begins with the rapture of all true Christians to heaven, where they are united with Jesus Christ. Those who are left behind must endure the seven years of plagues, natural disasters, and tyranny that precede Christ's return to earth and his establishment of the Millennial Kingdom. In this tribulation period Old and New Testament prophecies (particularly the book of Revelation) are fulfilled, and the forces of good (evangelical Christians) battle those of evil (nonconverts and worshippers of Satan). God's earthly followers form a militia group, the Tribulation Force, which carries out God's fight against Satan. At Christ's Glorious Appearing its surviving members, like all evangelicals, are reunited with their loved ones. The forces of evil are led by the Romanian statesman Nicolae Carpathia—who graduates from secretary general of the United Nations to Satanic Supreme Potentate—and by his False Prophet, Leonardo Fortunado.

The series can be roughly divided into five parts.

Novels one and two (*Left Behind, Tribulation Force*) depict the rapture and its effects. Millions are swept up into heaven, and life around the globe spins out of control. The first two of the 21 judgments announced in the book of Revelation occur: war and bloodshed (World War III), followed by famine and disease. Major characters such as pilot Rayford Steele, his daughter Chloe, journalist Cameron "Buck" Williams, and Pastor Bruce Barnes are introduced. Left behind in the rapture, they are born again when they recognize God's master plan and plead to Christ for their salvation, while Carpathia's rise to political power marks him as the Antichrist. A peace treaty with Israel, the appearance of prophets Eli and Moishe ("My God" and "Moses"), the relocation of the UN (renamed the "Global Community") to Babylon, the rebuilding of the temple in Jerusalem, and the establishment of the Enigma Babylon One

World Faith all signal the beginning of the period of tribulation.

Installments three to six (*Nicolae, Soul Harvest, Apollyon, Assassins*) continue the execution of biblical judgment. Natural disasters (earthquake, hail and fire from heaven, meteors, darkening of the sun, an invasion of locusts) and supernatural horsemen decimate the world's population. Such biblical scenarios are combined with action sequences in which members of the Tribulation Force are captured and escape, and these sequences are themselves interspersed with vividly described conversion experiences. Jewish scholar Tsion Ben-Judah, for instance, embraces Jesus as the Messiah and replaces Pastor Barnes (who was poisoned by Carpathia's men) as the spiritual leader of the Tribulation Force. In the sixth novel, *Assassin*, Carpathia himself is assassinated by Jewish scientist Chaim Rosenzweig, who has not yet converted (he will do so eventually and join the Tribulation Force) but is enraged by Carpathia's persecution of Jews.

The third segment, novels seven to 10 (*The Indwelling, The Mark, Desecration, The Remnant*), the most reminiscent in tone and narrative structure to the secular Matrix trilogy, describes the shattered and seemingly endless continuum of the tribulation, commencing dramatically with the resurrection of Carpathia, now Satan incarnate. Carpathia forces people to display a sign of loyalty on their foreheads (the mark of the beast), but believers are sealed by their own mark, a sign on their foreheads that protects them from the judgments and is visible to fellow believers only. Yet more of God's judgments come to pass: Nonbelievers suffer from sores and are burned by the sun; oceans and rivers turn to blood; New Babylon is destroyed. The Tribulation Force continues to oppose the Global Community, enlisting new members painstakingly and at great risk—members like pilots Mac McCullum and Abdullah Smith, nurse Leah Rose, former black marketer Al B., computer genius David Hassid (who is eventually murdered), as well as siblings Ming Toy and Chang Wong. The American branch of the Tribulation Force moves from various safe houses (suburban Mt. Prospect; Chicago) to an underground shelter on a San Diego military base. After Carpathia has desecrated the Jewish Temple in Jerusalem, Ben-Judah and Rosenzweig (now called Micah) lead a group of Jews (God's remnants) and believers to Petra, their anointed safe haven. Here Carpathia's nuclear weapons prove ineffective, and the refugees are fed by manna from heaven. Many of them convert, fulfilling the prophecy that a third of the remnant Jews will come to Christ before his Glorious Appearing.

The series closes with novels 11 and 12 (*Armageddon, Glorious Appearing*), which portray the events leading up the Battle of Armageddon (including the deaths of Chloe, Buck, and Ben-Judah), depict the battle between Carpathia's armies and the forces of God, and narrate Christ's return to earth. At their climax a worldwide earthquake rends the earth, Satan and his False Prophet are cast into a lake of fire, and Christ rules the Millennial Kingdom from Jerusalem. The prequels (*The Rising, The Regime, The Rapture*) trace the lives of central characters before the rapture. The sequel, *Kingdom Come*, depicts life in the Millennial Kingdom, Satan's uprising, and his final defeat.

Bibliography

LaHaye, Tim, and Jerry B. Jenkins. *Left Behind: A Novel of the Earth's Last Days.* Wheaton, Ill.: Tyndale, 1995.

———. *Tribulation Force: The Continuing Drama of Those Left Behind.* Wheaton, Ill.: Tyndale, 1996.

———. *Nicolae: The Rise of Antichrist.* Wheaton, Ill.: Tyndale, 1997.

———. *Soul Harvest: The World Takes Sides.* Wheaton, Ill.: Tyndale, 1998.

———. *Apollyon: The Destroyer Is Unleashed.* Wheaton, Ill.: Tyndale, 1999.

———. *Assassins: Assignment: Jerusalem, Target: Antichrist.* Wheaton, Ill.: Tyndale, 1999.

———. *The Indwelling: The Beast Takes Possession.* Wheaton, Ill.: Tyndale, 2000.

———. *The Mark: The Beast Rules the World.* Wheaton, Ill.: Tyndale, 2000.

———. *Desecration: Antichrist Takes the Throne.* Wheaton, Ill.: Tyndale, 2001.

———. *The Remnant: On the Brink of Armageddon.* Wheaton, Ill.: Tyndale, 2002.

———. *Armageddon: The Cosmic Battle of the Ages.* Wheaton, Ill.: Tyndale, 2003.

———. *Glorious Appearing: The End of Days.* Wheaton, Ill.: Tyndale, 2004.

———. *The Rising: Antichrist Is Born.* Wheaton, Ill.: Tyndale, 2005.

———. *The Regime: Evil Advances.* Wheaton, Ill.: Tyndale, 2005.

———. *The Rapture: In the Twinkling of an Eye.* Wheaton, Ill.: Tyndale, 2006.

Daniel Stein

Leonard, Elmore (1925–)

Elmore Leonard has done as much for the genre of crime fiction as any author in the past 50 years, his character-driven novels marked by sharp, snappy dialogue and a distinctive, intelligent style, elevating the crime novel above the level of pulp fiction.

He began writing at an early age, continuing at the University of Detroit, which he entered in 1946. After graduating, he joined the Campbell-Ewald advertising agency and began writing short western stories, published in *Argosy, Zane Grey Western,* and the *Saturday Evening Post.* His first novel was *The Bounty Hunters,* also a western, and he followed that with four more novels over the next eight years. In 1961 he left advertising to devote his full time to writing. During the 1970s, after the western market dried up, Leonard switched to crime fiction, his first great success being *Glitz* in 1985; most of his novels since have been both popular and critical successes. He has also written screenplays, as well as a host nonfiction articles for magazines and contributions to encyclopedias.

Leonard's novels stand out for their gritty realism and strong dialogue. His 10 rules of writing keep his style simple yet vigorous: never open a book with the weather; never use a verb other than *said* to carry dialogue; keep your exclamation points under control; use regional dialect sparingly; do not go into great detail describing places and things; all have served him well over the years, keeping his work taut, focused, and always moving.

His most distinctive feature, however, is his strong and memorable characterization. At times the plot of a Leonard novel almost seems inconsequential, except as a means to learn more about his characters: Chili Palmer the mob moviemaker in *GET SHORTY* (1991); Jackie Brown, the air stewardess who fights back in *Rum Punch* (1992); Blackbird, the Canadian hitman in *Killshot* (1989); Chris Mankowski, the vice cop confronting a pair of hippie bombers in *Freaky Deaky* (1988); Jack Delaney, the ex-con who never should have worked in a funeral home or gone up against the Contras in *Bandits* (1988). All illustrate in their attitude, diction, and sheer moxie the sort of character that compels and rewards attention throughout a Leonard novel.

Leonard uses a subtle, indirect manner to build his characters that seems almost inappropriate for a novel. There is usually one defining scene for each character. In his recent novel *The Hot Kid,* set during the Roaring Twenties in Oklahoma, Leonard uses simple scenes to speak volumes about his characters. We first meet Carl Webster as a 15-year-old boy who has his peach ice cream cone stolen by Emmett Long, a robber who just murdered deputy sheriff Junior Harjo. This simple action polarizes Carl's view of justice with immediate results: Carl shoots Wally Tarwater for trying to steal cattle from his father's ranch. When asked by the U.S. marshals about what happened, Carl tells the story but is more fascinated by the badges that the marshals carry. His obsession with justice has found an outlet, and he becomes one of the youngest marshals in Oklahoma.

Carl's new job for justice is the complete opposite of Jack Belmont, who is determined to become Public Enemy Number One, and he'll do it in a hurry. Jack is a spoiled rich kid who never gets everything he wants from his daddy, and after he is accused of many crimes as a youth but never really proven guilty, he winds up cleaning out oil tanks on his father's oil rig. Norm Dilworth, a slow-witted worker on the rig, explains how cleaning the tanks is a long, suffocating job, where you have to breathe toxic fumes from the oil, and you have to step out every 10 minutes to get air, and you're not paid for the time that you actually breathe clean air. But Jack has better ideas: He interrupts Norm and suggests a life of crime. Norm, suspicious at first, decides it is a good idea. But as they leave the rig:

> Jack pulled a pack of cigarettes and a silver lighter from the overalls that felt stiff on

> him. Norm looked back to see him lighting the cigarette and yelled out, "No!" and said Jesus Christ, no, a few more times, and looked towards Rossi's office, looking at Jack puffing on the butt, before he flicked it to arch into the stream of sludge.
>
> Fire flashed and spread over the ooze out on the ground—they were both running now—the fire wooshing into the tank to ignite the gas and there was a boom inside, an explosion that buckled steel plates, blew the roof off the tank and rolled black oil smoke into the sky (38).

This scene shows exactly what Jack Belmont is capable of, and there is much worse as he moves on to kidnapping, bank robberies, and murder.

Leonard never really describes his characters; he just lets them talk. And talk they do, about the big score, about the past, the present, and the future; they tell stories, they lie, they cheat; they talk about love, love lost, and love that could be found. Leonard grabs attention with his characters because their characters come through their conversations. When Chili Palmer is talking to his movie producer friend Elaine in *Be Cool,* their conversation is not just about the movies but also about how they love each other. Max Cherry goes along with Jackie Brown's con in *Rum Punch* not only because he does not like Ordell Robbie, but because he has found a woman he has never known before, and the only way he can truly show his love is to try to swindle one of the toughest players on the streets. These characters have their own agendas and their own experiences that define them, and Leonard is able to express this in a few turns of dialogue.

Leonard has been writing novels since the 1950s, and he shows no signs of stopping. He has been recognized as a master crime writer, but he is still expanding his oeuvre by writing stories about American history, including *Cuba Libre* (about the Spanish-American war) and *The Hot Kid* (about prohibition and the golden age of gangsters). His love for writing has gained him a wide variety of fans, from writers such as Martin Amis to filmmakers such as Quentin Tarantino. His novels pull one in, and they become almost impossible to set down. Start one and get set for one wild ride.

Bibliography

Leonard, Elmore. *Glitz.* New York: Arbor House, 1985.
———. *Bandits.* New York: Arbor House, 1987.
———. *Freaky Deaky.* New York: Arbor House, 1988.
———. *Killshot.* New York: Arbor House, 1989.
———. *Get Shorty.* New York: Delacorte, 1991.
———. *Rum Punch.* New York: HarperCollins, 1992.
———. *Out of Sight.* New York: Delacorte, 1996.
———. *Cuba Libre.* New York: Dell, 1998.
———. *Be Cool.* New York: HarperTorch, 1999.
———. *The Hot Kid.* New York: HarperTorch, 2006.

Samuel Harr

The Life and Hard Times of Heidi Abromowitz Joan Rivers (1984)

Comedian, actor, entrepreneur, and author, Joan Rivers has been a fixture in American pop culture since the 1960s. As successful in her authorship as in her other pursuits, Rivers writes with often surprising insight and pathos, in addition to the verve and wit for which she is famous. *The Life and Hard Times of Heidi Abromowitz* (1984) is Rivers's spoof biography of a fictitious high school friend with a hyperactive libido, written as a tell-all of the secret life of the buxom bimbo, whom the author claims "entrusted to me details of her life that I gave a sacred vow never to reveal" (7). However, after catching her hot-blooded friend "in the bushes with my German shepherd for the third time" and with a hefty offer from a publisher, the author sets about a thorough chronicle of Heidi's many conquests (7).

Having grown up with Heidi, the narrator can recollect abnormal behavior all the way back to her friend's infancy. "The Early Years" recalls Heidi "[doing] things with a pacifier that most women still haven't done with their husbands" (10) and "[jumping] out of her own birthday cake" (12); she strips for show-and-tell (14), takes "Flintstone's chewable birth control pills" in the sixth grade (16), and starts fires at summer camp by rubbing her thighs together (19); all sharply contrasted to the narrator's (typically) deprecating self-portrait: "In her sweater she looked like a walking dairy state. I was more underdeveloped than most third world nations. My training bra had taught me nothing . . ." (24); "that bitch had got a wrist corsage for the prom, and all I got was a flea collar with a daisy" (36).

After high school Heidi takes off to see (and be seen in) Europe, and Rivers's narrative, coupled with snippets from Heidi's diary, tell of the traveler's disappointment in learning that "Big Ben was a clock" and her failure to comprehend why Paris is known as "Gay Paree" when she finds no shortage of paramours (42). Of Spain Heidi observes, "I like a place where you can go to bed in the middle of the afternoon and no one asks any questions" (49). Upon her return to the States, Heidi survives a short-lived marriage ("The night before the wedding she entertained twenty-five [men]! She was having her going out of business sale" [55]), a brief stint as a career woman ("*Consumer Reports* asked her to rate Vaseline" [60]), and motherhood (". . . her son . . . had evidently been named after his father. The kid's name was Trick" [75]).

Peppered with references to contemporary pop culture, the novel also deftly invokes controversial issues, such as energy conservation, *The Hite Report,* and arms control, by having them knock repeatedly on Heidi's rarely opened bedroom door; while James Sherman's comical illustrations of Heidi—baby Heidi as an aspiring sadomasochist with whip in hand (11), teenage Heidi as a cheerleader with "Anytime" scrawled across her panties (1), middle-aged Heidi with "Now Serving" sign above her bed (92)—merely heighten the title's double entendre. Rivers's thoughtful inclusions of Heidi's Little Black Book, a collection of Abromowitzisms (who knew that the Women's Movement is "best from the waist down" [56]?), an interview with *Playboy* that made even their writers blush, and a *Cosmo*-like quiz entitled "What's Your Tramp Potential," all add to the humorous realism of the piece; and by the end Rivers has bequeathed us a Moll Flanders for the age of reality TV.

The public's enthusiastic embrace of Heidi's tale inspired an hour-long TV special, *Joan Rivers and Friends Salute Heidi Abromowitz* (1985), a celebrity roast with personalities such as Howie Mandell, Brooke Shields, Kris Kristofferson, and Robin Leach.

Bibliography

Rivers, Joan. *The Life and Hard Times of Heidi Abromowitz.* New York: Delacorte, 1984.

Susan E. Ray

Life Expectancy Dean Koontz (2004)

Life Expectancy opens with the birth of its protagonist, Jimmy Tock, amid the chaos, violence, and surprising good luck that will mark his progress throughout the story. On a dark and stormy night—Koontz plays with many such clichés throughout—Jimmy's father finds himself sharing a hospital waiting room with fellow father-to-be Konrad Beezo, a bitter, fuming, and soon-to-be-homicidal circus clown. In another part of the same hospital Jimmy's grandfather makes a deathbed prediction that his grandson will experience five terrible days, the dates carefully copied down on the back of a circus ticket bearing the legend "Prepare to Be Enchanted."

Suddenly the novel's strange mixture of dark fantasy and black humor explodes in action. When Konrad's wife does not survive the birth of his son, the enraged clown goes on a killing spree, barely sparing the lives of the Tock family, and then absconds with his newborn son, whom he names Punchinello. On each of the five terrible days in Jimmy's life the killer clown or his son returns to seek revenge. With the playful coincidence of a story about storytelling, these days also mark conventional turning points in Jimmy's life, commencing with the day he meets his wife and the day his first child is born.

The five terrible days evolve into a feud between the Tock family and the Beezos (a kind of antifamily, though neither clan is strictly normal). The Tocks are bakers, and as such keep the odd hours needed to run a bakery, going to work just after midnight and sleeping through noon. Konrad and Punchinello, ostensibly circus clowns, are, in fact, fantastically ruthless and monomaniacal killers, gifted with extraordinary criminal abilities and appetites, while the Tocks form a sort of collective that nurtures and protects its eccentric members. In the fragmented style characterizing his narrative Jimmy professes, "[A]s I write about the Tock clan, its members seem odd and singular. Which they are. Which is one of the reasons why I love them" (200). In a reverse image of the Tocks' collective individuality, Konrad Beezo brainwashes his son to carry out various family vendettas, forbidding Punchinello to follow his natural talent and join the clown's hated rivals, the aerialists.

The Tock home is characterized by an unusual yet not unfamiliar brand of gothic whimsy. Their upbeat, offbeat point of view becomes a source of strength in the face of the relentless assaults they must endure. Jimmy's wife, Lorrie, explains their cohesive bond as "living for each other," a quality even more important than love (283); even Jimmy's slapstick narrative style is attributed to his family's particularity: "I have learned the structure of story from a family that delights in narrative and understands in its bones the magical realism of life" (211).

Scenes from the Tock home are overtly warm and fuzzy, but Koontz, as Jimmy, insists that they never blind themselves to the cold, hard world around them. They confront very real and violent bodily threats with eyes wide open, but their most effective way to cope with such is laughter and another round of pastries. As circus clowns the Beezos are inherently and inescapably ridiculous, yet at the same time given to narcissistic rage and pathological violence. Jimmy's five terrible days are marked with the utmost graphic violence and terror, but the explosions are timed for effect, the psychological terror plays for laughs, and even the most grievous wound has the panache of a pratfall. Koontz deliberately draws these elements together and presents their juxtaposition as a moral stance:

> Insanity is not evil, but all evil is insane. Evil itself is never funny, but insanity sometimes can be. We need to laugh at the irrationality of evil, for in doing so we deny evil's power over us, diminish its influence in the world, and tarnish the allure it has for some people (139).

In order to win the war of ideas (if not the battle for their lives), the Tocks must retain their capacity for comic happiness no matter what the world, or an insane clown, can do to them.

The occupation of each family thus becomes identified with opposed worldviews: The bakers make everything pleasant and comforting, while the clowns constantly turn the world upside down. Their thematic qualities even surpass at times their importance as narrative characters: "Simply by existing . . . Konrad Beezo made the world a darker place, but we lived in light, not in his shadow" (317). The success or failure of the Tocks lies in their ability not to avoid tragedy—which has in a sense been predestined—but to maintain their cheerful point of view in the light of nearly incomprehensible malevolence.

The novel does not suggest, however, that evil can be physically laughed away; Jimmy and his wife respond to violence with violence. After a particularly brutal encounter leaves Konrad much the worse for wear, Jimmy simply states that "a restrained response to evil is not moral" (277). But even the most violent moments of the tale are undercut, or perhaps supported, by a persistent irony and understatement. When reflecting on how best to respond to the evil at hand, Jimmy muses that "any moral dilemma" can be made easier "if one consumes abundant quantities of sugar" (472).

This kind of humor irked some reviewers, who seemed especially displeased by dialogue that transforms into screwball repartee in extreme moments of terror and violence, when "real" people would be unable to assemble a sentence, let alone a snappy comeback. But none of the characters—or the novel's plot—are meant to be strictly believable, and Koontz has often explicitly (as above) called the novel a work of magical realism. The narrator is equipped with a keen sense that the story's alterations between laughter and screaming take some getting used to:

> In this account of my life, I will resort at every turn to amusement, for laughter is the perfect medicine for the tortured heart, the balm for misery, but I will not beguile you. I will not use laughter as a curtain to spare you the sight of horror and despair. We will laugh together, but sometimes the laughter will hurt (31).

Though the book has not appealed to suspense/horror purists, its zany humor makes an uncustomary and serious moral statement, amounting in the end to a first-person parable of how to cope with life's inevitable, inescapable tragedies.

Koontz, as Jimmy, constantly reflects on the process of writing *Life Expectancy*, often breaking away from the most suspenseful moments in order to tell a joke or play a trick on the reader. The characters are only believable as "make believe," and at one point Jimmy offers up fiction as a metaphor for the human condition: "Sometimes . . . I get the weird feeling that someone is writing my life as I write about it. If God is an author and the universe is the biggest novel ever written . . . I am a supporting player" (232). If human beings are something like God's fiction, then the process of writing and reading stories becomes critical to self-understanding:

> I wrote this to explain life to myself. The mystery. The humor, dark and light, that is the warp and weft of the weave. The absurdity. The terror. The hope. The joy, the grief. The God we never see except by indirection (438).

DEAN KOONTZ has often said that his optimistic point of view and his belief in the human capacity for good sets him apart from other horror and suspense writers. *Life Expectancy* celebrates this spirit on every page, incorporating it into the very act of writing itself.

Bibliography

Koontz, Dean. *Life Expectancy*. New York: Bantam, 2004.

Charles Tedder

Light from Heaven Jan Karon (2005)

Light from Heaven, the final novel in JAN KARON's well-loved Mitford series, chronicles one year in the lives of Father Timothy Kavanagh, his wife, Cynthia, and the many friends (both old and new) they encounter. The novel finds Father Tim retired after many years of serving as priest for the Lord's Chapel Episcopal Church in Mitford and happily married to Cynthia for seven years. They have moved 20 miles into the country to "farm-sit" at Meadowgate Farm for their friends Hal and Marge Owens, who are in France for a year. Their young charge, Dooley Barlowe, is 21 and away at college, but their pets, Violet and Barnabas, and a farm full of animals keep things lively. Still, the rural life finds Father Tim searching for more to occupy his time, while Cynthia sets out her own goals:

> "She'd decided to accomplish three lifetime goals: learn needlepoint, make perfect oven fries, and read *War and Peace*" (4).

Father Tim's restlessness is soon replaced with the hustle and bustle he is more accustomed to, when his friend Bishop Stuart McCullen offers him an assignment for one year to serve as vicar of a small mountain church called Holy Trinity. Father Tim discovers that Holy Trinity has stood empty for nearly 40 years and fears the worst. Instead, he finds an immaculate, well-tended church that has been maintained for three decades by a lady named Agnes Merton and her son, Clarence. In time Agnes recounts her life story to Father Tim and introduces him to many of the mountain folk during the priest's evangelical visits, some of whom are at first recalcitrant. One of these is Jubal Adderholt, a man close to nature but wary of strangers and religion, who retorts, when introduced by Agnes to the priest:

> "Don't ye bring no God people in m' place, you're all th' God people I can swaller" (102).

Others residents are more receptive to the idea of rejuvenating Holy Trinity, and the priest stays busy getting acquainted with them all and preparing the church for its first service in 40 years.

In addition to his growing responsibilities at Holy Trinity, Father Tim also encounters issues at the farm. Dooley's younger brother, Sammy, 16, has moved to the farm to get away from his abusive alcoholic father, and the couple's attempts to mold him into an upstanding young man require patience and love. They must also deal with a collapsed brick chimney in the old farmhouse that results in a lengthy repair, excessive dust and dirt, and workmen constantly underfoot. All of this chaos threatens to interfere with Cynthia's work, creating 12 watercolors of her cat Violet for a calendar, and she eventually agrees to hire the flamboyant and amusing Flower sisters to assist with housework and cooking. Two other significant subplots concern Father Tim's continued attempts to locate Kenny Barlowe, Dooley's brother, whose mother once traded him for a gallon of whiskey, and Father Tim's decision to finally divulge to Dooley that Miss Sadie had left him close to $2 million at the time of her death.

While the main narrative is centered 20 miles from Mitford, Father Tim is not isolated from the vicissitudes of town. His regular visits to Mitford reveal that Uncle Billy Watson and Gene Bolick are both very ill; JC's marriage is in need of a boost; Puny's two sets of twins are flourishing; and Edith Mallory is beginning to utter some words after her head injury earlier in the year. And it is here that he learns from Louella that Miss Sadie may have hidden a large sum of money before her death. Even though he is away at the farm, Father Tim continues to be the glue holding Mitford together.

Holy Trinity, which has a capacity of 40, reopens to seven, but a potluck dinner, new children's Sunday school class, and weekly sign language lessons to aid communication with a deaf member all endear the mountain people to the little church. This, combined with word of mouth and encouraging visits by Father Tim and Agnes, help to quickly quadruple the size of their congregation.

Like all of Karon's Mitford novels, *Light from Heaven* is sprinkled with inspiring scriptural passages, hymnal verses, lively society, and mouthwatering meals, centered on the endearing love between Father Tim and Cynthia but anchored always in unshakeable faith in God. Redemption is, as ever, a recurring theme, with several of the mountain people confessing sins (murder, adultery, alcoholism) to Father Tim and finding salvation in the church.

Karon brings her characters to life through their colorful and resonant experience, employing vivid dialogue and humor to animate the mountain congregants of Holy Trinity and the citizens of Mitford. The jokes of Uncle Billy Watson, the comical e-mails from Emma Newland, Father Tim's former church secretary, the uncouth behavior of Sammy Barlowe, or the crazy antics of the Flower sisters all take on a greater life than ordinary. Facing their quotidian trials and tribulations and recounting stories of their lives, they become people her readers relate to and care for, more with each successive story.

While *Light from Heaven* ends the Mitford series, Jan Karon has began a trilogy that follows Father Tim as he travels to Mississippi, England, and Ireland; the first book, *Home to Holly Springs*, appeared on 2007.

Bibliography

Hellmich, Nanci. "Karon's Father Tim to Leave Mitford." *USA Today*, 10 November 2005. Available online. URL: http://www.ebscohost.com. Accessed December 2, 2006.

Karon, Jan. *Light from Heaven*. New York: Viking, 2005.

Mary Chesnut

The Lincoln Lawyer Michael Connelly (2005)

The legal thriller has a long history, but it was SCOTT TUROW in the 1980s who galvanized the genre with his riveting formula of lawyer-as-sleuth; MICHAEL CONNELLY's first such attempt, *The Lincoln Lawyer*, has been favorably compared to the work of that master, as well as to that of the equally successful JOHN GRISHAM.

The germ of Connelly's novel lies in a conversation he had with a defense attorney who practiced in the Los Angeles area from the backseat of his car, and Connelly's great love and detailed knowledge of that city comes to life in his fiction. *The Lincoln Lawyer's* Mickey Haller is equally at home in the city's Chandleresque streets and sanitized law courts. Traditional legal thrillers tend to focus on the courtroom drama rather than the solving of a mystery, with their protagonist-lawyer often young and idealistic overcoming all obstacles to bring the guilty to justice. Haller is no such idealistic attorney, and *The Lincoln Lawyer*, no such thriller. Connelly's protagonist is a cynical and rather seedy defense attorney taking on ugly cases in Los Angeles, his clients including motorcycle gang members, prostitutes, and small-time criminals. Knowing the defendants are guilty, Haller works the system by finding loopholes, negotiating and manipulating, working out of the backseat of his Lincoln town car, reviewing cases and cutting deals as he is chauffeured from one to another widespread Los Angeles courthouse. Appearing in the courtroom as the ultimate image of the sleazy defense lawyer, Haller is terrified by the thought that in the end he would not know an innocent man if he met one. In fact, his famous lawyer father, J. Michael Haller, once said, "the scariest client a lawyer will ever have is an innocent client. Because if [. . .] he goes to prison, it'll scar you for life" (146).

With the appearance of Louis Roulet, what Haller calls a franchise client—one able to pay his defense high fees—Haller's nightmare threatens to come true. Roulet has been accused of assaulting a young woman, and Haller initially suspects that his client has been framed, but the more he and his partner, Ray Levin, dig into the case, the darker and more ambiguous things become.

Maggie McPherson, deputy district attorney, is Haller's estranged first wife and mother of his daughter. To her the law is a calling, and she considers reprehensible Haller's jaundiced sensibility: "There was nothing about the law I cherished anymore," he muses, "[. . .] The law was not about truth. It was about negotiation, amelioration, manipulation. I didn't deal in guilt and innocence, because everyone was guilty. Of something" (39). Connelly's verisimilitude, based on years of journalistic work and meticulous research, is exemplary, but it is his development of Haller's character that most distinguishes *The Lincoln Lawyer.* Though a supreme and supremely cynical manipulator of the court system, Haller is depicted as a conflicted soul behind his venal persona, soliloquizing, "I hate being inside a jail. I'm not sure why. I guess it's because sometimes the line seems so thin. The line between being a criminal attorney and being a *criminal* attorney. Sometimes I'm not sure which side of the bars I am on" (23).

Even Connelly's handling of minor, seemingly extraneous characters, typically the cartoonish foils for a thriller protagonist, is marked by subtlety and wit, with several becoming instrumental in helping Haller put Roulet away. Following his father's example, Haller has often assisted Gloria, a prostitute, pro bono, while another client, a Road Saints motorcycle gang leader, had his case dismissed with Haller's help. After Haller's assistant Levin is murdered and Haller himself is considered a suspect, ex-wife Maggie, Gloria, and the biker are among those who help him bring Roulet to justice.

As the case of Roulet unfolds, however, the manipulator becomes the manipulated, with Haller struggling to preserve not merely his career but his own life; when Roulet poses a threat to Haller's hitherto neglected family, the latter's crash course in priorities is all but complete. Injured finally in a shoot-out in the novel's concluding confrontation, the chastened Haller is granted both motivation and means to assess a misspent life, and the story ends on an ambivalent but enlightened note, with him showing nascent signs of deserving the title of his own tale.

The book has been optioned by Lakeshore Entertainment films. Connelly has not ruled out a return appearance of Mickey Haller.

Bibliography

Connelly, Michael. *The Lincoln Lawyer.* New York: Little, Brown, 2005.

———. "The Lincoln Lawyer—Behind the Writing." Available online. URL: http://www.michaelconnelly.com/Other_Words/Behind/behind.html.

Patricia Bostian

The Little Drummer Girl

John le Carré (1983)

The Little Drummer Girl deviates from JOHN LE CARRÉ's typical cold war spy novels, focusing instead on the Israeli-Palestinian conflict in the early 1980s. It opens with investigations into terrorist bombings of Israelis in the Diaspora but soon centers on Charlie, a politically radical British actress who is recruited to serve as an operative for the Israelis. As their operative Charlie is first trained by Israelis in western Europe and then undercover by Palestinians in London and South Lebanon, with the novel's first half devoted to a detailed narration of the former. She is recruited from the midst of a Greek holiday by a mysterious stranger named Joseph, who is in fact an Israeli agent, Gadi Becker. With Joseph to train her, Charlie the actress now prepares for a play performed in the "theater of the real" (106), "directed" by Marty Kurtz, an Israeli version of le Carré's Control, and his partner, Mike Litvak. But reality itself begins to waver as Charlie is trained to pose as the girlfriend of a Palestinian terrorist, Michel, with le Carré skillfully interweaving elements of the Israeli operation, Charlie's actual experience, and the elaborate romance of her imaginary relationship with Michel.

The novel's second half begins in London and explores Charlie's now complex and altering perceptions of reality as she operates among the Palestinians. Neither the novel nor she clearly distinguishes between events in the imaginary romance with Michel, her sublimated desire for a relationship with Joseph, and the daily reality of London in the early 1980s. le Carré's technique forces the reader to either pay most careful attention to the different narrative threads or be abandoned to Charlie's seemingly schizophrenic confusions of time, place, and identity. The terrorist associates of Michel now connect with Charlie and take her to a Palestinian training camp in the south of Lebanon. Here Charlie imperceptibly succumbs to the rhetoric of the Palestinian cause, but the narrative schizophrenia continues, indicating her continued allegiance to Joseph and her Israeli assignment while she outwardly expresses that allegiance as devotion to Michel. As she simultaneously follows the Israeli and Palestinian directives, Charlie gradually loses her identity to the "theater of the real," while desperately clinging to the ideals that tie her to her sense of humanity.

While exploration of humanity in a morally ambiguous world pervades le Carré's spy fiction, his cold war novels are unambiguously anti-Communist, the reader well aware that Smiley, Control, and their colleagues represent the heroes, and the Communist operatives, the villains. *The Little Drummer Girl,* however, does not clearly label either side of the conflict, and le Carré formally expresses this complication in his acknowledgments, thanking both the Israelis who "left me with my own judgments" (2) and the Palestinians who "knew nothing of my intentions" (2). The Israelis initially appear as the heroes, with their investigation into the bombings done in cooperation with the West German government, le Carré's traditional good side. But the novel presents both the Palestinian frustrations and motivations more clearly and sympathetically than those of the Israelis', who, unlike the Palestinians, do not try to recruit Charlie to their cause but merely to their operation, their moral position never being satisfactorily justified. When Charlie questions them about their authority to decide innocence or guilt, Kurtz is forced "to turn [the] question around a little . . . and say that in [their] view somebody has to be very guilty indeed before he needs to die" (107). As the Israelis emerge as stoic, Control-like operatives caring above all for the success of the operation, the Palestinians become sympathetically disorganized underdogs, fighting against hyperorganized Israeli forces. Joseph predicts that Charlie will easily fall in love with the Palestinian cause (327), especially since she mostly meets sympathetic, Western-educated Palestinians like Salma, who shows her the land, the children, and "where the Zionists will come from to kill us" (345). The narrative's rapid transition between Charlie's contrasting perspectives and attitudes further confuses the sense of the good and the evil, imbuing *The Little Drummer Girl* with far greater moral ambiguity than is found in le Carré's earlier work.

The narrative devices creating this moral confusion are only sharpened by his exploration of themes of theatricality, performance, and the creation of identity. In addition to Charlie, the professional actress, all the agents, whether Israeli or Palestinian, play roles in "the theatre of the real" (106), confirming the novel's far-reaching assumption that "no true drama can ever be a private statement. . . . Drama must have an application to reality. Drama must be useful" (95). Le Carré effectively confounds theater with reality, layering the different narratives to show every character playing multiple roles simultaneously. And such layers and roles suggest, in the end, that no identity is stable or simple enough to be identified as wholly good or evil, whether it belongs to an individual or a culture.

Typically, le Carré focuses on questions of individual identity, especially as these questions shift in the morally ambiguous environment he deftly describes; but *The Little Drummer Girl*'s protagonist is especially illustrative, since Charlie differs both from the traditional le Carré protagonist and the traditional le Carré female. As exemplified in his best known novel, *The Spy Who Came in from the Cold,* his usual protagonist is a male willing to change his persona in the service of his country; the traditional le Carré female is the site of ideological conviction: a character blinded by one ideology and devastated when that ideology—whether political or emotional—is undermined by the drama of the narrative. Charlie, however, is a female protagonist without a firm ideological center, having pursued radical extremes to the point of contradicting herself—a trait that allows her to work for the Israelis while sympathizing with the Palestinian cause. As Kurtz later acknowledges, Charlie falls in with the Israelis because, even within the framework of the schizophrenic personality she must take on, "They knew her through and through; they knew her fragility and her plurality. And they still wanted her" (138). This is the type of identity that le Carré explores through the novel, where characters and the world they live in are composed of intersecting and overlapping realities in want of a core group or conviction as a defining center—the "homeland at last" (138) that Charlie thinks she finds with the Israelis.

The Little Drummer Girl was made into a film in 1984 directed by George Roy Hill and starring Diane Keaton.

Bibliography

le Carré, John. *The Spy Who Came in from the Cold.* 1963. Reprint, London: Pan, 1964.

———. *The Little Drummer Girl.* London: Hoddor & Stoughton, 1983.

Malcah Effron

Lives of the Mayfair Witches

Anne Rice (1990–1994)

Lives of the Mayfair Witches is a horror trilogy consisting of *The Witching Hour* (1990), *Lasher* (1993), and *Taltos* (1994). Best known for her Vampire Chronicles, Rice decided in the mid-eighties to venture into a new realm of horror, and the so-called Mayfair Legacy was born, a series chronicling 13 generations of the Mayfair family, and one which, for all its novelty, is clearly shaped by the usual Ricean themes of alienation, eroticism, and the duality of good and evil.

The Witching Hour begins in San Francisco and tells the story of a young architect, Michael Curry, and Rowan Mayfair, a young woman who saves Michael from drowning in San Francisco Bay. After the accident the couple meets again in New Orleans, fall in love, and begin the unveiling of the Mayfair Legacy that began in the 17th century in Donneleith, Scotland, with Rowan learning that she is the 13th generation of the Mayfair witches. Throughout the early stages of the novel Rice evokes salient elements of each epoch of the Legacy, allowing her readers to visualize what life was like at that particular moment in time and to gain a synoptic grasp of the Legacy as a whole; on the Great Depression, for example: "The Roaring Twenties came to an end. Wealthy people everywhere lost their fortunes. Multimillionaires jumped out of windows. And in a time of new and unwelcome austerity, there came an inevitable cultural reaction to the excess of the twenties" (*WH* 548). Rice typically researches for months in advance of writing to ensure that all details related to the novel's historical time and place are accurate and memorable.

Michael and Rowan learn that Rowan's family legacy began with one Suzanne Mayfair, a young woman who, unaware of the seriousness of her action, roused Lasher, a morally ambivalent spirit of the extinct Taltos species, who ever since has appeared to one "designated witch" in each generation, bestowing upon him or her great wealth and prosperity.

Deeply rooted in this Legacy, the couple grows increasingly alienated from the world in which they live, Michael because of a unique ability to see past events related to a person or object simply through touching it, which produces the usual media storm and reclusion on behalf of the "gifted" one. Rowan is alienated for several reasons: first, because she is adopted by a family that removes her from her biological mother, thereby depriving her of the organic connectedness of family support, and second, because unlike in the past, when the designated witch had power only derived from Lasher, Rowan can heal and kill without Lasher's assistance.

Typically, unbridled eroticism is drawn into the vacuum of such alienation, a dynamic first evident in Rice's earliest, erotic writings under the pen names A. N. Roquelaure and Anne Rampling and rampant among the androgynous, sexually charged beings that dominate the Vampire Chronicles. Likewise, many of the witches are described as attractive to both men and women and are defined by a total lack of sexual restraint or inhibition. Even the character of Lasher is described as an attractive incubus who sexually satisfies the designated witch of each generation, whether male or female. All three novels in the trilogy are notable for their visceral depictions of rape, incest, sexual prowess, and domination.

Such acute, intransitive passion, housed on the very margins of human society, naturally leads to profound moral ambivalence, to actions and perspectives seemingly beyond good and evil. Thus Rowan, a skilled neurosurgeon, who has saved lives through her conventional surgical abilities, has both given life and taken it away with her telepathic power, having once killed a pedophile, for example, as an innocent girl, merely through her anger and desire to see him dead.

Lasher, too, is defined by ambivalence, protecting and benefiting the Mayfair family, but (readers later learn) with the ultimate object of finding a Mayfair witch strong enough to handle him entering her womb and possessing the body of her baby so that he can be incarnated, populate the world with Taltos, and destroy the human race. In spite of his malevolent designs, however, in *Lasher,* the second novel of the Mayfair trilogy, the eponymous spirit is portrayed rather sympathetically as one who merely seeks the stability and continuity of a family and the company of like souls. As he tells his story, he even at times appears harmless and vulnerable; after all, the only thing he wants is to be born in a physical body and surround himself with others who are like him. Yet at the end of *The Witching Hour,* when Rowan and Lasher leave Michael behind, Lasher takes her prisoner and constantly rapes her in order to produce an offspring. Finally he succeeds, but just as Rowan is giving birth to their daughter, Emaleth, she falls into a coma from the traumatic birth and Michael returns.

Later on, Lasher finds Michael at the side of the comatose Rowan and tells his story to him, explaining that he was stillborn to Queen Anne of England, the second wife of Henry VIII, that he never meant to be evil, and that now he just wants to be left alone. Michael, sufficiently apprised of Lasher's misdeeds, listens, denies, and kills the incarnate spirit.

After returning from burying Lasher, Michael is stunned to find Emaleth nursing Rowan back to health (the Taltos are born in adult form). Rowan comes out of the coma but is so terrified when she sees her daughter that she begs Michael to kill Emaleth, then shoots her herself when Michael recoils from the thought. Now Rowan is devastated by what she has done, recalling the self-torment of Christopher Marlowe's *Dr. Faustus* and Mary Shelley's *Frankenstein* (Rout).

In *Taltos,* the third installment of the Mayfair trilogy, Rice provides a vivid and detailed history of the Taltos species. In earlier novels Rice had described them as immensely long-lived creatures over seven feet tall, which are born as adults but with some critical childlike characteristics. The species was thought to have been killed by the Romans, but two Taltos escaped, Ashlar and Tessa. Tessa, however, could not bear children, so it appears that the species will be extinct when Ashlar and Tessa die. Ashlar is an extremely wealthy doll-maker, living in New York. He, too, is a Taltos, but whereas Lasher wanted to populate the earth with his own species and eventually destroy the human race, Ashlar, like many of Rice's vampires, is gentle, lonely, and deeply sympathetic, yearning only for the company of another Taltos and to revive his dying species, happy to live in peace with humans. Over the course of the novel he shares his loneliness with Rowan and Michael and begins to trust them. Yet as he tells his solitary tale, another Taltos is being born. Mona Mayfair, who had an affair with Michael, is now pregnant and soon realizes that the child she is carrying is a female Taltos, Morrigan. Despite the distrustful human efforts to keep her hidden, Ashlar at last finds Morrigan and is stricken to learn of the humans' betrayal. The end of the novel sees the two Taltos leaving together to refound their own species, which Rice intimates will one day, in an ironic climax to the trilogy's fundamental moral ambivalence, multiply and destroy the human race.

Rice ended the Lives of the Mayfair Witches with *Taltos,* but recalls some of its central characters in *Blackwood Farm* (2002) and *Blood Canticle* (2003), where they mingle with the lives of her notorious vampires.

Bibliography

Ramsland, Katherine. "Introduction." In *The Anne Rice Reader: Writers Explore the Universe of Anne Rice.* New York: Ballantine, 1997.

Rice, Anne. *The Witching Hour.* New York: Knopf, 1990.

———. *Lasher.* New York: Knopf, 1993.

———. *Taltos.* New York: Knopf, 1994.

———. *Blackwood Farm.* New York: Knopf, 2002.

———. *Blood Canticle.* New York: Knopf, 2003.

Rout, Kay Kinsella. "The Least of These: Exploitation in Anne Rice's Mayfair Trilogy." *Journal of American Culture* (winter 1996) 19:4. Retrieved from EBSCOHOST.

Candace Henry

London Bridges James Patterson (2004)

JAMES PATTERSON's *London Bridges* opens with the killing of a young prostitute in Brazil. The girl is not the intended victim, however, at least not for the men who shoot her; their target in fact is her would-be murderer, Colonel Geoffrey Shafer, a.k.a. the Weasel, who is soon being tortured and begging for his own life. This is how "the Wolf," a criminal described in an FBI profile as an "executive type" (109), recruits key players in his ultimate plot to blackmail the U.S., British, and German governments.

Meanwhile, Alex Cross, a former police detective and now FBI agent, is on a much needed trip to the West Coast to visit his youngest son and rendezvous with his current love interest, Jamilla Hughes, when he gets the call: An entire town in Nevada has been blown off the map. He must discover who is behind an act of terrorism made only more disturbing because the men who committed it were in the guise of U.S. soldiers. Cross quickly recognizes the Weasel from a photo snapped by a civilian but just as quickly that this civilian is working for the Wolf, mastermind behind the bombing, a villain so shadowy and evasive that no one—not even the criminals who work for him—knows who he is. The Wolf has pulled together an extensive and powerful network to carry off the crime of a lifetime and has seen fit to pull in Cross himself, making the detective as much a pawn in his plans as the ruthless men he employs. Cross must lead the FBI Terrorism Task Force to find the Wolf and prevent him destroying four major cities (one of which is Cross's own Washington, D.C.) if his demand of $2 billion is not met. Increasing the pressure on Cross is a warning against evacuating the target cities (New York, London, Washington, and Frankfurt), and he cannot convince his Nana Mama to leave their home in D.C. With his children at least sent away from the city for temporary safety, Cross must travel to England, France, and finally Zurich to track down—and stop—the Wolf.

Readers of mysteries and thrillers are familiar with the convention of recurring protagonists, but in the Cross series Patterson brings back not only Cross but a number of the criminals with whom he has previously tangled. While readers already familiar with Cross will discover new information about these enemies, as well as new details about Cross himself, *London Bridges* also serves new readers as an excellent introduction to the world of this multifaceted, likeable, and very real detective.

Cross is unusually well drawn for such a protagonist, deeply committed to his family, even as it is breaking apart. While in the midst of a custody battle with his former lover and mother of his youngest son, his two other children, Damon (12) and Janine (10), live with him and his Nana Mama, and these characters become as well known to readers as the protagonist himself. This very human aspect of Cross's personality only adds to the suspense of the novels, as the demands of his investigations and sometimes the criminals themselves constantly threaten the peace and safety of his family.

Fictional detectives often have strange quirks or eccentric mannerisms, but Patterson's readers are genuinely intrigued by Cross's passion for the piano and popular music and share many of his interests in popular culture; he plays classical music and Gershwin, listens to Jill Scott, quotes *The Karate Kid,* and cheers his favorite teams on TV with his kids. His adversary, the Wolf, is an equally multifaceted—even multifaced—character: Red Mafia or former government agent, man or woman, no one can say. What Cross has been able to ascertain is that something bad happened to the Wolf in Paris, and his desire for revenge drives him. He, too, is a man who (once) had a family he cared for. But the Wolf has a "need for complete control and power . . . he wants to do things on a large scale, work a big stage. He's a creative, obsessive planner . . . he organizes, delegates well, doesn't have problems making difficult decisions. But most of all, he's vicious. He likes to hurt people. He likes to *watch* people get hurt" (109).

The Wolf manipulates powerful heads of state and governmental agencies like puppets—a not inappropriate cliché; at one point he forces the top agents and two heads of the CIA and FBI to call out set responses in unison, like a hapless drill team on a training field. He has spies in the FBI and employs former military operatives to commit his crimes, dispatching them when they have outlived their usefulness. He toys with his prey, creating red herrings for Cross, leaving him clues that may or may not be reliable, but which, even when ruses, reveal his complicated psychological makeup.

Everywhere Cross looks there is corruption, from the streets where crime runs rampant but goes largely unnoticed because of poverty and indifference to agents who have turned, been bought, or been betrayed by their own government. Throughout, what is reaped has been sown, either by the careless nature of people or by the agencies meant to protect and serve them, which become the agent of their own disablement through the corruption of power. But Patterson plants the seed of hope that what is most powerful of all, love of the sort Cross feels for his family, his country, and fellow man, will not fail in the war, even though battles may be lost.

Two novels from the Cross series have been adapted into film, *Kiss the Girls* (1997) and *Along Came a Spider* (2001), both starring Morgan Freeman as Alex Cross.

Bibliography

Patterson, James. *London Bridges.* New York: Little, Brown, 2004.

Susan Lynne Beckwith

The Lonesome Gods Louis L'Amour (1983)

One of the most prolific and popular American writers of all time, LOUIS L'AMOUR was born Louis Dearborn LaMoor (his family had anglicized the name but L'Amour reclaimed the original French-Canadian version) in Jamestown, North Dakota, in 1908. He started writing only in his 40s but soon was wealthy and famous enough to travel among the glitterati of Southern California, and by the time he died in 1988 he had written more than 100 novels, short stories, poems, and pieces of nonfiction. Many of his stories have been made into movies, starring luminaries such as John Wayne, Sean Connery, Anthony Quinn, and Brigitte Bardot. He was more beloved and widely read than his closest rivals in the western genre, Larry McMurtry, Zane Grey, and Max Brand, and he outsold them all.

The Lonesome Gods is typical of L'Amour's coming-of-age stories, in which a youngster grows to manhood against a backdrop of the American frontier, but was seen by some as less accomplished than earlier works such as *Hondo, How the West Was Won* and *LAST OF THE BREED.* Some disliked what they saw as the excessive length of the novel, feeling the discursive approach detracted from the central story, while others criticized the inclusion of so much historical data about Southern California's past. Other critics, however, proclaimed the novel L'Amour's masterpiece, praising it as an unusually realistic depiction of an earlier America. All agreed that the novel introduced new elements into L'Amour's fiction: strong social comment still relevant today and a first-person narrative that encourages readers to form their own picture of the young protagonist.

The Lonesome Gods is the story of six-year-old Johannes Verne (certainly not a randomly chosen name), whose dying father takes him to California to be entrusted to his maternal grandfather, the patriarch of a proud and ancient Spanish clan. The old don, however, despises the Anglo-Hispanic background of his grandson and would rather see the child die in the desert than let him grow up to transmit his mixed-blood heritage. While learning such hard lessons, Johannes is helped by outlaws and befriended by Indians, but it is the latter who arrest one's attention. In contrast to the self-indulgent indolence of the Hispanic Californios and the violent greed of recent Anglo settlers—the two groups struggling for control of Southern California—the Cahuilla Indians are marked by uncommon civility and humanity, not only steeped in ancestral wisdom about the world and its people, but honorable, of strong moral fiber, and with high ethical standards. As Zachary Verne, Johannes's father says, "[t]hey respect truth, and they respect strength" (41).

Against a backdrop of conflicts involving Californios, Mexicans, Boston Yankees, and assorted Anglos, Johannes's life is profoundly influenced by two women, Miss Nesselrode (her first name is never used) and a younger girl, Meghan, who both play important roles as he struggles toward manhood. Whereas Miss Nesselrode nurtures the young boy, Meghan becomes his first love. At the end of the novel Johannes has learned not only to survive but even to thrive in the small, dusty Southern Californian town of Los Angeles: "I am Johannes Verne, and I was not afraid" (McMurtry 412).

The title of the work refers to the many gods that have been worshipped in the past and then forgotten. As the Indians tread ancient, well-worn trails, they leave pebbles in tribute to those forgotten gods. The pebbles in turn become signposts for other travelers as they search for routes to various destinations, both symbolic and real; the underlying metaphor is that a man's importance lies not in pride, purity of bloodline, or material conquests but in respect for the past, repayment of debts, and cooperation.

Marked by affinities with the epic works of JAMES MICHENER, L'Amour's saga has also much in common with the more modern westerns of Cormac McCarthy and Larry McMurtry. But the frontier violence and lawlessness so evident in McCarthy's Border Trilogy novels, and especially his later *Blood Meridian,* find a much more discreet expression in *The Lonesome Gods.* Nonetheless, like L'Amour's novel, McCarthy's coming-of-age stories include unsuitable matches between Anglo youths and Hispanic girls, some high-born, others long-fallen; in both cases the crossing of ethnic lines spawns hatred and retribution. McMurtry's acclaimed *Lonesome Dove* follows the growth of a young boy in the unpredictable wilderness of an earlier America. But in contrast to the wisely spiritual Cahuilla of *The Lonesome Gods,* McMurtry's Comanche, Blue Duck, is a bloodthirsty demon, leading a band of companions intent on kidnapping, rape, and mayhem: "They lay by the trails and murder travelers for whatever they've got on 'em" (412). While L'Amour's work acknowledges the dangers and roughness of the early American West, he appears in the end to subscribe more closely to the traditional romantic mythos associated with the frontier than do either McMurtry or McCarthy.

Today most evaluations of L'Amour's work mention *The Lonesome Gods* only in passing, but it can be argued the work is in fact his magnum opus, the novel that most accurately reveals the well-read, kind, and spiritual man underlying the popular writer. Not only is it rich in fascinating historical and cultural data of an earlier West, but it can be seen as a genuine and often luminous morality tale, an American frontier version of the eternal struggle between the enduring strength of goodness and surging forces of evil.

Bibliography

L'Amour, Louis. *The Lonesome Gods.* New York: Bantam Books, 1983.

McCarthy, Cormac. *The Border Trilogy.* New York: Everyman's Library, 1999.

———. *Blood Meridian: or the Evening Redness in the West.* New York: Random House, 1985.

McMurtry, Larry. *Lonesome Dove.* New York: Simon & Schuster, 1985.

Annette Olsen-Fazi

The Lovely Bones **Alice Sebold** (2002)

The Lovely Bones opens with a shocking event: the rape, murder, and dismemberment of a 14-year-old girl on December 6, 1973, in Norristown, Pennsylvania. The novel, however, explores the crime and its aftermath from an unusual perspective, that of the victim, Susie Salmon, who narrates from heaven, watching life continue without her and attempting to come to terms both with what she has lost and what the loss of her has meant to her loved ones.

While a murder early in a novel might lead readers to expect a mystery, Susie emphasizes that her story is not a traditional whodunit. "Don't think," she insists, "that every person you meet in here is a suspect" (6), and soon after reveals the identity of her killer, a nondescript neighbor named George Harvey. The novel is more about healing from trauma than about trauma itself. Nevertheless, it generates considerable suspense, for it is uncertain whether Harvey will be caught. Also uncertain is the fate of the family Susie is taken from: her father, Jack; mother, Abigail; sister, Lindsey; and brother, Buckley. Initially, Susie can only watch as they try to adjust to life without her.

Susie's heaven is nontraditional, no pearly gates or angelic choirs. She likens it to a snow globe sitting upon her father's desk, a closed environment that leaves inhabitants cut off from the world. Still, it is in many ways delightful, reflecting Susie's "simplest desires" and "dreams on Earth" (325, 17). Nor is she entirely isolated, but has a roommate, Holly, as well as an "intake counselor," Franny, whose goal is to help her find peace (18). Susie learns from Franny that her "heaven" is merely a rest stop of sorts, an intermediate place on her journey away from life. But before she moves on, Susie must give up on the living, something she is not immediately prepared to do. A passionate observer, she attempts to appreciate vicariously what growing older would have been like and to play a part, however small, in what happens to the people she cares for, feeling somehow "that if I watched closely, and desired, I might change the lives of those I loved on earth" (20).

From her vantage point beyond the world, Susie enjoys omniscience, which makes her a powerful and intriguing narrator. Bound by neither time nor space, she moves freely into the heads of characters, occasionally even shifting into the past or the future. Before her far-seeing eye, the once healthy Salmon family falls apart. Shaken by Susie's murder, her mother and father seek comfort in radically different ways. Abigail enters into an affair with Len Fenerman, the head detective on Susie's case, and decides at last that she cannot remain with her broken family, moving first to New Hampshire then to California. Jack, obsessed with finding Susie's killer, suspects George Harvey but cannot convince the police to pursue him. One night Jack stumbles on two young lovers, one of whom he mistakenly believes to be Harvey, and he is seriously injured in the ensuing encounter. Lindsey, while gifted, becomes hard, bold, and rebellious after her sister's death. Her relationship with a young man named Samuel anchors her somewhat, but she still takes great risks, the greatest of which is seeking evidence, through a break-in to Harvey's home, that he has murdered her sister. Susie's brother, Buckley, the youngest Salmon, is affected by the turmoil into which his family is thrown and by subsequent alternations of neglect and overprotectiveness.

The focus of *The Lovely Bones* extends beyond the Salmons when Susie turns her attention toward individuals whose lives she touched while on earth. She follows, for example, the difficult adolescence of Ruth, a young woman whom Susie's spirit grazed while leaving her body. Brilliant and sexually ambiguous, Ruth becomes preoccupied with Susie's memory and begins to believe in the enduring presence of the dead. Susie also observes Ray Singh, a boy in love with her before she was killed. An aspiring doctor, Ray is the intellectual equal of Ruth and grows close to her through their mutual interest in Susie. They become a couple of sorts in high school, though each sees in the other not a lover so much as a reflection of Susie.

The bridge Susie creates between Ray and Ruth underlines one of the central concerns of the book, relationships between the living and the dead. The book's title refers not just to Susie's remains but to such relationships, the disembodied narrator coming to appreciate "the lovely bones that had grown around my absence: the connections—sometimes tenuous, sometimes made at great cost, but often magnificent—that happened after I was gone" (320), connections that invariably include Susie's murderer, who touches so many, albeit in dark and dangerous ways.

As Susie plumbs the psyche of Harvey—whom she calls (as she did in life) "Mr. Harvey"—she finds he has in fact killed a host of young women, several of whom she meets in heaven. But instead of recoiling in censure, she explores the abuse Mr. Harvey suffered as a child and the primal urges within him that he himself barely understands, both of which are at the root of his becoming a serial killer. Rather like her own heroine, ALICE SEBOLD confessed in an interview with Terry Gross, discussing the challenge of writing about Harvey, that she discovered

> . . . a great deal of compassion for him. There are moments where he attempts to do things other than what his drive or instinct is telling him to do. . . . So he resists up until the point where he's no longer able to resist. And you know . . . you can have compassion without forgiveness (Sebold).

Despite Sebold's compassion, Harvey does meet with a kind of retribution near the end of the novel.

Yet it is not Susie's murderer being served justice that ultimately enables her to ascend to "the place I call this wide wide Heaven" (320). During her time as "a watcher" she finds that she can, if she exerts herself, still touch the living. Indeed, years after Susie's death Ruth offers her body to her so that she can make love with Ray (246). This experience, along with the realization that her loved ones will in time get over her death and again "become whole," allows Susie to let go, "to see things in a way that let me hold the world without me in it" (320). She thus recalls her aquatic namesake, completing an effortful journey—part of a greater life—even as she herself passes away.

A film adaptation of *The Lovely Bones* directed by Peter Jackson is planned for release in 2009.

Bibliography

Sebold, Alice. "Interview." *Fresh Air with Terry Gross.* National Public Radio (10 July 2002).

———. *The Lovely Bones.* New York: Little, Brown, 2002.

Noel Sloboda

Ludlum, Robert (1927–2001)

Most famous for his Bourne series, Robert Ludlum was the author of 21 novels, all of which made it to the *New York Times* best-seller list. They have been translated into 32 languages, and tens of millions of copies are in print worldwide. Many of his works have been produced for film and television, the most popular of which have been adaptations of the Bourne novels, starring Matt Damon. Some of his earlier work appeared under the pseudonyms of Jonathan Ryder or Michael Shepherd.

Ludlum was born in New York City in 1927 but raised in the suburbs of New Jersey. His mother sent him to attend private schools in Connecticut following the premature death of his father. He later became the first fine arts major to graduate from Wesleyan University, his wide-ranging studies including courses in fine arts, history, literature, and philosophy. Before beginning his career as an author at the age of 40, Ludlum was first an actor and producer for the Broadway and Off-Broadway stage and did a host of commercial voice-overs, the royalties for one of which, consisting only of the words, "Plunge works fast," put one of his children through two years of college. During World War II he enlisted in the marines.

The Scarlatti Inheritance, published by World Publishing in 1971, was Ludlum's first novel but already evinces some of the signature features of his style, including the dramatic opposition of well-drawn personalities in the form of its hero, Matthew Canfield, Department of the Interior employee, and villain Ulster/Kroeger, who provides financial backing for the young Nazi organization at the center of its destructive action. Also typical is the plot's well-balanced evolution through a complex dynamic of international intrigue and travel. In an interesting contrast Ludlum's follow-up, *The Osterman Weekend* (1972), is firmly set in suburban New Jersey, the hub of "Omega," a Soviet plan designed to destroy the American economy. Otherwise replete with traditional elements of mystery, suspense, gunfights, secret agents, and a brooding and pervasive CIA presence, the atypical suburban drama is resolved with a painstakingly logical explanation, which would also become a signature feature of Ludlum's oeuvre.

His 1977 work, *The Chancellor Manuscript,* explores the notion that a nation's history may in crucial respects be more accurately depicted in fiction than in the common truths learned by its citizenry. Here Ludlum plunges an unsuspecting graduate student into a tangle of intrigue when he attempts to uncover the truth of multinational corporations who backed the Nazi "wolfpack" from 1926 to 1939. Chancellor worms his way so dangerously close to the truth that higher powers insist that the doctoral committee fail his dissertation. A former ambassador visiting the university suggests that the young man turn his attention to fiction writing, an attempt to disarm and discredit Chancellor's ideas. However, through fiction the writer only draws closer to the truth. The plot is set in motion by the assassination of J. Edgar Hoover, planned and carried out by a secret group called Inver Brass, made up of five members who have been influencing the economy and society of America for decades. At first manipulated and then nearly eliminated by them, the young author yet survives, and in the very act of surviving he inscribes in his fiction the truths immanent in their corruptive power.

The AQUITAINE PROGRESSION (1985) stands out as one of Ludlum's richest and most complex tales, not merely in the subtlety of its plot, which tells a convoluted tale of international conspiracy and intrigue, but in the sheer number of its characters and the complexity of their allegiances. Moreover, the pervasive political paranoia that forms its thematic focus is so suffocating and believable that only the most skillful of resolutions can make plausible its eventual demise.

The ICARUS AGENDA (1988) illustrates Ludlum's masterly handling of historical realities, exploring the volatile relationship between the Arab world and the American-Israeli alliance, while thematically focused on questions of personal responsibility in the midst of dangerous political events and the tensions involved in the operation of secret organizations within a democratic society.

All these thematic and stylistic elements of Ludlum's fiction are epitomized in the novels of his Bourne series (1980–90), describing the struggle for justice, truth, and self-awareness of Jason Bourne, a CIA-trained covert assassin and amnesiac who begins the series with only the faintest, most dangerous grasp of his former self and then must survive escalating attempts on his life from a host of assailants whom he cannot at first even identify.

In the series' original and most famous installment, *The* BOURNE IDENTITY (1980), a confused and desperate Bourne enlists the aid of Marie St. Jacques, a Canadian finance official who later becomes his lover and helps him avoid capture while he searches for answers both to his identity and need to survive. Although Bourne is trained as a killing machine, fluent in three languages, and proficient in martial arts combat, Marie is convinced, principally through a heroic rescue he effects, that he is not a ruthless murderer. Bourne takes on disguises as he seeks to trace his past, taps into his secret Swiss bank account that contains millions of dollars, and attempts to isolate Carlos the Jackal, a powerful yet faceless assassin who operates from Paris. His quest for identity leads him through Switzerland, France, and the United States as he is hunted by both Carlos's minions and the U.S. clandestine services. While the ending of *The Bourne Identity* provides answers to some of its animating questions, Ludlum skillfully raises yet more probing quandaries with the novel and propels the reader into its two equally successful sequels.

Matt Damon starred as Jason Bourne in all three Universal adaptations of the Bourne novels—*The Bourne Identity* (2002), *The Bourne Supremacy* (2004), and *The Bourne Ultimatum* (2007)—and the tremendous box-office success of the films has both resulted in the release of new Bantam paperback editions of the novels and attracted new readership and interest to other Ludlum novels. While the screenplays have been significantly modified from the novels, especially to include more contemporary political references, the films capture admirably the essential elements of Ludlum's literary success.

In addition to his own novelistic output Ludlum created and coauthored the Covert-One series of books, a detailed anatomy of the nature and workings of a benign clandestine American security organization, commencing with the *The Hades Factor*, written with Gayle Lynds and published by St. Martin's Press in 2000. He also wrote *The Paris Option* (2002) and *The Altman Code* (2003) with Lynds and *The Cassandra Compact* (2001) with Philip Shelby. When he died of a heart attack in

2001, Ludlum left notes and manuscripts, which have themselves been used to construct two additional novels in the Covert-One series, *The Lazarus Vendetta* (2004) and *The Moscow Vector* (2005), written by Patrick Larkin.

Bibliography

"The Covert-One Series." Available online. URL: http://www.ludlumbooks.com/covert-one.html. Accessed July 10, 2007.

Greenberg, Martin H., ed. *The Robert Ludlum Companion.* New York: Bantam, 1993.

Martin, Douglas. "Robert Ludlum, Best-Selling Suspense Novelist, Dies at 73." *New York Times*, 14 March 2001, Section B, p. 9.

"Other Robert Ludlum Novels." Available online. URL: http://robertludlumbooks.com/othernovels.html#bournelegacy. Accessed July 10, 2007.

Elizabeth Whitehead

M

Mary, Mary James Patterson (2005)

Mary, Mary is the 11th novel in JAMES PATTERSON's "nursery rhyme" series about psychologist Alexander Cross. Having transferred to the FBI from the Washington, D.C., police force two novels earlier in *The* BIG, BAD WOLF, Cross is discovered on his first real family vacation since joining the FBI, taking his family, including Cross's grandmother, Nana Mama, to Disneyland. But typical of the series, he and his family appear only after the appearance of the criminal, here a serial killer in Hollywood who calls himself "the Storyteller" but signs himself as "Mary Smith" in the e-mails he sends to a film reviewer at the *L.A. Times*. Smith targets "perfect" mothers in the film industry, murdering them and slashing their faces. Though in Disneyland, Cross is called in to consult on the case, which leads to his eventual assignment to it after he returns from his vacation. In addition to following Cross's transcontinental investigation, the novel focuses on his painful custody battle for his youngest child, Alex, Jr., who lives in Seattle with his ex-wife, Christine. And to further complicate matters, Patterson also inscribes the narrative voice of Mary Smith, whose role remains ambiguous to the reader and whose identity remains unknown to Cross for most of the narrative.

As in all of his novels, Patterson interweaves several different narrative voices, providing a multilayered story from varying perspectives, including both criminal and detective. As usual, Alex Cross narrates his sections in the first person but in this novel emphasizes his role as a father and dedication to his son in passages that elsewhere would describe his dating experiences.

Another distinctive feature of the novel lies in the technical nature of his investigation, with Cross often resorting to literary analysis, comparing the e-mails that "Mary Smith" sends to the *Times* journalist with forensic data, in order to understand the killer's psychology. As Cross analyzes the Storyteller's narrative in the e-mails, the reader, too, builds a complex but limited narrative picture of the Storyteller's existence, coming to recognize that he is a male, though always writing as and with the perspective of the woman "Mary Smith"—two conflicting elements that equally confuse Cross as he struggles to reconcile the grotesque violence of the crimes with the female of the letters. While Cross does not employ procedural psychological practices as he does in other novels such as *Along Came a Spider*, the case again hinges on aspects of psychosis, as in the very confusion between the Storyteller and Mary Smith—a confusion prompting Patterson to produce an arrest that, far from solving, merely complicates the enigma.

But despite its psychological convolutions, *Mary, Mary* focuses predominantly on the issues of family, parenting, and parenthood itself. Both the crime and the criminal narratives revolve around motherhood since the Storyteller chooses only successful Hollywood career women who are involved in raising children, and his e-mails focus relentlessly on how their deaths will affect their children; while in her own narrative, Mary Smith appears obsessed with her children. These accounts of working mothers parallel Cross's own attempts to redeem his reputation as a good father, even though he is a single parent with a demanding job. Indeed, the novel foregrounds Cross as a father rather than as an FBI agent, and he spends much of the tale merely protecting his family from the intrusions of journalist and true-crime author James Truscott and fighting the custody suit for his youngest son. Moreover, since his target coincidentally operates in Hollywood, Cross uses his trips to the West Coast to visit his son, viewing the criminal investigation, in fact, as secondary to his familial troubles: "the Mary Smith case was as a backdrop to my entire life" (157). In fact, in an interesting inversion of the usual formula, Cross uses his work to distract him from familial concerns, rather than using his family to relieve the stress of his police work.

Another departure from form may be seen in *Mary, Mary*'s comparative lack of interest in racial issues, which regularly arise in the other novels about Cross, an African American working in the capital and living in its often troubled southeast neighborhood. Instead, the narrative's moral focus rests more on issues of gender, especially with the case dominated by sexual confusion and even psychosis. The Los Angeles Police accept the name and the murdered mothers as proof that "Mary Smith" is a woman, but Cross cannot easily accept the gender identification, recalling that "[a]ccording to the statistics [. . .] something like 89 per cent of known female serial killers used poison [. . .]. Less than ten per cent of various killers employed a gun [. . .] and none [. . .] on record used a knife" (130). While the male pronouns used in the Storyteller's narrative, as well as the detective's suspicions, suggest to the reader that "Mary Smith" is a man, Patterson maintains readerly confusion by highlighting the cogency and apparent veracity of Mary Smith's narrative, which is both distinct from that of the Storyteller and internally coherent. And by even conceiving of the possibility of a female serial killer, the novel explores the margins of accepted understanding of gender and its dispositions, an exploration only deepened by Cross's custody battle, in which the typical pattern of maternal stability and paternal instability is reversed. Nevertheless, Cross's refusal to accept the female serial killer assumption ultimately leads to solving the case and the novel's resolution.

Bibliography

Patterson, James. *Along Came a Spider.* London: HarperCollins, 1993.
———. *Cat and Mouse.* London: Headline, 1997.
———. *Mary, Mary.* London: Headline, 2005.

Malcah Effron

Masquerade Kit Williams (1983)

Masquerade is a charming yet perplexing fairy tale, seemingly created more for adults than for children, detailing the adventures of Jack Hare, a brown rabbit who serves with the Frog as the Moon's messenger. The Moon charges them to deliver to the Sun a jewel she has fashioned as a token of her affection: a rabbit made of gold and precious stones. In the course of his delivery Jack encounters riddle after riddle, presented to him by such colorful characters as Penny-Pockets Lady, Tara Tree-Tops, and the Practical Man, but while his progress is marked by correct answers to these enigmas, such answers are very rarely shared with the reader because they also provide clues to the discovery of a jeweled rabbit hidden somewhere in England. Such are the essential elements both of *Masquerade*'s great appeal as a novel and its phenomenon as a media event.

Williams offers his first clue to treasure hunters in a bit of rhyming verse on the title page:

> Within the pages of this book there is a story told,
> Of love, adventures, fortunes lost, and a jewel of solid gold.
> To solve the hidden riddle, you must use your eyes,
> And find the hare in every picture that may point you to the prize.
> (iii)

The full solution requires a painstaking analysis not merely of the novel's many literary puzzles but of its 16 intricate and enigmatic illustrations as well, also created by the author, more than fulfilling his original aim to generate a work that would—indeed could—not be "just flicked through and put down" (1) and which, at the same time, would in a sense redeem his own "lost childhood" (2).

The prize lay unclaimed for almost two and a half years, during which time Williams was barraged with prospective solutions and requests for hints, receiving up to 200 letters per day (this *before* the Internet), and was finally forced to request an unlisted phone number due to all-hours phone calls and in-person visits from manic "Masqueraders" (Gascoigne 2). Plagued by worries that his puzzle would prove insoluble, Williams was relieved to receive a letter on February 18, 1982, signed simply "Ken," which provided a sketch of the hiding place and the location's name but no solutions to the various puzzles. Before learning that the riddles themselves had not in fact been solved (the solution being purportedly based mostly on research of the author's own background), Williams contacted the puzzler and revealed that the general location was correct and a physical search should begin. On February 24 a clay coffer bearing the legend "I am the Keeper of the Jewel of Masquerade waiting for you or Eternity" (Gascoigne 10) was unearthed from soil apparently loosened by other puzzlers and later opened by Williams himself on television in the evening of March 11. In his appearances, photo-ops, and interviews, the solver used the evident pseudonym Ken Thomas and concealed his face from view, purportedly to protect his privacy but only encouraging suspicions that he had somehow cheated. Meanwhile, only days after the critical broadcast, Williams received a letter from Mike Barker and John Rousseau, two physics teachers who had genuinely solved all of the book's riddles months earlier but had not contacted Williams. They had also been digging in the same location and apparently dug up the hare late one night but stunningly overlooked the small clay container containing the confirmation of success (Gascoigne 167–178, Amrich).

For six years Thomas exploited the prize and his fame, using the jewel as collateral to found the video game company Haresoft and its 1985 two-part release, *Hareraiser*, a puzzle game featuring the Masquerade hare as the prize. But in 1988 the London *Times* published a story revealing that Dugald Thompson, a.k.a. Ken Thomas, and business partner John Guard had conspired to pressure Guard's own girlfriend, Veronica Robertson, Williams's ex-girlfriend and one of the only people who knew of the prize's location, to aid them in finding the hare, promising that the proceeds would benefit animal rights causes. The company was soon liquidated, and the golden hare was sold at auction for £31,900.

Williams followed up *Masquerade* in 1984 with *Book Without a Name*, a puzzle book whose object was to determine the volume's title; he has since claimed he will produce no other such work (Amrich).

Nonetheless, the astonishing success of *Masquerade* has spawned countless puzzle books and contests, perhaps the most intriguing of which is *Menagerie*, created by amateur puzzler/artist Dillon Waugh as a 25th-anniversary homage to *Masquerade*, featuring artwork and text similar in style and design to Williams's own but freely available online. Waugh's prize is also similar in design to Williams's but crafted of silver to commemorate the 25th anniversary.

Bibliography

Amrich, Dan. "Masquerade and the Mysteries of Kit Williams: About Ken Williams." In *Masquerade and the Mysteries of Kit Williams*. Available online. URL: http://www.bunnyears.net/kitwilliams/aboutkit.html. Accessed April 29, 2007.

———. "Masquerade and the Mysteries of Kit Williams: Frequently Asked Questions." In *Masquerade and the Mysteries of Kit Williams*. Available online. URL: http://www.bunnyears.net/kitwilliams/faq.html. Accessed April 29, 2007.

Gascoigne, Bamber. *Quest for the Golden Hare*. London: Jonathan Cape, 1983.

Waugh, Dillon. "Menageriehunt." *Menagerie: A Tribute to the Original Hunt*. Available online. URL: http://www.dillonwaugh.com/pages/menagerie.htm. Accessed April 29, 2007.

Williams, Kit. *Masquerade: The Complete Book with the Answer Explained*. New York: Workman, 1983.

———. *Out of One Eye: The Art of Kit Williams*. New York: Harmony Books, 1986.

———. *Book Without a Name* (a.k.a. *The Bee on the Comb*). New York: Knopf, 1984.

———. *Engines of Ingenuity.* Corte Madera, Calif.: Gingko Press, 2001.

Solomon Davidoff

McCullough, Colleen (1937–)

Colleen McCullough is a researcher, founder of the department of neurophysiology at the Royal North Shore Hospital in Sydney, and author of a biography, two cookbooks, musical lyrics, and 17 novels, including the seven-volume series *The Master of Rome* and the internationally successful romance novel *The Thorn Birds.* Although she writes in a variety of narrative forms, all of her books rely on meticulous historical research and detailed psychological interpretations of everyday characters.

McCullough was born in 1937 in the Australian outback of Wellington, New South Wales; however, she has lived most of her life outside of Australia. The child of a notably dysfunctional family that savored athletics, McCullough was a voracious reader and avid student of science. She studied at Holy Cross College and the University of Sydney, where she read widely in the humanities, especially in Roman history. Preferring sure employment to the uncertain vocations of the humanities and arts, she pursued a career in medicine, but a soap allergy forced her to leave medical school and turn to neurophysiology. Alternately employed as teacher, librarian, bus driver, and journalist, McCullough eventually settled into work as a neurophysiology researcher in Sydney, London, and finally the Yale University School of Internal Medicine, where she remained from 1967 to 1976.

Underpaid but determined, McCullough wrote fiction for extra money after her workdays at Yale, with the sales of her first novel, *Tim* (1974), bringing her enough to pay off her father's debts. Her second novel's success astounded even her. Escapist fiction like *Tim,* but far greater in scope, *The Thorn Birds* (1977) follows the lives, loves, and deaths of one family—the Clearys—through three generations, from 1915 to 1965, and provided McCullough with enough money to leave Yale for England to train as a nurse at St. Bartholemew's Hospital. Her fame quickly outgrew her trainee position, particularly when *Tim* appeared as a movie starring Piper Laurie and Mel Gibson and *The Thorn Birds* as a television miniseries starring Richard Chamberlain and Rachel Ward. McCullough sought relief from the press and her fans by moving in the late 1970s to idyllic Norfolk Island in the South Pacific, 1,000 miles away from her native Australia. There she met Ric Robinson, a former house painter and descendant of the *Bounty* mutineers, whom she married in 1984. She became stepmother to his two children; he, her most important critic.

McCullough continues as a member of the New York Academy of Sciences and a fellow of the American Association for the Advancement of Science and serves (with Henry Kissinger and others) on the Board of Visitors of the International Programs Center of the Department of Political Science at the University of Oklahoma. In 2006, at the celebration of Queen Elizabeth II's birthday, McCullough was awarded the Officer of the Order of Australia for her service to the arts as an author and to the community through her support of national and international educational programs, medico-scientific disciplines, and charitable causes.

Since McCullough's resettlement to Norfolk Island, she has written a host of works, including *An Indecent Obsession* (1981), *A Creed for the Third Millennium* (1985), *The Ladies of Missalonghi* (1987), *The Song of Troy* (1998), *Morgan's Run* (2000), *The Touch* (2003), *Angel* (2004), *On, Off* (2006), as well as her monumental *Master of Rome* series: *The First Man in Rome* (1990), *The Grass Crown* (1991), *Fortune's Favorites* (1993), *Caesar's Women* (1996), *Caesar: Let the Dice Fly* (1997), *The October Horse* (2002), and *Anthony and Cleopatra* (2008), some of which have garnered only modest sales and mixed reviews. The *Master of Rome* series, however, with its engrossing narrative and vivid historical detail, has been well received by readers and critics alike. McCullough was drawn to the republic of Rome because she saw it as an immensely significant area of history that novelists have largely ignored. McCullough loves to break new ground in her work, which is why she does not write sequels, commenting to interviewer Andrew Denton that she tends "not to write the same book twice because it's no challenge."

The Thorn Birds, which made Colleen McCullough's name a household word, is Australia's answer to Margaret Mitchell's *Gone with the Wind,* but without the Civil War. Like Scarlett O'Hara, the central character, Meggie Cleary, dominates the narrative and highlights the central theme of female suffering with her frustrating lifelong love for a handsome but unavailable Roman Catholic priest, Ralph de Bricassart. Although she marries unhappily and has a daughter, Justine, Meggie has a brief affair with Father Ralph from which comes a son, Dane, who later enters the priesthood unaware that his spiritual tutor is also his biological father.

The sweeping tale illustrates many of McCullough's best and worst characteristics as a novelist. Its plot is engrossing; its characterization entertaining if not highly nuanced; its settings adroit; and its central thematic concern, like most of McCullough's work, hinges on a complex and ennobling conflict between love and duty. The plot, however, is often driven by startling coincidences and constantly finds characters making simplistic emotional responses to complex circumstance. These almost cartoonish features of her writing, along with the huge television success of *The Thorn Birds*—the second-highest rated adaptation in the United States behind *Roots*—tend to overshadow McCullough's reputation as a serious novelist. McCullough, however, disregards such criticisms, arguing that she does not aim to write literary fiction. Her goal is to entertain readers, incorporating and enhancing the conventions of popular romance and historical fiction.

Throughout her career, McCullough has planned and researched, often for years, the material for her fiction, and this habit contributes to her speedy composition. More important, her ability as a storyteller and her wide-ranging interests make even her somewhat melodramatic work compelling. In later years McCullough has become increasingly reliant on a wheelchair, due to hemorrhagic macular degeneration, but she continues to live a full and creative life.

Bibliography

DeMarr, Mary Jean. *Colleen McCullough: A Critical Companion.* Westport, Conn.: Greenwood Press, 1996.

Denton, Andrew. "Enough Rope: Colleen McCullough." Available online. URL: http://www.abc.net.au/tv/enoughrope/transcripts/s2041318.htm. Accessed September 24, 2007.

LynnDianne Beene

McLaughlin, Emma (1964–) and Nicola Kraus (1974–)

McLaughlin and Kraus are the coauthors of *The* NANNY DIARIES (2002) and *Citizen Girl* (2004). The two women work as a writing team in New York City. Both graduated from New York University, where they first met at the Gallatin School of Individualized Study, and between the two they spent eight years nannying for wealthy families in Manhattan's Upper East Side. Over those years they worked for more than 30 such families, and it is their experiences in these nanny jobs that they drew upon to craft their first novel, *The Nanny Diaries,* which remains their biggest success both critically and commercially.

Within a few months of the first printing of *The Nanny Diaries* in 2002, half a million copies of the novel had been sold, with more than a million copies sold by the end of the year. A film version of the book starring Scarlett Johansson, Laura Linney, and Paul Giamatti was released in 2007. The rights to the book were sold to Miramax for a reported $500,000. Julia Roberts was selected to record an abridged audio-book version of the novel.

The two women originally signed with St. Martin's Press under editor Jennifer Weis for $25,000, but the success of *The Nanny Diaries* saw McLaughlin and Kraus receive a new two-book deal with Random House for $3 million. The first of these books was intended to be *Citizen Girl,* but the literary world was shocked when Random House rejected the manuscript. The book deal was rescinded, and the Random House president who authorized the deal, Ann Godoff, was fired. McLaughlin and Kraus revised the manuscript for *Citizen Girl,* and it was published in 2004 by Atria Books, a division of Simon & Schuster. Atria reportedly paid McLaughlin and Kraus $200,000 for the manuscript.

Though occasionally criticized for their choice to write as a team rather than individually, McLaughlin and Kraus draw from their combined experience to create their novels. While *The Nanny Diaries* and *Citizen Girl* are both clearly works of fiction, autobiographical elements are most certainly present, the two women employing details from their personal and professional lives to create vibrant, realistic protagonists.

Known for their broad satire and cutting social commentary, McLaughlin and Kraus have developed a reputation as clever, funny writers within the chicklit genre, which includes such best sellers as Sophie Kinsella's *Shopaholic* series and HELEN FIELDING'S BRIDGET JONES books and films, all focusing on the lives and work of women, as well as romantic relationships. The books are easily read and humorous and shape their plots out of the common experiences of contemporary women. McLaughlin and Kraus conform to the basic requirements of the genre, their novels being generally light and quick reads, funny, and rooted in the lives of everyday women.

The two differ from the bulk of chicklit writers, however, in their heightened use of irony to criticize social conventions. In *The Nanny Diaries*, for instance, McLaughlin and Kraus focus their satiric lens on rich New York parents who lack connection to their own children. The two women were initially nervous about the reception their book would receive (and indeed some critics took issue with a perceived antielitist tone in the novel), but it has proven an overwhelming success nonetheless. Their sharp comedy, combined with effective scenes of pathos and fundamentally compassionate, fallible characters, make for a witty and appealing mix that should survive their second effort.

Bibliography

"The Bumpy Ride from *The Nanny Diaries* to *Citizen Girl*." *New York* magazine, 15 November 2004. Available online. URL: http://nymag.com/nymetro/arts/columns/longstory/10330/.

McLaughlin, Emma, and Nicola Kraus. *The Nanny Diaries*. New York: St. Martin's, 2002.

Southey, Tabatha. "Review of *The Nanny Diaries*, by Emma McLaughlin and Nicola Kraus." *The Globe and Mail*, 20 April 2002.

"2002 Breakthroughs: Nicola Kraus / Emma McLaughlin." *People*, 30 December 2002, 136.

Warner, Judith. "Review of *The Nanny Diaries*, by Emma McLaughlin and Nicola Kraus." *Washington Post*, 10 April 2002.

Brenna Clarke Gray

McMillan, Terry (1951–)

Terry Lynn McMillan was born in 1951, the oldest of five children, in Port Huron, Michigan, near Detroit, to Edward and Madeline McMillan, coming of age at the height of the civil rights era. Early on she found the small town atmosphere of Port Huron stifling; however, the city could not contain her ambition, sparked by her lifelong love of reading and writing. McMillan later memorialized the town in the fictional Port Haven of her debut novel, *Mama*. In 1969 she left Port Huron for Los Angeles, enrolling first in Los Angeles City College, then the University of California, Berkeley, and eventually completing a bachelor's degree in journalism in 1976. Ishmael Reed, who first met McMillan when he taught her in a fiction-writing class at UC Berkeley, encouraged the young writer to develop her unique voice. She continued writing, beginning, but not completing, an M.F.A. in screenwriting at Columbia University in New York. Over the next decade McMillan worked as an administrative assistant in several New York law firms, all the while developing her craft as a writer. In 1984 she gave birth to her only child, Solomon, but within three years had ended her relationship with the child's father, Leonard Welch, and signed her first book deal for *Mama*.

McMillan's work is noted—sometimes praised, sometimes vilified—for its vivid realism. Like most authors she has drawn on her personal life for inspiration and material, but few have done so as intensely or successfully. *Mama* (1987), which chronicles the struggle of Mildred Peacock to raise five children and maintain a personal life after kicking out her alcoholic and abusive husband, was loosely based on the colorful life of McMillan's own mother, Madeline. *Disappearing Acts* (1989) was inspired in part by her relationship with Leonard Welch. WAITING TO EXHALE (1992), set in Phoenix, Arizona, where McMillan made her home at the time, grew out of her frustration with dating and finding a professional black man to marry. *How Stella Got Her Groove Back* (1996) is said to be a thinly veiled celebration of her relationship with Jamaican-born Jonathan Plummer, 20 years her junior. Plummer and McMillan married in Hawaii in 1998, but in 2005 their marriage ended in a rancorous divorce after Plummer revealed his homosexuality. In recent interviews McMillan has hinted at a future novel, *Don't Pity the Fool,* inspired by the tumultuous breakup.

Much of McMillan's success stems from her uncanny ability to gauge the pulse of African-American women. Through hard work and untiring self-promotion, McMillan tapped into a market of young, female, black professionals whose reading had been primed by the works of Alice Walker, Toni Morrison, and Gloria Naylor. While her work, impolitic and often profane, has been criticized as lacking gravity, it answers a real need for stories about the lives of contemporary, upwardly mobile, educated black women; many consider McMillan, along with E. Lynn Harris, Connie Briscoe, Tina McElroy Ansa, Eric Jerome Dickey, and Benilde Little, a force behind the Black Popular Literature boom of the 1990s. Their stories of romance, work, friendship, and "the good life" appeal to a growing cadre of young professional black readers whose organized book clubs and reading groups consume the latest offerings as quickly as they are released. McMillan has traveled extensively to speak to such clubs and read at bookstores, cultivating this market and establishing a template for the black writer as celebrity, not just intellectual. While her celebrity is partly the result of just such hard work and shrewd marketing, she herself acknowledges the dangers of overexposure. In particular she has criticized the recent crop of urban or "street lit" writers who, inspired by her financial success, offer up books that shock and titillate in order to make a quick dollar.

McMillan's novels share a preoccupation with the difficult process of finding and maintaining a romantic partnership. In *Mama* she depicts a strong, complicated mother struggling to hold her family together while dealing with her own desire for love and companionship. *Disappearing Acts,* which follows the up-and-down relationship of Zora Banks and Franklin Swift, was praised for its authentic representation of Franklin's struggle to maintain the relationship. Her most successful novels, *Waiting to Exhale* and *How Stella Got Her Groove Back,* chronicle the adventures of young "buppies" (black urban professionals) trying to find love. *A Day Late and a Dollar Short* returns to the theme of family, while *The Interruption of Everything,* in a natural progression, tells of a woman's struggle to keep her marriage and life together at midlife. While McMillan deals with realistic themes and concerns, she does so in a way that complicates and challenges conventional depictions of the black family, and she captures the angst of professional black women in a voice that is familiar without being preachy or self-consciously literary.

Two of McMillan's novels, *Waiting to Exhale* and *How Stella Got Her Groove Back,* have been adapted for the big screen; a third, *Disappearing Acts,* was produced for HBO. She has also published several short stories, including the often anthologized "Quilting on the Rebound," which originally appeared in 1976 in *Yardbird,* a journal edited by Ishmael Reed and Frank Chin. She has also developed a reputation for nourishing young writers, publishing *Breaking Ice,* an anthology of contemporary black writing, in 1990. In 2006 McMillan released *It's OK If You're Clueless—and 23 More Tips for the College Bound,* based on her remarks at her son's high school graduation. Recently McMillan has also begun to exhibit her creations as a fabric designer and painter, crediting these new creative outlets with helping her to heal from the trauma of the very public dissolution of her marriage.

Bibliography

McMillan, Terry. *Mama.* Boston: Houghton Mifflin, 1987.

———. *Disappearing Acts.* New York: Viking, 1989.

———. *Waiting to Exhale.* New York: Viking, 1992.

———. *How Stella Got Her Groove Back.* New York: Viking, 1996.

———. *A Day Late and a Dollar Short.* New York: Viking, 2005.

———. *The Interruption of Everything.* New York: Viking, 2005.

———, ed. *Breaking Ice.* New York: Penguin, 1990.
Patrick, Diane. *Terry McMillan: The Unauthorized Biography.* New York: St. Martin's, 1999.

Rychetta Watkins

Memories of Midnight **Sidney Sheldon** (1990)
Memories of Midnight is the only sequel in SIDNEY SHELDON's oeuvre, returning to characters and themes first introduced in Sheldon's second novel, the 1973 blockbuster *The Other Side of Midnight,* which quickly topped the best-seller list and stayed there for 52 weeks, securing Sheldon's position as a leading popular author despite lackluster reviews. The former tale established what would become Sheldon's stock in trade over the next three decades: complex female protagonists and battles for power among the rich and famous. Sheldon's settings are drawn with the assurance and veracity of a writer who has experienced for himself places frequented by the jet set. But even exotic details such as the making of wartime propaganda films or the traffic in heroin are carefully researched. What stays with readers, however, are Sheldon's characters, for he is a consummate student of the human psyche, as evidenced even in his prize-winning first work, the detective novel *The Naked Face* (1969).

The Other Side of Midnight follows the lives of two of Sheldon's most memorable women, Catherine Alexander and Noelle Page, from their foundational but ultimately disappointing relationships with their fathers to the point at which their paths catastrophically intersect. Catherine's father is a traveling salesman from Chicago, full of dreams that Catherine learns all too soon will never come true; Noelle's French fisherman father tells her she is a royal princess but is quick to exploit her beauty for his own benefit. Taking up residence in Washington, D.C., Catherine hides her inexperience in the realm of physical love behind a keen mind and acerbic wit and commences a promising career—especially for a woman in the 1940s—in public relations for the State Department; Noelle relies on her exceptional beauty, cultivating a sexual prowess with which she captivates the increasingly powerful men in her life.

Both women fall under the spell of the dashingly handsome Larry Douglas, who embodies much of the charm, as well as the shallowness, of the fathers whose love and approval both women still seek. Noelle is ecstatic when the charming American soldier proposes and eagerly awaits his return, until it becomes clear that he is never coming back for her. Meanwhile, Larry proposes to Catherine, and their romance and impetuous wedding for a time make life seem too good to be true, until Larry is called off to war once again, returning larger-than-life but unable to adjust to the routine of civilian life.

After Larry becomes the personal pilot for Constantin Demiris, one of the most powerful men on the world, his wartime affair with Noelle, who has established herself as Demiris's mistress merely to manipulate the events of Larry's life and bring him back to her, is predictably rekindled. Catherine is the only barrier now to Noelle's happiness, and Noelle convinces Larry that Catherine must be eliminated.

Noelle has underestimated Demiris, however. He is not a man to forgive or forget a wrong, and Noelle's betrayal wounds his masculine pride deeply. Demiris destroys both her and her lover, but his triumph does little to assuage the hurt he feels at realizing that Noelle has deceived him. Ultimately everyone in the novel is betrayed and left unfulfilled. Sex and power are not enough, and there seems to be nothing else to fill the void. As glamorous and successful as these characters are, they are not happy, and the novel ends on a haunting, open-ended chord that would be resolved only 17 years later when Sheldon took up the story in *Memories of Midnight.*

Sheldon's female characters are his signature and strength. They are immensely varied, interesting and provocative, endearing and repulsive, and ultimately memorable; but all trace their fictive roots to one or both of these two women. Catherine's compelling combination of intellectual power and sexual naïveté is rediscovered in Elizabeth Roffe (*Bloodline,* 1977), Jennifer Parker (*The Rage of Angels,* 1980), and Mary Ashley (*Windmills of the Gods,* 1987). Traces of Noelle reappear in Jill Castle (*The Stranger in the Mirror,* 1975) and Lara Cameron (*The Stars Shine Down,* 1992), though neither possess Noelle's single-mindedness of purpose. Conversely, Sheldon's male characters are far less developed and usually appear as one of four types: the self-made man of power, the self-absorbed womanizer, the malevolent but colorful and ever suave villain, and his counterpart, the upstanding but somewhat vapid man of principle.

The 1990 sequel to *The Other Side of Midnight,* Sheldon's 10th version of his familiar blend of glamour and intrigue, enjoyed a record-breaking first publishing of 1.1 million copies. *Memories of Midnight* more than picks up where the 1973 novel left off, as extensive flashback passages are quoted verbatim from the earlier novel. But where *The Other Side of Midnight* successfully focused on the contrasting female protagonists, *Memories of Midnight* less successfully focuses on the men, who are predictably neither as deep nor as richly drawn as Catherine and Noelle—or for that matter even Larry. Constantin Demiris, whose pivotal role was nonetheless overshadowed by the women in *The Other Side of Midnight,* is the central character in *Memories of Midnight.* His relationship to the now amnesiac Catherine could have provided the sort of intrigue that drove *The Other Side of Midnight* so compellingly, but Sheldon does not allow Cathy to significantly develop beyond her role in the previous work. She seems here only a faint echo of the dynamic woman who had the potential to prove a worthy adversary for Demiris as she struggles to escape the memories that haunt her. Equally undeveloped is the vivid sensuality characteristic of Sheldon's female characters in general, as well as a significant element of Catherine as readers came to understand her in *The Other Side of Midnight.* An unwitting target for Demiris's revenge, Catherine develops a crush on her supposedly infatuated boss, but there is no real chemistry there, or indeed between her and any of the men with whom she becomes involved.

Constantin Demiris himself is a thinly veiled model of Aristotle Onassis, who was much in the public eye during the time Sheldon was writing *The Other Side of Midnight* but who here exhibits few of the qualities such men of power famously yield with such precision and restraint. The revenge already exacted by Demiris on Larry and Noelle in the first novel make his actions seem merely petty and predictable as he seeks to destroy everyone connected to his manipulation of their trial, especially Catherine. Instead of employing someone equal to him in cunning and finesse, he hires accomplished but morally flawed hit men, and the plot moves from one murder to the next as Demiris tries to control the consequences of having exacted retribution on the lovers.

Despite his limitations, Demiris establishes the type for Sheldon's rags-to-riches heroes, and his nemesis, brother-in-law Spyros Lambrou, whom the reader only glimpses in *The Other Side of Midnight,* provides the contrast: "Where Constantin Demiris had come from the gutter and fought his way to the top, Spyros Lambrou was born an aristocrat" (*Memories* 88). But where the twin narratives of the nuanced female characters were deftly intertwined in *The Other Side of Midnight,* Spyros Lambrou here is simply the mirror image of his brother-in-law, out to avenge the abuse his sister suffers as Demiris's abused and neglected wife. What one man does, the other must do better, until one destroys the other.

Anthony Rizzoli, another street fighter clawing his way to the top, has neither the class of Spyros nor enough of Demiris's cunning to successfully play the two men off against each other. The other characters employed by Sheldon to distract attention from the man Demiris has hired to kill Catherine are virtually indistinguishable from one another, and the killer himself is so underdeveloped that the information Sheldon does reveal about him seems gratuitously grotesque. The role of Bill Fraser is reprised in two quite predictable characters: Kirk Reynolds, another Demiris employee with whom Catherine contemplates a brief affair, which is interrupted before it begins when Demiris has Kirk killed in a skiing accident; and Alan Hamilton, the psychiatrist who helps Catherine regain her memory and inevitably falls in love with her but who conveniently never registers on Demiris's radar as a threat and is thus still around to provide Catherine's happy ending.

One male character stands apart not merely from this clichéd pantheon but from all that Sheldon created. Even he is underdeveloped, but this flaw is remedied to some extent in the 1991 film version, in which under the direction of Gary

Nelson Paul Sand plays mathematical genius Wim Vandeen with enough subtle suggestion of emotions he appears to lack as to make him someone worth caring for; his platonic relationship with Catherine is potentially one of the most complex in the novel.

Some of the less predictable plot developments in *Memories of Midnight* revolve around its minor characters. Demiris's treacherous affairs have not gone unnoticed by his wife, Melina, who responds in kind when she sets him up to take the blame for a murder she herself commits. Her efforts, though considerably clumsier than her husband's, are almost enough to convict him; but in a surprising reappearance, Napoleon Chotas, the lawyer who helped Demiris destroy Larry and Noelle in *The Other Side of Midnight*, brokers a deal that he tells Demiris will cost him his fortune but spare his life. Demiris accepts, only to have Chotas deliver an ironically appropriate coup de grace, and even if the rest of the sequel evokes only a faded memory of the earlier page-turner, this finale delivers an unforgettable and immensely satisfying ending.

Sheldon's readership has always been sufficient to generate cinematic backing for his work despite lack of critical acclaim. Most of his works have been adapted for film, and this pair of novels is no exception. Indeed, Twentieth Century Fox had such high hopes for the 1977 film version of *The Other Side of Midnight* starring John Beck, Susan Sarandon, and Marie France Pisier that they refused to let theater chains book it unless they also booked an unpromising space adventure called *Star Wars*. *Memories of Midnight*, however, never made it to the big screen. It premiered in 1991 as a TV miniseries with a stellar cast that included Jane Seymour as Catherine, Omar Sharif as Constantin Demiris, and Theodore Bikel as Napoleon Chotas.

Bibliography

Internet Movie Database. "Trivia for *The Other Side of Midnight*." Available online. URL: www.imdb.com.

Sheldon, Sidney. *The Naked Face*. 1969. Reprint, New York: Morrow, 1976.

———. *The Other Side of Midnight*. 1974. London: Pan Books, 1976.

———. *The Stranger in the Mirror*. New York: Morrow, 1976.

———. *Bloodline*. New York: Morrow, 1977.

———. *The Rage of Angels*. New York: Morrow, 1980.

———. *Windmills of the Gods*. New York: Morrow, 1987.

———. *Memories of Midnight*. New York: Morrow, 1990.

———. *The Stars Shine Down*. New York: Morrow, 1992.

———. *The Other Side of Me: A Memoir*. New York: Warner Books, 2005.

Dawn Ellen Jacobs

The Memory Keeper's Daughter

Kim Edwards (2005)

The Memory Keeper's Daughter is KIM EDWARDS's first novel and is based on a true story told to her by her pastor. It begins in 1964 in a snowbound Lexington, Kentucky, with Dr. David Henry driving to the hospital with his pregnant wife, Norah. Running out of time, he stops at his own clinic to deliver the baby himself. A boy is safely delivered, but to the surprise of the doctor and his nurse, Caroline, there is a twin, a girl who is born with Down syndrome. Having witnessed the difficult life and death at 12 of his own sister and the terrible grief these caused for those who loved her, he makes the fatal decision to give the baby to his nurse to be placed in an institution and tells his wife that she has died.

Norah rapidly descends into postpartum depression, struggling to cope with the loss of her daughter. She plans a memorial service for the daughter she never saw and begins to turn to alcohol and long drives to ease her pain. David and Norah's marriage suffers under the weight of the secret as David copes with his deception by working long hours to build his practice. In the meantime Caroline is unable to leave Phoebe at the institution and decides to keep her, choosing to leave town and start a new life. She sends confessional letters to David, who sends money for his daughter's support without ever trying to find her.

Years pass, and Norah's anniversary gift of a camera, the Memory Keeper, becomes an obsession for David as he devotes more and more of his time to his study of photography; but this new passion only drives a further wedge between David and his wife. Caroline, meanwhile, continues to raise Phoebe while always keeping David apprised of their whereabouts.

As their son, Paul, becomes a teenager, David and Norah's estrangement grows deeper. David remains guilt-ridden and dedicated to his work, and Norah turns to extramarital affairs before taking a job and eventually buying a business to fight her loneliness. David reenacts the very pressures often foisted upon him by his own family as he tries to force Paul away from the career in music that Paul so badly wants. David finally expresses a desire to know Phoebe and for Paul to know his sister, but Caroline severs all contact at this request.

Only after Norah and David divorce do they find peace. David confronts and accepts his past through the help of a pregnant teenager named Rosemary, and Norah finds recuperative love in the arms of a man named Frederic. David's sudden death of a massive heart attack brings the truth to light, and Norah and Paul meet and try to become involved in the life of the daughter and sister they share.

The novel chronicles with great insight and sensitivity the alienation and suffering felt by David's family as each of its members deals with the apparent loss of the girl. Increasingly anguished by his secret and the deterioration of the very family he had meant to protect with it, David turns to still-life photography, a medium which in its static perfection is unburdened by the weight and cares of more vibrant but flawed life. Meanwhile, Caroline finds both strength and unexpected happiness in the raising of the girl, whom she has called Phoebe (recalling the Greek "phoebus," "bright," as in Phoebus Apollo, the god of healing), benefits that stand in stark and even tragic contrast to Norah's unsought and unwitting deprivation.

Searching and sensitive in its treatment of the often contradictory attitudes to disability, the novel thrives on obliquity and indirection, tracing the many, often unintended effects of a single, simple act (here the father's abandonment of his child); "the event of the story being like a stone thrown in water," Edwards notes, citing Katherine Anne Porter; "it's not the event that's interesting, but rather the ripples the event creates in the lives of characters." Among the ripples explored here are the sheer irreversibility of the act itself, the role of art (David's photography) in making sense of a life shaped by destructive unknowing, and the paradoxical tragedy of suffering being only magnified by human attempts to ameliorate it. But for all the implacable grief it depicts, the novel issues in a hopeful conclusion that truth, properly respected, has the power not merely to shatter but to heal.

Such themes reflect Edwards's most prominent influences, from Dostoevsky's *Crime and Punishment* and Hawthorne's *Scarlet Letter*—novels anatomizing the profound, often tragic effects of secrets hidden at their core—to the careful and sympathetic analysis of family trauma in the works of Marilynne Robinson and Alice Munro.

The Memory Keeper's Daughter was a number-one *New York Times* best seller and won the Whiting and Algren awards.

Bibliography

Edwards, Kim. *The Memory Keeper's Daughter.* New York: Penguin, 2005.

Cynthia M. VanSickle

Michener, James A(lbert) (1907–1997)

One of the best-selling authors of the 20th century, James Michener wrote 50 books in the final 50 years of his long life, including blockbuster historical novels such as *The Source, Iberia, The Drifters, Centennial, Chesapeake, The* COVENANT, *Space,* POLAND, TEXAS, *Alaska, Caribbean,* and *Mexico*—several of them household names for readers of popular fiction. His very first literary effort, the best-selling collection of short stories entitled *Tales of the South Pacific* (1947), earned him the Pulitzer Prize and served as the basis for the classic Broadway musical *South Pacific,* which also became a hit film—a representative summary of the Michener phenomenon. A host of his other novels, such as *The Bridges at Toko-Ri, Sayonara, Hawaii,* and *Caravans* were also adapted into popular films. Despite his influence and popularity, however, Michener characteristically refused to accept the "too pretentious" label of "best-selling author," emphasizing in his 1992 autobiography, *The World Is My Home: A Memoir,* that he was just a hardworking "writer of good books that people like to read." In addition to writing fiction Michener worked successfully as a teacher, journalist, essayist, scholar, and editor.

Michener's own life story is so rich, complex, and multifaceted that it would seem an appropriate subject for one of his expansive historical novels. He was born in New York City in 1907, and though in later life claimed to have been an orphan, his mother seems to have been Mable Michener, an impoverished Quaker widow who struggled to raise him and several other children. Michener grew up amid financial hardship in Doylestown, Pennsylvania, and the poverty of his youth made him frugal to the end of his days. A gifted student, upon graduation from high school Michener received a prestigious scholarship to Swarthmore College and inspired by professors there devoted the next decade and a half to academic education, first as student and then instructor. Though perhaps most interested in studying history, he earned a B.A. summa cum laude in English in 1929. After college Michener received grants allowing him to travel in Europe, where he studied cultural history, art, folklore, and music. During the early 1930s he taught in private schools before entering Colorado State Teachers College as a graduate student, where he earned a master's degree and became a member of the teaching faculty. In 1940 he accepted a position as visiting assistant professor of history at Harvard University, and a year later he took a job as associate editor at the Macmillian Publishing Company in New York, editing social studies textbooks.

Michener speculated that he probably would have remained "almost content" as a professor and editor, but the United States's entry into World War II dramatically altered his life's course. A Quaker, and thus exempt from military service, Michener was nevertheless an outspoken patriot and felt he could not forgo contributing in some way to his country's war effort, so in 1942 he enlisted in the U.S. Navy. Given the rank of lieutenant commander, Michener was assigned to report on the war in the Pacific theater as a naval historian and traveled widely through often spectacular and exotic venues, witnessing the remarkable cultural and personal diversity of soldiers and civilian populations thrown together in war and experiencing the mortal intensity of wartime existence. During this period, besides the copious and detailed observations in his military reports, he produced the aforementioned Pulitzer Prize–winning *Tales of the South Pacific*.

Creative writing proved to be the ideal outlet for Michener's restless, industrious, and hypercurious nature, and he produced a dozen more books about the Pacific area in the decade following the end of World War II. While *Tales of the South Pacific* earned him critical success, it was the 1959 blockbuster novel *Hawaii* that established him as a public figure and household name. After the war Michener had moved to Hawaii—at the time still a U.S. territory—and living among its diverse peoples, inspired by its extraordinary landscape, spent five years amassing a huge trove of cultural, historical, and natural-historical information. He then took a year and a half to write the thousand-page epic of its evolution from geological beginnings, through Polynesian habitation, to European, Chinese, Japanese, and American colonization. Then he took skillful advantage of the excitement and controversy surrounding the Hawaiian statehood issue to gain publicity for the new work, finally publishing it in the very year in which Hawaii became the 50th state of the Union.

Michener's method of writing *Hawaii* would serve as a model for the dozens of historical novels that followed, many of them as skillfully timed to coincide with national and international news events. A trained historian, he produced many revealing biographical accounts of historical figures but was also a gifted fabricator of fictional lives; his characters, both historical and fictional, interact dynamically and convincingly over the course of the panoramic tales. In later years he would draw upon the work of a considerable team of research assistants to amass the background detail for his novels, and while reviewers often criticized his "more-is-better" approach to epic storytelling, the reading public embraced it with enthusiasm.

An inveterate traveler, Michener liked to recall how before he was 20 he had hitchhiked through almost every state of the United States; in the course of his lifetime he visited countless varied and often remote regions of the world, exhibiting what may be seen as an almost obsessive desire to know the world in which he lived and to know it as one. "I take everything seriously" was one of his catchphrases, and one often has the impression that he attempts to observe and involve himself, at least imaginatively, in every facet of human experience, as interested in the lives of peasants as of kings, and viewing human life as part of a seamless continuum from the inanimate landscape that so profoundly informs it to the mysteries that forever escape and yet encompass it. His novelistic geography ranges from the South Pacific to Eastern and Central Asia, Europe, the Middle East, Africa, the Caribbean, much of North America, and even outer space.

His literary fame, capacity for hard work, and fascination with learning involved him in many public activities as well. In 1962 he ran as a Democrat for a U.S. House of Representative's seat in Pennsylvania but lost in the election. He served as the secretary of the Pennsylvania Constitutional Convention in 1968 and held longstanding positions on a host of important boards and advisory committees, among them the U.S. Department of State Committee for the Arts, the U.S. Information Agency, the National Aeronautics and Space Administration (NASA), even the U.S. Postal Service and the International Broadcasting Board.

For both his literary and humanitarian contributions Michener received countless awards and distinctions, including some two dozen honorary academic degrees, the Navy Gold Cross, the Franklin Award, the Einstein Award, and the Presidential Medal of Freedom. Though notoriously parsimonious in his everyday life, he could be extravagant in expenditures for works of art, and he assembled a large and significant private collection of modern paintings. He provided the Texas Center for Writers at the University of Texas with a $30 million endowment, donated his multimillion-dollar art collection to various museums, and gave his entire personal collection of letters, working papers, and literary documents to the Library of Congress.

Having married and divorced twice, he adopted a child before marrying his third wife, Mari Yokiko Sabusawa, in a union that lasted 39 years until Mari's death in 1992. Blessed with an unfailing literary imagination even into his 90s, Michener maintained a rigorous, systematic schedule of writing until shortly before his death. After giving instructions to terminate his attenuated medical treatment for renal disease, James Michener died of kidney failure in his adopted home of Austin, Texas, on October 16, 1997.

Bibliography

Day, A. Grove. *James A. Michener.* 2nd ed. Boston: Twayne, 1977.

Groseclose, David A. *James A. Michener: A Bibliography.* Austin, Tex.: State House Press, 1996.

Hayes, John P. *James A. Michener: A Biography.* Indianapolis, Ind.: Bobbs-Merrill, 1984.

Michener, James A. *Tales of the South Pacific.* New York: Macmillan 1947.

———. *The Bridges at Toko-Ri.* New York: Random House, 1953.

———. *Sayonara.* New York: Random House, 1954.

———. *Hawaii.* New York: Random House, 1959.

———. *Caravans.* New York: Random House, 1963.

———. *The Source.* New York: Random House, 1965.

———. *Iberia: Spanish Travels and Reflections.* New York: Random House, 1968.

———. *The Drifters.* New York: Random House, 1971.

———. *Centennial.* New York: Random House, 1974.

———. *Chesapeake.* New York: Random House, 1978.

———. *The Covenant.* New York: Random House, 1980.

———. *Poland.* New York: Random House, 1983.

———. *Space.* New York: Random House, 1982.

———. *Texas.* New York: Random House, 1985.

———. *Alaska.* New York: Random House, 1988.

———. *Caribbean.* New York: Random House, 1989.

———. *The World Is My Home: A Memoir.* New York: Random House, 1992.

Cliff Toliver

A Million Little Pieces James Frey (2003)

A Million Little Pieces is a largely fictionalized "memoir" detailing the time its author spent in a drug and alcohol rehabilitation center when he was 23 years old. The manuscript for this book was first pitched to multiple publishers as an autobiographical novel, and its reliance on considerable fabrications and exaggerations resulted in a messy public scandal in early 2006. Confronted by Oprah Winfrey on her television show, Frey admitted that he had lied in representing the work as wholly factual.

Editions of the book published after the scandal broke contain a "note to the reader," which contains Frey's apology for deceiving his audience. Frey admits here that he "embellished many details [. . .] and altered others in order to serve what I felt was the greater purpose of the book" (Frey "note"), while adding that he hopes "these revelations will not alter [readers'] faith in the book's central message—that drug addiction and alcoholism can be overcome, and there is always a path to redemption if you fight to find one."

AMLP opens with Frey, wounded from a drunken fall and dazed by drug abuse, alone on a plane to meet his parents. Horrified by the condition of their son, Frey's parents pay for him to enter an expensive treatment center in Minnesota. What follows is a description of Frey's six-week stay in rehab, with occasional flashbacks to events leading up to it. The major events of the narrative are Frey's romantic relationship with a fellow patient named Lily, his befriending of a Mafia don named Leonard, his adoption of the writings of the sixth-century philosopher Lao-Tzu as his spiritual guide, and his rescue of Lily from a crack house when she temporarily leaves the facility. As Frey learns to live without drugs and alcohol, he forges an exceptional sense of self-reliance that rejects the dominant paradigm of "victimhood" associated with many self-help groups. By the end of the book Frey is in control of his addiction and able to face the world while managing his aggressive and self-destructive impulses.

Frey's prose style is highly idiosyncratic. Some nouns are capitalized, apparently according to their emotional importance to the narrator, and several phrases are often linked together to form a sort of poetic, stream-of-consciousness style: "I can see trees and Woods and Swamps and Lakes and birds and animals and men and women and the Buildings of the Clinic and the Sky and whatever is beyond the Sky" (203). Furthermore, Frey abandons conventional paragraph structure, omitting indentation and often using a series of paragraphs of only one line. Quotation marks around characters' dialogue are also omitted. The deliberate strangeness of these techniques is intended to create a reading experience that in some sense mimics the disorderliness of drug-addled life while also signifying the author's fierce individualism.

A major part of the allure of Frey as a protagonist is his self-interpretation throughout the narrative as a rebellious and dangerous young man, an outlaw who has broken every social rule. Frey describes his early delinquency as an adolescent, when he responded to feelings of alienation "by declaring War on [authority figures] and their Town and by fighting that War with everything inside of me. I didn't care whether I won or lost, I just wanted to fight" (74). As an adult he confesses that he "Drank smoked got arrested doled out a beating or two took a beating or two cheated lied deceived used women slept with prostitutes took more money my best friends were drugs and alcohol those who tried to stop me were told to fuck off and leave me alone" (351). Frey explains how his dependence on drugs developed into a means of coping with what he terms "the Fury," a "murderous rage" (44) directed at others as well as himself. While the extent of these feelings are obviously unusual in him, Frey suggests that masculinity involves, at its deepest psychological levels, an attraction to violence: "Whether they will admit it or not, all men love fighting. Watching it or engaging in it ignites in us our true selves, the selves that have been diluted by thousands of years of culture and refinement, the selves that we are constantly told to deny for the greater good. To stand alone in front of another man and to either hurt him or be hurt is what men were built to do" (335). One of the crimes described by Frey near the end of the book involves the attempted murder of a French priest who about 18 months before Frey entered rehab made a homosexual advance toward him. Controversially, Frey writes that he does not "feel regret or remorse" about the brutal attack, and that he considers that the man "deserved it" (360).

Another element of Frey's narrative allure has to do with the fantastic courage he shows himself demonstrating in a variety of harrowing situations. One of the book's most famous episodes, which has since been debunked as a fabrication, involves Frey's endurance of dental surgery without anaesthetic:

> Doctor Stevens lowers the chair. I put my feet on the floor. I am cold and I am shaking and everything hurts. I'm sick of Doctors and Dentists and Nurses and chairs and tests and halogen lights and instruments and clean Rooms and sterile sinks and bloody procedures and I'm sick of the attention the weak and the injured and the needy receive and I don't want to go a Hospital. I have always dealt with pain alone. I will deal with it alone now.
>
> Get Hank and get me back to the Clinic.
>
> You need Medical Attention.
>
> I'll be fine.
>
> If you leave here, it will be against my direct advice.
>
> I understand.
>
> I push myself from the chair. The muscles in my legs are twitching and my legs are unsteady. I take a small, slow step and I stop. I take the blanket off and I drop it on the chair and I take another small, slow step and I stop.
>
> Can you make it?
>
> Yeah.
>
> Do you need help?
>
> No (65).

Frey's essential message about his experiences in rehab is, in short, that he did not need help other than what he could summon from within. His doctrine of self-reliance, which owes something to the writings of the 19th-century American philosopher Ralph Waldo Emerson as well as the 20th-century author Ernest Hemingway, demands a rejection of institutional methods of self-improvement that stress individual humility in favor of a strictly personal, heroic process of redemption. Frey, again controversially, dismisses the now common idea that addiction is "a genetic disease," insisting instead that taking drugs or alcohol is always, ultimately, a "choice," a matter of free will (258).

Frey's approach to his material emphasizes—ironically in light of the scandal surrounding the book—his authenticity in telling the gritty truth about the spiritual desolation caused by addiction. When he attends a lecture given by a famous musician, he becomes enraged by the falseness of the man's claims about the amount of his drug consumption. As Frey explains: "I don't like this man. I don't like what he has to say or how he's saying it. I don't believe him and his Rock Star status isn't enough to make me buy the shit he's trying to sell" (159). Much of the success enjoyed by *AMLP* had to do with its status as a believable account of one man's struggles that delivered a hard, but finally uplifting, truth about the perils of addiction.

The macho elements of the outlaw figure Frey constructs are balanced in him by a strong emotional sensitivity and capacity for empathic understanding. As Frey develops friendships in the rehab center, he learns to recognize the ways in which other wounded men have endured suffering similar to his own. Leonard in particular becomes an important mentor to Frey and even asks to "adopt" him as a kind of surrogate son. By the end of the book loving bonds between the men have been forged, representing a superior alternative to the destructive impulses they have battled to control.

AMLP ends with Frey leaving rehab and heading directly to a bar. After ordering a pint glass full of hard liquor, he stares down "the Fury" and tests his resolve. As he puts it, "I have a decision to make. It is a simple decision. It has nothing to do with God or Twelve of anything other than twelve beats of my heart. Yes or no" (381). Able to withstand temptation, Frey sends the liquor back and declares that he is ready to face life sober. The main part of the book ends with the narrator's victory over his addictions, followed by a brief epilogue that describes the fates of other characters in the book.

Bibliography

Frey, James. *A Million Little Pieces*. New York: Doubleday, 2003.

Geoff Hamilton

Misery Stephen King (1987)

Misery is a horror novel differing in two significant ways from most others in the genre. First, its scale is very small and contained, revolving around just two characters, mostly in one room. Second, while it features a considerable amount of physical torture, its focus is on psychological abuse, and of a unique kind: The victim is tormented by being forced to do something he excels at.

The story focuses on Paul Sheldon, a best-selling author who has earned a fortune from a series of historical romances, overblown bodice rippers involving a brave darling named Misery Chastain. Over time, however, he has come to hate his heroine. Thus he has tied up that series by killing her off and tried his hand at something new, a taut, lean novel that features much profanity and focuses on the harsh realities of modern urban life.

Having finished *Fast Cars,* Sheldon celebrates by getting thoroughly drunk and heading west for a wild time. Bound for Las Vegas, he crashes his car in the remote Rocky Mountains. When *Misery* opens he is drifting in and out of consciousness, but rather than awakening in a hospital, he finds himself in an isolated Colorado farmhouse with both legs shattered and in the hands of a madwoman.

His captor is Annie Wilkes, a former nurse who has fled society. Having rescued him from the wreck, she has done what at first seems a charitable thing, treated his injuries and given him powerful pain medication. It rapidly becomes apparent, however, that she does not have Paul's best interests at heart. Aware of her incessant fawning, Paul finally intuits who she is: his number-one fan. But Annie not only hates *Fast Cars* (to the extent that she forces him to burn his only copy of the manuscript), she is absolutely outraged that Misery has died in the last of his romance novels, *Misery's End,* and insists that Paul write her a new book, a book just for her, which will bring Misery back to life.

By this time the nature of their relationship has been established. Annie wants to believe that Paul is a good man—of whom she believes there are few—but instead has come to see him as a "dirty bird," a man of low moral character (33). Nonetheless, she is still enthralled by his writing talent. For his part Paul begins with a negative impression of Annie, based principally on her appearance, finding her physically unattractive and hating the stench of her breath. But he rapidly comes to fear her, learning at last that she is, in fact, a deranged serial killer. What causes her to kill he will never find out (King hints she suffers from bipolar disorder), but it is clear she cannot control her emotions; whenever he disappoints her in the slightest she becomes enraged and exacts from him a terrible price. Of course he schemes to escape her clutches, but at the same time he acquiesces to her demand that he write her Misery book.

At first he works—simply out of fear, knowing he needs to please her—but in time realizes that the stakes have become outrageously high. A state patrolman coming to her door to ask whether she has seen the novelist is immediately dispatched. Knowing that the law is now likely soon to catch up with her, Annie talks of killing Paul and herself. Paul, however, realizes she cannot do it until she has learned how her novel is going to turn out, so he begins to see himself as a kind of Scheherazade, keeping himself alive by feeding her crumbs of his story. But in a twist typical of King, he becomes wrapped up in his own novel, at one point becoming so engrossed in telling his story that he pictures himself falling through a hole in the paper. Ironically, by this very means he finds the strength to kick his addiction to the pain pills Annie has been feeding him, and he writes what he himself realizes is a stellar novel, while in the process devising a way both to finish off the book and—with it—Annie herself.

Misery was written when STEPHEN KING's fame was already well established, critics and fans alike having come to expect extremely long novels, usually featuring people confronting the supernatural. The novel was a surprise, therefore, coming in at just more than 300 pages and including no trace of the usual "demons, ghosts, vampires, beasts [or] seemingly ordinary folk who control extraordinary powers" (Katzenbach). Equally notable was the framework of the book. Although written in the third person, it is told entirely from Paul Sheldon's point of view, with King employing not merely flashbacks but the occasional flash-forward to tell his story, and with the focus centered on Sheldon's state of mind even in the midst of the narrative's generally fast pace.

This same focus enhances King's exploration of the novel's major themes, the significance and forms of captivity, the role of fiction in defining the self, and above all the role and responsibilities of the author. Sheldon states early on that he "had spent most of his adult life thinking the word writer was the most important definition of himself" (29). Yet it is only after being taken prisoner by Annie and forced to write that he begins to reflect sincerely on what he considers worth writing, as well as the worth of writing itself. Such reflection is shared by the author's author, as King meditates on his own place and responsibility as a now-famous best-selling writer.

King wrote the book he later confessed (in *On Writing*) at a time when he was himself addicted to drugs like his protagonist and notes that writing *Misery* actually helped him come to terms with the fact that he was an addict. He also expresses great pride in the book, which he considers his best to date.

Viking Press, the publisher of *Misery*, was so sure of its success that the first print run was a million copies. Sales actually exceeded expectations, in part because of favorable reviews. In 1990 the novel was made into a successful movie of the same name starring James Caan and Kathy Bates, who received an Oscar as best actress for her portrayal of Annie Wilkes.

In a bizarre footnote, in 1991 a man named Eric Keene broke into the King residence in Maine, claiming that Stephen King had stolen *Misery*'s plot from him. He hoped to force King to help him write a sequel.

Bibliography

Katzenbach, John. "Sheldon Gets the Axe." *New York Times*, 31 May 1987. Available online. URL: http://www.nytimes.com/books/97/03/09/lifetimes/kin-r-misery.html.

King, Stephen. *Misery*. New York: New American Library, 1988.

Ann Graham Gaines

Mistral's Daughter Judith Krantz (1982)

Mistral's Daughter is JUDITH KRANTZ's third novel, following *Scruples* (1978) and *PRINCESS DAISY* (1980). Like her earlier novels it centers on the rising success, temporary setbacks, and eventual victory of a female protagonist, here Magali (Maggy) Lunel. But unlike the former works, *Mistral's Daughter* is a multigenerational saga, focusing not only on Maggy's own journey from rags to riches but also on the lives of Maggy's daughter Theodora (Teddy) and Maggy's granddaughter, Fauve. Together, the Lunel women—grandmother, daughter, and granddaughter—are further connected by their common association with Julien Mistral, an artist whose life and work exerts a profound influence on all.

The novel opens with a bold fictive splicing on Krantz's part: Maggy is a poor but celebrated model for artists, who has established herself at the height of the Roaring Twenties as "the one and only Maggy" (28), an indispensable muse for the era's most famous painters:

> Pascin painted her with roses in her lap, an icon of sensual authority; Chagall painted her as a bride flying in wonder through a purple sky; Picasso painted her over and over again in his monumental neoclassic style and she became the preferred odalisque of Matisse (27).

Soon she finds herself in front of Mistral's easel and in his bed. He is her first lover, and their affair is passionate but short as Mistral's focus on his work is all-consuming. Neglected, Maggy stays with Mistral for months after his attention to her wanes. At his first exhibition, however, Mistral openly betrays Maggy by selling his first painting of her to Kate Browning, an American heiress "born with the painful capacity to appreciate the best, to aspire toward it, but without the ability to produce it" (52–53). For Maggy, "the loss of the painting, as no other event could ever have done, show[s] her his true manner" (76), and she leaves him.

While Mistral's first exhibition proves decisive for his reputation as a rising artist akin to Picasso, the event is equally life-changing for Maggy; for here she meets Perry Kilkullen, an American banker in a loveless marriage to a devout Catholic unwilling to divorce him. In contrast to Maggy's passionate but painful affair with Mistral, Maggy's relationship with Kilkullen is marked by his generosity and kindness, and when Maggy becomes pregnant he arranges for her to join him in New York with her daughter, Teddy.

Unfortunately, while Maggy and Teddy are in transit to New York, Kilkullen suddenly dies, leaving Maggy alone in a new country, with her infant daughter and without financial provision.

Krantz's heroines are often noted for their strength and ability to rise above tremendous setbacks and terrible circumstances, and Maggy is no exception. Despite her initial setback, and the depression sweeping the United States, Maggy's beauty and ingenuity soon land her work as a model, and eventually she creates the Lunel Agency, representing the world's finest, most sophisticated models.

Mistral, meanwhile, has married his financial backer Kate Browning and has fathered their daughter, Nadine. His reputation is greatly enhanced under Kate's management, but their relationship is businesslike, not romantic, and Mistral has little or no feelings even for Nadine. He remains consumed by his work, even ignoring the cataclysmic events of World War II raging at his doorstep. Early in the novel Krantz notes that "All 'isms' were equally loathsome to [Mistral], and in that group he included political parties of every type, all religious groups and anyone who believe in some clearly formulated system of morals" (32). Thus, when Mistral's Jewish art dealer seeks refuge from the Nazis, Mistral simply dismisses him so that the Nazi officers he has befriended for paint supplies will not interfere with his work—a decision that will later come back to haunt him.

After the war the novel shifts its focus briefly from Maggy's sophisticated confidence to Teddy's radiant but unstable energy. "[R]eality was never enough for Teddy" (209), who at 18 finds herself expelled from Wellesley College (Krantz's own alma mater) and modeling for Maggy. Teddy's legendary beauty brings her to Paris, where she is selected for a fashion shoot featuring Julien Mistral.

Mistral and Teddy's initial meeting witnesses the birth of an "irrevocable" (255) love at first sight, and Mistral abruptly leaves Kate for Teddy, who now bears a third generation of illegitimate Lunel women (Maggy, too, is the product of an illicit love affair). Fauve, named by Mistral for her emergence from the womb like "a little wild beast" (267), is the eponymous Mistral's daughter, who grows to embody all her rich and complex heritage, taking her beauty from her mother, her business savvy from her grandmother, and her innate artistic talent from Mistral.

Unable to bear his grief after Teddy's sudden death in a boating accident, Mistral gives Fauve to Maggy, returns to his painting and, by default, resumes his relationship with Kate. When Fauve is eight, however, Mistral reestablishes contact, sharing Fauve's custody with Maggy. Fauve thus grows up torn between the opposing worlds of New York and France, of her grandmother and her father. Oscillating between Mistral's and Maggy's worlds, Krantz, through Fauve, showcases another well-known theme in her work, what Grace Glueck calls her "Cosmopolitan Girl fantasies," centered on the posh lifestyle of "clothes, home furnishings, the French countryside, French society, the modeling business, painting, food and sex" (12).

At a local dance Fauve, now 16, meets and falls in love with Eric Avigdor, the son of Mistral's former art dealer, who has survived the Holocaust. Increasingly interested in the Lunel family's own Jewish ancestry—as well as in Eric—Fauve feels betrayed when she learns from a jealous Kate about Mistral's wartime complicity with the Nazis. Confronting him, then abjuring any further contact, Fauve returns to New York and becomes a partner in Maggy's agency, sacrificing her relationship with Eric in the process.

In atonement Mistral creates a final series of paintings depicting Jewish themes, and under the new French laws he is able to leave these works as well as his studio home in Avignon to Fauve. Accepting at last both her spiritual and physical inheritance from Mistral, Fauve resumes both her painting and her relationship with Eric, finally marrying him at the novel's conclusion.

Here, as in her other works, Krantz masterfully evokes what Rita Felski calls the "Krantzian heroine," a woman able to balance both feminine and masculine traits in a form of "striving corporate femininity" that became a model for other 1980s popular fiction centered on the lives of ambitious women (Felski 100). These traits are most apparent in the novel's three generations of Lunel women, whose search for a healthy balance between love and success, ambition and happiness, forms both the narrative and thematic core of the work.

Mistral's Daughter was adapted into a 1984 CBS miniseries starring Stephanie Powers, Lee Remick, and Stacy Keach. The series has also been released in VHS format.

Bibliography:

Felski, Rita. *Doing Time: Feminist Theory and Postmodern Culture.* New York: New York University Press, 2000.

Glueck, Grace. "Absolutely the Most." *New York Times Book Review,* 2 January 1983, 10+.

Krantz, Judith. *Mistral's Daughter.* New York: Crown, 1982.

Kristin Brunnemer

Mitla Pass Leon Uris (1988)

The many fans of LEON URIS's *Exodus* (1958) and *The Haj* (1984) welcomed the best-selling author's return to Israeli history in *Mitla Pass.* The novel opens at the turning point of the Suez War in 1956, with Israeli prime minister David Ben-Gurion initiating a military strike into the Sinai after Egypt has seized the Suez Canal and blocked Israeli shipping. The tension is heightened because Ben-Gurion knows other Arab states are likely to fight alongside the Egyptians, and while the French and British have promised the Israelis air support, both the United States and the Soviet Union will pressure them not to interfere. Ben-Gurion believes "*Israel must win the war in the first four days!*" (3), and "the linchpin of the entire operation" (5) is parachuting the Lion's Battalion into Mitla Pass, deep in the Sinai, where they will be "exposed to a disaster, a sacrificial force" (5). Accompanying the Israeli paratroopers is American novelist Gideon Zadok, who has been in Israel for some months researching a novel depicting the horrors European Jews endured before and during World War II and their heroism in establishing a Jewish state encircled by hostile Arab nations. During the climactic battle Gideon actively joins the fight, directing artillery against entrenched Egyptian forces in the pass.

While Israel's 1956 incursion into Egypt provides its historical framework, most of the novel focuses on the personal history of Gideon Zadok, with the events of 1956 interspersed with descriptions of his career as a writer and his rocky marriage with his wife, Val, gradually expanding to encompass tales of his ancestors from their roots in 19th-century Ireland and early 20th-century Russia to their experiences as immigrants in the United States. Uris colorfully and reverently details the childhood and youth of Gideon's father, Nathan, in the Jewish "Pale of Settlement" in Tsarist Russia, where he survives danger and indignity at the hands of anti-Semites to become a renowned Zionist activist. He is made a translator for the Germans in World War I, and afterward he immigrates to Palestine, only to discover he is unsuited for kibbutz life and so moves to Baltimore, Maryland, in 1921. In the United States Nathan becomes an ardent communist and marries Gideon's mother, Leah; his often carping letters to his son, Gideon, form a major thematic element in the novel.

Another narrative strand explores the lives of Gideon's maternal ancestors beginning in Ireland with Jewish tailor Moses Baliban, Gideon's grandfather, who also moves to Baltimore, where he marries Hannah Diamond, a strong woman who protects and provides for her children with grit and ingenuity. Hannah's daughter, Leah, marries Nathan Zadok but has a series of lovers as well. Between Nathan's misguided dedication to the Communist Party and Leah's philandering, Gideon's childhood is difficult, and he ends up running with street gangs and failing out of high school, despite his love of literature and his ambition to become a great writer. Gideon escapes his troubled home and life by enlisting in the U.S. Marines shortly after Pearl Harbor, but much of the later novel explores the influence of that difficult childhood on his adult life, even after he has achieved success as a novelist and Hollywood screenwriter. For example, though a loving parent to his daughters, Penelope and Roxanne, he is a notorious womanizer, apparently more concerned with his career than his marriage. When the family moves to Herzlia in 1956 for Gideon to research his novel on Israel, he has an affair with concentration-camp survivor Natasha Solomon, which threatens to end the marriage entirely.

The novel is uncharacteristic of Uris's oeuvre. While he typically develops memorable characters in order to bring history to life—the Warsaw Ghetto uprising in *Mila 18* (1961), the Irish troubles in *Trinity* (1976), the World War II Pacific campaign in *Battle Cry* (1953)—*Mitla Pass* is primarily a study of character, in which history provides a vehicle for a searching exploration of Gideon's own life and personality. Thus, while it turns out that the climactic historical battle of Mitla Pass is in fact a tragic mistake, as the Israeli command realizes the pass has no strategic value in the end, the experience is crucial in the maturation of Gideon Zadok because only by these violent means does he finally come to terms with the haunting loss of his Marine friend Pedro on Tarawa when confronted with the death of his Israeli aide, Shlomo. While the novel's point of view deftly alternates between third- and first-person narratives by a host of different characters, all are ultimately significant only insofar as they illuminate different shades in Gideon's character.

Nonetheless, a number of familiar Uris themes recur in *Mitla Pass*. Most obvious is his spirited indictment of the East European anti-Semitism that spurred the Herzlian Zionist movement, conveyed here through Nathan Zadok's story and dominating his earlier masterpiece *Exodus*. That novel has been considered as a critical factor in countering negative Jewish stereotypes by depicting Jews as strong and admirable warriors; but in *Mitla Pass* Uris portrays a much broader spectrum of Jews, from the eminently admirable to the thoroughly despicable, though those who immigrated to the United States tend to be portrayed less positively than those who settled in Palestine.

Another common Uris theme is that of writing itself. Writers—often reflecting aspects of Uris's own life and character—are significant characters in most Uris novels; indeed, just as novelist Abraham Cady is the hero of *QBVII* (1970), so Gideon is at the moral and narrative center of *Mitla Pass*. In addition, the novel illustrates his familiar negative portrayal of communists, seen also in *Armageddon* (1963) and *Topaz* (1967); "survivor guilt" (here felt by both Natasha Solomon and Gideon) as in *QBVII*; the trials of early Israeli statehood (*Exodus* and *The Haj*); and the kinship of men and women in combat (*Battle Cry*).

Uris novels are often overtly autobiographical. *Battle Cry* is clearly based on Uris's own experience in the Marine Corps, for example, and the slander trial at the heart of *QBVII* has obvious origins in the lawsuit brought against Uris for claiming in *Exodus* that a certain doctor performed human sterilization operations without anesthetic in Nazi concentration camps. But of all his fiction, *Mitla Pass* is by far the most autobiographical, with its description of Gideon/Uris's European ancestors and their immigration to Baltimore, his father's devotion to the Communist Party and his mother's infidelities, his experiences as a Marine and a struggling writer in San Francisco, his success at last with a Marine novel and subsequent screenwriting experiences, his bringing his family to Israel while researching a novel about Israel, and his evacuating them because of the 1956 Sinai campaign. Thus *Mitla Pass* offers to Uris fans not merely a compelling variation on his narrative formula but a virtual window on the writer and the man.

Bibliography

Cain, Kathleen Shine. *Leon Uris: A Critical Companion*. Westport, Conn.: Greenwood Press, 1998.

Uris, Leon. *Battle Cry*. New York: Putnam, 1953.

———. *Exodus*. New York: Doubleday, 1958.

———. *Mila 18*. New York: Doubleday, 1961.

———. *Armageddon*. New York: Doubleday, 1964.

———. *Topaz*. New York: Doubleday, 1967.

———. *QB VII*. New York: Doubleday, 1970.

———. *Trinity*. New York: Doubleday, 1976.

———. *The Haj*. New York: Doubleday, 1984.

———. *Mitla Pass*. New York: Doubleday, 1988.

Chip Rogers

My Friend Leonard James Frey (2005)

My Friend Leonard is James Frey's second published account of his recovery from alcoholism and drug addiction. A mixture of fiction and memoir, this follow-up to *A MILLION LITTLE PIECES* (2003) traces the author's supposed experiences after he leaves the treatment center that served as the setting in the earlier work. As the narrative opens,

Frey is depicted as finishing a three-month stint in an Ohio jail, his punishment for having assaulted a police officer—one of the events that prompted him to seek help for his addictions in the first place. Upon his release Frey drives to Chicago to meet a woman he fell in love with at the rehab center in *Pieces,* a former prostitute named Lilly, but on arriving he learns that she has hanged herself. Traumatized, he contemplates drinking but just manages to resist the urge thanks to the improbable support of a fellow substance abuser, a middle-aged Las Vegas gangster named Leonard, who like Lilly had met Frey in treatment.

Deciding to stay in Chicago, Frey finds work as a nightclub doorman, a job that troubles Leonard: "You're an alcoholic," the mobster explains, "and you're a drug addict. You've only been clean a couple months. You can't work at a bar. It's crazy and stupid and dangerous" (92). He persuades Frey to work for him, dropping off bags of money to shady characters throughout the Midwest. The risky nature of the work frightens Frey, however, and he finally quits, taking up writing instead and turning out film scripts that eventually draw the interest of people in Hollywood. Encouraged again by Leonard, Frey relocates to California, where he finds considerable success writing and directing movies. But Leonard then mysteriously disappears, and several months pass before Frey meets up with him again, this time in San Francisco. His once robust friend now looks "like a skeleton, like a dead man" (324), and he reveals to Frey that he is homosexual and ill with AIDS. Wanting to help, Frey moves into the mobster's apartment, staying there until the older man dies.

Stylistically and thematically, *My Friend Leonard* has much in common with *A Million Little Pieces.* Again the author's fondness for highly charged sentence fragments and eccentric punctuation is in evidence, calling to mind the expressive prose of writers such as Jack Kerouac and Hunter S. Thompson. Frey gives voice to the same unorthodox views about recovery from addiction he had expressed in the first book. An atheist, he believes that popular programs like Alcoholics Anonymous and Narcotics Anonymous, which ask their followers to seek assistance from a higher, spiritual power for their problems, cannot help people like him. Instead of asking God to relieve his desires to drink and use, he believes in fighting the compulsions on his own, exposing himself to temptation constantly and using self-will to control his cravings.

This intensely individualistic approach to recovery, tapping into the roots of the American mythology, at once frightens his acquaintances and wins their admiration. Frey's insistence upon keeping liquor in his home, for example, initially upsets Leonard, much like his willingness to work in the nightclub. But the confidence that develops in Frey because of his readiness to court danger convinces Leonard that he must himself become more fearless about the way he leads his life, eventually prompting him to enjoy and be open with, rather than secretive about, his homosexuality. He tells Frey:

> I started watching you and watching how you took responsibility for the mess you had made of your life, and how you rejected everything you were told would save you in favor of what you believed, which was that you had the power to make the decisions that would decide the course of your existence. What I learned from . . . you was that . . . I could decide to do anything I wanted to do (328).

Just as in *A Million Little Pieces,* friendship not only has the ability to make one's life more pleasant but can imbue it with new meaning and purpose as well.

Frey's friendship with Leonard also plays a major role in his recovery from his addictions, and as the memoir progresses and his affection for the gangster deepens, his desire to use controlled substances first diminishes significantly and then disappears entirely, the death of Leonard arousing none of the urges that beset him after Lilly's suicide. Much of the narrative, in fact, is more concerned with chronicling Frey's pursuits of financial security and a writing career than his efforts to overcome his addictions, a trait that distinguishes it from *Pieces,* as well as other recent recovery memoirs such as Pete Hamill's *A Drinking Life* (1994) and Augusten Burrough's *Dry* (2003). At the same time, the sustained attention the book gives to Frey's literary ambitions recalls James Joyce's *A Portrait of the Artist as a Young Man* (1916), Sherwood Anderson's *Winesburg, Ohio* (1919), and Philip Roth's *The Ghost Writer* (1979), which are likewise interested in depicting the creative and moral evolution of young male protagonists who long to be writers.

Shortly after its release in May 2005, *My Friend Leonard* landed on the best-seller lists, thanks in large part to the commercial and critical success of *A Million Little Pieces.* Its popularity enjoyed another boost when television personality Oprah Winfrey selected *Pieces* for her on-air book club in the fall of that year. But in January 2006, when the veracity of the earlier book was called into question by the Smoking Gun, an investigative Web site, and Winfrey charged Frey with lying about his past, suspicions also began to swirl around *My Friend Leonard,* in particular the author's assertion that he was sentenced to jail, something which turned out never to have happened. In response to the controversy an author's note was added to the paperback edition of the text, which Riverhead Books first published in June 2006, and in it Frey confessed:

> Many of the . . . characters' names have been altered or fictionalized as have major events in their lives. To call this book pure nonfiction would be inaccurate. It is a combination of fact and fiction, real and imagined events.

Bibliography

della Cava, Marco R. "Truth Falls to 'Pieces' after Suspect Memoir." *USA Today*, 16 January 2006, D1.

Frey, James. *A Million Little Pieces.* New York: Anchor Books, 2003.

———. *My Friend Leonard.* New York: Riverhead Books, 2005.

———. "Author's Note." From *My Friend Leonard.* New York: Riverhead Books, 2006.

Stephen B. Armstrong

N

The Nanny Diaries

Emma McLaughlin and Nicola Kraus (2002)

The Nanny Diaries tells the story of Nanny, a New York University student paying her way through university by looking after the children of rich families in Manhattan. Nanny takes a job looking after Grayer Addison X—only son of New York financier Mr. X and his socialite wife, Mrs. X—and progressively emerges as the only force for good in Grayer's life: taking him to family days at school, supervising his playdates, cooking his meals, and indeed, finally becoming his only source of protection from his parents' dissolving marriage and the sexy, mysterious challenge to family security that is Mr. X's latest mistress, Ms. Chicago. In her effort to keep the pieces of Grayer's world from falling apart, however, Nanny must discover where her own boundaries lie, all while trying to finish her thesis and graduate from NYU, find her first real job, and court the illusive Harvard Hottie (referred to throughout the novel as H.H.). With the help of her patient parents, her loving grandmother, and two devoted best friends, Nanny learns how to parent Mrs. X's child and, even more important, how not to.

EMMA MCLAUGHLIN and NICOLA KRAUS approach their novel from a position of rich experience, both having been students at NYU and having paid for their education by nannying. In a disclaimer preceding the story, however, the authors distance their novel from that experience:

> The authors have worked, at one time or another, for over thirty New York City families, and this story was inspired by what they have learned and experienced. However, *The Nanny Diaries* is a work of fiction, and none of those families is portrayed in this book. Names and characters are the product of the authors' imagination. Any resemblance to actual events or persons, living or dead, is coincidental. Although some real New York City institutions—schools, stores, galleries, and the like—are mentioned, all are used fictitiously. (McLaughlin and Kraus, "A Note to Readers.")

Nonetheless, devices like their use of generic ciphers for characters' names, along with the intensity of detail, toy with tell-all conventions and heighten readers' sense of the story's verisimilitude, encouraging them both to feel they have gained access to a real and private world and to sympathize more intimately with the protagonist.

The Nanny Diaries deals thematically with boundaries in professional and personal relationships and the perils of domestic service. For Nanny her frustration with life as a presumed slave to the Upper East Side is tempered by her devotion to Grayer. Originally hired by Mrs. X to work 12 hours a week, she soon finds herself logging 16-hour days as Grayer's sole caretaker. Her devotion to Grayer makes Nanny incapable of drawing a line in her relationship with her boss, even when she feels she is being taken advantage of. At Christmas, for example, Nanny is sent all over town to purchase designer purses for the domestic staff of the house, and a Christmas bonus is placed within each one. Nanny, however, receives "only earmuffs" for her troubles as Grayer's primary caregiver (121).

In this context of commodity and exchange the novel's central theme emerges: the worth of childcare itself. Parenting is not valued by the rich socialites of the novel, and they are incapable of understanding the true cost—emotional and financial—of raising their own children. In a world of housekeepers and butlers, doormen and cooks, parenting, too, can be outsourced. As the Christmas gifts illustrate, however, the outsourced childcare is the least valued employment. Nannies are underrespected, overworked, and underpaid because the work they do is perceived as superfluous. Nanny tries to tell her employers, "Raising your child is hard work! Which you would know if you ever did it for more than five minutes at a time!" (303). However, it is never clear that the message gets through to Mr. and Mrs. X. In this way McLaughlin and Kraus invite the reader to question a point of view that puts children below designer shoes and personal wish fulfillment.

Because the entire novel is focalized through Nanny, and the authors offer no reason to question her credibility, the reader is finally encouraged to condemn the behavior of Mr. and Mrs. X and their kind. Nanny becomes a victim of circumstance and their venal indifference, torn between doing the right thing for Grayer and asserting her own right to be treated fairly. In the end Nanny realizes that within the X family these two competing values may always be mutually exclusive.

The Nanny Diaries was an immediate phenomenon upon its release. Within a few months of the first printing half a million copies of the novel had been sold, with over a million sold in the first year. Julia Roberts recorded an abridged audiobook version of the novel, and a film version starring Scarlett Johansson, Laura Linney, and Paul Giamatti was released in 2007. Though their second novel, *Citizen Girl,* failed to repeat the success of their debut, in Nanny McLaughlin and Kraus have created a character of enduring appeal—a Mary Poppins for the 21st century.

Bibliography

McLaughlin, Emma, and Nicola Kraus. *The Nanny Diaries.* New York: St. Martin's, 2002.

Brenna Clarke Gray

Niffenegger, Audrey (1963–)

Audrey Niffenegger is the author of one novel, *The* TIME TRAVELER'S WIFE (2003), and two graphic novels (or novels in pictures), *The Three Incestuous Sisters* (2005) and *The Adventuress* (2006). She has also authored several short stories, among them "The Night Bookmobile" (2004).

Niffenegger was born in 1963 in South Haven, Michigan. She is currently an artist and professor in the Interdisciplinary Book Arts M.F.A. Program at the Columbia College Chicago Center for Book and Paper Arts, which she helped found in 1994. She teaches writing, letterpress printing, and fine-edition book production and holds a B.F.A. from the School of the Art Institute of Chicago (1985) and an M.F.A. from Northwestern University (1991). Niffenegger has received several awards for her printmaking, including an Isabella A. Brown Travelling Fellowship from the School of the Art Institute of Chicago. Her art is represented at the Printworks Gallery in Chicago, Illinois.

As Niffenegger has explored varying formats in her work—novel, short story, graphic novel, printmaking—it is difficult to make broad statements about her style. However, Niffenegger's works often exhibit tragic themes, with fantastical situations, romance, and a quaint, gothic atmosphere. She often mentions works of literature, music, or art, and these interests are strongly associated with the characters. For instance, both Henry De Tamble of *The Time Traveler's Wife* and Robert Openshaw of "The Night Bookmobile" are librarians, while both of Henry's parents and his daughter are musicians.

The Time Traveler's Wife became a phenomenal success, thanks largely to the purchase of its film option even before the book was signed by independent publisher MacAdam/Cage. It was subsequently chosen as a *Today Show* Book Club selection. The novel tells the love story of Clare, an artist, and Henry, a librarian with a strange genetic disorder that causes him to time-travel involuntarily. The novel is told in the first person by both Henry and Clare, and each chapter is prefaced by a note telling the date and ages of each character. Henry's age fluctuates throughout as he travels forward and backward in time.

Niffenegger says of the novel, "I wanted to write about waiting, but since waiting is essentially a negative (time spent in the absence of something) I wrote about all the things that happen around the waiting" (Flanagan). The book is peppered with references to art, literature, and music, both popular and classical.

The Three Incestuous Sisters tells of three sisters living together by the sea and what happens when a lighthouse keeper's son enters their lives. The book includes spare prose, relying primarily on vivid full-page aquatints to tell the story.

The Adventuress is similarly constructed. Its protagonist is an alchemist's daughter who undertakes a dreamlike adventure in which she is kidnapped, transformed into a butterfly, and falls in love with Napoleon Bonaparte.

Niffenegger's visual style, exhibited in her graphic novels, has been compared to that of Edward Gorey; she also cites Aubrey Beardsley as a major influence in her work. Authors who share Niffenegger's sense for gothic fantasy in a real-life setting include Roald Dahl, Keith Donohue, and SUE MONK KIDD.

Bibliography

Flanagan, Mark. "Audrey Niffenegger Interview." Available online. URL: http://contemporarylit.about.com/cs/authorinterviews/a/niffenegger.htm.

Niffenegger, Audrey. *The Time Traveler's Wife*. San Francisco: MacAdam/Cage, 2003.

———. *The Adventuress*. New York: Harry N. Abrams, 2006.

Starr Hoffman

Niven, Larry (1938–)

Laurence Van Cott "Larry" Niven is one of the most popular science-fiction writers alive today, and he has won numerous literary awards, including the Nebula, Hugo, Locus, and Australian Ditmar. Most famous for his Ringworld series, Niven usually writes "hard" science fiction, much of which takes place in a universe called Known Space, a 60-light-year sphere of the galaxy thus far explored by humanity. However, he has also written in many other genres, including rational fantasy (*The Magic Goes Away*), comic books (*Green Lantern*), and television (*Land of the Lost*). Furthermore, he has collaborated on dozens of novels with other SF writers, most notably Jerry Pournelle (*The Mote in God's Eye* and *Lucifer's Hammer*) and Steven Barnes (*Dream Park*). Niven's most critically acclaimed book is *The Integral Trees*.

Niven has confessed to having been ill-suited for school. Though now recognized as a gifted thinker, and with the liveliest interest in science and technology, he admits to having constantly daydreamed in class, sensing he was destined to be a writer. Born in Los Angeles (where he still resides), he attended the California Institute of Technology in 1954–55, then "flunked out," returning to school years later and graduating from Washburn University (Topeka, Kansas) in 1962 with a B.A. in mathematics. He also completed a year of graduate work at the University of California before abandoning studies to write full time.

In 1964 his first published short story, "The Coldest Place," appeared, and in 1970 the book that established his fame, *Ringworld*, was published. It was set in Known Space, his personal universe, which had first appeared in his mid-1960s work. The Ringworld itself is an artificial world, in effect a massive band on whose interior surface are land, water, and atmosphere, surrounding a star at about the orbit of Earth and spinning in order to create artificial gravity. This elegant, iconic science-fiction concept is Niven's more efficient alternative to a Dyson sphere and has been repeatedly used by others in science fiction, including culture author Iain M. Banks. *Ringworld* won worldwide acclaim and spawned an immensely popular series of the same name, featuring many of the most popular characters, races, and concepts of Known Space, including human adventurer Louis Wu; a fierce, alien feline race, the Kzin (who would later appear in *Star Trek* and spawn an entire series of their own called the Man-Kzin Wars); and the three-legged, cowardly Puppeteers, with their famous technology, including the indestructible General Products spaceship hulls.

Niven is also known for a series of canonical rules called Niven's Laws, including "There is no cause so right that one cannot find a fool following it," "It is easier to destroy than to create," and "History never repeats itself," some of which have emerged as an unspoken set of rules for science-fiction writers.

Though famous for his science fiction, Niven was most influenced by early pulp-adventure and detective writing, allusions to which often crop up in his works, such as *The Barsoom Project* (with Steven Barnes); many of his tales reveal strong mystery influences, such as the Hugo Award–winning story "The Hole Man," where a man is murdered with a quantum black hole. His chosen names often inscribe real, mythological, or fictional heroes and events or involve semi-metaphorical plays on words, and he borrows freely from elements of popular culture. In *The Ringworld Throne,* for example, which chronicles a war against vampires, some Protectors are named Bram, Anne, Lovecraft, and King. The compliment is frequently returned, as the creative community acknowledges Niven; Greg Bear's *The Forge of God,* for example, has a character named Lawrence Van Cott. Moreover, both Niven and his provocative concepts appear often in video games, TV, anime, or other SF outlets. The game *Wing Commander II,* for example, features a "Niven Sector," where players fight feline enemies called Kilrathi (based on the Kzinti). *The Gathering* card game has a spell called Nevinyrral's Disk (Larry Niven spelled backward); *Stars!* generates a planet named Nevinyrral in its maps; and *Netrunner* has an AI named Nevinyrral.

A hallmark of Niven's writing is his matter-of-fact style. A formidable theorist of the imagination, he is nonetheless capable of presenting extremely complex concepts and advanced scientific theories in accessible and enjoyable ways; nor is his prose convoluted or burdened by scientific jargon. All of which illustrates one of his aforementioned writing laws, which states, "If what you have to say is important and/or difficult to follow, use the simplest language possible." Niven has a straightforward narrative delivery, and his mysteries unravel in a way that usually hinges on action with a touch of humor while revealing profound scientific concepts at the heart of its logic. His wit is celebrated among fans and has led to some bawdy ersatz work, such as "Man of Steel, Woman of Kleenex," which explores the horrific real-world consequences of Superman and Lois Lane mating.

One of Niven's most dominant themes is the advancement and even salvation of mankind through science and technology, a conviction very much alive in the author's own life. He has long advocated the exploration of space and has worked for decades as an adviser to NASA, various astronomical organizations, and politicians, even helping as a consultant on the Star Wars defense concept championed by President Reagan. In addition he was a guest, among other SF visionaries, in the Jet Propulsion Laboratory for the Viking One landing on Mars.

Niven also introduced the concept of a "flash crowd" in a 1973 story of that name, and this has evolved into the current "flash mob" form of public protest. Indeed, given the topical yet philosophical vitality of his thought and its great significance for the influential community of science-fiction readers, Niven's work promises to exert a lasting influence not merely on popular fiction but on the broader society reflected in and defined by it.

Bibliography

Fletcher, Marilyn, and James Thorson, eds. *Reader's Guide to Twentieth-Century Science Fiction.* Chicago: American Library Association, 1989.

Niven, Larry. *Ringworld.* New York: Ballantine, 1970.

———. *N-Space.* New York: Tor, 1990.

———. *Scatterbrain.* New York: Tor, 2003.

———, and Steven Barnes. *Dream Park.* New York: Ace, 1981.

———, and Jerry Pournelle. *Lucifer's Hammer.* New York: Fawcett, 1977.

Thomas Fortenberry

Noble House James Clavell (1981)

JAMES CLAVELL's fourth novel is one of the six books of historical fiction that constitute his Asian

Saga, depicting the life and events of seminal moments in Asian history, with the protagonist always a European living in and coming to terms with the culture and traditions of the Asian world.

Shogun (1975) takes place in feudal Japan of 1600, while *Gai-Jin* (1993) returns to Japan in 1862. *Tai-Pan* (1966) is set in Hong Kong in 1841 and is the direct precursor to *Noble House,* set in Hong Kong in 1963. *King Rat* (1962) tells the story of life in a Japanese prisoner-of-war camp in 1945, while the final book of the series, *WHIRLWIND,* is set in the Near East context of Iran in 1979. *Tai-Pan* and *Noble House* are the two most closely related, together describing the founding of the Noble House mercantile concern (purported to be based on real-life company Jardine Matheson Holdings) and how it survives over a century of Hong Kong's volatile financial and meteorological climate.

Although all the novels stand firmly on their own, by reading the Asian Saga as a whole and in chronological order the reader is afforded the added pleasure of recognizing locales, characters, and families that resurface throughout the novels. In *Noble House,* for example, Riko Anjin Gresserhoff details her family history as the descendant of the hero of *Shogun;* Paul Choy appears in *Whirlwind* as the most powerful Chinese businessman in Hong Kong; Peter Marlowe and Robin Grey travel to Hong Kong after their appearance in *King Rat.*

Marlowe, the hero of *King Rat,* mirrors Clavell himself in many ways, and in *Noble House* he has become a famous writer who has published an ostensibly fictional book about being held in a Japanese prisoner-of-war camp. When asked how true his book is, he replies, as would Clavell: "[the book is] as true as any telling about any happening fifteen years after the event. As best as I can remember the incidents are accurate. The people in the book didn't live, though people like them did and said those sort of things and did those deeds" (854).

One of *Tai-Pan*'s plotlines, in particular, figures prominently in *Noble House.* In 1841 Dirk Struan accepted a loan of silver in order to save his business from financial ruin, and the merchant who made this possible, Jin-Qua, took four bronze coins and split them in half, making Dirk swear that whenever he or his descendants received one of the half-coins they would do the holder a favor, whether legal or illegal. Wu Fang Choi brings Dirk the first of these half-coins in *Tai-Pan,* while the location and control of a second half is a major element in the narrative of *Noble House,* wherein John Chen learns of the coin's power, steals it from his father (the compradore of the Noble House, Philip Chen), and tries to sell it to businessman Lincoln Bartlett but is kidnapped and killed, with underworld boss Four Finger Wu finally emerging with the powerful trinket.

More than 1,200 pages in length, yet taking place over only 10 days, the novel is a massive epic in miniature, melding together dozens of characters and plotlines involving espionage, murder, seduction, natural disasters, corporate takeovers, as well as intricate convolutions of honor and family. Written when the British colony of Hong Kong still had more than 30 years until reverting to Chinese authority, the novel insightfully explores the tensions and complexities of the coming transition, governed by a fundamentally pragmatic wisdom: "[Y]ou learn the hard way when you're in China that it's best to act a little Chinese. Never forget that though Hong Kong's British it's still China" (62).

A deadly rivalry played out in *Tai Pan,* between Straun and Tyler Brock, is rekindled in *Noble House* by their descendants, Ian Dunross and Quillian Gornt. The novel opens with American businessman Linc Bartlett, CEO of Par-Con Industries, and his beautiful vice president, Casey Tcholok, visiting Hong Kong with the intent to make a business deal with one of the large *huongs,* or companies. Bartlett makes separate promises to both Dunross and Gornt, then engineers a run on all the banks, waiting to see which company will survive the week. Through a flurry of deals, counterdeals, threats, favors, and negotiations, the three powerful men pledge all that they own, much they do not, and the reputations and future of their companies in the attempt to bring each other down and emerge (or remain) the Noble House of Hong Kong. The character of K.C. (Casey) Tcholok provides a focal point for discussions about the difficulty experienced by women in business, especially in the traditional Hong Kong, where men have first wives, second wives, and mistresses, and sex is often seen as a tradable commodity.

Interwoven with the corporate machinations of the Noble House, Rothwell-Gornt, Par-Con, and the banks of Hong Kong is a complex tale of international espionage and intrigue, as Dunross finds himself in possession of secret documents desired by British, Chinese, and Russian agents and becomes embroiled in the politics of the cold war—Hong Kong's position as the gateway to Asia drawing agents of the KGB, CIA, FBI, MI5, and MI6, all operating on important missions.

Clavell deftly employs various Chinese dialects, elements of Asian culture, and a supporting cast of hundreds to flesh out the world he has created, with the notion of "face," and the honor it implies, being a thematic focus of all. Words like *quai loh* (foreigner), *joss* (luck), *h'eung yau* (bribery money), and *dew neh loh moh* (a curse) are all used untranslated after their initial explanation, and Clavell writes from a shifting first- or third-person narration, maintaining the idiosyncratic voice of whichever character is thinking, at times in an almost stream-of-consciousness style.

As Marlowe warns Bartlett in describing Dunross, Gornt, and the mores of Hong Kong business, "there's a marvelous strain of violence that passes from generation to generation in these buccaneers—because that's what they are. This is a very special place—it breeds very special people. . . . I understand you may be going into business here. If I were you I'd be very, very careful" (256). *Noble House* is ultimately a kind of fable about how people gamble with life, whether in business, politics, or love, trying to outwit and dominate one another in an endless attempt to gain face, as well as their desires.

Most of the Asian Saga has been adapted for film or television: *King Rat* was released as a feature-length film in 1965 and starred George Segal; *Tai-Pan* starred Bryan Brown and Joan Chen and was released in 1986. Due to their complexity and length, some producers have seen the merit of adapting Clavell's books as TV miniseries. *Shogun* starred Richard Chamberlain and was aired on NBC in 1980 over nine hours; a critical and commercial success, the miniseries won three Emmys and three Golden Globe Awards. The miniseries of *Noble House* starring Pierce Brosnan was shown in 1988 and extended the tale from 1963 to the 1980s.

Bibliography

"The Asian Saga." Available online. URL: http://en.wikipedia.org/wiki/The_Asian_Saga. Accessed October 4, 2007.

Clavell, James. *King Rat*. New York: Dell, 1999, first published 1962.

———. *Tai-Pan*. New York: Dell, 1993, first published 1966.

———. *Shogun*. New York: Dell, 1986, first published 1975.

———. *Noble House*. London: Hodder, 2006, first published 1981.

———. *Whirlwind*. Flame, 1999, first published 1986.

———. *Gai-Jin*. New York: Dell, 1994, first published 1993.

Julie Barton

The North and South Trilogy

John Jakes (1982–1987)

Vividly delineating the central characters, locations, and themes in Jakes's trilogy about the American Civil War, *North and South* functions as both overture and introduction to that epic saga. The tale begins by focusing on two young men, George Hazard from Pennsylvania and Orry Main from South Carolina, who meet on the way to the U.S. Military Academy at West Point. Though they differ profoundly both in background and temperament and are sometimes at loggerheads, the friendship they forge in the crucible of antebellum West Point as they struggle against the machinations of power hungry cadet Elkanah Bent proves to be a lasting one—as does Bent's desire for revenge. On graduating, Hazard and Main are caught up in the Mexican-American War, during which Main is injured and Hazard falls in love with the surgeon's daughter, Constance. Main returns home to find that his only love, Madeline, has married the cruel slave owner Justin LaMotte. Relationships between the Hazards and the Mains are strained by cultural differences and the issues of slavery and human rights, yet like the sons, the families remain entwined through friendship and love, and George's brother, Billy Hazard, marries Orry's sister, Brett Main.

Jakes is a master of the art of what is often called the *clanback* novel, a copiously detailed chronicle tracing the history of a particular family, such as the Kents in his *The Kent Family Chronicles,* which has been compared to the Sackett history of western writer, LOUIS L'AMOUR. Hailed as "the godfather of the historical novel," Jakes was asked by his publisher to write a *clanback* tale for the underrepresented period of the Civil War, and the result was a critical and popular phenomenon in the 1980s, with even scholars contributing to the wave of interest and the media treating the latter in the manner of front-page news. Such a rich combination of instruction and entertainment has well-merited Jakes's informal title as "the history teacher of America."

Love and War (1984) is the second novel in the trilogy and follows the two families' fortunes through the outbreak and cataclysm of the Civil War itself. Cousin Charles Main now takes up study at West Point, along with Billy Hazard. Bent continues to seek revenge against the families, aided by the ubiquitous hardship of the war, while conniving sisters Ashton Main and Virgilia Hazard continue to make themselves a nuisance. Her eyes at last opened to the cruelty of her husband, Madeline abandons Justin LaMotte and takes refuge with Orry Main. The racial and religious bigotry, raised to a dramatic pitch by the trauma of war, are counterbalanced and even remedied on a humble, human scale by the supervenient force of friendship and love.

As if the earthly opposition of love and war were not dramatic enough, Jakes flirts with eschatology in his concluding work in the saga, *Heaven and Hell* (1987), whose title may be seen as an intimation of the posthumous existence not merely of the many victims of the war's savagery, like Orry Main, but of the societies and cultures of which they had been a part, especially that of the slave-owning South. Here again Jakes's stalwart narrative device, the intimate dialogue between the fates of the disparate families, provides an ideal structure for his exploration of the moral, religious, political, and economic conflicts of Reconstruction. For neither the South nor the North survived the war, the novel suggests, but out of the death of both arose a new being altogether, never fully healed but always healing, assuaged by love, from the wounds of the war.

The third volume in particular was assailed by critics for its shallow characterization and seemingly facile resolution of the many conflicts depicted so skillfully in the narrative; but none failed to acknowledge its masterly plotting, vivid ambience, telling detail, and compelling interest for readers.

The North and South Trilogy was made into a TV miniseries starring James Read as George Hazard and Patrick Swayze as Orry Main, with its three parts airing in 1985, 1986, and 1994, respectively. Unsurprisingly, the television version focused on the love story of Orry and Madeline, altering important events in the novels for the sake of their romance, such as having them meet much earlier than they do in the trilogy. Moreover, when Swayze chose not to reprise his role as Orry for Part 3, the character was forced to meet his death offscreen at the hands of the fiendish Elkanah Bent, and Cooper, an older brother of Orry, who was invisible in the first two parts, takes on a leading role in the third.

Bibliography

Jakes, John. *North and South.* New York: Signet, 1982.

———. *Love and War.* New York: Signet, 1984.

———. *Heaven and Hell.* New York: Signet, 1987.

Geraldine Cannon Becker

No Time for Tears Cynthia Freeman (1981)

CYNTHIA FREEMAN's sixth novel, *No Time for Tears,* follows the life of Chavala Landau and her family over four decades, from their 1905 flight from Russian pogroms to the founding of Israel in 1948. Chavala and her husband, Dovid, leave Odessa together for Palestine but end up leading mostly separate lives, Chavala moving to America, where she raises her family and builds a successful jewelry business, Dovid remaining in Palestine to fight for "Eretz Yisroel," the Jewish homeland.

Written in the simple style of the American realist tradition, Freeman's book at times approaches allegory. Although the plot is complex, each character represents a different aspect of 20th-century Jewish life. Chavala is the matriarch, providing for and protecting her family at great personal cost, while Dovid typifies the sort of men who created Israel. Chavala's siblings represent other choices, from Sheine's repudiation of Judaism and marriage to a German doctor to the opposite extreme in Raizel's marriage into an Orthodox Jewish community in Jerusalem. Between these ends of the Jewish spectrum are Dvora, who helps her American husband found a kibbutz in Galilee, and Chia and Moishe, both of whom assimilate into American culture while retaining their Jewish heritage.

Like Freeman's other novels, *No Time for Tears* focuses on the Jewish family, the choices available to Jews during the 20th century, and questions of Jewish identity and cultural assimilation, especially that of the struggle between a desire for safety, represented by Chavala's move to America, and for a Jewish homeland, represented by Dovid's transformation from farmer to soldier and eventually politician. Chavala sums up the division, symbolic of a larger one among Jews over the creation of Israel, when she explains to a new American friend, "I want to secure my family and he loves the land. *His* land. Our needs, our dreams are so different . . ." (231). Ultimately, these dreams come together as Chavala uses her increasing wealth to support Haganah (a clandestine military organization devoted to the creation of Israel), realizing near the end of the novel that Dovid's war is hers as well, "A war not only for her family but the whole Jewish family" (370).

Since the primary conflict of the novel revolves around the need for a Jewish state, the formation of Israel and the reunion of the Landaus suggest a happy ending. Unfortunately, Freeman's understanding of the difficulties faced by Jews in America, Europe, and the Middle East fails her when she writes about other peoples. This is especially true of Muslims in general and Palestinians in particular, who are presented as stereotyped caricatures. The "Oriental mind" is characterized by greed, laziness, and deceit; the Palestinians live "in a backwash of ignorance" (53), being variously described as "Arab marauders and Bedouin murderers" (131), "barbarians" (138), "locusts" (275), and "vermin" (276).

Underlying these mal-descriptions is another prevalent theme: the assumption of Jewish entitlement to the land. The only time a Palestinian speaks of his relationship to the land, saying to Dovid that what the settlers have claimed "is our spring grazing land" (279), Dovid justifies the new ownership by saying "we *worked* it" (278), the language reminiscent of American narratives of Manifest Destiny, with the Jewish settlers improving what the Arabs are too apathetic to "work." The Arabs, says Freeman, had "lived without lifting a hand to redeem the land" (262), their farms characterized by "women working in rock strewn fields (while men sat in the coffeehouses playing backgammon and sleeping in the sun)" (268). In contrast, the settlers have, by farming what had previously been used for grazing, "redeemed the eroded earth" (270). Although Freeman paints the British and Germans in equally sweeping terms, the novel pivots on the simplistic contrast between Palestinians and Jews, epitomized in the remark of Chavala and Dovid's American-born son that the conflict is like "cowboys and Indians" (361).

Beyond its superior storytelling, Freeman's book is most interesting as a historical and cultural document. A foundation myth about Israel, it depicts the horrors and persecution that compelled Jewish settlers to fight for a homeland, but it also perpetuates stereotypes and antagonisms that continue to plague the Middle East today.

No Time for Tears was 10th on the *New York Times* best-seller list for 1981.

Bibliography

Freeman, Cynthia. *No Time for Tears*. New York: Bantam Books, 1981.

Sarah Perrault

One Richard Bach (1988)

Readers familiar with earlier RICHARD BACH works such as *Stranger to the Ground, Biplane, A Gift of Wings,* and *Nothing to Chance,* will find *One,* at first glance, a significant departure from the aviation-oriented stories of his earlier career. However, a closer examination of those earlier works, and particularly his *Jonathan Livingston Seagull* and *Illusions,* reveals the same fundamental premises that underlie *One.*

In *One* Bach and his real-life actress wife, Leslie Parrish, leave their island home for a Los Angeles conference. Flying their amphibious Martin Seabird, they encounter a flash of golden light and are transported over a boundless sea with a network of golden underwater lines. Trying to determine where they are, they land on the water and are suddenly transported to their past. They see themselves before they met, passing in the halls of a hotel.

Each time the plane touches down they have a glimpse of another lifeline, a path branching from the previous line and determined by choices made. In a typical sequence in *One* Richard is stationed in Europe, flying with the Air National Guard in the 1960s. The world is near nuclear confrontation and tensions are high. In this reality Richard does not drop atomic bombs on the USSR; yet in another dimension he and Leslie are a Russian couple living just before a catastrophic nuclear attack takes place, an attack triggered by Richard dropping the first bomb. Bach's handling of the time transitions, as well as his feelings about the world situation prior to the collapse of the Soviet Union, are intimated in the second scenario, Richard's discussion with a fellow Russian:

> Leslie and I stood in helpless despair on that street in Moscow, watching the nightmare come true, not caring if we got away, not caring if we lived or died. Why tell our world, I thought. It's not that your world didn't know, Ivan, but that it knew and killed itself anyway. Would our world be different? (182)

The farther they fly, the more deeply into the future they venture. At one point they are in a distant future world where only one person occupies an entire planet, another simulacrum of Leslie, named Mashara. Mashara is the keeper of an earth renewed after being destroyed by environmental neglect and carelessness, and her view is perhaps the most direct statement of Bach's commitment to environmental issues:

> "But is it bad for a civilization that wrecks the planet from seafloor to stratosphere . . . is it terrible for that civilization to pass away? Is it bad for a planet to heal itself?"
>
> For the first time I felt unsettled with this place, imagining what its last days must have been, screaming and whimpering death.
>
> "Is it good for any life to perish?" I asked.

> "Not to Perish," she said after a moment, "but to change. There are aspects of you who chose that society. Aspects who reveled in it, aspects who worked desperately for change. Some won, some lost, all of them learned."
>
> "But the planet recovered," said Leslie, "look at it! Rivers and trees and flowers . . . it's beautiful."
>
> "The planet recovered, the people didn't." She looked away (226).

The story's complex logic is based on a theory proposed in quantum physics that describes the possibility of an infinite number of dimensions in different space-times coexisting simultaneously. Each scene, either future or past, reinforces this philosophy, one found throughout Bach's works, particularly in *Illusions.* It is a philosophy of unbounded existence, where one is neither born nor dies but exists in all dimensions at once.

One is also a love story on two levels. First, it is a tale of the physical and spiritual love between the real-life Richard and Leslie Bach, who had been together more than a decade when they collaborated on *One.* On a broader level, however, *One* is a story of love for the environment, the planet, and all things living—in the end, love of life in all its infinite possibilities:

> "Remember what Pye said?" I asked. "The pattern is psychic but the way back is spiritual. She said guide yourself by hope."
>
> I frowned, though, thinking about it. How do we guide ourselves by hope? We hoped to go home, why weren't we there?
>
> "She didn't say hope, wookie," Leslie said at last. "She said love! She said guide yourself by love" (334).

Illustrating the underlying spirit of fun and adventure native to Bach's work, having found a way to return home the couple instead decides to travel farther along the unknown avenues of alternate possibility. Typically, Bach carries the reader along on his journeys, painting word pictures of things that might be—whether flying on the wings of a wistful and wishful seabird in *Jonathan Livingston Seagull,* barnstorming about the country in a biplane in *Nothing to Chance,* winging over Europe's war-threatened skies in *Stranger to the Ground,* or traveling through alternate universes in *One*—always challenging preconceived notions and creating a sense of delight and wonder.

Bibliography

Bach, Richard. *One.* New York: Dell, 1988.

Warren Graffeo

On the Way to the Wedding

Julia Quinn (2006)

On the Way to the Wedding, a romance set in early 19th-century Britain, forms the conclusion of JULIA QUINN's popular Bridgerton series, which focuses on the love life of eight siblings. This last installment deals with the youngest son of the family, Gregory, who falls madly in love with the beautiful Miss Hermione Watson at a country house party hosted by his older brother. Yet as Gregory sets out to court Hermione, he is dismayed to find that his feelings remain unrequited. From her decidedly less beautiful friend, Lady Lucinda Abernathy, he learns that Hermione is already in love with another, namely her father's secretary. But because Lucy wants to save her friend from a mesalliance, and because Gregory strikes her as a charming, intelligent man, she agrees to help him win Hermione's heart. In the end, however, her efforts are all for naught: Gregory is not the right man for Hermione after all, and when Lucy finally realizes he would have been the right man for her, it is already too late. She is whisked away to London in order to marry the man to whom she has been engaged for years. By the time Gregory catches up, she is literally on her way to the wedding. In the aftermath they both learn that sometimes love is not enough; only with the sustained aid of their family and friends do they finally reach their happy end.

The novel explores the nature of love by contrasting mere infatuation with love based on friendship and affection. In a comic doubling, Hermione and Gregory both fall in love with the back of somebody's head:

> He couldn't see her face, not even her profile. There was just her back, just the breathtakingly perfect curve of her neck, one lock of blond hair swirling against her shoulder.
>
> And all he could think was—*I am wrecked* (13).

Here it is already obvious they are smitten with an ideal, not a person, as Gregory later realizes: "'I had been waiting so long to fall in love that I wanted the love more than the woman. I never loved Hermione, just the idea of her'" (337), a fact emphasized by disrupted communications between the lovers. As her social inferior, her father's secretary can admire Hermione only from afar by sending her secret letters, while Gregory in turn finds it impossible to draw Hermione into a real conversation. His inability to converse with her is contrasted with the easy friendship between him and Lucy. Friendship and affection, however, form the basis for real love in this novel, and thus both Hermione and Gregory eventually find happiness with a friend. When Gregory falls in love with the back of Lucy's head, it is therefore not a simple repetition of what he has experienced before: "But this time—it wasn't quite the same. With Hermione it had been dizzying, new. There had been the thrill of discovery, of conquest. But this was Lucy" (241), whom he already knows, and as a result he does not fall for an ideal this time but for the woman herself.

In keeping with its nuanced exploration of love, the romantic relationships in *On the Way to the Wedding* are set against the backdrop of broader familial relationships, Lucy's lonely teenage years in the house of her cold uncle being contrasted to the large family of the Bridgertons. Even though, as the youngest son of the family Gregory feels compelled to prove his worth, he nevertheless is aware of the security his family provides, and indeed throughout the novel he can count on their help. Lucy knows no such comfort; her parents are dead, her uncle happily barters her off, and her brother as well as Hermione, "the sister of [her] heart" (50), are not perceptive enough to realize something is amiss.

Yet, true to her reputation as an author of lighthearted romances, Quinn presents other humorous elements, culminating in a gentle dig against romance conventions in the epilogue, where traditionally protagonists are shown with their first child as a symbol of their love and their new life together. In this epilogue, captioned "In which our Hero and Heroine exhibit the industriousness of which we knew they were capable" (368), the reader does not witness the birth of Lucy and Gregory's first child, but of their eighth and ninth child:

> Love existed, Gregory thought to himself.
> And it was grand. [. . .]
> Nine times grand.
> Which was very grand, indeed (371).

Bibliography

Quinn, Julia. *On the Way to the Wedding.* New York: Avon-HarperCollins, 2006.

Sandra Martina Schwab

Outlander Diana Gabaldon (1991)

Outlander begins in Scotland, 1945. Claire Beauchamp Randall, an English combat nurse during World War II, has been reunited with her husband, Frank. Separated by war for most of their marriage, they are now enjoying a second honeymoon in Scotland, enhanced by the charms of their location, Claire indulging her interest in botany, Frank pursuing genealogical inquiries about his 18th-century Scottish ancestor. The prospect of witnessing ancient rites performed by local citizens on the eve of Beltane prompts Claire and Frank to go in secret to the stone circle at Craigh na Dun. Though the ceremony itself proves uneventful, Claire comes across a rare blue-flowered vine and is induced to return alone. This time she hears strange sounds emanating from the stones and, drawing nearer, loses for a moment her sense of time and place.

At first she does not understand what has happened to her. Even when assaulted by a Redcoat looking disturbingly like Frank, and when later captured by a gang of kilted Scotsmen on horseback, she assumes she has stumbled onto a group of reenactors of 18th-century battles, an assumption still as she tends to the battle wounds of one of the Scots, a swashbuckling young warrior named Jamie Fraser. Not until the next morning, when she arrives at Castle Leoch and observes the workings of an 18th-century stronghold, does she finally comprehend what has happened: She has traveled in time through the stone circle and arrived in Scotland, 1743.

Though she rapidly establishes herself as a healer, she is encompassed by danger. She is a "Sassenach," an outlander in a strange new world. She wants to escape back to the stones and her normal life, but her captors watch her closely. They suspect she is a British spy, while Frank's sadistic ancestor (the Redcoat who assaulted her) pursues her as a spy of the Scots. Even in the domestic world of the castle, Claire, who is posing as a widow, faces the jealousy of the young women, who resent her growing friendship with the handsome Jamie and try to put spells on her. Soon Jamie is the only one she can rely on.

The action only broadens and intensifies as Claire faces the many challenges of 18th-century life, clan intrigue, British oppression, and a love she did not expect to find. The secondary characters are numerous but well-rounded: Geillis Duncan, who may be a true witch (Claire is taken for one for her healing powers); Laoghaire, the young girl who wants Claire out of the way; Collum MacKenzie, the crippled laird who still rules his clan with an iron hand, and Dougal, his brother, who enforces his rules; as well as Murtagh, a swarthy, laconic warrior. But it is the love story of Claire and Jamie that drives the novel as a whole.

The pair first meet when Claire is captured by the Highlanders and, finding that Jamie has been hurt during a raid, applies her modern nursing skills to heal him, appalled equally by the unhygienic conditions and by his friends' apparent disregard for his injuries. Dougal asks,

> "Well, can ye keep one foot on each side of the horse, man?"
>
> "He can't go anywhere," I protested indignantly. "He ought to be in hospital! Certainly he can't—"
>
> My protests, as usual, went completely ignored.
>
> "Can ye ride?" Dougal repeated.
>
> "Aye, if ye'll take the lassie off my chest and fetch me a clean shirt" (79).

Their friendship is strengthened by their time at Castle Leoch, where Jamie explains to Claire the rituals of Highland life—and prevents her from attempting an escape from the castle during the clan gathering. On overtaking her, he asks in a scene typical of their entertaining relationship,

> "How far d'ye think you'd get, lassie, on a dark night and strange horse, wi' half the MacKenzie clan after ye by morning?
>
> I was ruffled in more ways than one.
>
> "They wouldn't be after me. They're all up at the Hall, and if one in five of them is sober enough to stand by morning, let alone ride a horse, I'll be *most* surprised."
>
> He laughed, and standing up, reached down a hand to help me to my feet. He brushed the straw from the back of my skirt with somewhat more force than I thought strictly necessary.
>
> "Well, that's verra sound reasoning on your part, Sassenach," he said, sounding mildly surprised that I was capable of reason. "Or would be," he added, "did Colum not have guards posted all round the castle and scattered through the woods. He'd hardly leave the castle unprotected, and the fighting men of the whole clan inside it" (179–180).

Jamie and Claire's relationship becomes one of trust, up to a point; she cannot explain to him why she so wants to escape.

Their marriage, for all its suddenness and seeming calculation, epitomizes both their intriguing and understated love and the dramatic necessities of the time. As an Englishwoman, Claire has no recourse if Captain Randall wishes to question her, and he has already shown his penchant for causing pain in his interrogations. If she marries a Scotsman, however, she becomes a Scot and is protected by the fragile independence of the clans. Dougal elects Jamie to wed her, and Claire, though already married in the 20th century, sees no way to refuse. She does have one question to ask him first:

> "Does it bother you that I'm not a virgin?" He hesitated a moment before answering.
>
> "Well, no," he said slowly, "so long as it doesna bother you that I am." He grinned at my drop-jawed expression, and backed toward the door.
>
> "Reckon one of us should know what they're doing," he said. The door closed softly behind him; clearly the courtship was over (255).

Bibliography

Gabaldon, Diana. *Outlander.* New York: Dell, 1991.

LuAnn Mars

P

Patterson, James (1947–)

James Patterson is the author of three detective fiction series, one children's series, and several independent novels. Three of his "nursery rhyme" or Alexander Cross novels have been adapted for film (*Along Came a Spider, Kiss the Girls,* and *Roses Are Red*), and his first Women's Murder Club novel (*1st to Die*) has been adapted for a television miniseries. He won an Edgar Allan Poe Award for his first novel, *The Thomas Berryman Number* (1976), which introduced his technique of writing from the perspectives of both detective and criminal; for his longstanding success as a popular thriller writer he received the 2007 ThrillMaster Award from the International Thriller Writers.

Patterson was born in Newburgh, New York, to insurance salesman Charles Patterson and teacher Isabelle (née Morris). He earned his B.A. (1969) summa cum laude from Manhattan College and his M.A. (1970) from Vanderbilt University, after which he pursued a successful career with the advertising company J. Walter Thompson, where he is said to have been the youngest CEO in the company's history. Though publishing his first novel in 1976, Patterson did not leave the advertising agency until 1996; but since then he has published at least one novel every year, including two epistolary romance novels, *Suzanne's Diary for Nicholas* (2001) and *Sam's Letters to Jennifer* (2004). Nevertheless, he is best known as a detective thriller writer, especially for his Alex Cross series. In addition to writing his own novels, Patterson collaborates with other writers, having already coauthored novels with six other writers.

Patterson's distinctive style is evident even in his earliest work, with the narrative of *The Thomas Berryman Number* (1976) alternating between the consciousness of the criminal and detective, the principal detective's narration being in the first person. In addition, short chapters switch rapidly between different narrative perspectives, so the text is often fraught with dramatic irony, as the reader frequently knows more than the detective himself. Patterson also tends to attenuate and nuance the suspense by complicating the initial arrest, proving it incorrect, incomplete, or psychologically untenable.

His first series, dubbed the "nursery rhyme" series for the titles taken from the lines of nursery rhymes, features African-American psychologist Dr. Alexander Cross, who progresses from deputy chief of detectives in the Washington, D.C., police department in his introduction in *Along Came a Spider* (1993) to FBI senior agent. While pursuing serial killers around the country and even across international borders with his childhood friend and partner on the force, John Sampson, Cross also cares, and cares deeply, for his family, which to date includes his grandmother Nana Mama, son Damon, daughter Jannelle, son Alex, Jr. and cat Rosie. His wife, Marie, is murdered three years before the start of *Along Came a Spider,* allowing Cross to pursue a series of relationships with different women.

As a forensic psychologist Cross employs psychological as well as physical evidence in pursuing the killers, who are serial not only in the sense that they murder multiple victims but also in the sense that they appear in multiple novels. Focusing on the life and work of an African-American, single-parent, detective-psychologist, the Cross series also explores many social concerns in contemporary American culture, among them the moral ambiguities involved in multiculturalism, increased psychological and psychiatric understanding, and the redefinition of the nuclear family.

Patterson himself wrote the first two novels of his next series, the Women's Murder Club series, but from the third novel (*3rd Degree*) onward, he has coauthored the entries with either Andrew Gross or Maxine Paetro, making most of the series a collaborative project. Set in San Francisco, the novels feature four women whose careers all relate to criminal investigation and who work together to solve the cases. In the first novels the group includes San Francisco homicide detective Lindsay Boxer, medical examiner Claire Washburn, assistant D.A. Jill Bernhardt, and crime reporter Cindy Thomas, but after Bernhardt's death in *3rd Degree,* she is replaced in *4th of July* by Yuki Castellano, another district attorney. In this series the police detective has the first-person narrative, making Lindsay Boxer's the principal perspective on the events in the plot; but with the narrative ultimately woven out of the experience of four women, the series also focuses more closely on gender issues than do the "nursery rhyme" novels. In both the multitude and concertion of its protagonists the series offers an interesting variation on the already interesting phenomenon of the female detective who creates "new forms outside the boundaries of patriarchal nuclear families, a striking departure from the solitariness of male hard-boiled detectives" (Reddy 183), for it establishes a cohesive network of female detectives needed to solve each crime, rather than the solitary hero or even the hero-sidekick combination generally associated with male-detective narratives, including those of the Alex Cross series.

In 2005, with *The Angel Experiment,* Patterson introduced a children's book series, *Maximum Ride,* featuring a group of mutant children, Max, Fang, Iggy, Nudge, the Gasman, and Angel, who are part-human, part-bird and have been bred in a laboratory. As in much children's fiction the group members are separated from their parents and must find or protect their families while defending themselves against the Erasers, wolflike beings that stalk them as prey; all are narrated with the brisk pace and sure handling that characterizes Patterson's adult fiction.

In February 2007, with *Step on a Crack,* Patterson commenced a new collaborative project with coauthor Michael Ledwidge, introducing New York detective Michael Bennett, a less exotic but more complex figure than Alexander Cross. The adoptive father of 10 children and with an ailing wife, Bennett must solve a crime affecting economic and political superstars while single-handedly caring for his large family. At the time of publication there is only one Bennett novel, but the official Patterson Web site promotes the first novel as "the beginning of a brand-new electrifying series."

The year 2008 saw Patterson collaborate with Gabrielle Charbonnet on the romance *Sundays at Tiffany's* and with Howard Roughan on *Sail,* a mystery involving a dysfunctional family lost at sea.

Patterson enjoys his popularity and has commented that he has no wish to be a literary writer—"I read *Ulysses* and figured I couldn't top that" (Womak). Indeed, reviewer Patrick Anderson suggests that part of Patterson's success as a popular writer comes from his success as an advertising agent: "[he] spends a great deal of time on the design, marketing, and advertising of his books" (248). Patterson acknowledges his popular status by dedicating the fifth Cross novel, *Pop Goes the Weasel* (1999), to "the millions of Alex Cross readers who so frequently ask 'Can't you write faster?'" (Contemporary Authors Online). He has taken advantage of such popularity to encourage literacy, developing educational guides to accompany the *Maximum Ride* series that suggest a new way for children to engage with popular texts. In addition, he promotes the charitable organization First Book, which works to promote literacy and provide children in low-income families with new books.

Bibliography

Anderson, Patrick. *The Triumph of the Thriller: How Cops, Crooks, and Cannibals Captured Popular Fiction.* New York: Random House, 2007.

Contemporary Authors Online. "James Patterson." Available online. URL: http://galenet.galegroup.com/servlet/LitRC. Accessed May 3, 2007.

James Patterson. *The Thomas Berryman Number.* 1976. Reprint, New York: Warner Books, 1996.

———. *Along Came a Spider.* London: HarperCollins, 1993.

———. *Pop Goes the Weasel.* New York: Warner Books, 1999.

———. *Roses Are Red.* New York: Warner Books, 2000.

———. *1st to Die.* New York: Warner Books, 2001.

———. *Suzanne's Diary for Nicholas.* New York: Warner Books, 2001.

———. *Sam's Letters to Jennifer.* New York: Little, Brown, 2004.

———. *3rd Degree.* New York: Little, Brown, 2004.

———. *The Angel Experiment.* New York: Little, Brown, 2005.

———. "The Official Website." Available online. URL: www.jamespatterson.com. Accessed May 3, 2007.

———. "Stretching the Boundaries of the Thriller." Interview with Stephen Womak. *Book Page* (June 2000). Available online. URL: http://www.bookpage.com/0006bp/james_patterson.html. Accessed May 3, 2007.

———, and Maxine Paetro. *4th of July.* London: Headline, 2005.

———, and Michael Ledwidge. *Step on a Crack.* New York: Little, Brown, 2007.

Reddy, Maureen T. "The Feminist Counter-Tradition in Crime: Cross, Grafton, Paretsky, and Wilson." In *The Cunning Craft: Original Essays on Detective Fiction and Contemporary Literary Theory,* edited by Ronald G. Walker and June M. Frazer. Macomb: Western Illinois University, 1990.

Scaggs, John. *Crime Fiction.* London: Routledge, 2005.

Malcah Effron

Pilcher, Rosamunde (1924–)

Born Rosamunde Scott in Cornwall, England, in 1924, Pilcher began writing novels in 1949 under the name Jane Fraser. In 1955 her first novel as Rosamunde Pilcher was published, but it was not until *The Shell Seekers* appeared in 1987 that her international reputation was established. It is a novel of grand proportions, narrating the life of Penelope Keeling and her family from pre–World War II England to 1980s London, and Pilcher once said that if she had died the day after writing it, everyone would know exactly what happened in her own life. However, she later qualified this, noting that the story is not truly autobiographical but about things that she had known and done, a foray into the past—her chance to write about things as she remembered them. And indeed, the places, people, and experiences she has known intimately and firsthand have always been her exclusive novelistic material. Thus her native Cornwall and Scotland, where she has lived for many years, figure prominently in her work. Even her look at wartime England is based on personal experience as she worked in the Women's Royal Naval Service from 1943 to 1946.

Pilcher has written numerous short stories and novels, several of which have been adapted for the stage and television, but is best known, perhaps, for her four major sagas, *The Shell Seekers,* SEPTEMBER (1990), *Coming Home* (1995), and *Winter Solstice* (2000). Each of them is a sensitive and affectionate gaze into the heart of family relationships, love, and sometimes grief and despair, all illustrating her authorial credo: "To be a successful writer you have to touch people, you have to make people want to turn the page."

Her work begins with the characters—Pilcher spends a lot of time with them, talking to them, learning about them, living with them before she ever begins to write. Once she knows them intimately, their tale unfolds with seamless ease and authenticity, no doubt a large part of the immediacy and strength of their appeal to readers. Their houses are filled with the tantalizing odor of sausages sizzling on the Aga and hot coffee for breakfast, furniture shining with fresh polish, deep comfortable chairs covered in loose coral slipcovers next to a roaring open fire, plenty of whiskey and soda on hand. Yet Pilcher skillfully intertwines such homely domestic details with arching themes of human emotion to create an English world most readers would hardly recognize and yet feel intensely at home in. Her landscapes are similarly deft and entrancing, rich with color and vitality, full of sweeping vistas of the north Cornish coast, enormous Scottish estates, urban London, and the sweet Gloucestershire countryside.

Bibliography

Authorized Web site. Available online. URL: http://www.kiswebdesigns.com/rosamundepilcher. Last updated January 28, 2006.

Pilcher, Rosamunde. *The Shell Seekers.* New York: Dell, 1987.

———. *September.* London: Hodder & Stoughton, 1990.

———. *Coming Home.* London: Hodder & Stoughton, 1995.

———. *Winter Solstice.* London: Hodder & Stoughton, 2000.

Robin Musumeci

The Pillars of the Earth Ken Follett (1989)

KEN FOLLETT's sixth major novel, *The Pillars of the Earth,* marks a departure from his usual fare of spy thrillers and World War II adventures. It is an improbable but immensely successful historical epic set in the 12th century, dealing with politics, romance, and revenge. Spanning more than 40 years—and well over a thousand pages—the tale is centered in the fictional English town of Kingsbridge, and its principal narrative focus rests on the efforts of the prior, the townspeople, and a series of master-builders and masons to build a cathedral.

Follett's depiction of the tumultuous reign of King Stephen skillfully connects the machinations and struggles of those in power to the everyday existence of the poorest of the king's subjects. He investigates the implications of political instability for all of his principal characters, who form an impressive ensemble cast in the multiple dramas enacted in the novel: Aliena, the displaced noblewoman and merchant; Richard, her brother and the displaced heir to the earldom of Shiring; Tom, the master-builder; Ellen, the outlaw and witch-figure; Alfred, Tom's son and a builder in his own right; Philip, the prior of Kingsbridge; Waleran, the ambitious bishop of Kingsbridge; and Jack, Ellen's son and Aliena's lover, the architectural genius who takes over the building of the cathedral after traveling to the great Gothic cathedrals of continental Europe. Amid the complex and multifaceted drama, however, two key narrative strands may be discerned: the efforts of Philip, the prior of Kingsbridge, to build a cathedral, and the struggles of Aliena to reclaim her father's earldom for her brother, Richard, and to be united with her lover, Jack.

Much of Follett's exploration of power and its abuse is concentrated in the figure of William Hamleigh, the usurping earl of Shiring (a town next to Kingsbridge). A thoroughly vile character, he neglects his lands, abuses his tenants, and rapes almost every woman with whom he comes into contact, including the noble Aliena, whom he is due to marry at the outset. He is, effectively, the antagonist of every major character in the novel, and the acts he perpetrates against them are often horrendous, culminating in his eventual attempt to burn the entire town of Kingsbridge, its priory included, to the ground. His continual and opportunistic attempts to stay in favor with those in power lead to his switching political sides on numerous occasions during the civil war between supporters of King Stephen and Empress Maud. Eventually, he becomes one of the favored knights in the subsequent court of Henry II, and Follett casts him as one of the overenthusiastic nobles who historically murdered the archbishop of Canterbury, Thomas à Becket. For this crime William is hanged, but after his extraordinary career of rape, pillage, and destruction, it seems almost too little a punishment, as if Follett were making the point that with power, at least in the Middle Ages, came very little ultimate accountability.

Philip, the prior of Kingsbridge, is essentially set up as a foil to the mendacious depravity of William's character. He is both a deeply devout monk and an astute politician, and his political strategies typically have more to do with forging alliances than deploying force (like William) or cunning (like Waleran), and he is unafraid to make unpopular decisions if he believes them to be right, which often sets him in conflict with others in this scheming time. For example, he persistently refuses to let Aliena marry Jack—although her first marriage (to Alfred) is never consummated—because Bishop Waleran will not grant her an annulment, though the latter is an obvious political ally of William (who has never recovered from her rejection). This refusal to bend the letter of the law, even in the face of injustice, profoundly affects Aliena's ability to interact with him on a daily basis:

> Her inability to marry Jack had blighted everything [. . .]. She had come to hate Prior Philip, whom she had once looked up to as her saviour and mentor. She had not had a happy, amiable conversation with Philip for years. Of course, it was not his fault that they could not get an annulment; but it was he who insisted they live apart, and Aliena could not help resenting him for that (871).

The depiction of Philip's painstaking negotiation of the needs of the Church and the needs of his community—both the monks and the townspeople of Kingsbridge—demonstrates considerable skill on Follett's part, both in dividing the loyalties of his reader and in capturing the complexities of the division Philip himself feels between the personal and the political. He is the only character in the novel to feel this division acutely, many of the others being motivated, for good or ill, primarily by their own interests, wherever they find themselves on the social scale; this, more than any significant action, makes Philip the most complex and interesting character in the novel.

Like Follett's other works, *The Pillars of the Earth* is thoroughly researched and replete with a wealth of historical detail, most notable in its description of medieval European cathedrals, with copious and fascinating bits of architectural information woven throughout the narrative (according to his Web site, the Kingsbridge cathedral is actually an imaginary amalgamation of the English cathedrals of Wells and Salisbury). Moreover, through the inspired efforts of the young architect Jack, Follett captures a sense of the seismic shift in English ecclesiastical architecture at that time, from solid, fortresslike Saxon strongholds to soaring Gothic structures filled with light; his descriptions convey a vivid sense of wonder both at the building itself and at the architectural achievements of the craftsmen who designed and built it.

Although an immense best seller, the novel has never been adapted for film. However, Follett has written a sequel entitled *World without End,* which continues the story of the Kingsbridge Priory and the community surrounding it, and though none of the characters from the first book will appear in the second—since, as Follett himself observes on his Web site, "by the end of *Pillars* they are all very old or dead"—many of their descendants feature in the second book. *World without End* appeared in 2007.

Bibliography

Follett, Ken. *The Pillars of the Earth.* London: Macmillan, 1989.

"Ken Follett." Available online. URL: http://www.kenfollett.com. Accessed January 23, 2007.

Claire Horsnell

Pirsig, Robert M. (1928–)

Robert Maynard Pirsig was born in Minneapolis, Minnesota, in 1928 and moved with his family to England when his father's law studies took him from Harvard to the Middle and Inner Temple Inns of Court in London. While in England his father and his mother would take him for trips on a motorcycle with a sidecar. A precocious child with an IQ of 170 at the age of nine, Pirsig accelerated rapidly in school and originally thought to study biochemistry, but he was troubled that science never took itself as an object of study—a serious intellectual and spiritual oversight in Pirsig's view, explored at length in the semi-autobiographical *Zen and the Art of Motorcycle Maintenance*; so in 1948 he enrolled in the University of Minnesota to study philosophy, gaining his B.A. in 1950.

By 1961, after having undertaking various studies and jobs, Pirsig—or Phaedrus as he is known in *Zen*—began to experience mental illness, and in 1963 his father signed a court order committing him to the Veterans Hospital in Minneapolis, where he underwent the shattering electroshock therapy described in *Zen.* He describes his treatment and recovery (in the novel) in terms of a profoundly ambivalent compromise, disassociating him from critical elements of his self and life (including his relationship to his own son), noting in the introduction to the 25th anniversary edition of the novel, "the narrator doesn't want to be honest anymore, just an accepted member of the community, bowing and accommodating his way through the rest of his years" (*Zen* xv).

In July 1968 Pirsig began a cross-country motorcycle trip with his son, Chris, and two friends, John and Sylvia Sutherland, the narrative trope supporting the plot and meditations of *Zen*. Pirsig kept notes for the book during this trip, and the resulting book, an epochal work of the late century, was published by William Morrow in 1974 after many failed attempts to find a publisher.

In August 1975 Pirsig began a similar trip, this time by boat, which is narrated in *Lila: an Inquiry into Morals* (1991). During this trip Pirsig met with Robert Redford to discuss the possibility of turning *Zen* into a film, but they could not agree on production terms and the project fell through.

Both *Zen* and *Lila* met with critical and popular success, but *Zen* was a phenomenon in both respects. Pirsig noted in an interview, "Sequels are almost never as popular as their predecessors, so a diminution of sales was expected. Also, while *Zen and the Art of Motorcycle Maintenance* is a skeleton of a philosophy enclosed within a full-bodied novel, *Lila* is a skeleton of a novel enclosed within a full-bodied philosophy. Since many more people read novels than philosophy books, this also explains the lower sales" (*The Philosophers Magazine Online*).

In a poignant yet strangely congruous epilogue to the events described in *Zen,* Pirsig notes in the afterword to the 25th anniversary edition, with characteristically haunting plainness, that his son, Chris, had been violently killed: "Chris is dead. He was murdered. At about 8:00 p.m. on Saturday, November 17, 1979, in San Francisco, he left the Zen Center, where he was a student, to visit a friend's house a block away on Haight Street" (*Zen* 535). On his way he is mugged, it would appear, and left to die, an otherwise anonymous victim of an otherwise anonymous crime.

At present the author, philosopher, and craftsman (especially in steel-welding) lives quietly in Portsmouth, New Hampshire, but a cottage industry has emerged around his system of Quality (the aforementioned philosophy inscribed in the two novels), most notably on the Web site entitled *Metaphysics of Quality* (www.moq.org). He continues to be interviewed and is working on several projects.

Bibliography

American Society of Authors and Writers. Available online. URL: http://amsaw.org/amsaw-ithappenedinhistory-090604-pirsig.html. Accessed July 16, 2007.

Baggini, Julian. "An Interview with Robert Pirsig." *The Philosophers Magazine Online*. Available online. URL: http://www.philosophersnet.com/magazine/pirsig_transcript.htm. Accessed July 16, 2007.

"Biographical Timeline of Robert Pirsig." Psybertron.org. Available online. URL: http://www.psybertron.org/timeline.html. Accessed July 16, 2007.

Gent, George. "A Successful Pirsig Rethinks Life of Zen and Science." *New York Times*, 15 May 1974, 36. Available online. URL: http://www.psybertron.org/pirsig%201974%20interview.htm.

Metaphysics of Quality. Horse. Available online. URL: http://www.moq.org. Accessed July 16, 2007.

Pirsig, Robert M. *Zen and the Art of Motorcycle Maintenance: An Inquiry into Values*. 1974. New York: Harper Torch, 1999.

———. *Lila: An Inquiry into Morals*. New York: Bantam, 1991.

Valerie Holliday

The Poisonwood Bible

Barbara Kingsolver (1998)

The Poisonwood Bible is an epic novel in seven books about the family of Reverend Nathan Price, a Baptist missionary who transplants his family from Bethlehem, Georgia, to the isolated hamlet of Kilanga in the Congo. Set within the context of the Congo's actual history—beginning just before independence from Belgium in 1960—the story traces the family's experiences during their 18-month mission in Africa and the subsequent 25 years of separation following that period. The novel was developed from an earlier Kingsolver short story, "My Father's Africa," published in *McCall's* in August 1991.

The title of the book derives from the species of lethal flora—the poisonwood tree, *bängala* in the local Kikongo language—that gives the reverend a terrible rash in his early days in Africa. "Tata Jesus is *bängala,*" Nathan Price sermonizes to the indigenous Congolese, mispronouncing the similar word *bangala*—"precious"—and thus failing in not his only attempt to serve his brand of redemption to the Africans.

The main body of the story is advanced by not one but four alternating narrators, the four Price daughters. Through their eyes, and in each girl's unique vernacular, is revealed their discovery of Africa, a development of the sense of place and the idea of home, and ultimately the displacement of the ideals of belonging and kinship. And from each girl the reader gets a different piece of the enigma of Nathan Price, whose very existence is finally no more than an assemblage of the perspectives of his family.

The eldest daughter is Rachel, 15 at the time her family arrives in Africa. For her the Congo is a kind of parlor game, a temporary distraction from her teenage pursuits back in Georgia. Leah Price is first of the two twins. Striving for godly forbearance and obedience to her father, she is nonetheless too inquisitive of her environment to follow any doctrine blindly. Adah is the other twin, physically crippled with hemiplegia but mentally and emotionally an unlikely superior. Though she is practically mute, her mind reveals great complexity in the form of her palindromes and an acutely rational perspective on her family and Africa. Ruth May Price is the little child of the family and the unfettered discoverer of things innocent and small. "Noah cursed all Ham's children to be slaves for ever and ever," she says, echoing her father's teachings. "That's how come them to turn out dark" (20). For Ruth May there are only subtle differences between life in Georgia and in Africa.

Introducing each of the first five books of the novel is Orleanna Price, the modest yet resolute wife and mother, whose reflections from the story's future foreshadow the events of the past as told by the girls. "Imagine a ruin so strange it must never have happened" (5), she opens the novel; later introducing herself simply as "Orleanna Price, Southern Baptist by marriage, mother of children living and dead" (7).

In Africa headstrong Nathan Price sets to work futilely building a congregation in the village, leaving the women to explore and reveal the environs. Their discovery of Africa includes weekly quinine tablets and bartering for goods, as well as encounters with characters such as Mama Tataba (the housemaid), Tata Ndu (the polygamist village chief), Anatole (a handsome, visionary schoolteacher), Pascal (a curious playmate), and Methuselah (a foul-mouthed parrot). Through the girls' narrative voices—tinged with humor and intrigue, suspense and primal fear—readers witness a Congolese parade of drought, famine, child soldiers, a military coup, lions, malaria, and even an invading army of ants. The Prices learn how the laws of God blend with the laws of nature, culminating in a village-wide referendum on Jesus and a deadly encounter with a mamba-wielding witch doctor.

In the last third of the book the narrative falls away abruptly from the 18-month chronicle in Kilanga. Years pass, the family is cleaved, and the tone of the storytelling in the final two books turns to reflection and overcoming. Ultimately, there is a sense among the remaining narrators that what binds them is not family but the separation of family, not Africa but the rupture that Africa carved upon them, not the Reverend but each woman's own composition of him as he slowly became indistinguishable from the environment he sought to tame.

The Poisonwood Bible is a theme-driven work, echoing the broad strokes of BARBARA KINGSOLVER's work as a whole. Her characters' narratives double as allegories for the uneasy colonial marriage between the West and Africa and the postcolonial divorce in which each side, like each of the Price girls, is left with a kaleidoscopic perspective of what happened. Themes that follow Kingsolver's earlier work—the rupture of the family ideal, the conflict of attachment to place, womanhood's parallel exhibitions of dependence and independence—are also woven throughout the novel.

Also characteristic is Kingsolver's employment of her setting as both a character and moral absolute. In her earlier works the personified place was commonly the American West; here it is Africa—abused, mysterious, alluring, and exhibiting the irresistible dual promises of fulfillment and horror, not unlike Conrad's Africa in *Heart of Darkness.* And like Conrad's Kurtz, Nathan Price is seduced by Africa and loses himself in its mystery, leaving others to try to retrace an image of him. The oppressed but enduring Africa, like Orleanna Price, is the steadying axis around which the various perspectives, such as those of the Price girls, revolve as they try to achieve an equilibrium between clashing cultures and between past and present.

Kingsolver spent more than two years researching and writing this novel. She traveled in central Africa, recording the sights, sounds, and smells that provide the precious details of the story's setting. She learned the essentials of the Kikongo language and the contemporaneous lingo of 1950s Georgia, which feature prominently in the novel. She also studied the King James Bible to buttress the protestant/missionary references in her characters' speech. Kingsolver's background as a biologist likely prepared her for such strenuous research. She writes, "sometimes, reading a whole, densely-written book on, say, the formation and dissolution of indigenous political parties during the Congolese independence, or an account of the life histories of Central African venomous snakes, would move me only a sentence or two forward in my understanding of my subject. But every sentence mattered" ("Barbara"). Following the novel, she provides her readers with a bibliography of her many sources.

The Poisonwood Bible was an international best seller and was named among the "Best Books of the Year" by the *New York Times, Los Angeles Times,* and *Village Voice.* The novel also won the American Booksellers Book of the Year (ABBY) top award for 1998, the Patterson Fiction Prize (1999), and was a finalist for the PEN/Faulkner Award and the Pulitzer Prize.

Bibliography

Kingsolver, Barbara. *The Poisonwood Bible.* New York: HarperCollins, 1998.

"Barbara Kingsolver." Available online. URL: http://www.kingsolver.com/faq/answers.asp#question11. Accessed January 23, 2007.

Richard Alexander Johnson

Poland James A. Michener (1983)

Poland is an epic historical fiction following the development of three families, the Lubonski (count), Bukowski (petty noble), and Buk (peasant), from the 1200s up until the 1980s, their members representing three important classes of Polish society and their experience woven through actual historical events to provide a panoramic view of Poland and its history. In a testament to Michener's storytelling skill, while the actual historical events often seem remote and sometimes bizarre, the joys, hardships, and suffering of the fictional characters appear always authentic and immediate. Consequently, the real and the imaginary intertwine to create a mesmerizing saga of Poland, a country often referred to as "the doormat of Europe."

Breathtaking vistas, rolling landscapes, and imposing castles peopled with indefatigable serfs, magnates, and puppets of foreign rule bind the land and its people in a knot that threatens to unravel at every political disaster yet remains mysteriously intact. As the borders of Poland wax and wane, and the nation faces one hardship after another, the Poles repeatedly rise to the challenge without self-pity or fanfare, picking themselves up from ruination to plant crops, mend walls, and rebuild castles, communities, and nation. JAMES MICHENER gleans from this vast history a unique Polish identity, which he defines in terms of a love of land, labor, and freedom; an absolute refusal to despair or indulge in self-pity, along with an indefatigable spirit to rebuild; an extraordinary individualism, crystallized in the parliament's *liberum veto,* where one "I object" can kill a piece of legislation; and most striking perhaps, a hatred of central authority so intense that the people prefer foreign to Polish kings, lest the latter should become dictatorial or establish dynasties.

The novel is narrated through a series of episodes bookended by two short chapters with mirrored titles, "Buk versus Bukowski" and "Bukowski versus Buk," beginning and ending at the same point: the dawn of the Solidarity movement and Poland's true freedom. Enclosed by this frame is the long and long-suffering history of Poland, covering eight major historical periods. Vast amounts of information are effectively presented through categories of attack from four geographical directions.

From the East come the marauding Tartars on horseback, their sole purpose to loot, pillage, and destroy. From the West come the Teutonic Knights on the invitation of a Polish King, ostensibly to Christianize the pagans, a mission the Poles bitterly resent, having long been Christianized already, and having developed their own thriving universities, music, and art. From the North come the ravaging Swedes, again pillaging and destroying the wealth of Poland. Later in the same (17th) century, from the South come the Ottoman Turks, for whom Poland is a hurdle on their way to Vienna. The Turks are not as ruthless as the Teutonic Knights, whose chosen method of Christianizing is by wiping out whole populations. The Turks instead make slaves and janissaries of those they conquer and do not leave utter destruction behind, as do the Swedes.

What enable the Poles to endure and finally prevail over these repeated assaults are their thick forests of birch, providing a safe haven for retreat and resistance, and their own indomitable capacity to organize, reorganize, strategize, and rebuild; for as they say, "A Pole is a man born with a sword in his right hand, a brick in his left" (522). Two decades of 20th-century respite follow these ceaseless oppressions, covered in a chapter appropriately titled "The Golden Freedom," when Poland was more democratic than any nation in Europe. But self-serving autocratic neighbors such as the Hapsburgs of Austria, the Romanoffs of Russia, and the Hohenzollerns of Prussia view Poland's democratic aspiration as a threat to their dynastic ambitions. In the face of this Poland's visionary leaders, chief among them the fictional Count Lubonski, repeatedly try to consolidate Poland's security by forging alliances with the Lithuanians and Ukrainians. Distrust, however, and an equally fierce desire for independence on the part of these nations make such consolidation impossible. Consequently, Poland is defeated by the Russian Communists at the Battle of Zamosc, then falls victim to the terror of Nazi occupation.

This harrowing occupation molds the ideological differences between Buk the farmer and Bukowski the Communist. But just as it seems their division is so deep that no compromise is possible, Bishop Marski, himself a survivor of Auschwitz, through his tolerance, faith, and compassion persuades them to overcome their differences in order make the compromises necessary to the political health of Poland. The two sworn enemies' dehumanizing experience in the Nazi camp has sharpened their differing positions, yet the same experience makes it necessary for them to get past such differences for the greater good.

While the unionization of factory workers and the bargaining power it provided is a well-known fact of modern history, the potential power of farmers unionizing to demand their due has rarely been realized, though such peasants have been exploited from time immemorial. In *Poland,* however, the vital strength and industry of the farmers remains at the center of Polish life. Their elemental energy, deriving from proximity to the land, and their continuous experience of the cycle of life, growth, bounty, and death shapes for Michener the national identity of patience and hope. So tied are the Polish people to their land that in a central ritual of marriage the bride bakes bread and offers it to the groom as she repeats, "I give you the soil of Poland. I give you the grain of Poland. Eat this good bread and be strong. Eat this good bread and be my husband" (111).

Characteristically, Michener has written a novel both historically accurate in its detail and immensely entertaining and interesting in style. The politics of the profitable amber trade, for example, provide intrigues and adventures on the "amber road" that stretches from the Black Sea to the Baltic Sea; amber, with its "subtle, woodland sunset beauty," acts a metaphor for the muted and unassuming beauty that is Poland itself (68). Amusement and laughter, meanwhile, infuse pastoral weddings, with Polish cooking and practical, prudent husbandry providing relief—for Poles and readers alike—from the ceaseless, often devastating struggles.

Michener began writing about contested lands with *The Bridges of Toko-ri* (1953), about Korea, and followed this with *Caravans* (1963), about Afghanistan, *The Source* (1965) about Israel, and *The Covenant* (1980) about South Africa. All, with the possible exception of the last, are as relevant today in engaging and instructing interest as they were at the time of publication. Although he consistently follows the same formula, of time line, flashbacks, and episodes of heroic deeds and everyday life, the formula works in *Poland* as elsewhere because of Michener's vivid and comprehensive historical imagination and his timeless skill as a storyteller.

Bibliography

Michener, James A. *The Bridges of Toko-ri.* New York: Random House, 1953.

———. *Caravans.* New York: Random House, 1963.

———. *The Source.* New York: Random House, 1965.

———. *The Covenant.* New York: Random House, 1980.

———. *Poland.* New York: Random House, 1983.

———. *Caribbean.* New York: Random House, 1989.

———. *Mexico.* New York: Random House, 1992.

Sukanya Senapati

Politically Correct Bedtime Stories

James Finn Garner (1992)

JAMES FINN GARNER's first and most popular book is a deft rewriting of some of the best-known and loved fairy tales, penned by such legends as the brothers Grimm and Hans Christian Andersen. Appalled to learn that children's classics were being revised and edited, sometimes even fully suppressed to accommodate contemporary political sensitivities, Garner began to "mimic that overreaction," first in improvisational comedy at "The Theatre of the Bizarre" in Chicago's Elbo room and later in this compilation of stories, which graciously concedes that their authors meant well but were sadly benighted by their times. After more than 30 rejections, the collection of thirteen "corrected" stories was published and became a runaway best seller, translated into 20 languages.

In Garner's updated tales readers meet characters who are vertically challenged, economically disadvantaged, or who appear to come "from some world other than (but certainly not unequal to) our own." Chicken Little is "cranially underenhanced," Snow White "melanin-challenged," and the three bears, an anthropomorphic nuclear family. Here girls and "womyn," having graduated from self-assertiveness courses, speak out against injustice without losing sight of the victimhood of their oppressor: "The wolf said, 'You know, my dear, it isn't safe for a little girl to walk through these woods alone.'" To which Red Riding Hood replies, "'I find your sexist remark offensive in the extreme. But I will ignore it because of your traditional status as an outcast from society.'"

Rumpelstiltskin's Esmeralda is similarly enlightened, declaring she need not, in fact, give up her firstborn child to the dwarf (the man of nonstandard height) who taught her to spin gold from straw: "I don't have to negotiate with anyone who would interfere with my reproductive rights!" Instead, putting her wealth to good use, she opens a birth control clinic to show that womyn need not be defined by their reproductive capacities.

Stereotypes of size, ability, beauty, and gender are obviously in need of correction, but so too are inappropriate attitudes to the environment and health. Referring to the Three Pigs, Garner reveals that the bad wolf's real crime was a lifetime of bad nutrition: "So he huffed and puffed, and huffed and puffed, then grabbed his chest and fell over dead from a massive heart attack brought on from eating too many fatty foods."

Garner's comic send-up of contemporary discomfort with traditional tales of sadism and irrationality is not just buffoonery. In his retelling of the Pied Piper story, for example, he shows how the wish to sanitize the world can be cruel and sadistic in itself. The inhabitants of Hamelyn have everything an enlightened community could wish for, "non-polluting industries, effective mass transit and a well-balanced ethno-religious diversity." They feel menaced, however. On the outskirts of town there is an ugly trailer park inhabited by "murderers of non domestic animals, former clients of the correctional system and off-road bikers." The age-old irony of utopia needing policing is treated comically here as the Pied Piper lures these undesirables out of town by playing country music and the "Ballad of the Green Berets." To be sure, the bourgoisie get their own comeuppance, but the real target of this satire is the desire to excise rather than engage with undesirable elements in society.

The lighthearted collection remains, nonetheless, a loving homage to traditional fairy tales in all their strange immorality and absurdity. Garner speaks of his childhood love of Pinnochio, "especially when he got his feet burned off," explaining, "it was such a thrill to think of a kid skipping school, being kidnapped by the cat and the fox and turned into a donkey. That's just a ball of psychologically damaging material." *Politically Correct Bedtime Stories* is a sharp reminder that altering the language and content of the best stories trivializes the real effort needed to address social inequality. It is also, as Garner says, "annoying."

Excerpts from *Politically Correct Bedtime Stories* can be found everywhere in popular culture, from calendars and Internet sites, to computer games and television pilots. The success of this first book spawned two others: *Once Upon a More Enlightened Time* and *Politically Correct Holiday Stories,* as well as *Apocalypse Wow: A Memoir for the End of Time.* A complement to *Politically Correct Bedtimes Stories* could be found in Frederick Crews's *Postmodern Pooh,* a send-up of efforts to read this childhood classic under the rubric of complex literary theory.

Bibliography

Garner, James Finn. *Politically Correct Bedtime Stories.* New York: Macmillan, 1994.

O'Conner, Patricia T. "Jack, the Beanstalk and His Marginalized Mother." *New York Times Book Review,* 15 May 1994.

Andrea Sauder

Predator Patricia Cornwell (2005)

PATRICIA CORNWELL's immensely popular Kay Scarpetta series is best known for its brilliant and flawed detective, Kay Scarpetta, longtime chief medical examiner of Virginia. Through the first dozen novels of the series Kay works for the state, often consulting on federal matters with the FBI and usually collaborating with a cadre of secondary characters also in traditional law enforcement positions. But *Predator,* the 14th book of the series, finds the characters in new roles at the National Forensic Academy, a Florida-based institution founded and directed by Lucy Farinelli, Kay's genius niece. Kay works as the director of forensic science and medicine, while Pete Marino, former police officer and Kay's longtime sidekick, is head of investigations. Benton Wesley, Kay's lover and former FBI profiler, consults for the academy and is engaged in a Harvard-based research study that gives the novel its title: Prefrontal Determinants of Aggressive-Type Overt Responsivity (P.R.E.D.A.T.O.R.). The novel examines both the characters' personal struggles and their investigations of several seemingly unrelated murders. Narrated from numerous perspectives, it is fast-paced and complex in its plotting and character development.

The team of Kay, Benton, Lucy, and Marino works together unofficially, across geographical distances, on five separate but related murders. A phone call to Marino from a caller identifying himself as Hog connects the Johnny Swift case to the Christians. Swift, either a suicide or murder victim, also happens to be Lucy's personal physician, while the Christian family—two middle-aged sisters raising two adopted boys—is missing, sought by the detectives while the reader watches them being brutalized by Hog. Their neighbor, Mrs. Simister, is herself eventually found murdered; in addition, Benton, in the course of interviewing a serial killer for the PREDATOR study, learns of "the Christmas Shop murder," while at the same time at work on a case in which a mutilated woman is marked with painted handprints—markings that Lucy has herself noted on a young woman during a one-night stand. When Scarpetta says to Lucy, "'I'm getting tired of coincidences. There seem to have been a lot of them lately'" (263), the reader may well agree. Such coincidences, though, skillfully deployed, only build tension and weave personal and professional elements of the story together.

Even as the details of the criminal investigation are narrated, the characters face personal struggles that highlight ongoing themes in the series, in particular those involving traditional law enforcement. Lucy, for example, who has worked in a number of federal agencies, often gets into trouble for her lack of respect for traditional authority; but thanks to her remarkable gift for solving crimes, her National Academy is presented as a positive alternative. In *Predator,* however, she must confront a life-altering illness that sends her spiraling into dangerous behaviors, thus jeopardizing the future of her promising institution.

Cornwell's series has often presented traditional law enforcement as engendering problematic models of masculinity, generally through the character of

Pete Marino. But Marino reached a turning point in *Trace* (2004) when sexually assaulted by a woman, and *Predator* reveals his masculinity as painfully complex: He becomes ultra-masculine in his appearance, riding a Harley and working out relentlessly, but also struggles with this same masculinity in visits to a psychiatrist and in dealing with the sexual side effects of antidepressants.

Throughout the novel Marino continually jockeys for power with Joe Amos, a forensic fellow at the academy and a man who exemplifies the worst of traditional law enforcement, demonstrating a deep disrespect for victims that goes against the fundamental principles of Kay and her team. "One of life's fables," he opines,

> is that dead bodies can't be sexy. Naked is naked if the person looks good and hasn't been dead long. To say a man has never had a thought about a beautiful woman who happens to be dead is a joke. Cops pin photographs on their corkboards, pictures of female victims who are exceptionally fine. Male medical examiners give lectures to cops and show them certain pictures, deliberately pick the ones they'll like (75).

Joe, in fact, imitates this behavior when he designs "Hell Scenes" for teaching new recruits, while in addition to such lack of professionalism, it turns out that his application to the academy was itself fraudulent, and as such he represents the potential for corruption as well as for depravity in law enforcement situations.

Thematically, *Predator* explores the question whether detectives should focus on victims or criminals, a debate clearly articulated by Benton, who characterizes typical forensic psychologists as "more interested in the details of the offender than in what he did to his victim, because the offender is the patient and the victim is nothing more than the medium he used to express his violence" (29). This idea is diametrically opposed to the attitudes shaping Kay's beliefs and her works. And yet, despite her insistence on placing the dead first, even Kay is drawn into the trap that detectives often fall into: doubling the criminal. At a crime scene, for example, Kay "isn't ready yet, her approach to a scene similar to a predator's. She moves from the outer edge to the inside, saving the worst for last" (165–166). Benton also struggles with overidentification with the criminals he studies, worrying "that maybe he has been spending too much time in Basil's [a serial killer's] head" (268), and Kay's displeasure with the whole project suggests that such intense focus on criminals is somehow profoundly misplaced.

Like many detective novels, *Predator* ends in ambiguity, neatly closing the multiple murder investigations but leaving open questions about law enforcement attitudes and practice, about criminal responsibility (the murderer having turned out to be a victim of sexual abuse and psychological illness), and about people's own ambivalent, sometimes irresponsible attitude to crime. But with most of the main characters confronting major life decisions at the end, the novel also ensures that readers will look forward to the next work of the series.

Bibliography

Cornwell, Patricia. *Trace.* New York: Putnam, 2004.

———. *Predator.* New York: Putnam, 2005.

Pamela Bedore

Presumed Innocent Scott Turow (1987)

Presumed Innocent is Scott Turow's compelling first novel, an early legal thriller that helped invent the genre, and one providing compelling evidence of the author's belief that "the crime novel . . . has a philosophical purpose beyond what it often gets credit for" (Interview 165). Written in the first person, the complexly plotted novel subtly renders both Rusty Sabich's experience as he is accused of murder and the murky world of political intrigue framing that experience. A former chief deputy district attorney for the fictional Kindle County (loosely based on Cook County, which includes Chicago), Sabich gets a firsthand look at his own legal system from the defendant's perspective.

The novel begins with the brutal murder of Sabich's coworker and former lover, Deputy District Attorney Carolyn Polemus. Complicating matters further, Sabich's boss, District Attorney Raymond Horgan, is in the midst of a hotly contested bid for reelection. Because Polemus was a beautiful and up-and-coming prosecutor with a penchant for sleeping her way into the next political appointment, her murder and the subsequent investigation quickly become election topics, especially when the district attorney's investigation, headed by Sabich, fails to produce a viable suspect. Despite pressure from Horgan for fast results, the investigation stalls, and it becomes apparent that Horgan will now lose the election to Nico Della Guardia, his longtime political adversary. After Della Guardia's own investigation reveals that Sabich may have had an affair with Polemus—may in fact have been in her apartment on the night she was murdered—Sabich is himself charged with the murder, and most of his former friends, including Horgan, turn against him. The circumstantial evidence quickly mounts: his fingerprints appear on a glass found at the crime scene; carpet fibers match those from his home; and most damning, a sperm sample matches his blood type.

Confronting the largely circumstantial case against him, Sabich hires Sandy Stern, a noted defense attorney, and the ensuing section of the novel provides a fascinating look at the legal system in action. As he reviews the evidence against him, Sabich reflects on latent vulnerabilities, both to violence and punishment: "I have made league with the all-stars of crime. John Dillinger, Bluebeard, Jack the Ripper, and the million lesser lights, the half-mad, the abused, the idly evil, and the many who surrendered to a moment's terrible temptation, to an instant when they found themselves well-acquainted with our wilder elements, our darker side" (149). It is these wilder elements that the legal system attempts to make sense of and contain, and from voir dire to final verdict, the trial is the highlight of the novel. Turow vividly renders trial procedure, capturing Stern's brilliant cross-examination of key state witnesses, the jury's reactions, and the constant bickering between prosecution, defense, and judge.

Indeed, the trial itself reveals one of the novel's major themes. Behind the veneer of seemingly objective, neutral legal guarantees such as the presumption of innocence afforded all criminal defendants lies real human beings, complete with complex and all-too-human motivations, temptations, and foibles. District Attorney Nico Della Guardia seems driven largely by political motivations rather than a desire to find the truth; Deputy District Attorney Tommy Molto may have tampered with the evidence to increase the chances of a conviction; even Judge Larren Lyttle, though known as a defendant's judge, in eventually dismissing the case, may be doing so out of fear that if the trial were to continue, evidence might reveal his own role in a bribery case involving Polemus.

Consider Turow's deft handling of the last, for example. Early in his investigation Sabich discovers the "B-file," a mysterious case Polemus was apparently investigating when she died. Launching an interesting subplot of its own, the B-file reveals that in their early days in the legal system Polemus solicited bribes for Judge Lyttle. Stern apparently recognizes the file's significance and repeatedly references it during the early stages of the trial, creating the impression that the defense will use the file to prove that Sabich was framed for Polemus's murder. At the end of the prosecution's presentation of the evidence against Sabich, Judge Lyttle dismisses the case. Given the specter of the B-file, Lyttle's motives remain unclear: Did he dismiss the case due to inadequate evidence or Stern's subtle blackmail?

Noting such ambiguity, Turow nevertheless explains in an interview that "the trial in *Presumed Innocent* comes out in exactly the right way. . . . It's not for all the right reasons, it never is, but in a rough, approximate way the justice system labors on. It's nearsighted, it's awkward, but it's not totally blind" (Interview 164). Significantly, neither the novel nor Sabich's troubles end with the trial's conclusion. Afterward he finds it difficult to return to a normal life. His marriage, already shaken by his affair with Polemus, finally disintegrates, and his wife leaves him, taking their son with her. At last, in a shocking twist, Sabich reveals the killer's identity to his longtime friend, Detective Lipranzer, whose skepticism provides the final gloss on Sabich's world. Noting Lipranzer's doubt, Sabich comments, "But there is that flicker there, the bright light of idle doubt. What is harder? Knowing the truth or finding it? Telling it or being believed?" (418).

These questions shape Turow's morally ambiguous terrain and suggest another of his major themes. *Presumed Innocent* does more than simply provide a potboiler's whodunit plot; it delves into complex philosophical questions about the nature of truth and morality, carefully explored through struggles of central characters that rise above mere types. In her review of the novel, ANNE RICE explains that most of the characters strive "for his or her own ethical balance in a world in which morality and purpose do, indeed, count. Characters defend themselves and each other in light of sound values and disillusioning realities." For Rice "the resulting complexity is as engrossing as it is challenging." Employing Sabich's own narrative voice throughout, the novel captures the emotional turmoil of this once-powerful chief deputy district attorney as he confronts his own legal system from the other side. Faced with the prospect of a prison sentence if he is convicted, Sabich's desperation is palpable: "Dear God, dear God, I am in agony and fear, and whatever I may have done to make you bring this down upon me, release me, please, I pray, release me. Release me. Dear God in whom I do not believe, dear God, let me go free" (194).

Sabich's lack of religious faith provides a profound comment on his and, for Turow, our situation: He lives in a world devoid of faith of any kind, a world of chaos and chance. Noting that "if luck, and luck alone, spares us the worst, life nonetheless wears many of us down." Sabich rationalizes his affair with Polemus: "Every life, like every snowflake, seemed to me then unique in the shape of its miseries, and in the rarity and mildness of its pleasures. The lights go out, grow dim. And a soul can stand only so much darkness. I reached for Carolyn" (398).

Such darkness permeates much of Turow's fiction, and in the case of *Presumed Innocent* translated well to the big screen. In 1990 the novel was successfully adapted into a film starring Harrison Ford as Rusty Sabich and Brian Dennehy as Raymond Horgan. The film was the 10th-highest grossing movie of 1990 and helped establish Turow's national reputation.

Bibliography

Rice, Anne. "She Knew Too Many, Too Well." *New York Times,* 28 June 1987, 7: 1.

Turow, Scott. "Interview with Scott Turow." In *Conversations with American Novelists: Best Interviews from the Missouri Review and the American Audio Prose Library.* Edited by Kay Bonetti, Greg Michalson, Speer Morgan, Jo Sapp, and Sam Stowers. Columbia: University of Missouri Press, 1997.

———. *Presumed Innocent.* New York: Warner Books, 1987.

Alicia M. Renfroe

Pretend You Don't See Her

Mary Higgins Clark (1997)

Pretend You Don't See Her tells the story of Lacey Farrell, a New York real estate agent who finds herself in the FBI's witness protection program after nearly walking in on the murder of her client Isabelle Waring. Before Isabelle dies, she passes on a clue to the previous murder of her daughter, Heather Landi, in the form of a cryptic and bloodstained journal. Lacey reluctantly enters the witness protection program after an attempt on her life results in the serious wounding of her young niece, Bonnie. Relocated to Minneapolis and renamed Alice Carroll, she finds it impossible, however, to accept her new, artificial life. Although she attracts the romantic interest of local radio celebrity Tom Lynch, she cannot commit to a life of constant deception and struggles to avoid giving away her identity. When the killer finally tracks her down, she chooses to return to New York and solve Heather's murder in order to end the threat to her family and reclaim the life she knew.

Lacey Farrell is firmly situated in MARY HIGGINS CLARK's tradition of strong female protagonists, yet her success and self-reliance are never translated into arrogance or seclusion. She constantly questions her own motives and actions, carefully negotiating what to do with Heather Landi's journal, debating whether to develop her relationship with Tom, agonizing over how to reassure her worried mother without revealing too much. As Linda Pelzer has pointed out, a basic honesty and strong self-identity lie at the core of Lacey's crises, and these traits make it impossible for her to wait passively in the witness protection program, deceiving everyone she meets as well as her family back in New York (Pelzer).

The qualities defining Sandy Savarano, the killer hunting Lacey down, serve as a precise foil to her virtues. A cold and arrogant Mafia hitman, Savarano is a characteristically incorrigible Clark villain. Whereas Lacey's integrity cannot accept any deception or compromise with evil, the man hunting her exists beneath multiple layers of false identities, cons, and disguises (including plastic surgery). Clark emphasizes this changeability and falsehood by repeatedly switching between his real name and the pseudonym Curtis Caldwell. Driven out of hiding to hunt down the one person who knows his true face, Savarano is bent on avoiding a return to prison. While readers might have sympathized if his desperation were presented differently, Clark allows for no such feeling, emphasizing the homicidal thrill he enjoys while tracking down his prey.

Most of the trauma in the novel occurs in the context of a parent-child relationship. Lacey witnesses the murder of a grieving mother, a crime that itself is meant to cover up the murder of the daughter a year before. Lacey's decision to enter the witness protection program is cemented by the shooting of her own young niece, Bonnie. She undertakes the risks and personal challenges of the program and, later, the dangers of leaving it for the sake of her immediate and extended family, in order to avenge and prevent violence. But Lacey herself can be seen as an imperiled child, and her concern for her mother's anxiety plays a major role in undermining Lacey's security in her anonymous new life. Clark compresses the roles of protective elder female and imperiled child into one character and then places her at the center of overlapping networks of peril and obligation.

There are three family groups in the novel. The Farrell-Taylors—built around the trio of Lacey, her sister, and their mother—take center stage as the family at risk. The Landi-Warings, driven apart by the death of their daughter, present an already shattered family in deep grief and anger. In direct contrast, however, to these two "good" groups—the one broken, the other in danger of breaking—the Parkers, who own Lacey's real estate firm, illustrate the depths of family dysfunction. The patriarchal hegemony of Parker Sr. contributes directly to the corruption and downfall of Parker Jr., and it is the mother Priscilla Parker who finally steps in to rehabilitate her son and mitigate some of the wrongs he has committed. (Rick Parker, as a damaged son, shares in the children-at-risk motif.) In all three groups the women serve to protect and maintain the family: Isabelle Waring the tenacious advocate, Lacey Farrell the selfless champion, and Priscilla Parker the reconciliatory healer.

The drive and protectiveness of these women do not necessarily result, however, in a reversal of conventional ideas of male protection and stewardship. Lacey's deceased father counsels her throughout the novel in the form of flashbacks and memories, and the male detectives and federal marshals competently serve their roles as Lacey's protectors, even though she must disobey their direct orders in order to survive as herself. In effect, she thwarts them in order to achieve their own goals. This idea of a woman facilitating the man's role as protector or guardian also characterizes Lacey's burgeoning romance with Tom Lynch. Without undermining their conventional masculine/feminine roles, she takes responsibility for his safety as a consequence of their relationship:

> He cupped her face in his hands, forcing her to look up . . . at the firm line of Tom's jaw, the way his forehead was creased with concern for her—the expression in his eyes.
>
> The expression you give someone special. Well, I won't let anything happen to you because of it, she promised (220–221).

Lacey rejects an immediate relationship until she can be safe and honest and welcome him into her real family. She undertakes her return to New York in the hope that by confronting the violent and deceptive criminal forces arrayed against her she can restore a safe, normal environment for herself and her loved ones.

Clark often develops novels from a core idea or current event, and she attributes her work here to her longstanding interest in the FBI program. Like many of her books, *Pretend You Don't See Her* takes its title from a song of the same name. In 2002 the PAX television network produced a movie adaptation starring Emma Samms as Lacey and Hannes Jaenicke as Savarano.

Bibliography

Clark, Mary Higgins. *Pretend You Don't See Her.* New York: Simon & Schuster, 1997.

Pelzer, Linda C. "Mary Higgins Clark." In Critical Companions to Popular Contemporary Writers Online. Greenwood Press, 2002. Available online. URL: http://www.gem.greenwood.com.

Charles Tedder

The Prince of Tides Pat Conroy (1986)

"My wound is my geography," begins Tom Wingo in *The Prince of Tides,* referring to the South; Tom shares both this geography and its wounds with his author, PAT CONROY. Indeed, this opening line establishes the central theme not merely for the novel but for virtually all of Conroy's work, which is often described as autobiographical fiction because of its close ties to his own life. Thus, the following passage from its opening chapter may serve also to introduce his oeuvre:

> I wish I had no history to report. I've pretended for so long that my childhood did not happen. [. . .] Because I needed to love my mother and father in all their flawed, outrageous humanity, I could not afford to address them directly about the felonies committed against all of us. I could not hold them accountable or indict them for crimes they could not help. They, too, had a history—one that I remembered with both tenderness and pain, one that made me forgive their transgressions against their own children. In families there are no crimes beyond forgiveness (8).

The narrative revolves around this "history" and those "transgressions" as Wingo attempts to help his suicidal sister, Savannah, by working with her psychiatrist. In the course of their sessions and, ultimately, an intimate relationship between Tom and the psychiatrist herself, readers discover that Tom's mental health issues are as daunting and complex as those of his sister. A series of flashbacks reveals the often outré incidents in the Wingo family's past that have created the adults of the present: Tom and his mother being gang-raped (saved by Tom's brother, Luke, letting their pet tiger loose to kill the rapists); the siblings' rescue of an albino dolphin; and Luke's attempt to save an island that results in him getting shot and killed.

Between the frequent and unsettling flashbacks to the South and the drama taking place in present-day New York, readers are induced to share with Tom an anxious and baffled sense of harm and incomprehension. And similar to those of other novels, Conroy's protagonist here represents the author himself in various stages of his life, reflecting his love/hate relationship both with his family and with the South itself. In addition to the very prevalent theme of place, and the rest of Conroy's typical thematic coterie—the dysfunctional family, disordered sensibility, and distressed coming-of-age—*The Prince of Tides* is concerned with nuclear proliferation, governmental encroachment on small communities, racism, and even the Vietnam War.

While many critics focus on the father-son relationships in Conroy's work, here the relationship of mother to son is in fact more interesting and worthy of analysis. While the father is depicted as a type, a typically abusive but weak male character, the mother is far more complex and nuanced, alternating between a loving parent and manipulative almost Medean heroine who ultimately betrays her own children; thus Tom's "I have spent a lifetime studying my mother, and still I am no expert" (110), and "The Wingo line produced strong men, but none of them were a match for the Wingo women" (152).

In addition to *The Prince of Tides,* Conroy has written *The Boo, The Water Is Wide* (nonfiction), *The Great Santini, The Lords of Discipline,* and *Beach Music;* his most recent work includes the nonfiction (but equally passionate) *My Losing Season,* about his senior year playing basketball at the Citadel. All of them revolve around solitary central protagonists evoking different stages of Conroy's own life.

As a student Conroy was introduced to Thomas Wolfe's *Look Homeward Angel,* and the latter's potent mix of humor, passion, and almost elegiac melancholy proved to be a key influence in his life and his writing. Although he actively denies such comparisons, Conroy's work has been likened to that of Wolfe, William Faulkner, and even Margaret Mitchell.

Reception of the novel was mixed, with some reviewers celebrating and some denouncing the same thematic and stylistic idiosyncrasies; Brigitte Weeks describing it as "long, yet a pleasure to read" (1), but Gail Godwin, echoing the sentiment of many, disparaging the narrative touch as "heavy-handed and inflated" (14). In 1988 Judith Fitzgerald, a Charleston, South Carolina, teacher at St. Andrews High School, placed *The Prince of Tides* on her reading list, creating a storm of controversy within the town and on the school board. The local newspaper favored censoring the book, drawing Conroy into the debates through letters to the editor. Conroy later lectured to Fitzgerald's class on the duty of the writer in issues of censorship and First Amendment protections ("Pat Conroy" 77–78), and he has continued to be outspoken concerning censorship issues.

The novel was made into a very successful movie in 1991 directed by Barbra Streisand and starring herself and Nick Nolte. It received seven Oscar nominations.

Bibliography

Conroy, Pat. *The Prince of Tides.* Boston: Houghton, 1986. Reprint, New York: Bantam, 1987.

Godwin, Gail. "Romancing the Shrink." Review of *The Prince of Tides. New York Times Book Review*, 12 October 1986, 14.

"Pat Conroy." In *Encyclopedia of Southern Literature,* edited by Mary Ellen Snodgrass. Santa Barbara, Calif.: ABC-CLIO, 1997.

Weeks, Brigitte. "Pat Conroy: Into the Heart of a Family." Review of *The Prince of Tides. Washington Post Book World*, 12 October 1986, 1, 14.

Susie Scifres Kuilan

Princess Daisy Judith Krantz (1980)

Princess Daisy is the story of Princess Marguerite Alexandrovna Valensky, or Daisy. This second novel by JUDITH KRANTZ improves on the detailed descriptions of the customs, possessions, and sex lives of the rich and famous that marked her debut, *Scruples* (1978), by distinguishing between Daisy as a White Russian princess, a working woman, and a marketable good. Thematically, the novel is unusual in its sexual politics, which reward female financial and sexual aggression, and in its simultaneous critique and celebration of glamour and conspicuous consumption. Daisy creates illusions of wealth and romance to sell products but resists being a product herself until financial need forces her to be a celebrity figurehead. Glamour is presented as a construction, something Daisy would rather make than be. Yet the novel also presents a world entirely composed of the owning, manufacturing, and promotion of luxury goods. The novel therefore verges on the self-referential, though Krantz eventually succumbs to genre requirements and provides a fairytale ending. A 1983 miniseries adaptation was a popular and artistic disappointment.

Princess Daisy begins in Manhattan in 1975 with Daisy scouting locations for a shampoo commercial. Though she is a producer, not a model, her hair is "silver-gilt," her eyes "the color of the innermost heart of a giant purple pansy," and her skin "like the particular part of the peach into which you bite first" (2, 4). The novel then flashes back to the 1951 meeting of her parents, Academy Award–winning actress Francesca Vernon and Prince "Stash" Valensky. When Francesca's hat blows off at a polo match, Stash sweeps her off her feet onto his pony and retrieves it. Francesca is overwhelmed: "She wanted him to fall to the ground with him in her arms, just as he was, flushed, steaming, still breathing heavily from the game, and grind himself into her" (13). Their relationship is consummated in the stables after Stash gives Francesca some ancestral Fabergé jewels. He proposes the next morning.

Stash's mother, Princess Titiana, had tuberculosis, and so his father moved his household to Switzerland—and thus kept his money despite the Russian Revolution. At 14 Stash is seduced in a tumultuous sex scene by the Marquise de Champery, on "the rose satin upholstery she knew was in bad taste but nonetheless permitted herself in private apartments" (47). He grows into a premier polo player, master aviator, and playboy.

Stash has a son from a first marriage but is not close to Ram, whose mother remarried into British aristocracy. Stash and Francesca have twins, Marguerite (Daisy) and Danielle, who is brain-damaged. Stash, traumatized by Titiana's illness, tells Francesca that Danielle is dead and institutionalizes her. But Francesca retrieves Dani and goes into hiding in Big Sur, where Daisy grows up convinced that she caused her sister's disability by being born first.

Stash finds comfort in Anabel de Fourment, who abandoned a secure future as a dowager marchioness to become a "great modern courtesan" (99). Anabel owes her success not to sex but to the ability to make men entirely comfortable. Only she can reach Ram, who is emotionally disturbed. When Francesca dies, the six-year-old twins move to Stash's London home. Dani is reinstitutionalized, and Daisy starves herself until Stash allows regular visits, though he insists she keep her twin secret. Daisy acquires a gypsy dog, a lurcher named Theseus, and becomes notorious at 12 for organizing an impromptu horse show in Belgrave Square. When Stash dies, Anabel, Ram, and Daisy retreat to La Marée, a *manoir* near Honfleur. The grieving 15-year-old Daisy is seduced then raped by Ram. Anabel banishes him and sends Daisy to UC Santa Cruz with General Motors heiress Kiki Kavanaugh, soon Daisy's best friend.

Daisy and Anabel's inheritance is in Rolls-Royce stock; when Rolls is nationalized, Anabel converts La Marée into a hotel, and Daisy leaves school to become a production assistant, as well as a child-and-pony portrait artist for the horsey set. Thus she supports herself and Dani without Ram's help.

The novel now returns to its opening, with Daisy rooming with Kiki and resplendent in 40-year-old Schiaparelli unearthed from jumble sales. Wild Kiki is tamed by creative director Luke Hammerstein (allowing for the comparison of WASP and Jewish upper-class cultures), and Daisy has an affair with North, her exacting, unsentimental boss, a director of spectacular commercials (described at some length). Though she knows physical pleasure, Daisy will not know emotional rapture until she meets the Black Irish orphan and self-made financier Patrick Shannon.

Daisy meets Shannon in Kentucky, where she is subtly scoring up portrait commissions. There she also meets the chic, homosexual, and married Robin and Vanessa Valerian. In a tangential sex scene Vanessa seduces her and Daisy's hostess, Topsy. Meanwhile, back in Manhattan, Shannon hires North and Hammerstein to resuscitate Elstree cosmetics. Shannon proposes Daisy as a figurehead: "A blonde . . . a face . . . a title. . . . Princess Daisy" (347). Daisy is horrified; she treasures her privacy and has:

> a profound fear of being perceived as a particular personality who was called Princess Daisy and who would be photographed and manipulated to sell Elstree in commercials, in ads and on display counters, until her Princess Daisy-ness would be burned permanently into the consciousness of the consumers of the Western world (355).

She is still hiding from Ram.

Now one of London's most eligible bachelors, Ram mortally insults the season's lead debutante, Sarah Fane, by screaming out "*Daisy! Daisy! Daisy, I love you!*" as he takes her virginity painfully and at length (352). In revenge, Fane blackens his name throughout the English upper class. Ram finagles himself and Daisy aboard the Valerian yacht, but when Daisy finds herself at sea with Ram, she demands that Vanessa dock. Anabel develops leukemia, and as Ram refuses to pay for treatment, Daisy becomes "Princess Daisy." Now she is on the other side of the camera, the star of a $20 million advertising campaign (described in depth), both bored and afraid.

Daisy grows close to Shannon, who had a similarly difficult childhood and also owns a lurcher. She tells him about her past, as she has no other man, and he assures her that she did not cause Dani's disability. They consummate their passion at La Marée . . . but does he love her or "Princess Daisy?" Vanessa—still smarting from the yachting fiasco—and Ram arrange to reveal Dani's existence in *People* magazine. How will Daisy react to the exposure of her secret twin? These questions and Ram's incestuous obsession are resolved as the novel climaxes with the launch of Princess Daisy cosmetics in Central Park, complete with troikas, artificial snow, gypsy fiddlers, candlelight, and a million daisies.

Bibliography

Krantz, Judith. *Scruples*. New York: Warner, 1978.
———. *Princess Daisy*. New York: Crown, 1980.

Jeff Solomon

Puzo, Mario (1920–1999)

Mario Puzo is best known for his novel *The Godfather* (1969), a phenomenally successful literary work that launched a series of other novels, films, and American icons. Although the original *Godfather* consisted of a single novel, Puzo collaborated with filmmaker Francis Ford Coppola to produce a film trilogy. The original book sold more than 21 million copies before the first film even appeared, and it stayed at the top of the best-seller list for 67 weeks. Beyond the novels and films, selections from the works often appear in *Bartlett's Quotations*, and even isolated phrases have entered the American vernacular, such as the line immortalized by Marlon Brando in the first film, "I made him an offer he can't refuse."

Born in New York City in 1920, Puzo weathered a difficult childhood typical of many first-generation Italian Americans. Raised in New York's Hell's Kitchen, an impoverished section of New York City, he was surrounded by Italian and Irish immigrants. His father abandoned the family when Puzo was 12, and his mother managed to raise her seven children despite numerous hardships, a feat that left a deep impression on the nascent author. Puzo enlisted in the army in World War II and met his future wife, Erika, when he was stationed in Germany. Their 1946 marriage produced five children, and he remained with her until her death in 1978 from breast cancer. Puzo also suffered from chronic illnesses, including heart problems and diabetes. Beyond his famous Mafiosi novels and a number of more traditional thrillers, Puzo's frequent trips to Las Vegas resulted in his fourth novel, *Fools Die*, in 1978, recalling his gambling experiences and the entire Las Vegas milieu and exploring gambling's significant influence on the U.S. economy and society during the 1950s and 1960s. Just before his death in 1999 he produced his last novel, *Omerta*, an extended eulogy for the conventions of obedience and loyalty that supported the Italian people in the early days of America's Italian immigration.

The astonishing realism of Puzo's Mafiosi characterization resulted in rumors that some key characters actually represented famous historical or contemporary figures, both from Sicily and America. However, Puzo, who typically demurred, interestingly stated in an interview with Larry King that the seminal Don Corleone actually represented Puzo's mother, the abandoned Italian immigrant mother of seven children who raised her children with love and an "iron hand." And indeed, in 1964, prior to his writing *The Godfather*, Puzo created another fictionalized version of his mother in *The Fortunate Pilgrim*. His great respect for his mother was revealed there in the character's phenomenal ability to negotiate a bicultural world, incorporating old-world values into the often violent wisdom of the American streets. Puzo knew that without these traits his family would not have survived the economic and social plights of the 1920s and 1930s. The typical Puzo Mafia plot revolves around a vivid depiction of Italian-American lifestyles, especially those of stereotypical figures of organized crime. Himself a first-generation Italian American, Puzo classically introduces readers to memorable cultural elements of this particular group and to the people, so intrinsic to the evolution of American urban life, who loved, hated, and died for them.

Capitalizing and expanding on his *Godfather* success, Puzo wrote *The Last Don* (1996) and *The* SICILIAN (1984). Set in 1950 at the end of the two-year Sicilian exile of Michael Corleone (the youngest son of Vito in the Godfather series), the latter focuses on the exploits of legendary Sicilian bandit Salvatore Giuliano.

The Fourth K, written in 1990, marked a significant, and in the circumstances, risky departure from Puzo's strong suit but deftly captures the intrigues of international terrorism on America's home turf. Written almost a decade before the horrific September 11 Twin Towers tragedy in New York City, the novel is at times, both in theme and tone, chillingly prophetic.

Puzo's novels center on human failings and weaknesses that ironically emerge from the acquisition of immense and often fatal power. As a student at Columbia University, where he focused on social and economic courses, the future author fused his academic knowledge with observations from his rich and often violent personal experience, and this union proved a fecund basis for his later fictive explorations of the abuses consequent on greed and acquisitiveness. For example, the call to the young Michael Corleone to forsake his ordinary world of quotidian decency in order to aid his family in their "special" world of organized crime finally results, for all its spectacular gain, in the loss of everything he truly valued. Indeed, his own family, the very family that had embraced him as its leader, finally abandons him when he needs it most. Stylistically, Puzo's entire oeuvre, from its depiction of the island enclaves of *The Sicilian* and through the seething streets of Italian-American New York to the vast international stage of *The Fourth K* reveals an exceptional storyteller's instinct for rendering immanent in even the most minute details of unreflective life resonant and far-reaching, almost mythological elements of universal human experience—and fixing those elements in the reader's imagination with unforgettable force and piquancy.

Known mainly for his famous Italian-heritage novels, Puzo is often overlooked for his excellent work as a screenwriter for such successful films as *Earthquake* (1972), *Superman* (1972), *Superman II* (1981), *Cotton Club* (1984), and *Christopher Columbus: The Discovery* (1992).

Bibliography

Puzo, Mario. *The Fortunate Pilgrim.* New York: Lancer Books, 1965.

———. *The Godfather.* New York: G.P. Putnam's Sons, 1969.

———. *The Sicilian.* New York: Simon and Schuster, 1984.

———. *The Fourth K.* New York: Random House, 1991.

———. *The Last Don.* New York: Random House, 1996.

JoNette LaGamba

Quinn, Julia (Julie Pottinger) (1970–)

Julia Quinn is one of the most popular authors of Regency-set historical romances. She has published 16 books with Avon. In addition, she has contributed several novellas to anthologies, and "Second Epilogues" to some of her novels have been released as e-publications.

A graduate from Harvard and Radcliffe, Quinn had originally planned to enter medical school. Before she could, however, her first two novels, *Splendid* (1995) and *Dancing at Midnight* (1995), had become the subject of a fierce bidding war between two publishers, and the medical career yielded to that of best-selling author, who has been featured in *Time* magazine and whose novels have been nominated for several prizes, including the RITA Awards of the Romance Writers of America. In 2001 she debuted on the *New York Times* best-seller list with *An Offer from a Gentleman*, her 10th novel.

Quinn was one of the authors who opened the market for lighter, wittier Regency-set historical novels, her heroes less dark and less dangerous than the typical alpha-male of historical romance and her plots enlivened by sparkling dialogue. Since 1998, when *To Catch an Heiress* was published, the titles of several of her books have referenced film titles, an idea originating, in fact, with her colleague Candice Hern, who had planned to call one of her novels *How to Marry a Duke*, referring to the 1953 film *How to Marry a Millionaire*. Her own editor disapproving of the title, however, Hern allowed Quinn to use the idea for her stories.

Quinn's best-loved books are those of the Bridgerton series, launched with *The Duke and I* (another film reference) in 2000 and ending with *On the Way to the Wedding* (2006), which focuses on the love life of eight siblings in Regency Britain, where, indeed, all her stories are set. Due to this unity of her fictional world, several character crossovers occur, and a number of secondary characters have become highly popular in their own right. Examples include the formidable but lovable Lady Danbury; the Smythe-Smith girls with their terrible annual musicale, first appearing in the non-Bridgerton novel *Minx* (1996) but reappearing in *Romancing Mr. Bridgerton* (2002); and, the witty Lady Whistledown, the mysterious gossip columnist who knows all of the *ton's* secrets and scandals and writes about them in "Lady Whistledown's Society Papers," which themselves frame two spin-off anthologies Quinn wrote with Suzanne Enoch, Karen Hawkins, and Mia Ryan: *The Further Observations of Lady Whistledown* (2003) and *Lady Whistledown Strikes Back* (2004).

Quinn's official Web site can be found at www.juliaquinn.com.

Bibliography

Quinn, Julia. *Dancing at Midnight*. New York: Avon, 1995.

———. *Splendid*. New York: Avon, 1995.

———. *Minx*. New York: Avon, 1996.

———. *To Catch an Heiress.* New York: Avon, 1998.
———. *How to Marry a Marquis.* New York: Avon, 1999.
———. *The Duke and I.* New York: Avon, 2000.
———. *An Offer from a Gentleman.* New York: Avon, 2001.
———. *Romancing Mr. Bridgerton.* New York: Avon, 2002.
———. *The Further Observations of Lady Whistledown.* New York: Avon, 2003.
———. *Lady Whistledown Strikes Back.* New York: Avon, 2004.
———. *On the Way to the Wedding.* New York: Avon, 2006.
———. Interview by Pia Lämmerhirt. *Die romantische Bücherecke.* Available online. URL: http://www.diebuecherecke.de/quinn1.htm. Accessed November 7, 2006.

Sandra Schwab

Rainbow Six Tom Clancy (1998)

TOM CLANCY's 10th novel continues the story of former CIA operatives John Clark and Domingo "Ding" Chavez, who emerge from the sidelines of earlier Clancy novels such as *Clear and Present Danger* and DEBT OF HONOR to occupy central positions here. The events of *Rainbow Six* follow those of Clancy's *Executive Orders,* in which Clark and Chavez worked with then President Jack Ryan to bring about the assassination of the Iranian ayatollah who had unleashed a series of terror attacks on the United States. Once again the threat of bioterrorism looms, but in *Rainbow Six* the enemy is within—a radical environmental movement whose members plan to save Mother Earth by eliminating all but a handful of human beings.

As the novel opens, Clark and Chavez are traveling with their wives and British operative Alistair Stanley by air to Hereford, England, where Clark, under the code name Rainbow Six, will assume command of Rainbow, a "blacker than black" (27) antiterrorist squad comprising elite American, British, and selected NATO personnel. The flight is hijacked by a group of amateurish Basque terrorists, providing Clark, Chavez, and Stanley with an opportunity to demonstrate the crack skills and cool professionalism that will mark the new Rainbow squad. Rainbow's two teams have barely begun to train together when their first mission arises: a hostage-taking in a bank in Bern, Switzerland. Another mission follows shortly after, another hostage-taking, this time at the home of a wealthy financial trader in Vienna. The proximity of the two incidents raises suspicions about a possible connection since both involved perpetrators who were once known as hard-core ideologues; the Bern group were erstwhile members of the German Baader-Meinhof Red Army Faction, while the couple behind the Vienna incident claimed membership in the Marxist Red Workers' Faction. None had been heard of for some time, suggesting that someone is waking up Europe's dormant terrorists. A third incident, in a Spanish theme park where French and Basque terrorists take 35 children hostage and demand the release of Il'yich Ramirez Sanchez, the notorious Jackal, appears to confirm the existence of a very dangerous pattern.

Two of the three incidents have been instigated by one man, Dimitriy Arkadeyevich Popov, a former KGB agent now in the employ of charismatic American multimillionaire John Brightling, whose motive for stirring up these terrorist cells is only later revealed to Popov and to the reader. Brightling has made his fortune as head of the Horizon Corporation, a private company engaging in genetic research, including a nefarious secret project to engineer a viral epidemic that will wipe out most of the human race. In Horizon's labs researchers are experimenting on unknowing human subjects to ensure that their new strain of Ebola—dubbed "Shiva"—will annihilate all but a chosen few. The virus is named for the Hindu god who is "by turns the Destroyer and Restorer" (125), an apt designation for a plan not simply to destroy the human race but to restore the world's natural harmony by doing so—ridding it of its most deadly parasite, humankind. A handful of carefully chosen human survivors, the beneficiaries of Brightling's "Project Lifeboat," will remain to enjoy a natural world restored to its proper balance.

As Rainbow comes uncomfortably close to discovering Brightling's furtive operation, his resident terrorism expert, a former FBI agent, decides to strike directly at Clark's group. Through Popov he hires a handful of Marxist IRA operatives to storm the Hereford community hospital where Clark and Chavez's wives both work; but owing to the overwhelming superiority of the Rainbow unit, the plan goes badly awry, and some of the terrorists, as well as their leader, are captured and interrogated, providing information that points in the direction of the elusive Popov and his equally elusive employer. Meanwhile, Brightling's plans move ever closer to fruition, and Popov, a guest in Project Lifeboat's Kansas facility, finally learns of the planned holocaust. Horrified by the plan, he flees and makes contact with Jack Ryan, who is thus able to foil the terrorist plot. Brightling and his followers destroy all the evidence of the Shiva project and flee to a second facility in the Brazilian jungle, where they expect to remain free from prosecution. However, Jack Ryan and his Rainbow team have other plans.

Clancy's depiction of the terrorist mindset is a key theme of *Rainbow Six,* with each of its violent episodes offering a similar lesson in the moral pathology of the terrorist, whose humanity is overridden by ideology, frequently the ideology of the extreme political left, a favored target of Clancy's fiction. Of the Marxist Irish republican Sean Grady, the contemptuous Popov thinks he "had replaced his humanity with a geometrically precise model of what the world should be—and he was too wedded to that vision to take note of the fact that it had failed wherever it had been tried" (577). The environmental movement, as Clancy portrays it, is a similarly lunatic fringe, and its apparently harmless supporters are mocked by a range of characters as naive "tree huggers" or risible vegans. But lurking behind this nonthreatening facade is a sinister potential for mayhem, as becomes clear when one environmentalist after another is easily recruited into Brightling's deadly club. In the world of *Rainbow Six* long-established and relatively mainstream organizations such as Friends of the Earth and the Sierra Club are barely distinguished from the considerably more radical Earth First organization, and all rest on a continuum that leads to the Horizon experimenters, who murder their human subjects and plan the greater annihilation of their race with equal lack of compunction. Whatever their particular cause, Clancy's terrorists are uniformly zealots dehumanized both by simplistic and inflexible thought as well as automatonic existence.

According to Rainbow's resident expert, psychiatrist Paul Bellow, theirs is a way of thinking entirely at odds with "his own supremely rational outlook on reality" (332). However, the dividing line between the "good guys" and "bad guys" may not be quite so clear to all of the novel's readers, and the author seems both aware of that possibility and keen to refute it. Like the terrorists they pursue, Clark, Chavez, and the other members of the Rainbow squad occasionally take it upon themselves to operate well beyond the restrictions of the law, administering rough justice, for example, to the man who killed the sole child victim of the Worldpark incident and using deceptive measures and intimidation to interrogate two of the Irish terrorists behind the hospital attack. Most dramatically, in the novel's climax, Clark coldly and deliberately abandons the survivors among Brightling's followers to what promises to be a cruel death in the Brazilian jungle. To Bellow, however—and it would appear to the author of *Rainbow Six*—the distinction is clear, and it resides in each group's chosen cause: Where Clark's agents break the rules, they do so in order ultimately to protect them. Far from the moral minefields in which wander the fictional creations of Graham Greene or JOHN LE CARRÉ, Clancy's warriors are, on the whole, impervious to self-doubt and—at least for their creator—invulnerable to critique.

Rainbow Six has inspired a very popular series of video games of the tactical-shooter variety, with the first appearing in 1998 and four more following between 1999 and 2006.

Bibliography

Clancy, Tom. *Rainbow Six*. 1998. Reprint, New York: Berkley, 1999.

Brian Patton

Red Dragon **Thomas Harris** (1981)
Red Dragon is a detective/thriller novel featuring Dr. Hannibal "The Cannibal" Lecter, a brilliant but deranged psychiatrist who, after committing a series of murders, has been incarcerated at the Chesapeake State Hospital for the Criminally Insane. Will Graham, an investigator formerly employed by the FBI, captured Lecter several years earlier but was both physically and psychically wounded in the process. Graham is lured out of retirement in order to solve another serial killing, this time involving the grisly murders of two families. The case proves difficult, and Graham is forced to rely on Lecter's assistance in order to understand the mind of the killer. He eventually succeeds, capturing a disfigured man named Francis Dolarhyde, who calls himself the "Red Dragon" after William Blake's watercolor *The Great Red Dragon and the Woman Clothed in the Rays of the Sun*. As Graham discovers, Dolarhyde works at a video transfer company and has thus gained access to the personal details as well as the security vulnerabilities of the families he murders. Though most of the novel is devoted to the respective struggles of Graham and Dolarhyde, Lecter is the story's overwhelming presence and indeed THOMAS HARRIS's lasting fictional legacy. The author's next three novels, *The* SILENCE OF THE LAMBS, *HANNIBAL*, and *Hannibal Rising* continue the story of Lecter's twisted dealings with law enforcement.

Besides the descriptions of outrageously brutal murders, perhaps the most disturbing element of Harris's work is its insistence on the blurry line separating the law-abiding from the criminal. This troubled boundary is made explicit in the characterization of Graham, who is haunted by the feeling that he is fundamentally very similar to the killers he tracks. A fellow investigator, Jack Crawford, notices that Graham has a tendency to mimic the person he is speaking with, and that this happens "involuntarily," for "sometimes he tried to stop and couldn't" (4). Graham, according to Crawford, has "Imagination, projection, whatever" (10), an exceptional empathy that makes it possible for him to assume, often without wanting to, the malevolent perspectives of killers. Lecter, who is always sensitive to any opportunity for manipulation, repeatedly tries to unbalance Graham by reminding him of this affinity:

> "Do you know how you caught me?"
>
> Graham was out of Lecter's sight now, and he walked faster toward the far steel door.
>
> "The reason you caught me is that we're just alike" was the last thing Graham heard as the steel door closed behind him (86).

Late in the novel Lecter continues his taunting of Graham by insinuating in a letter that they both have taken pleasure in killing (earlier in his career, Graham had gunned down a killer named Hobbs in the line of duty):

> I want to help you, Will, and I'd like to start by asking you this: When you were so depressed after you shot Mr. Garrett Jacob Hobbs to death, it wasn't the act that got you down, was it? Really, didn't you feel so bad because killing him felt so good? (348).

What frightens Graham, and readers, is the difficulty in denying Lecter's claim. The ferocious dark side of the human mind cannot be wholly disowned by the novel's hero, who is also, apparently, the only hope the authorities have for catching those who have fully succumbed to evil.

Dolarhyde himself is an intriguing mix of dark and light. Though he is detestable for having tortured and murdered whole families, Harris makes clear that the killer has been a victim himself, having suffered appalling childhood abuse. Dolarhyde's potential for some kind of redemption is seen in his relationship with Reba McLane, a blind coworker able to "see" beyond his disfigurement and social awkwardness. The tenuous love Dolarhyde finds with McLane holds the promise of delivering him from his grotesque calling, and he even tries to sever his connection to the lethal "Dragon," the dark power he worships, by gaining access to the Brooklyn Museum and devouring the original Blake watercolor itself. Dolarhyde is, we are to understand, controlled by monstrous urges but still recognizably human and all-too-similar to average people.

Another key subplot in the novel concerns the sleazy tabloid reporter Freddie Lounds, who is eventually murdered by Dolarhyde for writing unflattering descriptions of him. Harris further explores here the blurry separation of the normal and the deviant, as he points out the dark similarities between serial killing and its serial mediation. The public's fascination with and trivialization of the lurid details of violent crime is linked to the killer's own perverse imagination. Just as Graham cannot help watching and rewatching the same videos of the slaughtered families that fascinated Dolarhyde, the public obsessively consumes the lurid details of violent crimes. The difference between ordinary and pathological spectatorship becomes very uncertain as anyone can be implicated in a fascination with the particulars of sadistic acts.

The problem of this intimacy between the civilized and the barbaric is resolved, if a little uneasily, at the conclusion of the novel, when Graham considers that his own murderous impulses—when acknowledged, controlled, and put in the service of humanity—may be a necessary means for protecting civilized existence:

> Graham knew too well that he contained all the elements to make murder; perhaps mercy too.
>
> He understood murder uncomfortably well, though.
>
> He wondered if, in the great body of humankind, in the minds of men set on civilization, the vicious urges we control in ourselves and the dark instinctive knowledge of those urges function like the crippled virus the body arms against.
>
> He wondered if old, awful urges are the virus that makes vaccine (454).

By the novel's end it is this slim hope that Graham must cling to when contemplating his difference from those who give in to evil.

Lecter, who occupies the imaginative center of the novel, is a remarkably compelling character. His appeal has much to do with the way he combines extreme viciousness with a finely polished veneer of high-cultural sophistication. Trained as a psychiatrist to penetrate the human psyche and knowledgeable about a seemingly infinite number of subjects, Lecter represents a sort of parody of the hypercultivated human: His murderousness is concealed behind all the markings of a civilized existence. By manipulating others and, when he can, literally consuming them, Lecter pursues his calling as an aesthete, forging an idiosyncratic artistic vision through violently transgressive acts. Even when confined in a heavily secure mental institution, with very limited access to resources, he is able to script a number of bloody dramas in the outside world. The most impressive of these involves his discovery of Graham's home address and his goading of Dolarhyde into an attack on Graham and his family.

While Dolarhyde's psychopathology is to some extent explained away as the product of an abusive childhood and physical disfigurement, Lecter remains by the novel's end a compelling mystery. Dr. Frederick Chilton, the chief of staff at the state hospital where Lecter is being held, calls his patient "a pure sociopath," though that tag hardly does justice to the complexity of the man. Chilton reveals that he had hoped to study Lecter and gain some insight into his inner workings but laments that even after years of scrutiny, "I don't think we're any closer to understanding him now than the day he came in" (77). This unfathomable quality is essential to Lecter's enduring allure. Though physically captured, he is somehow beyond the comprehension of all those who would seek to know what motivates him.

Dolarhyde idolizes Lecter and is himself an aspiring aesthete. Shunned by others for his physical disfigurement and social awkwardness, he cultivates a private world of beauty and esoteric wisdom. The name he has chosen for himself, which distinguishes him not just as a powerful figure but as a connoisseur of fine art, as well as his knowledge of technology and Asian languages, separates him from the ordinary mass of men. As Dolarhyde sees it, his personal growth, or "Becoming," involves exercising his rare powers in a predatory campaign against those who oppose him. The basis of this campaign, which finds its inspiration in Lecter's forbidding example, is the assumption of a radical artistic license:

> [. . .] In Dolarhyde's mind, Lecter's likeness should be the dark portrait of a Renaissance

> prince. For Lecter, alone among all men, might have the sensitivity and experience to understand the glory, the majesty of Dolarhyde's Becoming.
>
> Dolarhyde felt that Lecter knew the unreality of the people who die to help you in these things—understood that they are not flesh, but light and air and color and quick sounds quickly ended when you change them. Like balloons of color bursting. That they are more important for the changing, more important than the lives they scrabble after, pleading.
>
> Dolarhyde bore screams as a sculptor bears dust from the beaten stone (121).

In such a scheme the world becomes this dark artist's canvas, its inhabitants mere material for the realization of his grand vision.

A good deal of Harris's novel is concerned with the techniques used by investigators in tracking down Dolarhyde. Among these are the analysis of tooth marks made by the killer at the crime scenes, fingerprints left on the cornea of a victim, and a psychological profile of the killer delineating his secret psychological motivations. The FBI's massive technological apparatus is ultimately shown to be inferior, however, to the eerie empathy Graham is able to conjure for Dolarhyde. While institutional forces contribute to the capture of the killer, it is a remarkable individual standing outside the official channels who proves to be the decisive factor in the case.

Harris's novel has been adapted into two films: the first, *Manhunter,* appeared in 1986; the second, which kept the title *Red Dragon,* appeared in 2002 and starred Anthony Hopkins and Edward Norton.

Bibliography

Harris, Thomas. *Red Dragon.* 1981. Reprint, New York: Dell, 1990.

———. *The Silence of the Lambs.* New York: St. Martin's, 1991.

———. *Hannibal.* New York: Dell, 2000.

———. *Hannibal Rising*: New York: Delacorte, 2006.

Geoff Hamilton

Redfield, (Brian) James (1950–)

Redfield is a therapist turned New Age author whose novels have sold millions of copies worldwide. Born to a Methodist home near Birmingham, Alabama, in 1950, he earned a bachelor's degree in sociology and a master's in counseling at Auburn University. While attending the university, he became interested in Eastern religions, especially Taoism, Hinduism, and Buddhism, as well as the Human Potential movement. In 1974 he began his career as a therapist for abused children and adolescents in Auburn, later in Birmingham, applying the ideas of psychic phenomena and intuition to counseling practice. As an author, now of international reknown, he has written about human spiritual awareness, blending insights from Eastern and Western traditions. He is also actively involved in the global campaign to protect the remaining wilderness areas.

In 1989 Redfield began to write full time with a novel embodying his New Age philosophy, self-published two years later as *The* CELESTINE PROPHECY: AN ADVENTURE, in which an unnamed American protagonist discovers "the Nine Insights" from an ancient Peruvian manuscript and comes thereby to understand how an individual can obtain a connection to the Divine and use sacred energy for the betterment of human society. Redfield sold 100,000 copies of the novel from his car before it drew the attention of Warner Books, which purchased the copyright and published it in 1993. It became an instant publishing sensation, selling millions of copies both in the United States and abroad, and was number one on the *New York Times* best-seller list, remaining there for three years.

The Tenth Insight: Holding the Vision, the best-selling sequel to *The Celestine Prophecy,* was published in 1996. Set in the Appalachian Mountains, the novel describes an adventurous search for the "Tenth Insight," taking readers into other dimensions, memories of past experiences and other centuries, to death and the afterlife, to heaven and hell, and finally to what Redfield calls "the World Vision."

In his first nonfiction book, *The Celestine Vision: Living the New Spiritual* (1997), Redfield discusses the historical and scientific background of the global renaissance of new spirituality, focusing on mysterious coincidences, the relationship between Eastern spirituality and Western science, and the purposefulness of human history, finally offering an optimistic vision of human destiny in which miracles and scientific discoveries are complementary and thus can be combined to create a better world.

Redfield's third adventure novel, *The Secret of Shambhala: In Search of the Eleventh Insight* (1999) is set in Shambhala (also known as Shangri-La), in the Tibetan Mountains, where residents maintain their ancient spirituality untainted by modern lifestyle. Here the protagonist obtains his "Eleventh Insight," according to which intentional, positive prayer can be materially beneficial to society as well as individuals. Redfield's latest major work, *God and the Evolving Universe: The Next Step in Personal Evolution* (2002), written with Michael Murphy and Sylvia Timbers, examines the history of human consciousness, the emergence of the new spiritual potential, and the need to transform culture through exercising a will beyond ego and experiencing integration and the synchronistic flow.

The commercial success of the Celestine series has led to the production of several guidebooks and adaptations. *The Celestine Prophecy* itself evolved into a sound recording (1996), a video recording (2006), and two hands-on guides, *The Celestine Prophecy: An Experiential Guide* (1995) and *The Celestine Prophecy: A Pocket Guide to the Nine Insights* (1996). Works accompanying *The Tenth Insight* include a sound recording (1996), *The Tenth Insight: Holding the Vision: An Experiential Guide* (1996), and *The Tenth Insight: Holding the Vision: A Pocket Guide* (1997). *The Song of Celestine* (1998) is an adaptation of *The Celestine Prophecy* designed for children.

Redfield's works have been translated into many languages—as of this writing *The Celestine Prophecy*, for example, has 37 foreign editions—and Redfield has received several notable honors. In 1997 he was awarded the Medal of the Presidency of the Italian Senate at the XXIII Pio Manzu International Conference in Rimini, Italy. He also received the Humanitarian of the Year Award from Auburn University in 2000 and the World View Award from the Wisdom Media Group in 2004.

Bibliography

The Celestine Prophecy. Directed by Armand Mastroianni. Sony Pictures Home Entertainment, 2006.

Franke, Christopher. *The Celestine Prophecy: A Musical Voyage*. Priority Records, 1996.

Redfield, James. *The Celestine Prophecy: An Adventure*. New York: Warner, 1993.

———. *The Celestine Prophecy: An Experiential Guide*. New York: Warner, 1995.

———. *The Celestine Prophecy: A Pocket Guide to the Nine Insights*. New York: Warner, 1996.

———. *The Tenth Insight: Holding the Vision*. New York: Warner, 1996.

———. *The Tenth Insight: Holding the Vision*. New York: Time Warner AudioBooks, 1996.

———. *The Tenth Insight: Holding the Vision: An Experiential Guide*. New York: Warner, 1996.

———. *The Celestine Vision: Living the New Spiritual Awareness*. New York: Warner, 1997.

———. *The Tenth Insight: Holding the Vision: A Pocket Guide*. New York: Warner, 1997.

———. *The Secret of Shambhala: In Search of the Eleventh Insight*. New York: Warner, 1999.

———, and Carol Adrienne. *The Celestine Prophecy: An Experiential Guide*. New York: Warner, 1995.

———, and Dee Lillegard. *The Song of Celestine: Inspired by The Celestine Prophecy*. Boston: Little, Brown, 1998.

———, Michael Murphy, and Sylvia Timbers. *God and the Evolving Universe: The Next Step in Personal Evolution*. New York: Jeremy P. Tarcher/Putnam, 2002.

John J. Han

Rice, Anne (1941–)

Best known for her intriguing gothic tales of vampires, witches, ghosts, and other supernatural exotica, Rice has a devoted following of readers who have created Web sites, organized book clubs, and even camped outside her Louisiana mansion. Many critics, in fact, have attributed the popularity of the "goth" lifestyle to the direct and indirect influence of her writings, which, though they include genres other than horror, are most notable for the immensely popular Vampire Chronicles; these alone have created a cultlike following and made her one of the leading contemporary American novelists.

Rice was actually born Howard Allen O'Brien in 1941 in New Orleans to Katherine (Allen) and Howard O'Brien, but abruptly (and perhaps understandably) changed her name at the age of five just as her mother was preparing to introduce her to her first-grade teacher. Before Katherine could state her daughter's name, the young girl introduced herself as "Anne O'Brien." Even during her elementary school days Rice's interest in writing was pronounced as she produced several short plays and stories, and the practice would take on an almost therapeutic aspect as her life became more difficult.

During Rice's teen years the O'Brien household was under financial stress. Her father was working two jobs, and her mother, finding money worries, running the household, and taking care of her four daughters to be overwhelming, turned to alcohol, which led to her death in July 1956, when Anne was only 15. Anne's father then remarried and relocated the family to Texas in 1958, where Anne would meet her future husband, Stan Rice.

In 1959 Anne enrolled at Texas Woman's College but left after a year and moved to San Francisco, where Stan and Anne would later be married in 1961. Shortly thereafter Anne returned to college and earned a B.A. in political science from San Francisco State University in 1964. A year later she had her first short story, "Oct. 4, 1948," published in *Transfer.*

In 1966 a daughter Michele was born, and four years later Anne enrolled in a master's program in creative writing at San Francisco State University. In the same year Anne was frightened one morning by a dream in which her daughter was dying because of a problem with her blood, a dream frighteningly realized several months later when Michele was diagnosed with leukemia, dying two years later in 1972. Michele's death devastated the Rices, and both turned to drinking; yet even in the midst of this troubled time Rice wrote her first novel, *Interview with a Vampire* (1976), the first in the Vampire Chronicles, in only five weeks. The novel, framed as an interview between a young reporter and Louis, a 25-year-old man who became a vampire in 1790, establishes with great authority the central themes of alienation, hypereroticism, and profound moral ambivalence that dominate her oeuvre.

In 1979 Anne gave birth to her second child, a son named Christopher, and both Anne and Stan decided to quit drinking because they did not want their child to grow up with alcoholic parents. It was also around this time that Anne took a break from her vampire tales and turned to her love of history, publishing *Feast of All Saints* (1979), *Cry to Heaven* (1982), and *The Mummy, or Ramses the Damned* (1989), historical novels rich in local ambience and detail but thematically similar to her supernatural narratives. While writing the historical novels, Rice also wrote a number of erotic novels under the pseudonym A. N. Roquelaure: *The Claiming* (1983), an erotic version of *Sleeping Beauty; Beauty's Punishment* (1984); and *Beauty's Release* (1985). Using the name Anne Rampling, she wrote *Exit to Eden* (1985) and *Belinda* (1986).

Returning to her vampire novels, Rice followed *Interview with a Vampire* with *The Vampire Lestat* (1985), in which Lestat is now a famous 1980s rock star who dresses as a vampire and whose fans do not realize he is telling them the truth in his songs and autobiography, truth that his fellow vampires violently attempt to suppress. The third novel in the chronicles is *Queen of the Damned* (1988), which describes Akasha, the mother of all vampires, who wants to kill all men and have the earth populated only by females.

Around this time Anne and Stan, himself now a well-published poet, returned to live in the Garden District of New Orleans. In the early nineties, after the death of her father in 1991, Rice commenced a new fictional venture, which again echoes her overarching thematic concerns but explores them with greater and more philosophical penetration. LIVES OF THE MAYFAIR WITCHES includes *The Witching Hour* (1990), *Lasher* (1993), and *Taltos* (1994) and chronicles the subtle, far-reaching, and ultimately catastrophic interaction over several millennia between humankind and the Taltos, a near immortal but dying race of powerful but childlike homunculi, one of whom, the complex almost Shakespearean Lasher, seeks to populate the earth with his own kind and rid it of the human species.

Even in the midst of this prodigious enterprise, almost as if she were returning to her fictive home, Rice resumed her vampire tales with *The Tale of the Body Thief* (1992), in which Lestat, at last utterly alienated from his fellow vampires, attempts to relearn how to be human.

In 1994 the movie versions of *Exit to Eden* (October) and *Interview with a Vampire* (November) were released, and Rice's popularity climbed to new heights. Her output kept pace with the release of *Memnoch* (1995), *Servant of the Bones* (1996), *Violin* (1997), *The Vampire Armand* (1998), and *Pandora* (1998), a fictional spin-off of the chronicles, itself followed by a sequel, *Vittorio* (1999).

Then, found in a coma, Rice was rushed to the hospital in December 1998, and after numerous tests she was diagnosed with diabetes mellitus or type 1 diabetes. Near to death and paralyzed for a time, Rice has since become a strong advocate for diabetes testing. The writing and its salutary effects continued, however, with further entries in the chronicles: *Merrick* (2000), *Blood and Gold* (2001), and *Blackwood Farm* (2002).

But then came another medical emergency, a ruptured appendix; and now, at last, even the author's hardiest secular habits and convictions yielded to a sense of divine force and fatality. After years of skeptical (but never cynical) apostasy, Rice returned to Catholicism in 1998, and to signify the return, she and Stan were married again in the very church that Anne attended as a young girl. In that same year Stan was diagnosed with a brain tumor. He would die four years later.

Devastated by this latest blow, Rice nonetheless continued to write, publishing *Blood Canticle* in 2003. But her health, particularly her weight, crucial to the delicate balance demanded by diabetes, became disordered, and Rice decided to have gastric bypass surgery. In 2004 she left New Orleans, the scene of so much of her life and work, and moved to California to be closer to her son, a published novelist. Yet once again she was struck down and rushed into surgery for an intestinal blockage.

In October 2005 Rice announced in a *Newsweek* article that she would "write only for the Lord" (Gates 35) and soon published *Christ the Lord: Out of Egypt* (2005), the first in a trilogy about Jesus, narrating the Passion from Jesus' perspective. The second installment, *Christ the Lord: The Road to Cana*, was published in 2008 as well as the memoir *Called Out of Darkness: A Spiritual Confession*.

She currently lives and writes in California with her five Siberian cats.

Bibliography

Gates, David. "The Gospel According to Anne." *Newsweek*, 31 October 2005.

Roberts, Bette B. *Anne Rice*. New York: Twayne, 1994.

Wadler, Joyce. "Anne Rice's Imagination May Roam Among Vampires and Erotica, but Her Heart Is Right at Home." *People Weekly*, 5 December 1988, 3.

Candace Henry

Ripley, Alexandra (1934–2004)

The author of seven popular works of historical fiction between 1981 and 1996, Ripley achieved her greatest fame and commercial (if not critical) success when selected by the Margaret Mitchell estate to write the long-awaited sequel to Mitchell's *Gone with the Wind*. SCARLETT appeared in 1991 accompanied by huge publicity (it was excerpted in *Life* magazine) and massive sales but largely unfavorable reviews.

A native of Charleston, South Carolina, Ripley (the surname of her first husband) was born Alexandra Braid. Attending Charleston's Ashley Hall finishing school and then Vassar on a scholarship funded by the United Daughters of the Confederacy, she knew well the social conventions and mindset of her fellow descendants of the Old South, and she deployed this knowledge, writing with great assurance and seeming effortlessness in her first historical novel, *Charleston* (1981). Beginning in 1864 and tracing the varied fortunes of the Tradd family from the last year of the Civil War through Reconstruction and beyond, *Charleston* proved a memorable best seller, demonstrating Ripley's skill with dialogue and multilayered narrative, as well as her intimate familiarity with her native Charleston, its history, traditions, and landmarks. A sequel, *On Leaving Charleston*, appeared in 1984 and picked up the Tradd saga in the early 20th century; for her third major effort Ripley remained in her native South but switched locales for the antebellum *New Orleans Legacy* (1987).

The result of these three best-selling novels led to her being tapped for the *Scarlett* assignment, reigniting a project that had first been given a go-ahead by the Mitchell heirs in the 1970s (originally assigned to biographer Anne Edwards). Largely unknown to readers outside of historical fiction/romance circles, Ripley suddenly found herself the object of intense media attention. But lacking Mitchell's sensitivity or psychological insight, Ripley's interpretations of Scarlett, Rhett, and company reduced the characters to stock romantic types, while her rendering of the O'Hara-Wilkes-Butler world seemed safe and sanitized. Perhaps most telling was her own assessment: "I really don't know why Scarlett has such appeal. When I began writing the sequel, I had a lot of trouble because Scarlett is not my kind of person. She's virtually illiterate, has no taste, never learns from her mistakes" (Brainy Quote).

Nonetheless, the book was a huge commercial success, selling 8 million copies in five years, and was loosely adapted into a four-hour miniseries that premiered in the fall of 1994, garnering high ratings and again critical derision.

Ripley would return to the pre-20th-century South once more for her 1994 novel, *From Fields of Flowing Gold,* set against the backdrop of Virginia's tobacco industry following the Civil War. Less than enthusiastic reviews and limited sales may have prompted Ripley to look elsewhere for her final novel. Having earlier left the South in *The Time Returns* (1985), centered in Medicean Florence, Ripley here ventured even further—and further back in time to biblical days—for *A Love Divine* (1996), which imagines the life and struggles of Joseph of Arimathea.

Ripley's last published writing was a chapter of the cooperative murder mystery *The Sunken Sailor,* coauthored with 13 others.

Bibliography

Ripley, Alexandra. *Charleston.* New York: Doubleday, 1981.

———. *On Leaving Charleston.* New York: Doubleday, 1984.

———. *The Time Returns.* New York: Doubleday, 1985.

———. *New Orleans Legacy.* New York: Macmillan, 1987.

———. *Scarlett: The Sequel to Margaret Mitchell's Gone with the Wind.* New York: Warner, 1991.

———. *From Fields of Gold.* New York: Warner, 1994.

———. *A Love Divine.* New York: Warner, 1996.

———, et al. *The Sunken Sailor.* New York: Berkley, 2004.

"Alexandra Ripley," obituary in *The Telegraph,* 26 January 2004. Available online. URL: http://www.telegraph.co.uk/core/Content/display. Accessed May 26, 2007.

Brainy Quote. "Alexandra Ripley Quotes." Available online. URL: http://www.brainyquote.com/quotes/authors/a/alexandra_ripley.html. Accessed May 26, 2007.

Michael McMurray

Ripley under Water

Patricia Highsmith (1991)

The fifth and final installment in a series commonly referred to as the "Ripliad," *Ripley under Water* concludes the chronicle of the reprehensible exploits of Tom Ripley, first introduced in *The Talented Mr. Ripley* (1955), who remains the same amoral sophisticate with sadistic tendencies, struggling with neurotic fantasies and violent inclinations.

Compared to the two other amoral and sophisticated serial killers famous in 1991—Hannibal Lecter in *The* S*ILENCE OF THE* L*AMBS* and Patrick Bateman in *American Psycho*—Highsmith's character seems at times almost quaint. Ripley misses his lovely wife, Héloïse, when she is away, enjoys his small village community without condescension, relishes the company of his friends, and sympathizes with one of his antagonists. And while Highsmith's narratives are rarely as explicit or violent as those of other celebrated thriller writers, *Ripley under Water* seems especially demure, with no murders committed and with the only violence occurring between Ripley and his neighbor after tea.

The story takes place five years after the events featured in *Ripley under Ground.* There Ripley and several collaborators scheme to sell forged paintings, and when Thomas Murchison, an American art collector, confronts Ripley about the scam, Ripley kills him and dumps his body in a canal near Ripley's French chateau. Five years later, Ripley still lives at his "Belle Ombre" ("Beautiful Shadow") in Villeperce, a French village with a "comforting main street" in the scenic Fontainebleau region (18). However, his leisurely bucolic lifestyle of tending his flower garden, playing old English ballads on his harpsichord, and painting landscapes begins to fall apart when Murchison's murder comes back to haunt him in the persons of his new neighbors, David and Janice Pritchard. Ripley notices the Pritchards around town, and their strange, vaguely American behavior encourages him to dub them the "Odd Pair." He comes to believe they are stalking him (and with good reason), so that when he receives a phone call from someone claiming to be Dickie Greenleaf, his first victim, he immediately suspects the Pritchards; his suspicions are confirmed when he visits their house (by invitation) and David mentions Greenleaf before threatening Ripley with his judo skills. Observing their cheap furniture and inferior manners, however, and dismissing David as "an overweight, everyday, mediocre bore," Ripley leaves feeling more annoyed than afraid (42).

But David also mentions Cynthia Gradnor, the fiancée of the artist who forged paintings for Ripley five years before. She hates Ripley and blames him for the suicide of her lover, and Ripley infers a conspiracy between her and David, following up his inference with a call to Jeff Constant and Ed Banbury, friends in London who helped him with the painting swindle. Their inquiries reveal that an American has recently been asking questions about Thomas Murchison, and Ripley decides that the Pritchards are allied with Gradnor against him, with the intent of exposing his role in Murchison's mysterious disappearance. But in typical Ripley fashion, he seems only amused and intrigued by these malicious machinations, and when the Prichards channel Greenleaf through the phone a second time, Ripley "laughed aloud. Games, games! Secret games and open games. Open-looking games that were really sly and secret" (63).

Most of the Ripley novels feature their hero taking some significant jaunt, and *Ripley under Water* is no exception. Though concerns about his nosy neighbors are causing him some minor apprehension, Ripley and Héloïse nonetheless take a long-planned trip to Morocco. But before they leave, he meets with Janice at a local café, and his ingratiating manner eventually encourages her to confide in him that David beats her and is in fact a serial stalker, obsessed with Ripley after seeing him and his fancy clothes in an airport. This disclosure is abundantly confirmed by his following the Ripleys to Tangier, intending to intimidate Ripley but merely being humiliated by him. After a cup of mint tea in a café overlooking the Strait of Gibraltar, Ripley gives David a beating that culminates in conduct self-consciously unbecoming of a gentleman: "Never kick a man when he's down, Tom thought, and gave Pritchard another kick, hard, in the midriff" (106). Then Ripley leaves his wife traveling round the Mediterranean while he quickly progresses to London in order to meet with his old collaborators and further investigate the connection between Pritchard and Gradnor.

Ambiguities of identity, consciousness, and morality may be considered the most prominent themes of PATRICIA HIGHSMITH's Ripley novels, and they are all emphasized here. While in Morocco, for example, Ripley wears a *djellaba* to conceal his identity and twice impersonates a French policeman on the phone in London by disguising his voice; throughout the novel he has difficulty recalling details of his previous crimes, almost as if he had committed them unconsciously or as someone else. In a nostalgic reverie Ripley tries to remember old adventures and wonders why he finds this task so challenging:

> Sometimes his imagination was as clear as a remembered experience. And some remembered experiences faded. . . . There was indeed a screen between fact and memory, Tom realized, though he could not have given it a name. He could, of course, he thought a few seconds later, and it was self-preservation (120).

During his meeting with Gradnor to discuss the Pritchards, Ripley repeats the public record of the Murchison case, proclaiming his innocence. But in his testimony, and finally in his own mind, distinctions between truth and fiction waver and finally collapse: "Tom believed himself, now at any rate. He would go on believing, until any undeniable evidence was put in front of him" (160); his growing inability to distinguish between reality and his own imagining highlights his chronic detachment from the moral codes of society. Highsmith may allude to this metaphorically in describing his meditation on a coming painting: "He thought of his composition, dark, intense, with a focus on a still darker area in the background which would remain undefined, like a small room without a light" (210). Yet in this final chronicle Ripley remains ostentatiously untroubled by his crimes, even as these crimes seem to be taking their toll on his psyche, marking a disassociation even from himself so complete as to be terminal.

The narrative climaxes with Ripley returning to Villeperce, only to find David dragging the canals with large hooks, looking for Murchison's corpse. In due time the body appears on Ripley's doorstep, and Ripley identifies it by Murchison's wedding ring, which he removes before dumping the corpse in the Prichards' pond. David and Janice hear the splash, see the body, and both somehow drown in the murky water attempting to retrieve it. Perhaps it was the pond's cement sides: "'You can't see the cement at grass level,'" Ripley suggests, "'it doesn't come up that high, so perhaps it's easy to slip at the edge and fall in'" (273). And so for his own moral trajectory; but Highsmith only leaves readers with an image of the last piece of evidence, Murchison's ring, slipping beneath the surface of the canal, out of the sight of an approaching policeman, dropped from Ripley's hand.

Bibliography

Highsmith, Patricia. *Ripley under Ground.* 1970. Reprint, New York: Vintage, 1992.

———. *Ripley under Water.* 1991. Reprint, New York: Knopf, 1992.

Michael Mayne

Rivers, Joan (1933–)

Rivers's prolific and eclectic literary output includes eight books—most notably the best-selling novel The LIFE AND HARD TIMES OF HEIDI ABROMOVITZ (1984); several plays, including *Fun City* (1971) and *Sally Marr and Her Escorts* (1994); the film *Rabbit Test* (1978); a column for the *Chicago Tribune* (1973–76); and even a mother/daughter advice column for *McCall's* magazine (1999–2000) along with her daughter, Melissa, with whom she also coauthored a fashion column for *Star* magazine (2002–03).

Born Joan Molinsky in Brooklyn, New York, Rivers was the daughter of Russian immigrants Beatrice and Meyer Molinsky. She attended Barnard College, where she appeared onstage in many college productions and graduated Phi Beta Kappa with majors in English and anthropology. After graduation she worked as a buyer for a department store, marrying the owner's son and divorcing him six months later. She then returned to acting and worked for nearly a decade at comedy clubs in New York City and Catskill Mountains resorts until her famous 1965 appearance on *The Tonight Show* with Johnny Carson. From that point on Rivers's career in show business accelerated as she made numerous television appearances, hosted her own daytime syndicated television show in 1968, became the first permanent guest host for *The Tonight Show,* and was honored with a star on the Hollywood Walk of Fame in 1989.

Rivers's books draw liberally from her own rich life experience, usually presented with a comedic twist, as in the discussion of potty training in *Having a Baby Can Be a Scream,* with its chapter titled, "There's No Such Thing as Kiddy Litter." *The Life and Hard Times of Heidi Abramowitz* (1984) is a short fictional biography filled with quips about its raunchy female protagonist, with chapters such as "Baby Bimbo." *Enter Talking* (1986), written with Richard Meryman, explores Rivers's relationship with her parents, their disapproval of her career choice, and the difficult early years of her career before her breakthrough appearance on *The Tonight Show. Still Talking* (1991) continues the autobiography, reflecting on her personal and business relationship with producer husband, Edgar Rosenberg, and his suicide in 1987. In it she details the extraordinary ups and downs of her career, while offering numerous anecdotes and opinions about celebrities ranging from Michael Landon to Elizabeth Taylor. *Jewelry* (1995) is a departure from her previous books. Although incorporating a host of personal stories, it recounts the history of jewelry designers such as Fabergé and Tiffany, advises how to wear and create jewelry, highlights her own "Classics" collection of jewelry, and includes many color photographs of individual pieces. *Bouncing Back* (1997), a motivational and self-help tool for dealing with grief, offers both humorous and practical advice gleaned from the experience of her own personal losses; a typical reflection:

> When you make your list of things that you believe could make you happy, you may find more than one dream in each category. For instance, you may want to be a surgeon *and* a concert pianist. You probably can't name too many of those, someone who might be fixing a hernia in three-quarter time, but it's all right to let your fantasies fly (190).

From Mother to Daughter: Thoughts and Advice on Life, Love and Marriage (1998), written on a lighter note, incorporates advice on relationships, prompted by her daughter Melissa's wedding. In *Don't Count the Candles: Just Keep the Fire Lit* (1999), Rivers declares, ". . . when it comes to our faces and our bodies, age is a weapon of mass destruction" (162), and advises readers on how to stay young at any age by utilizing a mix of positive attitude and plastic surgery.

While best known for her role as a female comic with an irreverent and sometimes caustic wit, Joan Rivers has also been successful as an entrepreneur (with her own lines of jewelry and cosmetics), motivational speaker, best-selling author, Tony-nominated actress, and fashion critic. She is featured on the cover of Susan Horowitz's *Queens of Comedy* along with famous comedians Lucille Ball, Phyllis Diller, and Carol Burnett; her trademark "Can we *talk?*" as well as the red-carpet fashion question "What are you wearing?" have become part of the jargon of popular culture.

Bibliography

Collins, Nancy. *Hard to Get: Fast Talk and Rude Questions Along the Interview Trail.* New York: Random House, 1990.

Henderson, Kathy. "Joan Rivers' Most Beloved Role." *Child* magazine, 2001.

Horowitz, Susan. *Queens of Comedy.* Amsterdam: Overseas Publishers Association, 1997.

"Joan Rivers' Biography." Available online. URL: www.joanrivers.com.

Pogrebin, Abigail. *Stars of David: Prominent Jews Talk about Being Jewish.* New York: Broadway Books, 2005.

Rivers, Joan. *Bouncing Back: I've Survived Everything . . . and I Mean Everything . . . and You Can Too!* New York: HarperCollins, 1997.

———. *Don't Count the Candles: Just Keep the Fire Lit!* New York: HarperCollins, 1999.

Wagner, Maryanne and American Jewish Historical Society. *American Jewish Desk Reference.* New York: Random House, 1999.

Elizabeth Whitehead

Robbins, Harold (1916–1997)

During a five-decade career as a writer of popular fiction, Harold Robbins sold more than 750 million copies of his 32 novels—nearly half of which have been adapted to film, and in doing so, popularized a genre of fiction characterized by brash dialogue and unapologetic portraits of ruthlessness and ambition.

JACKIE COLLINS, who describes Robbins as "a big inspiration" for her own work, notes that "Really successful writers give their readers a world they know intimately, and Harold certainly knew his world" (31). Born Harold Kane in 1916, Robbins was promptly left at an orphanage in Hell's Kitchen, New York. Although there are conflicting accounts of his early years, Robbins told his biographer and friend Ian Parker that between the ages of eight and 11 he was adopted by a Jewish family called Rubin, whose name he took in 1927, only later legally changing his name to Robbins. At 15 he dropped out of George Washington High School and ran away from home. Having lied about his age, he spent two years in the U.S. Navy, reportedly enjoying the lifestyle he would later explore in *Dreams Die First* (1976), which features a bisexual hero who works in the pornographic magazine business. After the navy Robbins worked in various low-paying jobs, including a brief stint running numbers for a bookie, but by the age of 30 he had already built and lost a fortune speculating in produce and been promoted from shipping clerk to executive director of budget and planning at Universal Studios. At 32 he bet a studio executive that he could write a captivating story, and the result of his winning gamble was his first novel, *Never Love a Stranger* (1948). Its protagonist, who shares Robbins's original surname, is forced to leave a Catholic orphanage at age 16 when it is discovered that like Robbins he is of Jewish parentage, a crisis in identity so destabilizing that he turns to a life of violence and crime, beginning with low-level bookmaking but culminating in wealth and power, all in a climate of racism most egregious to his own psyche.

In the words of his biographer, Andrew Wilson, "As decadent as his fiction was," his lifestyle was "just as profligate. Over the course of his career Robbins spent money as quickly as he earned it, reportedly expending $50 million on everything from booze and drugs to yachts and prostitutes." Thus, it is not surprising that Robbins reached the height of his success when he turned to fictionalizing the debauched Hollywood icons he courted in his own life. Married six times and constantly exposed to celebrity culture at its wildest, he explored the disillusioned, self-interested, often violent impulses lurking beneath the glamorous facade of the Hollywood glitterati. Though always deftly dodging slander, Robbins maintained that his most infamous characters were based on real celebrities he knew, such as Howard Hughes, Marilyn Monroe, and Lana Turner. Thus, a large part of the thrill of reading a Robbins novel lies in the voyeuristic pleasure of observing larger-than-life individuals in their least guarded and most outrageous moments. Given such a lifestyle, he died at the remarkably advanced age of 81 in 1997 in Palm Springs, California, one of the best-selling writers of popular fiction in the 20th century.

Exclusive as the glamorous, often dangerous social circles were that he himself navigated, the cliques featured in a Harold Robbins novel can nevertheless be infiltrated by ordinary men and women. With often shocking audacity, tenacity, and ruthlessness, Robbins's protagonists routinely claw their way from poverty and insignificance to the back rooms where deals are made—the board rooms of the powerful and the playgrounds of high society. The result is a mythic Gatsby-like antihero who in his ascent from rags to riches offers a voyeuristic glimpse into the lives of actual and imagined celebrities, served up with plenty of sex and dialogue astonishingly frank for its day. In *The Lonely Lady* (1977) readers meet Jerilee Randall, small-town innocent, whose quest to make it as a Hollywood screenwriter leads her from a failed marriage through a series of exploitive affairs to both creative and personal independence, as well as fame on a scale even she has some difficulty comprehending. *The Predators* (1998) features the ruthless rise of Jerry Cooper from obscurity in depression-era Hell's Kitchen, pitting his street smarts and will against his relatives, the Mafia, and his own reckless impulses to success in international trading. In *The Storyteller* (1985) screenwriter Joe Crown, irresistible to women and willing to exploit the attraction, trades a life of poverty in the Brooklyn slums for the bedrooms and playgrounds of the Hollywood jet set. As one critic astutely noted as early as 1952, in a review of *A Stone for Danny Fisher*, Robbins's characters "resemble the common man even as their bizarre exploits, fascinating sex lives and heroic struggles exude an air of Walter Mitty" (Lane).

Robbins varied the formula brilliantly in his most successful work, *The Carpetbaggers* (1961), which sold more than 8 million copies and was made into a successful film starring George Peppard. In it the heir to an industrial dynasty, Jonas Cord, loosely based on the aviator and industrialist Howard Hughes, struggles to escape the shadow of a cold and overpowering father. Rich enough to buy everything but the acceptance he most desires, Cord is driven at last to a near hysterical frenzy of domination, crushing some and alienating all whom he encounters, not merely his many enemies, but friends and lovers as well. Graphic, even lurid for its time, the novel was published just at the onset of the sexual revolution, illustrating Robbins's uncanny knack for testing and finally shaping the margins of the permissible. When Michael Korda, an editor at Simon & Schuster, described Robbins's manuscript for *The Storyteller* as "the dirtiest book" he had ever read, Robbins merely responded, "Don't take it so seriously[. . .]. Enjoy it."

By that time he had inspired a generation of other best-selling writers, such as Jackie Collins and SIDNEY SHELDON, whose sensationalistic plots and brash dialogue came to typify the now ubiquitous popular novel.

Thirteen of Robbins's novels have been adapted to film—many of which star screen luminaries such as Elvis Presley, Steve McQueen, Robert Duvall, and Leslie Ann Warren. Since his death in 1997, seven novels attributed to Robbins have been posthumously published, six of which were coauthored by Junius Podrug.

Bibliography

Brennan, Sandra. "Harold Robbins." *New York Times All Movie Guide*, 5 July 2007. Available online. URL: http://movies2.nytimes.com/gst/movies/filmography.html?p_id=108429&mo d=bio.

Collins, Jackie. "Eulogy for Harold Robbins." *Time*, 27 October 1997, 31.

Lane, James B. Review of *A Stone for Danny Fisher*, by Harold Robbins. *Journal of Popular Culture* (fall 1974). Available online. URL: http://galenet.galegroup.com.ezproxy.lib.usf.edu. Accessed June 13, 2007.

Lochte, Dick. "Peccadilloes of the Rich and Infamous: Remembering Harold Robbins." *Salon*, 16 October 1997. Available online. URL: http://www.salon.com/media/1997/10/16robbins.html. Accessed July 5, 2007.

Parker, Ian. "Making Advances." Available online. URL: http://www.publicity4u.com/newyorkermagazine. Accessed July 8, 2007.

Robbins, Harold. *Never Love a Stranger*. New York: Knopf, 1948.

———. *A Stone for Danny Fisher*. New York: Knopf, 1952.

———. *The Carpetbaggers*. New York: Pocket Books, 1961.

———. *Dreams Die First*. New York: Pocket Books, 1976.

———. *The Lonely Lady*. New York: Pocket Books, 1977.

———. *The Storyteller*. New York: Simon & Schuster, 1985.

———. *The Predator*. New York: Forge, 1998.

Wikipedia. "*The Carpetbaggers*." Available online. URL: http://en.wikipedia.org/w/index.php?title=The_Carpetbaggers&oldid=136534668. Accessed July 8, 2007.

Wilson, Andrew. *Harold Robbins: The Man Who Invented Sex*. New York: Bloomsbury, 2007. Available online. URL: http://www.amazon.com/gp/product/product-description/1596910089/sr=1-%20%20%20%20%201/qid=1179671034/ref=dp_proddesc_0/102-3605191-5396912?ie=UTF8&n=283155&s=books&qid=1179671034&sr=1-1.

Priscilla Glanville

Roberts, Nora (1953–)

With more than 160 novels to her credit, 124 having made the *New York Times* best-seller list, Nora Roberts is one of the most prolific and successful writers in America today. Averaging five novels a year, she has seen more than 30 of her novels, including her 2006 release, *Angels Fall*, debut at number one on the *New York Times* list. Currently, there are more than 300 million copies of her books in print.

Born Eleanor Marie Robertson in 1953 in Silver Spring, Maryland, to an Irish-American family, Nora Roberts grew up with four older brothers. She attended parochial school until high school, when she transferred to a public school and met Ronald Aufdern-Brinke, her high school sweetheart and first husband. After graduation they married, moved to Keedysville, Maryland, and had two sons, Jason and Dan. Roberts describes this time as her "Earth Mother" years, a phase when everything was homemade. During this period Roberts started reading romance, especially Harlequin novels. Trapped inside with her small children during a 1979 snowstorm, Roberts sought sanity by "scribbling" her first story on a legal pad, and over the course of the next year she wrote six more manuscripts, all rejected by Harlequin.

However, in 1980 Roberts submitted a manuscript to a new publisher of romance, Silhouette, and *Irish Thoroughbred* appeared in 1981. While not a huge success, it opened the floodgates on her writing career. She published five books in 1982 and 10 in 1983. Divorced from her husband in 1983, Roberts married Bruce Wilder, a local carpenter she hired to build bookshelves, in 1985. The two still live in rural Maryland, where Bruce owns a local bookstore in nearby Boonsboro.

While her first surge in popularity came with the publication of her MacGregor series in the mid-1980s, the novel often credited with bringing Roberts to the attention of the mainstream fiction community is *Montana Sky* (1996). Her first hardback publication, this novel features three sisters brought together after their father's death. The women, previously unknown to each other, find themselves in a perilous situation when an unknown figure begins to terrorize them and the ranch they have inherited. Roberts's more detailed characterization of the women sets this novel apart from her previous works. While most of her novels featured one heroine, *Montana Sky* has three, each of whom represent a type: professional, victim, loner. Each is flawed but through love learns how to see herself differently, and their appeal to readers as convincing types of the average woman accounts in large measure for the novel's success.

Under the pseudonym J. D. Robb, Roberts penned *Naked in Death* in 1995, set in New York City in 2058 and introducing Lieutenant Eve Dallas, a fiery homicide detective. The story describes a postwar society in which science-fiction advances like droid servants and auto-chefs exist alongside a dark world of drugs and murder; the series originates for Roberts an experiment in creating her own world. Readers had no idea that J. D. Robb was Nora Roberts (the "J.D." having been formed from the initials of her sons' names), but while her identity was never a closely guarded secret, the publisher, Berkley, wanted to let readers form a separate allegiance to Robb before publicizing the connection. To date there are 27 J. D. Robb *In Death* novels, 12 making the *New York Times* best-seller list.

According to published reports, Nora Roberts grosses approximately $60 million a year from her writing and owns all the copyrights to her work, yet she continues to maintain a rigorous schedule, writing five to seven hours a day; though perhaps the most famous face of romance, she recognizes the importance of her fans in the form of a Web site (www.noraroberts.com) that sees approximately 2 million hits a month. In addition, dedicated fans have created an online community for "Noraholics" called ADWOFF—the acronym formed from part of a famous Roberts quote: "A day without french fries is like a day without an orgasm." As a member of Romance Writers of America, "The Nora" is the standard of excellence, and she was the first inductee to the Romance Writers Hall of Fame. Publishing novellas with fellow writers and lending her time and talent to charity, Roberts is seen by contemporaries as both a colleague and role model, her unparalleled achievement being recognized with the 2003 release of *The Official Nora Roberts Companion*, a compendium of her published works with commentary from publishers, colleagues, and fans.

Nora Roberts's appeal is multifaceted. Typically employing culture and heritage to shape characters, she is also fascinated by the paranormal, several of her books featuring elemental forms of witchcraft. Her characters are fictional everymen, whether holding blue-collar or white-collar jobs, claiming degrees from the Ivy League or the School of Hard Knocks. Her heroines are spunky, independent, and instantly recognizable; her heroes both manly and sensitive. Marrying dark suspense with clear and accessible character development, Roberts explores the themes of sisterhood, friendship, and personal awareness. By creating realistic yet romantic characters, she creates a vision of the world that is both. She gives voice to both villain and hero, testing her characters by time, circumstance, and crisis. While the relationship between the hero and heroine is inevitably sexual, the heart of the novels is the characters' emotional journey; so that even in works revolving around a psychotic villain or unsolved mystery, the strength of love fosters equally the union of heroine and hero, the resolution of the danger, and the hope for a fulfilling future.

Bibliography

Roberts, Nora. *Irish Thoroughbred*. New York: Silhouette Books, 1981.

———. *Montana Sky*. New York: Putnam, 1996.

———. *The Official Nora Roberts Companion*. New York: Berkley Trade, 2003.

———. *Angels Fall*. New York: Putnam, 2006.

Kelly Rivers

Rollins, James (1961–)

James Rollins is the pseudonym for James Czajkowski. Under the Rollins name he has written eight novels in the action-adventure genre: *Subterranean, Excavation, Deep Fathom, Amazonia, Ice*

Hunt, Sandstorm, Map of Bones, and BLACK ORDER. He is also known to fantasy fans as James Clemens, author of the Banned and the Banished fantasy series and the Godslayer series.

Rollins was born in Chicago, Illinois, and grew up in the Midwest and rural Canada. He attended the University of Missouri with an undergraduate focus on evolutionary biology and received a doctorate of veterinary medicine in 1985. He later opened a veterinary clinic in Sacramento, California, but eventually sold it to become a full-time novelist. His writing career began in earnest at the Maui Writers Conference in 1996, when he entered a manuscript into a writers' contest. He garnered the attention of best-selling author Terry Brooks and this led to the publication of his first fantasy novel, *Wit'ch Fire,* under the pseudonym James Clemens.

Tales of fantastic worlds and dynamic characters have always interested Rollins, who counts Jules Verne, H. G. Wells, Edgar Rice Burroughs, and H. Rider Haggard among his literary influences, along with the old pulp novels featuring heroes such as Doc Savage, Tarzan, the Shadow, and the Avenger. Interested in creating modern versions of these old favorites, Rollins entered the thriller genre in 1999 with *Subterranean.* This story about an expedition into an underworld labyrinth beneath Antarctica has been compared to Jules Verne's *Journey to the Center of the Earth.* He quickly followed up with his second thriller, *Excavation,* which was constructed as a lost-world novel about a forgotten Incan tribe still surviving in the Andes. *Amazonia,* published in 2002, was his hardcover debut and tells the story of a group of scientists and military specialists searching through the Amazon rain forest to find a lost biopharmaceutical exploratory expedition and uncover the secret of a mysterious contagion. It is described by *Publishers Weekly* (March 4, 2002) as "old-fashioned rugged adventure in the tradition of Haggard and Crichton, told with energy, excitement, and a sense of fun"—a typical response to Rollins's adventure fiction.

While his first six novels were considered stand-alones, *Map of Bones* launched a series featuring the Sigma Force, an elite special operatives team for the U.S. Department of Defense. The novel, with its tale of stolen biblical artifacts, killers dressed in monk robes, and a medieval secret society within the Catholic Church has been compared to Dan Brown's *The* DA VINCI CODE.

Although Rollins is noted for his fast-paced plots, it is his seamless blending of scientific concepts, historical mystery, and suspenseful adventure that has become his hallmark. Among the most recurrent themes in his works is the exploration of the physical and ethical dangers of unchecked technological advancements, and Rollins's background in evolutionary biology plays a critical role in his thrillers: *Subterranean* explores the evolution of a species discovered in an underground world; *Amazonia* revolves around animal mutations caused by a tribe's use of a protein that both creates and kills cells; *Ice Hunt* features prehistoric predators roaming an abandoned Russian polar station; *Black Order* tackles the controversy between the theory of evolution and creationism.

Map of Bones was a nominee for the 2006 Barry Award in the Best Thriller category, and *Sandstorm* was named one of the best mystery/thrillers by Readers Read 2004.

Bibliography

James Rollins's Web site. Available online. URL: http://www.jamesrollins.com.

Rollins, James. *Subterranean.* New York: Avon, 1999.

———. *Excavation.* New York: HarperTorch, 2000.

———. *Deep Fathom.* New York: HarperTorch, 2001.

———. *Amazonia.* New York: Morrow, 2002.

———. *Ice Hunt.* New York: Morrow, 2003.

———. *Sandstorm.* New York: Morrow, 2004.

———. *Map of Bones: A Sigma Force Novel.* New York: Morrow, 2005.

———. *Black Order: A Sigma Force Novel.* New York: Morrow, 2006.

White, Claire E. "A Conversation with James Rollins." *The Internet Writing Journal* (June 2005). Available online. URL: http://www.internetwritingjournal.com/jun05/rollins.htm.

Donna Smith

Rowling, J. K. (1965–)

Rowling (pronounced "row" as in boat) is the author of the incredibly popular Harry Potter series, seven novels narrating the extraordinary life of the orphan Harry Potter, who discovers at the age of 11 that he is a wizard. The first four—*HARRY POTTER AND THE SORCERER'S STONE* (*Philosopher's Stone* in Britain), *Harry Potter and the Chamber of Secrets, Harry Potter and the Prisoner of Azkaban,* and *Harry Potter and the Goblet of Fire*—have been made into highly successful films, with the fifth installment, *Order of the Phoenix,* currently in production.

So widespread and enduring is its popularity, the Potter series is held by some to be single-handedly responsible for reversing the decline in reading among children in the last 10 years. While this may be debated, its appeal is clearly unrivaled among contemporary children's literature and has contributed to the success of even faintly similar series, such as the Lemony Snicket novels (A Series of Unfortunate Events, vols. 1–13). The Potter books were as eagerly awaited as installments of Dickens novels over a century ago, with parties held at midnight on the date of release in bookstores around the world and first-run printings of the Potter novels reaching into the millions.

Although there are several unauthorized biographies about Rowling, none benefit from even a single interview with the author herself or her family and so must be read with caution. Rowling maintains a Web site, however, with biographical information and a diary with regular entries about her writing progress and other activities. The site is also designed to entertain younger visitors, with clever hunts for hidden information and "prizes" such as a look at early manuscript drafts or sketches of characters as they developed. The Biography section is both informative and personal, without little obvious bowdlerizing of her past (though some areas are quickly glossed over, most likely to protect her privacy and because her readership is young—she gives very little information, for example, on her first marriage). No pictures of her children are on the Web site, and any other personal glimpses into her life are cleverly hidden among the site's bulletin-board-style background, with its concert tickets, notes on upcoming birthday parties, etc., changing over time. The Web site records that she was born near Bristol and that even as a child her ambition was to become a writer, often creating stories to entertain her younger sister, Di. During her teen years Rowling's mother was diagnosed with multiple sclerosis, which had devastating consequences for the family as they coped with her steady decline. Rowling further records that she studied in Paris as part of her course work during university and lived in London working for Amnesty International after graduating. In 1990 her mother died, affecting Rowling deeply; she states that she moved to Portugal to ease the unhappy memories and took a job as a teacher so she could write in the afternoons. While in Portugal she married but soon divorced, and with an infant daughter in tow she returned to the U.K. to live with her sister. Rowling now lives in Edinburgh with her second husband, with whom she has had two more children.

The popular legend surrounding the creation of the character that would make Rowling the richest woman in Britain is well known—a young single mother living on the dole, writing at coffee shops while her infant daughter slept in the carriage—and has been well publicized in magazine articles and news stories. However, on her Web site she reveals that she began writing about Harry in 1990 and was steadily revising and expanding her manuscript long before her coffee shop days. Nonetheless, she describes her creation of Harry in almost magical terms:

> It was after a weekend's flat-hunting, when I was travelling back to London on my own on a crowded train, that the idea for Harry Potter simply fell into my head [. . .]. To my immense frustration, I didn't have a functioning pen with me, and I was too shy to ask anybody if I could borrow one. I think, now, that this was probably a good thing, because I simply sat and thought, for four (delayed train) hours, and all the details bubbled up in my brain, and this scrawny, black-haired, bespectacled boy who didn't know he was a wizard became more and more real to me.

Rowling's first attempt to get an agent for *Harry Potter and the Sorcerer's Stone* was a failure, but on her second she found one who spent a year trying to find a publisher for the novel, and in August 1996 Bloomsbury Press agreed to publish it, inaugurating the Harry Potter phenomenon.

The Potter world is vividly realized, with wizards, witches, dragons, and other mythical creatures existing unbeknownst to the Muggles (nonmagical folk). Harry is orphaned as a one-year-old and left to be raised by his Muggle relatives, Aunt Petunia and Uncle Vernon Dursley, along with their odious son, Dudley. Harry's parents have been murdered by Lord Voldemort, or "You-Know-Who" as he is fearfully called in the wizarding world. Mysteriously, Harry survives this attack but is left with a lightning bolt–shaped scar on his forehead. Voldemort is somehow defeated by the backlash of the attack and disappears for 10 years, but it is clear he is not dead—only waiting to regain his strength so that he may finally kill Harry and once again wreak havoc on wizards and Muggles alike. On Harry's 11th birthday he receives an invitation by owl post (the wizards' preferred system of mail) to enter Hogwarts, which the Dursleys try to prevent through an amusingly Roald Dahl–like series of misadventures. He enters the school and becomes friends with Ron Weasley, from a large and poor wizarding family, and Hermione Granger, from a Muggle family of dentists. Each book covers one year at Hogwarts, with Harry, Ron, and Hermione facing increasingly dangerous manifestations of Lord Voldemort's growing power; each year also reveals more of Harry's mysterious past as well as his apparent destiny to face Voldemort in a final battle during which one of them must die. In addition, as Harry grows older he must face the usual trials of adolescence, including bullies, girls, loneliness, and other issues of maturation. And his fame as "The Boy Who Lived" creates an extra burden, as some shower him with fawning adulation but the jealousy of others results in sneering and abuse. Typical of heroes in fantasy quests, Harry receives special help from unexpected quarters on his journey and must finally come to terms with who he is—and who he wants to be.

Perhaps Rowling's masterstroke lies in her decision to make Harry ignorant of his wizard heritage so that the reader learns of it along with Harry and identifies with him that much more. Thus, for example, instructions about the intricacies of Quidditch (a sport combining soccer, rugby, and lacrosse while flying on broomsticks) becomes an organic part of the narrative rather than an expositional interruption of the plot. Setting the stories at a boarding school for wizards and witches provides another clever narrative device, explaining and describing via the students' class work the many fanciful spells and magical plants, creatures, and potions that make the Potter world so rich.

Rowling grounds much of her magical world in classical mythologies, particularly those of Britain's Celtic past, skillfully ensconcing these elements in a gothic setting of imposing castles, dark forests, and mysterious circumstances the hero must unravel. In fact, one of the many reasons for the series' success is Rowling's clever blend of narrative elements from many well-known categories and styles, among them English boarding school novels, plucky-orphan tales, Dickensian names and places, gothic mysteries, adolescent coming-of-age stories, and magical fantasy. Comparisons to Dickens are particularly inevitable, both in terms of the series' literary antecedents—*Oliver Twist, The Old Curiosity Shop,* and *Great Expectations* come to mind—and of its cultural phenomenon.

Nor have the Potter novels merely garnered massive sales and critical acclaim; they have spawned a multitude of academic works and conferences as well. "Pottermania" tends to ebb and flow with the release of the books and films so that as fans awaited the final installment of the series; for example, they argued and speculated endlessly on the Internet about the fate of Harry and his friends. But Rowling preserved strict secrecy regarding her work in progress and had great fun both prompting and puncturing the more ridiculous rumors surrounding its outcome. Already having killed off several major characters, for example, in the struggles against the forces of Lord Voldemort, Rowling dropped hints in the media before the publication of the last installment that others would also die.

The films of Rowling's novels have made international stars of the lead actors: Daniel Radcliffe as Harry, Rupert Grint as Ron, and Emma Watson as Hermione, who were all unknown when originally cast. Rowling was reportedly adamant that the films be cast with British actors; a host of British institutions, such as Richard Harris (who played Dumbledore until his death), Maggie Smith, Robbie Coltrane, Alan Rickman, Kenneth Branagh, Gary Oldman, Fiona Shaw, John Hurt, and Ralph Fiennes, have all made appearances in the series.

Bibliography

Dickens, Charles. *Oliver Twist*. 1837–1839. Reprint, London: Penguin Classics, 1985.

———. *Great Expectations*. 1861. Edited by Janice Carlisle. Reprint, Boston: Bedford Books, 1996.

Harry Potter and the Sorcerer's Stone. Directed by Chris Columbus. Warner Brothers Studios, 2001.

Harry Potter and the Chamber of Secrets. Directed by Chris Columbus. Warner Brothers Studios, 2002.

Harry Potter and the Prisoner of Azkaban. Directed by Alfonso Cuaron. Warner Brothers Studios, 2004.

Harry Potter and the Goblet of Fire. Directed by Mike Newell. Warner Brothers Studios, 2005.

Harry Potter and the Order of the Phoenix. Directed by David Yates. Warner Brothers Studios, 2007.

Helquist, Brett and Lemony Snicket. A Series of Unfortunate Events, vols. 1–13. New York: HarperCollins, 1999–2006.

Rowling, J. K. *Harry Potter and the Sorcerer's Stone*. New York: Scholastic, 1998.

———. *Harry Potter and the Chamber of Secrets*. New York: Scholastic, 1999.

———. *Harry Potter and the Prisoner of Azkaban*. New York: Scholastic, 1999.

———. *Harry Potter and the Goblet of Fire*. New York: Scholastic, 2000.

———. *Harry Potter and the Order of the Phoenix*. New York: Scholastic, 2003.

———. *Harry Potter and the Half-Blood Prince*. New York: Scholastic, 2005.

———. *Harry Potter and the Deathly Hallows*. New York: Scholastic, 2007.

———. "Biography." *J. K. Rowling Official Website*. Available online. URL: http://www.jkrowling.com. Accessed November 7, 2006.

Steege, David K. "Harry Potter, Tom Brown, and the British School Story: Lost in Transit?" In *The Ivory Tower and Harry Potter: Perspectives on a Literary Phenomenon*, edited by Lana Whited. Columbia: University of Missouri Press, 2002.

Julie Brannon

The Rule of Four

Ian Caldwell and Dustin Thomason (2004)

The Rule of Four is a skillfully constructed intellectual thriller in which the scholarly pursuit of knowledge is transformed into detective work. The plot revolves around two friends who become perilously embroiled in a centuries-old mystery as they attempt to unravel the secrets of a mysterious Renaissance book; the text intertwines history, philosophy, literature, art, and film, playfully invoking various genres, including the campus novel, the coming-of-age story, murder-mystery, thriller, and romance.

The narrator, Tom Sullivan, and his close friend Paul Harris are roommates in their final semester at Princeton. Both are struggling with the demands of academia and with professional, peer, and romantic relationships; both share a keen interest in a rare and inscrutable book, the *Hypnerotomachia Poliphili*, a puzzling 15th-century text of uncertain authorship that has attracted and perplexed scholars for hundreds of years. Ostensibly a story of love and faith as the hero Poliphilo quests for his beloved Polia, the work encodes in its seven languages, series of illustrations, and preoccupations with eroticism, allegory, and mythology a mathematical labyrinth and powerful secret.

Tom's connection to the text is a deeply personal one; his father had attempted to uncover the novel's mysteries until his untimely death six years earlier. Paul, by contrast, has a scholarly obsession with the Renaissance text, writing his senior thesis on the seemingly unfathomable work. When a key to unlocking the text—a lost diary—is found and a fellow *Hypnerotomachia* scholar is murdered, the two friends' scholarly and personal obsessions conjoin, and they collaborate in order to decipher the text's secrets.

Central to the novel is its nuanced portrayal of the complexities inherent in male relationships; indeed, its title not only refers to a mathematical principle underlying the *Hypnerotomachia Poliphili* but also gestures toward the four friends at the center of the story. In *The Rule of Four* Tom and Paul are assisted and supported throughout their detective work by two other close friends, Charlie and Gil, and as their graduation approaches, the four share common anticipations and doubts, each in their way facing an uncertain even problematic future. Moreover, both Tom and Paul are surrounded by male mentors and father-figures in their work to decode the *Hypnerotomachia Poliphili,* and both are troubled by an obsessive desire to understand the text that disrupts their relationship with each other, with their friends, and with their romantic interests. In fact, as Tom notes:

> My father, who understood the way the *Hypnerotomachia* had seduced him, once compared the book to an affair with a woman. *It makes you lie,* he said, *even to yourself* (98).

Here Tom begins to recognize the immense and multifaceted power of the text, and the tale gradually becomes a suspense-filled struggle to understand not merely the complexities of the book but those of adult life as well.

A dominant theme in the novel concerns the nature of reading and interpretation, which is not surprising given the story's academic setting and the overweening importance of the scholarly work. However, this process of reading texts proves to be anything but straightforward. In one instance Tom describes how, following his father's death, various acquaintances prescribed the reading of particular novels in order to alleviate his grief. However, he questions this notion and reflects upon the limits of interpretation itself:

> My father's death had a nasty finality to it, and it made a mockery of the laws they lived by: that every fact can be reinterpreted, that every ending can be changed. Dickens had rewritten *Great Expectations* so that Pip could be happy. No one could rewrite this (45).

Nonetheless, though at this early stage Tom stresses the limitations of art to shape reality, by the novel's end the recuperative power of texts and art is affirmed, and the intersection of reality and its representations becomes profoundly blurred.

Beyond these sober thematic concerns *The Rule of Four* is a playful and self-aware murder mystery that emphasizes hybridity and complexity as it resists fixed interpretation. Such hybridity is illustrated early on when Tom notes that his dissertation reinterprets Mary Shelley's *Frankenstein,* and the reader gradually becomes aware that he and his friend are coming to resemble the self-isolated scientist of that work as they toil obsessively at their dangerous exploration. And when Tom states, "There's an old saw in Frankenstein scholarship that the monster is a metaphor for the novel," one cannot help but think that similarly the *Hypnerotomachia Poliphili* is a monstrous metaphor for IAN CALDWELL and DUSTIN THOMASON's own work, with the labyrinthine and sinister nature of the medieval text echoed in the complex layering of the *The Rule of Four* itself.

The publication of *The Rule of Four* in 2004 followed the sensational release in the previous year of DAN BROWN's *The DA VINCI CODE,* and their similar themes of history, art, mystery, scholarship, and conspiracy, as well as their narrative focus on portentous, encoded texts, have prompted inevitable comparisons.

Bibliography

Caldwell, Ian, and Dustin Thomason. *The Rule of Four.* London: Century, 2004.

Alison Jacquet

The Runaway Jury John Grisham (1996)

The Runaway Jury is a legal thriller set in Biloxi, Mississippi, about a civil litigation case involving a recent widow and a tobacco manufacturer. The case of *Wood v. Pynex* is far from groundbreaking, just one in a line of many in which actual as well as punitive damages are sought from a cigarette maker; the result would appear to be all but guaranteed, as up until now no jury has ever found in favor of the plaintiff. Nonetheless, Celeste Wood has lost her husband, Jacob, to lung cancer after he has spent all of his adult life smoking, and she chooses to sue Pynex with the help of Biloxi's renowned litigation lawyer Wendall Rohr. Pynex is part of the Big Four, a tight cabal of cigarette manufacturers who have almost unlimited resources to fight any civil case, pooled in The Fund, which has helped them (and other companies indirectly) to be so successful until this time. Rohr, however, believes that he finally has what it takes to win and set an all important precedent in this controversial sphere.

Unknown to Rohr and his team, the Big Four have hired Rankin Fitch, a hardened veteran of judicial venality; manipulative and unscrupulous, he works behind the scenes for vast sums of money to secure a jury that will "work," vote the way he wants it to. It is primarily because of Fitch that the Big Four have yet to lose a trial. Fitch's own crack team is tasked with secretly photographing and researching potential jurors, digging up whatever dirt they can about their past, to either exclude or, better, twist them in the right direction. One man troubles Fitch: potential juror number 56, Nicholas Easter. Easter's past is shrouded in mystery; all that is known about him is that he is a student, works in a computer game store, and is registered to vote in Biloxi. What his real name is, where he came from, what he is studying and where are all unknown to Fitch, who realizes that having Easter on *his* jury is a gamble that he can ill afford.

But Easter has a game of his own: He has a personal interest in tobacco trials and wants to be on the jury, which he achieves due to a stroke of good luck. Working subtly but shrewdly from the inside, he gradually gains control of most of his fellow jurors and manipulates them, and even the judge, without their realizing it. Fitch becomes aware that someone is controlling the jury from the inside but only has contact with Easter's sidekick on the outside, the mysterious Marlee. Marlee baits Fitch by repeatedly calling him prior to the days' proceedings and informing him of what will happen in the jury on a given day, offering to "deliver" his jury for $10 million. At first dismissive, then skeptical, then at last forced to deal, Fitch nonetheless believes he finally has the runaway jury back in hand. But Marlee and Easter have no interest in serving his aim.

Unlike other novels by Grisham, such as *A Time to Kill* or *The Rainmaker*, in which the trial is central to the plot and the courthouse to the setting of the story, *The Runaway Jury*'s complex narrative weaves in and out of the courtroom as if to suggest that in a world saturated with manipulable yet potent information, the traditional, discreet courtroom is no more and its justice a far more complicated affair. There is no detailed narration of testimonies and cross-examinations. The two lawyers, Rohr and Pynex's Durwood Cable, are minor characters, largely acting as legal constants for the true variables of the plot: Fitch, Easter, and Marlee, and the central action of the novel informs the trial from without, instead of being informed by it.

In this way JOHN GRISHAM poses several searching questions to the reader: Should juries remain the essential means of deciding such critical cases when they are vulnerable to corruption? Are children being subtly victimized by cigarette advertisements? Should plaintiffs receive compensation for damage done by cigarettes? And how much and how legitimate is the power that big corporations can exert in juried trials?

Most central is the question of jury corruption, which reaches into the very heart of Western jurisprudence. The novel asks whether the intrinsic trust that societies have in juries is warranted in high-profile cases where both sides will do whatever it takes to win, a very real concern in the United States, at least since the trial of O. J. Simpson. The idea of a randomly selected jury that is representative of the community is already undermined by the jury consultants, who seek to weed out those least congenial to the aim of their paying client. Each of the stories concerning the corruption of jurors in the Pynex case is both compelling and credible. Lonnie Shaver, for example, a black store manager whose goal is to mount the employment ladder, is approached by a sister company of one of the Big Four corporations and induced to vote in favour of Pynex in exchange for his dream job; the Duprees are coerced by pressure from two fake FBI agents hired by Fitch. Easter, meanwhile, answers Fitch's external corruption of the jury with a subtler, but even more effective (and believable) manipulation from the inside, eventually "disposing" of two jurors merely to prove to Fitch his supremacy in the jurors' room.

The Big Four argue that it is the person's free choice to smoke and that because they do not force anyone to buy and consume their products, they cannot be held liable for any damage that the products may inflict on the person's health.

But the effect of advertising on vulnerable children would appear to contradict this argument, and it, too, is searchingly explored in the novel. Typical of Grisham's writing, the novel is short on character description and development but clear and penetrating in its depiction of the machinery and susceptibilities of the American legal system, especially in its reliance on the jury as the essential arbiter of justice. With the steady increase of individual lawsuits against the tobacco companies and the staggering threat of a nationwide class-action suit, *The Runaway Jury,* besides providing a compelling read, promises to be relevant for years to come.

The novel was adapted to film in 2003, but interestingly the film altered the focus of the narrative from cigarette ligation to gun control, probably to simplify the narrative lines. But the essential moral lineaments and characterization of the novel are impeccably preserved, with Gene Hackman delivering a crackling performance as the godlike Fitch, Dustin Hoffman as a somewhat blurry Wendall Rohr, and John Cusack in a minor tour de force as the acutely ambiguous Nicholas Easter.

Bibliography:

Grisham, John. *A Time to Kill.* New York: Wynwood Press, 1989.

———. *The Rainmaker.* New York: Doubleday, 1995.

———. *The Runaway Jury.* New York: Doubleday, 1996.

Victoria Nagy

The Russia House John le Carré (David John Moore Cornwell) (1989)

The Russia House is the last of JOHN LE CARRÉ's explicitly cold war–based novels and the work in which he introduced glasnost into espionage. Typically, le Carré presents the West's ideological confrontations with the Soviets as both personal and reciprocal, the two powers differing little in their willingness to employ the other's methods. If the British have any moral edge, it is only because of their professed support for individual freedom, and even that declaration is often compromised. With *The Russia House,* le Carré indicts both the means and ends of the cold war confrontations, depicting the Western allies—particularly the Americans—as naive when challenged to hope and petulant when faced with a 40-year sham. Rather than celebrating the end of the cold war and its costly, useless arms race, his novel has the quality of a sobering cartoon, casting the West as the Keystone Cops and the Soviets as the Big, Bad Boogie Man.

Typical of le Carré, these revelations are buried in a labyrinthine narrative centered on an unlikely romance. Packing his wares at the end of a Moscow audio fair "for the teaching of the English languages and the spread of British culture," Niki Landau is approached by an attractive Russian woman, Katya. Apprehensively, she persuades him to secretly take "a novel . . . [with a] message . . . important for all mankind" to the English publisher Bartholomew Scott "Barley" Blair, who did not come to the conference.

The setup is vintage cold war, and Niki, eager to be a player, complies. Naturally, he cannot find Barley, who is off getting drunk in Europe, so Niki reads the manuscript, panics, and turns it over to the Foreign Office. FO agents are baffled and, in turn, give the manuscript to the denizens of "the Russia House," a "stubby brick out-station in Victoria."

As the narrator, Horatio Benedict de Palfrey (a.k.a. Harry Palfrey), and other Russia House functionaries discover, Barley is entirely clueless. A middle-aged, heavy-drinking, jazz aficionado, he heads a modest family-owned publishing company and is given to expounding loudly when he has an audience. But on one such drunken occasion, at a Moscow dacha, Barley unknowingly impresses a Russian scientist named Yakov (codenamed Göethe in Operation Bluebird) with his bold affirmations of patriotism and courage, of a democratic New World Order, and of the end of cold war tensions. Yakov is persuaded by Barley's bravado and prepares a manuscript that may, if understood, confirm the Soviet nuclear capabilities as a mere facade. Yakov sees himself as serving Russia and his countrymen by hastening Barley's predicted emancipation; however, all he does in handing over the document is endanger himself, his former lover Katya, and the unsuspecting, reluctant Barley.

In possession of the confusing document, the Russia House officials and their American "Cousins" want Barley, Katya, and more information—but only if it fits their biased outlook. Yakov's notebooks, in essence, divulge that "the Russians can't shoot straight." In fact, the Soviet military behemoth is just that: a fanciful, mythical construct that is eroding from the inside out, with the Soviet Union going broke trying to sustain it.

Captive in the Russia House, Barley naively welcomes the news: "Fortress America should be jumping for joy!" But Russell Sheriton and his fellow CIA interrogators react with disbelief and acrimony. If true, Yakov's information makes the arms race gratuitous: "The entire American military might is invested in the belief that the Soviet hardware is accurate as hell . . . the idea of Soviet supremacy in the matter of ICBMs is the main argument in favour of Star Wars, and the principle strategic fun-game at Washington cocktail parties." Harry, Ned, Walter, and Barley's other British handlers share the American's hostility. After all, Britain cannot continue to profit from the Pentagon's largesse if America discovers the Soviet deception.

Unwilling to get involved, Barley is pressured into finding the unstable scientist/author through Katya, but rather than serving the West, he proceeds to fall desperately in love with Katya. Now, assuming rightly that both sides' intelligence services are following him, he faces E. M. Forster's impossible dilemma: Does he betray his country or the woman he loves? When Yakov is mysteriously "hospitalized," Barley knows that he and Katya are in danger and agrees, therefore, to deliver "a final and exhaustive" list of questions about the manuscript's assertions for Yakov to answer, even though he believes Yakov is dead. During the meeting with Yakov's KGB handlers, however, Barley uses the list to bargain for Katya and her family. His and Katya's future now depend on these shadowy Soviet agents and Barley's naive faith. Barley disappears, letting Sheriton, Ned, and the others believe the KGB took him. Months later, when he appears in Portugal, sober and hopeful, Russia House officials ignore him. Barley then waits, unsure if the Soviets will honor their bargain and release Katya, consoling himself with the conviction that, like any institution, he, too, can justly manipulate and betray when the goal is important.

The Russia House ends with "spying is waiting," a leitmotif that le Carré uses to underscore the boredom and inevitable disenchantment all agents face. But the theme extends beyond a description of geopolitics to characterize the novel and its players. Characters linger or encounter one another in dark, shabby halls, hidden phone booths, rooftop hideaways, and isolated cabins. Every character seems worn out, whether from professional or personal demands. Harry, Ned, Walter, and the other British agents lack enthusiasm for the truth or even for the Great Game, in stark contrast even to le Carré's archetypal reluctant hero, George Smiley. Harry, for example, continually laments his failing relationship with a woman named Hannah; Ned realizes that Barley's defection means his further demotion in the service. Meanwhile, the alternately cynical, brutal, and naive Americans who take over running Barley resent the idea that their demonized Evil Empire may cease to be. The CIA's Sheriton correctly realizes the West's untenable position—after all, "how do you peddle the arms race when the only [fool] you have to race against is yourself"?—yet he knows that the military-industrial agents will likely continue the arms race whether anyone needs the weapons or whether the weapons even work.

Barley and Katya are outlined rather than complex characters, but there is complexity in the outline nonetheless. Barley tells Katya he is an iconoclastic, world-weary man but works vigorously to double-cross the intelligence services by using their methods for his own ends. As a public figure he embraces his irresponsible persona, but when he falls for Katya her love ennobles him. Indeed, their relationship is one of le Carré's most optimistic. Yakov, however, is little more than an ambiguous presence in the novel. He could be a mad scientist driven to his misconceptions by deprivation, or he could be a Russian force for idealism and morality, his character depending on a manuscript that readers never see.

Le Carré summed up the melancholy brought on by the end of the cold war in an address read into the *Congressional Record* (October 4, 1989).

Rhetorically, he asks, "is it possible that after 40 years of being locked into the ice of the cold war, some of us in the West have lost the will, even the energy, to climb out and face a more hopeful future? That after believing so long we could improve nothing inside the Evil Empire, we have to pinch ourselves before we can accept that we really can write tomorrow's script, and help to make it play." His novels after *The Russia House* show him answering his own questions.

Bibliography

le Carré, John. *The Russia House*. London: Hodder & Stoughton, 1989.

LynnDianne Beene

S

Sagan, Carl (1934–1996)

The most popular astronomer of the 20th century, Carl Sagan was also the author of the best-selling CONTACT (1985), a science-fiction novel about first contact with alien intelligence. He had previously won a Pulitzer Prize for nonfiction in 1978 for *The Dragons of Eden,* and his 1980 book, *Cosmos,* was the best-selling science book ever published in English, while the television series of the same name won both Emmy and Peabody awards and was the most-watched series in PBS history.

Sagan earned his undergraduate and graduate degrees at the University of Chicago, then was on the faculty at Stanford and Harvard before gaining a full professorship at Cornell, where he directed the Laboratory for Planetary Studies. He was an active participant in NASA's unmanned space exploration programs, including Mariner, Viking, Voyager, and Galileo, and he served as Distinguished Visiting Scientist at the Jet Propulsion Laboratory, receiving numerous awards, including the National Academy of Sciences' Public Welfare Medal, its highest honor.

His launch into the public eye came when he began appearing on *The Tonight Show with Johnny Carson* in 1977; Carson was an astronomy buff and Sagan a recurring guest on the program. Sagan was also a contributing editor for *Parade* magazine and wrote numerous articles on science topics for the Sunday newspapers.

In his nonfiction writing he explored a broad range of topics, from a mathematical understanding of the probabilities for intelligent life in the universe to the nature of human intelligence, the origin of life, and the intersection of science and philosophy in the public consciousness, all of them themes evident in *Contact.*

The novel's lead character, Dr. Ellie Arroway, is a scientist working in the Search for Extra-Terrestrial Intelligence (SETI) project, using the field of radio astronomy to seek signals that may emanate from intelligent life instead of natural sources. When such a signal comes through, just as she is about to lose her funding, Arroway is thrust into the competing and often conflicting worlds of science, faith, government, and business. Characteristically, rather than design a faster-than-light spacecraft for the adventure that follows, Sagan conceives of an extra-dimensional transport system, noting that he consulted with gravitational physicists to make the science fiction grounded in possibility.

Sagan had originally created *Contact* in 1980–81 as a movie treatment with collaborator and future wife, Ann Druyan, but the feature film starring Jodie Foster as Arroway was released only in July 1997, seven months after Sagan died from cancer caused by a rare blood disorder. The film had the simple dedication "For Carl."

Bibliography

Sagan, Carl. *The Dragons of Eden: Speculations of the Evolution of Human Intelligence.* New York: Random House, 1977.

———. *Cosmos.* New York: Random House, 1980.
———. *Contact.* New York: Simon & Schuster, 1985.

Ronald C. Thomas

Sanders, Lawrence (1920–1998)

Sanders is the author of 38 crime and mystery novels that span a wide gamut of subgenres in the field, from the caper novel and the police procedural to the society mystery and private-eye series. He created a host of popular recurring characters who, though not achieving the status of pop culture icons, have exerted a considerable influence over authors as diverse as THOMAS HARRIS and JANET EVANOVICH, while his books have sold more than 60 million copies in 15 different languages. He also published under two pseudonyms, Mark Upton and Lesley Andress, and his McNally series has been continued by Vincent Lardo since his death.

Lawrence Sanders was born in 1920 in Brooklyn, New York. He was raised in the Midwest and attended Wabash College in Indiana, where he earned a B.A. in 1940. After a three-year stint in the U.S. Marines during World War II, Sanders moved to New York City, where he spent the next 25 years working as a copy editor and writer for *Mechanix Illustrated* and *Science and Mechanics* while also churning out pulp stories and humorous jokes and captions for a wide variety of magazines. Sanders had no children and reportedly never married, though he lived with Fleurette Ballou for more than 40 years. Eventually he retired to Pompano Beach, Florida, where he died in 1998.

A lifelong fan of police and detective fiction, Sanders finally grew tired of editing others' work and decided to write his own. The year was 1968, and the technical magazine Sanders was working for had been printing a host of articles on high-tech spy gadgetry, including surveillance devices. Intrigued, Sanders combined this cutting-edge technology with a classic but ambitious caper premise and wrote *The Anderson Tapes* (1970), which tells the story of a Mafia-backed plan to case and rob an entire luxury apartment complex. Sanders's unique twist on the genre was to tell the entire story through the very police surveillance records that ultimately prove decisive in thwarting the heist.

His second major work, *The First Deadly Sin* (1973), cemented his reputation as a leading crime author and established some of the hallmarks of a Lawrence Sanders novel: graphic scenes of sexuality and death and striking intimacy with the mind of the novel's antagonist to the point that the reader almost sympathizes with the killer. Even the protagonist, retired New York City chief of detectives Edward X. Delaney, is something of an antihero. Gruff, sloppy, opinionated, but dogged, Delaney first appeared as a minor character in *The Anderson Tapes* and was promoted to protagonist because of his popularity with readers, especially female readers. In *The First Deadly Sin* Delaney hunts a killer who uses an ice-ax to slaughter his victims. But the book renders so vivid the perspective of both policeman *and* killer that the antagonist is now seen as a forerunner of Hannibal Lecter.

Sanders often wrote in a quasi-series style, with several novels loosely related by recurring characters or motifs. The Sin series, for example, employed the seven deadly sins as inspiration for the motives behind the crimes; likewise, his Commandments series, commencing with *The Sixth Commandment* (1979) and concluding four books later with *The Seventh Commandment* (1991), clustered crimes and motivations around certain representative transgressions. Others, such as the Tangent series (*The Tangent Objective* [1976] and *The Tangent Factor* [1978]) utilize a particular setting, in this case Africa, as a unifying factor. Still others employ a central protagonist, such as the Wall Street financial detective introduced in *The Timothy Files* (1987).

In 1992 Sanders combined most of these elements in launching the longest series of his career. *McNally's Secret* (1992) introduced Archy McNally, a rakish playboy sleuth who through seven adventures solves crimes for his father's Palm Beach law firm while dining and dating his way through Palm Beach society. Archy represents the antithesis to Delaney, and the McNally novels in general represent a departure from Sanders's earlier series, though his distinctive writing style is everywhere evident.

Sanders, too, has a distinctive way of using setting in his works. The New York of the Sin series;

Africa in the Tangent novels; Washington, D.C., in *The Tomorrow File* (1975); and the posh Florida coast in the McNally series are all as important to the shape and movement of the narrative as the characters themselves, a feat that Vincent Lardo has been unable to reproduce in his generally competent extension of the series.

Bibliography

Grella, George. "Lawrence Sanders." In *St. James Guide to Crime & Mystery Writers*. Edited by Jay P. Pederson. Detroit: St. James Press, 1996.

Kernan, Michael. "The Methodical Master." *Washington Post*, 11 August 1985, G1.

Nelson, Bill. "Expiatory Symbolism in Lawrence Sanders' *The First Deadly Sin*." *Clues* 1, no. 2 (fall 1980), 71–76.

Ringle, Ken. "The Author's Killer Instincts." *Washington Post*, 12 February 1998, D01.

Sanders, Lawrence. *The Anderson Tapes:* New York, Putnam, 1970.

———. *The First Deadly Sin*. New York: Putnam, 1973.

———. *The Tangent Objective*. New York: Putnam, 1976.

———. *The Second Deadly Sin*. New York: Putnam, 1977.

———. *The Tangent Factor.* New York: Putnam, 1978.

———. *The Sixth Commandment*. New York: Putnam, 1978.

———. *The Third Deadly Sin*. New York: Putnam, 1981.

———. *The Timothy Files*. New York: Putnam, 1987.

———. *The Seventh Commandment*. New York: Putnam, 1991.

———. *McNally's Secret*. New York: Putnam, 1992.

Michael Cornelius

Santmyer, Helen Hooven (1895–1986)

As a child Helen Hooven Santmyer yearned to become a writer. Born in 1895 into a family of modest means, she grew up in Xenia, Ohio. Her mother encouraged her ambition, and Santmyer planned on attending college, an unusual goal for a female of the time. She graduated from Wellesley College with a bachelor's degree in literature and composition in 1918.

After graduating, she worked briefly for a suffragette organization in New York City, then became secretary to an editor at *Scribner's* magazine, but she returned to Xenia in 1921 when her mother became ill. She taught English at the local high school, and when her mother recovered, she taught at Wellesley before traveling to England in 1924 as one of the first female Rhodes scholars. She completed a bachelor of letters degree at Oxford in 1927 with a thesis on minor 18th-century novels. Her first novel was published while she was in England. The semi-autobiographical *Herbs and Apples* (1925) concerns an Ohio girl whose plans to go to New York City to become a writer are disrupted by family responsibilities. Santmyer returned to Xenia and finished a second book, *The Fierce Dispute,* in 1928. This tale of the feud between a mother and grandmother over the future career of a young girl had fewer autobiographical elements but was also set in Xenia.

Santmyer moved with her family to California in the 1930s, but her interest in Ohio continued, particularly focusing on Xenia during the period 1860–1932. She returned to the state to become dean of women and head of the English department at Cedarville College, staying until 1953, when the college became a fundamentalist Baptist institution. She then worked as a librarian in the Dayton and Montgomery County (Ohio) Public Library until retiring and returning to Xenia in 1959.

Ohio State University Press published Santmyer's Xenia essays, *Ohio Town,* in 1963, which were well received but did not find a wide audience. The main work of her retirement years, however, was a novel about small-town life in midwestern Waynesboro (a fictionalized Xenia). Unlike earlier satires by Sinclair Lewis and others, she celebrated the timeless, sustaining details of middle-class life. She completed the manuscript in 1975 and submitted it to Ohio State University Press. Before publication, Santmyer had to shorten the manuscript by almost 700 pages, bringing . . . *AND LADIES OF THE CLUB* down to 1,300 pages in two volumes. Sales were modest until it was republished in 1984 by G.P. Putnam's Sons. This time it remained on the *New York Times* best-seller list for 37 consecutive weeks and was made a Book of the Month selection. A novella, *Farewell Summer,* which deals with a love affair between cousins in Sunbury, Ohio, around the turn of the 20th century, was published in 1988.

In the 1980s Santmyer's major work, combined with her amiability (in spite of ill-health) and her extraordinary life story, made her a favorite of the press and the public, and her celebration of small-town middle-class life found a ready audience in a culture wearied by social upheavals and rapid technological change.

Bibliography

Quay, Joyce Crosby. *Early Promise, Late Reward.* Manchester, Conn.: Knowledge, Ideas & Trends, 1995.

Santmyer, Helen Hooven. *Herbs and Apples.* New York: Houghton, 1925. Reprint, New York: Harper, 1985.

———. *The Fierce Dispute.* New York: Houghton, 1929. Reprint, New York: St. Martin's, 1987.

———. *Ohio Town: A Portrait of Xenia.* Columbus: Ohio State University Press, 1963. Reprint, New York: Harper, 1984.

———. *. . . And Ladies of the Club.* Columbus: Ohio State University Press, 1982. Reprint, New York: Putnam, 1984.

———. *Farewell, Summer.* New York: Harper, 1988.

James A. Kaser

Saul, John (1942–)

John Saul is the best-selling author of 28 psychological horror novels, including *Suffer the Children, Cry for the Strangers, Punish the Sinners,* and *Comes the Blind Fury,* his trademark protagonist an innocent child led through a labyrinth of evil by a sinister child from beyond the grave.

John Saul III was born on February 25, 1942, in Pasadena, California. His father, John Saul II, worked at an oil refinery, and his mother, Elizabeth, was a homemaker. He grew up in Whittier, California, a small suburb of Los Angeles that is a short drive from the ocean, a frequent location in his novels. Saul has one older sister, and the two lived a normal childhood, never experienced by the children in his stories.

He was encouraged to write by two of his high school teachers, and after graduating in 1959, he attended Antioch College, Cerritos College, Montana State University, and San Francisco State University, but never attained a degree, having difficulty finding a major that suited him. After working a string of odd jobs and writing short adult novels to pay the rent, Saul's break came when his agent, Jane Rotrosen, encouraged him to write a psychological thriller like those of major authors in the genre at the time, particularly STEPHEN KING. Also, Saul had the good fortune to meet Michael Sack, a psychologist who became his friend and collaborator on many of his books. The result was *Suffer the Children,* published in 1977, which became a huge best seller.

Saul's novels are often set in small rural towns along lonely back roads or bordering remote ocean beaches. Following the gothic literary tradition, the houses in his novels are often haunted, and old schools or asylums hide horrifying memories, whispered in the ears of the living. The child-in-peril, supernatural incursion, revenge, twisted coming-of-age, and slow psychological descent into madness dominate the thematic landscape, almost all of the books featuring children or teens battling the supernatural.

In *Suffer the Children* a small child plays her fantasy tea party over and over inside a cave to which she lures and murders local children. In *Punish the Sinners* (1978) a young boy is traumatized and grows up to visit that experience on others. Many of Saul's novels begin with a prologue describing an incident in the distant past that then reemerges in the novel's present, as in *Comes the Blind Fury* (1980), where a child's teasing a century before, which resulted in death, is revenged in the present. Two of Saul's most recent novels, *Manhattan Hunt Club* (2001) and *Midnight Voices* (2002), depart from the small-town setting and venture into the dark places of New York City. With *The God Project* (1982) and *Brainchild* (1985), Saul expands on his theme of children and the supernatural with technological detective fiction that centers on medical experimentation, a form revisited in his most recent novels, *Perfect Nightmare* (2005) and *In the Dark of the Night* (2006).

To date, only one of Saul's novels, *Cry for the Strangers,* has been made into a film (a 1982 TV movie), though two others, *Creature* and *The God Project,* are optioned.

Bibliography

Saul, John. *Suffer the Children.* New York: Dell, 1977.

———. *Punish the Sinners.* New York: Dell, 1978.
———. *Cry for the Strangers.* New York: Dell, 1979.
———. *Comes the Blind Fury.* New York: Dell, 1980.
———. *The God Project.* New York: Bantam, 1983.
———. *Brainchild.* New York: Bantam, 1985.
———. *Creature.* New York: Bantam, 1990.
———. *Manhattan Hunt Club.* New York: Ballantine, 2001.
———. *Midnight Voices.* New York: Ballantine, 2002.
———. *Perfect Nightmare.* New York: Ballantine, 2005.
———. *In the Dark of the Night.* New York: Ballantine, 2006.

Debbie Clare Olson

Scarlett Alexandra Ripley (1991)

Scarlett, the much anticipated sequel to *Gone with the Wind* commissioned by the estate of Margaret Mitchell, centers on the continuing story of Scarlett O'Hara, the heroine of Mitchell's novel, picking up the story where *Gone with the Wind* leaves off, just after the death of Melanie Wilkes, with Scarlett's belated realization that she does not love Ashley Wilkes and the disenchanted departure of her husband, Rhett Butler, for his hometown of Charleston. The sequel details Scarlett's move to Charleston and her attempts to rekindle Rhett's love for her, but the novel's entire second half takes place in Ireland, where Scarlett flees after failing in her attempts to regain Rhett's affections. After many convolutions, both of plot and emotion, Rhett and Scarlett are reunited at the novel's end.

Thematically the novel may be seen as a further exploration of Scarlett's character, tracing the continuance of her painful, often halting, but empathetic maturation. In much the same way that Scarlett's stubborn love for Ashley was the unifying thread of *Gone with the Wind,* her love for Rhett provides the narrative core of the sequel, around which evolves her broader development as a woman, as a person, and as a southerner. In the course of her brief stay in Charleston, for example, where she's gone in search of Rhett, she bonds with many of the characters whose counterparts she had shunned during her years of luxury in Atlanta; through lengthy conversations with Rhett, Rhett's mother, and various other Charleston inhabitants she continues to grow in understanding and wisdom concerning both the conditions of the South and those of her own soul. And while Scarlett's lengthy stay in Ireland seems at times little more than a convenient plot twist to keep her away from Rhett, the time there affords her an opportunity to learn about her father's past and to develop loving family relationships, again in ways entirely foreign to the Scarlett of *Gone with the Wind.*

Writing a sequel to any novel penned by another author would be difficult enough, but to create a credible follow-up to a popular masterpiece like *Gone with the Wind* would seem next to impossible, especially given Mitchell's own oft-quoted claim that she herself would never write a sequel to the novel because it ended as it was supposed to end. From a generic standpoint *Scarlett* is a historical romance in the tradition of Alexandra Ripley's other successful novels such as *Charleston* (1981) and *New Orleans Legacy* (1987). It was her evident skill as a writer of historical fiction of the Old South that attracted the attention of the heirs of Mitchell's estate. But *Gone with the Wind* is no simple historical romance. In the end, like most great folk art, it defies categorization, belonging as it does to any number of genres, including the historical novel and the bildungsroman, and contextualizing Scarlett's coming of age in the fall and reconstruction both of the South and of the southern psyche. Its love stories are subtly inscribed with elements of Scarlett's own development and the narrator's meditations on southern identity, while its ending alone, steeped in pathos and hard-won wisdom, eschewing all the conventions of historical romance, renders foolish any attempt to label it along generic lines.

As a historical romance *Scarlett* can stand on its own, remaining true to the conventions of the genre and culminating with the obligatory happy ending, albeit after almost 900 pages of attenuated delay and deflection. But the narrative never rises *above* the conventions of romance as its predecessor so famously does. It is true, and unsurprising, that Ripley hits her narrative stride in the Charleston portion of the novel, and its descriptions of life in the Charleston of the Reconstruction era are lively and engaging. But even at its most entertaining, with its lush descriptions of historical material, the narrative fails to integrate the characters' respective developments into their rich historical and geographical milieu as Mitchell consistently does. In *Scarlett* milieu provide window dressing and little more, and when Ripley has Scarlett forgo life in America for Ireland, the novel pales even further in the light of its antecedent. Stiff and wooden at best, with fabricated simulations of Irish brogues and clichés about Irish love of whiskey and step dancing, the narrative's greatest failing finally lies in its never actually accounting for her being there in the first place, let alone staying there for half the tale.

Unsurprisingly perhaps, the 1994 TV miniseries of *Scarlett* starring Joanne Whalley as Scarlett and Timothy Dalton as Rhett played fast and loose with Ripley's novel, inserting a trial in which Scarlett is indicted for murdering a sadistic lover, as well as lengthy scenes depicting Rhett's marriage to Anne Hampton.

Bibliography

Ripley, Alexandra. *Scarlett: The Sequel to Margaret Mitchell's "Gone with the Wind."* New York: Warner, 1991.

Kathryn Kleypas

Sebold, Alice (1963–)

Born in Madison, Wisconsin, Sebold moved as a child to Malvern, Pennsylvania, when her father began teaching at the University of Pennsylvania in 1968. From her earliest days Sebold knew that she wanted to be a writer. However, her first novel, *The* LOVELY BONES (2002), was not published until she was 39.

After graduating from Great Valley High School in 1980, Sebold enrolled at Syracuse University in order to study writing but was temporarily and strikingly deflected from her purpose when near the end of her freshmen year she was raped on campus. She comments on this experience, and her college years, in the memoir *Lucky* (1999), the only book she has brought forth besides *The Lovely Bones* and *The Almost Moon* (2007). The title of her memoir was chosen because, after reporting her attack, Sebold was told by the police that she was "lucky" since another young woman had been murdered in the place where Sebold herself was raped. This other woman and her fate haunted Sebold, and the narrator of *The Lovely Bones,* murder victim Susie Salmon, recalls her in a host of ways. Sebold suggests such a connection between her life and her art in an interview with Dave Weich, stating that "*Lucky* was part of the process of writing *Lovely Bones*."

Sebold returned to Syracuse for her sophomore year and eventually helped with the capture and prosecution of her attacker. During her time at Syracuse she also studied under an illustrious faculty that included writers Tess Gallagher, Raymond Carver, Hayden Carruth, and Tobias Wolff. Despite her training, talents, and ambition, however, Sebold did not immediately succeed as a writer after graduating from college.

She began an M.A. at the University of Houston, focusing on poetry, but did not complete the degree. Instead, she moved to Manhattan and during the next 10 years wrote little, working in restaurants and as an adjunct at Hunter College. During this period she drifted through a series of relationships and dabbled in drugs. As she tells Weich, "for fifteen or twenty years before I was published I was floating in and out of the atmosphere where everyone else was getting published. . . ." Her own rape continued to haunt her, and she wrote about it in the *New York Times* and spoke about it on the *Oprah Winfrey Show.* "It is not just forcible intercourse," she explains in *Lucky,* "rape means to inhabit and destroy everything," including the very fabric of victims' lives (12).

Sebold finally realized that she suffered from posttraumatic stress disorder from her attack. Seeking to heal and gain independence from her past, she moved to California and became caretaker of the Dorland Mountain Arts Colony. Shortly thereafter she renewed her passion for writing and entered the M.F.A. program at the University of California, Irvine. There Sebold completed her degree and also met the man she would marry, fellow author Glen David Gold, described in *Lucky* as her "one true love" (245). After graduating, she published *The Lovely Bones,* which earned great critical acclaim for a debut novel and sold more than 1 million copies. Today Sebold lives with her husband outside of Los Angeles, where she is at work on her next novel.

Bibliography
Sebold, Alice. *Lucky.* New York: Little, Brown, 1999.
———. *The Lovely Bones.* New York: Little, Brown, 2002.
———. "Interview. Dave Weich." Available online. URL: http://www.powells.com/authors/sebold.html. Accessed December 26, 2006.

Noel Sloboda

The Secret Life of Bees

Sue Monk Kidd (2002)

The Secret Life of Bees is a poignant coming-of-age novel that celebrates the transformative power of love and family, as well as the strength and divinity of sisterhood. Working through personal emotions of guilt, rejection, uncertain love, and forgiveness, SUE MONK KIDD intertwines with these national emotions—racial tensions, social wounds, and political uprisings—to demonstrate the inseparable and universal need for love and redemption in both private and public relationships.

In early July 1964 President Johnson signs the Civil Rights Act, and bees swarm through the cracks of the bedroom walls of a 14-year-old white girl, Lily Owens—two seemingly unrelated events that set the tale in motion. Living on a rural South Carolina peach farm with T. Ray, her abusive and ignorant father, Lily is sustained by her wit and latent strength of character but at the same time by a profound need to make sense of powerful and confusing memories concerning her mother, Deborah, who died when she was four years old. In addition to the despair of being a motherless child, Lily must deal with her father's brutal insistence that she herself had accidentally killed her mother, a memory Lily can neither fully confirm nor escape. She is, however, supported by the love—sometimes sharp, sometimes tender—of Rosaleen, the determined African-American woman who has been caring for her since her mother's death.

Typical of T. Ray's behavior is his punishment of Lily by making her kneel on Martha White grits until her knees are "swollen with hundreds of red welts, pinprick bruises that would grow into a blue stubble" (25). Yet despite such abuse, wit and resourcefulness are typical of Lily's worldview:

> You can tell which girls lack mothers by the look of their hair. My hair was constantly going off in eleven wrong directions, and T. Ray, naturally, refused to buy me bristle rollers, so all year I'd had to roll it on Welch's grape juice cans, which had nearly turned me into an insomniac. I was always having to choose between decent hair and a good night's sleep (3).

In her attempt to register to vote for the first time, Rosaleen is hatefully attacked by a cluster of white men and thrown in jail, an incident Lily witnesses. Determined to help Rosaleen, and simultaneously escape life with T. Ray, Lily orchestrates a comical jailbreak, and the two set off for a new life in Tiburon, South Carolina, a destination they know only by name; among Deborah's few surviving artifacts that Lily secretly possesses is a mysterious picture of a Black Virgin Mary glued to a block of wood, on the back of which is handwritten, "Tiburon, South Carolina." Lily feels certain this cryptic scrawl holds a secret to her mother's life and death. Upon their arrival in dusty, nondescript Tiburon, three wildly eccentric sisters—the "Calendar Sisters," who not only keep bees but worship the Black Madonna—welcome Lily and Rosaleen into their home. Life in the pink house, complete with the wisdom of these African-American women, the mystical hum of bees, the all-soothing power of honey, and the strength and comfort of the Queen Bee herself, the Black Madonna, gradually heals Lily's broken spirit and enables her to settle into a loving and sacred colony of new mothers.

Kidd's development of place, of the homestead of the Calendar Sisters, is richly nuanced; but the novel's most endearing quality is the full-bodied texture of the southern female characters, each crackling with individuality. Lily herself is an enchanting combination of childlike innocence and adult suffering, always trying to muster up a shred of self-worth:

> . . . no one, not a single person, had ever said, "Lily, you are such a pretty child," except for Miss Jennings at church, and she

> was legally blind. . . . I had thought my real chance would come from going to charm school . . . , but I got barred because I didn't have a mother, a grandmother, or even a measly aunt to present me with a white rose at the closing ceremony. Rosaleen doing it was against the rules. I'd cried till I threw up in the sink (8–9).

Having fled T. Ray, filled with self-hatred, Lily enters a loving, compassionate world of the feminine divine, a black sisterhood grounded in worship of the Black Madonna. The strength and wisdom of these women—the Calendar Sisters with their resonant traditions, the Daughters of Mary with their outrageously fancy hats, and Rosaleen with her will as strong as her snuff—are juxtaposed not merely to the cruelty of T. Ray but to the broader background of negative racial sensibilities that pervade society. Young Lily's relationship with the sisters exemplifies one of the book's most important themes—truth, family, love, and spirituality can and should be all-inclusive.

While *The Secret Life of Bees* is Kidd's debut novel, her body of published work is rich and extensive, this first work of fiction having been preceded by a host of personal, inspirational, and nonfiction essays, as well as three books, all contemplative spiritual memoirs exploring her turn to Christian spirituality and discovery of feminist theology. This earlier work clearly served to hone and enrich Kidd's later novelistic depiction of sisterhood and spirituality, as well as the lush, authentic southern voices that permeate the dialogue in *The Secret Life of Bees.* Winning multiple awards both nationally and internationally, *The Secret Life of Bees* has sold more than 4.5 million copies, been published in more than 20 languages, and spent more than 80 weeks on the *New York Times* best-seller list. It has been produced on stage in New York City by the American Place Theater and was adapted to film by Focus Features in 2008.

Bibliography

Kidd, Sue Monk. *The Secret Life of Bees.* New York: Penguin, 2002.

———. *The Mermaid Chair: A Novel.* New York: Viking, 2005.

———. *Firstlight: The Early Inspirational Writings of Sue Monk Kidd.* New York: Guidepost Books, 2006.

Judy L. Isaksen

September Rosamunde Pilcher (1990)

The second of ROSAMUNDE PILCHER's sweeping family sagas, *September* follows the Aird and Blair families through the summer and fall of a very special year, culminating in a huge birthday ball. Pilcher tells her story cinematically, cutting freely from the Scottish Highlands to London to Majorca and back again, focusing on different family members and friends and weaving her story in and through their lives.

Invitations go out to friends scattered far and wide, calling them home to Scotland for the celebration of Katie Steynton's 21st birthday; this invitation prompts Pandora Blair to think back on her family and childhood home, the sprawling estate of Croy. Beautiful and impetuous, Pandora ran away from home at 18 and has never been back, never even thought of returning, simply moving from one relationship to another in search of fun and freedom. She is now living alone in a Spanish villa in Majorca when a call comes through from her niece, Lucilla Blair. Lucilla and her friend Jeff have been traveling through Europe and suggest a visit, to which Pandora unexpectedly responds with open arms. Pandora and Lucilla have both received invitations to the party, forwarded by Archie Blair, (Lord Balmerino, Pandora's brother and Lucilla's father); even more surprising Pandora herself proposes going to the party, saying it would be a good excuse to go home to Croy. Lucilla is stunned, but no one can know what Pandora's thoughts are, her reasons for leaving Scotland 21 years ago, or her motives for going back.

Meanwhile, in Strathcroy, the Highland village surrounding the Croy estate, life proceeds much as usual; however, Violet Aird senses problems ahead as the time approaches for her young grandson to be sent away to boarding school. Violet's son, Edmund, and his young wife, Virginia, are slowly growing apart, deeply divided as to whether eight-year-old Henry is ready for such a move; Edmund, accustomed to getting his own way, insists the boy should be sent away, while Virginia believes he is still too young. In London Edmund's daughter, Alexa, receives her invitation, and a decision must be made about how to deal with a momentous and fragile relationship in her own life. Noel Keeling, one of the main characters of Pilcher's first best-selling novel, *The Shell Seekers,* makes an appearance here as well, and the continuation of his story, besides its appeal to fans, adds to the vivid sense of the familiar, which is such an attractive feature of Pilcher's work.

Indeed, the novel is replete with comforting images of home and the beauty of the Scottish countryside. Pilcher has a knack for capturing the essence of place, so that readers feel rooted in the setting and sensitive to its nuances. From the turquoise sweep of the Mediterranean and the blinding sunbaked terraces of the Casa Rosa in Majorca to a gentle mist soaking into the heathery moors and tumbling brown burns of the Scottish highlands, to the warm glow of dying embers and heavy curtains drawn against a stormy night, readers can settle into the novel like a snug hearth and soak up its atmosphere.

Also characteristic of Pilcher's style, a special bond is established between reader and characters, which sustains interest even through long and static passages of description or exposition. She explores the power of guilt, misunderstanding, and unhappiness in life but sets against this the redemptive power of love in all its forms, the assurance of home, and the draw of nature. In *September* readers journey with Pandora, Archie Balmerino, Edmund, Virginia, Alexa, and the others through heartache and unhappiness, trauma, and even death. But in the end, as in life, the residents of Strathcroy and all those making their way home there learn to make of life what they can, find what joy and peace they can.

The day and night of the ball brings all these disparate elements into sharp and memorable focus as each of them in his or her own way must find the grace to live with the critical decisions that constitute a life, to accept the consequences of mistakes made and opportunities lost, and to understand what, in the end, means the most and is most worth fighting for.

Bibliography

Pilcher, Rosamunde. *The Shell Seekers.* New York: Dell, 1987.

———. *September.* London: Hodder and Stoughton, 1990.

Robin Musumeci

Seuss, Dr. (Theodor Seuss Geisel) (1904–1991)

Theodor Seuss Geisel, better known by his pen name "Dr. Seuss," is arguably the most influential and beloved U.S. children's author of the 20th century and an American icon. Writing and illustrating more than 40 books known for their delightful use of rhyme, nonsense words, and lively often surrealist illustrations, Dr. Seuss is a fixture in both U.S. children's literature and American popular culture. Even his lesser-known books remain perennially in print, while his more popular titles such as *Hop on Pop* (1963), *The Lorax* (1971), and *one fish two fish red fish blue fish* (1960) have become part of the American literary landscape and cultural imagination. Indeed, Herb Cheyette has relayed this astonishing statistic: "One out of every four children born in the United States receives as its first book a Dr. Seuss book."

To date, Dr. Seuss's writings have sold more than 400 million copies worldwide and have been translated into more than 15 languages. In 1984 Seuss was awarded a Pulitzer Prize for "his special contribution over nearly half a century to the education and enjoyment of America's children and their parents." His books have been made into 10 television specials, some of which—e.g., Chuck Jones's animated *How the Grinch Stole Christmas!* (1966)—continue to be broadcast every year and have become a holiday tradition in their own right. As a further indication of Seuss's iconic status, in 2002 his birthplace of Springfield, Massachusetts, completed a $6.2 million Dr. Seuss National Memorial. The following year the U.S. Postal Service unveiled a stamp honoring him. Challenging assumptions that his work is exclusively for children, his 1990 narrative, *Oh, The Places You'll Go!,* has become a common gift for graduates. Likewise, his 1986 narrative, *You're Only Old Once!: A Book for Obsolete Children,* is a frequent sight at parties celebrating those entering middle age as well as those beginning retirement.

Theodor Seuss Geisel was born in 1904 in Springfield, Massachusetts, to a middle-class German family. Encountering both financial hardship with the devastating impact of Prohibition on his family's brewery and anti-German prejudice with the outbreak of World War I, his childhood was marked by adversity. Attending Dartmouth College as an undergraduate, Seuss adopted his middle name as an occasional pen name for columns in the campus newspaper. After graduation he departed for Oxford, where he planned to earn his doctorate. Although Seuss would drop out of the institution after finding graduate studies dull, this desire earned him the nickname that he would later adopt has his official nom de plume, Dr. Seuss.

Upon returning to the United States, Seuss began a career as a writer and illustrator, enjoying early success in the advertising field with his "Quick, Henry, the Flit!" campaign for a brand of household insect repellent. During this period he also tried his hand at creating children's books, releasing *And to Think That I Saw It on Mulberry Street* (1938), *The 500 Hats of Bartholomew Cubbins in New York* (1938), and *The King's Stilts* (1939). All three texts contained elements of his signature line drawings accompanied by lines of rhyming couplets. Interestingly, Seuss would credit the rhythmic sound made by the ship's engines during his 1936 return voyage from England with inspiring his poetic style. Of his drawings he would assert that his images had such a distinct appearance because he knew little about modern art and his talents as an illustrator were limited.

Too old to be drafted into the military during World War II but still longing to contribute to the war effort, Seuss accepted a position with *PM,* a left-wing political newspaper in New York City, penning more than 400 political cartoons for it between 1943 and 1945. The publication of many of these in Richard H. Minear's *Dr. Seuss Goes to War* (1999) demonstrated the importance of this period on his later writing for children. Indeed, these cartoons not only contain some of his most famous later characters—including the Cat in the Hat, Yertle the Turtle, and Horton the elephant—but often address the same social issues spotlighted in his books for children, most notably the inanity of military one-upmanship, the subject of *The* BUTTER BATTLE BOOK (1984), and the dangers of prejudice, addressed in both *Horton Hears a Who!* (1954) and *The Sneetches* (1961). Through these works Dr. Seuss challenged existing assumptions about the purportedly innocuous nature of children's writing. Instead of using his picture books to shelter children from social, economic, and political realities—as in the contemporaneous Dick and Jane series—Seuss harnessed them as a means to introduce young people to important issues.

One might say, however, that Dr. Seuss became "Dr. Seuss" during the 1950s. After a *Life* magazine article cited the dull nature of current children's books as contributing to the declining literacy rates among young people, his publisher challenged him to pen a story that first-graders would be unable to put down. The result was *The Cat in the Hat* (1957), which uses only 225 words designed for beginning readers and was an instant success. Several other similarly crafted books followed, including *Green Eggs and Ham* (1960), which strikingly employs only 50 different words.

Through these texts Dr. Seuss changed the way children's books were written, read, and illustrated in the United States. For many, his memorable rhyming couplets ("I do not like them, Sam-I-am. / I do not like green eggs and ham"), playful use of nonsense words (he coined the term *nerd,* for example), and distinctive illustrative style (whimsical line drawings and restricted color palates) remain a benchmark of writing for children. His work has inspired as many imitators as admirers, giving rise to literary parodies such as Johnny Valentine's *One Dad Two Dads Brown Dad Blue Dads* (1994), along with such television tributes as *Dr. Seuss on the Loose* (1974).

Since his death in 1991 Dr. Seuss's writings have come under increased scrutiny and even criticism. Literary critics have noted the dearth of female characters in his narratives, and parents and teachers have lamented the increased commercialization of his writings by the executors of his estate, from the authorization of over-the-top films of *How the Grinch Stole Christmas!* and *The Cat in the Hat* to the opening of the "Seuss Landing" section of Universal Studios theme park in Orlando, Florida.

These issues notwithstanding, Dr. Seuss's place in American culture is secure. Indeed, given the depth and breadth of his influence, one can say without exaggeration that it is impossible to imagine either the field of U.S. children's literature or the experience of American childhood without him.

Bibliography

Cheyette, Herb. *An Awfully Big Adventure: The Making of Modern Children's Literature.* Directed by Roger Parsons. London: BBC, 1998.

Dr. Seuss' The Cat in the Hat. Directed by Bo Welch. Universal, 2003.

Dr. Seuss' How the Grinch Stole Christmas! Directed by Ron Howard. Universal, 2000.

Dr. Seuss National Memorial. Available online. URL: http://www.catinhat.com/drseuss.

Dr. Seuss on the Loose. Directed by Hawley Pratt. Universal, 1974.

How the Grinch Stole Christmas! Directed by Chuck Jones. Warner Bros, 1966.

Lurie, Alison. "The Cabinet of Dr. Seuss." *The New York Times Book Review* (December 20, 1990): 50–52.

MacDonald, Ruth. *Dr. Seuss.* New York: Twayne, 1988.

Minear, Richard H. *Dr. Seuss Goes to War: The World War II Editorial Cartoons of Theodor Seuss Geisel.* New York: The New Press, 1999.

Nel, Philip. "The Disneyfication of Dr. Seuss: Faithful to Profit, One Hundred Percent?" *Cultural Studies,* 17, no. 5 (September 2003): 579–614.

———. *Dr. Seuss: American Icon.* New York: Continuum, 2004.

Seuss, Dr. *The 500 Hats of Bartholomew Cubbins.* 1938. Reprint, New York: Random House, 1989.

———. *And to Think That I Saw it on Mulberry Street.* 1938. Reprint, New York: Random House, 1989.

———. *The King's Stilts.* 1939. Reprint, New York: Random House, 1970.

———. *Horton Hears a Who!* New York: Random House, 1954.

———. *The Cat in the Hat.* New York: Random House, 1957.

———. *Yertle the Turtle and Other Stories.* New York: Random House, 1958.

———. *Green Eggs and Ham.* New York: Random House, 1960.

———. *one fish two fish red fish blue fish.* New York: Random House, 1960.

———. *The Sneetches.* New York: Random House, 1961.

———. *Hop on Pop.* New York: Random House, 1963.

———. *The Lorax.* New York: Random House, 1971.

———. *The Butter Battle Book.* New York: Random House, 1984.

———. *Oh, The Places You'll Go!* New York: Random House, 1990.

Seussville. Available online. URL: http://www.seussville.com.

Valentine, Johnny. *One Dad Two Dads Brown Dad Blue Dads.* Los Angeles: Alyson Wonderland, 1994.

Michelle Ann Abate

Sheldon, Sidney (1917–2007)

In many ways Sidney Sheldon epitomized the American storyteller, selling more than 300 million books in his lifetime (all 18 of his novels hit number one on the *New York Times* best-seller list) and winning both Oscar and Tony awards for his screenwriting (25 motion pictures) and playwriting (six Broadway plays), respectively. His novels are sold in more than 180 countries, and he has been translated into 51 languages, a Guinness World Record; yet he only took up novel-writing in his 50s. At the time of his death *Variety* magazine estimated his net worth at $3 billion.

Sheldon was born Sidney Schechtel in Chicago in 1917 to Ascher "Otto" Schechtel, a jewelry store manager, and Natalia Marcus, both of Russian Jewish ancestry. As best-selling authors go, his beginnings were not auspicious:

> I was born in Chicago during the Depression and both my parents were third grade dropouts. . . . My Father never read a book in his life and I was the only one in the family to complete high school.

Yet at the age of 10 he made his first literary sale, $10 for a poem. Still in his teens and working at one of many depression-era jobs in the checkroom at the Bismark Hotel, he gave the hotel's orchestra leader, Phil Levant, a song he had written. Levant liked it, arranged it, and played it regularly within earshot of the anonymous coat-check boy.

After a brief stint at Northwestern University he moved to Hollywood in 1937, promising his parents he would return in three weeks if he failed to find a job. He neither found a job nor returned. His aspirations as a screenwriter temporarily forestalled and hearing that the studios often needed script readers, Sheldon distributed a synopsis of Steinbeck's *Of Mice and Men* to the major studios and heard from all within three days, finally accepting a job with Universal for $17 a week. While there he collaborated with an equally junior colleague named Ben Roberts and had a number of screenplays accepted by Republic Studios for B movies that vanished without a trace, except in the seasoning of their young author.

After serving as a pilot in World War II, Sheldon returned not to Hollywood but to Broadway, achieving instant and memorable success—with three musicals running simultaneously at one point—and winning a Tony for *Redhead* starring Gwen Vernon; all the while he continued to write increasingly significant screenplays for MGM and Paramount. Soon he returned to Hollywood and immediately scored one of his greatest successes, winning an Academy Award for best original screenplay in 1947 for *The Bachelor and the Bobby Soxer* starring Cary Grant and Myrna Loy. He also penned *Easter Parade* starring Judy Garland and Fred Astaire, *Annie Get Your Gun, Jumbo,* and *Anything Goes* starring Bing Crosby.

Keenly attuned to technological developments in his craft, he turned his sights to television in its infancy and dominated the medium from its early years, with the *Patty Duke Show* and *I Dream of Jeannie,* right through until the 1980s with *Hart to Hart* starring Robert Wagner and Stephanie Powers. In the last year of his work on *I Dream of Jeannie,* Sheldon recalls, he "decided to try a novel":

> Each morning from 9 until noon, I had a secretary at the studio take all calls. I mean every single call. I wrote each morning—or rather, dictated—and then I faced the TV business.

In 1969 his first novel, the mystery *The Naked Face,* was sold to William Morrow after being rejected by five publishers. As instant a success as his first efforts in theater and film, the novel was nominated for the prestigious Edgar Allan Poe Award for best first novel from the Mystery Writers of America and was described by the *New York Times* as "the best mystery novel of the year."

His second work, and the first of Sheldon's signature successes, *Another Side of Midnight* (1973) is a flawlessly crafted narrative dialogue between the lives of two extraordinary and beautiful women, one from Marseilles, one from Chicago, who surmount a welter of difficulties—most notably men—on their way to brilliant careers and dazzling lives. The book was received with wild enthusiasm, especially on behalf of women, who would remain Sheldon's most faithful readers. Asked why, the author suggested that it was owing to his focus on "women who are talented and capable, but most important, retain their femininity. Women have tremendous power—their femininity, because men can't do without it." It would be 17 years and eight best-selling novels later before he would return to take up the story of Catherine Douglas (now in a convent) and Noelle Page (now the mistress of a ruthless Onassis-styled tycoon) in *MEMORIES OF MIDNIGHT* (1990).

Bold not merely in their focus on such independent women, but in their sensuality, violence, and excess, for three decades Sheldon's novels drew the ire of reactionary moralists like Jerry Falwell and Tom Williams, which was ever good for sales and which provided the author with a lively backdrop for his lifelong crusade against censorship. Equally passionate was his support of literacy and reading; he was a national spokesman for the Freedom to Read Foundation and Libraries for the Future.

In addition to his 18 novels he also wrote a recent memoir, *The Other Side of Me* (2005), in which he first reveals his lifelong struggle with a bipolar condition so acute that he verged on suicide at the age of 17, only to be discovered and dissuaded by his father.

After the failure of his first, impulsive marriage, Sheldon in 1951 married Jorja Curtwright, a prominent interior designer who had enjoyed a successful career on the stage and screen before meeting the author and who shared more than three decades of happily married life with him until her death in 1985. In 1989 Sheldon married Alexandra Kostoff, a former child actress and advertising executive, and remained with her until his death.

In its obituary on the critically maligned but perennially popular author, the *New York Times* delivered a peerless summary of his fictional palette:

> A Sidney Sheldon novel typically contains one or more—usually many more—of these ingredients: shockingly beautiful women, square-jawed heroes and fiendish villains; fame, fortune and intrigue; penthouses, villas and the jet travel these entail; plutonium, diamonds and a touch of botulism; rape, sodomy, murder and suicide; mysterious accidents and mysterious disappearances; an heiress or two; skeletons in lavishly appointed closets; shadowy international cartels, communists and lawyers; globe-trotting ambassadors, supermodels and very bad dogs; forced marriages and amnesia; naked ambition and nakedness in general; a great deal of vengeance; and as The New York Times Book Review described it in 1989, "a pastoral coed nude rubdown with dry leaves."

Bibliography

Associated Press. "Author Sidney Sheldon Dies at 89." 30 January 2007.

"Sidney Sheldon, Author of Steamy Novels, Dies at 89." Available online. URL: http://www.nytimes.com/2007/02/01/obituaries/01sheldon.html. Accessed January 30, 2007.

"Sidney Sheldon Biography." Available online. URL: http://www.hachettebookgroupsusa.com/features/sidney/bio.html.

Nemo Ouden

The Sicilian Mario Puzo (1984)

Michael Corleone, youngest son of Godfather, Don Vito Corleone, is lying low in Sicily while the rap for his murder of an American police captain blows over. The week before his two-year exile is to end and he is to return to America, he receives a special request from his father to escort home a romantic outlaw hero of the Sicilian peasantry—"the Sicilian"—Salvatore Guiliano. So begins MARIO PUZO's *The Sicilian*, a novel describing events that occur in the two-year interregnum in Sicily that plays mostly offstage in Puzo's more famous *The Godfather* (1969).

Born and raised in the Sicilian town of Montelepre, Salvatore "Turi" Guiliano is idolized as a young man by everyone in his hometown for his Grecian good looks, his sturdiness, athletic prowess, and most of all for that vengeful and ethically questionable strain of honor so famous in Puzo's depictions of Sicilian culture: "He was a man of honor. That is to say, a man who treated his fellow man with scrupulous fairness and one who could not be insulted with impunity" (49). Turi's story begins on the day of Montelepre's Festa, the most important celebration of the year. He and his cousin and right-hand man, Aspanu Pisciotta, are in the middle of smuggling a great cheese wheel out of town (for the support of their families) when they are stopped by a small patrol of *carabinieri* (the Italian national police). In an action sequence reminiscent of John Woo's baroque fury, Turi attempts a diving escape into the underbrush, receiving a rifle blast in the side. Still rolling, and with his body "awash in blood" (69), the Sicilian takes quick aim and sees his bullet "shatter the enemy's face into a mask of blood" (69)—an archetypical moment in the Guiliano legend, heightened by Puzo's prologue to the event: "They disappeared in the late morning mist around the mountaintop. They were vanishing into the beginning of their myth" (61). Such figuration of the Sicilian's mythopoeic rite of passage is typical of his characterization in *The Sicilian*, which is conspicuously located in epic-romance traditions like the medieval legends of Robin Hood and Roland. Perhaps the most striking doubling may be seen in the parallels between the Sicilian and his American counterpart and potential savior, Michael Corleone. Michael and Turi both murder (crooked) policemen in their catalyzing acts of heroic banditry, and both are banished for it, Michael to Sicily and Guiliano to the hills surrounding his hometown of Montelepre, from which vantage point he builds his noble empire of outlaws and wrestles for the spiritual control of Sicily with his most formidable opponent, the Mafia.

Though exiled to the mountains, Guiliano and Pisciotta boldly serve notice both to the Mafia and the Italian government that they are the new kings of Sicily, kidnapping and extorting money from aristocrats and politicians, brutally silencing opponents and traitors, and even stealing from American Army installations, rich landowners, and the Mafia rulers themselves, all in the name of the Sicilian peasantry; for though he pays his lieutenants well and seems himself to live a luxurious if rustic mountain existence, Guiliano insists on distributing all his profits to the poor villagers who have suffered for so long at the hands of organized crime and corrupt government. This campaign earns him the everlasting love of the Sicilian people and the cautious curiosity of the *Capo di Capi* (the big boss) of the Sicilian Mafia, Don Croce Malo. Don Croce initially sees Guiliano as a potential heir to his criminal empire (his own unworldly son having become a missionary in Brazil, to the eternal shame of his father); however, Guiliano's continuing gracious but firm refusal even to meet with the *Capo di Capi* rapidly erodes Don Croce's goodwill, and the balance of the narrative chronicles Guiliano's fortunes in his mountain hideout, through his growing tension with Don Croce and the Mafia and the escalating pressure from the Italian government and *carabinieri* to capture the "Italian Robin Hood" (33) and his not entirely merry men (including murderers, rapists, and the ever-menacing Aspanu Pisciotti). The gathering storm finally breaks in a thrilling and tragic climax that tests once and for all the character of Guiliano and his devotion to his people and confirms his place in popular legend.

Though Puzo firmly locates the tale in the epic-romance tradition, the events and characters constituting the narrative are in fact based on the real-life rise and fall of the Sicilian bandit Salvatore Giuliano, a story documented in *Time* magazine from 1948 to 1956 in a rather less laudatory account, describing the often brutal slayings of 75 *carabinieri*, 25 local policemen, and 40 civilians over the course of the Sicilian's seven years in the mountains.

But it is the mythic treatment of Guiliano by Puzo that marks his most striking divergence from the real-life account. The devastating violence perpetrated by the Sicilian is consistently glossed over or justified in the name of his righteous mission on behalf of the Sicilian people, and the novel clearly lionizes the young bandit, with his youth, beauty, and idealism constantly juxtaposed against the ugly mien, brutal greed, and pragmatism of Don Croce. Equally gorging his belly and his bank accounts on the fat of the Sicilian land, the latter is a repugnant caricature of the Mafiosa as greedy, calculating capitalist, in relative contrast to the almost noble restraint of Puzo's American Godfather, Don Vito Corleone. Yet as Don Croce seems to get older, fatter, and more repellent each time he appears in the novel, Guiliano retains an archetypal and impossible youth, never corrupted by greed or psychologically damaged by his own acts of extraordinary violence. And here one is tempted even to add Huck Finn to the list of outlaws recalled by Puzo's Sicilian: less a man than a boy, living in a fantasy wilderness populated only by other boys—far away from women, parents, and social and domestic concerns.

Guiliano seems thus both a double and a foil to Puzo's more famous Michael Corleone, but Michael's characterization in *The Sicilian* retains a psychological realism not present in the archetypal rendering of Guiliano. Michael feels doubt, fear, and loneliness, as well as a profound sense that the myth of Guiliano, however attractive, is just that. Thus, in one of the final scenes of the novel Michael returns to America, disillusioned by the greed and pragmatism not only of the Sicilian Mafia but of his own father and nostalgic for the heroism of figures like Giuliano. Witnessing his son's displeasure, Don Vito sits Michael down and offers him in a sense the ironic lesson of the novel as a whole: "A man's first duty is to keep himself alive. Then comes what everyone calls honor . . . Always remember that and live your life not to be a hero but to remain alive. With time, heroes seem a little foolish" (397). The scene foregrounds the broader role of *The Sicilian* within the context of Puzo's fictional universe, namely, to sharpen and complicate the characterization of Michael Corleone in *The Godfather* novel and trilogy (produced mostly before but set mostly after *The Sicilian*). Though an awkward bit of loose-end tying concludes the novel, its emotional ending (and perhaps its proper end) comes with Puzo's final word on the aforementioned advice:

> It was the first lesson Michael learned from his father and the one he learned best. It was to color his future life, persuade him to make terrible decisions he could never have dreamed of making before. It changed his perception of honor and his awe of heroism. It helped him to survive, but it made him unhappy. For despite the fact that his father did not envy Guiliano, Michael did (398).

Michael Cimino directed a film adaptation of *The Sicilian* in 1985 starring Christopher Lambert as Turi Guiliano, with the Michael Corleone subplot removed for copyright reasons; however, like the novel itself, the film was far less successful than the seminal *Godfather* novel and films.

Bibliography

"Bandit's End." *Time,* 17 July 1950.

"Beautiful Lightning." *Time,* 12 September 1949.

"Executioner." *Time,* 30 April 1951.

Puzo, Mario. *The Godfather.* New York: Putnam, 1969.

———. *The Sicilian.* New York: Ballantine, 1984.

Sean McAlister

The Silence of the Lambs

Thomas Harris (1988)

The Silence of the Lambs is THOMAS HARRIS's third novel and the second in the influential Hannibal Lecter series; it is a thriller chronicling the efforts of FBI trainee Clarice Starling to track down and subdue a psychopath who skins his victims after killing them. For assistance, Starling turns to Hannibal Lecter, a once distinguished forensic psychiatrist who killed—and ate—many of his patients and now spends his days confined in the Baltimore State Hospital for the Criminally Insane. Impressed by the young trainee's intelligence but attracted equally to elements of her complex character that far exceed it, Lecter agrees to help under one condition: In exchange for his insights, Starling must reveal her most intimate memories.

Thanks to his counsel, Starling and her associates at the FBI begin to make progress in their pursuit of "Buffalo Bill," so named, Starling tells Lecter, "because he skins his humps" (19). The investigation grows more complicated and the stakes rise when Bill abducts one Catherine Martin, the daughter of a U.S. senator. Frustrated by what she regards as the bureau's turgid progress, the senator decides to join in the investigation and has Lecter transported to Memphis, Tennessee, where she solicits his advice—misleading in this case, though Lecter again gives aid to Starling. Unaware just how dangerous the doctor is, the authorities in Tennessee fail to secure their prisoner adequately, and he manages to escape. Undeterred, Starling, her supervisor Jack Crawford, and several FBI agents carry on with their search for Buffalo Bill, but it is the young trainee who, partly through her brave exposure to Lecter's interrogations, eventually lands the killer.

Structurally and thematically, *The Silence of the Lambs* shares much in common with Harris's previous books, *Black Sunday* (1975) and RED DRAGON (1981). In each a government operative races to stop a madman from completing his murderous plans; in *Black Sunday* Mossad agent Kabokov has only days to head off a terrorist attack on a football stadium filled with people; in *Red Dragon*—the novel in which Hannibal Lecter makes his first appearance—FBI investigator Will Graham must apprehend a serial murderer before the arrival of the next full moon; in *The Silence of the Lambs* Starling and the others at the FBI have just a day or two at the most to find Buffalo Bill and his victim. Starling's willingness to expose herself to great danger in the pursuit of her aim also recalls the heroism of Kabokov and Graham. Like these characters, she is wounded when she confronts her opponent. But while the Israeli commando is blown up, and Graham has his face destroyed by a knife, Starling emerges from her own violent confrontation with only a gunpowder scar on her cheek.

Her real tribulations are psychological, and the most striking and memorable difference in the third novel lies in Starling's risking her safety in each encounter with Hannibal Lecter. "Be very careful," Crawford warns the trainee before she leaves for the asylum where the doctor is kept.

"If Lecter talks to you at all, he'll just be trying to find out about you. It's the kind of curiosity that makes a snake look in a bird's nest" (5–6). As the critic Robert Winder has suggested: "The genius of Harris's conception [is] that Lecter remain[s] dangerous even when incarcerated. The briefest conversation with him [is] a perilous *pas de deux* with something monstrously clever and malign" (44).

Despite Crawford's warnings, Starling finds that she lacks the ability to protect herself from Lecter's influence when she meets with him. Even in her first interview "she felt an alien consciousness loose in her head, slapping things off the shelves like a bear in a camper" (24). But rather than retreating from the danger, Starling continues to meet the doctor, each time furnishing him with increasingly personal knowledge in exchange for the mere possibility of information vital to her investigation. A typical encounter, shortly after Bill kidnaps the senator's daughter:

> "What's your worst memory of childhood?"
> Starling took a deep breath.
> "Quicker than that," Dr. Lecter said. "I'm not interested in your worst *invention*."
> "The death of my father," Starling said.
> "Tell me."
> "He was a town marshal. One night he surprised two burglars, addicts, coming out of the back of the drugstore. As he was getting out of his pickup . . . they shot him" (137).

But for all his aggression Lecter appears unwilling to damage Starling, explaining in a critical letter that "[the world is] more interesting with you in it" and even suggesting that he and Starling are kindred spirits: "Some of our stars are the same" (337). Harris reveals in his subsequent novels Hannibal (1999) and *Hannibal Rising* (2006), that Lecter's childhood was itself traumatized, like Starling's, by the murder of a beloved family member—in his case a sister named Mischa who was killed and eaten by bandits.

In many respects, however, and greatly increasing the tension and interest in their exchanges, the personalities of doctor and trainee could not be more different. Lecter, for example, thrives on suffering. "I collect church collapses, recreationally," he tells Starling early in their friendship. "Did you see the recent one in Sicily? Marvelous! The façade fell on sixty-five grandmothers at a special Mass" (19). Starling, in contrast, feels an almost obsessive desire to ease pain, a need emerging from her own similar suffering as a child. After her father's death she spent several months on an aunt and uncle's farm where horses and sheep were kept. One morning, she recalls to Lecter, she woke to the sound of "lambs screaming." The doctor asks her:

> "They were slaughtering the spring lambs?"
> "Yes."
> "What did you do?"
> "I couldn't do anything for them."

The experience has a lasting effect on her. Not only does its memory dominate her dreams but it fosters her desire to join the FBI and bring serial killers to justice, something Lecter recognizes in the course of their discussions:

> "Do you think if you caught Buffalo Bill yourself and if you made Catherine all right, you could make the lambs stop screaming, do you think they'd be all right too and you wouldn't wake up again in the dark and hear the lambs screaming? Clarice?"
> "Yes" (211).

By turns a hyperrealistic police procedural and a work of gothic horror—novelist STEPHEN KING once described Lecter as the "great fictional monster of our time"—*The Silence of the Lambs* stands out as one of the most celebrated works of popular fiction published in the latter part of the previous century. It is also the source for one of the last century's most successful films, director Jonathan Demme's similarly titled film, which won the 1991 Academy Award for best picture.

Bibliography

Harris, Thomas. *Black Sunday.* 1975. Reprint, New York: Dell, 1990.

———. *Red Dragon.* 1981. Reprint, New York: Dell, 2000.

———. *The Silence of the Lambs.* 1988. Reprint, New York: St. Martin's, 1998.

———. *Hannibal.* 1999. Reprint, New York: Dell, 2000.
———. *Hannibal Rising.* New York: Delacorte, 2006.
King, Stephen. "Hannibal the Cannibal." *New York Times Book Review*, 13 June 1999, 4–6.
Winder, Robert. "A Contemporary Dracula." *New Statesman*, 21 June 1999, 44–45.

Stephen B. Armstrong

S Is for Silence **Sue Grafton** (2005)

S Is for Silence is the latest installments in the Alphabet series featuring Kinsey Milhone as a hard-boiled private detective, this time hired by Daisy Sullivan to find out what happened to her mother, Violet, who disappeared 34 years before. Daisy's motive for hiring Kinsey is to get closure: "If she's alive, I want to know where she is and why she's never been in touch. If she's dead, I might feel bad, but at least I'll know the truth" (16). While Violet was a neglectful mother, her disappearance caused even more harm to Daisy's psychological well-being, and the latter is now struggling to get her life on track.

Violet Sullivan was a flirt who had affairs with various men in the town, including a leading car salesman (this for a new Chevy Bel Air that disappeared with her). Her husband, Foley, was a drunkard known for his violent temper, and besides being the town flirt, Violet defied convention by never attempting to hide the abuse he had inflicted upon her. While Foley was never charged with murder when his wife disappeared, he was the leading suspect, which has only added to Daisy's sense of loss. Foley claimed that Violet had run off with a lover but could not prove it, and neither explanation was any comfort to his daughter.

Kinsey tells Daisy she will work for five days, and if she finds no answers by the end of that time she will give up. But as she is investigating, her motel room is searched and her tires slashed, leading her to realize she must be onto something. The novel then follows the traditional path laid down by Chandler and Hammett, where the hard-boiled detective interviews the people involved with a character who has disappeared, only to uncover the scandals that these (often prominent) people have been hiding since the disappearance—Kinsey, meanwhile, coming perilously close to becoming a missing person herself.

However, the novel is the first in the Alphabet series to deviate from the typical first-person narrative. While Kinsey still narrates the present case, her story is intertwined with third-person narratives about the other characters from Violet Sullivan's past in the days before she disappeared, and these vignettes provide alternate perspectives on Violet, from the men with whom she had affairs, the women who hated her, even the teenage babysitter who worshipped her. Furthermore, *S Is for Silence* focuses more on the details of the mystery itself than do the other novels, devoting little time to any social commentary, beyond some indirect statements on the effects of parental neglect and spousal abuse. It also pays less attention to Kinsey's personal life and relationships, limited though they are. Beyond brief mentions of her friends such as Henry Pitt—and the ever-present descriptions of her eating habits—readers see very little of that personal side of Kinsey, which has played an increasing role as the series has evolved.

Some reviewers have commented on the abrupt nature of the ending, arguing that it falls short of SUE GRAFTON's newer, more nuanced narrative style. Connie Fletcher in *Booklist,* however, claims that in *S Is for Silence* Grafton "presents strong character portrayals, a mosaic of motives, and a stunning climax" (6). The novel had a rare million-copy run in its first printing and was chosen for the Literary Guild, Book of the Month Club, and Mystery Guild main selections.

Bibliography

Fletcher, Connie. *Booklist*, 15 September 2005, 6.
Grafton, Sue. *S Is for Silence.* New York: Putnam-Penguin, 2005.
Harris, Karen. *Booklist*, 1 May 2006, 52.

Susie Scifres Kuilan

The Sisterhood of the Traveling Pants **Ann Brashares** (2001)

The Sisterhood of the Traveling Pants is a young-adult novel about four teenage girls whose friendship, both symbolized and supported by a shared pair of jeans, enables them to weather the storms of adolescence. They call themselves the Septembers because they were all born in that month within 17 days of one another, their mothers meeting in a maternity aerobics class. Carmen, whose narration begins and ends the novel, explains:

> Sometimes it seems like we're so close we form one single complete person rather than four separate ones. We settle into types—Bridget the athlete, Lena the beauty, Tibby the rebel, and me, Carmen, the . . . what? The one with the bad temper. But the one who cares the most. The one who cares that we stick together (7).

The four friends have already survived major crises together, including the death of Bridget's mother and the divorce of Carmen's parents, but this summer the girls will be apart for the first time in their lives: Lena is visiting her grandparents in Greece; Bridget is going to soccer camp in Mexico; Carmen will be with her dad in South Carolina; Tibby is stuck at home in boring Bethesda.

The day before going their separate ways, the Septembers discover the Pants, a pair of faded blue jeans Carmen bought secondhand but never wore. The other girls are amazed when the jeans not only fit but flatter each of them in turn, despite their very different shapes, and they insist that Carmen try them on too. Self-conscious about her full figure, Carmen is hurt when her friends suddenly fall silent, but Bridget finally cries out:

> "Carmen, that's not it at all! Look at yourself! You are a thing of beauty. You are a vision. You are a supermodel."
>
> Carmen put her hand on her hip and made a sour face. "That I doubt."
>
> "Seriously. Look at yourself," Lena ordered. "These are magic pants."
>
> Carmen looked at herself. First from far away, then from up close. From the front and then the back.
>
> The CD they'd been listening to ended, but nobody seemed to notice. The phone was ringing distantly, but nobody got up to get it. The normally busy street was silent.
>
> Carmen finally let out her breath. "These are magic pants" (18).

Thus, the Sisterhood of the Traveling Pants is born. Although they believe the Pants are lucky, each girl experiences a major crisis during her turn to wear them. Lena, for example, is troubled by the attention her beauty attracts and afraid of opening herself to love. Distressed by a handsome Greek boy's interest, she makes a vague accusation that leads to a terrible misunderstanding between their respective families but is too ashamed to apologize or admit her growing attraction to Kostos.

Tibby decides to document her lame summer in a "suckumentary," but her focus shifts when Bailey, a mouthy 12-year-old with leukemia, appoints herself as Tibby's assistant and teaches the older girl about courage and compassion. Bailey confesses to the camera: "I'm afraid of the quick judgments and mistakes that everybody makes. You can't fix them without time. I'm afraid of seeing snapshots instead of movies" (174). Tibby, whose sarcastic judgments mask her own fears of change and loss, is inadvertently convicted by Bailey's words.

Carmen could not wait for "the summer of Carmen and Al" (61), but is shocked to learn that her dad has moved in with his fiancée and her two teenage children. Angered by her father's secrecy and neglect, but unable to confront him directly, Carmen heaves a rock through the dining room window and catches the next bus home.

Bridget becomes enamored of a soccer coach and recklessly pursues him even after he warns her to stop. She expects the encounter to be a purely physical thrill but is overwhelmed by the emotional intimacy of sex and the pain of rejection.

During the second rotation of the Pants, the girls draw closer together as they attempt to resolve their respective dilemmas. Back in Bethesda, Carmen and the Pants give Tibby the strength to visit Bailey in the hospital and accept the death of a beloved pet. Inspired by Tibby's courage, Carmen wears the Pants to her father's wedding and sends them on to Lena, who confesses her love for Kostos before flying to Mexico to rescue Bridget and bring her home. Reunited, the Septembers hold a ritual in which they literally record their experiences on the Pants, now a silent witness to the secrets they keep as well as the stories they share.

The central message of the novel is summed up in Rule 10 of the Sisterhood: "Remember: Pants = love. Love your pals. Love yourself" (25). And despite the invocation of magic, *The Sisterhood of the Traveling Pants* is not a fantasy novel; the Pants do not bring the wearers luck or make the girls wiser or better versions of themselves. Rather, Carmen describes the Pants as both a promise and a challenge: "It's not enough to stay in Bethesda, Maryland, and hunker down in air-conditioned houses. We promised one another that someday we'd get out in the world and figure some stuff out" (8), ANN BRASHARES reminding readers that true friendship is in the end no more or less miraculous and essential as a pair of soft, comfortable, well-fitting jeans.

The novel was adapted into a 2005 film starring Amber Tamblyn (Tibby), Alexis Bledel (Lena), America Ferrera (Carmen), and Blake Lively (Bridget). *The Sisterhood of the Traveling Pants 2,* a film version of the novelistic sequel, *The Second Summer of the Sisterhood,* was released in 2008. The series also includes *Girls in Pants: The Third Summer of the Sisterhood* and *Forever in Blue: The Fourth Summer of the Sisterhood.*

Bibliography

Brashares, Ann. *The Sisterhood of the Traveling Pants.* New York: Delacorte, 2001.

———. *The Second Summer of the Sisterhood.* New York: Delacorte, 2003.

———. *Girls in Pants: The Third Summer of the Sisterhood.* New York: Delacorte, 2005.

———. *Forever in Blue: The Fourth Summer of the Sisterhood.* New York: Delacorte, 2007.

Internet Movie Database. "The Sisterhood of the Traveling Pants." Available online. URL: http://www.imdb.com/title/tt0403508. Accessed May 15, 2007.

April N. Kendra

Slow Waltz in Cedar Bend

Robert James Waller (1993)

ROBERT JAMES WALLER's second novel, a middle-aged love story, is aimed at the same audience that made his *THE BRIDGES OF MADISON COUNTY* such a resounding success and employs much the same formula, with the addition of an element of mystery in the heroine's secret past. (Waller reports that he wrote his first book in two weeks and *Slow Waltz* in only 10 days.)

Michael Tillman, a college professor with a working-class background, is a bit of a rebel among his colleagues at an Iowa campus. He is a tenured full professor, so even though often deliberately annoying the administration, and especially his dean, Michael is fully aware that unless "the dean could prove professional incompetence, which he couldn't, or charged Michael with moral turpitude, which he wouldn't," his job is safe (84). At 43 he has lost "the awe he once experienced contemplating the great sweep of time and space" (32) but on the whole is satisfied with his life, "a life of slightly unsettled contentment, all right in general but cut through with an aloneness he simultaneously treasured and disliked"(34). Then a woman with the unlikely name of Jellie Braden walks into his life.

Michael first sees Jellie, the wife of a new faculty member, at the dean's annual faculty reception and is immediately so attracted to her beauty that he begins fantasizing about flying to the Seychelles with her and plunging naked into a waterfall. An economics professor, Jellie's husband just returned from a Fulbright in India, and Michael soon learns that Jellie had lived there with him for three years. However, Michael "picked up something strange about her India days [. . .] that made her reluctant to go into it other than acknowledge she'd been to India" (69).

During the next few months a strong friendship and mutual attraction grows between the two. Surprisingly, Michael finds he also likes Jellie's husband, the "standard issue, [. . .] earnest and boring" Jim Braden (11). Sensitive to the dangers of their budding attraction for each other, Jellie leaves Michael to go to London with Jim when he accepts a semester-long visiting professorship. But when the new school year begins Jim and Jellie return to Iowa, and after a brief struggle of conscience, Jellie and Michael begin an intense and deeply felt affair. That Thanksgiving Jim and Jellie visit their parents in New York, but when Jim returns, Jellie is not with him, and no one knows when or if she will return.

Michael soon learns that Jellie has gone to India, and it is he, not Jellie's disconsolate husband, who sets out to find her and discover what secrets from her past lie hidden there. The book opens with him boarding the Trivandrum Mail train in Villupuram, India, following clues he has gleaned concerning Jellie's whereabouts, but knowing "it was easy to get lost in India if that's what you wanted" (169). Shifting between past and present, the story then unfolds through Michael's flashbacks until he catches up with Jellie and begins to learn her secrets.

Waller vividly evokes the atmosphere of university life, a life he knows well, having been a dean of the Business School at Northern Iowa University; but he is equally adept at bringing to life the sights and sounds of the cities and countryside of India, a country he has only visited. Moreover, there are a number of interesting parallels between the novelist and his protagonist: As young men both had played basketball because their fathers enjoyed the sport; both won college scholarships to play, and "somewhere around [the] sophomore year, discovered [they] didn't really like playing" (66); and both move to ranches in the West after leaving university positions. There he is also a teasing intertextual reference to Robert Kincaid, the fictional *National Geographic* photographer and protagonist of Waller's *The Bridges of Madison County*: As Michael is registering at a hotel where he hopes to find Jellie, he notices a particularly striking photograph of a tiger behind the desk, a photo autographed by Robert Kincaid, whom Tillman learns often spent time at the same hotel. (Waller is also a professional photographer.)

Beyond its colorful protagonists, *Slow Waltz* is peopled with decent individuals endeavoring to do the right thing, and even Michael's jabs at the stodginess of the university are never aggressive or made in a spirit of malice. He is an intellectual and individualist who relishes his eccentricities but who does not throw away all convention. He is also a dutiful and loving son, and most important, he loathes the thought of being an instrument of marital breakup, his relationships have always have been with women as free to make such choices as he. Moreover, he develops a genuine, if reluctant, regard for his colleague Jim Braden. If he *is* missing anything in his life, it is not of any consequence—until he meets Jellie. At Thanksgiving at the Bradens Michael becomes "a little sad . . . in a way he couldn't grasp. Sad for her, for him, for Jimmy, and for where this might all lead" (60).

Nonetheless, though sensitive, Michael is the epitome of masculinity: Jellie's father, a man who was "all right, as long as you didn't cross him" (54), thinks Michael has "got some fiber to him" (71); the dean's wife, Carolyn, says, "Michael Tillman frightens the hell out of Arthur" (122); and all the other middle-aged, balding, and out-of-shape men (whom Carolyn classifies as eunuchs) are envious of Michael's athletic body, his free spirit, and his attractiveness to women. Even in an early morning encounter with a tiger in India, Michael remains coolheaded and unafraid.

Meanwhile, Jellie, even with her scarred past, has come to accept her life as it is. She is not unhappy but has settled into a marriage with Braden because she "couldn't think of any good reason not to" (18). Jim, in Jellie's words, "would have agreed to anything, just to get me to marry him. . . . He's never complained once about my visits to India, and he's never asked any questions about what it is I do when I'm over here" (212). Like the list of guests Jim wants to invite for Thanksgiving, he is "predictable, safe" (47) and has provided Jellie with the sense of security she sought in marrying him. It is only when she meets Michael that she begins to think of the possibility of real happiness.

Notwithstanding such nuances, *Slow Waltz in Cedar Bend* follows closely the narrative trajectory of Waller's previous blockbuster: A solitary but essentially decent man meets and falls in love with a good woman who is married, and they are forced to confront difficult choices about their love and the remainder of their lives, the message of each being that one cannot choose the person with whom one falls in love, or as Woody Allen famously put it, "the heart wants what it wants."

On the heels of the success of *The Bridges of Madison County*, *Slow Waltz in Cedar Bend* quickly became a best seller but did not attain the success of the first novel. Critical reviews were mixed, but more negative than positive. The movie rights to the book were purchased, and Eric Roth worked on an original screenplay, but a film has not yet been undertaken.

Bibliography

Waller, Robert James. *Slow Waltz in Cedar Bend* (Large Print Basic Series). Thorndike, Maine: Thorndike Press, 1993.

Jean Shepherd Hamm

Smith, Martin Cruz (1942–)

Martin Cruz Smith was born Martin William Smith in Reading, Pennsylvania, in 1942 and worked as a journalist before taking up a career in fiction. He is of Native American origin (Pueblo) from his mother's side, and his first fictional work, *The Indians Won* (1970), an alternative science-fiction Native American history, as well as the novel *Nightwing* (1977) with its Native American setting, reflect this side of his complex background (the latter was made into a film in 1979 directed by Arthur Hiller). Smith has also written mysteries, horror and spy stories, detective fiction, and suspense stories.

Much of his work has been written under various names and pseudonyms. Before his fame with the success in 1981 of *GORKY PARK*, he published three novels as Martin Smith (*The Indians Won*, *Gypsy in Amber* [1971] and *Canto for a Gypsy* [1972]), and in his early career he published two volumes of formulaic thrillers as Nick Carter, two as Jake Logan, seven as Simon Quinn, and one as Martin Quinn. He also wrote two novels as Cruz Smith: *Nightwing* and *The Analog Bullet* (1978), while in the 1990s there came another 30 volumes as Jake Logan (especially the Slocum series).

Smith is, however, best known for his tightly woven political thrillers centered on the brilliant, dogged, and incorruptible Arkady Renko, a Soviet-era investigator harkening back, for all his differences (and the third-person narrative) to Raymond Chandler's iconoclastic Phillip Marlowe, navigating his melancholic way through the murk of noir Los Angeles. Renko is a man of high morals but not a moralist, obstinately, even recklessly seeking justice where there seems none to be found. The series, which bridges several crucial epochs in modern Soviet history, began with the highly acclaimed *Gorky Park*, set in the late 1970s Soviet Union at the coldest of the cold war. The story opens with the discovery of three mutilated bodies in Gorky Park in central Moscow and revolves around corruption, international crime, and conflicts between various law enforcement units of Soviet Russia. It was adapted into a film by the same title in 1983 directed by Michael Apton.

Smith followed with *Polar Star* (1989), *Red Square* (1992), *Havana Bay* (1999), *Wolves Eat Dogs* (2004), and *Stalin's Ghost* (2007).

Polar Star finds Renko in the late 1980s, now in hiding from the KGB on a trawler sailing the Bering Sea, reluctantly investigating the death of a member of the crew. As in *Gorgy Park*—indeed throughout the whole series—the grim reality of everyday Soviet life is set in stark and sometimes morbid contrast to the alluring dazzle of the capitalist West. In *Red Square* Renko has been recalled to his post as a militia investigator to confront the Chechen black-market mob and commences an implacable exploration into the murder of his informant. Set in 1991, the novel chronicles the breakdown of the Soviet state and the ensuing corrupt capitalist escalation of black marketeering.

In *Havana Bay* the setting changes dramatically. Renko is mourning his dead wife, Irina, and contemplating suicide in Cuba, where he has been sent to investigate the death of his friend Sergei Pribluda, who had been working for the Russian foreign intelligence service there. By now, unfolding in a suffocating and yet strangely liberating atmosphere, the "Communist world has shrunk to Cuba," and the former Cuban affection for the Russians (sweetened by billions of rubles) has turned to bitterness. With his Cuban aide Ofelia Osorio, a detective in the Policia Nacional de la Revolucion, Renko cracks the case, revealing in the course of his investigation a massive and complex conspiracy.

In *Wolves Eat Dogs* Renko (now a senior investigator) travels to Ukraine to look into the death of two eminent Russian business moguls. Set in 1996, 10 years after the Chernobyl nuclear plant disaster, the tale focuses on the abandoned city of Pripyat, firmly inside the "zone of exclusion" around the

Chernobyl plant. Accompanied by the insistent ticking of the dosimeter, Renko navigates the shadowy avenues of corruption, greed, and betrayal in the shadow of nuclear catastrophe to solve one of his most convoluted cases.

Stalin's Ghost, the most recent installment in the series, finds Renko back in now contemporary Moscow in a setting reminiscent of the series' inception in *Gorky Park*:

> Winter was what Muscovites lived for. Winter knee-deep in snow that softened the city, flowed from golden dome to golden dome, resculpted statues and transformed park paths into skating trails. . . . And, in Arkady's experience, when the snow melted, bodies would be discovered.

A case involving contract killings and corruption sets him investigating his own colleagues who had previously served as Black Berets in Chechnya. Stalin's ghost is said to appear regularly in the Moscow metro as, in this brave new Russia, the past haunts the present, love appears inseparable from betrayal, and crime is about to pay.

The three other novels written in between the Renko books—*Stallion Gate* (1986), *Rose* (1996), and *December 6* (2002)—differ significantly from Smith's thriller prose and illustrate the author's eclectic interests and skills. The first is centered on the character of a Pueblo Indian, Joe Pena, and tells a story about the atomic bomb tests of 1944 in Los Alamos; *Rose* is about coal mining in Victorian England from a feminist point of view; *December 6* (published in the Great Britain as *Tokyo Station*) is a sensitive exploration of Japanese life on the eve of Pearl Harbor.

Smith has been nominated four times for the Edgar Award of the Mystery Writers of America: 1972 (for *Gypsy in Amber*), 1976 (for *The Midas Coffin* as Simon Quinn), 1978 (for *Nightwing*), and 1982 (for *Gorky Park*). In 1982 he was awarded the Gold Dagger prize by the Crime Writers Association for *Gorky Park*. He has also twice received the Dashiell Hammett Award from the International Association of Crime Writers/North America in 1997 (for *Rose*) and in 2000 (for *Havana Bay*).

Bibliography

Smith, Martin Cruz. *Gorky Park*. London: William Collins, 1981.

———. "The Salon Interview: Working in a Coal Mine." Interview by Sophie Majeski. Available online. URL: http://www.salon.com/weekly/interview960520.html.

Van Dover, J. K. "Martin Cruz Smith: Overview." In *St. James Guide to Crime & Mystery Writers*, 4th ed. Edited by Jay P. Pederson. Farmington Hills, Mich.: St. James Press, 1996.

Joel Kuortti

Sparks, Nicholas (1965–)

Sparks is the author of 12 best-selling novels distinguished by their sensitive and moving portrayals of love and loss, often shadowed by tragedy. He was born in Omaha, Nebraska, in 1965, and his earliest memories include moving from city to city as his father pursued various academic degrees. Because of this, the family often struggled financially, but Sparks was never much aware of their poverty as a child. In high school he excelled both in both academics and athletics and graduated as valedictorian in 1984, receiving a full track scholarship to the University of Notre Dame, where as a freshman he set a track record yet to be broken.

While recovering from an injury the following year, Sparks was encouraged by his mother to write a book to pass the time, and though this first novel remains unpublished, it marked the beginning of an interest in writing that, though long deflected, would eventually result in an extraordinary career. Sparks went on to graduate with a degree in business finance from the University of Notre Dame in 1988, and that year he met his future wife, Cathy, whom he married in 1989.

The family suffered several blows during the following years. Sparks's mother died in a horseback-riding accident, and his younger sister, Danielle, was diagnosed with cancer. Unable to find his niche in the business world, Sparks dabbled in real estate, waited tables, sold dental products over the phone, and even opened his own manufacturing company. During this time he wrote a second novel and collaborated with Olympic gold medalist Billy

Mills on a book entitled *Wokini: A Lakotan Journey to Happiness and Self-Understanding,* which did well in the regional market and was later reprinted by both Random House and Hay House Books.

At the age of 28, while working as a pharmaceutical salesman, Sparks penned *The Notebook,* found an agent, and through their offices was offered a million-dollar advance from Warner Books only months after completing the manuscript. But as Sparks was preparing for a grueling 45-city book tour in the fall of 1995, he received word that his father had been killed in an automobile accident. Despite this latest trial he managed to promote the novel, which spent 56 weeks on the *New York Times* hardcover best-seller list and 54 more on the paperback list.

Over the next few years Sparks moved his growing family to North Carolina and produced a string of national and international best sellers, often drawing inspiration and material from the very misfortunes he had known. Characters fall in love and are separated by tragedy or disease; others suffer silently until discovering a love that makes them stronger. The misdiagnosis of his son's autism anchors the narrator of *The Rescue* (2000); his sister's courageous but unsuccessful battle with cancer, that of *A Walk to Remember* (1999).

Several of his novels also became box-office hits. In 1999 *Message in a Bottle* premiered starring Kevin Costner and Robin Wright Penn and eventually grossed $120 million in total sales. *A Walk to Remember* starring Mandy Moore and Shane West premiered in 2002, just as filming for *The Notebook* began. Starring James Garner, Gena Rowlands, Rachel McAdams, and Ryan Gosling, *The Notebook*'s premiere in 2004 was followed by 11 award wins, including a Screen Actor's Guild best actor in a supporting role for James Garner and seven other nominations. It went on to gross more than $80 million in the United States alone, making it Sparks's most successful movie adaptation.

Today Sparks lives in New Bern, North Carolina, with his wife, Cathy, and their five children. He is still an avid athlete who runs daily, competes in Tae Kwon Do, and coaches the track team at a local high school. He is also a major contributor to the Creative Writing Program at the University of Notre Dame.

Bibliography

Message in a Bottle. Directed by Luis Mandoki. Warner Home Video, 1999.

Mills, Billy, and Nicholas Sparks. *Wokini: Your Personal Journey to Happiness and Self-Understanding.* Quiney Calif.: Feather Publishing, 1991.

The Notebook. Directed by Nick Cassavetes. New Line Home Video, 2004.

Sparks, Nicholas. *The Notebook.* New York: Warner, 1996.

———. *Message in a Bottle.* New York: Warner, 1998.

———. *A Walk to Remember.* New York: Warner, 1999.

———. *The Rescue.* New York: Warner, 2000.

———. *A Bend in the Road.* New York: Warner, 2001.

———. *Nights in Rodanthe.* New York: Warner, 2002.

———. *The Guardian.* New York: Warner, 2003.

———. *The Wedding.* New York: Warner, 2003.

———. *Three Weeks with My Brother.* New York: Warner, 2004.

———. *At First Sight.* New York: Warner, 2005.

———. *True Believer.* New York: Warner, 2005.

———. *Dear John.* New York: Warner, 2006.

———. *The Choice.* New York: Grand Central Publishing, 2007.

———. *The Official Nicholas Sparks Website.* Available online. URL: http://www.nicholassparks.com. Accessed May 19, 2007.

A Walk to Remember. Directed by Adam Shankman. Warner Home Video, 2002.

Erin Brescia

The Spike

Arnaud de Borchgrave and Robert Moss (1980)

The Spike focuses on the behind-the-scenes interactions of Soviet KGB agents and the U.S. government as they struggle to manipulate the media and public opinion. The events of the story begin in May 1967 at the height of protests against the Vietnam War, follow the election and later resignation of Nixon, and conclude with the rise and fall of a fictional, ineffective president unwittingly controlled by the KGB. Robert Hockney, 22, although supposedly "embarrassed by slogans" (3) criticizing U.S. involvement in Vietnam, yearns to break into journalism by exposing covert actions of the CIA His hunger for journalistic success drives him to uncover abuses of government power but also leads him directly into the path of dangerous "revolutionaries" who want to use him as an outlet for their own propaganda. The KGB and Soviet Union are the novel's main villains, along with those characters who agree to assist them in weakening America, both from within and without.

ARNAUD DE BORCHGRAVE and ROBERT MOSS avoid stock characters and simple motivations. Michel Renard, a French journalist morose from his lack of professional advancement and dysfunctional marriage to Astrid, is lured into the services of the KGB through its offer of money and power. Tessa Torrance, a famous Hollywood actress, becomes increasingly involved in calls for America to cease what she views as aggression all over the globe. Her naïveté, however, blinds her both to the brutal tactics implemented by guerrilla groups and to the reality that not all "counter-revolutionary" organizations are trustworthy and just. Viktor Barisov, although initially seeking advancement and recognition from the KGB, later defects, and his knowledge of KGB spies within the U.S. government and subsequent testimony before a Senate Intelligence Committee shakes Washington, including the White House, to its core.

The same themes are at play in Moss's earlier *Death Beam* (1982) and de Borchgrave and Moss's *Monimbo* (1983), in which Hockney returns to investigate Fidel Castro's involvement with the Sandanistas in Nicaragua.

The "spike" of the title refers to a newspaper editor's ability to kill a story; the articles suppressed in *The Spike* having the potential to embarrass either the United States or the Soviet Union. *The World*, Hockney's newspaper, has close ties to the Foundation for Progressive Reform, heavily involved in KGB operations in America, and when he begins to uncover the extent of the KGB presence in Washington, he finds himself unceremoniously out of a job. Personal loyalty quickly gives way to perpetuating propaganda, and Hockney discovers that many of those he counted on as friends and mentors have either betrayed him outright or fed him misinformation all along, forcing him to reconsider his entire career.

Hockney's progress toward a realistic yet not cynical maturity emerges as *The Spike*'s primary focus, and late in the novel a friend recognizes this maturity in Hockney's refusing to author a sensationalistic story, telling him, "It means there are values and loyalties that you care about more than a quick headline" (306). Now in his late 20s, he has become a man of some integrity and honor, and his eventual reconciliation with Julia Cummings, the love of his youth, whom he has avoided in his quest for fame, represents the final stage in this progress. It is only when he overcomes his blind ideological idealism and decides to pursue truth over headlines that he can appreciate the values of stability and fidelity offered by Julia and rise above the sophisticated mendacity of his milieu.

The specific events of the novel became dated with the fall of the Soviet Union and the end of the cold war. However, the larger issues it raises are still relevant in the current political climate. It may be said as much of the present-day situation in Iraq as of the novel's Vietnam that "a growing body of Americans had come to accept that the war could not be won" (65); and journalists embedded with a given platoon must decide whether to report what they see or sanitize their stories to satisfy government officials who control their ability to remain there. Most searchingly, while reporting from Vietnam, Hockney discovers that all sides in the conflict have reasons for their actions, which he feels the American people deserve to understand, one of the lessons being that precisely in proportion to the power of the media, damage occurs when truth is subjected to "the spike."

Bibliography

Borchgrave, Arnaud de, and Robert Moss. *The Spike*. 1980. Reprint, New York: Avon Books, 1981.

Amy M. Green

State of Fear Michael Crichton (2004)

State of Fear is a curiously inverted thriller describing the efforts of its protagonist to thwart a group of violent ecoterrorists seeking to create environmental disasters to advance their own cause. Though Crichton frequently shifts the point of view, most of the novel centers on Peter Evans, a young lawyer working for philanthropist George Morton. As it opens, Morton's most important contribution is the money he provides to the National Environmental Resource Fund (NERF), a group pursuing a lawsuit against the Environmental Protection Agency, blaming the U.S. government for its decisive share in global warming and the resulting rise in sea level that threatens a poor island nation.

Early on, however, Morton begins to suspect that the grounds for the suit may not be as solid as he had assumed, and following a meeting with the mysterious Professor Kenner, he becomes increasingly skeptical of NERF's aims, finally denouncing the organization at a banquet that the group itself has arranged in his honor. Following the banquet, the wreck of his car is discovered on a mountain road, Morton himself apparently having been cast into the sea.

Meanwhile, Evans himself becomes increasingly disturbed as he learns more about the lawsuit. When the lawyers involved ask him about his knowledge of global warming, concerned about their ability to sway the jury, he is repeatedly forced to admit that his knowledge on the subject is less precise or more limited than he thought, or simply inaccurate. These concerns continue to mount when Evans meets the mysterious Professor Kenner himself and learns that Kenner is, in fact, a government agent on the trail of an international terrorist group called the Environmental Liberation Front (ELF). With Morton, whose death had been faked, and an informally assembled team, Evans circles the globe, locating ELF cells and foiling their plans to create natural-looking disasters that will help draw media attention to the dangers of global warming. Along the way he repeatedly confronts the polymathic Kenner, whose incisive logic and seemingly comprehensive knowledge of climatology finally convinces him that global warming is not the problem he had been convinced it was.

The climax of the novel comes when Evans, Kenner, their team, and George Morton work together to stop the most devastating attack of all, the creation of a tsunami that would devastate the California coast. The novel ends with Morton proposing the creation of a new kind of environmental organization altogether, one that will address real problems based on genuine science.

In many ways *State of Fear* is a conventional thriller featuring the kinds of characters and scenes that readers of the genre would easily recognize. The opening scenes, for example, describe a beautiful femme fatale luring an unsuspecting young scientist to his doom. There are car chases and gunfights, as well as the stalwart device of the genre—when the villains are ready and able to kill the heroes, they do not kill them outright but leave them in positions where they must "surely" be killed and then depart, allowing the heroes to narrowly escape. Thus, Evans and Morton's assistant, Sarah, escape from an Antarctic crevasse, while Kenner and Sarah manage to evade electrocution because the villains cannot abide the smell of burning flesh (280). In some instances, however, Crichton deliberately invokes the genre's clichés only to work interesting variations on them, as he does in the novel's most dynamic scene, a car chase in which Peter and Sarah are attacked by lightning controlled by the villains' technology.

The novel's overarching thematic interest, characteristic of Crichton's oeuvre, lies in the nature of scientific understanding in the modern world, particularly the popular understanding of global warming. The central thesis of the novel is summed up by the eccentric genius Professor Hoffman when he is refused admittance to a conference on climate change: "Fearmongers!" he cries, "Immoral fearmongers [. . .] False fears are a plague, a modern plague!" (447–448). As Crichton depicts it, global warming, far from being a clear and dangerous trend created by human action, is a grand hoax perpetrated on a public only too eager to have something to fear. Hoffman blames "the politico-legal-media complex" who, at the end of the cold war, needed a new enemy to inspire fear in the masses. Global warming, the novel suggests, was "a setup from the beginning" (245) but gained ground because it provided an adequately and conveniently terrifying enemy. The false threat was propagated not only by self-serving bureaucrats but also by greedy scientists eager to cash in on newly available funds to research the faux crisis (315–316). As the novel concludes, Crichton via Morton, makes a sweeping denunciation of science as it is presently done, condemning it as effectively worthless, at least when it comes to addressing real problems of public policy: "Because if you solve a problem, your funding ends. All that's got to change" (565)—a change Crichton describes in a striking author's message after the novel's conclusion, followed by an appendix, "Why Politicized Science Is Dangerous."

One of Professor Kenner's principal functions in *State of Fear* is that of a Socratic master, humiliating the feckless simpletons who have swallowed the global warming lie whole, the most memorable being celebrity Ted Bradley, a thinly veiled portrait of actor and activist Martin Sheen. Bradley's bravado, honed by playing the president on television, is undermined by his stupidity and ignorance, and Kenner continually makes a fool of him.

Bradley is the most benighted environmentalist in the novel, but he is typical of the novel's view of the modern environmentalist movement in general, which it sees as self-serving and out of touch with reality. Indeed, every committed environmentalist in the novel is either a dupe like Bradley or a Machiavellian con man like NERF director Nicholas Drake, who is revealed late in the novel to be in league with the terrorists all along (467). There is not a single character in the novel who is both committed to global warming *and* who knows the facts, implying that it is impossible to know the truth and still be a global warming advocate. Intellectuals, the novel suggests, have abandoned their posts as seekers of truth and have allowed universities to become "factories of fear" (458). Somewhat paradoxically, while Kenner cites reams of scientific papers to make his case, the novel nevertheless suggests that science, at present, is never to be trusted. Surprisingly, the banning of the chemical DDT ("so safe you could eat it") is lamented because it has spurred the resurgence of malaria (487). Even more surprising, the novel implies that the harmful nature of tobacco smoke has never been adequately proven and that antismoking laws are a travesty of justice (438).

Unsurprisingly, such a polemical work provoked vigorous response when it was published, some praising it for exposing the "scam" of "global warming alarmism" (Ebell 22), others accusing Crichton of mixing misleading half-truths with "straightforward error" to make his case against global warming while still admitting that Crichton's larger claims about scientific objectivity were worth taking seriously (Allen 198). Still others have gone further, attacking *State of Fear* as "one-sided [and] error-ridden," even dangerous in so far as its author "has been treated as if he actually possessed a deep understanding of climate science" (Miller 94).

Bibliography

Allen, Myles. "A Novel View of Global Warming." *Nature* 433, 20 January 2005, 198.

Crichton, Michael. *State of Fear.* New York: HarperCollins, 2004.

Ebell, Myron. "Politically Incorrect Thriller Exposes Global Warming Scam." *Human Events,* 10 January 2005, 22.

Miller, Allen. "Bad Fiction, Worse Science." *Issues in Science and Technology* (winter 2006): 93–95.

Todd H. J. Pettigrew

Steel, Danielle (1947–)

Steel is a romance author with more than 70 titles to her credit. She has been on the *New York Times* best-seller list for an impressive 390 consecutive weeks, has 560 million in sales, and has had her work translated into 28 languages, with many of her romances adapted for television. She has also written three books of nonfiction and 14 children's books.

Danielle Fernande Dominique Schuelein-Steel was born in 1947, the only daughter of John Schuelein-Steel, a German immigrant of some means who fled the Nazis during World War II, and Norma da Camara Stone des Reis, the daughter of a Portuguese government representative. Both of them appear to have been more interested in parties and traveling than in the young Danielle, who was raised for the most part by nannies and sent away to boarding schools and summer camps at a very young age. This estrangement from her parents led to a very lonely early life and left its imprint on the young author. As a student she excelled in literature and the arts but did poorly in math and science. At the age of eight she attended the exclusive Lycée Français de New York and thrived in its highly regimented and academically rigorous environment; yet, though she flourished academically, physically she was beset with difficulties, suffering from asthma, allergies, a mild case of polio, and hepatitis from eating contaminated food. Though illness often kept her out of class and at times in the hospital, her parents rarely, if ever, came to visit.

In 1963 she attended the prestigious Parsons School of Design in New York but did not enjoy it much, transferring after a year to New York University, where she majored in French and minored in Italian. However, she dropped out four months from graduation and has never gone back to finish her degree. Some biographers speculate that she dropped out to anger her parents, who divorced when she was still a child, though Steel herself has said that she felt she had been educated and that the diploma was of no consequence (Bane 14).

After leaving college at 18, she married her longtime boyfriend, Claude-Eric Lazard, the son of an international banking family; his controlling personality eventually led to the couple's divorce but not until they had produced a daughter, Beatrix, in 1968, Steel's first of seven biological children. Though Steel was wealthy even before marrying Lazard, she quickly grew bored with the life of a socialite and started working, while still pregnant, for an advertising and public relations firm, a move that in part led to the first of her five divorces, in 1974. In the midst of all this upheaval Steel published her first romance, the moderately successful *Going Home* (1973).

No sooner had she gained such hard-won independence, however, than she embarked on a stage in her life as improbable and riveting as those of her best novels, marrying in 1975 a convict named Danny Zugelder in a jailhouse ceremony. Zugelder, in prison for bank robbery, was paroled shortly after they married, but by 1978 the marriage had fallen apart; they divorced, and Zugelder was shortly thereafter charged with a series of rapes. In that same year Steel married William Toth, a recovering heroin addict, with whom she had become pregnant. Though Toth had been clean for two years when he met her, he quickly relapsed into his drug habit and they divorced in 1981. However, in 1978 they had had a son, Nick, whose life would itself read like a peculiarly sensational subplot in the Steel romance. Struggling to raise a newborn and her teenage daughter, Steel had known John Traina for some time, and after both their divorces were finalized in 1981, hers from Toth and Traina's from his wife, Dede, they were married in that same year. Traina formally adopted Nick, as Toth had given up all parental rights, and Steel adopted Traina's two teenage sons, Trevor and Todd. Together Steel and Traina had five more children.

In the early 1990s two biographers, Vickie Bane and Lorenzo Benet, wrote a biography of Steel's life entitled *The Lives of Danielle Steel: The Unauthorized Biography of America's #1 Best-Selling Author.* Steel did not endorse the book, and when she discovered that it would reveal that Nick was not Traina's biological son, she sued to keep the book from being published and won in the California lower courts—the judge going so far as to seal the case and the adoption records, but the Supreme Court of California overturned the decision because of Steel's fame, and the book was published in 1994. Fifteen at the time, Nick had been fighting bipolar disorder all his life, and at the age of 19 in 1997 he committed suicide, the discovery of his true parentage, though far from the only cause, undoubtedly a contributing factor. In response, Steel wrote a work of nonfiction, *His Bright Light* (1998), about Nick and his battles with bipolar disorder and also created the Nick Traina Foundation, whose mission is to help manic depressives in all areas of life. But the stress, the legal battles with the biographers, and the revelations those battles brought to light had done irreparable damage to the marriage, and in 1996 Steel and Traina divorced.

Steel, however, had already fallen in love again, this time to Silicon Valley financial guru Tom Perkins. They married in 1997 but two years later divorced, at which point it would appear that some lesson finally came home to the author, who has remained single ever since, devoting her time to her children and writing—the latter leaving little room for much else. According to her official Web site, "She works on three books at a time—researching one storyline, writing another, and editing the third. Still, she often spends two to three years researching and developing a single project. In the heat of a first draft, it is not uncommon for her to spend eighteen to twenty hours a day glued to her 1946 Olympia manual typewriter."

Unsurprisingly, much of Steel's romance oeuvre reflects elements of her own romantic life: *Passion's Promise* (1977) concerns a woman who marries an ex-con; *Remembrance* (1981) has a heroin-addicted husband; *The Klone and I* (1998) recalls Steel's marriage to Tom Perkins and was apparently a joke between the two of them. But Steel also illustrates a true storyteller's gift for vivid historical description: *Jewels* (1992) relates the tale of a family of jewelers who are financially decimated during World War II and then successfully rebuild their empire; ZOYA (1968) unfolds during the cataclysmic events of the Russian Revolution. But whether the setting be domestic or exotic, the same recurring themes emerge, among them childhood struggles, abandonment, unhappiness, hard-won personal realization, love, lust, abuse, and overcoming.

Steel is often criticized for her thin plotting and outré portrayals of character and place. Certainly an inordinate number of millionaires and exotic settings are found throughout her work. But her immense and long-standing popularity, the intense loyalty of her fans, and above all the page-turning appeal of her narratives all bear the unmistakable mark of a first-class storyteller.

Bibliography

Bane, Vickie L. and Lorenzo Benet. *The Lives of Danielle Steel: The Unauthorized Biography of America's #1 Best-Selling Author.* New York: St. Martin's, 1994.

Danielle Steel The Official Website. "Biography." Available online. URL: http://www.randomhouse.com/features/steel/index.html.

Steel, Danielle. *His Bright Light.* New York: Delacorte, 1998.

Wikipedia. "Danielle Steel." Available online. URL: http://en.wikipedia.org/wiki/Danielle_Steel. Accessed May 17, 2007.

JJ Pionke

The Stephanie Plum Mystery Series

Janet Evanovich (1943–)

The release of *One for the Money* in 1994 marked JANET EVANOVICH's move from romance writing to mystery writing and the introduction of her heroine, Stephanie Plum. Evanovich, born and raised in South River, New Jersey, employs nearby Trenton, and more specifically a blue-collar neighborhood called "the burg," as the setting for her humorous mystery novels. The numerically titled series chronicles Plum's escapades as an incompetent bounty hunter, having been laid off from her position as a low-end lingerie buyer. The series has proven highly successful with its diverse cast of appealingly eccentric characters engaged in delightfully madcap plots. Stephanie Plum, a big-haired and trash-mouthed Jersey girl, devours pizza and doughnuts but can still squeeze into tight jeans or a spandex miniskirt. Though entirely inexperienced as a bounty hunter, she somehow manages to solve her cases with a mix of native intelligence, self-deprecating humor, and the help of her oddball family and friends.

One for the Money introduces most of the characters that populate the Plum novels, as well as the polluted and usually murderous setting for Stephanie's adventures in crime-solving. Unable to pay her rent and having lost her car to repossession, Stephanie bribes her sexually deviant cousin Vinnie, a bail bondsman, into hiring her as a bounty hunter. Vinnie's assistant, Connie, gives Stephanie her first case, apprehending Joseph Morelli, a sly and sexy Trenton cop accused of fatally shooting an unarmed suspect and then failing to appear in court. Stephanie's task is complicated by the fact that she has a history with Morelli, having lost her virginity to him at 16 and then struck him with her father's Buick. Despite these complications, the $10,000 for apprehending Morelli proves too much to refuse, so she apprentices herself to Ranger, a Cuban-born bounty hunter with no address, lots of weapons, and the seeming ability to appear out of nowhere. As she delves further into the Morelli case, she encounters a psychotic boxer and his creepy manager, two prostitutes who serve as her most reliable informants, Morelli's imposing mother, and at last Morelli himself, charming and volatile, who becomes more appealing the more she gets to know him.

In the second novel of the series, *Two for the Dough* (1996), Stephanie pursues bail-jumper Kenny Mancuso, accused of shooting his friend in the knee. Her investigation leads her into a morass of murder, missing caskets, and weapons stolen from an army base. Joe Morelli is also investigating the case, which gives Evanovich the opportunity to further the romantic tension between Morelli and Stephanie. In addition, Stephanie's unbalanced Grandma Mazur, from whom Stephanie clearly inherits her love of intrigue, insinuates herself into the case as it involves the funeral parlor where she enjoys attending wakes—her primary social outlet.

In *Three to Get Deadly* (1997) Stephanie faces the unpopular task of apprehending Uncle Mo, a beloved candy-store owner, who has skipped bail on a charge unlikely to earn him any serious legal punishment. While the community is unwilling to help her in her investigation, Stephanie does have the rather clumsy assistance of Lula, one-time prostitute and current filing assistant, with a love of spandex, guns, and criminal takedowns.

Stephanie again teams up with Lula and Grandma Mazur in *Four to Score* (1998) as she attempts to recover Maxine Nowicki, a waitress accused of stealing her boyfriend's car. What seems like a simple apprehension quickly becomes complicated, though, and requires her to call on Sally Sweet, a gigantic transvestite and rock singer with a penchant for cracking codes. Meanwhile, the loss of yet another vehicle and her apartment causes Stephanie to move in with Joe Morelli, kindling marriage talk in her family and his. In the hunt prompted by coded messages received by Nowicki's boyfriend, Stephanie witnesses mutilation and murder, as well as an adventure in Atlantic City before solving the crime.

High Five (1999), Evanovich's her first hardcover best seller, finds Trenton's accused largely showing up for their court dates, again seriously crimping Stephanie's income. She agrees to work for her mysterious and sexy mentor at RangeMan Enterprises and also agrees to do some private snooping to find her missing uncle after discovering photos of garbage bags full of body parts at his home. Stephanie finds herself tailed by a bookie also looking for her uncle and stalked by the psychotic boxer, Ramirez, with whom she tangled in *One for the Money.* Evanovich here intensifies the sexual tension between Stephanie and Ranger and the love triangle involving Morelli.

In *Hard Eight* (2002) Stephanie pursues not a criminal who has jumped bail but a mother and daughter who have disappeared in violation of a child custody bond. Her investigation leads to dangerous entanglements with a sadistic mobster obsessed with Napoleon. Her relationship with Joe Morelli is strained by his belief that her career is too dangerous for her, and Stephanie finds herself more vulnerable to her attraction to Ranger. Evanovich introduces a new character to the cast, an incompetent lawyer named Albert Kloughn (pronounced "clown"), who becomes her sister's romantic interest.

Confronted with the dangers of being a bounty hunter at the opening of *Eleven on Top* (2005), Stephanie decides to pursue a safer career, successively working in a button factory, dry cleaner, and fast-food restaurant. However, trouble pursuing her to each of these establishments, along with the disappearance of several local businessmen, threatening notes from a stalker, and an attack by the stalker on Joe Morelli all combine to lure Stephanie back into investigating crimes with Lula, who has taken over her bounty-hunting duties.

Twelve Sharp (2006) finds Ranger once again the suspect in a crime, this time the kidnapping of his own daughter. As she seeks to help him, Stephanie must deal with a female stalker claiming to be his wife, as well as a psychotic Ranger imposter, all while trying to keep Grandma Mazur, who has joined a rock band, from causing too much damage at the funeral parlor.

Evanovich has also published two holiday-themed Plum novellas, *Visions of Sugar Plums* (2003) and *Plum Lovin'* (2007). In each Stephanie teams up with Diesel, an attractive blond mystery man who seems to have supernatural powers which he employs to help Stephanie solve their cases.

Bibliography

Evanovich, Janet. *One for the Money.* New York: Scribner's, 1994.

———. *Two for the Dough.* New York: Scribner's, 1996.

———. *Three to Get Deadly.* New York: Scribner's, 1997.

———. *Four to Score.* New York: St. Martin's, 1998.

———. *High Five.* New York: St. Martin's, 1999.

———. *Hot Six.* New York: St. Martin's, 2000.

———. *Seven Up.* New York: St. Martin's, 2001.

———. *Hard Eight.* New York: St. Martin's, 2002.
———. *Visions of Sugar Plums.* New York: St. Martin's, 2002.
———. *To the Nines.* New York: St. Martin's, 2003.
———. *Ten Big Ones.* New York: St. Martin's, 2004.
———. *Eleven on Top.* New York: St. Martin's, 2005.
———. *Twelve Sharp.* New York: St. Martin's, 2006.
———. *Plum Lovin'.* New York: St. Martin's, 2007.

Michelle Greenwald

The Summons John Grisham (2002)

Unlike the typical JOHN GRISHAM legal thriller, pitting an individual lawyer-hero against some vast and sinister force, *The Summons* foregrounds a dysfunctional southern family and eschews the trademark courtroom drama. Though two of the main characters are lawyers, the law remains in the background for most of the novel, Grisham focusing instead on an old Mississippi family full of secrets and in decline. A cancer victim on his deathbed, retired Judge Reuben Atlee requests that his sons, Ray and Forrest, return to Maple Run, the family home in Clanton, Mississippi, to resolve the judge's estate before he dies.

Ray Atlee, a recently divorced law professor, is reluctant to return to his father's world, but the judge's summons forces him to confront the past he wants to leave behind. As a young lawyer he refused to join his father in private practice in Clanton, opting instead for an academic career at the University of Virginia. Ray's world is Charlottesville, where he lives an urban lifestyle in a downtown apartment surrounded by coffee shops, bars, and jogging trails. His return to Clanton forces him to deal with his latent sense of guilt: "he should've stayed, should've gone in with the old man and founded the house of Atlee & Atlee, should've married a local girl and sired a half-dozen descendants who would live at Maple Run, where they would adore the Judge and make him happy in his old age" (42).

Like Ray, Forrest Atlee is reluctant to return, but for different reasons. He is the family's black sheep, "a living, walking disaster, a boy of thirty-six whose mind had been deadened by every legal and illegal substance known to American culture" (11). When Ray arrives at Maple Run, he finds his father dead (apparently of complications from cancer or an accidental morphine overdose) and a new handwritten will directing Ray to serve as executor and the estate to be divided equally between Ray and Forrest, which revises an earlier one filed with the judge's attorney, Harry Rex Vonner (a returning character from Grisham's earlier novel *A Time to Kill*). Ray also finds almost $3 million in cash stashed in a cupboard, and this discovery sets the plot formally in motion.

In addition to its melodramatic story line, *The Summons* evokes the same moody southern atmosphere of Clanton that Grisham so richly detailed in his first novel, *A Time to Kill*; the reader is rewarded for grasping the significance of Clanton landmarks such as Claude's Restaurant, with its classic southern catfish special and predominately African-American clientele, and the Tea Shoppe, with its white-collar patrons. But Clanton in *The Summons* combines elements of the Old and New South, a juxtaposition highlighting both the romanticized decline of the Old South and the gaudy materialism of the New. Judge Atlee represents the Old South that Ray has spent most of his life trying to escape: "The Atlee bloodline was thinning to a sad and inevitable halt, which didn't bother Ray at all. He was living life for himself, not for the benefit of his father or the family's inglorious past. He returned to Clanton only for funerals" (8). Descriptions of the judge's study and personal effects create a picture of a benevolent aristocrat, a southern gentleman who lived in the past, refighting key Civil War battles from his front porch. A portrait of Confederate general Nathan Bedford Forrest presides over his desk, and detailed financial records list his many contributions to local causes, including "crippled children, sick folks with no insurance, black kids he sent to college, every volunteer fire department, civic club, all-star team, [and] school group headed to Europe" (66). The Atlee family home, Maple Run, mirrors the decline of the judge and the South he held so dear: "It was still a handsome house, a Georgian with columns, once a monument to those who'd built it, and now a sad reminder of a declining family" (7–8). The once-grand home, though a historical site, has fallen into disrepair; even the maples once lining its driveway have vanished.

Though the story revolves around the family drama and Ray's attempts to come to terms with his past, *The Summons* also offers a sustained and searching critique of the legal system, particularly its complicity in corporate excess. Indeed, greed is the theme that unifies several subplots. Ray's ex-wife has left him because she "found a better deal, like an athlete swapping teams at the trading deadline"; she trades up for Lew the Liquidator, a "corporate vulture whose raids had netted him half a billion or so" (16). Ray eventually learns that attorney Patton French gave the 3 million to the judge as a gift after the judge ruled in French's favor in a huge products-liability suit against a pharmaceutical company. Grisham makes clear that such lawsuits bring huge profits to lawyers with little justice for the plaintiffs themselves. For instance, Forrest briefly works "for some local ambulance chasers, a bunch of sleazy bastards who advertise on cable, and hang around hospitals" (29). French, "a shameless ego pit" (274), conspicuously displays his wealth while laughing at the injured people he purportedly represented.

The money provides the ultimate test of Ray's understanding and character as he confronts questions of where the judge got the money and what he, as executor of the estate, should do with it. To answer the first, Ray investigates several possibilities, all of which, however, call into question the judge's ethics, and he concludes that bribery or gambling are the most logical sources; but the money does not appear in any of the judge's financial records. Desperate to find out if it is even real but loathe to visit the local bank with potentially counterfeit funds, Ray tours the underworld of casino gambling, itself vivid evidence of his own materialistic New South. Once having determined that the money is real, unmarked, and untraceable, he must decide what to do with it, but as he wrestles with this question, a series of break-ins suggests that someone else knows and may be willing to kill for the cash. Driven by a heady mix of paranoia and greed, Ray spends most of his time moving the money from his car to his apartment in Virginia, then to numerous self-storage units scattered throughout the South, and eventually back to Maple Run, where Grisham stages one of his most ambiguous endings.

Within a carefully constructed world of excess, Ray must come to terms with the consequences of his greed, and much like *The* FIRM's Mitch McDeere, he finally risks his life in order to keep the money. In *The Summons* the line between Ray Atlee and Patton French or Lew the Liquidator is blurred, a point Grisham stresses through a trademark surprise twist. Thus, though the novel eschews the legal intricacies and courtroom theatrics characterizing Grisham's typical work, it compensates with a more searching exploration of the morally ambiguous terrain that informs that work.

Bibliography

Grisham, John. *A Time to Kill.* New York: Bantam Doubleday Dell, 1989.

———. *The Firm.* New York: Bantam Doubleday Dell, 1991.

———. *The Summons.* New York: Bantam Dell, 2002.

Pringle, Mary Beth. *John Grisham: A Critical Companion.* Westport, Conn.: Greenwood Press, 1997.

Alicia M. Renfroe

T

Tara Road Maeve Binchy (1998)

Tara Road, a best-selling Oprah Book Club selection, is another of MAEVE BINCHY's engrossing tales of women who must come to grips with some profoundly unexpected turn in their lives. The protagonist, Ria Lynch, marries well and builds a comfortable, lively home with her real estate agent husband, Danny, and two children. She is content with her life, but her world is shattered when Danny tells her he is having an affair with a younger woman who is carrying his baby. To avoid the attention and pity of her close-knit community, Ria impulsively enters into a house swap with an American woman, Marilyn Vine, who is dealing with a devastating situation of her own.

Characteristically, the novel centers on family and friendship. When it opens, Ria Johnson is 16 years old and living at home with her mother, Nora, and older sister, Hilary. Nora is still angry that her late husband died without insurance, leaving her to struggle and with one overriding wish for her daughters: "She would die happy if Hilary and Ria had nice respectable men and homes of their own. Nice homes, in a classier part of Dublin, places with a garden even. Nora Johnson had great hopes that they would all be able to move a little upward. Somewhere nicer than the big sprawling housing estate where they lived now" (2).

First, Hilary marries Martin, a teacher, and then Nora's wish comes true for both her daughters when Ria becomes a secretary at a real estate office and meets Danny Lynch. For her it is love at first sight, but Danny seems equally taken with her, and when he proposes marriage, Ria, Nora, and Hilary are equally surprised as he is a decided catch. Hilary warns Ria: "'But you'd have to watch him; he's a high flier. He's not going to be content with earning a living like normal people do; he'll want the moon. It's written all over him'" (37).

Tara Road becomes a community after Danny and Ria move into a house he inherits from an uncle; and they renovate it extensively. Eventually, Nora and Rosemary, a friend from the real estate office, move there. Another friend of Ria's, Gertie, lives and works nearby, and in time Colm Barry opens a restaurant on the corner of the street.

Ria turns the house into a home and social center where friends and family constantly visit and of which she is very proud. Danny, as a real estate agent, looks to improve the house with a view to resale, which frightens Ria since she loves the house so. The kitchen is the hub of Tara Road: "A big kitchen where everyone gathered, something always cooking in the big stove, the smell of newly baked cinnamon cakes or fresh herb bread" (119). Just as Danny is not as fond of the house as Ria is, he is not as enamored with the constant bustle in it, at one point suddenly exclaiming of Rosemary's house, "I love going to that house [. . .]. It's so calm and peaceful, there are no demands on you." (201)

Binchy skillfully brings together characters that are not alike but who nonetheless form strong and lasting bonds. In Tara Road Ria's closest friends are Rosemary and Gertie. The former, who worked with Ria at the real estate office, leaves there to open her own business, which proves quite successful. Immaculately attired and perfectly made up, she never marries but has a string of lovers, many of whom are married, following her own adage, "career first, fellows later" (8). In contrast, Gertie is less successful both in her personal and professional life. Married to an abusive alcoholic, she must work in a laundromat and clean in Ria's home to support both her children and his drinking habit. But despite their striking lack of commonality, the women develop a deep friendship that is sustained over many years and stands out all the more vividly for the contrast. Ria, meanwhile, forges a new friendship when Danny tells her about his affair and she agrees to swap houses with an American, Marilyn Vine. Communicating by phone, they do not meet face-to-face until the end of the novel, but Marilyn turns out to be a truer friend than even Rosemary has been.

Binchy once said in an interview, "Some of my books end either in death or with someone taking a different route in life. If I have any philosophy it is that we have to be in charge of our own lives." Thus, though Ria suffers great disappointment when her life does not work out as she had imagined, she gains new respect for herself, as well as new and lasting friends, when she herself takes charge of her life.

The novel was adapted for film in 2005 but has not yet been released in the theatres or on DVD for the North American market.

Bibliography

Binchy, Maeve. *Tara Road.* New York: Dell, 2000.

Burns, Mike. "Maeve Binchy." *Europe* 345 (April 1995): 22–25.

Karen Bell

Texas James A. Michener (1985)

One the most popular, commercially successful, and critically acclaimed of his two dozen historical novels, *Texas* is also one of JAMES A. MICHENER's longest and most expansive literary projects, a 1,100-page saga chronicling 450 years in the human history of the geographic area that constitutes the modern-day state of Texas, from its exploration by a party under the Spanish conquistador Francisco Vásquez de Coronado in 1539 until its (apparent) cultural domination by a mixture of cattle barons, oil tycoons, real estate moguls, society belles, and football aficionados in 1985. Given the state's reputation as a land of larger-than-life figures and epic events, Texas proved a naturally fitting subject for the panoramic, episodic, multicharactered, multigenerational narratives Michener was renowned for; but it may also fairly be regarded as one of his most personal projects. Many of the diverse figures portrayed in his novel immigrate to Texas to begin a new life, lured by the area's vast natural wealth, rugged beauty, wide-open spaces, and promise of opportunity. Born in New York City and raised in Pennsylvania, Michener moved temporarily to Texas in 1983, as he had previously moved to many other locations around the world, to do research for his next book project. But like so many of the historical and fictional characters he portrays in the book, Michener was himself deeply attracted by Texas's rich landscape and cultural uniqueness, and after completing the novel, he made Texas his permanent home, residing in Austin, a Texan by choice, until his death in 1997.

Michener researched and wrote *Texas* between 1983 and 1985, its publication strategically timed to coincide with the popular interest stirred by the public sesquicentennial remembrances of the Texas struggle for independence from Mexico, the Battle of the Alamo, and the founding of the Republic of Texas in 1836. Directing a team of researchers and editorial assistants, Michener produced the text of *Texas* in 30 months while working out of quarters on the University of Texas campus within sight of the Texas State Capitol and its governor's office and at the behest of Texas governor William Clemens.

The novel's narrative is constructed around a group of five prominent Texans who have been appointed by the governor of Texas to a task force to study Texas history and make recommendations on how Texas schoolchildren may better be instructed about the rich and complex culture of their state. The task force is headed by Dr. Travis Barlow, a professor of cultural studies, who is proud that his ancestors were present at the Battle of the Alamo. A second member, multimillionaire Ransom Rusk, traces his Texas lineage back to a 19th-century Quaker Indian agent. Miss Lorena Cobb, the only woman appointed to the task force, traces her heritage to plantation owners who rose to prominence in the 1840s, when Texas became an independent republic. Lorenzo Quimper, a wealthy businessman whose ancestors emigrated from Tennessee as homesteaders in the 1820s, boasts that Texas has "made" him, and he is an ardent supporter of all things Texan. The fifth member, Professor Efrain Garza, who becomes the representative of Hispanic-heritage contributions to the state, claims his descent from ancestors who explored Texas in 1539 with Coronado. Each of the five holds strong opinions as to what should be considered the seminal elements of Texas history, and these opinions initially, dramatically—and apparently irreconcilably—conflict.

The major portion of the novel, and the one of most interest and creative merit—indeed a model of Michener's skill in hybrid storytelling—narrates at great length the historical accounts that Barlow, Rusk, Quimper, Cobb, and Garza themselves narrate, or have "guest lecturers" narrate, as a justification of their personal perspectives on Texas and the nature of its historical development. These "history lessons" are arranged into 14 largely independent but resonant chronological sections, each of which tells the story of a coherent group of characters in a historical period of a decade or two in length and the geographical area they inhabited. At the conclusion of each section the members debate the merits and importance of the historical events presented; the full collection, combined with the debates, finally provides the reader with an astonishingly detailed, comprehensive, and well-examined summary of five centuries of Texas history.

A brief sketch reveals much about Michener's mastery in historical selection and construction. The first, titled "Land of Many Lands," traces the early European exploration of Texas under Coronado and the futile search for the "Seven Golden Cities of Cibola" during the late 1530s. "The Mission" describes the initial efforts to establish Christianity among the native peoples of Texas in the early 1700s. "El Camino Real" concerns the last attempts by Spanish settlers in the later 1700s to impose a European Spanish character on "Tejas." "The Settlers" introduces Stephen F. Austin and represents his efforts in the early 1800s to found a colony of American settlers in Mexican Texas. "The Trace" continues the story of the influx of settlers from the United States into Texas. "Three Men, Three Battles" is the obligatory Texas set piece describing figures such as Sam Houston, Davy Crockett, Jim Bowie, and Mexican general Santa Anna, as well as the revolutionary events at the Alamo, Goliad, and San Jacinto in the 1830s. "The Texians" depicts the development of the newly independent Republic of Texas in the late 1830s and 1840s. "The Ranger" recounts events in the Mexican War of 1846–48, after Texas's annexation by the United States. "Loyalties" deals with slavery and the secession of Texas from the Union to join the Confederacy. "The Fort" deals with attempts by the U.S. and Texas governments to subdue the native Comanche Indians. "The Frontier" recounts the passing of the Wild West and the beginning of civilized life in late 19th-century Texas. "The Town" recounts the establishment of a Texas economy and culture based upon cattle ranching, cotton growing, and oil production in the early 1900s. "The Invaders," set in the post–World War II 1940s, explores pressures put on "native Texans," both by newcomers from the American North and immigrants from south of the Texas border. "Power and Change," the concluding section, depicts Texas as a dynamic, diverse, still-evolving economic power in the 1980s. The scope and depth of each of the 14 narrative sections would merit a novel unto itself, and it is a tribute to Michener's extraordinary skill that they nonetheless form part of a single, coherent, and deeply engrossing narrative.

Michener maintains in the front matter to *Texas* that he has striven to present an "honest blend of fiction and historical fact"; his interrelated narratives of diverse, complex, resilient characters swept along in the unpredictable currents of evolving, often violent history are engaging, veracious, and often compelling. As part of his extensive research for his book, Michener traveled throughout the state and interviewed dozens of subjects; the personal expertise he gained lends to the novel great vitality, convincing specificity of detail, and the unmistakable stamp of authenticity.

Bibliography

Michener, James A. *Texas.* New York: Random House, 1985. Reprint, New York: Fawcett Crest, 1987.

Cliff Toliver

The Third Deadly Sin

Lawrence Sanders (1981)

The Third Deadly Sin is a crime-thriller and police procedural featuring Edward X. Delaney, a retired detective in the New York City police department who first appears in Sanders's *The Anderson Tapes* (1970) (awarded the Edgar for best first mystery from the Mystery Writers of America) and then plays a central role in his Deadly Sin series: *The First Deadly Sin* (1973), *The Second Deadly Sin* (1977), *The Third Deadly Sin* (1981), and *The Fourth Deadly Sin* (1985).

This third installment is a fast-paced and emotionally charged novel focusing on that rarity in fiction as in life: a female serial killer, here named Zoe Kohler, with whom the reader becomes intimately acquainted in the course of her grisly murder of seven men. Zoe has come to New York City from the Midwest after the end of her failed marriage. A quiet, plain-looking, compulsively neat woman employed in the security office of a New York hotel, she is nonetheless filled with rage. Obsessed with her health and given to consuming large dosages of vitamins, tranquilizers, barbiturates, pain killers, and assorted other medications, she is especially plagued by debilitating menstrual cramps just before her period. At these moments in a striking instance of gender specificity on Sanders's part, she is overwhelmed with the compulsion to murder. Then this mousy, unattractive woman transforms herself with makeup, a wig, and provocative clothing and haunts hotels that are holding large conventions most conducive to anonymity. She meets a man in the bar, agrees to go to his room, then stabs him in the neck with a Swiss army knife and mutilates his genitals. By the end of the novel she has butchered seven men, six in hotel rooms.

After a few murders the city becomes obsessed with the "Hotel Ripper" case, and the police are under great pressure to find the killer. At this point Delaney is called out of retirement and asked to be a special consultant. As he studies the case, and as the police begin to develop a profile of the killer, Delaney perspicaciously observes that the killings occur at intervals approximating the menstrual cycle of an average woman. Speculating that the killer is a woman, he soon comes into conflict with his feminist wife, Monica, who is certain no woman could commit such atrocities; his conversations with her become a significant thematic and narrative element in the tale.

The novel's considerable momentum stems from two primary sources: the readers' increasing familiarity with the extraordinary workings of Zoe Kohler's mind as she prepares for her murderous forays, and Delaney's solitary efforts to put the pieces of the puzzle together and identify this quiet, unassuming woman as the "Hotel Ripper." Sanders's psychological portrait of Zoe is both convincing and compelling. She is so unobtrusive that "sometimes she had a fantasy that she was an invisible woman" (13). She lives alone, has few friends, and is almost never noticed in her office or on the street. But after her malignant metamorphosis, now clad in fancy dress, wig, and makeup, she is noticed: "Men in the lobby stared at her. Men passing on the sidewalk outside stared at her" (35); in a sense her killings provide her, in their twisted way, with precisely what is lacking in her daily life. She is "exhilarated by the fearful excitement she had caused. More than that, the secret that she alone knew gave her an almost physical pleasure, a self-esteem she had never felt before" (313). This woman who had found sex with her husband so repulsive now finds the physical pleasure she had been missing, through murder and mutilation. Ultimately, in her mind, only in such murderous "adventures" does she acquire an authentic and autonomous life:

> It came to her almost as a revelation that this was the reason she sought adventures. They were her only opportunity to try out and to display her will.

She knew that others—like the Son of Sam—had blamed their misdeeds on "voices," on hallucinatory commands that overrode their inclination and volition.

But her adventures were the only time in Zoe Kohler's life when she listened to her own voice (323).

Zoe's complex psychological portrait is further nuanced by her relationship with her doctor, whom she visits monthly even though he insists such visits are unnecessary. She demands regular Pap smears and breast examinations yet withholds the truth about her dysfunctional eating and drug habits; he is constantly mystified by the state of her health. Moreover, as the novel develops, the reader learns that Zoe suffers from Addison's disease, a fact that ultimately leads to her detection. So great, indeed, is the almost deific presence of dysfunctionality in her world, Zoe effectively comes to define herself by her diseases. Thus, when the doctor wants to send her to a hospital for tests, she adamantly refuses: "There was also a secret fear that, somehow, in a hospital, she might be restored to perfect health, but in the process be deprived of those private pains and pleasures that were so precious to her" (389–390).

Sanders's portrayal of Delaney is equally masterly, with the detective's stalwart restraint and decency set in the starkest contrast to the repressed and twisted passions of his quarry. Sanders describes this contrast in theatrical terms:

> It was not the first time that Edward X. Delaney had been struck by the contrast between the drama of a heinous crime and the dry minutiae of the investigation. The act was (sometimes) high tragedy; the search was (sometimes) low comedy.
>
> The reason was obvious, of course. The criminal acted in hot passion; the detective had only cold resolve. The criminal was a child of the theater, inspired, thinking the play would go on forever. But along came the detective, a lumpish, methodical fellow, seeking only to ring down the curtain (302–303).

Lumpish and methodical he may be, but it is through his keen (as well as stolid) intellect and shrewd calculations that the killer is finally brought to justice.

Beyond its dramatic plot, *The Third Deadly Sin* offers a searching and uncommonly sensitive exploration of the feminine psyche through its evolving contrast of the respective sensibilities of Zoe (diseased and malignant) and Delaney's wife, Monica (healthy and benignant). Sanders is especially adept in explaining the source of emotional suffering in a person like Zoe, with his sympathetic description of her treatment by her parents, her failed marriage to a very difficult man, and her attitudes toward sex and men in general, all enabling the reader to better understand and empathize with this brutal serial killer. The presentation of Monica is equally deft, encouraging readers to reason with her—as they feel for her—in the face of such unfamiliar and uncanny evil. The result is a narrative compelling both in action and meditation, a rarity in its genre.

Bibliography

Sanders, Lawrence. *The Third Deadly Sin.* New York: Putnam, 1981.

Howard A. Mayer

Timeline Michael Crichton (1999)

Timeline is a science-fiction thriller concerning three historians, André Marek, Kate Erickson, and Chris Hughes, who travel through time to 14th-century France in order to save their mentor, Professor Edward Johnston. Johnston and a group of researchers, including the protagonists, are excavating ruins along the Dordogne River under the corporate sponsorship and supervision of International Technology Corporation (ITC). Following the visit of a journalist to the site, Johnston learns that ITC has been making covert land purchases surrounding the area, and this, combined with prodding from an ITC representative who demands quicker progress on the research, causes Johnston to suspect that the company has ulterior motives. At ITC's headquarters, he is candidly informed that the corporation has developed time-travel technology and that its interest in the historical site stems from this capacity. Johnston refuses to believe and demands a demonstration, which in typical science-fiction style eventually involves *him,* and as typically, involves him being separated from the time machine and finding himself unable to return to the present.

Meanwhile, Johnston's assistants uncover a document at the site reading "HELP ME," along with a bifocal lens, both lens and language being utter anachronisms for the time period. The message is at first thought to be a hoax, as well as the bifocals a contamination at the site, but they are finally authenticated and the handwriting identified as Johnston's. Amid this bitemporal confusion, Marek, Kate, Chris, and colleague David Stern are brought to ITC in order to help save Johnston. They are debriefed on the situation and the time-travel technology and though likewise skeptical are soon convinced of its reality after viewing the technology in action. They then travel back in time to save Johnston and the two ITC employees with him, security personnel named Susan Gomez and Victor Baretto. But David refuses to go. Gomez and Baretto are quickly killed by marauding knights, and in the melee a live grenade is accidentally returned to the present, where it devastates the fragile equipment in the laboratory.

With only 37 hours before the historians must return to the present or be trapped in the past forever, Marek, Kate, and Chris strive to locate their mentor, needing to get all four historians together in one place before (as they believe) they can summon the time-travel machine and return to the present. Meanwhile, David and the ITC personnel work to rebuild their laboratory so that the return of the historians can be effected. The balance of the novel then chronicles the exploits of the three historians as they journey through the past, becoming embroiled in a battle between the warlord Sir Oliver de Vannes and his attacker Arnaut de Cervole, all the while trying to rescue Johnston.

Thematically, *Timeline* examines the disastrous effects of powerful technology in the hands of corporations and individuals whose pride and ambition cause them to ignore the dangers of such technology and the likely possibility that something could go wrong—a common theme in MICHAEL CRICHTON's novels (as in *JURASSIC PARK*). Such self-serving ignorance is here exemplified in the character of Robert Doniger, a brilliant quantum physicist who founds ITC and is primarily responsible for the development of the time-travel technology. Doniger is depicted as petulant, uncaring, and crass, with little regard for the feelings or safety of the people around him. Although at first appearing to have an honest and selfless interest in history (at odds, nonetheless, with his private personality), while rehearsing a speech for potential investors Doniger reveals his true motives:

> In other centuries, human beings wanted to be saved, or improved, or freed, or educated. But in our century, they want to be entertained. The great fear is not of disease or death, but of boredom (443).

He explains that after becoming bored of television and movies, people turn to participatory activities, such as computer interaction or attending amusement parks (like Jurassic Park); and then extrapolates:

> "*Authenticity* will be the buzzword of the twenty-first century. And what is authentic? Anything that is not devised and structured to make a profit. Anything that is not controlled by corporations. Anything that exists for its own sake, that assumes its own shape. But of course, nothing in the modern world is allowed to assume its own shape. [. . .] Where, then, will people turn for the rare and desirable experience of authenticity? They will turn to the past" (444).

Although at first it seems that Doniger merely wants to use time travel in order to profit from establishing and controlling a tourist trade in the past, his motives soon appear considerably more sinister—to control not merely a tourist trade but the past itself:

> "The purpose of history is to explain the present—to say why the world around us

is the way it is. History tells us what is important in our world, and how it came to be. It tells us why the things we value are the things we should value. And it tells us what is to be ignored, or discarded. That is true power—profound power. The power to define a whole society.

"The future lies in the past—in whoever controls the past. Such control has never before been possible. Now, it is" (480).

This idea that the modern world has been defined by the events of the past is a major theme of the novel, and Crichton places suggestive and convincing emphasis on the medieval period as a decisive and unacknowledged influence on the modern world. Allied to this is the suggestion that cherished notions of social progress are illusory, that the contemporary vision of the past is too simplistic, and that the medieval period was in fact a dynamic time of rapid technological development. Crichton elaborates in the book's acknowledgments:

> In fact, the conception of a brutal medieval period was an invention of the Renaissance, whose proponents were at pains to emphasize a new spirit, even at the expense of the facts. If a benighted medieval world has proven a durable misconception, it may be because it confirms a cherished contemporary belief—that our species always moves forward to ever better and more enlightened ways of life. This belief is utter fantasy, but it dies hard (490).

Although Crichton's education is primarily medical, *Timeline* provides ample evidence of meticulous historical research, as well as a competent grasp of the philosophical implications of quantum mechanics; even by Crichton's unique standards the book bristles with corroboration, including a bibliography of 91 supporting texts.

But typically, fact never mars fiction. Just as in his other speculative scenarios, like those of *Jurassic Park* and *The Andromeda Strain*, Crichton skillfully blurs the lines between established scientific fact and original fiction in order to heighten believability and suspense. So while *Timeline* opens with an introduction citing extant books and articles to provide an overview of the development of quantum physics and research into quantum technology, the same passage ends with a note on the rise of the fictitious company ITC; the book is prefaced by three quotations, one by Winston Churchill, the others by Johnston and Doniger.

Timeline was adapted into a computer game in 2000 and into film in 2003 by director Richard Donner (best known for his work on the *Lethal Weapon* and *Superman* franchises) starring Paul Walker, Frances O'Connor, Gerard Butler, Billy Connolly, and David Thewlis.

Bibliography

Crichton, Michael. *Timeline*. 1999. Reprint, New York: Ballantine, 2000.

Timeline. Directed by Richard Donner. 2003. DVD. Paramount Home Video, 2004.

Timeline. CD-ROM. Eidos Interactive, 2000.

Jonathan Ball

The Time Traveler's Wife

Audrey Niffenegger (2003)

The Time Traveler's Wife is a novel portraying the love story of Clare Abshire, an artist from a wealthy Michigan family, and Henry DeTamble, a librarian at the Newberry Library in Chicago, who has a genetic condition causing him to travel through time uncontrollably and spontaneously. The book begins by describing the first time the two met, which for Clare was when she was six and Henry, 36 (having traveled from a future time in which he and Clare are married), and for Henry when he was 28 and she, 20. The novel then traces their love story from each of these perspectives, centering on key moments in their lives—from their respective childhoods to their meeting as adults, to their married life—arranged in a loosely linear order that roughly follows Henry's time line, with nonlinear episodes interspersed to follow specific story lines or themes. Each chapter opens with the date and respective ages of Henry and Clare to clarify when Henry is time traveling, and the story is told in the first person, alternating between Henry and Clare, often in the same chapter.

Although the book's plot hinges on time travel, a common feature in science fiction, it is not properly a science-fiction novel, employing the travel as it does in a thoroughly unsensational manner and rooting its characters firmly in present-day Chicago, with vivid descriptions of concerts, restaurants, and quotidian life, as well as brimming with references to music, literature, art, and popular culture. This is due in no small part to the history and interests of the characters themselves: Henry's father is a violinist, his mother a singer, and he himself a librarian; Clare and her friend Charisse are artists, and Clare's sister Alicia is a cellist. Quotations from literature and popular music appear at the beginning of each chapter and frequently in the dialogue. Moreover, AUDREY NIFFENEGGER naturalizes her conception of time travel, characterizing it as a genetic condition in an ordinary world and describing it in terms of concrete physical sensations and reactions. Henry's time travel is often brought on by emotional or physical stress, and he experiences symptoms similar to those of migraine sufferers: nausea, trouble seeing or hearing, "vertiginous falling sensations," tingling limbs, seeing bright auras around objects (2); or it may be caused by the typical epileptic triggers: bright flashing lights, for example, such as those caused by televisions.

But his time travel exhibits another, more profound relation to stress; never able to control his destination, he tends to travel toward stressful or otherwise eventful periods, most often to that of the traumatic death of his mother when he was six. He describes it as a kind of gravitational pull on his life: "My mother dying . . . it's the pivotal thing . . . everything else goes around and around it" (113). Niffenegger also details the practical complexities of time travel. Henry cannot take anything with him when he travels, including clothing, and thus arrives naked and hungry, creating problematic episodes in which he is chased, beaten, arrested, or exposed to severe weather. Upon his arrival, therefore, he usually tries to steal clothing and money in an attempt to blend into his surroundings. He masters the art of picking locks and pickpocketing, which he later teaches to his younger self in a dizzying display of time paradox; when his younger, more morally abiding self suggests begging instead of stealing, his older self replies pragmatically, "Begging is a drag, and you keep getting carted off by the police" (50).

The plot principally revolves around a particular time paradox, which the novel's characters themselves ponder and attempt to test: Henry is compelled to travel back in time to Clare's childhood because they are married in his present. Clare grows up, meets, and marries Henry precisely because she knew him in her childhood; a rather complex case of the chicken-and-egg conundrum, prompting numerous absorbing discussions about free will and determinism. Several scenes reinforce the idea upheld by Henry that all of history is written once and cannot be changed, even by him; but the young Clare is reluctant to embrace this idea, though she begins to accept it the more time she spends with him.

There is also the more subtle theme of fate, which by turn complements and contradicts these deterministic ideas. For instance, when Clare is 11, a Ouija board spells out the name Henry and indicates he will be her husband. Clare's perspective reveals that she has not pushed the board, and no one else present knows about Henry's existence. Another recurring theme is that of familial tragedy: Henry's mother dies in a car accident when he is a child, severing his relationship with his father and propelling them both toward self-destructive alcoholism; Henry's family's landlord, Mrs. Kim, lost a child to leukemia; Clare's mother is a manic-depressive whose moods rule her entire household and who eventually loses her life to ovarian cancer; Clare and Henry's attempts to conceive a child result in tragedy and profound strain on their relationship.

Niffenegger's other works, primarily graphic novels such as *The Adventuress,* are shorter than *The Time Traveler's Wife* and rely more on art than prose to tell the story. What defines all her work, however, is the use of gothic fantasy elements in an everyday, realistic setting. While thematically *The Time Traveler's Wife* might seem to suggest similarities to H. G. Wells's fanciful *The Time Machine,* Niffenegger's novel has more in common with the everyday fantasy of Keith Donohue's *The Stolen Child* or the fantastic everyday of SUE MONK KIDD's *The* SECRET LIFE OF BEES.

The film option to the novel was famously purchased by Brad Pitt and Jennifer Aniston's production company, Plan B, before the book itself was published.

Bibliography

Donohue, Keith. *The Stolen Child: A Novel.* New York: Nan A. Talese, 2006.

Kidd, Susan Monk. *The Secret Life of Bees.* New York: Penguin, 2003.

Niffenegger, Audrey. *The Time Traveler's Wife.* San Francisco: MacAdam/Cage, 2003.

———. *The Adventuress.* New York: Harry N. Abrams, 2006.

Wells, H. G. *The Time Machine.* New York: Penguin Classics, 2005.

Starr Hoffman

True Believer Nicholas Sparks (2005)

True Believer is NICHOLAS SPARKS's attempt to produce a fresh twist on the classic love story. Introducing a big-city journalist into a small-town ghost story, the tale recasts in an improbable but affecting form the pleasing fatalities of love.

As the novel opens, Jeremy Marsh is an investigative journalist and self-proclaimed scientific debunker with a regular column in *Scientific American.* Born in New York, Jeremy delights in all the city has to offer, living the life of a divorcé waiting for a career-making break. Taking a breather from his usual fare of groundbreaking exposé, Jeremy decides to head south in search of the truth behind a mysterious ghost story in the small town of Boone Creek, North Carolina. Once there he is introduced to a myriad of southern characters that alternately confuse, confound, and warm his heart, in particular Lexie Darnell, the town librarian, with whom he spends a weekend that changes his life.

Typical of Sparks's romance novels, readers are thrust into a quaint little town and swept up in the lives of two engaging characters who must overcome seemingly intractable obstacles in order to realize what love is meant to be. What is most striking about *True Believer,* however, is that neither character is looking for love. Both Jeremy and Lexie are content with their lives and happy in the place they call home. That is, until the lights of Cedar Creek Cemetery find them together.

Seven years before the novel begins, Jeremy's divorce to his ex-wife, Maria, is made final. Why she divorced him comes much later, but Sparks hints at the reason throughout the first half of the novel; the catalyst ironically turns out be a crucial factor in Jeremy and Lexie's story of enduring love, the prime element in the former's conversion to a true believer.

As the only one of six brothers to go to college, and the first in all his family to graduate, Jeremy is an educated man, seemingly on the road to success; yet something is wanting, and he locates it in his career. Chasing his dream as a journalist, Jeremy wants to be recognized by the prominent figures in his profession and the public at large. Nate, his agent, is equally hungry for Jeremy's fame and energized by the recent developments and opportunities in his career.

But then the twist: Responding to a letter from one Doris McClellan of Boone Creek, North Carolina, Jeremy packs up for a long weekend and heads south in search of ghosts, or rather yet another, and yet more stinging demystification, for the benefit of the credulous inhabitants of Boone Creek. The legend behind Cedar Creek Cemetery says that it is haunted by the spirits of former slaves, and every winter when the fog rolls in, residents claim to have witnessed inexplicable blue lights dancing on the headstones.

Sparks brilliantly juxtaposes the settings of Manhattan and Boone Creek to heighten the contrast between her soon-to-be lovers, and as the tale unfolds the town itself becomes a kind of character, like a stodgy and eccentric parent opposed to their daughter's new fellow.

Upon driving into Boone Creek, Jeremy feels he has entered another world: The streets are quiet and deserted, the homes and buildings old and decaying; no sense of life, human or mechanical, decrepitude everywhere. And the cemetery appears emblematic, neglected, overgrown, and crumbling to pieces. Yet from this dying place of the dead, phoenixlike, a new, youthful and passionate life of love will rise.

The first impression of Lexie is deceptively simple: a clever, independent country woman, sure of herself; her adamant defense of small-town life renders all the more surprising that she had at one time lived just a few blocks from Jeremy in Manhattan. With characteristic subtlety and skill Sparks sculpts her persona to hide, almost like a code, the pain and loneliness she feels inside; only as the second half of the novel unfolds do readers realize the heartbreak she has suffered and the complex reasons for the wall she has built around herself.

Orphaned at the age of three, Lexie was brought up by her grandmother, Doris, the same Doris that sent Jeremy the letter about the mysterious cemetery lights. Doris owns Herb's Restaurant, one of the main restaurants in town, and claims to be the town psychic. While the famous debunker gives no credit to her psychic abilities, Jeremy must at last rely on her alone when Lexie disappears and cannot be found. Indeed, without the "mystified" Doris, the love of Lexie and Jeremy would never have come clear.

Typically, Sparks weaves into this grand, time-honored tale of two people destined to love a Dickensian cast of characters, such as the voluble Tully, a gas-station attendant who never stops talking, and Jed, the tall, intimidating taxidermist who has filled his guest rooms at Greenleaf Cottages with animals in attack postures. And like Dickens, in spite of all the obstacles that contemporary life throws in its way, and all the ineffable twists of fate that somehow circumvent these obstacles, he finally locates home very simply, in a loving heart.

Soon after the great success of *True Believer,* Sparks published an equally popular sequel, AT FIRST SIGHT (2005). Film rights for both have been sold.

Bibliography

Sparks, Nicholas. *True Believer.* New York: Warner, 2005.

Lori Dees

Turow, Scott (1949–)

Scott Turow is the author of several genre-crossing thrillers, including PRESUMED INNOCENT (1987), which became a blockbuster film starring Harrison Ford and established Turow's position as a formidable writer of popular fiction. His work defies easy classification, successfully combining elements of a host of genres, principally suspense mysteries and legal thrillers. Turow sees himself as a writer transcending genre expectations and bridging the gap between literary and popular fiction:

> I don't believe that the role of literature has been, or ought to be today, to confine itself to a tiny professional elite who are capable of understanding it. We all dream every night. We all tell ourselves stories and I am on the verge of rage when I listen to certain kinds of academics who believe literature is really the province of a select few. It's not. Storytelling is as innate to human experience as music, and some of us . . . feel a fundamental responsibility to recognize that and to seek as wide an audience as possible ("Interview" 169).

Turow was born in Chicago, Illinois, in 1949. His father, David, was a doctor, and his mother, Rita Patron Turow, was a teacher who graduated from the University of Chicago and published several nonfiction texts, including a well-received book about divorce, *Daddy Doesn't Live Here Anymore* (1977). He spent his childhood in Rogers Park, a predominantly Jewish neighborhood, before the family moved to the more affluent suburb Winnekta, where Turow attended high school. Despite his parents' desire that he become a doctor, Turow developed a passion for writing and majored in English at Amherst College, Massachusetts, completing his first novel during his freshman year. Though it was rejected by publishers, he continued to write, eventually receiving encouragement from Farrar, Straus & Giroux, which would become his longtime publisher. While he was still an undergraduate, his short story "The Carp Fish" was published by the *Transatlantic Review* and selected for the prestigious collection *Best American Short Stories* (1970). Upon graduation in 1970, Turow received a fellowship to study at Stanford, where he earned his M.A. in 1974 and was the E. H. Jones Lecturer in Creative Writing for three years. During this time he married Annette Weisberg. Despite the publication of another short story, "A Classic Case," in the *Transatlantic*

Review, Turow became discouraged after his second novel, *The Way Things Are*, was rejected, and he turned down an offer to teach at the University of Rochester, deciding instead to attend Harvard Law School.

The change, as it turned out, was the best thing he could do for his writing. His first published book, *One L* (1977), an immediate cult classic, is a semiautobiographical account of his experience in the grueling freshman year of Harvard Law (the "One L"); in it Turow vividly captures the cutthroat atmosphere of competition and distrust that would shape in many ways the sensibility evident in all his later works. Its exploration of the average person's capacity for violence and evil, for example, profoundly informs his first published novel, *Presumed Innocent* (1987), which he began while working full time as an assistant U.S. attorney in Chicago (Lundy 64–65). The novel made the *New York Times* best-seller list during its first week, and the sale of paperback and movie rights provided Turow with immediate financial security. However, rather than write full time, he continued his legal career, accepting a position with Sonnenschein, Nath, and Rosenthal, a prestigious Chicago firm, where he is now a partner specializing in white-collar criminal defense, doing much of his work pro bono (Scottturow.com).

He has written seven other thrillers to date: *The* BURDEN OF PROOF (1990), *Pleading Guilty* (1993), *The Laws of Our Fathers* (1996), *Personal Injuries* (1999), *Reversible Errors* (2002), *Ordinary Heroes* (2005), and *Limitations* (2006). He also wrote *Ultimate Punishment* (2003), a nonfiction work on the death penalty, and edited *Best American Mystery Stories* (2006) and *Guilty as Charged: The Penguin Book of New American Crime Writing* (1996). Turow currently practices law part time and lives in Chicago with his wife and three children.

Bibliography

Lundy, Derek. *Scott Turow: Meeting the Enemy.* Ontario: ECW Press, 1995. Scottturow.com. Available online. URL: http://www.scottturow.com/biography.htm. Accessed November 6, 2006.

Turow, Scott. *One L.* New York: Putnam, 1977.

———. *Presumed Innocent.* New York: Farrar, Straus & Giroux, 1987.

———. *The Burden of Proof.* New York: Farrar, Straus & Giroux, 1990.

———. *Pleading Guilty.* New York: Farrar, Straus & Giroux, 1993.

———. *The Laws of Our Fathers.* New York: Farrar, Straus & Giroux, 1996.

———. "Interview with Scott Turow." In *Conversations with American Novelists: Best Interviews from the Missouri Review and the American Audio Prose Library.* Edited by Kay Bonetti, Greg Michalson, Speer Morgan, Jo Sapp, and Sam Stowers. Columbia: University of Missouri Press, 1997, 153–169.

———. *Personal Injuries.* New York: Farrar, Straus & Giroux, 1999.

———. *Reversible Errors.* New York: Farrar, Straus & Giroux, 2002.

———. *Ultimate Punishment: A Lawyer's Reflections on Dealing with the Death Penalty.* New York: Farrar, Straus & Giroux, 2003.

———. *Ordinary Heroes.* New York: Farrar, Straus & Giroux, 2005.

———. *Limitations.* New York: Picador, 2006.

———, and Otto Penzler, eds. *Best American Mystery Stories 2006.* New York: Houghton Mifflin, 2006.

———, ed. *Guilty as Charged: The Penguin Book of New American Crime Writing.* New York: Penguin, 1996.

Alicia M. Renfroe

2010: Odyssey Two Arthur C. Clarke (1982)

2010: Odyssey Two is a novelistic sequel to ARTHUR C. CLARKE and Stanley Kubrick's groundbreaking film *2001: A Space Odyssey* (1968). Nearly a decade after the events of the movie, Dr. Heywood Floyd is asked to join a Soviet-American mission to return to Jupiter in order to salvage the *Discovery* and discover the reasons for the failure of the original mission. In *2001: A Space Odyssey*, the *Discovery* with its five-man crew had been sent to Jupiter to investigate the reason for the mysterious transmission sent by a monolith discovered buried on Earth's moon. During the mission the breakdown of the ship's intelligent onboard computer, HAL 9000, led to the death of nearly all the crew, except for David Bowman. Upon arriving at Jupiter, Bowman discovered an identical but more massive monolith orbiting the Jovian planet and was transported to a "beautifully appointed hotel suite containing nothing that was wholly familiar" (172), where he was transformed by the monolith's creators into "an embryo god" (173) and sent back to Earth, his state and situation at the beginning of *2010.*

Themes of transcendence and change are a hallmark of Clarke's fiction. In *Childhood's End* (1953), for example, Clarke explores mankind's transformation after an encounter with an alien race called Overlords. Over the course of the novel the Overlords are revealed to be working for a noncorporeal race of beings known as the Overmind. The Overlords help mankind evolve to a higher realm of existence and then merge with the Overmind. The title refers to Clarke's argument in the novel that mankind needs to evolve beyond its all-too human childhood—a childhood marked by bodily frailty, war, and colonialism—into a form of life that transcends such human limitations. In the *2001: A Space Odyssey* film, David Bowman's transformation into the embryo god is consonant with such themes of transcendence and transformation. He has evolved beyond his human limitations, with their emotional and physical frailties. It is further suggested that HAL 9000's breakdown is rooted in recognizably human pride; he refuses to admit that he is capable of mistakes, telling a BBC interviewer in the film that he is "Foolproof, and incapable of error."

2010: Odyssey Two, however, is a step back from Clarke's earlier position, suggesting that the very human traits overcome in *Childhood's End* and *2001* are crucial for mankind's long-term survival and evolution. This becomes apparent in Clarke's portrayal of David Bowman. While changed into something close to a demigod, Bowman is haunted by the loss of his human existence. Allowed to visit Earth before being tasked with the mission the monolith builders wish him to undertake, Bowman returns to the places and people of his childhood: the lake where his older brother died, his aged mother, and a former lover, Betty. The meeting with Betty allows Clarke to explore in some depth the theme that any advancement in human evolution, consciousness, or technology cannot be separated from empathy and contact with others:

> At least he understood what he was doing there, swept back by the tides of sorrow and desire to rendezvous with his past. The most powerful emotion he had ever known had been his passion for Betty: the elements of grief and guilt it contained only made it stronger (189).

It is hinted that, unlike the Overmind of *Childhood's End,* the creators of the monoliths, while having evolved beyond material existence, have not wholly lost the ability to empathize with others: "[D]espite their godlike power they had not wholly forgotten their origins in the warm slime of a vanished sea" (308). The monolith builders' intervention in human evolution is driven by loneliness, a need for communication and companionship with others in an immense universe (306). Curnow, one of Dr. Floyd's colleagues, remarks that HAL's own, often perplexing behavior after being reactivated seems driven by loneliness and a need for human contact (287).

Clarke's greatest strength as a writer was his ability to describe alien worlds, technologies, and life in terms of rigorous science and with an attention to detail. In *Rendezvous with Rama* (1972), for example, Clarke describes how life would exist inside a 30-mile long alien spaceship that passes through the solar system; in *The Fountains of Paradise* (1979) he outlines how a space elevator could be built using advanced carbon compounds, long before developments in nanotube technology had made such conceivable. In *2010* the description of the life encountered on Jupiter's great moon, Europa, is based on the then latest knowledge of Europa and on how life could evolve in such a hostile environment with little sunlight. Such life, Clarke suggests, would likely be based on processing energy and material from thermal vents deep within the moon's oceans, powered by the tidal forces exerted on the moon by Jupiter and Io; not as farfetched as it sounds, as unique life not based on sunlight has in fact evolved around thermal vents in the Earth's deep oceans. Clarke gives full flight to his imaginative and scientific speculations in describing how such life could survive and reproduce:

> One after another, they [the flowerlike petals on the creature] dropped off from the parent buds. For a few moments they flopped around like fish stranded on dry land—and at last I realized exactly what they were. Those membranes weren't petals—they were fins, or their equivalent. This was the free-swimming, larval stage of the creature. Probably it spends much of its life rooted on the seabed, then sends these mobile offspring in search of new territory. Just like the corals of Earth's oceans (78).

This life on Europa provides the novel's final coda. David Bowman is tasked by the monolith creators to watch over Europa's creatures after Jupiter is transformed into a small sun, and Clarke ends the novel with the Europan inhabitants, tens of thousands of years in the future, beginning to contemplate the universe about them. They are beginning to form theories about the origins of the cosmos and their own place within it, and they notice the strange movements of certain stars about their world, as well as the expanding number of lights on the worlds orbiting the Jupiter sun. These lights are in fact human spaceships and colonies. The Europans are not aware of mankind yet, as their world is protected from contact with humans by the monolith left on their world, which now contains a slumbering David Bowman. But Clarke suggests a time will come when Bowman will be awakened from his slumber inside the monolith and will foster the first tentative contact between mankind and the Europans, the goal of the monoliths' creators being ultimately to discover whether the two races, marked by two radically different forms of consciousness, can coexist (332). Clarke suggests such coexistence may be possible if both learn to empathize with the other to discover a common ground of fellow feeling, the lack of which doomed the *Discovery* mission. If there can be no such ground of empathy between humanity and the Europans, then only tragedy can result from the meeting of these, or any, two races.

Bibliography

Clarke, Arthur C. *2010: Odyssey Two.* New York: Ballantine, 1982.

Tom Venetis

U

Uris, Leon (1924–2003)

Author of 15 novels and several works of nonfiction, in addition to a number of screenplays for Hollywood films, Uris is best known for *Exodus* (1958), his sprawling historical tale of the founding of the state of Israel, which was translated into 50 languages and had sales equaling those of *Gone with the Wind.*

Uris was born in 1924 in Baltimore, Maryland, to Jewish parents of Russian-Polish extraction and attended public schools in Norfolk and Baltimore, failing English three times. He quit high school after Pearl Harbor was attacked and joined the Marine Corps, serving as a radio operator at Guadalcanal and Tarawa. Contracting malaria, he was sent home for the remainder of the war. His first novel, *Battle Cry* (1953), was based on his experiences in the Marines, and its success prompted a move to Hollywood to write the screenplay for the film, which was released in 1955. After writing the *Angry Hills* (1955), an account of a Palestinian Jewish brigade that fought with the British in Greece, Uris set out to work on what would become his masterpiece.

Exodus tells the eventful story of Ari Ben Canaan, a native born *sabra* modeled after a young Yitzhak Rabin, who leads the Jewish struggle to create a Jewish homeland in Palestine. Interspersed with a historical narrative stretching from the Jewish *shetls* of 19th-century Russia to the United Nations vote partitioning Palestine is Ben Canaan's romance with a Gentile American nurse whose husband perished in World War II, contrasted in a parallel romance between Dov, an embittered member of the underground Irgun, and Karen, a Holocaust survivor subsequently murdered by Arabs. The novel was the basis for the successful film of the same name by Otto Preminger, starring Paul Newman as Ben Canaan. Even the theme song from the film was a hit for Pat Boone.

One of the scenes in *Exodus* depicts the 1943 Warsaw Ghetto uprising, and Uris expanded on this episode in a subsequent novel *Mila 18* (1961), which takes its name from the address of the headquarters of the Jewish resistance in the ghetto. The protagonist, Andrei Androfski, is an underground leader reminiscent of Ben Canaan and based loosely on the uprising's real-life leader, Mordechai Anielewicz. Interweaving journal entries of a fictional Jewish historian and a sympathetic Italian-American journalist, the novel chronicles the rise, heroic resistance, and crushing fall of the Poland's Jewish population.

QBVII—Queen's Bench Seven—(1970) is the fictionalization of a real lawsuit filed against Uris by Dr. Wladislaw Dering for defamation, Dering claiming that the author had characterized him as a war criminal. As in real life, the court finds in favor of the doctor but awards him minimal damages. The novel was adapted into a television production with Ben Gazzara playing the Jewish novelist. *Topaz* (1967) also embroiled Uris in controversy when its primary source, an exiled French diplomat, sued Uris for reneging on a profit-sharing agreement.

Trinity (1976), recalling the plot of *Exodus* and enjoying only moderately less success, narrates the saga of the struggle for independence in Ireland, as well as a poignant romance between the Catholic protagonist Conor Larkin and a Protestant woman. Uris's other major works include *The Haj* (1984), which was broadly criticized for its unflattering depiction of the Palestinian Arabs; *God in Ruins* (1999); and MITLA PASS (1988), which describes the writing career of an ex-marine named Gideon Zadok and his experiences in California and Israel in what is in many respects a fictional autobiography of the author himself. His posthumous final novel, *O'Hara's Choice* (2003), returns to the theme of the U.S. Marine Corps.

Uris also wrote and collaborated on nonfiction works, including *Exodus Revisited* and two books written in collaboration with his third wife, Jill Peabody Uris, *Ireland: A Terrible Beauty* (1975) and *Jerusalem: Song of Songs* (1981). He is also known, improbably, for the original screenplay for the classic *Gunfight at the OK Corral* (1957) starring Burt Lancaster and Kirk Douglas.

As a novelist Uris's sweeping, humanistic, and well-researched style is perhaps most similar to that of JAMES MICHENER (Uris interviewed 1,200 people for *Exodus* and devoted three years researching postwar Berlin and the famous airlift for *Armageddon* [1964]); but he has been criticized far more than Michener for technical inadequacies and his larger-than-life characters. As a self-taught writer with no academic credentials, his tremendous success also provoked anger among some critics, most notably the writer Philip Roth, who challenged his depictions of Jewish warrior-heroes fighting back against their enemies. On the other hand, Ruth Wisse of Harvard University notes that "powerful currents within Zionism itself sought to create just the kind of un-Jewish farmer-warriors that Uris inadvertently caricatured in the form of Ari Ben Canaan." Wisse also notes that privately circulated translations of *Exodus* in the former Soviet Union are said to have revived Jewish identity for many Russian Jews. He may in the end, for all his meticulous research, be best seen more as mythographer of history than a proper historical novelist.

A full-length study of Uris's work, *Leon Uris, A Critical Companion*, was published in 1998 by Kathleen Shine Cain.

Bibliography

Gray, Madison, et al. "Leon Uris, 'Author of Exodus,' dies at 78." Associated Press. Available online. URL: http://obits.eons.com/national/feature/national_literature/9874.

Homberger, Eric. "Leon Uris" (Obituary). *The Guardian*, 25 June 2003.

Leon Uris Biography and List of Works (Litweb). Available online. URL: http://www.litweb.net/biography/156/Leon_uris.html.

Leon Uris, 1924–2003 Papers, 1939–1999 Preliminary Inventory. Available online. URL: http://www.hrc.utexas.edu/research/fa/uris.html.

Roth, Philip. "New Jewish Stereotypes." In *Reading Myself and Others*. New York: Farrar, Straus & Giroux, 1975.

Uris, Leon. *Battle Cry*. New York: Putnam, 1953.

———. *The Angry Hills*. New York: Random House, 1955.

———. *Exodus*. New York: Doubleday, 1958.

———. *Mila 18*. New York: Doubleday, 1961.

———. *Armageddon*. New York: Doubleday, 1963.

———. *Topaz*. New York: McGraw Hill, 1967.

———. *QB VII*. New York: Doubelday, 1970.

———. *Ireland, A Terrible Beauty*. 1975 (with Jill Uris).

———. *Trinity*. New York: Doubleday, 1976.

———. *Jerusalem: A Song of Songs*. 1981 (with Jill Uris).

———. *The Haj*. New York: Doubleday, 1984.

———. *Mitla Pass*. Doubleday, 1988.

———. *Redemption*. New York: HarperCollins, 1995.

———. *A God in Ruins*. New York: HarperCollins, 1999.

———. *O'Hara's Choice*. New York: HarperCollins, 2003.

———, and Dimitrios Harissiadis. *Exodus Revisited*. New York: Doubleday, 1960.

Willmann, Travis Leon. "Uris's Exodus." Harry Ransom Center for the Humanities, *Newsletter*, fall 2003. Available online. URL: http://www.hrc.utexas.edu/news/newsletters/2003/fall/19/html.

Wisse, Ruth R. *The Modern Jewish Canon, A Journey through Language and Culture*. New York: The Free Press, 1980.

Louis Gordon

Valhalla Rising Clive Cussler (2001)

In characteristic CLIVE CUSSLER style, the narrative of *Valhalla Rising* revolves around three strikingly disparate elements: the Vikings, Jules Verne, and America's oil supply. Dirk Pitt, Cussler's swashbuckling hero (and in some respects alter-ego), here a Special Projects Director for the National Underwater and Marine Agency (NUMA), is leading a deep-water survey of the Tongas Trench when he and his sidekick, Al Giordino, spot a cruise ship, *The Emerald Dolphin,* on fire and divert their NUMA ship to rescue the passengers. Pitt quickly discovers that the *Dolphin* has been sabotaged with much loss of life and vows to bring the perpetrator to justice; his resolve only increases when he meets the beautiful Kelly Egan, daughter of Dr. Elmore Egan, designer of the cruise ship's revolutionary engines.

Kelly's story of a mysterious black man who killed her father and tried to steal his seemingly empty briefcase intrigues Pitt, and he sets out to find out all he can about the secretive inventor. The mystery of the briefcase deepens considerably when Pitt discovers that it fills with oil out of nowhere every 14 hours; but his attempts to solve the mystery, as well as to learn more about the saboteurs, are cut short by the hijacking of his own NUMA survey ship, *Deep Encounter,* and the further sabotage of a cruise submarine also powered by Egan's engines. As Pitt tries to untangle the connections between Dr. Egan's research and the sabotage, he brings to light not only a plot by an oil cartel to drive the price of oil sky high but also a Viking treasure, a teleportation machine, and the actual *Nautilus* submarine from Jules Verne's *20,000 Leagues under the Sea.*

Thematically, and again characteristically, *Valhalla Rising* unashamedly celebrates the triumph of honesty, integrity, and humanitarianism over mendacity and greed, with Pitt and Curtis Zale, sinister head of the Cerberus Corporation, set in starkest contrast (Cerberus being the three-headed hound of hell). Thus, when the latter openly threatens him and his friends in a Washington, D.C., restaurant, Pitt summarizes: "You murder men, women and children. Al and I are just your common, law abiding, taxpaying citizens who became swept up in your scheme to create a domestic oil monopoly" (356). There are no shades of gray, no doubts about who the villains or heroes are, and part of the fun for Cussler fans is the simple and satisfying pleasure of cheering on the home team—a home team sure to win.

Zale and his heartless minions set about the murder of thousands of people by sinking two cruise ships and plotting to ram a liquid natural gas tanker into the World Trade Center to create a backlash against foreign oil; Zale himself is "a cold blooded sociopath without a shred of conscience. He could kill a child as easily as he would step on an ant" (313). And as in Fleming's Bond fantasies, Zale kills his own men, with perhaps even more relish, when they disappoint, reminding all that "Failure begets failure. When your senses dull it is time you be replaced" (316). Even when facing death by his own hand, Zale leaves "no final note expressing shame or regret" (482).

In contrast, Pitt is selfless to a fault, pushing himself to the brink of exhaustion to rescue the passengers of the burning cruise ship; nearly dying of asphyxiation when he chooses to remain aboard a sinking cruise sub until the proverbial last minute; deliberately subjecting himself to a vicious beating in his effort to rescue Kelly (who is being tortured to force her to reveal the location of her father's laboratory); haunted by every life he fails to save, and heroically striving not to kill—with notable exceptions in the case of the perfectly malignant, whose deaths he stoically, even gladly ascribes to justice done. Thus, when Kanai, Zale's rather unsavory right-hand man, is crushed in a minisub under the weight of the very tanker he was trying to sabotage, Pitt—effectively his executioner—"spread his lips into a smile that showed every tooth, and waved bye-bye" (468).

"My God! Is he for real?" (416) exclaims a typical witness to one of his feats, to which the beautiful Kelly Egan replies, "Take my word for it. He's bigger than life" (416). Indeed, as the personable yet indestructible hero of more than 16 Cussler novels, Pitt often does seem superhuman, but in *Valhalla Rising,* perhaps in keeping with its eponymous theme of Viking mortality, readers are afforded a rare glimpse of his inalienable humanity: "His face though was beginning to show the unstoppable result of aging. Deepening mirth lines spread from edges of his eyes. The skin did not have the elasticity of his younger years and was slowly achieving a weathered look to it" (100). Lost love has also taken its toll, as Pitt is tormented by the memory of one Summer Moran, the only woman he truly loved, yet whom even he could not save: "He always saw her swimming into the depths to find her father who was trapped in an underwater cavern, her lovely body and flowing red hair vanishing into the green water of the Pacific" (100). After her death Pitt has "lived only for his work on and under the water. The sea became his mistress" (100). In contrast to his earlier, more casual relationships with women, Pitt's love for Summer endures, even dooms his ongoing relationship with Congresswoman Loren Smith, whom Pitt asks toward the novel's end,

> "So where do *we* go from here?"
>
> She touched his hand lightly with her fingertips. "We go on as before."
>
> "You in Congress and me under the sea," he said slowly.
>
> A soft look came into her violet eyes. "I believe it was meant to be that way" (512).

Loren appears to have said it all when she notes, "It hasn't been easy competing with a ghost" (512), and Pitt himself jokes that his dreams of being a grandfather have died; yet one day two mysterious visitors arrive at his home (a converted aircraft hangar): one, a young man looking remarkably like him; the other, a beautiful young woman whose resemblance to Summer makes him stagger. They are, in truth, his own children, twin offspring of his only love (Summer survived her plunge into the sea, though disfigured and crippled for life). As both twins have degrees in marine engineering and oceanography, Pitt's long-suffering love ultimately results in an unthought-of reward: two grown children who will carry on his work and name.

Pitt's discovery of his son and daughter reinforces the novel's overarching Cusslerian theme: the intimate and often surprising interpenetration of past and present (and here, future). Characteristically, the novel's prologue describes two seemingly unrelated historical events—the destruction of a Viking village by Native Americans and the sinking of a warship by a strange submarine. Both are neatly interwoven in the novel's present-day adventures when a series of Viking runes found in Dr. Egan's notes leads Pitt and his friends to the inventor's hidden laboratory and his revolutionary teleportation device, which is hidden in a cave near the Hudson River. Here Pitt finds a treasure trove of valuable historic artwork and coins, which Egan had used to finance his experiments (another touch of the old as new). But Pitt also discovers several ships belonging to the Vikings who were slain centuries ago, as well as the very *Nautilus* of Jules Verne fame, which Dr. Egan had been using as his laboratory. As Giordino neatly puts it, "So this is where one great man lived and another great man created" (503).

Continuing a tradition that began with *Dragon* as a joke he (wrongly) thought his editor would remove, Cussler himself appears with a small but critical role in the tale, here both rescuing a starving Pitt and his friends from a drifting submersible abandoned when Zale's men hijacked the *Deep Encounter* and helping them save that ship's crew from the hijackers.

Bibliography

Cussler, Clive. *Valhalla Rising.* New York: Berkley, 2001.

Patti J. Kurtz

Vance, Jack (1916–)

John Holbrook "Jack" Vance is an American author best known for his work in science fiction, fantasy, and mystery. One of the most decorated writers alive—a SFWA Grand Master whose awards include the Hugo, World Fantasy, Jupiter, Nebula, and Edgar—he is in an elite class of authors who have won the major awards of different genres.

Vance himself, however, is something of an enigma, being notoriously quiet and reclusive. Refusing to promote himself, to divulge details of his biography, or to participate in the broader SF and fantasy communities, he remains "the least well-known master in the field," employing such a host of pseudonyms (Ellery Queen, Peter Wade, Jay Kavanse, Peter Held, and John Van See) that many of his greatest fans read works without knowing that they are his.

Vance was born (and still resides) in California. In 1942 he earned a B.A. from the University of California, Berkeley, afterward working at numerous jobs (merchant seaman, jazz musician, and carpenter) that would considerably enhance his later writing. He was also part of the bohemian San Francisco renaissance, an experimental arts and literature movement. He often lived on water—for a time enjoying joint ownership of a houseboat with close friends Frank Herbert and Poul Anderson and sailing the Sacramento Delta—a lifestyle mirrored in many of his stories, such as "Showboat World." He has been married to Norma Ingold for half a century.

After a stint in journalism Vance began his writing career in the pulp magazines of the 1940s, a seething hotbed of later genres such as science fiction, fantasy, horror, action, and detective fiction. The incredibly prolific Vance has since written in all these areas, often skillfully blending them so that his science-fiction work features the intricate and often outré cultures associated with fantasy. His fantasy often features advanced technologies that function as magic (he also invented what is called Vancian spellcasting—where one forgets magic spells once cast—which was used by Gary Gygax in the seminal Dungeon & Dragons game system), and most of his works revolve around a mystery and a rebel who acts as a reluctant hero against an unjust system. This iconoclastic archetype (Emphyrio), sardonic rebel in a picaresque world, is almost universally present in his protagonists.

Vance's style is intensely idiosyncratic, influenced, in the opinion of the author himself, by no one. He is a lyric wordsmith with an obvious and exuberant love of language, and his linguistic mastery with its elegant, stylized, and often elevated prose has become world-renowned. There is a distinct classicism, an Old World sensibility of taste, manners, and comedy in his writings, with farces such as *The Many Worlds of Magnus Ridolph* and flights of linguistic fancy such as *The Languages of Pao.*

Vance also has few peers in the world- and culture-creation so esteemed by fans of science fiction. Many of his SF tales exist in the Gaean Reach, a densely populated, far-reaching human universe. His stories often contain, but are not burdened by, staggering amounts of natural, linguistic, architectural, philosophical, and societal detail, with seemingly endless layers of mentioned worlds, races, and cultures resting beneath each illuminated scene—"a universe of infinite variety," as some have described it.

The manifold profusion of civilizations, the universe crowded to the point of chaos, contributes an operatic or epic sense of scale to his tales. But through them all the individual stands firm and tall, as if Vance were reminding readers that, however irrational may be the nature of our realities, people always have the capacity to make sense of them, to reason them out, much like the order lying beneath the often extravagant sensuality of music, at which Vance is also adept.

Some of his most famous SF books are *Big Planet* and *The Last Castle,* as well the novels comprising the Tschai, Demon Princes, and Dying Earth series. His most notable fantasy works include the Lyonesse trilogy and *Cugel's Saga.* And beyond the fame of Ellery Queen, with his award-winning *The Man in the Cage,* some of Vance's best mysteries are those that feature Sheriff Joe Bain (*The Fox Valley Murders, The Pleasant Grove Murders*).

Bibliography

Clareson, Thomas D. *Understanding Contemporary American Science Fiction. The Formative Period, 1926–1970.* Columbia: University of South Carolina Press, 1990.

Fletcher, Marilyn, and James L. Thorson, eds. *Reader's Guide to Twentieth-Century Science Fiction.* Chicago: American Library Association, 1989.

Gunn, James, ed. *The New Science Fiction Encyclopedia.* New York: Viking, 1988.

Prozini, Bill, and Marcia Muller. *1001 Midnights. The Aficionados Guide to Mystery and Detective Fiction.* New York: Arbor House, 1986.

Thomas Fortenberry

Velocity Dean Koontz (2005)

With characteristic wit, the opening pages of DEAN KOONTZ's *Velocity* appear to overlook entirely the protagonist, as bartender Billy Wiles keeps to himself in a quiet, small-town bar. Then a note appears on his car:

> If you don't take this note to the police and get them involved, I will kill a lovely blond schoolteacher somewhere in Napa County.
>
> If you do take this note to the police, I will instead kill an elderly woman active in charity work.
>
> You have six hours to decide. The choice is yours. (18)

Billy dismisses the note as a joke. But after a blond schoolteacher is found murdered, another note appears, this time with a five-hour deadline, the novel's velocity steadily increasing, even as the choices required of Billy become more and more impossible.

Koontz has long been concerned with what constitutes an ordinary person's proper response to extraordinary evil. In LIFE EXPECTANCY (2004), which immediately preceded *Velocity,* the hero espouses humor and cheer as an antidote to inevitable tragedy, but here there is nothing lighthearted about Billy's tribulations as he blames himself for the outcome of each note, believing that even the silence of not choosing is itself a choice for which he somehow bears responsibility. But when Billy begins to fight back, he also begins to reconnect with himself and those around him, and out of the excruciating perversity of his suffering comes a kind of redemptive normalcy he would otherwise, one assumes, never have known.

Koontz's characters often struggle with painful memories of familial tragedy (Koontz himself became familiar with the conventions of modern therapy and rehabilitation while caring for his once-abusive father), and Billy is no exception. Prior to the novel's opening, the sudden death of his parents when he was 14 and the near-fatal poisoning of his fiancée, Barbara, have together driven him into an isolated, friendless life.

Barbara lies comatose in the local hospital, and Billy visits her several times a week, always carefully noting the cryptic phrases she intermittently utters, the most frequent being "I want to know what it says, the sea" (30); his attempts to comprehend such sayings form part of a larger thematic focus in the novel on reading and listening. Billy must somehow read the killer's notes "correctly" in order to outmaneuver him, with a misread spelling certain tragedy; when evidence is planted to frame Billy, he must prevent the police from misreading him as the killer. In addition, Billy's coworker Ivy believes herself to be a haruspex, a person who reads the future from dead bodies; just as Billy attends to the words of Barbara and the killer, so Ivy listens for the voices of her deceased mother and grandmother.

In dramatic contrast to Ivy's watchful calm, Billy's fellow bartender Steve Zillis is a loudmouthed buffoon. Billy comes to suspect that his breezy style is just an act, and if Ivy represents an almost unnatural stillness, Steve comes to symbolize restless, even manic performance as an end in itself. Billy himself must learn to hold still long enough to understand the killer's performances, the multiple layers and inscrutable motivations of each elaborate crime scene. For most of the novel the one lead he has on his tormenter—whom he calls "the freak"—is that the serial killer sees his actions as a kind of beautiful, significant performance.

Compelling aspects of beauty and interpretation inscribe another major theme in the novel: the inexplicability of modern art. The bar where Billy works is located near an ongoing art installation, a giant animated mural that will be burned to the ground when completed. The thirties-modernist work represents a man surrounded by gears and pistons, apparently

> caught up in the machine and pressing forward with as much panic as determination, as though if he rested for an instant he would slip out of sync and be torn to pieces (40).

Although this image comes in many ways to symbolize Billy's own predicament, he views the mural as "either low art or high craftsmanship" (41), and the only thing less sensible than actually constructing it would be the act of destroying it needlessly. Throughout the novel both art and craftsmanship take on similar and often surprisingly sinister connotations. Artifice comes almost to represent a perverse, sadistic kind of self-gratification. When Billy arrives at one of two possible lairs for his tormentor, for example, he finds female mannequins that have been "mutilated" into disturbingly violent and hateful sculptures. Billy senses the care and purpose their maker put into these figures but believes "he didn't know, didn't care" what they might mean (283), concluding that the artist "nurtured a sick and vivid fantasy life" (285). At the second possible lair, which is as lavish and refined as the first is tawdry and dilapidated, Billy finds a collection of "Japanese bronzes . . . priceless examples of the finest Meiji-period work" (414); but this art collection only mimics the killer's own trophy case, an assortment of hands and faces preserved in clear jars, showcased with all the care of a museum exhibit.

The second lair also features custom furniture and expensive fabrics, and its craftsmanship recalls the nonsensical details Billy has painstakingly installed in his own home, notably coffered ceilings with hand-carved ornaments. Billy uses his carpentry skills to retreat from the world around him, hiding himself at his workbench. If art implies a kind of perversion or fetishism, craftsmanship comes to signify an almost autistic isolation, a narrow focus on material surfaces to the exclusion of a deeper, spiritual life.

There emerges a kind of anti-intellectualism aimed at both the spiritual poverty and the material wealth of the overeducated, but this is subtly mitigated throughout. The novel has little patience for "rarefied circles where the simplest thoughts are deep and where even gray has shades of gray" (455). When an otherwise noble doctor urges Billy to allow Barbara to die, the novel provides a mocking diagnosis: "unfortunately, the university . . . had infected him with what they called 'utilitarian ethics'" (254). But the novel also distances Billy from the masses, "the press and the public," who would romanticize the serial killer's genius (455). Its opening scene, for example, satirizes a local barfly who cruelly toasts the death of his pretentious neighbor, a local professor of contemporary literature. High culture is valued, at least of the right sort; Billy's thoughts in crisis often take the form of quotations from T. S. Eliot, and the lowbrow bartender is highbrow enough to recognize and interpret the killer's art, even offering a terse review in a recognizable art-critical style.

Billy himself is both artist and craftsman in his roles as writer and carpenter, and when he applies his carpentry skills to making his home more inviting, he is also able to begin writing again, the lesson seemingly being that rather than using art to nurse perverse fantasy, the good artist connects to common human experience—as per Dickens and Eliot, both of whom are quoted extensively in the novel (Barbara's above-quoted mantra, for example, is lifted straight from the former's *Dombey and Son*). The good craftsman, likewise, does not retreat to his workroom to escape the world but rather makes the world a more comfortable, more elegant place to live together with other people. Against the killer's zeal for surfaces and performance, Billy develops a deep appreciation of community in the genuine living moment.

Velocity recalls Koontz's earlier work *Intensity* (1996) in several ways: the style of its title, a time-compressed plot, a solitary hero with a dark past, and a seemingly insurmountable serial killer, while both titles derive from definitive qualities associated with the respective killers. But where the hero's struggle in *Intensity* is essentially a physical one (her adversary has nearly superhuman senses, strength, and reflexes), in *Velocity* Billy must triumph not only over a physically dangerous killer but over what might be termed a fatal inauthenticity in art and life.

Bibliography

Koontz, Dean. *Intensity.* Franklin Center, Pa.: Franklin Library, 1995. Reprint, New York: Knopf, 1996.

———. *Life Expectancy.* New York: Bantam, 2004.

———. *Velocity.* New York: Bantam, 2005.

Charles Tedder

Waiting to Exhale **Terry McMillan** (1992)

Waiting to Exhale chronicles the story of Savannah, Bernadine, Gloria, and Robin, four African-American sister friends juggling careers and relationships while struggling to find personal satisfaction. Set in 1991, the novel follows this circle of friends as they try to reconcile their life's dreams with reality.

TERRY MCMILLAN alternates the narration between the four, weaving together an engrossing tale that begins with 37-year-old Savannah, a marketing executive who works for a gas company in Denver but yearns to be a TV producer. After deciding that "Denver is dead," Savannah heeds the advice of her friend Bernadine and relocates to sunny Phoenix: "Nothing unforgettable has happened to me since I've been in Denver, which is why I'm getting the hell out of here" (3). Savannah is the bedrock for her family, providing financial support for her mother and emotional support for her sister. However, finding her own love proves difficult: "I worry if and when I'll ever find the *right* man, if I'll ever be able to exhale. [. . .] Never in a million years would I have ever believed that I would be thirty-six years old and still childless and single. But here I am" (14).

The plot hinges on the story of Bernadine, a 38-year-old accountant and mother of two, who has her life turned upside down when John, her husband of 11 years, announces that he is moving out and wants a divorce so that he can be with his secretary: "Right after Bernadine's husband told her he was leaving her for a white girl, she stood in the kitchen doorway, snatched the eighteen hot rollers out of her hair, and threw every last one of them at him" (23).

At the same time, Gloria, a 37-year-old hair stylist and salon owner, "got tired of waiting for love and divided all of her attention among God, hair, and her son" (69). As her teenage son, Tarik, approaches graduation and prepares to embark on his own life, Gloria, who struggles with her weight and self-image, wonders how she will define herself without her son to raise.

Finally, Robin, a 35-year-old insurance company analyst, consistently confuses sex with love. Her neediness leads her to overlook "a good man" for a string of noncommittal Lotharios.

In this circle of women and their respective struggles, McMillan manages to capture many of the concerns of the "Funk" generation—30-something professional black women who enjoy unprecedented levels of education and professional success but long for genuine, fulfilling, romantic relationships.

As the novel unfolds, each woman is forced to reassess her life in light of major personal disappointments. Savannah finds that moving to Phoenix (where the others live) in no way solves her problems. After one particularly forgettable night out with the other girls just a few weeks into her stay, Savannah decides, "Phoenix is as dead as Denver" and resolves to leave within a year if "nothing exciting happens" (179). Savannah serves as the down-to-earth, sarcastic, world-weary opposite to Robin's incurable romanticism. While Savannah also longs for love, she cannot understand Robin's neediness, observing, "Women who think like her really piss me off" (201). This very inability to be vulnerable seems to have lost her a relationship with her own "good man," Kenneth, with whom she broke up without explanation, not revealing her true feelings for fear of being hurt: "By the time I realized I was in love with him, I was too scared to tell him. I knew what he *thought* about me, but I didn't know how he *felt*. [. . .] I got tired of guessing. And I didn't feel comfortable questioning him about it. So one day I wrote him a letter and told him I didn't want to go out with him anymore" (206).

While Savannah struggles to keep her mask of invulnerability in place, Robin holds out hope that things will work out with the promiscuous deadbeat Russell: "I don't think I'll be satisfied until I get Russell, even though in my heart I know he's a dog. I just can't seem to get him out of my system. I'm probably living in a fantasy world or something" (177). At the same time she is blind to the quieter virtues of Michael, who promises, "I can give you everything you want, everything you need, if you'll let me" (58). Instead, Robin dismisses Michael because he is bad in bed and takes up with Troy, a 40-year-old crack addict and dealer she meets in a grocery store. In addition to this exhausting drama, Robin must deal with her father's gradual decline from Alzheimer's, which only compounds her longing for a man in her life.

Gloria, meanwhile, resigns herself to never having a man. At the same time as her own love life hits its nadir, Tarik emerges into young manhood, making plans to travel with a musical group, Up With People, after graduation and enjoying the pleasure of his white girlfriend in his bedroom. Midway through the novel, Gloria's new neighbor, Marvin, moves in, befriending her and fixing things around the house but little else. For her 38th birthday the girls treat Gloria to a nostalgia-filled party. Soon after, she suffers a massive heart attack and is forced to rethink her self-sacrificial, loveless life. Bernadine, meanwhile, refuses her husband's paltry initial offer and hires a lawyer and an investigator, who manage to uncover John's deceptive financial dealings. Despite her resolve, Bernadine faces a difficult adjustment. She aggressively enters the dating scene, only to end up in an affair with a married man, producing (and empathizing with) the same suffering that she herself had felt. While celebrating the finalization of her divorce at a resort outside of Scottsdale, she meets James, an African-American civil rights attorney who is taking care of his white wife who is virtually incapacitated by breast cancer. After the death of his wife James reconnects with Bernadine, his "soul mate."

The novel ends with each woman resolved to forge ahead with a new vision for her life. Robin learns that she is pregnant with Russell's child. Rather than pursue him, however, she resolves to take care of the child on her own: "If I don't do anything else right, I'm going to do this right. I'll finally have somebody I can love as hard as I want to. Somebody who needs *me*" (401). After her attack Gloria's relationship with Marvin blossoms, and she resolves to take care of her health, realizing she has everything she needs to be happy. Savannah, stung by a fling during a conference, resolves to quit falling for guys who seem to fit her picture of perfection and hold out for something truer. After lengthy and rancorous negotiations Bernadine receives almost a million dollars in her divorce settlement, enough for her to finally start her own business, Bernadine's Sweet Shop, which she had put off in order to raise her children and take care of her family according to her husband's wishes. Each woman has, in her own unexpected way, learned to exhale and live her life according to her own design rather than the expectations and demands of others.

Waiting to Exhale was made into a blockbuster Hollywood film starring Whitney Houston and Angela Bassett in 1995.

Bibliography

McMillan, Terry. *Waiting to Exhale.* New York: Viking, 1992.

Rychetta Watkins

Waller, Robert James (1939–)

Educator, lyricist, photographer, and author of 10 novels, Robert James Waller remains most famous for what he deems his "loosely-jointed trilogy," comprising *The* BRIDGES OF MADISON COUNTY, *A*

Thousand Country Roads (2002), and *High Plains Tango* (2005). Revolving around the introspective, hippie photographer Robert Kincaid and his son, Carlisle McMillan, these three novels, as *USA Today* reviewer Deirdre Donahue puts it, often "bypass the literary establishment," yet "nestle deep in the hearts of the general public." Indeed, the phenomenal popularity of *The Bridges of Madison County* precipitated a Steven Spielberg–produced film in 1995 starring box-office favorites Clint Eastwood and Meryl Streep, bringing Robert Kincaid to life on the big screen and solidifying his iconic status in the popular imagination.

The son of a modest produce businessman and midwestern housewife, Waller grew up in the small town of Rockford, Iowa, and was educated at the Iowa State Teachers College (now known as the University of Northern Iowa), obtaining a B.A. in business education teaching (1962) and an M.A. in education (1964). He married Georgia A. Weidemeier in 1962 and fathered a daughter with her, but they eventually divorced in 1997. After receiving his Ph.D. from Indiana University's School of Business in 1968, he began teaching as an assistant professor of management and economics at the University of Northern Iowa in Cedar Falls, where he would remain for 22 years, serving as dean of the School of Business between 1980 and 1986.

Though he published numerous scholarly pieces and essays during his tenure at the university, Waller did not turn his attention to fiction writing until a sabbatical in 1989. Inspired by a serendipitous combination of Iowan covered bridges and self-styled song lyrics about the dreams of a woman called Francesca, Waller took less than two weeks to write his debut novella, *The Bridges of Madison County,* which takes place in the 1960s and chronicles a passionate four-day love affair between a ruggedly handsome globe-trotting *National Geographic* photographer and a plain Iowa housewife stuck in a secure but numbing routine. Published globally in 36 languages, the novel spent more than three years on the *New York Times* best-seller list and excited such interest in Kincaid that *National Geographic* received thousands of inquiries about him in the years immediately following the book's release. David Lamb, a reporter for the *Chicago Times,* noted that letter writers spoke of "Kincaid with a reverence, as if Waller has created a character so believable he transcended fiction and became as real as the mythic loner of our legends."

Waller's succeeding novels, *SLOW WALTZ IN CEDAR BEND* (1993), *Border Music* (1995), and *Puerto Vallarta Squeeze* (1995), describe the same type of ardent love story complicated by one event or another, which garnered *Bridges* such popular success. None of them involves Kincaid and Francesca, but the last features a cameo appearance by an elusive photographer suspiciously resembling Kincaid. As the much anticipated next novel by the writer of *Bridges, Slow Waltz in Cedar Bend* sold more than 2 million copies, but critics continued to assail Waller's writing style, and sales for the other two books waned. In 2002 Waller finally heeded the overwhelming response from readers clamoring for more of Kincaid and wrote *A Thousand Country Roads,* an epilogue to *Bridges,* which fills in some of his earlier story and reveals what becomes of him after his Iowan tête-à-tête. Waller also introduces Carlisle McMillan, Kincaid's illegitimate son, who follows a series of clues to track down the father he has never known. Like Kincaid, McMillan proved so popular with readers that in 2005 Waller released *High Plains Tango,* centering on McMillan's efforts to remove himself from big-city environs and ethics, only to wind up embroiled in a battle against a profit-seeking land developer who wants to seize his Salamander, South Dakota, home.

Lampooned by critics as mere attempts at profit seeking on Waller's part, both *A Thousand Country Roads* and *High Plains Tango* nevertheless appealed to readers and sold well. However, in his latest work, *The Long Night of Winchell Dear* (2006), Waller abandons both Kincaid and McMillan to take up the story of Winchell Dear, an honest south Texas poker player who senses trouble one night as two Los Angeles thugs, a drug mule from Mexico, a Native American squatter, and a seven-foot rattlesnake all converge on the ranch he has won with a hand of two pair. Having remarried in 2004, Waller and his second wife currently reside in a 100-year-old stone farmhouse in Texas, a setting that may well have influenced his latest novel. Indeed, most of Waller's fiction is characterized by tacit biographical details, linked to places where he has lived or traveled, and peopled by characters that share commonalities with him or his family, friends, or acquaintances.

Bibliography

Donahue, Deirdre. "*High Plains Tango* Has Two Left Feet." *USA Today,* 29 June 2005, 5.

Lamb, David. "Magazine Tells *Bridges* Fans: It's Only Make-Believe." *Chicago Times,* 23 June 1995, 23.

Dana Nichols

Wambaugh Jr., Joseph Aloysius (1937–)

Wambaugh is an innovative writer of police procedurals and true-crime novels who revolutionized their form, content, and language. He has also garnered praise for his work as a consultant for television and feature films. Crime fiction and nonfiction should, Wambaugh believes, describe criminals, their victims, and the police realistically and with empathy.

The son of a police chief, Wambaugh was born in East Pittsburgh, Pennsylvania, in 1937. After having moved to California with his family at an early age, he enlisted in the U.S. Marine Corps and served from 1954 to 1957. In 1955 he married Dee Allsup, with whom he later had three children. Wambaugh's college education focused on English and American literature, and he earned a B.A. and an M.A. from California State College (now University), Los Angeles. Serving as a patrolman and detective sergeant in the Los Angeles Police Department between 1960 and 1974, Wambaugh began his writing career in 1970 with the publication of *The New Centurions.* Soon becoming famous, he found it increasingly difficult to function effectively as a member of the Los Angeles police force and resigned in 1974. During that same year he completed *The Onion Field,* his first work of nonfiction and one that he claims he felt driven to write. Devoting himself full time to his new career as an author in the years after leaving the L.A.P.D., Wambaugh developed his unique voice as a narrator of fiction and nonfiction highlighting police work. He began his work in the Hollywood entertainment industry, adapting his novel *The New Centurions* for film in 1972 and playing an instrumental role in creating and supervising the television series *Police Story* (1973–77). He has won a number of awards, including the Edgar Allan Poe Award in 1974 and 1981 and the Rodolfo Walsh Prize for Investigative Journalism in 1989. The author now lives with his wife in the San Diego area and spends his time writing and teaching. His most recent novel, *Hollywood Station,* appeared in 2006.

Wambaugh's life experience profoundly shaped his literary production. His training and work as a police officer acquainted him with the strengths and weaknesses of the American criminal justice system; service in the Marine Corps gave him an understanding of group discipline and a degree of tolerance and respect for authority figures; his early academic interest in the satire of Joseph Heller and Theodore Dreiser would later imbue novels such as *The Glitter Dome* (1981), *The Secrets of Harry Bright* (1985), and *Finnegan's Week* (1993) with comic elements bordering at times on the ridiculous or macabre.

The Blue Knight (1972), *The Choirboys* (1975), *The Blooding: The True Story of the Narborough Village Murders* (1989), and *Fire Lover: A True Story* (2002) illustrate his strong inclination toward realism and his desire and ability to portray victims, criminals, and police as human beings. Wambaugh helped revitalize the almost moribund police procedural in print and film, leaving his unique imprint on plotting, characterization, and setting. He is also credited with adding reliability and sophistication to nonfiction accounts of crime. Since 1970 his books have constantly appeared on best-seller lists, and his abilities as a screenwriter have been in strong demand. Although some of his prose is faulted for being too gritty or sexually charged, few readers would question his ability to capture the essence of crime and criminal investigation in his narratives, and even fewer would deny his skill as an entertainer.

Bibliography

Wambaugh, Joseph. *The New Centurions.* Boston: Little, Brown, 1970.

———. *The Blue Knight.* Boston and Toronto: Little, Brown, 1972.

———. *The Onion Field.* New York: Delacorte, 1973.

———. *The Choirboys.* New York: Delacorte, 1975.

———. *The Glitter Dome.* New York: Morrow, 1981.

———. *The Secrets of Harry Bright.* New York: Morrow, 1985.
———. *The Blooding: The True Story of the Narborough Village Murders.* New York: Morrow, 1989.
———. *Finnegan's Week.* New York: Morrow, 1994.
———. *Fire Lover: A True Story.* New York: Morrow, 2002.
———. *Hollywood Station.* New York: Little, Brown, 2006.

David Witkosky

War and Remembrance

Herman Wouk (1978)

War and Remembrance is a multifaceted historical chronicle featuring Victor (Pug) Henry, naval officer and presidential envoy during World War II. The novel serves as a sequel to *Winds of War* (1971), which commenced the saga of the Henry family as the nation prepared for war. Readers witness the drama and uncertainty of unfolding events in Europe and Asia, from Hitler's invasion of Poland to the attack on Pearl Harbor, always through the perspective of Commander Henry and his family.

The relationships forged in *Winds of War* help to locate the reader amid the welter of historical detail encompassing the lives of Wouk's many characters, while the events chronicled reflect with painstaking accuracy the major events of World War II. From the opening scenes of the Japanese attack on Pearl Harbor to the dropping of the atom bomb on Hiroshima, HERMAN WOUK provides a thorough analysis of the Japanese, American, and German political situations, as well as a full narrative exploration of the major land and sea battles, detailing the cultural tragedy of the concentration camps and the technological achievements surrounding the development of the atomic bomb. Through all these complexities, however, Wouk maintains a sure and balanced sense of the global dimensions of the war, its cataclysmic scale yet intimate effects.

A believer in the traditional values of depression-era America, Pug considers marriage and patriotism not as sacred ideals to which one should aspire but as sacred duties one must uphold and live by. His values, however, face strong challenges through his relationship with the young, bright, beautiful Pamela Tudsbury, as well as through the offer of a new military assignment. Pug Henry is a man who commands, an officer with experience, but when asked to serve as President Roosevelt's personal emissary to the Soviet Union, he does what his honor dictates, forgoing his personal ambitions and accepting the service to his country.

Byron Henry, like his father, Pug, views his friends, family, and fellow officers in the light of the highest moral standards. Acting as a sort of moral compass within the novel, Byron personally sees to the dissolution of his sister Madeline's affair with Hugh Cleveland, her boss and a married man; distances himself from his father over Pug's affair with Pamela; and openly disapproves of his captain's decision to shoot the Japanese soldiers of a disabled ship. Wouk's depiction of the Henrys as icons of upright American male behavior stands in dramatic contrast to the world around them in which the warring forces are everywhere corrupting civilized behavior.

The educator, Aaron Jastrow, serves as a prime example of such corruption, being led to believe, through the cunning deceptions of a former student, Werner Beck, that collaborating with the Nazis will save his niece Natalie's life while avoiding implication in the Nazi regime. Having compromised himself, he and his niece nonetheless fall victim to the persecution he had sought to avoid, illustrating a fundamental premise of the novel that compromising moral standards, even with the best intentions, is a loser's game.

Wouk creates a complex tapestry of the events of the war with his deft incorporation of historical figures, offering readers both accurate portraits and cultural background through which they may gain a deeper understanding of the times. Fully drawn characters like that of Roosevelt, Harry Hopkins, and the victorious admiral at Midway, Raymond Spruance, serve as vivid reminders that Wouk's tale has its roots in very real events.

Interspersed with the vignettes of such historical figures are the deeds of fictionalized characters, fleshing out the anatomy of war: Leslie Slote is a well-intentioned American foreign service worker who unsuccessfully attempts to uncover the truth about the events taking place within the European concentration camps; German general Armin von Roon's racial bias exemplifies the anti-Semitic climate of the time; Alistair Tudsbury is the British everyman who typifies Great Britain's vulnerabilities at the outset of war.

The novel suggests that America, too, was largely unprepared both morally and militarily for the global war but despite this was able to prevail through its spirited response and tremendous capacity to generate the resources critical to the defeat of her enemies. Wouk explores the brilliance of Roosevelt's Lend-Lease strategy, for example, which allowed the Soviets to battle the Germans while minimizing American casualties and allowing his country vital time to mobilize its forces. Forming a second central theme is the emergence of what might be termed the calculus of destruction: the Nazis "Final Solution" and the Americans' nuclear solution both demonstrating a catastrophic deconstruction of traditional views of the world and raising profound and perhaps unanswerable questions about mortality and justice in a time of technological supremacy.

Although novels concerned with World War II are legion, few offer a better balance of breadth, depth, accessibility, and complexity. Like its predecessor, *Winds of War, War and Remembrance* enjoyed tremendous success as a novel and was made into a historic television miniseries. Produced by Dan Curtis and broadcast over two weeks in 1988, the series ran for an astounding 30 hours and cost more than $104 million dollars, "the costliest and grandest single-story undertaking in medium history" (Directors). It starred Robert Mitchum, Jane Seymour, and Polly Bergen and received 15 Emmy Award nominations.

Bibliography

Davis, Don. *Appointment with the Squire.* Annapolis, Md.: Naval Institute Press, 1995.

Director's Guild of America. "Nothing Mini about the Mini-Series." Available online. URL: http://www.directors-guild.org/index2.php3.

Wouk, Herman. *War and Remembrance.* Boston: Little, Brown, 1978.

Christine Marie Hilger

Weisberger, Lauren (1977–)

Weisberger is the author of three novels, the first of which, *The Devil Wears Prada* (2003), stayed on the *New York Times* best-seller list for six months and was later adapted successfully to film. Although Weisberger has stressed the fictional nature of her work, *The Devil Wears Prada* is generally thought to be a roman à clef based on Weisberger's experiences working for *Vogue* editor Anna Wintour.

Weisberger was born in Scranton, Pennsylvania, and graduated from Cornell University in 1999 with a B.A. in English. She spent some time traveling through Europe before returning to the United States, where she took her first job as assistant to the editor in chief of *Vogue* magazine, Anna Wintour, a brilliant fashion editor whose hard-edged personality has earned her the nickname "Nuclear Wintour." Weisberger later moved to *Departures* magazine as an assistant editor. At night she attended writing classes, where she began writing *The Devil Wears Prada* as a series of nonfiction essays about the magazine world. Her instructor, Charles Salzberg, pushed her to keep the project going and develop it into her first novel, which she sold a year later.

The Devil Wears Prada chronicles the misadventures of recent college grad Andrea Sachs, a would-be writer who takes a "dream job" as personal assistant to the editor of a fashion magazine called *Runway* in the belief that it will bring her a step closer to her real dream of writing for the *New Yorker.* Despite the luxurious perks of her new position, Andrea finds her boss's outrageous demands difficult to handle. Meanwhile, her relationships with friends and family become increasingly strained due to the amount of time and attention she is devoting to her job. Realizing that she is on the point of becoming like her boss, Andrea quits her job and returns home to attend the bedside of a friend who is comatose following a car accident. The novel ends with Sachs making her first professional sale to *Seventeen* magazine in the wake of her very public departure from *Runway,* a move that helps rather than hurts her writing career.

The film adaptation of *The Devil Wears Prada* (2006) starring Meryl Streep as Miranda Priestly and Anne Hathaway as Andy Sachs followed the plot of the novel fairly closely and was a major success, inspiring the development of a possible TV series.

In Weisberger's second novel, *Everyone Worth Knowing* (2005), young Bette Robinson impulsively quits her Manhattan bank job and soon afterward starts a new career with an event-planning concern, Kelly & Company. A major component of Bette's new job involves partying in the VIP rooms of the city's most exclusive clubs, a career that seems made in heaven until her personal life starts appearing in the tabloids. As in *The Devil Wears Prada,* the protagonist finds that her "dream job" comes between her and the people she truly cares about, and she eventually leaves her job in dramatic fashion.

Weisberger's fiction has been alternately praised as frothy Cinderella stories offering gossipy exposés of the rich elite and denounced as the worst example of what Kate Betts calls "bite-the-boss fiction." However, given that Betts herself previously worked for Anna Wintour, many readers perceived her highly negative review of *The Devil Wears Prada* as participating in exactly the kind of workplace mud-slinging Betts criticizes.

Weisberger published a third novel, *Chasing Harry Winston,* in 2008. It concerns the lives of three female New Yorkers troubled by the onset of early middle age.

Bibliography

Betts, Kate. "Anna Dearest." *New York Times Book Review,* 13 April 2003. Available online. URL: http://query.nytimes.com/gst/fullpage.html?res=9507EED61F39F930A25757C0A9659C8B63.

Weisberger, Lauren. *The Devil Wears Prada.* New York: Broadway, 2004.

———. *Everyone Worth Knowing.* New York: Simon & Schuster, 2005.

Siobhan Carroll

West, Morris (1916–1999)

Morris Langlo West, Australia's most internationally successful author, was born in Melbourne in 1916, the eldest of six children. He attended St. Mary's College in St. Kilda, the suburb in which he was born, and the University of Melbourne, from which he received his B.A. in 1937. He spent 12 years as a member of the Christian Brothers order, which he compared to the training of a terrorist (Clancy 227), but left in 1941 without taking final vows. From 1933 to 1939 he taught at schools in New South Wales and Tasmania. During World War II from 1939 to 1943 he served as a cipher officer in the Australian Imperial Forces Corps of Signals, and while stationed in Queensland he wrote his first semi-autobiographical novel, *A Moon in My Pocket* (1945), based on his experiences in the Christian Brothers and published under the pseudonym Julian Morris (he used the pseudonym Michael East for two later novels). In 1943 West spent three months as the private secretary to William Morris "Billy" Hughes, former prime minister of Australia.

After leaving the army, he worked as a publicity manager at Radio Station 3DB in Melbourne for two years before founding and later becoming managing director of Australian Radio Productions (1945–54), where among other things he produced and wrote soap operas. After suffering a breakdown, he sold his stake in the business and settled near Sydney, where he worked as a film and dramatic writer for the Shell Company and the Australian Broadcasting Network. In 1953 West married Joyce Lawford and with her had three sons and a daughter; his previous marriage to Elizabeth Harvey produced a son and daughter.

In 1955 West left Australia and moved to Sorrento, Italy, to further his career as a writer, supporting his family with the royalties from his second and third novels, *Gallows on the Sand* (1955) and *Kundu* (1956). West's nonfiction account of the Naples slums, *Children of the Sun* (1957), attracted significant attention, but he became a best-selling international author and millionaire with *The Devil's Advocate* (1959), after which he remained extremely popular for 40 years, producing a long succession of best sellers. Between 1956 and 1958 West lived in England, then spent time in Austria, Italy, and the United States, serving while in Italy as the Vatican correspondent for London's *Daily Mail* newspaper. In 1980 West returned to live in Australia after 25 years abroad.

His best-known works are *The Devil's Advocate* (1959) and *The Shoes of the Fisherman* (1963), the latter launching West's Vatican trilogy. *The Devil's Advocate* (1959) describes an investigation by the Catholic Church into whether or not an army deserter, Giacomo Nerone, should be canonized. Monsignor Blaise Meredith, the investigator and "devil's advocate," is an English priest expecting to die shortly from cancer and is described as "the quintessential West protagonist, a man filled with guilt" (Clancy 228). *The Shoes of the Fisherman* (1963), describing the election of a pope, drew upon West's experiences as the Vatican correspondent for the *Daily Mail.* The novel, beginning with the sentence, "The Pope is dead," was published on the very day Pope John XXIII died, which led to tremendous publicity and sales. Moreover, it describes the election of a Slavic pope 15 years before Karol Wojtyła became Pope John Paul II and includes material regarding papal reforms that would also take place, such as the use of vernacular language, an emphasis on forgiveness, and the relaxation of clerical dress. West's Vatican trilogy continued with *Clowns of God* (1981) and *Lazarus* (1999).

His Catholicism and seminary training pervade all his works. Indeed, critics often refer to them as "religious thrillers" due to their frequent combination of religion and politics in a plot-driven narrative. His writerly interest tends toward serious moral issues, significant world events, and international locations, and throughout his work he argues for a Catholic Church that will place forgiveness before punishment, a stance described as "liberal Catholicism" (Clancy 228). In addition to the novels focused on the Catholic Church, West wrote political thrillers concerned with a number of major world events: *The Ambassador* (1965) is set in Vietnam; *Tower of Babel* (1968) focuses on the Arab-Israeli conflict; *The Salamander* (1973) deals with fascism and violence in Italy; *Proteus* (1979) is about an organization like Amnesty International, dedicated to the release of prisoners of conscience worldwide; *The Ringmaster* (1991) anticipates the imminent demise of the Soviet Union.

Utilizing a true case history from Jung's autobiography, *The World Is Made of Glass* (1983) draws parallels between confession and psychoanalysis and was adapted for the stage and performed in New York in 1982. *Masterclass* (1991) is set in the art world and reflects West's lifelong passion for art, both as collector and patron. Prior to the publication of his 24th novel, *The Lovers* (1993), West claimed to be finished as a novelist, but in 1998 he published *Eminence,* which again focused on the papacy, the Vatican, and the politics of the Catholic Church. His autobiography, *View from a Ridge: The Testimony of a Twentieth-Century Pilgrim,* appeared in 1996.

West wrote a total of 31 novels, nine dramas, five screenplays, and two nonfiction books. His novels have been translated into 27 languages and a number have been adapted into films. *The Shoes of the Fisherman* appeared in 1968 starring Anthony Quinn, Laurence Olivier, Leo McKern, and John Gielgud. A decade later, *The Devil's Advocate* was released with a screenplay written by West. His style has been compared to that of Graham Greene and Jeffrey Archer, and his plotting shares similarities in scope and seriousness with LEON URIS and JAMES MICHENER (whose success largely paralleled his own).

In addition to his writing career West served as chair of the National Book Council and the National Library Council in Australia during the 1980s. He received numerous awards, including the Royal Society of Literature Heineman Award (1960), National Conference of Christian and Jews Brotherhood Award (1960), and the Dag Hammarskjöld prize (1978). He was a fellow of the Royal Society of Literature and the World Academy of Arts and Sciences. In 1985 he was appointed a Member of the Order of Australia for services to Australian literature and in 1997 was appointed Officer of the Order of Australia for services to literature. In 1997 he was proclaimed an Australian National Living Treasure. In addition, West received several honorary degrees, including a D.Litt. from the University of California, Santa Clara.

Despite his phenomenal global success and continued popularity, he has been largely ignored by Australian literary critics and omitted from the Australian canon, his works being considered as alternately too formulaic, repetitive, homophobic, misogynistic, or clichéd. Only half a dozen articles on West have been published in academic journals, and he is the subject of just two books, both by Maryanne Confoy. Morris West died of a heart attack on October 9, 1999, at his home in Clareville, a suburb of Sydney, while working on the manuscript for his appropriately titled 31st novel, *The Last Confession* (2000), published posthumously. At the time of his death West was Australia's most successful writer, having sold approximately 70 million copies worldwide.

Bibliography

Clancy, Laurie. *A Reader's Guide to Australian Fiction.* Melbourne: Oxford University Press, 1992.

Confoy, Maryanne. *Morris West: A Writer and Spirituality.* Sydney: HarperCollins, 1997.

———. *Morris West: Literary Maverick.* Milton, Queensland: John Wiley & Sons, 2005.

Mote, David, ed. *Contemporary Popular Writers.* Detroit: St. James Press, 1997.

Morris, Julian. *A Moon in My Pocket.* Sydney: Australasian Publishing, 1945.

Pierce, Peter. "Morris West." In *Australian Writers, 1950–1975.* Edited by Selina Samuels. Detroit: Gale, 2004.

Vinson, James, ed. *Contemporary Novelists.* London: St. James Press, 1972.

West, Morris. *Gallows on the Sand.* Sydney: Angus and Robertson, 1955.

———. *Kundu.* Sydney: Angus and Robertson, 1956.

———. *Children of the Sun.* Garden City, N.Y.: Doubleday, 1957.

———. *The Devil's Advocate.* New York: Morrow, 1959.

———. *The Shoes of the Fisherman.* New York: Morrow, 1963.

———. *The Ambassador.* New York: Morrow, 1965.

———. *The Tower of Babel.* New York: Morrow, 1968.

———. *The Salamander.* New York: Morrow, 1973.

———. *Proteus.* New York: Morrow, 1979.

———. *Clowns of God.* New York: Morrow, 1981.

———. *The World Is Made of Glass.* New York: Morrow, 1983.

———. *Masterclass.* New York: St. Martin's, 1988.

———. *Lazarus.* New York: St. Martin's, 1990.

———. *The Ringmaster.* London: Heinemann, 1991.

———. *The Lovers.* New York: D.I. Fine, 1993.

———. *A View from the Ridge: The Testimony of a Twentieth-century Pilgrim.* San Francisco: HarperSanFrancisco, 1996.

———. *Eminence.* New York: Harcourt Brace, 1998.

———. *The Last Confession.* Oxford: Compass Press, 2000.

Nathanael O'Reilly

Whirlwind James Clavell (1986)

Whirlwind is the story of a group of helicopter pilots stationed in Iran flying missions under the guidance of their corporation, S-G Helicopters, for the Iranian government and the oil industry. As revolution breaks out across the nation, and Ayatollah Khomeini overthrows the government currently under the rule of the shah, the pilots find themselves in a dangerous position, caught between conflicting parties vying for control of the country.

Whirlwind tells the story of these pilots' internal and external struggles as each confronts the violent change taking place around them over a span of 24 days of the revolution, between February 9 and March 4, 1979; its title echoes the label attributed to the revolutionary Khomeini, "whirlwind of god." These expatriates have already been living and working in Iran alongside the Iranians for years before the revolution takes place, and several have married Iranian women; but they now find themselves suddenly isolated and in danger, in the midst of the chaos and rioting, and are forced at last to flee the country that they have made their home. With deception and fear on all sides, no one is sure who to trust, and friends find themselves at odds with one another; loyalties are tested, and families torn apart.

The interactions of these characters with one another, and the roles their cultural beliefs play in such interactions, become a significant theme in the novel, as JAMES CLAVELL depicts with great skill how rapidly in the escalation of the revolution their relationships evolve from those of common friendship and respect into almost surreal mutations of suspicion and distrust. At the core of the novel is struggle, individual and collective, not merely for survival, although this plays a fundamental role, but for some understanding of the chaos and for some human means to make things right. But moral and intellectual lines are rapidly blurred, and the reader is ultimately confronted with searching questions of just what right is, when put under extraordinary pressure, when the evident good of one group is simply irreconcilable with that of another.

While all of the characters in the novel's large and complex cast are purely fictional, *Whirlwind* is profoundly historical, and as such the activities and events set in motion by well-known historical figures, particularly those involved in Khomeini's ascension to power and the bloody overthrow of the current government, play an important role in the novel, even though their authors are not actually depicted. Additionally, Clavell's characters are drawn from a vast variety of cultures and backgrounds, both native and foreign to Iran, which allows the reader to understand and appreciate the significance of unfolding events from multiple viewpoints.

Complicating this already rich palette is Clavell's typically deft integration of characters from his other novels, here most notably from NOBLE HOUSE (1981). Among the novel's central characters are Duncan McIver and his wife, Genny; Andy Gavallan, the owner of S-G Helicopters (along with silent partner, Struan, whose story is told in *Noble House*); and the pilot, Charlie Pettikin, who is currently living with McIver and Genny following his recent divorce. Pilot Tom Loch is married to an Iranian woman and has promised to remain in Iran as a condition of her father's acceptance of their marriage. Scragger, the Australian, is known for his superior flying skills, particularly when operating CASEVAC missions, helping those who need emergency medical attention. Also important to the story is Finnish pilot Erikki Yokonnen, married to Azadeh, daughter of the Kahn of Azerbaijan, whose story was published in a shortened version of the novel entitled *Escape: The Love Story from Whirlwind.*

Each of these has a story line pertaining to their own situation and their place in the revolution, which is significant to the broader narrative; as the revolution unfolds, Clavell employs flashbacks to fill out their backgrounds and explores with great subtlety their thoughts and feelings. It is notable then that the novel, while seemingly sympathetic to the perspective of the people of Iran, is told from a traditionally Western viewpoint, and many of the Iranian characters lack depth and nuance.

Interwoven with the complex religious and political aspects of the revolution are the machinations of external forces vying for Iran's oil, from the Russians to the Japanese, French, and Americans, as well as the threat this oil hunger poses to a 3,000-year-old culture fighting for its life and integrity. At home in such foreign surroundings, yet always marked by the country that sent them, the pilots thus offer an ideal vantage point from which to explore the pathologies of cultural interaction, where one culture's business is another's hegemony.

This complex, often paradoxical socioeconomic perspective is typical of Clavell's Asian Saga, of which *Whirlwind* is the fifth novel. Also typical are the exotic locale, the profusion of local detail, and the welter of characters and subplots all skillfully handled by the author. While *Whirlwind* is the second-last novel in the saga, which also includes the titles *King Rat* (1962), *Tai-Pan* (1966), *Shogun* (1975), and *Noble House* (1981), it is actually the last chronologically, taking place over a century after the story told in *Gai-Jin* (1993), the concluding work in the series.

While the novel made the best-seller list and was as popular as any in the series, *Whirlwind* was not as critically acclaimed as Clavell's previous novels and is currently out of print. The novel was not adapted into film; however, it spawned the short novel, *Escape: The Love Story From Whirlwind,* and was the basis of a board game, "James Clavell's Whirlwind," which was released in 1986 through FASA.

Bibliography

Clavell, James. *Noble House.* New York: Delacorte, 1981.

———. *Whirlwind.* New York: Avon, 1986.

Angela Craig

Williams, Kit (1946–)

Williams is the author and illustrator of MASQUERADE (1979) and *Book without a Name* (1984), two children's picture books that encode captivating puzzles and hints leading toward a unique prize.

Williams was born in the Romney Marshes area of Kent, England, but raised in nearby Tenterden, his father a bicycle salesman, his mother a housewife. Although he had no formal training or background in writing, painting, or sculpture, he received a broad introduction to handicraftsmanship and design from Frederick Curl, a local artisan who specialized in porcelain repair. In 1961

Williams left school and joined the Royal Navy for a four-year term, during which he studied electronics and took up painting as a hobby but with an eye to become what he calls "... the first visual philosopher" (Williams). He currently resides in Gloucestershire, England, where he works on various paintings, woodcraft, and sculptures, most for private commissions but some sold through the Portal Gallery in London. He is known to make appointments with the general public once per year at his home studio, with all arrangements made through his Portal Gallery representative. He has also taken on larger public and private commissions, crafting pieces intended for public view, among them massive clocks for shopping centers and the celebrated Dragonfly Maze for Bourton-on-the-Water, Cheltenham, England.

Williams is best known for writing and illustrating *Masquerade,* a work credited with reinvigorating the "Treasure Hunt Book" genre, which contained clues for finding a golden bejeweled rabbit, also crafted by Williams, buried in England prior to the book's publication in 1979. *Masquerade* took the world by storm, selling more than 1 million hardcover and countless paperback copies internationally before the prize was discovered in 1982, which in turn prompted a revised version of the book, with the nominal solution included.

Williams' follow-up to *Masquerade* took into account various complaints his first work had received, ranging from the difficulty of the puzzle itself to the inability of some puzzlers to travel to and throughout England to hunt on site. The intriguing object of *Book without a Name* was to find the title of the book within its own pages and then communicate the answer to Williams without actually using the title itself. He set a firm deadline of one year and a day from initial publication, at which point a sealed box containing the only copy bearing the title would be opened on May 25, 1985. Rather than dig for the prize, puzzlers had to send to Williams a piece of art they created that would indicate the title without using words.

Williams has stated he will create no more puzzle books due to the barrage of hint requests *Masquerade* generated and the discouraging but not unsurprising revelation in 1988 that the winner had cheated. He has since published two philosophico-autobiographical albums of varied visual media creations, *Out of One Eye: The Art of Kit Williams* and *Engines of Ingenuity.*

Bibliography

Amrich, Dan, ed. "Masquerade and the Mysteries of Kit Williams: Frequently Asked Questions." In *Masquerade and the Mysteries of Kit Williams.* Available online. URL: http://www.bunnyears.net/kitwilliams/faq.html. Accessed April 29, 2007.

Gascoigne, Bamber. *Quest for the Golden Hare.* London: Jonathan Cape, 1983.

Williams, Kit. *Masquerade: The Complete Book with the Answer Explained.* New York: Workman, 1983.

———. *Book without a Name* (a.k.a. *Untitled*). New York: Knopf, 1984.

———. *Out of One Eye: The Art of Kit Williams.* New York: Harmony Books, 1986.

———. *Engines of Ingenuity.* Corte Madera, Calif.: Gingko Press, 2001.

———. "The Man of Masquerade." Interview with Susan Raven. *New York Times Magazine,* 20 June 1982. In *Masquerade and the Mysteries of Kit Williams.* Edited by Dan Amrich. Available online. URL: http://www.bunnyears.net/kitwilliams/aboutkit.html. Accessed April 29, 2007.

Woolf, Jenny. "Kit Williams: Roots." *The Sunday Express* (April 1986) 86. In *Masquerade and the Mysteries of Kit Williams.* Edited by Dan Amrich. Available online. URL: http://www.bunnyears.net/kitwilliams/kitarticle.jpg. Accessed April 29, 2007.

Solomon Davidoff

Wouk, Herman (1915–)

Herman Wouk has achieved extraordinary prominence and success in several genres, often telling his stories through the dominant medium of the time. In the 1930s he wrote for a popular national radio show hosted by Fred Allen, and in the succeeding years he has produced a vast and eclectic oeuvre of short stories, novels, and plays, as well as film and television scripts. He has also written a host of nonfiction works centered on the Jewish faith that has been an unshakable pillar of his life and work.

While some critics have criticized the perceived shallowness and simplicity of his characterization or his manipulation of extraordinary coincidences, all recognize him as a consummate storyteller and locate his work firmly on that fecund borderline between art and entertainment.

Wouk was born in 1915, the son of Russian Jewish immigrants, in New York City, attending high school in the Bronx and later graduating from Columbia University in 1934. After writing for radio shows, he went to work for the government when the United States entered World War II, eventually joining the navy and becoming an officer, like Willie Keith, the main character in *The Caine Mutiny* (1954). After receiving his commission, Wouk was assigned to the Pacific, where he served in several campaigns on a destroyer-minesweeper much like the fictional U.S.S. *Caine*. During his naval service he spent his off-duty hours writing a novel, again reminiscent of another character on the *Caine*, Tom Keefer. Wouk's naval service not only provided him with stories and experience that he would employ in his fiction well into the 1980s but also helped to define central themes that would dominate this fiction, such as a distrust of intellectuals and the fundamental value of service to others.

After the war Wouk returned to civilian life and married Betty Sarah Brown, a Catholic who converted to Judaism; they had three children, one of whom died at an early age. At home Wouk commenced a full-time writing career, working first on plays but soon publishing his debut novel, *Aurora Dawn*, to reasonable success. His follow-up, *City Boy*, was not well received, but it was followed in 1951 by the work that would become his most famous and, according to many, his greatest work, *The Caine Mutiny*.

The novel, a subtle yet gripping morality tale, tells the story of a small ship (a destroyer-minesweeper) assigned to pedestrian support tasks through the Pacific Theater during World War II. Illustrating vividly the workings of a community in miniature, the crew of the *Caine* gradually suffers a loss both of cohesion and morale as the result of inept, paranoid, and battle-wearied Commander Queeg. Finally, in the middle of a typhoon, when it seems the ship will sink, one of the officers forcibly relieves the captain and takes command; the ensuing trial examines all of the incidents leading up to the relief of Queeg, detailing his loss of control and alienation from the officers and crew of his ship. Although the description of the ship under Queeg's command induces the expectation that Queeg's removal will be a triumph of integrity and common sense, by the trial's end Wouk has shrewdly called into question the sincerity and good intentions of officers who thought, or said they thought, they were doing the right thing. The second half of the novel, the trial itself, was adapted into a play by Wouk, *The Caine Mutiny Court Martial*, which appeared on Broadway and was well received. A revival of the play starring David Schwimmer of *Friends* and Tim Daly of *Wings* played in New York in 2006. The play was also produced as a television show several years later.

Wouk followed up *The Caine Mutiny* with *Marjorie Morningstar* in 1955, a novel described by one critic as a "tragi-comic meeting of traditional Jewish culture and the American success myth." Its protagonist is a young Jewish woman in New York who wishes to become an actress, leaving behind her traditional upbringing, but eventually she gives up her dream of stardom and settles into suburban life as the wife of a rich lawyer in Westchester, New York. What might be seen by some as a small-scale, Flaubertian tragedy is, in Wouk's treatment, a gentle, forgiving, and ultimately comic exploration of benign conformity and the continuity of tradition. *Youngblood Hawke*, published in 1962, and based partly on the life and career of the American writer Thomas Wolfe as well Wouk's own experiences, tells the story of a young novelist who attains rapid and dazzling success, only to face the age-old quandaries of fame. The work was well received, although some reviewers found it rather drawn out at 700 pages (in the first edition) and somewhat contrived in both outcome and characterization.

The rest of the 1960s were spent in researching and writing the masterpiece whose scope and size would become so great that it would eventually be published as two separate novels, *The Winds of War* and *WAR AND REMEMBRANCE*, in 1971 and

1978, respectively. These covered essentially the same period as *The Caine Mutiny,* but while the story of the *Caine* was crafted on a tactical and personal scale, the latter works concerned the personal lives of individuals engaged in the highest strategic levels of policy making as well, including a host of real historical personalities. Because of the immense scope of the two novels, Wouk wanted them produced as miniseries rather than as films; as he had been very displeased with previous film adaptations of his work, he himself assumed production and writing responsibilities. Both series were enthusiastically received.

After this more secular phase in his prolific career, Wouk's fictional interests began to merge more explicitly with his religious concerns, with *Inside Outside* (1985), following the lives of a Jewish family from the turn of the 20th century to the 1970s, and *The Hope* and *The Glory,* chronicling the fate of families and military men in Israel from the late 1940s to the early 1980s. He also published the nonfiction *This Is My God: The Jewish Way of Life* in 1997.

Bibliography

Beichman, Arnold. *Herman Wouk, the Novelist as Social Historian.* New Brunswick, N.J.: Transaction Books, 1984.

Mazzeno, Laurence W. *Herman Wouk.* New York: Twayne, 1994.

Wouk, Herman. *The Caine Mutiny Court-Martial, a Play.* New York: Doubleday, 1954.

———. *Marjorie Morningstar.* Garden City, N.Y.: Doubleday, 1955.

———. *Youngblood Hawke.* Garden City, N.Y.: Doubleday, 1962.

———. *City Boy: The Adventures of Herbie Bookbinder.* Garden City, N.Y.: Doubleday, 1969.

———. *The Winds of War.* Boston: Little, Brown, 1971.

———. *War and Remembrance.* Boston: Little, Brown, 1978.

———. *The Caine Mutiny: A Novel of World War II.* New York: Doubleday, 1979.

———. *This Is My God: The Jewish Way of Life.* London: Souvenir Press, 1997.

Robert Stacey

Z

Zoya **Danielle Steel** (1988)

Zoya is a romance initially set against the backdrop of the Russian Revolution and advancing through time to post–World War II America. Zoya, a distant cousin of the czar, leads a privileged lifestyle as a child but must learn how to cope with and adapt to cataclysmic changes in her life and world. Typical of DANIELLE STEEL's fiction, family dynamics are at the heart of the story, as Zoya and her grandmother escape with their lives from war-torn Russia. The tale then follows Zoya's tumultuous coming of age, first in World War I Paris and then in America, through the depression, and World War II, with her resourceful struggle first to survive and then provide for her own children, revealing a family forced to constantly redefine itself over the course of two generations.

Zoya begins a shocking new life of poverty and uncertainty when she and her grandmother settle in Paris to wait out the war. The grandmother is shocked and upset when Zoya, a child of great privilege and high social standing, takes a job as a dancer with the Ballet Russe; but typical of the young at heart, Zoya enjoys a freedom she would never have known had her life remained the same. While poverty takes its toll on her grandmother, Zoya thrives in the new and hard-won life she is building for herself. When she meets Clayton Andrews, an American officer, this life takes a romantic turn.

As in many love stories set against the backdrop of war, the drama of world events swirling around Zoya's personal struggle is never far from the reader's imagination. When these events thwart the happily-ever-after that her marriage to Clayton seemed to promise, Zoya is forced once again to reshape her life along with that of their two children in order to survive the Great Depression. Indeed, Zoya reinvents herself many times throughout the story, lending her character an accumulated firmness, and yet suppleness, that will bend but not break before even the most adverse circumstances. She experiences the full range of happiness and tragedy through her two marriages—first with Clayton and then with Simon; the cultural riches sustained by wealth and the family values fostered by poverty all come together to produce a strong and resilient female character, both inspiration to and protector of her children and grandchildren.

As Zoya becomes Americanized and the depression strikes, her career as a ballerina is diminished to that of a burlesque dancer as she struggles to support herself and her two children; but she fights her way out of this potentially terminal decline by becoming a sales clerk for an exclusive New York fashion store, utilizing her royal status to entice the new, post-depression rich into the shop, ultimately garnering power and respect as an entrepreneur in her own right.

Even at the busy height of her success, however, Zoya's thoughts are never far from the homeland and traditions she left behind, and she zealously protects and passes on the one family heirloom that Grandmamma never sold during the lean war years: a Fabergé egg, a gift from the czar.

The fortune it would have fetched in the midst of Zoya's frequent distress utterly pales in comparison to its value as a tangible symbol of the life and family she has lost.

The novel was adapted for film in 1995 starring Melissa Gilbert, Bruce Boxleitner, and Diana Rigg, and the movie takes the story in several different directions, commencing in media res with Zoya and her grandmother fleeing Russia, dispensing with a number of telling subplots. But the same singular thematic focus on the courage and hard-won resiliency of the heroine, as well as the deep, sustaining, almost inarticulable strength of the family she centers and preserves, is well served in the film adaptation.

Bibliography

Steel, Danielle. *Zoya*. New York: Dell, 1988.

Zoya. Directed by Richard Colla. NBC Home Video, 1995.

Linda Dick

Selected Works by Major Writers of Popular Fiction

Adams, Douglas
The Hitchhiker's Guide to the Galaxy (1979)
The Restaurant at the End of the Universe (1980)
Life, the Universe and Everything (1982)
So Long, and Thanks for All the Fish (1984)
Dirk Gently's Holistic Detective Agency (1987)
The Long Dark Tea-Time of the Soul (1988)
Mostly Harmless (1992)
The Salmon of Doubt (2002)

Albom, Mitch
The Five People You Meet in Heaven (2003)
For One More Day (2006)

Asimov, Isaac
I, Robot (1950)
Foundation (1951)
Foundation and Empire (1952)
Second Foundation (1953)
The Caves of Steel (1954)
The Naked Sun (1957)
The Robots of Dawn (1983)
Robots and Empire (1985)
The Best Science Fiction of Isaac Asimov (1986)

Auel, Jean M.
The Clan of the Cave Bear (1980)
The Valley of Horses (1982)
The Mammoth Hunters (1985)
The Plains of Passage (1990)
The Shelters of Stone (2002)

Bach, Richard
Jonathan Livingston Seagull (1970)
Illusions (1977)
One (1989)

Baldacci, David
Absolute Power (1996)
Saving Faith (1999)
Wish You Well (2000)
Last Man Standing (2001)
Split Second (2003)
Hour Game (2004)
The Camel Club (2005)
Simple Genius (2007)

Barker, Clive
Books of Blood (1984–85)
The Essential Clive Barker: Selected Fiction (2000)

Benchley, Peter
Jaws (1974)

Binchy, Maeve
Light a Penny Candle (1982)
Circle of Friends (1990)
The Glass Lake (1994)
Evening Class (1996)
Tara Road (1998)
Scarlet Feather (2000)
Quentins (2002)
Whitethorn Woods (2006)

Borchgrave, Arnaud de, and Robert Moss
The Spike (1980)

Bradford, Barbara Taylor
A Woman of Substance (1979)
Hold the Dream (1985)
To Be the Best (1988)
Emma's Secret (2003)
Unexpected Blessings (2005)
Just Rewards (2005)
The Ravenscar Dynasty (2006)
The Heir (2007)
Being Elizabeth (2008)

Brashares, Ann
The Sisterhood of the Traveling Pants (2001)
The Second Summer of the Sisterhood (2003)
Girls in Pants: The Third Summer of the Sisterhood (2005)
Keep in Touch: Letters, Notes, and More from the Sisterhood of the Traveling Pants (2005)
Forever in Blue: The Fourth Summer of the Sisterhood (2007)
The Last Summer (of You and Me) (2007)

Brown, Dan
Digital Fortress (1998)
Angels & Demons (2000)
Deception Point (2001)
The Da Vinci Code (2003)

Brown, Sandra
French Silk (1994)
Fat Tuesday (1997)
Unspeakable (1998)
The Alibi (1999)
The Switch (2000)
Envy (2001)
The Crush (2002)
Chill Factor (2005)
Ricochet (2006)
White Hot (2004)
Hello, Darkness (2003)

Caldwell, Ian and Dustin Thomason
The Rule of Four (2004)

Clancy, Tom
The Hunt for Red October (1984)
Red Storm Rising (1986)
Patriot Games (1987)
The Cardinal of the Kremlin (1988)
Clear and Present Danger (1989)
The Sum of All Fears (1991)
Without Remorse (1993)
Debt of Honor (1994)
Executive Orders (1996)
SSN: Strategies for Submarine Warfare (1996)
Rainbow Six (1998)
The Bear and the Dragon (2000)
Red Rabbit (2002)
The Teeth of the Tiger (2003)

Clark, Mary Higgins
A Stranger Is Watching (1977)
A Cry in the Night (1982)
Stillwatch (1984)
Remember Me (1994)
Pretend You Don't See Her (1997)
No Place Like Home (2005)
I Heard That Song Before (2007)
Where Are You Now? (2008)

Clarke, Arthur C.
Childhood's End (1953)
The City and the Stars (1956)
Rendezvous with Rama (1973)
2001: A Space Odyssey (1968)
2010: Odyssey Two (1982)
2061: Odyssey Three (1988)
3001: The Final Odyssey (1997)
The Collected Stories of Arthur C. Clarke (2001)

Clavell, James
King Rat (1962)
Tai-Pan (1966)
Shogun (1975)
Noble House (1981)
Whirlwind (1986)
Gai-Jin (1993)

Coelho, Paulo
The Alchemist (1988)

Colfer, Eoin

Artemis Fowl (2001)
Artemis Fowl: The Arctic Incident (2002)
Artemis Fowl: The Eternity Code (2003)
The Artemis Fowl Files (2004)
Artemis Fowl: The Opal Deception (2005)
Artemis Fowl: The Lost Colony (2006)
Artemis Fowl: The Time Paradox (2008)

Collins, Jackie

The World Is Full of Married Men (1968)
The World Is Full of Divorced Women (1975)
The Bitch (1979)
Hollywood Wives (1983)
Chances (1981)
Lucky (1985)
Rock Star (1988)
L.A. Connections (1998)

Collins, Larry and Dominique Lapierre

Is Paris Burning? (1968)
O Jerusalem! (1972)
Freedom at Midnight (1975)
The Fifth Horseman (1980)
Is New York Burning? (2005)

Connelly, Michael

The Black Echo (1992)
The Black Ice (1993)
The Concrete Blonde (1994)
The Last Coyote (1995)
The Poet (1996)
The Narrows (2004)
The Lincoln Lawyer (2005)
Echo Park (2006)

Conroy, Pat

The Boo (1970)
The Great Santini (1976)
The Lords of Discipline (1980)
The Prince of Tides (1986)
Beach Music (1995)
My Losing Season (2002)

Cook, Robin

The Year of the Intern (1972)
Coma (1977)
Outbreak (1987)
Mortal Fear (1988)
Harmful Intent (1990)
Terminal (1993)
Invasion (1997)
Vector (1999)

Coonts, Stephen

Flight of the Intruder (1986)
The Cannibal Queen: A Flight into the Heart of America (1992)
Saucer (2002)
Deep Black (2003)
Liars and Thieves (2004)
The Assassin (2008)

Cornwell, Patricia

Hornet's Nest (1997)
Southern Cross (1999)
Isle of Dogs (2001)
The Scarpetta Collection Volume 1: Postmortem and Body of Evidence (2003)
The Scarpetta Collection Volume 2: All That Remains and Cruel and Unusual (2003)
At Risk (2006)

Crichton, Michael

The Andromeda Strain (1969)
The Great Train Robbery (1975)
Eaters of the Dead (1976)
Congo (1980)
Sphere (1987)
Jurassic Park (1990)
Rising Sun (1992)
Disclosure (1994)
The Lost World (1995)
Airframe (1996)
Timeline (1999)
Prey (2002)
State of Fear (2004)
Next (2006)

Cussler, Clive

The Mediterranean Caper (1973)
Raise the Titanic! (1979)
Deep Six (1984)
Treasure (1988)

Sahara (1993)
Flood Tide (1997)
Valhalla Rising (2001)
Golden Buddha (2003)

DONALDSON, STEPHEN R.

The First Chronicles
- *Lord Foul's Bane* (1977)
- *The Illearth War* (1978)
- *The Power That Preserves* (1979)

The Second Chronicles
- *The Wounded Land* (1980)
- *The One Tree* (1982)
- *White Gold Wielder* (1983)

The Last Chronicles
- *The Runes of the Earth* (2004)
- *Fatal Revenant* (2007)

EDWARDS, KIM

The Secrets of a Fire King (1997)
The Memory Keeper's Daughter (2006)

ERDMAN, PAUL E.

The Billion Dollar Sure Thing (1973)
The Silver Bears (1974)
The Crash of '79 (1976)
The Last Days of America (1981)
The Panic of '89 (1986)
The Palace (1987)
The Swiss Account (1992)
Zero Coupon (1993)
The Set-up (1997)

EVANOVICH, JANET

Elsie Hawkins series
- *Back to the Bedroom* (1989)
- *Smitten* (1990)
- *Wife for Hire* (1990)
- *Rocky Road to Romance* (1991)

Stephanie Plum series
- *One for the Money* (1994)
- *Two for the Dough* (1996)
- *Three to Get Deadly* (1997)
- *Four to Score* (1998)
- *High Five* (1999)
- *Hot Six* (2000)
- *Seven Up* (2001)
- *Hard Eight* (2002)
- *Visions of Sugar Plums* (2003)
- *To the Nines* (2003)
- *Ten Big Ones* (2004)
- *Eleven on Top* (2005)
- *Twelve Sharp* (2006)
- *Lean Mean Thirteen* (2007)
- *Plum Lovin'* (2007)
- *Plum Lucky* (2008)

The Barnaby series
- *Metro Girl* (2005)
- *Motor Mouth* (2006)

EVANS, NICHOLAS

The Horse Whisperer (1995)
The Loop (1998)
The Smoke Jumper (2001)
The Divide (2005)

EVANS, RICHARD PAUL

The Christmas Box (1995)
The Timepiece (1996)
The Locket (1998)
A Perfect Day (2003)

FAST, HOWARD

Conceived in Liberty: A Novel of Valley Forge (1939)
The Last Frontier, (1941)
The Unvanquished (1942)
Citizen Tom Paine (1943)
Freedom Road (1944)
Spartacus (1951)
April Morning (1961)
The Immigrants (1977)
The Second Generation (1978)
The Establishment (1979)
The Legacy (1980)
The Immigrant's Daughter (1985)
An Independent Woman (1997)

FIELDING, HELEN

Bridget Jones's Diary (1996)
Bridget Jones: The Edge of Reason (1999)

FOLLETT, KEN

Eye of the Needle (1978)
Triple (1979)

The Key to Rebecca (1980)
The Man from St. Petersburg (1982)
On Wings of Eagles (1983)
Lie Down with Lions (1986)
The Pillars of the Earth (1989)
Night over Water (1991)
A Dangerous Fortune (1993)
World without End (2007)

FORSYTH, FREDERICK
The Day of the Jackal (1971)
The Odessa File (1972)
The Dogs of War (1974)
The Devil's Alternative (1979)
The Fourth Protocol (1984)
The Negotiator (1989)
The Deceiver (1991)
The Fist of God (1994)
Icon (1996)
The Veteran (2001)
Avenger (2003)
The Afghan (2006)

FREEMAN, CYNTHIA
A World Full of Strangers (1975)
Come Pour the Wine (1980)
No Time for Tears (1981)
Seasons of the Heart (1986)
The Last Princess (1988)

FREY, JAMES
A Million Little Pieces (2003)
My Friend Leonard (2005)
Bright Shiny Morning (2008)

GABALDON, DIANA
Outlander (1991)
Dragonfly in Amber (1992)
Voyager (1994)
Drums of Autumn (1997)
The Fiery Cross (2001)
A Breath of Snow and Ashes (2005)

GARNER, JAMES FINN
Politically Correct Bedtime Stories (1994)
Once Upon a More Enlightened Time (1995)
Politically Correct Holiday Stories (1995)

GRAFTON, SUE
"A" Is for Alibi (1982)
"S" Is for Silence (2005)

GRISHAM, JOHN
A Time to Kill (1989)
The Firm (1991)
The Pelican Brief (1992)
The Client (1993)
The Chamber (1994)
The Rainmaker (1995)
The Runaway Jury (1996)
The Partner (1997)
The Street Lawyer (1998)
The Testament (1999)
The Brethren (2000)
A Painted House (2001)
Skipping Christmas (2002)
The Summons (2002)
Bleachers (2003)
The King of Torts (2003)
The Last Juror (2004)
The Broker (2005)
Playing for Pizza (2007)
The Appeal (2008)

HAILEY, ARTHUR
Hotel (1965)
Airport (1968)
Wheels (1971)
The Moneychangers (1975)
Overload (1979)
Strong Medicine (1984)
The Evening News (1991)
Detective (1998)

HAMILTON, LAURELL, K.
Nightseer (1992)
Guilty Pleasures (1993)
The Laughing Corpse (1994)
Circus of the Damned (1995)
Bloody Bones (1996)
The Lunatic Café (1996)
The Killing Dance (1997)
Blue Moon (1998)
Burnt Offerings (1998)
Obsidian Butterfly (2000)

Narcissus in Chains (2001)
Cerulean Sins (2003)
Cravings (2004)
Incubus Dreams (2004)
Bite (2005)
Danse Macabre (2006)
Micah (2006)
Strange Candy (2006)
The Harlequin (2007)

HARRIS, THOMAS
Red Dragon (1981)
The Silence of the Lambs (1988)
Hannibal (1999)
Hannibal Rising (2006)

HARRISON, KIM
Dead Witch Walking (2004)
Every Which Way But Dead (2005)
The Good, the Bad, and the Undead (2005)
A Fistful of Charms (2006)
For a Few Demons More (2007)
The Outlaw Demon Wails (2008)
White Whitch, Black Curse (2009)

HIGHSMITH, PATRICIA
Strangers on a Train (1950)
The Talented Mr. Ripley (1955)
Deep Water (1957)
The Sweet Sickness (1960)
The Cry of the Owl (1962)
Ripley under Ground (1970)
Ripley's Game (1974)
The Boy Who Followed Ripley (1980)
Ripley under Water (1991)
Nothing That Meets the Eye: The Uncollected Stories (2002)
Man's Best Friend and Other Stories (2004)

HOOPER, KAY
Lady Thief (1981)
The Delaney Historicals (1988)
All for Quinn (1993)
Elusive (2004)
Chill of Fear (2005)
Sleeping with Fear (2006)

HORNBY, NICK
High Fidelity (1995)
About a Boy (1998)
How to Be Good (2001)
A Long Way Down (2005)
Slam (2007)

IRVING, JOHN
Setting Free the Bears (1968)
The Water-Method Man (1972)
The 158-Pound Marriage (1974)
The World According to Garp (1978)
The Hotel New Hampshire (1981)
The Cider House Rules (1985)
A Prayer for Owen Meany (1989)
A Son of the Circus (1994)
A Widow for One Year (1998)
The Fourth Hand (2001)
A Sound Like Someone Trying Not to Make a Sound (2004)
Until I Find You (2005)

JAKES, JOHN
The Best of John Jakes (1977)
The Kent Family Chronicles
- *The Bastard* (1974)
- *The Rebels* (1975)
- *The Seekers* (1975)
- *The Furies* (1976)
- *The Titans* (1976)
- *The Warriors* (1977)
- *The Lawless* (1978)
- *The Americans* (1979)

The North and South Trilogy
- *North and South* (1982)
- *Love and War* (1984)
- *Heaven and Hell* (1987)

The Crown Family Saga
- *Homeland* (1993)
- *American Dreams* (1998)

JENKINS, JERRY AND TIM LAHAYE
Left Behind: A Novel of the Earth's Last Days (1995)
Tribulation Force: The Continuing Drama of Those Left Behind (1996)
Nicolae: The Rise of Antichrist (1997)
Soul Harvest: The World Takes Sides (1999)
Apollyon: The Destroyer Is Unleashed (1999)

Assassins: Assignment: Jerusalem, Target: Antichrist (1999)
The Indwelling: The Beast Takes Possession (2000)
The Mark: The Beast Rules the World (2000)
Desecration: Antichrist Takes the Throne (2001)
The Remnant: On the Brink of Armageddon (2002)
Armageddon: The Cosmic Battle of the Ages (2003)
Glorious Appearing: The End of Days (2004)
The Rising: Antichrist Is Born: Before They Were Left Behind (2005)
The Regime: Evil Advances: Before They Were Left Behind #2 (2005)
The Rapture: In the Twinkling of an Eye: Countdown to Earth's Last Days #3 (2006)
Kingdom Come: The Final Victory (2007)

Jong, Erica
Fear of Flying (1973)
How to Save Your Own Life (1977)
Fanny, Being the True History of the Adventures of Fanny Hackabout-Jones (1980)
Parachutes & Kisses (1984)
Shylock's Daughter (1987; a.k.a. *Serenissima*)
Any Woman's Blues (1990)
Inventing Memory (1997)
Sappho's Leap (2003)

Karon, Jan
A Common Life (2001)
Light from Heaven (2005)

Keillor, Garrison
Lake Wobegon Days (1985)
Leaving Home (1987)
We Are Still Married (1989)
Wobegon Boy (1997)
Lake Wobegon Summer 1956 (2001)
Pontoon: A Novel of Lake Wobegon (2007)

Kellerman, Jonathan
When the Bough Breaks (1985)
Blood Test (1986)
Over the Edge (1987)
Silent Partner (1989)
Time Bomb (1990)
Private Eyes (1992)
Devil's Waltz (1993)
Bad Love (1994)
Self-Defense (1995)
The Web (1996)
The Clinic (1997)
Survival of the Fittest (1997)
Monster (1999)
Dr. Death (2000)
Flesh and Blood (2001)
The Murder Book (2002)
A Cold Heart (2003)
Therapy (2004)
Rage (2005)
Gone (2006)
Obsession (2007)

Kidd, Sue Monk
The Secret Life of Bees (2002)
The Mermaid Chair (2005)

King, Stephen
Carrie (1974)
The Shining (1977)
The Stand (1978)
Firestarter (1980)
Cujo (1981)
Christine (1983)
Pet Sematary (1983)
It (1986)
Misery (1987)
The Tommyknockers (1988)
Gerald's Game (1992)
Dolores Claiborne (1993)
Desperation (1996)
The Girl Who Loved Tom Gordon (1999)
Dreamcatcher (2001)
Cell (2006)
Lisey's Story (2006)

Kingsolver, Barbara
The Bean Trees (1988)
Animal Dreams (1990)
Pigs in Heaven (1993)
The Poisonwood Bible (1998)
Prodigal Summer (2001)

Klein, Joe
Primary Colors (1996)

Koontz, Dean
Whispers (1980)
Midnight (1989)
The Bad Place (1990)
Cold Fire (1991)
Hideaway (1992)
Mr. Murder (1993)
Intensity (1995)
Ticktock (1996)
Life Expectancy (2004)
The Husband (2006)

Kostova, Elizabeth
The Historian (2005)

Kotzwinkle, William
The Fan Man (1974)
Doctor Rat (1976)
Fata Morgana (1977)
E.T., the Extra-Terrestrial: A Novel (1982)
E.T., the Book of the Green Planet: A New Novel (1985)

Krantz, Judith
Scruples (1978)
Princess Daisy (1980)
Mistral's Daughter (1982)
I'll Take Manhattan (1986)
Till We Meet Again (1988)
Dazzle (1990)
Scruples Two (1992)
Lovers (1994)
Spring Collection (1996)
The Jewels of Tessa Kent (1998)

L'Amour, Louis
Hondo (1953)
Flint (1960)
How the West Was Won (1963)
The Quick and the Dead (1973)
The Lonesome Gods (1983)
Last of the Breed (1986)
The Collected Short Stories of Louis L'Amour (2003–2006).

le Carré, John (David John Moore Cornwell)
The Spy Who Came in from the Cold (1963)
Tinker, Tailor, Soldier, Spy (1974)
The Honourable Schoolboy (1977)
Smiley's People (1979)
The Little Drummer Girl (1983)
A Perfect Spy (1986)
The Russia House (1989)
The Secret Pilgrim (1990)
The Night Manager (1993)
Our Game (1995)
The Tailor of Panama (1996)
Single & Single (1999)
The Constant Gardener (2001)

Leonard, Elmore
Hombre (1961)
The Big Bounce (1969)
Mr. Majestyk (1974)
Fifty-two Pickup (1974)
Swag (1976)
The Hunted (1977)
The Switch (1978)
Gunsights (1979)
City Primeval (1980)
Cat Chaser (1982)
Stick (1983)
Glitz (1985)
Bandits (1987)
Touch (1987)
Freaky Deaky (1988)
Killshot (1989)
Get Shorty (1990)
Rum Punch (1992)
Out of Sight (1996)
Be Cool (1999)

Ludlum, Robert
The Osterman Weekend (1972)
The Gemini Contenders (1976)
The Chancellor Manuscript (1977)
The Holcroft Covenant (1978)
The Matarese Circle (1979)
The Bourne Identity (1980)
The Parsifal Mosaic (1982)
The Aquitaine Progression (1984)
The Bourne Supremacy (1986)
The Icarus Agenda (1988)
The Bourne Ultimatum (1990)
The Road to Omaha (1992)
The Scorpio Illusion (1993)

The Apocalypse Watch (1995)
The Matarese Countdown (1997)
The Prometheus Deception (2000)

McCullough, Colleen

Masters of Rome series
- *The First Man in Rome* (1990)
- *The Grass Crown* (1991)
- *Fortune's Favorites* (1993)
- *Caesar's Women* (1996)
- *Caesar* (1997)
- *The October Horse* (2002)
- *Antony and Cleopatra* (2007)

The Thorn Birds (1977)
An Indecent Obsession (1981)
A Creed for the Third Millennium (1985)
The Ladies of Missalonghi (1987)

McLaughlin, Emma and Nicola Kraus

The Nanny Diaries (2002)
Citizen Girl (2004)
Dedication (2007)

McMillan, Terry L.

Waiting to Exhale (1992)
How Stella Got Her Groove Back (1996)
The Interruption of Everything (2005)

Michener, James A(lbert)

Tales of the South Pacific (1947)
The Bridges at Toko-Ri (1953)
Sayonara (1954)
Hawaii (1959)
Caravans (1963)
The Source (1965)
The Drifters (1971)
Centennial (1974)
Chesapeake (1978)
The Covenant (1980)
Space (1982)
Poland (1983)
Texas (1985)
Alaska (1988)
Caribbean (1989)
Mexico (1992)

Niffenegger, Audrey

The Time Traveler's Wife (2003)
The Three Incestuous Sisters (2005)
The Adventuress (2006)

Niven, Larry

Ringworld series
- *Ringworld* (1970)
- *The Ringworld Engineers* (1979)
- *The Ringworld Throne* (1996)
- *Ringworld's Children* (2004)

Rainbow Mars (1999)
Larry Niven Short Stories, Volumes 1–3 (2003)

Patterson, James

Along Came a Spider (1992)
Kiss the Girls (1995)
Jack & Jill (1996)
Cat and Mouse (1997)
Pop Goes the Weasel (1999)
Roses are Red (2000)
Violets are Blue (2001)
Four Blind Mice (2002)
The Big Bad Wolf (2003)
London Bridges (2004)
Mary, Mary (2005)
Cross (2006)
Double Cross (2007)

Pilcher, Rosamunde

The Blue Bedroom and Other Stories (1985)
The Shell Seekers (1988)
September (1990)
Coming Home (1995)
Winter Solstice (2000)

Pirsig, Robert M.

Zen and the Art of Motorcycle Maintenance (1974)
Lila: An Inquiry into Morals (1991)

Puzo, Mario

The Godfather (1969)
Fools Die (1978)
The Sicilian (1984)
The Fourth K (1991)
The Last Don (1996)
Omertà (2000)

Quinn, Julia (Julie Pottinger)

Everything and the Moon (1997)
Romancing Mister Bridgerton (2002)
To Sir Phillip, With Love (2002)
On the Way to the Wedding (2007)

Redfield, (Brian) James

The Celestine Prophecy (1993)
The Tenth Insight: Holding the Vision (1996)
The Celestine Vision: Living the New Spiritual Awareness (1997)
The Secret of Shambhala: In Search of the Eleventh Insight (1999)

Rice, Anne

Interview with the Vampire (1976)
The Feast of All Saints (1979)
Cry to Heaven (1982)
The Vampire Lestat (1985)
The Queen of the Damned (1988)
The Mummy (1989)
The Witching Hour (1990)
The Tale of the Body Thief (1992)
Lasher (1993)
Taltos (1994)
Memnoch the Devil (1995)
Servant of the Bones (1996)
Violin (1997)
Pandora (1998)
The Vampire Armand (1998)
Vittorio the Vampire (1999)
Merrick (2000)
Blood and Gold (2001)
Blackwood Farm (2002)
Blood Canticle (2003)
Christ the Lord: Out of Egypt (2005)
Christ the Lord: The Road to Cana (2008)

Ripley, Alexandra

Charleston (1981)
On Leaving Charleston (1984)
The Time Returns (1985)
New Orleans Legacy (1987)
Scarlett (1991)

Rivers, Joan

Fun City (1971)
The Life and Hard Times of Heidi Abramowitz (1984)
Sally Marr and Her Escorts (1994)

Robbins, Harold

The Carpetbaggers (1961)
Where Love Has Gone (1962)
The Betsy (1971)
The Lonely Lady (1976)
Dreams Die First (1977)
Memories of Another Day (1979)
Goodbye, Janette (1981)
The Storyteller (1982)
The Raiders (1995)
The Stallion (1996)
Tycoon (1997)
The Predators (1998)
Sin City (2002)

Roberts, Nora

The Heart's Victory (1983)
This Magic Moment (1984)
Untamed (1984)
A Matter of Choice (1985)
Opposites Attract (1985)
One Summer (1987)
Brazen Virtue (1989)
Night Shift (1992)
Divine Evil (1993)
Nightshade (1994)
Private Scandals (1994)
Hidden Riches (1995)
Born in Ice (1996)
Carolina Moon (2001)
Three Fates (2003)
Birthright (2004)
Remember When (as J. D. Robb; 2004)
Angels Fall (2006)
Survivor in Death (as J. D. Robb; 2006)
Blue Smoke (2007)

Rollins, James

Subterranean (1999)
Excavation (2000)
Deep Fathom (2001)

Amazonia (2002)
Ice Hunt (2003)
Sandstorm (2004)
Map of Bones (2005)
Black Order (2006)
The Judas Strain (2007)

ROWLING, J. K.
Harry Potter and the Sorcerer's Stone (1997)
Harry Potter and the Chamber of Secrets (1998)
Harry Potter and the Prisoner of Azkaban (1999)
Harry Potter and the Goblet of Fire (2000)
Harry Potter and the Order of the Phoenix (2003)
Harry Potter and the Half-Blood Prince (2005)
Harry Potter and the Deathly Hallows (2007)

SAGAN, CARL
Contact (1985)

SANDERS, LAWRENCE
The First Deadly Sin (1973)
The Tomorrow File (1975)
The Tangent Objective (1976)
The Tangent Factor (1978)
The Third Deadly Sin (1981)
The Timothy Files (1987)
The Dream Lover (1988)
Capital Crimes (1989)
McNally's Secret (1992)

SANTMYER, HELEN HOOVEN
. . . And Ladies of the Club (1984)

SAUL, JOHN
Suffer the Children (1977)
Punish the Sinners (1978)
Cry for the Strangers (1979)
Comes the Blind Fury (1980)
The God Project (1982)
Brainchild (1985)
The Right Hand of Evil (1999)
Nightshade (2000)
Manhattan Hunt Club (2001)
Midnight Voices (2002)
Perfect Nightmare (2005)
In the Dark of the Night (2006)

SEBOLD, ALICE
The Lovely Bones (2002)
The Almost Moon (2007)

SEUSS, DR.
Horton Hears a Who! (1954)
The Cat in the Hat (1957)
Green Eggs and Ham (1960)
one fish two fish red fish blue fish (1960)
The Sneetches (1961)
Hop on Pop (1963)
The Lorax (1971)
The Butter Battle Book (1984)

SHELDON, SIDNEY
The Naked Face (1970)
The Other Side of Midnight (1973)
A Stranger in the Mirror (1976)
Bloodline (1977)
Rage of Angels (1980)
Master of the Game (1982)
If Tomorrow Comes (1985)
Windmills of the Gods (1987)
The Sands of Time (1988)
Memories of Midnight (1990)
The Doomsday Conspiracy (1991)
The Stars Shine Down (1992)
Nothing Lasts Forever (1994)
Morning, Noon and Night (1995)
The Best Laid Plans (1997)
Tell Me Your Dreams (1998)
The Sky Is Falling (2001)
Are You Afraid of the Dark? (2004)

SMITH, MARTIN CRUZ
Gorky Park (1981)
Polar Star (1989)
Red Square (1992)
Havana Bay (1999)
Wolves Eat Dogs (2004)
Stalin's Ghost (2007)

SPARKS, NICHOLAS
The Notebook (1996)
Message in a Bottle (1998)
A Walk to Remember (1999)

The Rescue (2000)
A Bend in the Road (2001)
Nights in Rodanthe (2002)
The Guardian (2003)
The Wedding (2003)
Three Weeks with my Brother (2004)
At First Sight (2005)
True Believer (2005)
Dear John (2006)
The Choice (2007)

STEEL, DANIELLE
Zoya (1968)
Passion's Promise (1977)
Now and Forever (1978)
Remembrance (1981)
A Perfect Stranger (1983)
Family Album (1985)
Kaleidoscope (1987)
Daddy (1989)
Jewels (1992)
Mixed Blessings (1992)
Five Days in Paris (1995)
The Klone and I (1998)
The Wedding (2000)
Sunset in St. Tropez (2002)
Second Chance (2004)

TUROW, SCOTT
Presumed Innocent (1987)
The Burden of Proof (1990)
Pleading Guilty (1993)
The Laws of Our Fathers (1996)
Personal Injuries (1999)
Reversible Errors (2002)
Ordinary Heroes (2005)
Limitations (2006)

URIS, LEON
Exodus (1958)
Mila 18 (1961)
Armageddon: A Novel of Berlin (1963)
Topaz (1967)
QB VII (1970)
Trinity (1976)
The Haj (1984)
Mitla Pass (1988)
Redemption (1995)
A God in Ruins (1999)
O'Hara's Choice (2003)

VANCE, JACK
Big Planet (1957)
The Last Castle (1966)
Tschai series
- *City of the Chasch* (1968)
- *Servants of the Wankh* (1969)
- *The Dirdir* (1969)
- *The Pnume* (1970)

Demon Prince series
- *The Star King* (1964)
- *The Killing Machine* (1964)
- *The Palace of Love* (1967)
- *The Face* (1979)
- *The Book of Dreams* (1981)

Dying Earth series
- *The Dying Earth* (1950)
- *The Eyes of the Overworld* (1966)
- *Cugel's Saga* (1983)
- *Rhialto the Marvellous* (1984)

Lyonesse trilogy
- *Suldrun's Garden* (1983)
- *The Green Pearl* (1985)
- *Madouc* (1989)

The Jack Vance Treasury (2006)

WALLER, ROBERT JAMES
The Bridges of Madison County (1992)
Slow Waltz in Cedar Bend (1993)
A Thousand Country Roads (2002)
Call the Cops—Mario (2005)
High Plains Tango (2005)
The Long Night of Winchell Dear (2006)

WAMBAUGH JR., JOSEPH ALOYSIUS
The New Centurions (1971)
The Blue Knight (1972)
The Choirboys (1975)
The Black Marble (1978)
The Glitter Dome (1981)
The Delta Star (1983)
The Secrets of Harry Bright (1985)

The Golden Orange (1990)
Fugitive Nights (1992)
Finnegan's Week (1994)
Floaters (1996)
Hollywood Station (2006)
Hollywood Crows (2008)

Weisberger, Lauren

The Devil Wears Prada (2003)
Everyone Worth Knowing (2005)
Chasing Harry Winston (2008)

West, Morris

The Devil's Advocate (1959)
Daughter of Silence (1961)
The Shoes of the Fisherman (1963)
The Ambassador (1965)
The Tower of Babel (1968)
Sutnis (1969)
Summer of the Red Wolf (1971)
The Salamander (1973)
Harlequin (1974)
The Navigator (1976)
Proteus (1979)
The Clowns of God (1981)
The World Is Made of Glass (1983)
Cassidy (1986)
Masterclass (1988)
Lazarus (1990)
The Ringmaster (1991)
The Lovers (1993)
Vanishing Point (1996)
Eminence (1998)

Williams, Kit

Masquerade (1979)
Book without a Name (1984)

Wouk, Herman

The Caine Mutiny (1951)
Marjorie Morningstar (1955)
Slattery's Hurricane (1956)
Youngblood Hawke (1961)
Don't Stop the Carnival (1965)
The Lomokome Papers (1968)
The Winds of War (1971)
War and Remembrance (1978)

Bibliography of Secondary Sources

Anderson, Patrick. *The Triumph of the Thriller: How Cops, Crooks, and Cannibals Captured Popular Fiction.* New York: Random House, 2007.

Armitt, Lucie. *Fantasy Fiction: An Introduction.* London: Continuum International Publishing Group, 2005.

Badley, Linda. *Writing Horror and the Body: The Fiction of Stephen King, Clive Barker, and Anne Rice.* New York: Greenwood Press, 1996.

Bloom, Clive. *Bestsellers: Popular Fiction Since 1900.* Houndsmills, U.K.: Palgrave Macmillan, 2002.

———. *Gothic Horror: A Guide for Students and Readers.* Houndsmills, U.K.: Palgrave MacMillan, 2007.

Docherty, Brian. *American Crime Fiction: Studies in the Genre.* New York: Palgrave, 1988.

Drew, Barnard A. *100 Most Popular Genre Fiction Authors: Biographical Sketches and Bibliographies.* Westport, Conn: Libraries Unlimited, 2005.

Ferriss, Suzanne, and Mallory Young. *Chick Lit: The New Woman's Fiction.* New York: Routledge, 2005.

Gelder, Ken. *Popular Fiction: The Logics and Practices of a Literary Field.* New York: Routledge, 2005.

Hellekson, Karen, and Kristina Busse, eds. *Fan Fiction and Fan Communities in the Age of the Internet.* Jefferson, N.C.: McFarland, 2006.

Herald, Diana Tixier. *Genreflecting: A Guide to Reading Interests in Genre Fiction.* Westport, Conn: Libraries Unlimited, 2000.

Holland-Toll, Linda J. *As American as Mom, Baseball, and Apple Pie: Constructing Community in Contemporary American Horror Fiction.* Madison: Popular Press, 2001.

James, Edward, and Farah Mendelsohn. *The Cambridge Companion to Science Fiction.* Cambridge: Cambridge University Press, 2003.

Landon, Brooks. *Science Fiction after 1900: From the Steam Man to the Stars.* New York: Routledge, 2002.

Makinen, Merja. *Feminist Popular Fiction.* New York: Palgrave Macmillan, 2001.

Matthews, Richard. *Fantasy: The Liberation of Imagination.* New York: Routledge, 2002.

McCarty, Michael. *Giants of the Genre: Interviews with Science Fiction, Fantasy, and Horror's Greatest Talents.* Rockville, Md.: Wildside Press, 2003.

McCormick, Donald, and Katy Fletcher. *Spy Fiction: A Connoisseur's Guide.* New York: Facts On File, 1990.

McKee, Gabriel. *The Gospel According to Science Fiction: From the Twilight Zone to the Final Frontier.* Louisville, Ky.: Westminster John Knox Press, 2007.

Mizejewski, Lind. *Hardboiled and High Heeled: The Woman Detective in Popular Culture.* New York: Routledge, 2004.

Mort, John. *Christian Fiction: A Guide to the Genre.* Westport, Conn.: Libraries Unlimited, 2002.

Palmer, Jerry. *Potboilers: Methods, Concepts and Case Studies in Popular Fiction.* New York: Routledge, 1991.

Payant, Katherine B. *Becoming and Bonding: Contemporary Feminism and Popular Fiction by American Women Writers.* New York: Greenwood Press, 1993.

Priestman, Martin. *The Cambridge Companion to Crime Fiction.* Cambridge: Cambridge University Press, 2003.

Pugh, Sheenagh. *The Democratic Genre: Fan Fiction in a Literary Context.* Bridgend, U.K.: Seren, 2006.

Ramsdell, Kristin. *Romance Fiction: A Guide to the Genre.* Westport, Conn.: Libraries Unlimited, 1999.

Saricks, Joyce G. *The Reader's Advisory Guide to Genre Fiction.* New York: American Library Association, 2001.

Seed, David. *A Companion to Science Fiction.* Hoboken, N.J.: Wiley-Blackwell, 2005.

Smith, Myron J. *Cloak and Dagger Fiction: An Annotated Guide to Spy Thrillers*. New York: Greenwood Press, 1995.

Sutherland, John. *Bestsellers: A Very Short Introduction*. Oxford: Oxford University Press, 2007.

Swirski, Peter. *From Low Brow to No Brow*. Montreal: McGill-Queen's University Press, 2005.

Wisker, Alistair. *Crime Fiction: An Introduction*. London: Continuum International Publishing Group, 2008.

Wisker, Gina. *Horror Fiction: An Introduction*. London: Continuum International Publishing Group, 2005.

INDEX

Note: **Boldface** numbers indicate major treatment of a topic.

G

H

I

J

K

L

M

N

O